OREVER!!

EXIT

WE LOVE YOU
BEATLES

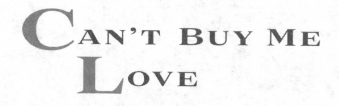

CAN'T BUY ME LOVE

CAN'T BUY ME LOVE

THE BEATLES, BRITAIN, AND AMERICA

JONATHAN GOULD

HARMONY BOOKS · NEW YORK

Published in the United States by Harmony Books, an imprint of the Crown
Publishing Group, a division of Random House, Inc., New York.
www.crownpublishing.com

HARMONY BOOKS is a registered trademark and the Harmony Books colophon is a
trademark of Random House, Inc.

Library of Congress Cataloging-in-Publication Data

Gould, Jonathan, 1951–
Can't buy me love: the Beatles, Britain, and America / Jonathan Gould.—1st ed.
1. Beatles.   2. Rock music—United States—History and criticism.
3. Rock music—Great Britain—History and criticism.   I. Title.
ML421.B4G68 2007
782.42166092'2—dc22   2007013240

ISBN 978-0-307-35337-5

Printed in the United States of America

Design by Lauren Dong

10 9 8 7 6 5 4 3 2 1

First Edition

In loving memory of my parents,
   Milton & Eleanor Gould

And loving appreciation of my children,
   Ellie & Oliver Gould

CAN'T BUY ME LOVE

John F. Kennedy Airport, New York, February 1964

PROLOGUE

They went to sea in Sieve, they did, in a Sieve they went
   to sea:
In spite of all their friends could say, on a winter's morn,
   on a stormy day,
In a Sieve they went to sea!

Edward Lear, "The Jumblies"

On a gray, blustery Friday afternoon in February 1964, the four young British musicians collectively known as the Beatles arrived on a gleaming Pan American Airways jetliner at Kennedy Airport in New York, where they were met by a crowd of two hundred jostling reporters and photographers and some four thousand fans, mostly teenaged girls, who lined the rooftop observation deck of the airport's International Arrivals Building in a great singing, shrilling mass.

The reporters and photographers were there because, over the preceding three months, news of a phenomenon that had consumed the attention of the British public since the summer before had been drifting across the Atlantic in reports filed by the London bureaus of American newspapers, magazines, and television networks. The British press had coined the term "Beatlemania" to describe the relentless and seemingly hysterical response of that country's teenagers to an indeterminate mixture of musical presence, public personality, and social significance that was projected by this pop group from the port city of Liverpool, whose fresh-faced exuberance and insouciant wit had endeared them to a substantial number of adult Britons as well. Beginning with a smattering of articles in the fall of 1963, early coverage of the Beatles by the American press had been playfully condescending. There were repeated references made to the stereotype of English "eccentricity" and much reliance placed on metaphors of infestation and epidemic: BEATLE BUG BITES BRITAIN read a headline in the show-business weekly *Variety*. The British had gone mad for—of all things—rock 'n' roll.

Rock-'n'-roll hysteria was considered old news in America in 1964.

Most people thought of it as something that had come and gone in the years since Elvis Presley had burst upon the national consciousness in the spring of 1956. By the early 1960s, the pop-singing teen idol had become a cliché epitomized by the character of Conrad Birdie in the 1963 Hollywood musical *Bye Bye Birdie:* a loutish, leering naïf, plucked from obscurity by a cynically manipulative manager and foisted on a needy, worshipful adolescent public. Though nobody had thus far been able to expose the hands that were pulling the strings, the American reporters who were assigned to cover the story took it for granted that "Beatlemania" was another spectacular example, with an unaccountably British twist, of an established promotional technique by which the hormones of pubescent femininity were milked for money and fame.

Having cleared the formalities of Customs and Immigration, the Beatles and their small entourage were escorted into the terminal's press room and grouped around a podium for an impromptu news conference. Uninitiated as to which of these slim, dark-suited figures was which, reporters directed their questions at the group, whose members seemed to vie with one another to come up with the most flippant or outrageous answer. They began by affirming their professionalism with a bluntness that was startling by the prevailing standards of show-business cant. "Won't you *please* sing something?" asked a woman reporter. "No!" said one. "Sorry!" said another. "We need *money* first!" said a third. And away it went from there: "Are you for real?" they were asked. "Come and have a feel." "How many of you are bald, that you have to wear those wigs?" "Oh, we're all bald . . . and deaf and dumb, too." "How do you account for your success?" "We have a press agent." What started as a press conference rapidly devolved into a parody in which the Beatles, speaking in the droll, hooded accents of their native Liverpool, seemed to gather up the banality of the entire proceeding and toss it back good-naturedly in the faces of the New York press. "What do you think of Beethoven?" "We love him—especially the *poems.*" Through it all, the four of them exuded an almost mysterious sense of solidarity and self-possession. They were their own show, and their own audience. Having attracted the sort of attention for which most people in their line of work would be willing to sell their souls, here they were, cracking dumb jokes for their own amusement, calling attention to the mercenary motives of their visit, and generally acting as if it really didn't matter what the newspapers and television stations reported about them after all.

And what of the thousands of fans who squealed on the roof and raced down the corridors and pressed like love-starved orphans against the doors of the room where this curious rite of transatlantic passage was taking place? By and large, their motivations were more complex, and their intentions more honorable, than those of the New York press. They were there because, for the past month, they had been listening to an incessant crescendo of Beatles songs on the radio and buying unprecedented numbers of Beatles records as fast as the group's American label, Capitol Records, could press them and ship them to stores. On the basis of what they had heard in the tough, bluesy rhythms and tender pop melodies of those songs, they were in thrall to a form of passionate enthusiasm that was, for most of them, unlike anything they had ever experienced before.

In a uniquely American gesture of hospitality, the four Beatles were then individually placed into four black Cadillac limousines and driven into midtown Manhattan. As they rode into the city, they listened with amazement to the sound of their own songs blaring forth wherever they turned on the radio dial, interspersed with the disc jockeys' simultaneous accounts of their trip into the city and their approach to the Plaza Hotel on Central Park South.

The Beatles spent their first weekend in New York holed up behind the imposing faux-Renaissance façade of the Plaza, insulated by a thickening blanket of police, press, and fans. "I don't want to talk to them. I just want to stand here and get *images*," announced a reporter from *The Saturday Evening Post*. "I don't want to interview them. I just want their autograph for my managing editor," echoed his colleague from *Life*. In the public square that adjoined the hotel, a crowd of several hundred teenagers maintained a constant vigil, their eyes riveted on the entrance to the Plaza, their backs pressed against the stonework of the Pulitzer Fountain, a gift to the city from the famous newspaper publisher, its granite basins topped by the statue of Pomona, the Roman goddess of abundance. Periodically the Beatles would reward the attention of these sentries by emerging from the hotel on one pretext or another—a photogenic stroll by the boathouse in Central Park, a visit to local night spots like the nearby Playboy Club, a television rehearsal at the CBS studios on Broadway at 53rd Street. Then, on Sunday evening, February 9, the group performed live on *The Ed Sullivan Show*, while an estimated 74 million Americans, or 34 percent of the population, watched from the comfort of their homes. According to the Nielsen rating service, this was the largest audience that had ever been recorded for an American television program. Included in the total was an extremely high percentage of the country's 22 million teenagers.

Looking like the world's most nervous substitute teacher as he faced a studio audience of 1,500 fans, the dour, square-shouldered Sullivan—a man renowned for the awkwardness of his stage presence—introduced the Beatles at the top of the show. Their appearance was greeted by a sustained screech from the audience that one New York television critic likened to the sound of a subway train rounding a curve in the track.

The Beatles went on to perform three songs. Two of these, "All My Loving" and "Till There Was You," were drawn from an album called *Meet the Beatles,* which had sold two million copies in the three weeks since its release. The third song, "She Loves You," had been issued as a single in the United States the previous summer and had sold negligibly at the time. That record now stood at number three on the American charts, two positions behind the Beatles' most recent single, "I Want to Hold Your Hand."

By the time of this performance, most of the material on the two albums and five singles the Beatles had released in Britain over the preceding year was familiar to their American fans. The saturational press coverage had helped to familiarize most teenage viewers with the faces and emblematic personality traits of the individual Beatles as well. (For many adult Americans, by contrast, it would take years to learn to tell them apart). What came as a complete revelation to the budding Beatlemaniacs who first saw them on *The Ed Sullivan Show* was just that: the sight of the group onstage. For the Beatles looked and acted like no performers they had ever seen. The four of them were dressed identically in dark suits, white shirts, and knit ties, the conventionality of which was subverted by the tight fit of their jackets and trousers and the sleek, almost reptilian line of their pointy-toed, Cuban-heeled boots. The band's defining physical feature, however, was the helmetlike profusion of hair that shook and bounced around their faces as they sang, longer and fuller than the hair on any males these kids had ever seen outside of storybook illustrations of the Middle Ages. In addition to the novelty of their physical appearance, another notable feature of the Beatles' performance involved the absence of any obvious leader or focal point. All three of the guitarists not only played but sang, while the two on either side, their guitar necks pointing in opposite directions, shared the lead vocals on the songs. The television cameras reflected this egalitarian arrangement by dividing their attention between shots of the group, shots of its individual members, and shots of the fans in the audience—shrieking, shouting, waving their arms, and careening in their seats. At the end of each number, the Beatles acknowledged the bedlam in the studio by performing a courtly, well-synchronized bow. The final chord of "She Loves You" was followed by the reappearance of a relieved-looking Ed Sullivan, who read a brief benedictory telegram from Elvis Presley before inviting his viewers to partake of "a word from Anacin."

The supporting acts on the program that night included the juvenile cast of *Oliver!*, a hit Broadway musical based on the story of Oliver Twist, and an impressionist named Frank Gorshin, whose routine was based on the then-ludicrous concept of Hollywood stars running for political office. Near the end of the hour-long show, the Beatles returned for two more numbers, "I Saw Her Standing There" and "I Want to Hold Your Hand," the two sides of their current number-one single. The girls in the audience now rewarded themselves for forty minutes of good behavior by completely cutting loose.

The press coverage redoubled on the morning after the broadcast with reviews in all the New York papers and a formal news conference at the Plaza that was likened by *Variety* to a White House briefing. (Capitol Records later claimed that its nationwide clipping service had collected 13,882 newspaper and magazine articles about the Beatles by the end of their two-week stay.) "How did you propose to your wife?" a reporter asked John Lennon, the acknowledged wit of the group, whose wife Cynthia had accompanied him to New York. "The same as anyone else," said Lennon, clearly irritated by the question. "I want to do it right," the reporter insisted. "You want to do it right?" Lennon responded coldly. "Then do it with both hands." Asked if they had found "a leading lady" for their upcoming film, the Beatle named George Harrison replied, "We're trying to get the Queen. She sells." "Obviously, these kids don't give a fig about projecting any sort of proper image," a reporter was heard to say.

On Tuesday a snowstorm forced the Beatles to travel by train to Washington, where they were scheduled to play their first live concert in America and attend a reception in their honor at the British embassy. The concert was held at a sports arena whose centrally located stage required the Beatles to pause after every few songs to physically reorient themselves and their equipment toward another quadrant of the eight thousand screaming participants. The embassy reception was attended by much of the Washington diplomatic corps and marred by an incident involving a scissors-wielding guest and the hair of Ringo Starr. After accepting a flustered apology from the wife of the British ambassador, Ringo turned to her husband and asked, "And what do you do?"

The following day the group returned to New York to play two concerts at Carnegie Hall, where they paid their respects to America's great shrine of classical music by opening their set with Chuck Berry's "Roll Over Beethoven" to the delight of two thousand fans and those members of New York's political, social, and cultural establishment who had the clout to demand and receive tickets. ("I loved it. They were marvelous," said Mrs. Nelson Rockefeller, wife of the governor.)

Next the Beatles flew to Miami Beach, where on Sunday, live from the Napoleon Ballroom of the Deauville Hotel, they performed before another 70 million viewers on *The Ed Sullivan Show.* (This time Sullivan introduced them as "four of the nicest youngsters we've ever had on the show.") Then, after several days of exceedingly well-reported relaxation in the Florida sun, the Beatles flew back to Britain. On American newsstands, their faces filled the covers of *Life, Look,* and *The Saturday Evening Post.* On the American record charts, their music occupied the first and second positions for both singles and albums. (The trade journal *Billboard* later estimated that the Beatles accounted for 60 percent of *all* the singles sold in the United States during the first three months of 1964.) At London's Heathrow Airport, a crowd of ten thousand British patriots turned out at seven o'clock in the morning to afford their heroes the sort of welcome that General Gordon might have received if Gordon had returned from Khartoum.

FOR ALL THAT came after, the events of February 1964 remain to this day the best-known chapter of their well-known story: the Beatles' "conquest" of America, a moment worthy of mention in the most cursory chronicle of the 1960s, preserved for posterity in a set of iconic photographs and grainy black-and-white video images whose familiarity has served, over time, to obscure the sheer *strangeness* of it all. Until this point, the influence of American and European models on their music and fashion sense notwithstanding, the Beatles' lives and their popular phenomenon had been bordered by the bounds of a British world. The outbreak of Beatlemania in Britain had marked the culmination of nearly seven years of self-improvement and self-promotion on their part, in a career that had progressed through distinct stages of success at the local, regional, and national level. Now this same crazed enthusiasm had leaped the borders of Britain to arrive in New York City, the world capital of mass culture and communications, where a state of full-blown pop hysteria had been achieved in five weeks' time, with most of it occurring before the group had set foot on American soil. In Britain the popularity of the Beatles was widely understood to be an expression of social and cultural forces that had been in motion for many years. In America, like princes in a fairy tale, they seemed to awaken some great, slumbering need.

Though the Beatles seemed utterly new to the millions of young people who first saw them perform on *The Ed Sullivan Show* in February 1964, two generations of American adolescents had already bestowed a similar form of frenzied adulation on musical heroes of their own, Frank Sinatra and Elvis Presley. At the first opportunity, both Sinatra and Presley had managed to parlay their initial success as teen idols into extraordinarily lucrative but otherwise conventional show-business careers. After weathering a celebrated "downfall" in the late 1940s, Sinatra went on to establish himself as the preeminent all-around entertainer of his generation: a best-selling recording artist, a major Hollywood movie star, a top-drawing Las Vegas headliner, and a paragon of middle-aged cool. (All told, in a career lasting half a century, he released more than seventy albums and starred in more than fifty films.) On a less artistically acclaimed level, Elvis Presley also assimilated eagerly into the world of conventional show business, making his mark as the best-paid B-movie star in the annals of Hollywood. Earning more than a million dollars a picture, Presley from 1960 onward settled into a numbingly remunerative routine that yielded two or three feature films and two or three best-selling soundtrack albums in every fiscal year. Though he, too, would experience a modest downfall and comeback during the second half of the 1960s, by the time of his death in 1977 he had recorded more than forty albums, released nearly a hundred hit singles, and starred in fifteen films.

With the Beatles, there would be no downfalls or comebacks, no scores of singles and albums, no headlining appearances in Las Vegas, no catalog of Hollywood films. With the Beatles, there would be nothing that could properly be described as a "show business career" at all. While the extent of their commercial success, artistic influence, and enduring popularity would qualify them as one of the greatest phenomena in the history of mass entertainment, by their own insistence they never considered themselves to be "entertainers" in the accepted sense of the word. Instead, February 1964 marked not only the climax of a pop craze, but also the beginning of a remarkable metamorphosis.

Over the next six years, drawing on untold reserves of creativity and ambition, the Beatles would play a leading role in revolutionizing the way that popular records were made, the way that popular records were listened to, the nature of popular songwriting, and the role that popular music itself would play in people's lives. They would preside over the transformation of the music business into the record business, and over the expansion of that business into a branch of the entertainment industry whose international sales and scope would come to rival those of Hollywood.

At the same time, from its frenzied, inchoate beginnings in Britain and the United States, the great upsurge of adolescent fervor that the press called Beatlemania would coalesce into one of the main tributaries of a broad confluence of pop enthusiasm, student activism, and mass bohemianism that would flood the political, social, and cultural landscape of much of the industrialized world during the second half of the 1960s, spinning off whorls and eddies—the women's movement, the gay liberation movement, the environmental movement—in its wake. In a manner that was inconceivable prior to an era when pop stars, film stars, and sports stars began to achieve the sort of fame and exert the sort of influence that had once been reserved for political, military, and religious leaders, the Beatles would serve as prominent symbols, spokesmen, or, as some would have it, avatars of this great international upheaval. Bridging nationalities, classes, and cultures, they became the common property of a generation of young people who idealized them, and then identified powerfully with that idealization of them—even as the Beatles themselves, in their music and their public lives, struggled to deflate those idealizations in an effort to retain their own grip on reality. Through it all, they would demonstrate an uncanny ability to be all things to all people while remaining true to themselves.

Nor would their influence wane. For a few years after the Beatles disbanded in 1970, pop critics tended to downplay their importance and compare their music unfavorably with the ruder styles of rock exemplified by their old rivals, the Rolling Stones. But throughout the 1970s, as each of the former Beatles released solo recordings of his own, a flame of hopeful speculation flickered around the possibility that the four of them would one day reunite and reassert the cultural power they had once wielded with such authority, humor, and grace. John Lennon's murder in 1980 put an end to that hope. (It also turned Lennon into an awkwardly sainted figure: an apostle of Peace and Love who bore little resemblance to the sardonic and mercurial Beatle the world had known.) Still, in the aftermath of that senseless tragedy, with all prospect of a triumphant reunion gone, the Beatles continued to sell vast numbers of their recordings—more than a *billion* at last count. In 2001, thirty years after their demise, a CD reissue of their hit singles sold an unprecedented 13 million copies in the first month of its release. Year after year, decade after decade, young listeners have continued to experience their own personal version of the sense of revelation that first gripped a generation of British and American adolescents in the fall of 1963 and the winter of 1964, while millions of older listeners have continued to experience the Beatles' music as an enriching and benevolent force in their lives. To this day they are widely regarded as the greatest concentration of singing, songwriting, and all-round musical talent that the rock-'n'-roll era has produced.

In February 1964, of course, all of this lay in the future. But, from the beginning, there were several attributes that distinguished the Beatles from anything that had happened in popular music before. The first of these was their nationality. Since the term was first coined in the 1920s, the very concept of a *superstar* had become synonymous with the burgeoning celebrity entertainment culture of the United States, which had colonized the world with its mythos of Broadway, Tin Pan Alley, and Hollywood. The Beatles in 1964 were the first unmistakably non-American performers in any mass medium to achieve the status of superstars on an international scale (unlike, say, Charlie Chaplin, who had lived in Hollywood and played a seminally American character on the screen). As the spearhead of a "British Invasion" of the American music scene, the Beatles posed an unprecedented challenge to the hegemony that America had exerted over the world of popular music (and popular entertainment in general) since the syncopated rhythms of ragtime first captured the fancy of Europe on the eve of World War I.

In mounting this challenge to America's domination of the pop world, the Beatles also succeeded in defying all the prevailing stereotypes of what it meant to be British in 1964—stereotypes that, until the recent dissolution of Britain's far-flung empire, had exerted not only influence but a direct form of political and cultural authority over a quarter of the earth's population. "From the start, the very cut of their limbs, the very glint in their eyes, showed that they were ironically detached from the grandeur of the British past," noted the writer Jan Morris at the time. Youthfulness, stylishness, unpretentiousness, and nonchalance—these were not the qualities the world had come to expect from the familiar and once-intimidating spectacle of Englishmen abroad. Yet by drawing on their origins in the Lancashire seaport of Liverpool, whose polyglot population of ethnic and religious minorities made it the least homogeneously "English" city in all of England, the Beatles personified an iconoclastic version of their national character that proved to be as compelling to the youth of North America, Europe, Australia, and parts of Asia as it was to their British fans.

Another attribute that distinguished the Beatles from the beginning was their identity as a *group:* the first such group in the history of mass entertainment to elicit the sort of romantic fascination and identification that defined the power of a *star.* Like the edge of defiance that Sinatra and Presley brought to their careers, the sense of unity and camaraderie the Beatles projected was rooted in their social origins, and it added an explicitly social dimension to their appeal. Teenagers in particular recognized that, whatever the nature of their professional association, these four young men were indeed a group of friends who had grown up in the same place, shared many of the same experiences, and owed one another the same unspoken loyalty that had bound young men together in groups since time began. From the outset, there was something atavistic about the Beatles' group identity. The most obvious expression of this (apart from their punningly totemic name) was their uniform yet idiosyncratic appearance: the matching clothes and hair that tied them to one another and set them apart from everyone else. Yet the most potent expression of the Beatles' collective nature was ultimately to be found in their music. For, unlike the vast majority of popular recording artists in 1964, the Beatles were not only singers (three of whom sang lead) but collaborative composers and ensemble instrumentalists who wrote their own material and provided their own accompaniment. This was something very different from the nondescript "vocal groups" and hierarchical "harmony groups" that popular music had known. The Beatles were a vision of self-sufficiency, interdependence, and shared ambition that supplied popular music with the archetype of a "rock group," a model of musical organization that would endure for decades to come.

As THE FOCUS of so much interest and appreciation over the last forty years, the Beatles have come to represent a bibliographical phenomenon as well as a musical one. The first real book about them, Michael Braun's astute account of Beatlemania titled *Love Me Do,* appeared in 1964. Since then they have served as the subject of more than five hundred books, running the full gamut of the publishing arts. These include a glut of memoirs by friends, family, and professional associates; multiple biographies of the individual Beatles; transcriptions of their interviews and treasuries of their quotations; anthologies of newspaper and magazine articles; photograph albums by the dozen; diaries of their day-to-day activities; chronicles of their individual recording sessions, concert tours, and even vacation trips; collections and concordances of their song lyrics; volumes of critical commentary and formal musicological analysis; and scrupulously notated scores of their recorded arrangements. There are Beatle encyclopedias, dictionaries, discographies, and at least two book-length bibliographies devoted to making sense of all the other writing about them. This output is all the more remarkable considering that, prior to the Beatles, not a single significant book had been written on the subject of rock 'n' roll.

Given this great effusion of words, it is interesting to note how few full-scale biographies of the Beatles as a group have been published over the years. The first such effort, written at the peak of their popularity in 1968 by the British journalist Hunter Davies, was an "authorized" biography that enjoyed the cooperation of the Beatles, their families, and their manager, Brian Epstein. The virtues of Davies's book included its unassuming style and its unequaled access to the group. As a biography, its main deficiency was that it ended before the Beatles did, leaving the final years of their association undocumented. Davies's work was also slightly compromised by his need to obtain the Beatles' approval of its contents, which led him to avoid or expunge a certain amount of material that was deemed objectionable. These omissions were amply redressed by the next major biography, Philip Norman's *Shout,* which was published in 1981, one year after John Lennon's death. A former colleague of Hunter Davies's at the London *Sunday Times,* Norman filled out the story admirably and carried it through to its end. The tone of his writing was by turns more elegiac and jaded than Davies's, but his approach was essentially the same. Both books relied heavily on extensive (and exclusive) interviews—in Davies's case, with the Beatles and their intimates; in Norman's case, with nearly everyone *but* the Beatles and their intimates. More recently, in 2005, the American journalist Bob Spitz published a compendious biography of the group that revisited many of Norman's sources (who spoke with both the benefit and detriment of hindsight) and further enlarged the picture by drawing on the huge body of published interviews, memoirs, and more-specialized historical sources that has accumulated over the years. All three of these books have reflected the ethos of feature journalism in seeking to penetrate the public image of these very public figures in an effort to reveal the "inside story" of their lives. Among other things, this meant that Davies, Norman, and Spitz devoted comparatively little attention to the Beatles' music; their records, after all, were known to everyone.

Over the last twenty-five years the vast bulk of the biographical writing about the Beatles has focused on the individual members of the group and on specialized aspects of their career. To some extent, this tendency toward individualization and specialization has reflected the way the Beatles' collective identity has made them resistant to the standard biographical treatment. Most biographies tell the story of a person's life from beginning to end. A biography of the Beatles, by contrast, is neither the story of a full life nor the story of a person. It is rather the story of a group of young men whose affiliation began in adolescence and effectively ended before any of them had reached the age of thirty. It is a story that defies individualization and, as a result, places more importance on the qualities the four of them shared than on the qualities that made them distinct.

This is a book about the Beatles, Britain, and America in the twenty-five years after World War II. It is drawn from widely diverse sources of information and imagination, and it seeks to combine three main perspectives—the biographical, the musical, and the historical—in an effort to convey the full import and interplay of the Beatles' lives, art, and times.

The first strand of the story—the biographical—comprises the narrative of their career, beginning with their individual childhoods and their collective adolescence in postwar Liverpool, and ending with their breakup in 1970. It is, by any measure, a remarkable success story, which has been told and retold so often that it has come to resemble a modern folktale. Like a folktale, it has been put to many different uses by its many different narrators. The goal in recounting it here again is to do so as vividly and accurately as possible, clearing away the ephemeral, the apocryphal, and the merely anecdotal in order to focus on what can truly be known about the lives of four people whose overnight success caused them to pass from obscurity to ubiquity with little transition in between. Here especially, this book benefits from the tremendous amount of material about the Beatles that has been published over the last twenty years. That a great deal of this information is contradictory, implausible, or, in some cases, simply incredible has required that none of it be taken at face value; instead, every assertion has been assessed for its plausibility and its concurrence with other accounts. Particular attention has been paid to the reliability of sources, since the many retellings of the Beatles' story do not lack for unreliable, self-serving, or reflexively revisionist narrators. In keeping with the conventional wisdom of writing about the past, greater weight has been given to primary sources and contemporary accounts than to memoirs and recollections—including those of the Beatles themselves. (As Paul McCartney once remarked, "I keep seeing pictures of myself shaking hands with Mitzi Gaynor [a minor celebrity of the time] and I think, 'I didn't know I met her.' It's that vague.")

The second strand of the story centers on the Beatles' music. This is an account of their early musical awakenings, idols, and influences, their apprenticeship as singers and accompanists in the clubs of Liverpool and Hamburg, their precocious flowering as songwriters, and their extraordinarily rapid and dynamic evolution as recording artists from 1963 onward. From the Beatles' perspective, this is closest thing to the "inside story" of their lives. For while their fans, the press, and the public may often have wanted to see them as something else or something more, it was always as musicians that the Beatles saw themselves. Music was the passion that linked them to one another and brought them to the attention of the world, and from 1960 to 1970, more than any other activity, music was what they *did*. This strand of the story also involves the many ways that millions of listeners, including fans, critics, and fellow artists, responded to the Beatles' music: what people experienced at their live performances and heard in the songs on their records, and how it was that they related this music to their own lives. An added virtue of putting the Beatles' music at the center of their story is that the relevant materials—the eleven albums and twenty-three singles they recorded between 1962 and 1969, containing their definitive performances of 182 original songs—are so readily available to listeners and readers, sounding just as they did at the time.

The third and broadest perspective of this book focuses on what might be termed "the real outside story." This comprises the social and cultural background, the conditions and developments that shaped the lives of the Beatles and determined the part they played in the history of their times. The years of their story coincided with a period of rampant social and cultural change in Britain and America, and throughout the industrialized world. In Britain this transformation began with the election in 1945 of a Labour government committed to dismantling the British Empire, reforming the British class system, and providing for the health and education of the populace through the creation of a socialist "welfare state." It continued during the 1950s with the efforts of Conservative governments to promote the growth of an American-style consumer economy stimulated by the enticements of an American-style consumer culture; and it culminated during the 1960s with the emergence of London as a world capital of pop culture, ruled by an unruly elite of former "war babies" who were bent on taking their country's new climate of expressive freedom to once unimaginable extremes. The Beatles began as creatures of this new social and cultural milieu; they wound up serving as the most prominent symbols of it for people all over the world.

The years of their story also coincided with a technological revolution, paced by advances in the field of electronics, that would transform the nature of everyday life during the second half of the twentieth century as dramatically as the utilization of electricity had transformed the nature of life during the first half of the century. To cite some obvious examples: the passenger jets on which the Beatles traveled to America, the long-playing records they sold in such profusion, and television shows like the one that allowed 74 million people to view them simultaneously from the comfort of their homes—all were freshly minted products of the postwar world. Tape recording, FM radio, and electrified musical instruments—these, too, were recent innovations whose creative potential remained largely unexplored. To a considerable extent, the Beatles' ability to exert a new form of cultural power would turn on their ability to capitalize on these new technologies, and on the consolidation of these new technologies into a new kind of parallel universe, combining information, entertainment, and commercial advertising, that ordinary people first began referring to during the early 1960s as "the media."

Finally, the years of the Beatles' story coincided with the historic shift in Anglo-American relations precipitated by World War II, when the leading imperialist nation of the nineteenth century conclusively yielded its power and influence to the leading internationalist nation of the twentieth century. In 1939, Britain still ruled over the greatest sovereign empire the world had ever known, and the British people retained a sense of their country (whatever else they may have thought about it) as the most powerful nation on earth. In 1939 the United States remained a country still preoccupied with its own internal development and its recent efforts to recover from the disastrous social and economic consequences of the Great Depression. Within ten years everything had changed. Now Britain—its cities scarred, its wealth depleted, and its vitality sapped by the war—was turning its gaze inward as it abdicated its status as a Great Power, while the United States, its economy booming, its confidence bursting, had triumphantly assumed the mantle of world leadership.

This historic reversal of fortune transformed not only the political relationship between the two great English-speaking nations, but the unique cultural relationship between them as well. Throughout the first half of the twentieth century, unimpeded by the need for translation, the dynamic and democratic sensibility of American popular culture had exerted a powerful influence on the imaginative lives of the British people, with American styles and American products dominating the British market for music and films. The Beatles themselves were a product of this influence, which intensified sharply in the years after World War II. But the democratization of postwar British society had given rise to a new generation of young people who were no longer content merely to watch and listen, and were now prepared to participate in this popular culture on their own terms. Just as Britain had once bequeathed one of the world's great literary traditions to America, where it became infused with the native genius of writers like Poe and Wharton and Twain, America was now bequeathing one of the world's great musical traditions to Britain, where a tight little band of young Liverpudlians stood ready to infuse that tradition with a native genius of their own.

1

Now, you've got to keep in mind that Elvis Presley was probably, innately, the most introverted person that came into that studio. Because he didn't play with bands. He didn't go to this little club and pick and grin. All he did was sit with his guitar on the side of his bed at home.

—Sam Phillips

"Well since my baby left me . . ." The voice, unaccompanied but for the tinny flourish of piano that anchors the end of each line, was somehow bigger and riper with feeling than any voice its young listeners had ever heard. "Well I found a new place to *dwell* . . ." It projected an authority and an insolence that reached beyond the words themselves, and it came from a place beyond the realm of "entertainment" as they had ever conceived of the term. Now joined by a doomstruck bass line, the sound of that voice seemed only to grow larger and more menacing, yet closer and more confiding as well, as if—given the lurching slow-dance tempo of the music—the singer's lips were pressed tight against the ear of the girl he now began to address, his words expressing a vengeful wish to make her feel the same way he was feeling in his room at the Heartbreak Hotel: "So lonely I could *die.*" Though such things had been said since time immemorial in the lives of ordinary people; and though similar expressions of such dire emotion could be found in a growing number of avowedly realistic novels, plays, and films; and though something very much like it had been available for years on the sorts of records that most people never heard (including earlier, more obscure records by this same singer)—the fact remained that no man had ever sounded this way, or spoken this way to a woman, in front of so many millions of listeners before.

Elvis Presley was the catalyst, not the originator, of the phenomenon called rock 'n' roll. Three years before he made his first recordings, the term was being promoted by a Cleveland disc jockey named Alan Freed as a race-neutral pseudonym for the black rhythm and blues that Freed began beaming across a wide swath of the North American continent in

1951. In 1954, the year that Freed moved his radio show, "Moondog's Rock 'n' Roll Party," to New York City, a white band singer named Bill Haley (himself a former disc jockey) recorded a pair of songs on the Decca label, one a novelty tune with a snappy tick-tock rhythm called "Rock Around the Clock," the other a sanitized "cover" version of a current rhythm-and-blues hit by Joe Turner called "Shake, Rattle and Roll." "Rock Around the Clock" failed to catch on at first, but Haley's pallid rendition of "Shake, Rattle and Roll" became a hit record, rising into the *Billboard* Top Ten in the fall of 1954. The following year, "Rock Around the Clock" was featured on the soundtrack of a film called *Blackboard Jungle*—one of a spate of Hollywood movies designed to exploit the rising tide of public anxiety about juvenile delinquency in America. Placed in a suitably inflammatory context, the song caught fire, reaching number one on the pop charts in the summer of 1955, turning the chubby, thirtyish, tartan-jacketed Haley into the world's first rock-'n'-roll star.

In the meantime, legend has it, an eighteen-year-old delivery truck driver named Elvis Aron Presley sauntered into the storefront offices of Sam Phillips's Memphis Recording Service in the summer of 1953 to make an acetate of a song called "My Happiness" as a birthday present for his mom. (That Gladys Presley was born in the spring only burnishes the myth.) Sam Phillips, who operated his studio in conjunction with a small independent record label called Sun, had concerned himself to date with recording such talented Memphis-area bluesmen as Howlin' Wolf and B.B. King. Elvis at first made little impression on him. But Elvis made enough of a pest of himself in the months ahead that Phillips eventually called up an aspiring guitarist he knew named Scotty Moore and asked him to work with the boy. In July of 1954, Presley, Moore, and a bassist named Bill Black came in for a recording test. Sam Phillips asked Elvis what he liked to sing. Elvis, it turned out, liked to sing most anything. He sang country songs in a keening tenor reminiscent of Bill Monroe, and pop ballads in a woozy baritone reminiscent of Dean Martin. Phillips started him out on a ballad, "I Love You Because." The performance, like that of nearly every ballad Presley would ever record, was cloying and overdrawn. Then, during a break in the session, Elvis began to fool around with a blues song he knew called "That's All Right"; Moore and Black fell in behind him, and Phillips rolled the tape.

Of the many astonishing things about Elvis Presley, nothing is more astonishing than the fact that Elvis "never did sing anywhere in public" (outside of a couple of high school talent shows) before he started making records with Sam Phillips at Sun. For all its romantic associations with dance halls and honky-tonks, rock 'n' roll was born and reared as the child of records and radio. That the prime exponent of this new style of music should be a singer who possessed no prior professional experience was an anomaly; but it was also a telling sign of the way that record-making would change the very nature of music-making in the years ahead. Presley's inexperience was all the more astonishing in light of the opinion held by many of his fans that he would never sound much better on a record than he did on "That's All Right." Not only were most of the mannerisms that would define his vocal style present at the creation—from the sudden swoops in register to the habit, derived from gospel singing, of starting his lines with a throat-clearing "well" that gave whatever followed the feeling of a retort; even more impressive was the extent to which his first professional recording was marked by the trait that has characterized every great popular singer: the absolute assertion of his personality over the song. From this it might be concluded that Presley was simply a "natural." But the truth, as ever, was more complex than that.

For one thing, the recording Elvis made with Sam Phillips on that hot summer night in Memphis was made in a manner that would not have been technically possible only a few years before. Up through the end of the 1940s, commercial recording had relied upon a "direct to disc" process that was essentially a reversal of what happened when a record was played on a phonograph: the sound in the studio was converted first into electrical signals by a microphone and then into mechanical impulses by a stylus, which cut a sinuous groove in the surface of a spinning wax or acetate disc. Though this method offered audio engineers little opportunity to edit or enhance the finished product, it was quite adequate to a philosophy of recording whose main goal was to produce as accurate a *record* as possible of the performance taking place. An alternative technology, involving the use of magnetized wire, had been around for decades, but it was not until World War II that German engineers (working on behalf of Nazi propagandists) developed an efficient means of recording sound on reels of magnetic tape. After the war, this new technology was quickly refined, and by the early 1950s it had all but replaced the direct-to-disc process.

Tape recording revolutionized record-making in several ways. On a purely economic level, tape equipment was so affordable, portable, and easy to operate that small storefront recording studios sprang up in cities and towns across the United States. Many of the people who operated these studios had backgrounds in commercial radio, and it wasn't long before they grew restless producing audio keepsakes of weddings and award ceremonies and began to think about trying their hand in the record business—drawing, like Sam Phillips, on the talent in their immediate area. A chain reaction occurred: tape spawned the storefront studios, the storefront studios spawned the independent labels, and the independent labels, by specializing in types of music the major labels (for various geographic, demographic, and aesthetic reasons) tended to ignore, spawned a record boom. This boom combined with a comparable trend toward decentralization and diversification in the radio broadcasting industry (caused by the advent of television) to propel the American music business into the Atomic Age.

Tape technology did more than decentralize the recording industry, however; it also helped to democratize record-making by adding a new kind of informality and flexibility to the recording process itself. The big commercial studios in New York and Los Angeles were owned by large corporations and run on a cost-effective basis that equated time with money. They relied on a professionalized cadre of engineers, arrangers, and sidemen who prided themselves, above all, on their efficiency. By comparison with these record factories, the owner-operators of storefront studios had a lot of free time on their hands—time to tinker with their equipment, audition and rehearse prospective talent, and, in the case of Sam Phillips, time to coax a historic performance out of a malleable young singer who had never sung in public before. What came to life in the course of that first Sun session was an entirely new vocal personality, as surprising to its creator as it would be to everyone else. "I never sang like [that] in my whole life until I made that record," Presley said later. Awed by the capacity of modern recording technology to enhance the sound of their voices, something similar would happen to a great many other young, unformed singers—including the boys who became the Beatles—in the years ahead.

Sun Records released "That's All Right" as a single in August 1954. Paired with an equally eclectic version of Bill Monroe's "Blue Moon of Kentucky" on its flip side, the record caused an immediate commotion on the radio in Memphis and sold enough copies to qualify as a local hit. In the year that followed, it was succeeded by four more Presley singles on Sun: "Good Rockin' Tonight," "Milkcow Blues Boogie," "Baby Let's

Play House," and "Mystery Train." All were blues that had previously been recorded by black artists; all were performed in the hybrid "rockabilly" style of "That's All Right"; and all were paired with country songs on their flip sides. Together with a weekly spot on the *Louisiana Hayride* radio show and live appearances at high school dances and county fairs throughout the South, these records established Elvis Presley as a regional sensation by the end of 1955. Yet the modest success of these singles—none of which prior to "Mystery Train" sold more than 25,000 copies—put Sam Phillips in a bind. Independent labels like Sun were dependent on a network of wholesale distributors who only paid for the records they handled if and when they sold. This meant that Phillips was constantly strapped for cash to pay for the pressing and promotion of a product whose cost he could only hope to recoup several months down the line. By the end of 1955, Presley's success in the South had drawn a whole pride of hillbilly cats to the Sun label—singers like Carl Perkins, Jerry Lee Lewis, and Johnny Cash—any one of whom, Phillips believed, could do what Elvis had done. So when RCA Victor offered him the princely sum of $35,000 for Presley's contract, Phillips jumped at the chance. The deal was brokered by a former carnival barker, pet-cemetery operator, and country music impresario named "Colonel" Tom Parker who was gradually assuming command of Presley's business affairs.

As one of the half-dozen major labels that dominated the American record market in 1955, RCA had a country music division based in Nashville. The label turned Elvis over to its Nashville production staff and in January 1956 he recorded "Heartbreak Hotel." Its release was coordinated with a series of appearances on network television shows that exposed the American public to the provocative visual image that complemented Presley's provocative musical style: the infamous pelvic gyrations, the outlandish clothes and pompadoured hair, the hurting eyes and the lopsided grin, poised between a leer and a sneer, that functioned as a kind of generational Rorschach test. The effect of this television exposure was overwhelming. "Heartbreak Hotel" vaulted to the top of the *Billboard* charts in April and held there throughout the spring. Over the next eighteen months, by never failing to have a record or two in the American Top Ten, Elvis Presley would completely redefine the amount of attention that a twenty-one-year-old white boy from a place like Tupelo, Mississippi, could expect to receive from the world.

As a matter of course, RCA offered "Heartbreak Hotel" to EMI, the major British label with which it enjoyed a reciprocal licensing deal. Released in May 1956, the record was an immediate hit in Britain, where its popularity was all the more remarkable for the fact that it received little direct airplay on BBC radio, which preferred to broadcast live renditions of current releases by in-house studio bands. This meant that Presley's performance of "Heartbreak Hotel"—the only performance that mattered—was first heard mainly on the jukeboxes of dance halls and coffee bars and on the nightly English-language broadcasts of Radio Luxembourg, a clear-channel commercial station that provided the youth of Britain with a service comparable to that of Radio Free Europe in reverse. It was five hundred miles from Luxembourg to Liverpool, but on most nights the signal carried tolerably well, accompanied by just enough static to enhance the aura of mystery that surrounded rock 'n' roll. Thirteen years after the release of "Heartbreak Hotel," a leading theorist of mass communications asked a leading practitioner of mass communications how he got his start. "I heard Elvis Presley," John Lennon told Marshall McLuhan. "There were a lot of other things going on, but that was the conversion. I kind of dropped everything."

THE SAME MONTH that "Heartbreak Hotel" entered the British Top Ten, John Osborne's play *Look Back in Anger* opened at the Royal Court Theater in London, marking the theatrical debut of a literary sensibility that would henceforth be known by the catchphrase "Angry Young Men." *Look Back in Anger* confronted its audiences with a new kind of English protagonist. "He is a disconcerting mixture of sincerity and cheerful malice, of tenderness and free-booting cruelty," John Osborne wrote of his character Jimmy Porter. "To some he may seem sensitive to the point of vulgarity. To others he is simply a loudmouth." Set in a shabby, one-room flat in an unnamed Midlands town, the play consists largely of Jimmy's sardonic tirades against the deadness and complacency of contemporary English life. He directs these outbursts at his timid wife, Alison, who irons while he rants, and at his best friend, Cliff, whose periodic pleas for peace and quiet set Jimmy off anew, since peace and quiet is the very thing that Jimmy is railing against. "It's such a long time since I was with *anyone* who got enthusiastic about *anything!*" he shouts in the opening act. "Nobody thinks. Nobody cares. No convictions, no beliefs, and no *enthusiasm!*" Over the course of the play, it emerges that this bilious character is the product of a middle-class mother and a working-class father (who died when Jimmy was ten); that he attended a provincial university, where he played the trumpet in a Dixieland jazz band; and that after trying his hand at journalism and advertising, he now prefers to scrape out a living by running a sweet stall in the town market, presumably out of contempt for the concessions he would have to make to get on in the middle-class world. His Oxford-educated wife is the symbol of that world; she is the daughter of a retired Indian Army colonel who left England on the eve of the First World War and didn't return until the end of the Second—a "sturdy old plant left over from the Edwardian Wilderness" whom Jimmy professes to despise but secretly rather likes. Embittered by the efforts of Alison's family to discourage their marriage, Jimmy treats his wife "like a hostage from those sections of society [he's] declared war on."

The dramatic impact of *Look Back in Anger* stemmed from the defiant authenticity of Jimmy's personality and the sheer abusiveness of his tirades, which exposed English playgoers to a type of strong language and bad behavior they had previously learned to associate with American drama and films. As such, the play was perceived as a frontal assault on the essential gentility (defined by one critic as the "belief that life is always more or less orderly, people always more or less polite, their emotions more or less decent and more or less controllable") that had prevailed in English literary culture since the end of World War I. John Osborne and his director, Tony Richardson, were strongly influenced by the work of Tennessee Williams, and Jimmy Porter (as played by the actor Kenneth Haigh) came off as a kind of anglicized Marlon Brando character, his verbal aggression analogous to the physical aggression Brando brought to the role of Stanley Kowalski in *A Streetcar Named Desire*.

The wider cultural impact of *Look Back in Anger* stemmed from the understanding that Jimmy Porter represented a new kind of social, as well as theatrical, type—an understanding facilitated by the Angry Young Man designation, which was applied by the press to the playwright and his character alike. "The salient thing about Jimmy Porter," wrote the critic Kenneth Tynan, "was that we—the under-thirty generation in Britain—recognized him on sight. We had met him; we had pub-crawled with him; we had shared bed-sitting-rooms with him. For the first time the theatre was speaking to us in our own language, on our own terms." Tynan went on to describe Jimmy as a spokesman for "the new intelligentsia created by free education and state scholarships . . . young

Britons who came of age under a Socialist government, yet found, when they went out into the world, that the class-system was still mysteriously intact." *Look Back in Anger* helped to turn the phenomenon of the working-class "scholarship boy" into a national talking point.

As an attack upon complacency and an expression of disillusionment among the educated young, the work of the Angry writers in Britain—a group that included, in addition to Osborne, the playwrights Arnold Wexler and Harold Pinter and the novelists Alan Sillitoe and John Braine—showed clear similarities to the work of the Beat writers in America. (A popular paperback anthology of the period was in fact predicated on the link between *The Beat Generation and the Angry Young Men*.) Notwithstanding his astonishing lack of cool, Jimmy Porter with his jazz trumpet and his verbal lust for life was the closest thing in Britain to the sort of existential hipster that embodied the Beat ideal: "mad to live, mad to talk, mad to be saved," as Jack Kerouac defined it in *On the Road*. Among the meaningful parallels between the Angries and the Beats was the tendency of both groups to extol a form of authenticity that was not only young and disaffected but also categorically *male*. Like the women in Kerouac's novels, the women in Osborne's plays exist purely as foils for the personalities of the men.

Considering the simultaneity of their arrival in the public eye, it would seem a short step from the defiant lower-class masculinity of Jimmy Porter to that of Elvis Presley, who didn't have to go to a university to learn how to use women as a foil for *his* personality. Yet in Britain at the time— as in America, where *Look Back in Anger* enjoyed a successful run on Broadway the following year—these two vivid cultural protagonists were seen to inhabit totally separate worlds. However great his admiration for the vitality of postwar American theater and prewar American jazz, John Osborne shared with most British writers, artists, and intellectuals of his day—young or old, angry or not—a disdain for such vulgar manifestations of American popular culture as rock 'n' roll. As yet, what Kenneth Tynan called "the new intelligentsia" was no more capable than the old of grasping the cultural affinities between Stanley Kowalski and Elvis Presley, or, for that matter, between "St. James Infirmary" and "Heartbreak Hotel."

"HEARTBREAK HOTEL" AND *Look Back in Anger* were only two of the cultural milestones that made 1956 a signal year in Britain, the sort of year that journalists and historians like to evoke by name: "the first moment in history after the Second World War," wrote one, "about which there is anything like a persistent myth." At the core of that myth, linking a great confluence of events and influences, was a coming-to-terms with the political, economic, and cultural imperatives of the new American Age. "The social revolution of 1945, though profound, took ten years to show its effects on spending," wrote the journalist Anthony Sampson. "Then, within two years, the credit squeeze ended, skyscrapers rushed up, supermarkets spread over cities, newspapers became fatter or died, commercial television began making millions. . . . After the big sleep many people welcomed any novelty, [and] any piece of Americanization seemed an enterprising change." Some signs of this "Americanization" were obvious, such as the fervid public welcomes given to visiting celebrities like the evangelist Billy Graham and the film star Marilyn Monroe. Others were more subtle, even furtive, like the theme of an art exhibition called "This Is Tomorrow" that opened in London in the summer of 1956, presenting work by a pair of artists, Richard Hamilton and Eduardo Paolozzi, whose mutual fascination with the hyperbolic aesthetics of American mass culture would eventually earn them recognition as two of the founding fathers of Pop Art.

For the average Briton, however, the most ubiquitous source of American influence emanated nightly from the jingle and jabber of commercial television, which came on the air in the fall of 1955, feeding its viewers a steady diet of American-made or American-inspired westerns, quiz shows, and crime dramas; subjecting a population long insulated by the government ban on commercial broadcasting to the full force of American-style advertising and its attendant consumer ideology. Within five years, three-quarters of all British households would possess a tiny window on the American Way of Life. To the despair of many intellectuals, this flood tide of American influence was embraced with seemingly boundless enthusiasm by the British populace. "The most compelling social characteristic of the British people today," wrote Alistair Cooke in the *Manchester Guardian,* "is not the wide gamut of native qualities and habits but the greater range of American habits, customs, and conventions they seem to have incorporated, without complaint, since the war." "There was a tremendous romance about America," recalled the novelist Ray Gosling. "America was the place we all wanted to be."

2

> I was bored on the 9th of Octover 1940 when, I believe,
> the Nasties were still booming us led by Madalf Heatlump
> (who only had one). Anyway, they didn't get me. I
> attended to varicous schools in Liddypol. And still didn't
> pass—much to my Aunties supplies.
>
> —John Lennon

In all but name, the Beatles began with the friendship of John Lennon and Paul McCartney, who met in July 1957 at a garden fête at St. Peter's Church in the Liverpool suburb of Woolton, where Lennon's skiffle group, the Quarry Men, had been invited to perform. There was a photograph taken of the Quarry Men that day. It shows a six-piece group—two guitars, banjo, washboard, tea-chest bass, and drums—standing on a low outdoor stage, surrounded by a crowd of young children. Five of the players are hunched over their instruments, oblivious to the camera. Alone at the microphone, dressed in his favorite plaid shirt, a tousle-haired sixteen-year-old John Lennon stares intently into the lens.

John Winston Lennon was indeed born in Liverpool in October 1940, the first and only child of Alfred and Julia Lennon, who had known each another casually for more than ten years and had been married, also rather casually, for two. Five feet four inches tall and twenty-seven years old at the time, Alf Lennon was a self-styled charmer and man of the world. As the youngest of five sons in an Irish Protestant family, he had been placed by his mother in Liverpool's Bluecoat Orphanage after his father died when he was nine. Since leaving the orphanage in 1927, he had worked as a busboy, waiter, and steward on the Atlantic passenger lines. Julia Lennon (or Julie as she was called) was two years his junior—the pretty, free-spirited daughter of George Stanley, a former marine salvage inspector, and his wife Annie, whose family came from Wales. The Stanleys considered themselves to be a respectable lower-middle-class family, and they thoroughly disapproved of Julia's choice in men.

Accounts differ as to how Alf Lennon came to be absent from Liverpool at the time of his son's birth. Alf's version was a stirring tale that began with his being stranded in New York at the start of World War II, interned for a spell on Ellis Island, pressed into service on a freighter bound for North Africa, falsely accused of pilfering liquor from the ship's stores, and unjustly sentenced to a term in jail—although somewhere in this saga he must have returned to Liverpool to play his part in the conception of his son, since possibly the only thing about Alf that was never in doubt was his paternity of John. The Stanley family's version of Alf's absence was somewhat more prosaic. It was always their contention that he simply ran away to sea. As for John Lennon's impression that the Luftwaffe was attendant at his birth, this portentous piece of Stanley family lore (later embellished by John's aunt Mimi with exploding parachute mines) is contradicted by every reliable account of the blitz in Liverpool. But together with Alf's version of his war experiences, it does suggest that a talent for self-dramatization ran strong in both bloodlines.

With Alf away at sea, Julia lived with her recently widowed father on a block of terraced houses on the south side of Liverpool, in the area known as Penny Lane. She cared for her child with the help of her four sisters, the eldest of whom, Mary, known in the family as Mimi, took a special interest in John. In 1944, Julia had a fling with a Welsh soldier that resulted in the birth of a daughter, Victoria, who was quickly put up for adoption and never heard from again. A year later, Julia took up with a man named Bobby Dykins and sent John to live with Mimi and her husband, George Smith, who had no children of their own. Though members of the Dykins family would later maintain that John was in fact *taken* by Mimi with the help of the local child-welfare authorities, there is nothing to suggest that either Julia or her new boyfriend, who worked as a hotel waiter, had any compelling interest in caring for her son. Not long after John moved in with the Smiths, however, in the summer of 1946, Alf Lennon showed up out of the blue and announced his intention of taking the boy on a holiday to Blackpool. Uncertain of her say in the matter, Mimi let them go. When Alf failed to return with John on the appointed day, Julia followed them to Blackpool and a traumatic scene ensued. According to Alf (who later recounted this story without a hint of shame), he told his five-year-old son to choose between accompanying his mother back to Liverpool or going "to New Zealand" with him. After a moment of hesitation, John opted for Liverpool, and returned to live with the Smiths. Though they never actually married, Julia and Bobby Dykins soon started a family of their own, and John saw his mother "sporadically" during the rest of his childhood years. Alf Lennon remained a model of parental discretion: John would be a millionaire before he heard from his father again.

George and Mimi Smith lived in a pleasant, four-bedroom, semi-detached house called "Mendips" on Menlove Avenue in Woolton, where George's family owned and operated a commercial dairy. (Prior to their marriage in 1939, Mimi had worked as a nurse in a convalescent hospital and as a private secretary to a Liverpool businessman.) Situated on gently rolling land about five miles southeast of the city center, Woolton was regarded as an upscale suburb; along with the neighboring areas of Allerton and Childwell, it had been incorporated into the city some forty years before, and parts of it retained a decidedly rural character. Though it fronted on a busy road, the Smiths' house was surrounded by fields and woods. The Allerton Municipal Golf Course lay directly across Menlove Avenue; down the street was Calderstones Park (so named for its druidic relics) with its boating pond and tennis greens. The neighborhood was dotted with grand old houses that had been built during the 1800s as the country estates of Liverpool's merchant class and converted during the 1900s to institutional use.

Living in Woolton, married to a man who owned his own business and home, Mimi Smith was the soul of lower-middle-class propriety, and her nephew, from the age of five, was brought up in material circumstances that were more than comfortable by the austere standards of postwar Liverpool. John seems to have found some measure of emotional security as well with Mimi and George. In the realm of daily life, he treated them as his parents and they treated him as their son. (As a child, John took after the Stanley side of the family, and his resemblance to Mimi was strong.) Yet the subject of John's real parents, and particularly Alf Lennon, was rarely if ever discussed. George Smith has remained something of a mystery, remembered by John and his childhood friends as a kindly, rather retiring figure who encouraged John's artistic interests and served as his ally on the domestic front. Mimi Smith was very much the matriarch, not only of her own household, but of the extended Stanley family as well. She was strong-willed, sharp-tongued, acutely class-conscious, and fiercely devoted to John.

A month before his sixth birthday, John entered the Dovedale Road Primary School, where he came to be seen as an intelligent, domineering child distinguished by his love of drawing and wordplay and his talents as a ringleader. Mimi Smith was an avid reader, and John grew up in a household filled with "Wilde and Whistler and Fitzgerald and all the Book of the Month Club stuff my auntie had around." By the time he was nine, he was well-read in the classics of children's literature, and much of his imaginative life was taken up with books. Like many future writers and artists, he started a personal magazine, *Sport, Speed & Illustrated,* which he filled with stories, sketches, and bits of whimsical verse. His favorite literary characters were Lewis Carroll's Alice and Richmal Crompton's William. John spent many hours copying the illustrations in Carroll's *Alice* books, writing doggerel in the style of "Jabberwocky," and fancying himself the embodiment of Crompton's archetypal English schoolboy, William Brown.

Anyone who doubts the capacity of life to imitate art would do well to consider John Lennon's identification with the young hero of *Just William* (first published in 1922) and its twenty-odd sequels—an incorrigible eleven-year-old who lives with his family in a quiet English village (not so different from Woolton) whose peace is shattered regularly by William and his gang, the Outlaws, comprising Douglas, Henry, and Ginger. With the ironclad consistency of a successful literary formula, each of William's adventures turns on a fundamental misunderstanding, usually stemming from the fact that he sees things differently from the grown-ups in his life. (He also hears things differently: "She's a real Botticelli!" one of his sister's suitors tells him. "Bottled cherry yourself!" is the boy's indignant reply.) By the time John himself attained the age of eleven, he had thoroughly assimilated William's incredulous disdain for the ways of the adult world. He had also assembled his own band of Outlaws, made up of three boys from his neighborhood named Pete Shotton, Nigel Whalley, and Ivan Vaughan. Their weekly adventures ranged from patrolling the woods and parks of Woolton to petty theft, minor vandalism, and other boyhood rites.

In 1952, John passed his "eleven-plus" entry examination and was admitted to the Quarry Bank Grammar School, which lay on the far side of Calderstones Park, a mile from his home. Placed in the A-stream of his class on the basis of his test results, he proved from the beginning a recalcitrant grammar-school boy. "He did not share in what we set out to do," his headmaster would recall—so much so that by his third year at Quarry Bank, John had descended to the bottom of the B-stream of his class and developed a reputation, along with his sidekick Pete Shotton (the only other Outlaw to accompany him to the school), as a seriously disruptive influence, the subject of frequent detentions and canings.

In the summer of 1955, when John was fourteen, his uncle George died suddenly of a liver hemorrhage at the age of fifty-two. John was visiting with his aunt Elizabeth in Scotland at the time, and though he showed little outward reaction, he was strongly affected by the death of his surrogate father. In the following term at Quarry Bank, his grades and his behavior went from bad to worse. By now his troubles at school were a source of constant tension between Mimi and him. Shaken by the death of her husband, Mimi was deeply embarrassed by the misconduct of a boy she had worked so hard to bring up right. Even more than most parents would have, Mimi saw John's adolescence as a battle between the forces of Nurture, as represented by herself, and Nature, as represented by the long-lost father whose face John's face resembled more with every passing day. It was at this critical juncture that John's mother, Julia, reentered his life.

Throughout John's years in Woolton, Julia, Bobby Dykins, and their two young daughters had been living nearby on a council-house estate in Allerton. John saw his mother at Stanley family gatherings, but there wasn't much casual contact between them until after George Smith's death, which seems to have had the effect of drawing Mimi and Julia closer together. Though John resented Bobby Dykins (whom he referred to as "Twitchy"), he now became fascinated by Julia, and she by him. The basis on which they renewed their relationship was not that of a mother and a son. Instead, John regarded this flighty, funny, flirtatious woman as more of "a young aunt or a big sister" to him. For her part, Julia had lived in the shadow of Mimi's disapproval for most of her adult life; now that John seemed intent on joining her there, she welcomed his company and offered a sympathetic ear. From the fall of 1955 onward, John became an increasingly frequent guest in the Dykins household, stopping off on his way home from school and staying the night on weekends. One of the things he shared with Julia—who loved to sing and could play a bit of banjo—was a taste for rock 'n' roll.

THOUGH ALL FOUR of the Beatles would date their serious interest in music from the epiphany of "Heartbreak Hotel," it took a more familiar, less intimidating figure than Elvis Presley to convince the youth of Britain that strumming guitars and singing the blues were things they themselves could do. Enter Anthony "Lonnie" Donegan, a frantic, nasal Scot who burst upon the scene in 1956 singing perhaps the world's worst version of the American folk song "Rock Island Line." Prior to this sudden emergence, Donegan had been the banjo player in the Chris Barber Band, one of Britain's foremost exponents of "traditional" New Orleans jazz. In the early fifties, the Barber band began to cater to the growing curatorial interest in the history of jazz by playing a short set of "skiffle" or jug-band music as a prelude to its faithful renditions of classic Dixieland. Skiffle was touted as an indigenous Southern folk music, played in a rag-tag manner on makeshift instruments, a variant of which was supposedly still performed by young panhandlers on the hallowed streets of Memphis and New Orleans. This made it a presumed progenitor of jazz and fair game for the purists in the Barber band. In 1954, with Donegan singing in a shrill tenor and breathlessly strumming a guitar, the group recorded several of these deliberately primitive arrangements. In January 1956, Decca Records released one of those tracks, "Rock Island Line," as a single under Donegan's name. The record became a hit, peaking at number eight on the pop charts. But what really caught the attention of British teenagers was its success in the United States, where "Rock Island Line" became one of the few British-made records of the decade to reach the Top Ten.

The sole redeeming feature of skiffle was that it was a form of music so artless that it planted the thought "I could do *that*" in the minds of adolescents throughout the British Isles. Donegan's mediocrity was a living inspiration, and over the second half of 1956, as skiffle groups formed by the dozens in every British town, merchandisers flooded the market with "genuine" washboards, tea-chest bass conversion kits, and flimsy mail-order guitars. In London the whole thing became institutionalized, with several Soho jazz clubs reconstituted as "skiffle cellars." Elsewhere, the hearty, participatory spirit of the craze made it irresistible to scoutmasters, social workers, and youth club volunteers.

It was not until the climax of the skiffle craze in the spring of 1957, with Donegan's recording of "The Cumberland Gap" riding high atop the charts, that John Lennon decided to try his hand at this wholesome form of fun. He began, like many others, with the purchase of a mail-order guitar. With Julia's help, he tuned it like a banjo (ignoring the bottom two strings) and picked up a handful of chords. He next recruited Pete Shotton on washboard, a classmate named Rodney Davis on banjo, a pair of acquaintances named Colin Hanton and Eric Griffiths on drums and second guitar, and an assortment of tea-chest bassists that included his fellow Outlaws Nigel Whalley and Ivan Vaughan. In a matter of weeks they worked up a repertoire that included the entire Donegan catalog of paeans to the Iron Horse—"Rock Island Line," "Cumberland Gap," "Freight Train," "Midnight Special," "Railroad Bill"—rounded out with a smattering of recent pop hits like the Del-Vikings' "Come Go with Me" and Gene Vincent's "Be-Bop-A-Lula." In May, following their debut at an Empire Day street party in Liverpool, they approached the new headmaster of the Quarry Bank school, William Pobjoy, to ask about performing at the sixth form's annual dance. Pobjoy, unaccustomed to receiving constructive offers of any sort from Lennon and Shotton, agreed to let them play—disarmed, no doubt, by the boys' decision to call themselves the Quarry Men. Next came the church fête in Woolton, where Paul McCartney entered the picture, invited by his grammar school classmate Ivan Vaughan.

COMPARED WITH THE parental neglect and uncertainty that scarred John Lennon's earliest years, Paul McCartney's childhood was a rock of constancy. Christened James Paul and born in Liverpool in June of 1942, he was the first child of James and Mary McCartney, who had married the year before. Jim McCartney was forty years old at the time of Paul's birth. He had grown up in the working-class district of Everton as the seventh of nine children—two of whom died young—in a close-knit family of Irish Protestant descent. His father was a tobacco cutter at a Liverpool firm called Cope's, where he proudly played the tuba in the company's brass band. At the age of fourteen, Jim found work as a sample boy at Hannay & Company, cotton brokers; fourteen years later, in 1930, he was promoted to salesman, a "black-coated" position that paid him a living wage. Prior to that, during the dance-hall craze that swept Britain in the 1920s, Jim had supplemented his income and enlivened his bachelorhood by playing the piano and trumpet in a semiprofessional group that billed itself as Jim Mac's Band—this despite a childhood accident that had left him deaf in one ear. His age and his disability disqualified him from military service in 1939; with the Cotton Exchange closed for the duration of the war, he was assigned to work as a lathe operator at a local aircraft plant. In 1941 he met a thirty-one-year-old nurse named Mary Mohin, and the two of them fell in love.

Paul's mother, Mary, was a second-generation Irish Catholic from the Fazakarley district of Liverpool. Her father had emigrated from Ireland as a boy and achieved success as a coal merchant, but his gains in business were eventually offset by his losses in gambling. When Mary was nine, her mother died in childbirth. At fourteen she went to work as a nurse's aide, and by the time she met Jim McCartney, she was running the maternity ward at Walton General Hospital—a post she left when she married, to attend to babies of her own. Following the birth of a second son, Michael, in 1944, Mary returned to work, first as a visiting nurse, then as a resident midwife. These jobs enabled the McCartneys to live rent-free in a succession of council houses that landed them eventually on the enormous Speke estate on the outskirts of Liverpool. In 1946, Jim returned to his post at Hannay's, but the decline of the textile industry ensured that he was barely earning what he had made before the war. Mary's salary and her housing benefits were essential to the family's well-being.

Looking back, Paul and Michael could never understand how their mother managed to care for them as attentively as she did while holding down a job that had her dashing out at all hours of the day and night to play her part in Britain's "baby bulge." But Mary McCartney was a woman of high standards and high expectations. She saw to it that her children were well-dressed, well-motivated, and, in her presence, well-behaved. When her boys began to affect the broad Scouse accent the inner-city migrants brought to Speke, she was quick to correct their speech.

Though Paul and Michael were baptized as Catholics, parochial education in Liverpool was notoriously poor, and it was taken for granted by Jim and Mary that the boys would attend state schools. Paul was sent to the primary school at Speke until the facility became so crowded that they began busing the overflow to Gateacre, a suburb to the east. From the first, he was a bright, conscientious student—of the sort who won a prize for his "Coronation Essay" in 1953. That same year, Paul scored well on his eleven-plus examination and was admitted to the Liverpool Institute, the city's best grammar school. There he continued to thrive, placing high in his class, becoming popular with his classmates, and furthering the hopes of his parents and teachers that he was headed for the university. One of his masters remembered Paul as "eminently like-able, charming, and pleasant"—a "keeny," in other words.

By the beginning of 1955 the McCartneys had had enough of life in Speke, which was rapidly degenerating into Liverpool's newest slum. Mary's return to health-visiting enabled the family to move into a brand-new block of council houses on Forthlin Road in Allerton, less than a mile across the golf course from Menlove Avenue. The McCartneys passed their first year there in a state of modest domestic bliss. Paul's brother had joined him at the Liverpool Institute, and their new house included such novel amenities as a backdoor garden and an indoor toilet. In the summer of 1956, however, while the boys were away at Scout camp, Mary's health began to fail. In October she was found to be suffering from advanced breast cancer, and a few weeks later, after a futile operation, she was dead. The family was devastated by the loss, but one of Jim McCartney's many maxims extolled the need to "soldier on." A host of relatives descended on Forthlin Road and nursed the boys and their father through the worst of their grief. Mary's diligent and devoted nature lent her death a tinge of martyrdom, and her memory would always serve as something for her sons to live up to.

For some years, Jim had been urging Paul and Michael to learn to play musical instruments, which he promoted as a "passport to popularity." During their first summer in Allerton, Paul was given a trumpet on his birthday, and both boys reluctantly submitted to lessons on the family piano. But when Elvis arrived the following year, Paul was seized by a sudden enthusiasm for the guitar. Once he determined the need to reverse the strings to account for his left-handedness, he made rapid progress on the instrument, which became a virtual obsession after his mother's death. Alone among the boys who became the Beatles, Paul McCartney possessed the combination of quick hands and a good ear that most people mean when they speak of musical talent. When he was introduced to John Lennon the following summer in Woolton, the mere fact that he knew how to tune a guitar properly amazed the Quarry Men. That he also knew the words and chords to Eddie Cochran's "Twenty-Flight Rock" and did a recognizable imitation of the American singer Little Richard was icing on the cake. A few days after their first meeting, John Lennon deputized Pete Shotton to approach this young virtuoso from Allerton about the possibility of his joining the Quarry Men. Paul readily accepted the invitation, although his actual debut with the group was delayed by his annual fortnight at Scout camp. In his absence, the Quarry Men played an inauspicious skiffle-night engagement at a Liverpool jazz club called the Cavern, where John's insistence on performing selections by Elvis Presley and Gene Vincent violated the club's strict policy prohibiting rock 'n' roll and earned the group a reprimand.

3

It was a port. That means it was less hick than somewhere
in the English Midlands. . . . The North is where the money
was made during the 1800s. That was where all the brass
and the heavy people came from, and that's where the
despised people were. . . . It was going poor, a very poor
city, and tough.

—John Lennon (1970)

In many ways the circumstances of John Lennon's and Paul McCartney's childhoods in the suburban milieu of Liverpool were similar to
those of millions of other children growing up in provincial cities and
towns throughout Britain in the years after World War II. But at least one
aspect of their experience was unique, for, as its residents liked to
remind themselves at every opportunity, Liverpool was a place like no
other in Britain. Situated on the coast of Lancashire, two hundred miles
northwest of London at the point where the Mersey River meets the
Irish Sea, the character of the city had been shaped for more than two
hundred years by the shifting tides of world history and geography. From
the mid-eighteenth century onward, only London had played a more
important role in the projection of British economic power around the
world, and no English city, including London, had played a more important role in the settlement and development of North America, or
enjoyed stronger, longer, or more direct ties with the United States. And
yet, until the Beatles, the vast majority of native-born Americans knew
nothing of the place.

In Britain it was different. There, everyone knew about Liverpool, if
only as a dot on the map, or as the site of the celebrated Grand National
steeplechase, or as the home of two of England's most belligerent professional football teams. Broadly speaking, Liverpool was identified in the
minds of most Britons with a string of cities, including Manchester,
Bradford, Leeds, Sheffield, and Hull, which together constituted the
region known as the Industrial North. Once, during the middle decades

of the nineteenth century, at a time when Britain was producing half the world's iron, half the world's cotton cloth, and half the world's coal, the North of England had been the home of a burgeoning provincial culture, flush with the new wealth of manufacturing and commerce, whose economic vitality and political influence challenged the dominance that London and the Home Counties of the South had traditionally exerted over every sphere of English life.

In Liverpool, reminders of that great upsurge of commerce and culture were visible at every turn: in the vast complex of granite docks and warehouses that lined the River Mersey for seven miles, whose "extent and solidity" the American novelist Herman Melville had once compared to the great pyramids of Egypt; in the ornate shipping, banking, and insurance company offices that squatted on the streets of the commercial district adjoining the dockland; in the outsized magnificence of St. George's Hall, Britain's largest Neoclassical building, which loomed like a brooding Acropolis over the squalid, jerry-built residential districts that had once made the city as famous for its slums as for its ships; and in the terraces and squares of Georgian and Regency townhouses that spread across the rising slope to the east of the commercial district, culminating in the mansions and villas on the heights of Mossley Hill, where the city's merchants and shipping magnates had once gazed (on the occasional clear day) across the Mersey to the Wirral Peninsula and the distant hills of Wales.

Over the first half of the twentieth century, however, this aura of civic grandeur had gradually assumed a deeply ironic cast. For the North of England had been in a state of precipitous economic decline since the end of World War I, as the many attributes that had once made it the cauldron of the Industrial Revolution—the fortuitous convergence of coal and cotton, steam and sail, together with access, via the port of Liverpool, to markets around the world—counted for little in the new industrial age of steel and electricity, motorized transport, and consumer goods that was rising from the wreckage of free-market capitalism in the wake of the Great Depression. The hard times of the interwar years had imparted a dazed quality to life in the North. With its obsolescent factories, congested cities, and anachronistic economic attitudes, the region was increasingly seen as an industrial dinosaur, and the preponderance of new investment gravitated toward the South. The Industrial Revolution had begun in the North of England at the turn of the nineteenth century, and it was there, in the middle decades of the twentieth century, that the world's first industrial nation entered a postindustrial age. And the city of Liverpool, as surely as its rise had mirrored the rise of Britain itself as a commercial colossus, came to symbolize the erosion of power, wealth, and status that applied to the nation as a whole.

The standard line, proudly repeated by natives to non-natives with the air of an original thought, was that life in the city was so hard that you had to be a comedian just to survive there. And indeed, Liverpool in the years after World War II was perhaps best known in Britain as the home-town of an exceedingly popular radio comedian by the name of Tommy Handley, who presided over the top-rated BBC comedy program of the 1940s, *It's That Man Again,* or "ITMA" as it was called, which poked holes in the social fabric of wartime Britain to the delight of a weekly audience of 16 million listeners. It was Handley who popularized the terms *Scouse* (rhymes with "mouse") and *Scouser* as synonyms for *Liver-pudlian,* and his fast-talking comic persona (which he modeled on the American radio comedians of the time) epitomized the brash, assertive, skeptical spirit that Liverpudlians prided themselves on. So great was Handley's popularity that when he died suddenly in 1949, memorial ser-vices were held at both St. Paul's in London and the Anglican Cathedral in Liverpool. "The death of a Prime Minister would obviously be a far greater disaster," noted *The Spectator,* "but there are millions of people in this country who would not regard it so."

By the late 1940s, when Tommy Handley was its best-known native son, and the boys who became the Beatles were growing up there, Liver-pool was the sprawling, soot-blackened home of 750,000 people, set in the middle of a metropolitan area called Merseyside, whose total popula-tion numbered a million and a quarter. In those years it was still Britain's fourth-most-populous city, its principal deep-water port, and its largest provincial center of banking and insurance. It was still the site of Europe's largest grain terminal and the world's largest cotton market. Yet Liverpool was *still* these things because it was well on its way to becoming *none* of these things. The dockyards that lined the banks of the Mersey now pro-vided work for barely a quarter of the sixty thousand men who had been employed there during the heyday of the port. The Depression-era merger of the Cunard and White Star shipping lines and the rerouting of luxury liner traffic to Southampton had robbed the city of its chief source of glamour and diminished its historic status as the eastern terminus of the

Atlantic crossing. Some of that status had been reclaimed during World War II, when Liverpool had served as the anchor of Britain's maritime lifeline and the naval headquarters of convoy operations on the Atlantic. But this brief reprise of glory had come at a terrible cost. In the spring of 1941, whole neighborhoods were reduced to rubble by German air raids that killed nearly four thousand people on Merseyside, destroyed eleven thousand dwellings, and damaged 125,000 more. Yet in contrast to other British cities (especially London, which sustained far worse bomb damage), block upon block of the wreckage remained uncleared, much less rebuilt, for several years after the war, as the Liverpool Corporation put all of its energy and resources into relocating tens of thousands of displaced families to the vast new housing estates that were springing up on the outskirts of the city. "A decaying corpse of Victorian self-satisfaction" was how one of the characters in John Brophy's 1946 novel *City of Departures* described his battered hometown.

Historically, the social quality that had always set Liverpool apart was a cosmopolitan character and outlook that were otherwise unknown among the great provincial cities of Britain. The population was a mixture of ethnicities exceeded only by that of London. In addition to the descendants of the hundreds of thousands of English, Welsh, Scots, and Irish who had converged on the city from all points of the compass during the great internal migrations that accompanied the Industrial Revolution and the Irish Famine of the 1840s, sizable numbers of Germans, Dutch, Scandinavians, and Jews from all over Europe had taken up residence, drawn by the traffic of the port. There was also a small but prominent presence in the city of West Indian, African, East Indian, and Chinese seamen, who had mingled and intermarried with the native population to an extent that was unprecedented in the rest of xenophobic England. As early as 1839, after encountering his ship's black steward "walking arm in arm with a good-looking English woman," Herman Melville had noted that "in New York, such a couple would have been mobbed in three minutes." For the most part, however, the diversity of the population did not translate into social harmony; with close to half the workforce dependent on some form of casual labor, the fierce, day-to-day competition for jobs generated prodigious levels of social tension. The fiercest of those tensions was the sectarian strife between the Protestant majority and the city's large Irish Catholic minority, which came to a head during the interwar years with the creation of the Irish Free State and the partition of Ulster. The old joke that there were two main religions in Liverpool, anti-Catholicism and anti-Protestantism, was borne out by ritualistic street fighting on nationalist holidays and institutionalized discrimination against Catholics. For its part, the Catholic archdiocese sought to preserve the bonds of ethnic identity by staffing its parishes with priests imported from Ireland, who came to the city, in the words of one observer, "in the role of missionaries."

The cosmopolitan character of the city reached its apex during World War II, which counted as Liverpool's swan song as a great international port. Following America's entry into the war, and especially during the year-long buildup to the invasion of France, the streets, pubs, cinemas, and dance halls of the city were crowded with Allied servicemen of a dozen nationalities. Here as elsewhere in Britain, the Americans were a special source of fascination. Everything about them—their well-nourished physiques, their ready cash, the cut and cloth of their uniforms, the size and variety of their vehicles as they rumbled in long convoys through the streets of the town—affirmed in the minds of Liverpudlians an image of unimaginable largesse. There had always been a strong American presence in the city; in addition to the constant flow of tourists and commercial travelers, returning seamen and stewards had provided a conduit for the latest American fads, fashions, and social attitudes, earning themselves the appellation "Cunard Yanks." Now a vision of America that had previously existed mainly as a Hollywood fantasy of fast-talking urban ethnics and lanky, laconic farm boys materialized in battalion strength on the streets of Liverpool. All told, 1.2 million U.S. servicemen passed through the port, including tens of thousands of airmen who were posted at nearby Burtonwood, which served as the chief maintenance and supply base for the American air force in Europe. Their presence inspired countless rows, romances, and rivalries, including some of the most overt racial tension the city had ever known, as white Americans reacted to the sight of their black countrymen consorting with Englishwomen much as Herman Melville had once predicted they would.

THERE WERE TWO main strands to the legacy that history had bequeathed to Liverpool in the years when the boys who became the Beatles were growing up there. The first was a beleaguered sense of regional identity that Liverpudlians shared with the residents of Manchester,

Sheffield, and the rest of the Industrial North. In a region synonymous with working-class attitudes, this could be seen as a geographical projection of the traditional working-class ethos of Us and Them, expressed as an opposition between the tough, pragmatic, proletarian North and the posh, pretentious, bourgeois South. "There exists in England a curious cult of Northernness," George Orwell observed. "A [Northerner] in the South will always take care to let you know that he regards you as an inferior. If you ask him why, he will explain that it is only in the North that life is 'real' life, that the industrial work done in the North is the only 'real' work, that the North is inhabited by 'real' people, the South merely by rentiers and their parasites. The Northerner has 'grit,' he is grim, dour, plucky, warm-hearted, and democratic; the Southerner is snobbish, effeminate, and lazy—that at any rate is the theory."

Yet if one strand of the Liverpudlian sensibility was derived from a sense of regional solidarity, a second and equally vital strand was derived from a fiercely local patriotism that drew on a long-standing sense of *difference* from the rest of the Industrial North. From the start of its rise to power and prominence in the eighteenth century, Liverpool had stood apart, geographically and otherwise, from the manufacturing centers of Manchester, Sheffield, and Leeds, not least in showing a singular regard for its own uniqueness and importance. "Liverpool gentleman, Manchester man" was the nineteenth-century maxim with which the venture capitalists of Merseyside had sought to differentiate themselves from the mere industrialists of "Cottonopolis" and the other manufacturing towns. Throughout the Victorian era, these merchant princes (who referred to themselves as Liverpolitans, not Liverpudlians) extolled their city as "the Gateway to the Empire," "the Modern Tyre," and even, incredibly, as "the Florence of the North." A century of exposure to this rhetoric of civic grandiosity had helped to institutionalize a sense of Liverpool's exceptionalism in the minds of its middle- and working-class population, whose competing tribes of English, Scottish, Welsh, and Irish seemed to be staging their own perpetual reprise of the last five hundred years of British history. Woven together, these two strands of sensibility resulted in a social character of uncommon complexity, and an urban folk culture of uncommon richness, in which the cosmopolitan and the provincial, the worldly and the insular, the outward-looking and the inward-turning, were combined in ways that truly *were* exceptional by comparison with other British cities and towns.

The city's social character found its ideal medium of expression in the unmistakable Scouse accent and dialect with which modern Liverpudlians trumpeted their identity to the world. Scouse was a comparatively recent and localized linguistic development, a hybrid variation on the standard Lancashire dialect that dated from the late nineteenth century and was initially confined to the dockland and its adjoining slum neighborhoods. It shared with the rest of Lancashire such traits as the pronunciation of *book* to rhyme with *fluke* and *singer* to rhyme with *finger*; the substitution of *me* for *my* and *yer* for *your*; and the use of *dead* and *right* as intensifiers ("dead right," "right dead"). Scouse's deviation from the standard Lancashire dialect began with its incorporation of such classic Anglo-Irishisms as *dat* for *that*, *tree* for *three*, and *youse* as the plural of *you*. The Celtic influence may also have contributed to the growth of a quasi-Joycean vernacular that included terms like *moodying* (for "wandering thoughtfully") and *earwiggen* (for "eavesdropping"), which merged easily with a Lancastrian tradition of puns and deliberate malapropisms. As the dialect spread from the waterfront neighborhoods, it also picked up some of the intonations associated with Welsh-English, assuming a faintly singsong quality that has variously been described as "plaintive" or "inquisitorial." "Intonation in Liverpool," wrote the linguist Peter Wright, carries "rising inflections at the ends of sentences [that] wrongly convey a background tone of mild surprise, as if the Liverpudlian is incapable of accepting calmly any obvious fact. With many a Scouser, nothing seems to be a statement." Still another trait of the Scouse idiom is its affection for diminutives, which resulted in coinages such as *sarney* for sandwich, *bevvy* for beverage (especially an alcoholic one, hence *bevvied* for drunk), and *ozzy* for hospital. During World War II, a bomb site became known as a *debby*, a term derived from *debris*.

Over and above these particularities, the true earmark of Scouse speech has always been its flat, "adenoidal" drone, caused by a phonetic technique called *velarization*, in which the back of the tongue is lifted toward the roof of the mouth, imparting a blurriness to vowels and a slurriness to consonants. Various explanations have been advanced to account for this accent, which sets Scouse apart from all of its influences. These range from the droll notion that the mouths of the city's residents are simply worn out from arguing and gossiping to the more scientific theory that the damp climate and polluted atmosphere exacerbated the chronic respiratory infections common to slum dwellers, producing "a mixture of Welsh, Irish, and catarrh," which, through a process of conscious and unconscious emulation, then influenced the rest of Merseyside. What is indisputable is that this initially stigmatized dockland accent not only survived the overall improvement in respiratory health and the efforts of the local grammar schools and the BBC to promote a more standardized form of English, but actually became more pronounced over the first half of the twentieth century as a badge of identity and a means of bridging the city's ethnic and sectarian divisions with a common tongue. By the 1950s, a broad range of working- and middle-class Liverpudlians spoke with at least some degree of Scouse inflection.

The nasality and uncertain intonation of Scouse could lend a deadpan or quizzical quality to the simplest of utterances, which made it the perfect medium for the rude, mocking humor on which Liverpudlians prided themselves. Long before Tommy Handley exposed the city's comic sensibility to a mass audience, Scouse humor specialized in the put-on, the put-down, and the sarcastic or deflationary retort. Its underlying motive was the management of social aggression—most often through the simple expedient of bringing everyone and everything down to the same level. Thus did Liverpudlians exact some small measure of revenge on the grandiosity of the nineteenth-century merchants and ship owners who had built the city on the backs of its laborers and seamen. "To understand Liverpool and its people," wrote Alun Owen, the Welsh-born playwright who featured the city in his work, "you have to get right with this basic fact that any form of pretentiousness must be punctured swiftly and mercilessly. Nobody must be allowed to get away with anything. If they do, you're the mug." "I was born in Liverpool," noted the critic Walter Redfern. "I would be flattering myself if I claimed that you need to be a comedian to survive there. But Liverpudlians do, like punsters, switch things about. They breathe through their mouths and talk through their noses. They are physiological, existential twisters."

The Quarry Men in Liverpool, November 1957 (Paul on the left, John on the right)

4

One of the first things I realized about John when I got to know him was that he came from a very different world to my working-class one. My family was from the housing estate. . . . John's relations were definitely middle-class. I remember being very impressed seeing the entire works of Winston Churchill on a bookshelf at Mendips. I was even more impressed when I learned he had actually read them.

—Paul McCartney

The musical friendship that started in the summer of 1957 began on unequal terms. Paul McCartney was twenty months younger than John Lennon and a year behind him in school—a small eternity in the time frame of adolescence. "In the beginning he was a sort of fairground hero," McCartney recalled. "[I was] younger, and that mattered. . . . I idolized John. He was the big guy in the chip shop. I was the little guy." From John's perspective, however, the part of the fairground hero was a familiar and comfortable role. All of the other members of his Woolton band of Outlaws (including his classmate Pete Shotton) were at least a year younger than he.

The difference in the two boys' social backgrounds was less immediately apparent than the difference in their ages; a generation or two before, when class status had been instantly advertised by speech and manner and dress, it would have counted for more. Paul's family epitomized the notion of upper-working-class respectability, John's family that of lower-middle-class propriety. Historically, on account of its largely ascriptive nature, this distinction had been more aggressively policed than any other social frontier. Yet for these two teenagers, the difference in their family backgrounds was substantially offset by their common identity as grammar-school boys. So strong, in fact, was the mark of their schooling upon them that the Beatles themselves can be seen as the product of a tension between two wildly conflicting visions of what life might hold in store. The one was derived from the glamorous world of American popular culture and symbolized by the charismatic figure of Elvis Presley; the other was derived from the sober world of British social policy and symbolized by the bureaucratic figure of R. A. Butler, the donnish Tory cabinet minister who lent his name to a landmark piece of reform legislation officially known as the Education Act of 1944.

As an instrument of social policy, the Butler Act was designed to create an expanded and democratized educational elite. Its most immediate effect, however, had been to expose a larger and more diverse group of young adolescents to the singular social and psychological environment of an English grammar school. Long before Butler, the state-supported grammar schools had modeled themselves as closely as possible on the venerable institutions like Eton and Rugby that had trained successive generations of Britain's ruling class. John Lennon's alma mater, Quarry Bank, was typical in this regard. The atmosphere was harshly authoritarian and relentlessly competitive. Instruction was by rote, and students were openly and minutely ranked in every course and school activity. Great stress was placed on the "character-building" attributes of team sports. During most of John's tenure there, the school was run by a stiff-necked headmaster named E. R. Taylor, who, like many postwar grammar-school heads, responded to the democratization of his student body by wielding a free hand with the cane and reminding his charges at every opportunity of how fortunate they were to be grammar-school boys.

Paul McCartney's alma mater, by comparison, offered a slightly less neurotic atmosphere. The Liverpool Institute had all the usual public-school trappings, but the tone of the place was more like that of an elite urban high school in the United States. Many of the masters were former scholarship boys who had gone on to study at Oxford or Cambridge and then returned to teach; they were more apt to ignore recalcitrant pupils than to deal with them as an affront to the school's authority. Yet, despite their differences in style, both Quarry Bank and the Liverpool Institute shared the same goal. Grammar-school students were taught to speak in a manner, think in a manner, and behave in a manner that was designed to obscure the vagaries of class and geographic origin and inculcate a set of attitudes and ideals that had been perfected during the late Victorian era at the better boarding schools—a set of attitudes and ideals that were inherently genteel.

By the early fifties, when John Lennon and Paul McCartney passed the eleven-plus examination and entered their respective grammar schools, a thick cloud of controversy had already gathered around the Butler Act reforms. Contrary to most expectations, the act turned out to be a boon for Britian's independent schools, as middle-class parents proved more willing than ever to pay for the sort of education that would provide their children with the academic credentials and social graces required for a middle-class career. This siphoning-off of the more afflu-ent students, together with a demonstrable bias in the eleven-plus selec-tion process against children from poorer homes, turned the state grammar schools of the 1950s into enclaves of adolescents drawn almost entirely from the lower-middle and upper working classes. This popula-tion of prospective Jimmy Porters was selected, moreover, on the basis of intelligence, not motivation, and to judge by the high proportion of dropouts, many pupils showed little inclination to apply themselves to the curriculum or submit to the grammar-school regime. Some of the working-class children came from families that viewed academic educa-tion with suspicion or outright hostility and offered them little support. Some of the middle-class children were resentful at being grouped with, and often surpassed by, their social inferiors.

Much as they shared the identity of grammar-school boys, John Lennon and Paul McCartney responded quite differently to the rigors of these "educational forcing houses." For a working-class boy like Paul, raised on a housing estate, grammar school came as a calculated form of culture shock. Certified "clever" by the eleven-plus and segregated by day from his peers, he became, in effect, a designated individualist in the col-lectivist culture of the English working class. "There weren't many other kids from the Institute living round our way," McCartney recalled. "I was called 'college pudding'—'fucking college pudding'—they said." Yet com-ing from a family that encouraged social and educational aspiration, Paul was better equipped than most to cope with the feelings of difference and isolation that came from shuttling daily between the worlds of school and home. (It was in part to relieve these pressures on their sons that the McCartneys had fled from Speke.) Paul's marks, his popularity, and his participation in a range of extracurricular activities all attested to his suc-cessful adaptation to grammar school. Especially telling was his ability to maintain his high standing with classmates and masters alike—a balanc-ing act that required considerable tact and social awareness. Though his academic performance suffered somewhat in the year that followed his mother's death, his teachers were sympathetic (one of them circulated a note asking his colleagues to cut the boy some slack). At the time he met John Lennon, there was still every reason to expect that Paul would fulfill the hopes of his parents and teachers and attend a university.

"But, good gracious, you've got to educate him first," wrote the satirist H. H. Munro. "You can't expect a boy to be vicious until he's been to a good school." In the case of John Lennon, who would turn out to be one of the more spectacular grammar-school rebels of his generation, the virulence of his clash with the system would seem to suggest that the problem ran deeper than, as Lennon once said, "whatever sociological thing gave me a chip on my shoulder." By the time he came to Quarry Bank, John had built a formidable shell of personality around the seeds of insecurity that were sown in his earliest years. He took inordinate pride in his self-assurance, and like other strong-willed children who have suffered rejection or neglect, his initial impulse was to dominate any social situation he encountered. "I was aggressive because I wanted to be popular," Lennon recalled. "I wanted everybody to do what I told them to do, to laugh at my jokes and let me be the boss." The transition required of every eleven-plus child—from top-dog status in primary school to underdog status in grammar school—was especially jarring to him. "I looked at all the hundreds of new kids, and I thought, Christ, I'll have to fight all my way through this lot," he said of his first day at Quarry Bank, "[but] the first fight I got in, I lost." Seeing little prospect of making a name for himself in the sanctioned fields of academics or athletics (as he grew older and more myopic, he developed a hatred of sports), John resolved to attain the status of a leader by other means. His careful study of William Brown and his own experience of growing up with an aunt who served as his mother and a mother who served as his aunt had left him with what he would later describe as a special feel for the limits of adult authority. In an environment as coercive and constricting as Quarry Bank, a boy could go far in the eyes of his peers by resisting the regime. Yet apart from his authorship of a broadsheet called *The Daily Howl,* which specialized in grotesque caricatures of his teachers and classmates, it would seem that the imaginative quality, if not the intensity, of John's rebellion has been exaggerated over the years. The many incidents recounted proudly in Pete Shotton's memoir, *John Lennon in My Life,* add up to little more than a catalog of typical schoolboy pranks.

From an intellectual standpoint, the effect of his schooling upon him was mainly negative. As an intelligent child with a serious interest in reading and writing, John came to mistrust the expressive world of literature on account of its association with the academic culture of the school. His years at Quarry Bank left him with a defensive, derisive, and at times defiantly philistine attitude toward a wide range of artistic and intellectual pursuits that would confound and inhibit him in his subsequent artistic career. In the near term, though, it merely ensured that there were no literary influences on his adolescence that compared with those exerted by writers like Lewis Carroll and Richmal Crompton on his childhood. Instead he had the Goons.

The Goon Show was a popular—and now legendary—BBC radio program that began in 1951 and ran through the end of the decade, attracting a weekly audience of four million devoted listeners who ranged from schoolboys like John to Oxbridge dons to members of the Royal Family. The Goons were Harry Secombe, Peter Sellers, and Spike Milligan, assisted by the singer and bandleader Ray Ellington and the jazz harmonica player Max Geldray, who provided the music for the show. Secombe, a Welshman, was a perfect ham. Sellers, a mix of Jewish Cockney and Yorkshire heritage, was a brilliant mimic. Milligan, an Irishman born in India, was an inspired comedy writer and guerrilla intellectual. The three of them were linked to one another by the shared experience of military service in World War II, and service humor, with its reflexive irreverence and its stoic acceptance of absurdity, was the wellspring of Goonery. Goon humor, wrote the poet L. E. Sissman, turned on "a constant conflict between fine words and mean intentions, a stripping away of the language of hope and glory to reveal the ruined institutions—and moral attitudes—beneath." For highbrow listeners, the show's popularity coincided with the vogue for the Theater of the Absurd that began with the first English-language productions of Beckett and Ionesco in London in 1955. For teenagers, the Goons' mockery of the conventions of popular entertainment served a function akin to that of *Mad* magazine in the United States. Their clashes with the BBC over Milligan's scripts and Sellers's ad-libs were closely followed by fans of the show, who liked to think of their heroes as living under a constant threat of cancellation or reprimand.

The Goons were John Lennon's first important heroes from the world of popular culture, and, as with his early literary heroes, he would revere them for the rest of his life. Their humor was both lighthearted and aggressive, nonsensical and polemic, and very much in tune with the spirit of deflation that reached a special intensity in the city of Liverpool. Picking up where the illogic of Alice and the impudence of William left off, the Goons served as the main inspiration for the droll banter that would distinguish John Lennon as a teenager and endear him to his friends. Goon humor was cult humor, and the essential principle of cult humor can be stated as follows: The more obscure the joke, the greater the intimacy that comes from sharing in it. This was a principle that Lennon grasped intuitively, and he used it to delineate and dominate his circle of friends. At the same time, *The Goon Show* also provided him with a practical education in Dada, Surrealism, and other aspects of avant-garde sensibility that he otherwise would have rejected as unacceptably highbrow.

Considering that the series ran until 1960, it is telling that John Lennon's own chronology of the Goons' influence—"I was twelve when the Goon Shows first hit; sixteen when they finished with me"—corresponded neatly with his five-year career in grammar school. The fate of that career had been quietly sealed in June of 1957, a few weeks before his first meeting with Paul McCartney, when John took the examinations (known as "O-levels") that determined whether he could advance into the sixth (or college preparatory) form. In August came the news that he had failed at every one. When Mimi Smith met with William Pobjoy to discuss her nephew's dwindling options, the headmaster noted that John had obvious intelligence, a thorough lack of motivation, and, to judge by confiscated copies of *The Daily Howl,* a certain propensity for art. Though he considered Lennon an intolerable nuisance, Pobjoy, unlike his predecessor, was not a martinet. John's one chance of continuing his education, he explained to Mimi, lay with the possibility of getting him into the Liverpool College of Art. The admission requirements for the college were blessedly subjective, involving little more than a perfunctory interview and the submission of some samples of artistic work. In short order, Pobjoy drafted a guarded recommendation, Mimi agreed to provide support in lieu of a government grant, and John became an art student in September 1957.

The journalist George Melly once described the art colleges of the 1950s (in words that mirror William Pobjoy's thinking at the time) as "the refuge of the bright but unacademic, the talented, the non-conformist, the lazy, the inventive and the indecisive: all those who didn't know what they wanted but knew it wasn't a nine-to-five job." Liverpool's local art college was a second-rate institution, overshadowed even within the region by its more dynamic counterpart in Manchester. The caliber of the faculty was compromised by the reluctance of practicing artists to live in a place so far removed from the museums and galleries of London, and an air of marginality prevailed. Yet for the students, most of whom commuted from their homes in the suburbs of Merseyside, the school and its surroundings were like a slice of Montparnasse. The college was located on Hope Street, on the edge of a neighborhood known by its postal designation, Liverpool 8, whose nondescript name belied a veritable cauldron of local color. It so happened that John Lennon's grandparents, George and Anne Stanley, had raised their five daughters in a house on Huskisson Street in the heart of Liverpool 8, back when the area was still a respectable place to live. But there was another feature of the Art College's location that held greater significance for John. Right next door, in a most felicitous coincidence, stood the gray granite pile of the Liverpool Institute.

At the time of Lennon's arrival, the prevailing style at the Art College was a provincial strain of 1950s student bohemianism. In dress, this meant duffle coats, drab corduroys, oversize sweaters, and school scarves; in culture, it meant American jazz, Continental films, Angry fiction, and Beat poetry; in politics, the Committee for Nuclear Disarmament, or CND. Among the students who professed a serious interest in contemporary art, the preferred alternative to the academic modernism espoused by the college faculty was the "kitchen-sink" school of social realist painting associated with younger English artists like John Bratby and Jack Smith. The influence of American Abstract Expressionism, having recently arrived in London, was still some years away. Nor was there any trace in the students' work of the early Pop motifs that were beginning to ruffle feathers at more-prestigious institutions like the Slade School and the Royal College of Art.

John Lennon's entry into this environment in September 1957 was a slightly less belligerent reprise of his arrival at Quarry Bank. From the first, he made no serious effort to apply himself to the work. Instead, preoccupied as ever with the need to assert his personality, Lennon simply carried on in his accustomed role, inspired for the first time in his avocation as a class clown by an audience that included girls. In time, his outlandish wit would earn him both the admiration and animosity of his classmates, but in his first term at the college he distinguished himself mainly by his clothes. Free at last from the strictures of a school uniform, John showed up each day on Hope Street in the provocative and rather preposterous guise of a Teddy boy.

As Lennon later described it, "We dressed in Teddy boy style—long jackets and all that—but we weren't [Teds]. We never got in trouble. We knew what we were doing." The *real* Teds were proletarian peacocks from the unfortunately named "secondary modern" system that constituted the nonacademic alternative to grammar school: working-class boys who filled the sorts of dead-end jobs that were plentiful for British teenagers during the early 1950s, when compulsory National Service turned the years between fifteen and eighteen into a period of occupational limbo. (Reinstated in 1947 to help the country deal with its Cold War and post-colonial commitments, the draft was sharply curtailed after the Suez crisis of 1956 and eliminated altogether in 1960.) The neo-Edwardian fashions that gave the Teds their name dated from 1949, when clothes rationing was finally lifted and the tailors on London's Savile Row sought to relieve the gloom of postwar austerity by reviving the longer suit jackets, narrower trousers, and brocade waistcoats that set the style of gentlemanly fashion in the halcyon era that ended with World War I. At a time when a Labour government was seeking to dismantle an empire abroad and a class system at home, the irony of young Mayfair blades aping the look of their imperial Edwardian forebears was perhaps a bit too rich, which may explain why the style never quite caught on with its intended clientele. Yet this same irony, turned on its head, may also explain why a caricatured version of this style went on to become popular among adolescent boys in the working-class strongholds of South London. There, in 1953, "Edwardianism" emerged as the first in a series of flamboyant fashion subcultures by which the youth of Britain would play a part in changing the look of youth all over the world.

Coming as they did from the tough "corner boy" milieu of South London, the first Teds were heirs to a tradition of petty criminality that went back many generations. For the police, the press, and the public, this made the conspicuous figure of the Teddy boy a perfect scapegoat for the genuine social problem of rising juvenile crime. For the Teds themselves, the sudden notoriety of their clothing conferred a degree of social power unlike anything they had ever known. As a result, what began as an individualistic impulse to appropriate an upper-class fashion was rapidly converted into a uniform of peer-group solidarity. Loose-knit gangs of Teds brawled with one another in London dance halls and transit stations; larger groups on football or bank-holiday outings convinced their anxious elders that Britain had been invaded by an alien uniformed force. The fashion itself evolved in response to this new notoriety, as the Teds assimilated motifs (and social attitudes) derived from the poker-faced Western gunslingers and gamblers they knew from American films. By the mid-1950s, teenage boys in frock coats, lace ties, and wispy "sideboards" strode the streets of Notting Hill and Shepherds Bush looking like desperadoes who had checked their hats and guns at the door, and the style had begun to spread from the "manors" of metropolitan London to provincial cities like Liverpool.

Though the Teds were an established presence before the advent of rock 'n' roll, they took to the arrival of this brash new music like the members of a cargo cult. Rock 'n' roll galvanized the Teddy boy subculture. It was the one form of popular entertainment that best expressed the ethos of excitement and aggression that ruled their leisure lives. In the fall of 1956, crowds of Teds greeted the first showings of the Bill Haley film *Rock Around the Clock* by jiving in the aisles of London cinemas, battling with ushers, and slashing theater seats.

It was precisely this aura of toughness and aggression and its association with rock 'n' roll that attracted John Lennon to the guise of the Teddy boy. In his final year at Quarry Bank, John had dabbled in the fashion, adopting a "Tony Curtis" hairstyle and letting his sideburns grow. But it was not until he arrived at the Art College that he actually tried to represent himself as a Ted. There the fashion not only advertised his passion for rock, but also served as a way of camouflaging his comfortable Woolton origins and distancing himself from the bohemian pretensions (the "artiness," as he called it) of his fellow art students. Lennon was not the only middle-class English teenager to complete the cycle of ironic appropriation by adopting this uniform of working-class solidarity as a mark of his own individuality, but he does seem to have been the first to do so in the context of the Liverpool College of Art. Unlike the proletarian dandies he was emulating, however, most of whom had jobs, John was hampered in his adoption of this persona by the fact that his only sources of discretionary income were the small allowance he received from Mimi and whatever he could cadge from Julia and Bobby Dykins.

Lennon's Teddy boy posturing could be dismissed as just that—mere posturing—if it were not so indicative of the spirit of romantic proletarianism that would influence his life in the years to come. Perhaps he simply reasoned that his failure in grammar school had earned him the right to identify with the world of the secondary modern. But John's attempt to cultivate a working-class identity must also be seen in the context of his increasingly triangulated relationship with Mimi and Julia. Of the five Stanley sisters, Julia alone had failed to advance the family's claim to middle-class status by means of marriage, education, and lifestyle. Instead, her weakness for waiters had led her first to marry Alf Lennon and then to abandon all claim to respectability by starting a second, out-of-wedlock family with her boyfriend Bobby Dykins in their Allerton council house. For John, the difference between a working-class identity and a middle-class one was thus personified by the difference between Julia and Mimi. And the choice posed by these two sisters was made much easier by John's impression that Julia had paid no obvious price for her downward mobility. On the contrary: whereas Mimi's frugal nature had only intensified since her husband's death, Julia and Bobby Dykins appeared to live life as a series of small indulgences for which there was always cash on hand.

JOHN'S FIRST TERM at the Art College marked the high point of the Quarry Men as a performing band. Nattily attired in matching gray jackets and Western string ties, the group—now composed, with the addition of Paul McCartney, of three guitars, a tea-chest bass, and drums—played as many as a dozen engagements at youth clubs, church halls, and private parties during the fall of 1957. Shortly thereafter, however, the zeal for skiffle began to wane.

In March of 1958, Buddy Holly and the Crickets became the first major American rock-'n'-roll act to perform in Liverpool. Though neither John Lennon nor Paul McCartney attended the concert, they became completely caught up in the enthusiasm generated by Holly's appearance at the Philharmonic Hall, which was right next door to the Art College and the Liverpool Institute. After a few more performances at a private club that was aptly called The Morgue, the Quarry Men, like most of their musical brethren on Merseyside, entered a period of extended hibernation, in an effort to make the transition from skiffle to rock 'n' roll.

The news that Paul McCartney had joined a skiffle group had not escaped the attention of a Liverpool Institute schoolmate whom Paul had befriended a few years before, when his family still lived in Speke. George Harrison was eight months younger than Paul and a year behind him in school. Born in February 1943, he was the fourth and final child of Harold and Louise Harrison, who at that time lived in the Wavertree district of Liverpool, not far from Penny Lane. Harry Harrison's father had worked as a builder before enlisting in the army and dying in France at the start of World War I. In 1925, at the age of sixteen, Harry had put to sea as a cabin boy with the White Star Line. He met Louise French in 1929 and they were married the following year. She was a second-generation Irish Catholic whose family came from Wexford and whose father had worked as a lamplighter in Liverpool. The Harrisons' first child, Louise, was born in 1931; their second, Harold junior, in 1934. Two years later, Harry senior lost his job with White Star, a victim of the merger with Cunard. He spent a year and a half on the dole before finding work as a bus conductor (and later as a bus driver) for the Liverpool Corporation. A third child, Peter, was born in 1940, followed at last by George.

Like many families in Liverpool, the Harrison household was an undeclared matriarchy that turned on the hub of its mum. Louise Harrison was a gregarious, fun-loving woman who encouraged her children to think and fend for themselves. As the baby of the family, George became her prize pupil in this regard, notable even as a small child for his well-developed sense of independence and privacy. Harry senior was more reserved than his wife, though hardly a stick-in-the-mud. Together the couple taught a class in ballroom dancing at the busmen's union hall, where Harry acted as the master of ceremonies at Saturday-night socials. Eventually he became an official of the busmen's union itself.

In 1948, when George was five, the Harrisons finally got their chance to join the great migration to Speke. "It was a brand-new house," Louise Harrison recalled of their lodgings on Upton Green, "but I hated it from the minute we moved in." By the time they arrived on the huge estate, even the schools in neighboring Gateacre were filled to overflowing, so George wound up taking a bus back into the city to the school he would have attended had his family remained in Wavertree—Dovedale Road Primary. There, for the next two years, he shared a schoolyard with John Lennon, though their paths never seem to have crossed.

In 1954, George passed the eleven-plus and was admitted to the Liverpool Institute, thus becoming the first of his brothers to attend a grammar school. Though George was a year behind Paul McCartney at the Institute, the boys became acquainted on the long bus ride into town. Unlike Paul, however, George despised the school. "I think it was awful; the worst time of your life," he said of his grammar-school days. "They were trying to turn everybody into little rows of toffees." His academic performance was summarized by a comment one of his teachers wrote on a term report: "I cannot tell you what his work is like because he has not done any." Harrison exemplified the resentment and resistance felt by many eleven-plus boys who came from families in which the identification with working-class values was strong. His father was a devoted union man, and George had seen both of his brothers leave school at the earliest opportunity to learn a trade and earn a workingman's wage. Harry junior was a car mechanic, while Peter had recently become an apprentice in an automotive body shop. Harry senior nursed the hope of one day opening a garage in partnership with his sons—a prospect unrelated to George's academic career. Nor did it help that the Harrisons lived in Speke, where, as Paul McCartney had learned, grammar-school attendance carried a serious social stigma. George had always been touchy about issues of autonomy; the Institute honed his resentment of authority to a fine edge.

The way he chose to express his disaffection (apart from ignoring his schoolwork) was couched in the symbolism of class. In Speke, nothing advertised his status as "college pudding" more openly than his school uniform of blazer, cap, and tie. Scrounging what he could from his brothers and their friends, George began to customize this staid ensemble with drainpipe trousers, orange socks, double-breasted waistcoats, and pointy-toed "winkle-picker" shoes—thus transforming himself into the Institute's tiniest Ted. Each eye-popping addition to his wardrobe provided a satisfying point of contention with the school authorities. An upswept quiff of thick brown hair (topped by his school cap worn in the precarious style popularized by Gene Vincent and his Bluecaps) added valuable inches to his height and completed the effect.

Like John and Paul, George had shown no more than a casual interest in music prior to the advent of skiffle and rock 'n' roll. His mother gave him the money and the encouragement to buy his first guitar, and she would remember his early efforts at learning to play it as an agony of frustration, complete with bleeding fingertips and outbursts of despair. From the first, George was drawn to the guitar as an instrument in its own right, rather than as a source of accompaniment for his own singing. He had never been a leader, or much of an extrovert; having grown up as the youngest member of a large, exuberant family, his tendency was to find a niche and settle in. The guitar became his new badge of identity. In addition to Carl Perkins, Buddy Holly, and other rock guitarists, his early musical heroes included jazz and country stylists such as Django Reinhardt and Chet Atkins.

Though he knew of the Quarry Men from Paul McCartney, Harrison didn't actually see the band perform until one of their last public engagements in the winter of 1958. For some time thereafter, he remained on the periphery of the group. It was enough of a stretch for a college student like John to associate himself with a grammar-school boy like Paul; George was even younger, "a bloody kid" in Lennon's eyes. But by focusing all of his energies on the guitar, George was able to make up for what he lacked in age and stature with musical proficiency. Gradually he was absorbed into the remnants of the Quarry Men, filling the vacuum left by the attrition of John's original recruits. With Louise Harrison's enthusiastic approval, George's house in Speke became a favorite rehearsal spot. By the summer of 1958, the nucleus of the future Beatles—Lennon, McCartney, and Harrison, two protons and a neutron—was formed. At this point they were not so much a band as a small circle of musical friends.

5

We started off by imitating Elvis, Buddy Holly, Chuck
Berry . . . we just copied what they did. John and I used to
sag off school and go to my house or to his house, and just
start trying to write songs like theirs. We'd put a Buddy
Holly record on, and then after we'd listened to it several
times, we'd sit around with our guitars and try to write
something like him. The people we copied were all American, of course, because there was no one good British.

—Paul McCartney

That the Art College was located directly next door to the Liverpool
Institute made it easy for Lennon, McCartney, and Harrison to stay in
touch on a regular basis. Trundling their guitars to and from their respective schools, the boys would meet at lunchtime in the Art College cafete-
ria or afterward at Paul's or George's or Julia Lennon's house to rehearse
and pass the time. An informal style was set in these early sessions that
would serve them for years to come—a loose routine of playing, joking,
smoking, and listening to records, sometimes working in unison, sometimes noodling away on their guitars as if in separate worlds.

It was of prime importance to their future careers as singers and
songwriters that most of what John Lennon and Paul McCartney
learned about music, they learned in each other's company. Although
collaboration has long been the rule in the writing of popular songs, it is
hard to name another pair of successful popular songwriters whose
musical educations were so closely intertwined from such an early age.
(Even George and Ira Gershwin did not start writing together until they
were past their teens.)

Prior to the advent of Elvis Presley, the two boys' actual experience of
music-making had consisted mainly of the singing they did as children at
church and school. Paul had toyed with the trumpet and taken a few
piano lessons; John had enjoyed a brief infatuation with a harmonica he

was given by his uncle George. Although Paul consulted some "method books" early on, and John may have taken an introductory lesson or two, neither of them sought out formal instruction on the guitar, nor would they ever learn to read or write conventional musical notation. Had they wanted to take lessons, it wasn't as if there was anyone in Liverpool who could have taught them much about the sort of rock-'n'-roll guitar playing they wanted to learn; as it was, they didn't consider the development of technique on the instrument to be an important goal. Rather, they valued the guitar as a means of accompanying their singing and, like Elvis, as a prop for performing. Practice for them did not consist of the usual attempt to master scales and chord inversions that has broken the spirit of generations of musical neophytes. It consisted instead of sitting together for hours, attempting to work out by ear (and often from memory) the songs they wanted to play. Like most of the performers they liked, they confined themselves to a handful of convenient keys, and every new chord or cadence they learned, even if it merely duplicated a harmonic relationship they already knew in another key, came as a small revelation to them. Only slowly did they begin to generalize from specific progressions to the underlying principles of pop composition: the movement between chords built on the tonic, subdominant, and dominant notes of the scale (referred to in musicians' parlance as the I, IV, and V chords); the addition of the flatted sevenths that constitute the most common form of harmonic embellishment used in blues and rock; and the intuitive eight-, twelve-, and thirty-two-bar patterns on which popular songs are built.

Their real teachers were thus the records themselves. They were generally available in Britain from 1957 onward, the success of Bill Haley and Elvis Presley having convinced the country's two major record companies, Decca and EMI, of the market for rock 'n' roll. There was a significant delay, however, in the release of records by some of rock's brightest stars, caused by the time it took for independent American labels like Atlantic, Chess, and Specialty to set up foreign licensing deals. Little Richard's first Top Ten hit on Specialty came in the spring of 1956; it was not released in Britain until the following year. Chuck Berry's first Top Ten hit on Chess came in the summer of 1955; his first success in Britain came nearly two years later, in the summer of 1957, barely a month before Buddy Holly's first record entered the charts. Yet this time lag only helped to sharpen the impact of rock by flooding the market with an abundance of music by the four performers—Presley, Richard, Berry, and Holly—who assumed the places of highest honor in the Quarry Men's pantheon of musical heroes.

That Elvis reigned as the King of Rock was widely recognized long before his fans defiantly bestowed this title upon him during the extended twilight of his career. (Early on, RCA tried to promote him as "The King of Western Bop.") Presley's influence on the Quarry Men and their contemporaries was compounded by his role as the charismatic figurehead of a new, commercialized youth culture that had taken root in the high schools of postwar America and was now spreading by means of records, radio, film, and television throughout the industrialized world. As with Sinatra before him, Presley's status as a culture hero threatened to overshadow the fact that he was also an extraordinarily gifted singer when he first burst on the scene.

Along with many other fledgling musicians in Britain and the United States, the Quarry Men belonged to a subspecies of Elvis aficionados whose initial enthusiasm was, if anything, stronger than that of the average fan, but who eventually came to regard Presley's musical career, in the words of his biographer Peter Guralnik, as a "long and continuing saga of perfect decline." Among this cadre of true believers, opinions varied as to when the fall from grace occurred. "Heartbreak Hotel" is widely acknowledged as a pop cultural milestone; its distinction as the first truly convincing example of white blues singing to broach the popular mainstream is less commonly recognized. "All Shook Up," released in Britain in the summer of 1957 (right around the time that Lennon and McCartney first met), may be Elvis's quintessential performance, in which the Presleyan ego and Presleyan id achieve a state of perfect comic equilibrium. Many of the tracks on his early albums (which included cover versions of songs by Little Richard, Carl Perkins, Clyde McPhatter, and Ray Charles) were similarly superb. The Elvis heard on these hit singles and album cuts is a different singer from the edgy young upstart heard on the Sun recordings. Emboldened by his success, Elvis in his early years at RCA projected an air of complete self-assurance and emotional self-sufficiency—a singer who never came close to losing his composure on a song.

As time went on, however, it became harder for discriminating listeners to overlook the rising proportion of dross to gold in Presley's work. "Jailhouse Rock," released in Britain in January of 1958 as the title track to his third film, was arguably his last great performance as a full-blown rock-'n'-roll singer. (Of the title track to Elvis's fourth film, the lyricist Jerry Leiber said, "If I ever have to write another song like 'King Creole,' I'll cut my fucking throat.") And though RCA continued to release material from its small stockpile of Presley masters during his two-year sabbatical in the army, these tracks, with one or two teasing exceptions, sounded like pale imitations of his earlier hits.

Fans devised their own theories about what had happened to "El." Many blamed the army, surmising that the rigors of military life had tamed Presley's defiant spirit (as symbolized by the Samsonesque crew cut he received as a raw recruit). Others assumed that his record company and his manager had prevailed upon Presley to turn away from rock. Yet the real reasons for Presley's artistic decline began with the nature of his ambition itself—with the fact that, much as Elvis loved to sing, it was never his goal to become a great singer as such. His goal was to become a great star. And the path to stardom in Elvis's day led inexorably to Hollywood. By any measure, the "record business" in the 1950s was still a nickel-and-dime operation compared with the "film industry"; hence the efforts of earlier, phenomenally successful singers like Bing Crosby and Frank Sinatra to broaden their appeal and enhance their prestige by appearing in Hollywood films. An appreciation of the millions to be made in movies was one of the traits that set "Colonel" Tom Parker apart from other country music managers of his time. From 1957 onward, under Parker's supervision, Presley's creative energies and aspirations were channeled into a succession of third-rate Hollywood musicals that were designed to transform a singing sensation into a legitimate star of the screen. As a promotional strategy it was unassailable, and Elvis himself was predictably entranced by the glamour of Hollywood. Yet, unlike Crosby or Sinatra, Presley proved hopeless as a screen actor.

Regardless, the great majority of fans would keep on buying his records and faithfully attending his films. Such was the extent of their fascination or identification with Presley that his transition from rockabilly rebel to pop sensation to the world's richest B-movie star was in no sense perceived as a letdown or a betrayal, for it was the sheer scale of his success and celebrity, not the nature of his art, that mattered most to them. But for rock-'n'-roll loyalists like the Quarry Men, whose lives were so touched by the power of records like "Don't Be Cruel" and "All Shook Up" that they began to dream of making such records themselves,

Presley's career from the late 1950s onward would be tinged with disappointment, until it gradually assumed the tenor of a cautionary tale.

IN A GENRE of popular music that was destined to be almost entirely dominated by male stars, it fell to Little Richard to play the Queen to Presley's King. Born and raised in Macon, Georgia, Richard Penniman left home at the age of fourteen (his departure hastened, he later said, by his father's intolerance of his homosexuality), adopted the moniker Little Richard, and bounced around the rhythm-and-blues circuit during the early 1950s, recording without success for labels as small as Peacock and as big as RCA. In 1955 a tape he submitted to Specialty Records in Los Angeles caught the ear of a producer named Bumps Blackwell, who was looking to sign a singer to emulate the new style of gospel-inflected R&B that Ray Charles was pioneering with great success for Specialty's rival, Atlantic. Thinking that Little Richard might be his man, Blackwell set up a recording date in New Orleans. In keeping with the standard script of the rock-'n'-roll discovery myth, the session went poorly at first. Richard turned out to be an almost freakishly flamboyant and effeminate young man whose singing remained oddly inhibited until, during a break in the session, he sat down at the piano and pounded out an obscene song that began with the exclamation "Awop-bop-aloo-mop-alop-bam-boom / Tutti-frutti, *good booty!*" Bumps Blackwell promptly commissioned some minor adjustments in the lyric and had him repeat this performance with a band.

Released in the fall of 1955, "Tutti-Frutti" was an immediate hit on the R&B charts; it crossed over into the pop Top Twenty in January 1956, two months before "Heartbreak Hotel." Over the next two years, Little Richard released a half-dozen hit singles, all of which relied on a frenetic formula of pounding piano, wailing sax, startling falsetto interjections, and convulsively phrased lyrics that seemed to walk the line between scat singing and talking in tongues. In a sense, Bumps Blackwell had simply overshot the mark in his search for the next Ray Charles. Instead of the soul-stirring black Baptist emotionality with which "Brother Ray" infused the blues, Richard's style was drawn from the histrionic fervor of the Pentecostal and Holiness sects. His records married the sound of the storefront studio to the spirit of the storefront church, and he came across, on the best of them, as if he were truly possessed. His wide, masklike face and wild, lascivious grin lent a crazed aspect to his physical appearance as well. He was precisely what parents and politicians across America had in mind when they declared the need to "do something" about rock 'n' roll.

John Lennon's introduction to Little Richard came in 1956, when a friend of his obtained a Dutch pressing of "Long Tall Sally" several months before its British release. At a time when John considered Elvis to be "bigger than religion in my life," it unnerved him to hear another singer who rivaled his idol's intensity. Lennon was subsequently relieved to learn that Richard was black, a trait that presumably gave him access to sources of musical energy that even Elvis couldn't tap. In Britain especially, Richard's popularity was furthered by his show-stopping, almost shamanistic performance in *The Girl Can't Help It,* the best of the rock-'n'-roll exploitation films. Paul McCartney's imitation of this performance was one of the first things about him that impressed the Quarry Men, and Paul went on to monopolize their efforts to reproduce Richard's songs.

ELVIS PRESLEY AND Little Richard were the two most distinctive singers of 1950s rock, but they were singers and singers only. (Though Richard co-wrote some of his material, neither his writing nor his piano playing was intrinsic to his appeal.) Chuck Berry, on the other hand, combined the talents of singer, songwriter, and instrumentalist in a more distinctive manner than any other 1950s recording artist with the inevitable exception of Ray Charles. Thirty years old at the time of his first success, Berry was the Homer of rock: the music's first and greatest epic poet. Almost single-handedly, he introduced the concept of *authorship* to a style of popular music whose lyric content otherwise consisted mainly of catch-phrases, base clichés, and childish counting rhymes. For this, Paul McCartney considered him "a ridiculous favorite" and John Lennon placed him "in a different class from the other performers." "He really wrote his own stuff," Lennon explained. "The lyrics were fantastic, even if we didn't know what he was saying half the time."

Born and raised in St. Louis, Missouri, Berry drew his influences from a broad spectrum of postwar black music, including the suave pop balladry of Nat "King" Cole; the witty, wordy jump blues of Louis Jordan; and the swaggering Chicago blues of Muddy Waters. In the spring of 1956 he released an anthem to rock, "Roll Over Beethoven," which updated the premise of a Judy Garland record from the 1930s called

"Swing Mr. Mendelssohn." "Beethoven" became the prototype for a series of moderate hits and memorable B-sides on which Berry regaled his teenage listeners with a sympathetic yet gently satiric commentary on their leisure lives. Many of these songs were set in juke joints and dance halls and celebrated what might be termed the existential moment of rock 'n' roll. With a fine sense of irony, Berry wrote about the music as if it were an epic cultural force: "Hail, hail rock 'n' roll," he sang in "School Days," "deliver me from the days of old." His career reached its commercial and creative peak in the spring of 1958 with a pair of Top Ten hits, "Johnny B. Good" and "Sweet Little Sixteen," on which he presented his definitive portraits of the rock-'n'-roll singer and fan.

By itself, Chuck Berry's songwriting was enough to make him a seminal figure in rock, but his influence on the Quarry Men extended to all aspects of music-making. As a singer he was the least affected of the early rock 'n' rollers. He sang in a clear, declamatory voice designed to put the words across, and he avoided the sort of exaggerated vocal mannerisms made famous by Presley and Richard. As an electric guitarist, Berry helped to establish the instrument as the defining *sound* of rock, employing a strident, heavily amplified tone and a muscular technique that allowed for fluid movement between rhythm and solo fills. A consummate showman, Berry was the first well-known rock guitarist to actually *play* the instrument in a sexually provocative manner (this in contrast to Elvis, who merely held it that way). His onstage antics entailed a real risk in America's racially charged social climate of the 1950s, when a whole complex of double standards made it unacceptable for a black man—though not for a black woman—to perform suggestively in front of a white audience. Little Richard managed to defuse this issue by maximizing his effeminate tendencies (at one point billing himself as the "Bronze Liberace"). But Chuck Berry would wind up paying a harsh price for his insistence on behaving, onstage and off, like a "brown-eyed handsome man."

COMPARED WITH THE work of Presley, Richard, and Berry, Buddy Holly's music sounded almost tame. Holly grew up in the postwar boomtown of Lubbock, Texas, at the western extremity of the country-and-western continuum. In 1956, after forming a band with some friends from high school, he landed a contract with the Nashville division of Decca Records (a distant relation of the British label), for whom he recorded several unsuccessful singles. The following year, Holly and his drummer Jerry Allison auditioned at a storefront studio in Clovis, New Mexico, that was run by a former disc jockey and lounge-trio organist named Norman Petty. Their first offering, "That'll Be the Day," was a song Holly had already recorded for Decca—a contractual complication that Petty finessed by selling the remade version to a Decca subsidiary called Brunswick Records as the work of a group called the Crickets. Rising to the top of the charts in the U.S. and Britain, "That'll Be the Day" marked the start of a short run of hits, some of which ("Oh Boy," "Maybe Baby") were released under the Crickets' name, and others of which ("Peggy Sue," "Rave On") were released under Holly's name.

Always more of an integrator than an innovator, Holly combined the giddy enthusiasm of a white boy singing the blues with the musical self-sufficiency of a singer-songwriter-guitarist. Considered individually, his talents were relatively modest, but his lasting contribution to the future of rock stemmed from his willingness to pool those modest talents with those of his fellow Crickets and his producer Norman Petty in the context of a collaborative recording *group,* whose members all contributed to the songwriting, the arranging, and the creation, in the studio, of a distinctive instrumental sound. Though their collective identity began as a marriage of contractual convenience, Holly and the Crickets became the prototype for the small, self-reliant bands of musical brothers that would colonize the landscape of pop in the decade ahead.

Holly's best records were medium-tempo love songs imbued with a tenderness and vulnerability that were rare in a musical genre that often seemed bent on dispensing with all distinctions, euphemistic or not, between the desire for sex and love. Like an insecure teenager fussing at the mirror in search of a distinctive look, Holly embellished his singing with a boyish idiom of yelps, bleats, breaks, growls, squeaks, and hiccupped vowels that turned affectation into a form of affection. Offsetting the innocence of the lyrics (and the occasional corniness of Norman Petty's production) was the instrumental toughness of the band. At their best, Holly and the Crickets presented conventional romantic sentiments in an unconventional setting of stinging guitar and snappy drumming that added a new kind of ardor and urgency to these shopworn professions of love.

Alone among the Quarry Men's quartet of primary influences, Holly and the Crickets were far more popular in Britain than they were in the

United States, and in the wake of their 1958 visit to Liverpool, the group was all but canonized as the city's patron saints of rock 'n' roll. Their influence on the Quarry Men and the other young musicians on Merseyside began with the more or less accurate perception that, while Holly was clearly their leader, the Crickets were truly a group. Their collective image had a special resonance among working-class teenagers in the North of England, where the social sanctions against individualistic behavior were traditionally so strong.

To the Quarry Men and their contemporaries, the prosaic-looking Holly seemed like a messenger from the gods, capable of moving back and forth between the world of ordinary mortals and some distant Olympus of rock. On record and in concert, Holly and the Crickets paid homage to their musical heroes, both by performing their songs, and, more important, by using riffs, rhythms, and arrangements from the records they liked as the basis for their own material. It was no accident that Paul McCartney cited Holly by name when describing the Quarry Men's early and unabashedly imitative efforts at songwriting. He served as their original tutor in the magpie art of musical appropriation.

BEYOND THESE FOUR bright constellations that stood at the center of the Quarry Men's musical universe lay a firmament of lesser-magnitude comets and stars. Prominent among them were the rockabilly singers Carl Perkins and Jerry Lee Lewis, both of whom recorded for Sam Phillips at Sun. Perkins was a gifted guitarist and songwriter whose one real hit, his signature recording of "Blue Suede Shoes," was overshadowed in Britain by Presley's cover version of the song. Perkins's career was dogged by bad luck and hobbled by his lack of sex appeal, but his records provided the Quarry Men, and particularly George Harrison, with a master class in rockabilly guitar. Jerry Lee Lewis fancied himself the heir apparent to Presley; in reality he was more like rockabilly's answer to Little Richard: a histrionic singer and piano player whose two best records, "Great Balls of Fire" and "Whole Lot of Shakin' Going On," took the link between rock 'n' roll and Bible Belt revivalism to its logical extreme. (Lewis's career was derailed in 1958 when it was revealed during an aborted tour of Britain that his third wife was also his second cousin, who was thirteen years old at the time.)

Kissing cousins of a different sort to the Sun rockabillys were the loutish Gene Vincent, whose 1956 recording of "Be-Bop-A-Lula" was a triumph of salacious inanity, and the boyish Eddie Cochran, a singer, guitarist, and songwriter whose knock-kneed performance of "Twenty Flight Rock" in *The Girl Can't Help It* made an indelible impression on an entire generation of aspiring English rockers. Though neither of these rather one-dimensional singers was able to sustain his initial success on the American record charts, both saw their popularity rise in Britain as the 1950s drew to a close. Another star of *The Girl Can't Help It* who won favor with the Quarry Men was Fats Domino, the genial sultan of New Orleans rhythm and blues. From 1955 to 1960, Domino established himself as America's most popular black recording artist, trailing only Presley in the number of records he sold.

Chuck Berry aside, the only other pop songwriters of the period to offer a comparable mixture of narrative and satire were Jerry Leiber and Mike Stoller, who were best known for their work with Presley but best appreciated for their work with the Coasters, a black vocal group who recorded for Atlantic Records. A classic combination of a word man and a music man, Leiber and Stoller exemplified the Jewish-hipster strain in the world of rhythm and blues. Their hits with the Coasters began in 1957 with "Searchin' " and continued with a pair of timeless teen protest songs, "Yakety Yak" and "Charlie Brown" (the second of which might have been written about John Lennon's school days). The hip humor of the Coasters' records and their use of caricature voices made them exceedingly popular with the Quarry Men, who regarded the group as a rock-'n'-roll equivalent of the Goons. Their songs were some of the very few on which Lennon, McCartney, and Harrison summoned the nerve to sing together at the start of their musical careers. Another distinctive group that inspired the Quarry Men to try their hand at vocal harmonies was the Everly Brothers, whose records conveyed an authentic sense of adolescent yearning similar to that of their close friend Buddy Holly.

The Quarry Men's listening at this point was largely confined to current pop, and within that broad category, they shied away from music that was not expressly identified with the sound and generational fury of American rock 'n' roll. John Lennon in particular was quick to label a record "soft" (meaning sentimental), thereby dismissing it from further consideration. Although they showed a certain preference for the flip side over the hit, they were not in any sense "record collectors," scouring shops in search of obscure or undiscovered gems. As a result, like most white teenagers in Britain and America, they remained unfamiliar with the earthier, adult-oriented styles of rhythm and blues associated with artists like Muddy Waters, Joe Turner, Howlin' Wolf, and B.B. King. Even the great Ray Charles they knew mainly secondhand, from covers of his songs by Elvis Presley and Eddie Cochran. Apart from George Harrison's appreciation of Django Reinhardt, instrumental jazz, be it "modern" or "traditional," they dismissed as a highbrow taste. Modern jazz intimidated them with its virtuosity and harmonic sophistication. Trad jazz, despite its connection to skiffle, they rejected as arty, outdated, and fake. They felt much the same way about most folk music, which in Britain at that time referred mainly to sea shanties, Scotch-Irish ballads, and pre-war American blues. Rock 'n' roll, by comparison, had a temporal as well as a visceral immediacy for them. Like its country of origin, it seemed to be in tune with the world to come.

6

A disconcerting mixture of sincerity and cheerful malice, of tenderness and freebooting cruelty; restless, importunate, full of pride, a combination which alienates the sensitive and insensitive alike. Blistering honesty, or apparent honesty, like his, makes few friends.

—John Osborne (on Jimmy Porter)

John Lennon's renewed relationship with his mother, Julia, continued to flourish during his first year at the Art College, as the emotional contrast between Julia and his aunt Mimi became more absolute. Where Mimi scoffed at John's musical interests, Julia encouraged them. Where Mimi scorned his Teddy-boy clothes, Julia fancied them. Where Mimi looked down at his working-class friends, Julia welcomed them. This at least was how John saw it—though if there was any overt rivalry between the two women for his affections, it doesn't seem to have compromised their own relationship. Along with a third Stanley sister, Harriet Birch, who lived around the corner from Mendips, Julia was now in the habit of stopping by Mimi's for an hour or two of idle chat nearly every day.

It was on a twilit evening in July of 1958, while returning home from one of these visits, that John's mother was struck by a car in the middle of Menlove Avenue. She died in an ambulance on the way to the hospital, at the age of forty-four. The car was driven by an off-duty policeman who claimed he hadn't seen Julia as she stepped out of the privet hedge that lined the median strip. Though Mimi maintained that the driver was drunk at the time, a coroner's inquest ruled the death an accident.

As it had been with his uncle George, John's outward reaction to his mother's death was muted, but there is no question that this searing loss marked a turning point in his escalating war with the world. In the months that followed, the aggression and hostility that had been building in him since childhood erupted with terrifying force in bouts of drunken anger and calculated cruelty. The rude repartee with which he habitually teased his friends and tested the strength of their affection now took on a dark, retributive edge. "I was in a sort of blind rage," Lennon recalled. "There was something the matter with me." When he wasn't abusing his friends, he was amusing them at the expense of unsuspecting strangers who happened to cross his path. He took particular pleasure in ridiculing the cripples and amputees who were a common sight on the streets of postwar Liverpool. Those who had no choice but to show their wounds on the outside evoked a special horror in an embittered seventeen-year-old who was now engaged in a daily struggle to keep his own wounds hidden.

For all the sense it gave him of being double-crossed by fate ("I lost my mother twice," Lennon later said), Julia's death did serve to bring the simmering crisis of her son's adolescence to a head. Prior to this tragedy, John's mask of self-assurance had been imperturbable. After Julia's death, the pose could no longer be held. The loss of his mother drew him closer to Paul McCartney, with whom he now shared a special emotional bond. Julia's death also seems to have had some bearing on a pair of new relationships John formed after he returned to the Art College in the fall of 1958.

The first of these was a friendship with a student named Stuart Sutcliffe, who was regarded by many of his classmates as one of the most gifted artists at the school. A sensitive, almost delicate child of Scottish descent, Stuart attended the local grammar school near his home by Sefton Park until his precocious artistic ability qualified him for early admission to the Art College, where he arrived the year before John. His talent and his quiet temperament set him apart from the other students and earned him the admiration of a tutor named Arthur Ballard, who became his mentor at the school. Well-mannered and serious-minded, Sutcliffe was an odd match for Lennon, but that was surely the point: each boy became fascinated by the extremes of the other's personality. Where John cultivated his defenses, Stuart cultivated his vulnerabilities. Inspired by the 1956 film *Lust for Life,* he had embraced the role of the alienated artist to the point of developing a strong identification with Vincent Van Gogh, which he expressed by painting disturbing self-portraits and signing his work using his first name only. Together with a bookish classmate named Bill Harry, Stuart had also familiarized himself with the available works of Beat poetry and the metaphysical musings of Colin Wilson, whose 1956 bestseller *The Outsider* served as a diffuse primer in romanticism, existentialism, and mysticism. Still another influence on Sutcliffe's *maudit* persona was the air of pained sensitivity associated with Method-trained actors like the late James Dean—to whom John's new friend, with his slight stature, small features, and swept-back pompadour, bore a distinct physical resemblance.

The second new relationship that graced John's second year of college was a love affair with a girl named Cynthia Powell, who commuted to the school from her home in Hoylake, on the Wirral Peninsula. Cynthia's family background was lower middle class, but because she came from Hoylake, acted demure, and dressed conservatively, she was presumed to be quite posh. Toward the end of the fall term, to the amazement of their classmates, these two seemingly disparate characters fell head-over-heels in love. In fact they had more in common than met the eye, for not only was Cynthia's social background similar to John's, but her father, to whom she was very close, had died two years before. On the face of it, however, their relationship looked like Jimmy and Alison Porter all over again: he the flamboyant lower-class rebel; she the proper middle-class girl entranced by his intensity.

John's grief over his mother's death and the pull of these new relationships left him with less time for the Quarry Men during his second year at the Art College. Though the group continued to rehearse on an irregular basis, their only known performances during this period came at a couple of Harrison family functions and, thanks to the efforts of Stuart Sutcliffe and his friend Bill Harry, as a supporting act at several Art College dances.

Paul McCartney was also preoccupied by matters other than music during the fall of 1958, having jeopardized his bright academic future by failing four of the five O-level examinations he had taken the summer before. Placed in a remedial form for the fall term and faced with the unappealing prospect of leaving school and having to get a job, Paul applied himself to his studies and retook his O-levels in December, passing them this time. In January 1959 he joined the Institute's sixth form, where he began preparing for A-level examinations in art, geography, and English literature. He had earned an eighteen-month reprieve.

By tradition and design, the sixth form was a world apart from the rest of the Institute. Its students were granted considerable autonomy in their studies and freedom of movement around the school. They were taught by the best masters, with whom they enjoyed a new kind of relaxed favor.

That Paul chose to specialize in English literature reflected his affection for a teacher named Alan Durband, who had studied literature at Cambridge with the firebrand critic F. R. Leavis. Durband introduced his sixth-form students to Leavis's great passion, the novels of D. H. Lawrence, along with works by such contemporary American writers as James Thurber and Tennessee Williams. But when he tried to impress upon McCartney the need to study hard in order to get ahead, he eventually concluded that Paul simply "wouldn't compete to become an Oxbridge type of person." To the extent that Paul retained higher academic aspirations, he now saw himself studying literature, or possibly art, at the Liverpool University. Yet he also knew that the most likely destination for a middling sixth-form student like himself was one of the many second-rate teacher-training colleges that had been set up during the 1950s to meet the staffing mandates of the Butler Act reforms.

George Harrison turned fifteen in February 1959. Three months later, without bothering to take any O-levels, he fulfilled his fondest ambition and withdrew from grammar school. His immediate plans consisted of dressing as he liked and playing his guitar. With the Quarry Men so idle, Harrison began to sit in with a guitarist he knew named Ken Brown at a private club in the West Derby section of Liverpool. Upon hearing that a new club called the Casbah was opening up the street, George and his friend persuaded the owner, a woman named Mona Best, to hire the Quarry Men (with new member Ken Brown) as the house band. Behind a cacophonous front of four guitars, the group played the Casbah a half-dozen times in the late summer of 1959—until Brown quit and promptly trumped the Quarry Men by forming a new house band with Mona Best's son, a neophyte drummer named Pete.

The opening of the Casbah coincided with an upsurge of grassroots musical activity on Merseyside—the first stirrings of an indigenous "beat music" scene (the term appears to have been native to Liverpool) that was centered on a circuit of dance halls and coffee bars. The dances were generally held on weekends and run by part-time promoters who operated on the fringe of organized show business. Depending on their location, they could be very rough affairs, providing rival gangs of Teddy boys with a weekly forum in which to settle issues of pride and turf. The coffee bars ranged from full-scale commercial establishments to informal membership clubs that operated, like the Casbah, in the basements of private homes.

The first local beat groups to gain a following in Liverpool were Cass & The Cassanovas, known for their powerful rhythm section, Derry & The Seniors, known for their West Indian lead singer, and Rory Storm & The Hurricanes, known for Rory Storm, a blond Scouse Adonis who cornered the local market in flashy showmanship. A former high school athlete, Storm (whose real name was Alan Caldwell) enlivened his performances with gymnastic stunts of such daring that they sometimes resulted in injuries. With the help of a devoted stage mother, he had turned his family home (henceforth known as "Stormville") into the center of a microcosmic pop cult. Each member of the Hurricanes was awarded a colorful stage name, derived from Hollywood Westerns by the image-conscious Storm. His guitarist was Johnny Guitar. His bassist was Lou Walters. His drummer was a doleful-looking character called Ringo Starr.

The Quarry Men were complete nonentities in this local music scene. Their brief residency at the Casbah had whetted their appetite for performing, but without a rhythm section they were not a viable band. Drummers and bass guitarists were in short supply on Merseyside, for the instruments were expensive, and neither had figured heavily in the skiffle craze. In any case, teenagers who could afford the monthly payments on a set of drums or an electric bass tended to be the sort of affluent young laborers who rarely had much contact with art college students and grammar-school boys.

So it was that in September 1959, Paul McCartney began his second term of sixth-form studies at the Liverpool Institute; George Harrison appeased his anxious father by finding a job as an electrician's apprentice at a downtown department store; and John Lennon moved out of his home on Menlove Avenue, joining with Stuart Sutcliffe and a classmate named Rod Murray in renting a flat near the Art College. In the judgment of his teachers, Lennon's second year at the college had been as dismal as his first; it was only due to the influence of Sutcliffe's tutor, Arthur Ballard, that John was allowed to stay on.

That fall, with Ballard's encouragement, Stuart Sutcliffe entered one of his paintings in a newly established biennial exhibition at the Walker Art Gallery that was sponsored by the prominent Liverpool businessman and art collector John Moores. When Moores himself bought Sutcliffe's painting for sixty pounds, the artist, at the urging of his friend John Lennon, used this windfall to purchase an electric bass guitar. Suitably equipped, Stuart became the newest member of Johnny & The Moon-dogs, as the Quarry Men, bowing to the current fashion in band names, had taken to calling themselves.

Sutcliffe's enrollment in the Moondogs was a fair indication of how much the group still functioned as an extension of John Lennon's social life, since Stuart's only qualification was his standing as John's friend. Neither Paul McCartney nor George Harrison was enthusiastic about the new member, whose complete lack of facility on the bass could only have served to reinforce their reputation as a bunch of dilettantes. Yet the surest sign of Sutcliffe's improbability as a rock musician was the oddly totemic name he now proposed for the group. Out of homage to Buddy Holly, whose tragic death in a plane crash nine months before had sealed his cult status in Britain, Stuart now suggested that the Moondogs follow in the entomological footsteps of Holly's Crickets by calling themselves the Beetles. His suggestion was met with uncertainty by his bandmates and derision by everyone else. Crickets, after all, are regarded as the most musical of insects. Beetles, by comparison, are generally seen as mute, ignoble creatures, one step up from a grub. (As a fan of *The Outsider*, Sutcliffe may also have been influenced by the book's repeated references to the protagonist of Dostoevsky's *Notes from the Underground* as a "beetle-man.") In an effort to salvage his friend's inspiration, John Lennon added a characteristic twist by suggesting that they spell it "Bea-tles," as a dual-edged pun on beat music and Beat writing. But the others remained dubious, and further tinkering ensued. It hardly mattered what they called themselves until they found some work.

Among the local haunts frequented by students at the Art College was a tiny shrine to the cosmopolitan character of Liverpool called the Jacaranda Club. Belying its South American name, the Jacaranda was an Italian-style espresso bar owned by a short, stout Welshman named Allan Williams, who ran the place with the help of his Anglo-Chinese wife, Beryl, a schoolteacher by trade. Like many such establishments on the edge of the city center, the "Jac" functioned as a lunch bar by day, a neighborhood hangout by night. Regular entertainment was provided by a gaggle of West Indians called the Royal Caribbean Steel Band; they were supplemented at odd moments by the owner himself, who liked to affirm his Welshness by bursting into song. Williams's own taste in music ran toward opera and ballads, but in March 1960 a rock-'n'-roll package tour headlined by the fading American stars Eddie Cochran and Gene

Vincent played a week at the Empire Theatre in Liverpool. Sensing the buzz of excitement that ran through the teenage population of Merseyside, Williams resolved to add the title "concert promoter" to the long list of short-lived occupations at which he had tried his luck. He boldly contacted the London impresario Larry Parnes and arranged with him to bring Cochran and Vincent back to town for a concert at the Liverpool Stadium, a six-thousand-seat boxing arena, later in the spring. The news of this booking vaulted Allan Williams into the forefront of pop promotion on Merseyside. Banking on their status as regular customers, John Lennon and Stuart Sutcliffe began to prevail on the Jacaranda's owner to do something nice for their group.

IN THE SPRING of 1960, Elvis Presley was honorably discharged from the United States Army and marked his return to civilian life by donning a tuxedo and appearing on a television special hosted by Frank Sinatra, who three years before (in a ghost-written magazine article) had denounced rock 'n' roll as "the music of every sideburned delinquent on the face of the earth . . . the most brutal, ugly, desperate, vicious form of expression it has ever been my misfortune to hear." Sinatra reportedly paid Presley $100,000 for his ten-minute spot on the show. In the two years since Elvis had last performed in public, the pantheon of rock had crumbled as, one by one, its occupants succumbed to miscalculation, misfortune, and misadventure. Buddy Holly was dead. Little Richard had been seized by a religious epiphany, retired from the music business, and enrolled in an Alabama Bible college. Jerry Lee Lewis's marital scandal had consigned him to a state of professional exile, and Chuck Berry had been indicted on federal charges after a teenage prostitute from Texas was found to be working in a St. Louis nightclub he owned. As if to herald the prospect of a return to normalcy in the music business, the hottest new show on Broadway that season was Bye Bye Birdie, in which Tin Pan Alley exacted its revenge on Elvis by expertly burlesquing his career.

That same spring in Britain, the pop charts were dominated by a blandly handsome, blandly competent singer called Cliff Richard (real name Harry Webb), who had gotten his start in skiffle and made the transition to a more rock-oriented sound with the help of a four-piece backup band called the Shadows. Onstage, Cliff and the Shadows moved in tight, synchronous motion. Offstage, Richard gave interviews in which he spoke of his ambition to follow in the footsteps of Sir Laurence Olivier by playing the part of Heathcliff in a film of *Wuthering Heights*.

Cliff Richard's chief rival for the affections of British teenagers was a singer named Billy Fury, who gave the impression that he didn't know Heathcliff from a hole in the ground. Fury affected a more pugnacious look than Richard and his voice had more of an edge. His real name was Ronald Wycherly, and though he made no effort to advertise it, he came from Liverpool. The man responsible for transforming him from a Wycherly into a Fury was Larry Parnes, who had codified the lessons he learned from managing Britain's first teenage idol, the Cockney singer Tommy Steele (real name Tommy Hicks), into what was widely seen as a surefire formula for the creation of British pop stars. Parnes would take a suitably representative working-class lad who could more or less carry a tune, dress him in Presleyan garb, and assign him an evocative name. Reginald Smith became Marty Wilde. Richard Kneller became Dickie Pride. By 1960, Parnes had assembled a contingent of young, bewildered-looking male singers who were invariably described (with a verbal leer) as his "stable."

Lennon, McCartney, Harrison, and Sutcliffe professed nothing but disdain for most of the singers corralled by Larry Parnes, much less for the process by which they were groomed for fame. Nevertheless, in May of 1960, when Allan Williams grandly announced that Larry Parnes and Billy Fury would shortly be coming to Liverpool in hopes of hiring a backing group for Fury's next British tour, the Silver Beetles (as they were calling themselves that month) signed up for the audition along with a half-dozen other bands.

As things turned out, Billy Fury chose not to hire any of the local talent, but Larry Parnes was sufficiently impressed with the Silver Beetles to offer them a job playing behind one of his lesser creations, a singer named Johnny Gentle, on a week-long "tour" of Scotland beginning right away. After recruiting a drummer named Tommy Moore, who was nearly twice their age (and convincing Jim McCartney that a week away from school would be good for his son), the Silver Beetles piled into a rented van and, with Johnny Gentle as their designated driver, headed northward in the general direction of John o' Groats.

The Johnny Gentle Tour was a musical and logistical fiasco, culminating in a minor van accident that put Tommy Moore in the hospital for a day. But the fans in Scotland were notoriously starved for live rock 'n' roll—eighteen months before, a crowd of Dundee teenagers had nearly dismembered Tommy Steele—and for the Silver Beetles, the whole experience smacked of high adventure. On the strength of the group's first professional credit, moreover, Allan Williams was able to get them some bookings at a pair of dance halls in Liscard and Neston, two of the *least* posh towns on the Wirral Peninsula. Relying on a succession of pickup drummers (even without the accident, a week in a van with John Lennon had been enough for Tommy Moore), the group played these tough, Ted-infested ballrooms twice a week during the summer of 1960. In the meantime, Williams accompanied another of his clients, Derry & The Seniors, on a trip to London in search of work. There he met a German promoter named Bruno Koschmider, who was looking to import some English beat groups to play at a Hamburg nightclub he owned. Williams persuaded Koschmider to hire Derry & The Seniors, who left for Hamburg in July. Two weeks later, Koschmider contacted Williams to request a second group for a second nightclub he owned. Williams's first choice was Rory Storm & The Hurricanes, but they were booked for the entire summer at a Butlin's Holiday Camp. After several other local bands declined the chance to go, Williams informed the Beatles (as they had finally decided to call themselves) that if they could find a drummer, they could have the job.

Right around the time that Williams made them this offer, Paul McCartney and George Harrison revisited the Casbah to check up on their former bandmate Ken Brown. Brown's drummer, Pete Best, was a handsome eighteen-year-old who had recently left grammar school with the vague intention of pursuing a career in show business. Pete's father, Johnny, was a well-known boxing promoter in Liverpool; his mother, Mona, was a feisty woman of Anglo-Indian background who was willing to do almost anything—like running a beat club in her basement—for the benefit of her son. Pete Best had been playing the drums for barely a year when the Beatles approached him in August 1960 to ask him to join their band, but that was four months longer than Stuart Sutcliffe had been playing the bass. Best looked the part, owned a set of drums, and, unlike anyone else the Beatles knew on Merseyside, was willing to accompany a group of virtual strangers on a month-long trip to Germany.

7

Many people ask what are Beatles? Why Beatles? Ugh, Beatles, how did the name arrive? So we will tell you. It came in a vision—a man appeared on a flaming pie and said unto them, "From this day forward you are Beatles with an A." Thank you Mister Man, they said, thanking him. And then a man with a beard cut off said—will you go to Germany (Hamburg) and play mighty rock for the peasants for money? And we said we would play mighty anything for money.

—John Lennon

Both in the way that others saw them and in the way they saw themselves, Hamburg was the place where the Beatles' story first tapped into what Joseph Campbell in his classic work *The Hero with a Thousand Faces* called the *monomyth*. The hallmark of the monomyth is the theme of a journey to a strange and distant land, in the course of which a young hero is tested by his encounters with various benevolent and malevolent forces, and from which the hero returns, sometimes in triumph, sometimes in flight, but either way transformed by the experience, and possessed of some new form of strength or knowledge that has the power to change the world. Had the Beatles never been heard from again, the three and a half months they spent in Germany in the fall of 1960 would have been for them the same lurid detour on a road to obscurity that it was for the Derry & The Seniors, Rory Storm & The Hurricanes, Kingsize Taylor & The Dominoes, and the many other Liverpool bands that performed in the nightclubs of Hamburg during the early 1960s. But for the Beatles—and of these many groups, for the Beatles alone—their first trip to Germany engendered a remarkable transformation. It was in Hamburg, far removed from the doubts of their families and the disbelief of their friends, that the Beatles began to subscribe to their own private mythology. That they were self-conscious and half-believing as they pursued this process of collective self-invention was apparent from the facetious tone of John Lennon's written account (published in 1961 in the music paper *Mersey Beat* under the title "A Short Diversion on the Dubious Origins of Beatles") of their meeting with a man on a flaming pie. But pursue it they did. And with the help of several benevolent figures they met along the way, the Beatles would transform themselves in Hamburg as musicians, performers, and personalities. Their trip to Germany was the first and most crucial in a series of initiatory journeys they would undertake in the years ahead. Each of these journeys would penetrate to a greater source of power, subject them to new trials and temptations, and reap them a richer return—until eventually their own collective rite of passage would come to symbolize the rites of passage for millions of adolescents in countries all over the world.

As for the setting of this metamorphosis, Hamburg in 1960 was the great commercial and maritime center of the German Federal Republic, a prosperous metropolis of just under two million people, straddling the banks of the Elbe River some sixty miles inland from the North Sea. Its history and geography presented numerous parallels with Liverpool, for Hamburg, too, had come into its own in the nineteenth century as a western-facing port. Its ships had carried hundreds of thousands of passengers and countless tons of cargo between the Old World and the New, forging commercial and cultural ties with Britain and the United States that made it the most Anglophonic and Anglophilic city in Germany. Remarkably, Hamburg's enthusiasm for things English had withstood the effects of both world wars, the second of which brought destruction of catastrophic proportions down on Germany's principal port. Yet the pace of the city's recovery from this devastation had been truly miraculous. By the time the Beatles arrived there, fifteen years after the last bomb fell, the high-spired Gothic churches had been exactingly rebuilt, the docks were expanded and modernized, hundreds of new mills and factories stood on the wreckage of the old, and vast tracts of notably well-designed housing spread amid a network of tree-lined boulevards and carefully landscaped parks. In starkly ironic contrast to its victorious rival Liverpool, Hamburg's traditional climate of bustling prosperity had been entirely restored.

Rebuilt along with everything else was the old St. Pauli quarter, close behind the dockyards on the northern bank of the Elbe, known the world over for a twenty-block area bisected by a street called the Reeperbahn

that had grown since the reign of Bismarck (whose gigantic granite like-
ness loomed above the treetops in a neighboring park) into what con-
noisseurs of vice regarded as the largest and most comprehensive
"amusement district" in all of Europe. What distinguished St. Pauli from
its equivalents in Liverpool or Marseilles was the same North German
genius for organization that distinguished Hamburg in general from
other, more chaotic ports. The Reeperbahn and its principal side street,
Grosse Freiheit ("Great Freedom"), were lined with a garish array of
neon-lit nightclubs, cafés, restaurants, cinemas, dance halls, cabarets,
strip joints, peep shows, gay bars, sex shops, flophouses, and brothels
where, side by side with more seemly forms of entertainment, every type
of erotic activity, from mere titillation to the most bizarre forms of copu-
lation, could be seen or had for a price. At the same time, a vigilant police
presence made the streets quite safe for passersby, ensuring that on any
given night the crowds along the Reeperbahn would include a substantial number of middle-aged, middle-class couples wandering wide-eyed
among the sailors, dockers, gangsters, grifters, transvestites, pimps, and
whores.

The Beatles' first venue in Hamburg was a converted strip joint on
Grosse Freiheit called the Indra Club. Their lodgings were a pair of
squalid rooms behind the screen at a nearby movie house, the Bambi
Kino. Their work consisted of performing six nights a week, for four to six
hours a night. Said Paul McCartney, "Our role in life was to make people
buy more beer. That's how we started out." Their employer, Bruno
Koschmider, was a forbidding figure with a gimpy leg and classic Teutonic demeanor. At a time when most of the live music played in the
amusement district was a debased variety of Dixieland jazz, Koschmider
had introduced beat groups into the Indra and the Kaiserkeller, his larger
club, in hopes of attracting a younger crowd. (His letterhead described
the Kaiserkeller as a *Tanzpalast der Jugend,* a "dance palace for youth.")
His interest in music was thus confined to its capacity to generate an air
of excitement and novelty that would draw people into his clubs. At first
he found the Beatles too sedate for this purpose, and exhorted them in
his pidgin English to "make show." They responded by doing their best to
make a spectacle of themselves onstage, adopting a clownish, frenetic
approach to performing that was quite at odds with their former, more
studied pretensions to cool. In October, satisfied with the group's new
level of showmanship, Koschmider extended the Beatles' contract and

moved them into the Kaiserkeller, where for the next two months they alternated sets with Rory Storm & The Hurricanes, who had just arrived from Liverpool.

The most tangible transformation that Hamburg worked on the Beatles was the improvement in their musical craft. In their first three weeks at the Indra Club, the group spent more time performing onstage than they had in three years of sporadic appearances in Liverpool, while the requirement that they play for up to six hours a night exhausted their meager repertoire. At first they filled the time by stretching out every number, repeating the verses over and over, vamping endlessly on the chords. Quickly, however, to ward off boredom, they began to introduce new songs into their act. These consisted mostly of recent hits and old standards they found on the local jukeboxes or picked up from other bands. Except for the occasional ballad, they applied the same hard, stamping beat to every new song they learned. This foursquare rhythm with its choppy double upbeat in the middle of each bar became the first principle of the Beatles' music in Hamburg. Its simplicity suited the dancing needs of their audience and went a long way toward camouflaging the deficiencies of their rhythm section. Varying only its tempo, they concentrated on playing it louder and harder than any other band.

The Beatles' efforts at musical self-improvement were facilitated by another of Bruno Koschmider's English imports, a grammar-school dropout from Norwich named Tony Sheridan. Sheridan was the most accomplished rock-'n'-roll guitarist the Beatles had ever met, and as vocally adept an Elvis imitator as Britain had yet produced. But a reputation for obnoxiousness and undependability had blighted his career at home. As a member of a group called Vince Taylor and the Playboys, he had arrived in Hamburg in the summer of 1959 and quickly established himself, at the age of twenty, as the dean of the Reeperbahn beat music scene. Soon after the Beatles moved to the Kaiserkeller, Sheridan and his band began to play at a rival club called the Top Ten, which had opened around the corner in a converted hippodrome. Sheridan felt an immediate affinity with the Beatles and took them under his wing. In addition to overseeing their musical educations, he introduced them to some of the finer points of the St. Pauli lifestyle, including a variety of amphetamine called Preludin whose popularity with West Germans in all walks of life had given a stiff pharmacological boost to the country's postwar economic miracle. Marketed euphemistically as "slimming tablets" and readily available from the waiters and barmaids in all the local clubs, these pep pills enabled their users to stay awake and skittishly engaged for hours, even days, on end. They also inspired a talkativeness and an edgy, excitable energy that would shortly earn them favor as the 1960s' first great intensity-drug.

If the most tangible benefit of the Beatles' stay in Hamburg involved the improvement in their musicianship and stagecraft, the more mysterious transformation involved the growth of their identity as a group. They came to Germany as five young Englishmen whose experience of the world beyond Liverpool had consisted of a week-long trip to Scotland and, before that, of family holidays in places like Blackpool and Edinburgh and sightseeing trips to London. Suddenly they were immersed in the Threepenny Opera underworld of one of Europe's great commercial cities, earning good money and spending all of it on themselves, living the life they had dreamed of living ever since Elvis Presley first presented them with an impossibly far-fetched alternative to the narrow vistas of grammar school. The Reeperbahn was the realization of all the lurid fantasies of freedom and pleasure they had absorbed from American music and films. Apart from the other English musicians on the scene, no one in Hamburg knew them, and no one cared what they did. This extended respite from the familiarity and reflexive debunkery of Liverpool, which blunted ambition as surely as it punctured pretension, granted the Beatles the license to be whoever they wanted to be. They responded by becoming almost entirely self-referential during their stay in Germany.

At first, in the insular manner of Englishmen abroad, they shunned all casual contact—apart from sex—with the native population. By day they hung out at the British seamen's mission near the St. Pauli Landing Stage. By night they performed in front of drunken, distracted patrons who regarded them as little more than loud props in the lumpen–Las Vegas glitter of the Reeperbahn. Emboldened by their mandate to "make show" (and shielded by Koschmider's goons), they stopped at nothing to get a rise from the crowd. "Where are your tanks now, you bastards!" John Lennon would shout at the jabbering "Krauts" (as the Beatles called them) in their audience, most of whom were too young or drunk or oblivious to take offense. The long days and nights of playing, clowning, arguing, and bantering among themselves gradually turned the Beatles into a kind of tiny self-governing society.

While this tendency is common (though by no means universal) among musical groups and theatrical troupes that spend time on the road, the Beatles' version of it was unusual on account of their youth, their inexperience, their immobility, and the lack of formal structure in their group. If anything, Hamburg helped to level the schoolboy hierarchy that had governed their relations in Liverpool, since the differences in their ages meant nothing in a place where, by local standards, all five were babes in the woods.

Hamburg also helped to level some of the differences in their personalities, which were now subsumed in their shared identities as Englishmen, Liverpudlians, and Beatles—none of which had counted for much back in Liverpool. Indeed, having finally decided to call themselves the Beatles, they began to dress the part, shedding the mauve suit jackets they had worn onstage in Liverpool for a thick new skin of shiny black leather, of the sort worn by Gene Vincent during his recent British tour, and favored by many of the young merchant seaman and *schlagers* ("toughs") who patronized the St. Pauli clubs.

Their developing sense of group identity did not necessarily translate into a sense of group harmony over the length of their Hamburg stay. Like any clique of male adolescents, their relations were coarse, their egos were fragile, and they were prone to rivalries. As the last to join, the taciturn Pete Best remained something of a stranger in their midst, for he did not share in their humor, and by nature kept to himself. Yet the other Beatles were so grateful at having found a steady drummer (and Pete was nothing if not steady) that they tended to leave him alone. A more serious source of discord arose from Stuart Sutcliffe's shortcomings as a bass player, which only became more glaring as the rest of the band improved. Sutcliffe's ineptitude (which no one has ever disputed) is a bit puzzling in light of his intelligence and creativity. Considering that a good many people of modest musical ability have learned to play the bass well enough for the purposes of rock 'n' roll, his failure to improve on the instrument suggests that Sutcliffe may well have been tone deaf, and forced to play from memory rather than by ear. Whatever the cause, as musical prowess became the standard by which the Beatles measured their worth, their bassist's failings became a flashpoint for the tensions in the group. Paul McCartney emerged as Sutcliffe's sharpest critic—his impatience quickened by the two boys' rivalrous relationship with John. But Lennon also picked on his close friend constantly. Had this been taking place in Liverpool, Sutcliffe most likely would have left the Beatles at this point. But in the third month of their Hamburg stay, Stuart's relationship with the rest of the group took a momentous and unexpected turn.

One evening shortly after the Beatles had moved to the Kaiserkeller in October, a young graphic artist named Klaus Voorman came into the club, attracted by the sound of the music blaring into the street. The son of a Berlin doctor, Voorman had lived in Hamburg as an art student since 1956, but he was an infrequent visitor to the Reeperbahn, and he was intimidated by the seamy atmosphere of the Kaiserkeller. The Beatles, however, enthralled him, and he returned a few nights later accompanied by his girlfriend, a twenty-two-year-old photographer's assistant named Astrid Kirchherr. Astrid lived with her widowed mother in Altona, an upscale suburb of Hamburg (her father had been an executive with the German division of Ford). She felt no more at home in the Kaiserkeller than did Klaus Voorman, but she, too, was electrified by the Beatles. From that night on, Astrid, Klaus, and a third friend named Jurgen Vollmer became fixtures at the club, sitting by themselves at a table near the stage, their attention riveted on the band. The three of them had met at a private art college in Hamburg, and though they moved in a scene that was essentially a more sophisticated version of the scene at the Liverpool College of Art, it would be some time before they understood that any of the Beatles shared such a background with them.

In the beginning, Astrid, Klaus, and Jurgen were simply three young German bohemians excited by the stylized presence of five young English proletarians. "I had always been fascinated in a way by Teddy boys," Astrid recalled. "I'd liked the look of them in photographs and films. Suddenly there were five of them in front of me. . . . I just sat there openmouthed." Contact between these two groups was inhibited at first by the language barrier and by the Beatles' insularity. Voorman and Vollmer spoke schoolboy English; McCartney and Best spoke schoolboy German. The others could barely converse. Yet this did not prevent Astrid Kirchherr from recognizing, as she studied these five apparitional Teddy boys, the one whose sensibility most closely matched her own. Within a few weeks of their first meeting, with Klaus Voorman's acquiescence, she and Stuart Sutcliffe had fallen deeply, wordlessly, in love. To Astrid, Stuart looked "like a character from a story by Edgar Allan Poe." This would prove to be more accurate than even she could know.

Astrid Kirchherr would play the Goddess in the Beatles' incipient myth. Her qualifications for this part began with the fact that she was a stunningly attractive young woman, with pale skin, softly inquisitive eyes, and close-cropped blond hair that caused her to resemble the American actress Jean Seberg, whose recent performance in the Jean-Luc Godard film *Breathless* had popularized a new, androgynous style of Euro-chic. Astrid's faintly boyish beauty combined with her forthright manner and her fiercely romantic temperament to generate a considerable mystique. Two years older than the oldest of the Beatles, she held stronger and more informed opinions about the visual arts and literature than anyone they knew. In her rebellion against the stolid burgher ethos of Hamburg, she and her circle of art-college friends had taken most of their stylistic and attitudinal cues from Paris—from French films, novels, and fashion, and from the café existentialism of Saint-Germain-des-Pres. Referring to themselves as "exis," they thrilled to Edith Piaf, lionized Camus, and allied themselves with a branch of aestheticism, eroticism, and modernism which, in Astrid's case, had led her to a special fascination with the work of Jean Cocteau. (Cocteau, that is, whose best-known film retold the legend of Orpheus, the divinely endowed musician who descended into an Underworld far more treacherous than Hamburg's Reeperbahn to rescue his beloved Eurydice.)

It is a safe bet that had the Beatles at this point in their lives encountered a similarly well-read, well-bred *English* girl whose taste in culture ran to the likes of Poe and de Sade, Camus and Cocteau, their class-consciousness alone would have prevented them from having anything much to do with her. But Astrid's artistic and intellectual pretensions were softened by her halting English, by her looks and stylishness, and, above all, by her forthright fascination with *them*. Over time, most of her influence on the Beatles would be channeled through her relationship with Stuart Sutcliffe. But she began to exert a profound effect even before the start of their love affair. One afternoon not long after their first meeting at the Kaiserkeller, Astrid escorted her five new English friends to a deserted fairground near the Reeperbahn. There, against a desolate backdrop of empty rides and shuttered carnival booths, she photographed them in a series of somber, informal poses, perched on the fenders of caravans and the beds of trailer trucks, cradling their guitars.

In years to come, these photographs would be so widely imitated that it is hard, in retrospect, to appreciate the singularity of Astrid's vision. One can search through whole archives of music-business portraiture taken prior to 1960 and find nothing resembling them. Technically

The Beatles in Hamburg, November 1960 (George, Stuart, John)

accomplished and elegantly composed, they are unquestionably some of the first art photographs (as opposed to news or publicity photographs) ever taken of rock musicians. Yet their real distinction involves something other than their purely aesthetic quality, for it remains that no photographer had ever attempted to play up the proletarianism of a rock group in the way that Astrid did. To have done so would have violated a prime convention of show-business portraiture, which had always sought to present performers (unless they were being expressly depicted "in character") as stylish, confident figures exuding an air of professional success. Astrid, however, was unconcerned with these conventions, which left her free to impose a grainy, documentary aesthetic—derived from New Wave cinema and the pioneering fashion photography of William Klein—onto the world of rock 'n' roll. Unwittingly at first, but quite consciously later on, the Beatles became her collaborators in this novel undertaking. They were, of course, acutely aware of being photographed, and determined to act as if this sort of attention were second nature to them. Unlike Astrid, they were perfectly aware of the conventions that dictated how they ought to appear. Yet some shared impulse caused them to balk at conformance with that ideal. Instead, written on their faces as they stare back at the camera—and at the beautiful German girl behind it—is the most affecting mixture of defiance, determination, vulnerability, and fatigue. Their ages, their scruffy appearance, their casual air of camaraderie, and the jaunty familiarity with which they brandish their guitars—all conspire with the derelict surroundings to make them look less like professional entertainers than like soldiers in the field. Which is what they were, in a manner of speaking: a tiny band of musical partisans, operating in an obscure theater of a culture war whose outbreak had barely been noticed at the time. Enlarged by Astrid to the size of exhibition prints, these photographs struck the Beatles with the force of self-revelation, providing them with an objective confirmation of the changes that Hamburg had wrought in their appearance and attitude. In an essay about the work of the German photographer August Sander that goes a long way toward explaining the mysterious power of these images, Golo Mann once wrote, "When someone is trying to be natural, or, better, when he does not even know he is being photographed, then he reveals character. But if he approaches the camera with a certain solemnity, with the intention of showing himself off, then he is revealing more than himself: he is revealing a secret self-image. There is no movement, no laughter, only deadly seriousness and the desire to be taken seriously by others."

THE BEATLES' EXTENDED contract with Bruno Koschmider ran through the end of 1960. Toward the middle of November, however, Koschmider became so annoyed with the group's new practice of sitting in with Tony Sheridan at the Top Ten Club during their hour-long breaks at the Kaiserkeller that he gave the Beatles their notice. Peter Eckhorn, owner of the Top Ten, responded by offering them a job at a significant raise in pay. Unsurprisingly, Koschmider took exception to this idea—such violent exception that he arranged with the police to have George Harrison, who at seventeen was legally underage to be working in Hamburg's bars, deported from Germany. When this shot across their bow failed to deter the others from accepting Eckhorn's offer, Koschmider arranged a similar fate for Paul McCartney and Pete Best, accusing them of trying to start a fire in their rooms at the Bambi Kino. McCartney and Best were arrested, jailed overnight, and put on a plane to London. A week later, lonely and broke, John Lennon joined this humiliating retreat to Liverpool. Stuart Sutcliffe remained in Hamburg through the end of January, under the protection of Astrid and her family.

Demoralized by the outcome of their great adventure in Hamburg, the four returning Beatles took a few weeks to regroup. A number of bridges had quietly burned behind them during the time they were away. John Lennon's misbegotten career as art student had officially ended with his failure to enroll at the college in the fall of 1960. Paul McCartney's academic career had ended in a similarly unceremonious manner. Despite the fact that he had earned an A-level pass in English Literature that would have qualified him for placement at a teacher-training college, Paul never considered this possibility. What he did instead, at his father's insistence, was to present himself at the local Labour Exchange, where he was assigned to a menial job with an electrical manufacturing firm.

In the three months they had been away, the beat music scene on Merseyside had exploded, with scores of newly formed bands performing in hired halls, coffee bars, and makeshift basement clubs. It took the Beatles until the end of December to line up some local bookings. The second of these was a spot on the bill with two other bands at a municipal ballroom in Litherland, a northern suburb of Liverpool. The

Beatles' performance there on December 27, 1960, was the fulfillment of the heroic cycle begun by their trip to Germany. Billed as "Direct From Hamburg" (which led the crowd to believe that they were indeed a German band), dressed in their black leather jackets, playing at a volume and with an intensity unlike anything that had ever been heard in Liverpool, the group brought down the house. Like a Merseyside version of the legendary scene at the Palomar Ballroom in Los Angeles in 1935 when the Benny Goodman Band first stirred the pandemonium that signaled the start of the Swing era, the Beatles' performance at the Litherland Town Hall was a catalyst for the whole phenomenon of beat music in Liverpool.

During the first three months of 1961, the promoter who hired them for the Litherland dance booked the group into ballrooms the length and breadth of Merseyside. (Prior to Stuart Sutcliffe's return at the end of January, they performed many of these dates as a quartet, with Paul McCartney on bass.) In February the Beatles played their first lunch-hour session at the Cavern Club in the city center of Liverpool. That same month George Harrison turned eighteen, making it legally possible for the group to return to Germany. In the interim, Peter Eckhorn had managed to get the deportation orders against McCartney and Best rescinded. By the time they left for Hamburg at the end of March to play a three-month stand at the Top Ten Club, the Beatles had transformed themselves in the eyes of Liverpool's beat-crazy teenagers from a bunch of suburban dilettantes into one of the city's most popular bands.

8

There was a feeling we all had, built into us, that something was going to happen. . . . It was just a matter of time
and how to get it happening.

—George Harrison

In the fall of 1960, while the Beatles were undergoing their metamorphosis in Hamburg, a celebrated trial was held at the Old Bailey court-
house in London. The defendant in the case was Penguin Books, and, by
extension, the writer D. H. Lawrence, whose final novel, *Lady Chatterley's Lover,* had been officially banned in Britain since its private publication in 1928. (Expurgated versions of the novel, shorn of its profane
language and its forthright descriptions of sex, had been commercially
available for years.) In 1959, after a similar ban on the book was over-
turned in the United States, Parliament had passed a new Obscene Publications Act that permitted British courts to consider, for the first time,
the redeeming "scientific, literary, or artistic" merit of works that previously would have been adjudged obscene on the basis of their content
alone. "The new legislation was designed to prevent, in future, prosecutions of such books as D. H. Lawrence's *Lady Chatterley's Lover,*" wrote
the journalist Bernard Levin. "This being the case, it naturally came
about that the Director of Public Prosecutions selected [*Lady Chatterley*]
as the first book to be prosecuted under the new law."

The most celebrated feature of the *Lady Chatterley* trial was the procession of thirty-five distinguished witnesses who testified for the
defense regarding the literary merit of the book. These included the
writers E. M. Forster and Rebecca West, the poet Cecil Day-Lewis, several members of Parliament (including Roy Jenkins, author of the new
Obscene Publications Act), and a half-dozen prominent Anglican and
Roman Catholic clerics. Yet the relevance of the *Lady Chatterley* trial to
the contemporary cultural climate in Britain centered less on these living luminaries than on the long-dead figure of D. H. Lawrence himself,
who was now revealed in retrospect as the seminal Angry Young Man of

English literature. Forty years before John Osborne, Lawrence had challenged the gentility of the English world of letters with a vehemence unmatched by any other writer of his time—nowhere more aggressively than in his account of the adulterous relationship between Lady Constance Chatterley and her gamekeeper, Oliver Mellors. As Lawrence's spokesman in the novel, Mellors came across as an utterly contemporary figure in the wake of the Angry Young Men.

For all the publicity they generated, the initial impact of the Angry writers had been limited by a paradox common to populist art: namely, that the audience for their work was confined to the comparatively small group of mostly upper-middle-class people who made a practice of reading contemporary novels and attending first-run plays. In 1958, in an effort to reach beyond this well-heeled constituency, John Osborne and his director Tony Richardson applied the proceeds of their theatrical success to the formation of Woodfall Films, an independent production company that was dedicated, in Richardson's words, to making movies with "the same sort of impact and sense of life that the Angry Young Man cult has had in the theatre and literary worlds." Woodfall's first production, an adaptation of *Look Back in Anger* that starred Richard Burton as Jimmy Porter, was released in the spring of 1959. After all the attention that had been lavished on the play, some critics were quick to dismiss the screen version as dated. But combined with the release of a film based on John Braine's novel *Room at the Top* that starred Laurence Harvey as Joe Lampton, a coldly ambitious office clerk who sets out to marry the boss's daughter, the Woodfall production of *Look Back in Anger* did succeed in bringing the sensibility of the Angry writers out of the world of the literary weeklies and into the popular mind.

Ironically, the most revolutionary feature of these films stemmed from their main concession to commercialism, for the casting of established male movie stars—Burton as Jimmy Porter, Harvey as Joe Lampton— endowed their protagonists with an aura of working-class virility that had little precedent in British popular culture. In contrast to Americans, who had a long history of projecting their sexual fantasies onto the lower strata of society, the British had tended to associate sexual prowess and adventurism with the upper classes, who were excused on the basis of power and position from the strictures of Victorian morality. The overt portrayal of working-class men as handsome, vital, sexually desirable figures was something new in British film, and it reached its fullest expression in

Albert Finney's electrifying performance as a randy young Nottingham factory worker in Woodfall's adaptation of the Alan Sillitoe novel *Saturday Night and Sunday Morning,* which was released in the fall of 1960—only a few weeks after the end of the *Lady Chatterley* trial. Unlike Burton, who was Welsh, and Harvey, who was South African, Finney was the genuine article: as a native of the Lancashire cotton town of Salton and a graduate of the Royal Academy of Dramatic Arts, he exemplified a new generation of English actors who had learned to talk "fine" as a function of their classical training, but who now, in their portrayal of working-class characters, went back to talking "broad." Capitalizing on the international success of *Saturday Night and Sunday Morning,* Woodfall and its emulators went on to produce a series of acclaimed and unsentimental films depicting the lives of young working-class people living in the North of England. Britain was undergoing an almost oxymoronic inversion of its traditional social geography: the birth of Northern chic.

It was in this sense that the trial of "Lady C" (as the tabloids dubbed the book) was in keeping with the current cultural trend, for the novel was the prototype, in modern English literature, of upper-class fascination with the sexual and emotional authenticity of the lower classes. Yet if the outcome of the trial was a posthumous vindication of D. H. Lawrence and a boon for Penguin Books (which sold more than two million paperback copies of the novel in the following year), the proceeding itself was anything but Lawrentian in tone. To the contrary: the real significance of the Lady Chatterley case as a cultural bellwether lay in the way the proceedings subverted the high seriousness of the Old Bailey courtroom with an air of unwitting, Goonish farce.

The lead actor in this regard was the prosecutor, a stereotypic High Court barrister named Mervyn Griffith-Jones, who set the stage in his opening remarks by railing against the effects of "unbridled sex" on the minds of British youth, and went on to ask the nine men and three women of the jury to consider whether Lawrence's novel was indeed the sort of book "you would even wish your wife or your servants to read." The stir of astonished laughter that rippled through the jury box in response to this query was the sound of a rift widening in the consciousness of the British public: between people who saw nothing to laugh at in the prosecutor's question, and people for whom this kind of paternalism had come to seem not just ludicrous, but dangerously absurd. The incredulity of the spectators (many of them defense witnesses who had stayed to see the show) was matched by the imperturbability of the jury in its finding for the defense. "I was not embarrassed by the book," one male juror told reporters, "and I was certainly not uneasy about reading it in the same room with the women."

> We have with us this evening the newly appointed Lord Chamberlain. Lord Cobbold, what is your opinion of censorship in the theatre?
>
> Censorship in the theatre. Well frankly I feel there's far too much sex and violence gets by in the name of entertainment these days. I mean, I go to the theatre to be entertained. I want to be taken *out* of myself. I don't want to see lust and rape, incest and sodomy—I can get all that at home.
>
> —Dudley Moore and Peter Cook, *Beyond the Fringe*

The laughter in the *Lady Chatterley* courtroom foretold the shape of things to come. If Britain in the 1950s had been stirred by the spirit of Anger, Britain in the 1960s would be ruled by the spirit of Farce, as exemplified by the theatrical revue *Beyond the Fringe,* written and performed by a quartet of young men—Alan Bennett, Peter Cook, Jonathan Miller, and Dudley Moore—which opened to rave notices in London in May of 1961; by the following fall, it was joined by a Soho nightclub called The Establishment, dedicated to the presentation of satiric comedy in a context unconstrained by Britain's strict theatrical censorship laws, and the satiric weekly *Private Eye,* which went on to become the country's most durable organ of sixth-form humor, scurrilous gossip, and political espionage. Taken together, *Beyond the Fringe,* The Establishment Club, and *Private Eye* described enough of a trend for the press to declare the advent of a "Satire movement." Presaged by this vanguard of jesters, public life in Britain in the years ahead would begin to assume the exaggerated form and frantic pace of a ribald comedy, replete with outlandish characters, compromising situations, and improbable events in which the high would sink low, the low would rise high, youth would triumph over age, impulse would reign over intellect, and the great postimperial shell of British society would suddenly start to ring out in a higher, brighter, more sardonic and fanciful key.

THE BEATLES ARRIVED in Hamburg in the spring of 1961 eager to pick up where they had left off the previous November at Peter Eckhorn's Top Ten Club, with Astrid Kirchherr, Klaus Voorman, and Jurgen Vollmer resuming their nightly vigil at a table near the stage. Yet the reunion of Astrid and Stuart Sutcliffe threw the group's internal dynamic into an immediate state of flux. Prior to Stuart's return to Liverpool in January, he and Astrid had become formally engaged. Now, while his four bandmates shared the Top Ten's drafty attic dormitory with their old friend Tony Sheridan and the members of his group, Stuart began living with Astrid and her mother at their home in the Altona district of Hamburg. He soon became assimilated into Astrid's wider circle of friends, several of whom were students at the Hochschüle für Bildende Künste, the state art college in Hamburg.

Within a few weeks of his arrival, one of those friends introduced Stuart to the British artist Eduardo Paolozzi, late of the Independent Group, who was in the midst of a two-year appointment as a visiting professor at the school. Paolozzi had been born, like Sutcliffe, in Edinburgh, where he and his Italian immigrant parents had been interned as enemy aliens at the start of World War II. Acutely impressed with his fellow Scot's intelligence and sensitivity, Paolozzi arranged for Stuart to receive a scholarship to the art college. Under Paolozzi's tutelage, Sutcliffe blossomed as a painter, working with an intensity his teacher viewed with awe. ("I always felt there was something desperate about Stuart," Paolozzi recalled.) After struggling for several weeks to balance his revitalized interest in art with his nocturnal existence as a nightclub musician, Sutcliffe gradually began to withdraw from active participation in the Beatles, ceding his role as the group's bassist to Paul McCartney.

The Top Ten Club was a much larger and more congenial venue than Bruno Koschmider's Kaiserkeller, and by promoting the place as a mecca for rock 'n' roll, Peter Eckhorn had succeeded in usurping and enlarging upon his rival's clientele. His prime attraction was Tony Sheridan. By now Sheridan's popularity in Hamburg had attracted the attention of German record scouts, one of whom, a well-known bandleader named Bert Kaempfert, worked as a producer for Polydor Records. Kaempfert was a native of Hamburg and a product of the intensely Anglophilic swing-jazz subculture that had thrived in the city prior to World War II in defiance of the Nazi regime. A savvy and resourceful record man, he had recently been responsible for a pair of international hits. In January 1961, Kaempfert's own recording of his soundtrack to the German film *Wonderland by Night* had risen to number one on both the singles and albums charts in the United States; three months later, Elvis Presley's recording of "Wooden Heart," an old German folk song that Kaempfert had adapted for the soundtrack of Presley's "comeback" movie, *G.I. Blues,* became a top-selling single in Britain and Germany. After hearing Sheridan perform at the Top Ten Club, Kaempfert offered him a recording contract. When Sheridan requested that the Beatles serve as his backing band for the session, Kaempfert signed them, too.

As the headquarters of Polydor Records and its estimable parent company, Deutsche Grammophon, Hamburg did not lack for professional recording facilities. But Bert Kaempfert saw no reason to devote expensive studio time to capturing the sound of a Reeperbahn rock-'n'-roller; he preferred to record Sheridan and the Beatles on portable tape equipment, set up in the auditorium of a local elementary school. Owing to the informality of the session, its details remain obscure, but it took place on a weekend (when school was out) and resulted in at least four finished tracks. The most polished of these were Tony Sheridan's rock-'n'-roll arrangements of "My Bonnie Lies Over the Ocean" and "When the Saints Go Marching In," both of which had the virtue, from a publishing standpoint, of existing in the public domain. (Rhythm-heavy versions of these songs had already been recorded by Ray Charles, Bill Haley, Jerry Lee Lewis, and Fats Domino.) Two additional tracks, featuring the Beatles alone, seem to have been recorded as something of an afterthought. On one, John Lennon delivers a throaty rendition of another old standard, Eddie Cantor's "Ain't She Sweet"; on the other, the group performs a jokey guitar instrumental called "Cry for a Shadow," written by Lennon and Harrison.

Though the two best tracks were dominated by Sheridan's singing and lead guitar—both of which were considerably more accomplished than anything his accompanists could manage at the time—these 1961 Polydor recordings provide the first real evidence of how the Beatles actually sounded during their two-year apprenticeship in the clubs of Hamburg and Liverpool. As such, they do little to support the group's own opinion that their music reached an unmatched peak of excitement and intensity during these formative years. What the Polydor recordings reveal is a quartet of drastically limited instrumentalists who seem to have focused all of their efforts on doing one thing well. Drummer Pete Best imposes on each of these tracks the same unyielding beat, broken at regular intervals by the same scampering fill. Lead guitarist George Harrison, consigned to the background on the Tony Sheridan cuts, sounds pinched and timid in his solo on "Ain't She Sweet"; George's playing is more confident on "Cry for a Shadow," but at no point does he show the slightest inclination to improvise. From an instrumental standpoint, the strength of the band consists of John Lennon's steady if unimaginative rhythm guitar and Paul McCartney's vigorous bass. Shortly before this session, McCartney had acquired the short-necked, violin-bodied Hofner electric bass that would become his musical trademark in years to come. It was the most compact and guitarlike of the models then available, and Paul began by playing it like a guitar, with a fluidity that contrasts sharply, on these recordings, with the rigidity of the rest of the band.

Despite its ad-hoc nature, this first professional recording session was the high point of the Beatles' second Hamburg trip. Polydor released the Tony Sheridan tracks on a single in July of 1961, copies of it having been sent to the Beatles shortly after they returned to Liverpool at the end of June. In all other respects, the band's three-month stay in Hamburg in 1961 was an extension of their first visit to the city in its effect on their music, their morals, and the refinement of their image as a group. Once again, their exposure to Tony Sheridan proved musically enlightening. And, once again, their exposure to Astrid Kirchherr and her circle had a determining influence on the Beatles' fashion sense.

Soon after Astrid and Stuart Sutcliffe began living together, the two of them began to dress identically in black leather jackets and pants; around the same time, at Astrid's suggestion, Stuart began to brush his hair forward into the tousled *pilzenkopf* ("mushroom head") style favored by university students in Germany and France. By the time they returned to Liverpool, all of the Beatles had taken to dressing onstage in leather from head to toe, and at least two of them, George Harrison and Paul McCartney, had begun to experiment with the softer, rounder hairstyle worn by Sutcliffe, Klaus Voorman, Jurgen Vollmer, and the rest of their artist friends. (The Beatles' conclusive adoption of this hairstyle would await the fall of 1961, when Lennon and McCartney spent a week in Paris with Vollmer, who had moved there to work as an assistant to the fashion photographer William Klein. Vollmer cut their hair for them, and this time the style stuck, although Pete Best, proud of his picture-perfect pompadour, resisted the new look.)

Photographs of the Beatles in their "Hamburg leathers" can come as a shock to modern eyes, not least because the outfits they wore during this period have since become widely identified with the "butch" regalia of male prostitutes. In 1961, however, this "leather boy" iconography, while certainly provocative, was stylistically up for grabs. The Beatles associated it mainly with the menacing stage persona that had recently been created for Gene Vincent by the British television producer Jack Good, and they adopted it, in part, as a sign of their allegiance to the uncompromising style of rock 'n' roll that Vincent epitomized. During the 1950s, Hollywood films like *The Wild One* and *Blackboard Jungle* had helped to establish the black leather bomber or motorcycle jacket as an international symbol of disaffected youth—so much so that, in Europe, the young toughs who trashed movie theaters during screenings of rock-'n'-roll films were often described by the press in their respective countries as *lederjakken, skinknuttes,* or *blousons noir.* In Britain, where importation of *The Wild One* had been banned by the Home Office, neo-Edwardianism remained the prevailing style among fashion-conscious teenagers during most of the 1950s. But by the end of the decade the secondhand romance of the American motorcycle outlaw had penetrated British popular culture to the point where a growing number of working-class youths had begun to apply their newfound affluence to the purchase of powerful motorcycles and the adoption of the distinctive garb and defiant social attitudes associated with their use. Sensationalized reports appeared in the press about the exploits of these leather-clad "ton-up boys" (a "ton" in biker parlance meant a speed of one hundred miles per hour), who congregated at truck stops on the ring roads surrounding London and proved their mettle by roaring up and down the newly completed A1 motorway to Birmingham. Most of these fledgling Anglo road warriors were gainfully employed young manual workers; many were former Teds who were looking to prolong their adolescent heroics into their adult years. This meant that the British biker cult, inspired as it was by the mystique of a 1954 Hollywood film that few of its members had ever seen, was imbued from the start with a strong sense of nostalgia for the pop culture and pop music of the 1950s. The very term they came to be known by, Rockers, confirmed this link to the past, for by 1961, rock 'n' roll was widely regarded as a musical style whose time had come and gone.

The embryonic Rocker subculture was centered in the working-class suburbs of London, with offshoots reaching as far as the Midlands industrial towns. As yet there was little sign of it in northern cities like Liverpool, and the Beatles did not overtly identify themselves with this group. Instead their relationship to the Rockers resembled the dilettantish pattern of their relationship to the Teds: they shared similar taste in fashion and music, but they drew the line at the point where taste left off and aggressive action—ganging, fighting, and, in this case, motorcycle riding—began.

9

Pop Art is: Popular (designed for a mass audience), Transient (short-term solution), Expendable (easily forgotten), Low Cost, Mass-Produced, Young (aimed at youth), Witty, Sexy, Gimmicky, Glamorous, Big Business.

—Richard Hamilton (1957)

As if the distinction between rock 'n' roll and rhythm and blues weren't confusing enough, another term that took on new meaning during the 1950s was "pop," which had previously served the music business as a casual abbreviation for "popular." In the sense that it came to be used from 1955 onward, pop was a marketing term. It referred to a wide range of music that was released on 45-rpm singles, played on mainstream radio stations, and indexed on the weekly sales charts that were published in American trade journals like *Billboard* and *Cash Box* and their British equivalents like *Melody Maker* and the *New Musical Express.* Since "pop singles" made up the segment of the record market that came to be dominated during this period by teenagers, the diminutive quality of the term also connoted the youth of this audience and the presumed immaturity of their taste. But "pop" was simultaneously taking on a set of aesthetic connotations as well, beginning in Britain, where Richard Hamilton, Eduardo Paolozzi, and their colleagues in the Independent Group had coined the term *pop art* to describe those products of American mass culture—comic books, sci-fi novels, and popular music, as well as advertising, packaging, and industrial design—that appealed to their artistic imaginations. By 1961, Pop Art (duly capitalized) was emerging in Britain as a new category of fine art, referring not only to the products of mass culture but also to the work of a group of young painters who were incorporating imagery derived from those products into their art. In the convergence of these two concepts of pop and Pop, the new decade of the 1960s would find its unifying aesthetic and its universal modifier.

. . . .

By the summer of 1961, with two grueling tours of duty in the clubs of Hamburg behind them, the Beatles' repertoire had ballooned to include nearly a hundred songs. Some of this material they played really well, some of it they could barely get through, but, either way, the great preponderance of it was derived from American records that had been released prior to 1960. On a given night, the Beatles could choose from any of a half-dozen numbers each by Elvis Presley, Little Richard, Buddy Holly, Gene Vincent, Jerry Lee Lewis, Eddie Cochran, Larry Williams, and the Coasters—even more by Chuck Berry and Carl Perkins, who were particular favorites of John Lennon and George Harrison respectively. Of the more current songs in their repertoire, many were recent releases by artists like the Everly Brothers, Buddy Knox, and the Crickets (without Buddy Holly), who had risen to prominence in the decade before. Though the category did not yet exist, the Beatles in 1961 were what would one day be described as a rock-'n'-roll oldies band.

They were hardly alone in their longing for the glory days of rock 'n' roll. Britain in the early 1960s was an elephants' graveyard of rock, where defunct or deceased stars like Gene Vincent, Eddie Cochran, and Buddy Holly continued to place records high on the pop charts. In America, too, as signaled by the release of the first LP collection of *Oldies But Goodies* in 1959, nostalgia for the popular music of the 1950s began to set in even before the decade was done. The early 1960s, by comparison, have gone down in pop history as the Dark Ages of Rock: an aimless interregnum when the airwaves and pop charts were cluttered with a hodgepodge of billowy ballads, mechanistic dance records, lush instrumentals, mindless novelty songs, and inconsequential singles by synthetic teen idols and faceless vocal groups. Orphaned by the attrition and defection of its brightest stars and the efforts of the music business establishment to reassert control, rock 'n' roll relinquished its influence on popular music during these years, degenerating into an empty set of musical and attitudinal clichés. In the words of the Herodotus of pop historians, the British writer Nik Cohn, "Tin Pan Alley was back in the catbird seat."

Leaving aside such gross aberrations as Brian Hyland's "Itsy Bitsy Teeny Weenie Yellow Polka Dot Bikini," the case against the pop music of the early 1960s can be summarized by a pair of records that rose to the top of singles charts in the summer of 1960. Exhibit A was Elvis Presley's

"It's Now or Never," a love ballad based on the Italian standard "O Sole Mio." Recorded a few weeks after his army discharge, "It's Now or Never" was a calculated departure for Presley, whose stentorian delivery combined with the song's turgid arrangement to create a quasi-operatic effect. Coming on the heels of his television appearance with Frank Sinatra, the record sounded like an attempt to court the acceptance of an older generation of listeners whose tastes had been formed by an older generation of mainly Italian-American singers who had dominated the pop charts during the early 1950s and continued to dominate the type of singing heard in big-city nightclubs, resort hotels and casinos, and on television variety shows. "It's Now or Never" could hardly have been more successful in this regard; it went on to become Presley's best-selling single of all time, and it was followed by his even more overbearing renditions of "Are You Lonesome Tonight," an old Al Jolson number with an insipid spoken-word middle, and "Surrender," which was based on another Neapolitan standard, "Torna a Sorrento." Thus was the great rock-'n'-roll protagonist of the 1950s conclusively reborn as a mainstream entertainer who would spend the rest of his career seeking, rather than setting, the denominators of popular taste. Yet the commercial success of these records unleashed a torrent of *opera adolescentia* into the pop world, inspiring a new contingent of melodramatic tenors like Roy Orbison and Del Shannon to strain for a similarly bombastic effect.

Exhibit B in the case against early-1960s pop involved the phenomenal success of a twenty-year-old Fats Domino impersonator called Chubby Checker (real name Ernest Evans) and a record called "The Twist," the original version of which had been issued in 1958 as the flipside to an R&B hit by Hank Ballard & The Midnighters. Checker's rendition of "The Twist" was closely patterned on Ballard's, but unlike the original, Checker's record enjoyed the patronage of the Philadelphia-based impresario Dick Clark, whose nationally syndicated *American Bandstand* television show had come to serve as America's premier showcase for teen-market pop. Taking their lead from the teenagers in the *Bandstand* studio audience, Clark and Checker promoted "The Twist" as the accompaniment to a simple gyrational dance whose hip-shaking suggestiveness was amply offset by the fact that the partners, for the first time in the recent history of social dancing, *never actually touched one another*. By September 1960, the song and the dance had become enough of a craze in the United States to propel the single to number one.

Up to this point, "The Twist" was merely an example of expert pop promotion, and it wasn't long before the record was descending the charts and Chubby Checker was applying his slender talent to other lucrative song-and-dance combinations with names like the Pony and the Fly. The real twist in the story concerned what happened next. Having all but faded from the consciousness of American teenagers by the summer of 1961, the Twist was adopted by a group of New York socialites who sought to emulate the current Parisian craze for *discothèque* dancing by patronizing a seedy Times Square nightclub called the Peppermint Lounge. Duly noted in the gossip and society columns of the New York tabloids, this jet-set version of the old upper-class phenomenon of "slumming" soon led to the sweaty spectacle of middle-aged celebrities twisting the night away in the pages of *Time* and *Life*. On the strength of this second wind of publicity, the Twist was embraced by socialites and suburbanites across America as a kind of national rite of disinhibition. Chubby Checker was invited to give a prime-time demonstration of the dance on *The Ed Sullivan Show,* and his record enjoyed an unprecedented resurgence. By the end of 1961, it was back at number one in the United States and high on the charts in much of Europe as well. Dozens of songs were recorded, or in some cases re-recorded, with the word "twist" substituted for the word "rock" in the title and lyric. (Checker himself reprised Bill Haley by starring in a film called *Twist Around the Clock.*) Twist classes were offered in commercial dance schools, and America's glamorous new First Lady, Jacqueline Kennedy, was reported to have performed the dance at the White House.

On every level—musical, commercial, and sociological—the Twist was a perfect travesty of the spirit of rock 'n' roll. Where Sam Phillips had once sought to set the music world on fire by recording "a white man who could sing like a black man," Chubby Checker was a black man who sounded uncannily, on record, like a white man imitating a black man. The dance craze he inspired took the same form of suggestive motion with which "Elvis the Pelvis" had scandalized America in 1956 and recast it, five years later, as an innocuous form of fun. And in contrast to the generational *Sturm und Drang* that had surrounded rock 'n' roll, the audience for Checker's song and dance extended not only to the young, but also to what advertising copywriters liked to call the "young at heart." Between them, "It's Now or Never" and "The Twist" were a blueprint for the process by which the American music business sought to return the Genie of Rock to the Lamp of Pop.

As its detractors never tired of saying, the appeal of rock 'n' roll, when it first captured the attention of teenagers in America and Britain during the 1950s, was based on something very simple. Rock 'n' roll arrived at a time when the prevailing Tin Pan Alley style of popular song had been burnished for half a century by the genius of its composers (nearly all of whom were natives of New York City) and the ascendant cultural power of Broadway and Hollywood to a degree of melodic and harmonic sophistication that was all the more remarkable considering the genre's increasingly narrow, mannered, and sentimental focus on the theme of romantic love. The sophisticated Tin Pan Alley style had assimilated the influence of black American music mainly in its use of rhythm, which from the 1930s onward had been strongly, albeit politely, indebted to swing. But there was nothing polite, much less sophisticated, about the rhythm of rock 'n' roll. Rock 'n' roll tapped into a vein of African-American rhythm that lay behind the supple syncopations of swing, beyond the cultural reach of New York City, and beyond the experience of most white Americans. By weighting upbeats and offbeats like downbeats, the jump, stomp, and boogie rhythms that rock derived from R&B turned the metric organization of European music on its head. Though every new style of popular music comes as something of an affront to the style that immediately precedes it, rock 'n' roll marked a break with the prevailing Tin Pan Alley style that was far more extreme than any that had come before. Rock rhythm reached up through the feet and the legs into the groin and the gut, and as Elvis Presley had been happy to demonstrate, it engendered a form of physical movement that had previously been taboo in nearly all precincts of white society. Early rock-'n'-roll songs accentuated this intense physicality by paring the melodic and harmonic content of the music down to a bare minimum, and by reducing the lyric content to a level that verged on nonsense rhymes: "Rock Around the Clock," "Tutti-Frutti," "Be-Bop-A-Lula." All that was left was a sense of urgency, immediacy, visceral intensity, and inchoate sensation. Through a process of elimination, rock 'n' roll became an unalloyed celebration of physical pleasure. Devoid of any narrative context, the music seemed to exist entirely in the present moment—an affective quality that it shared with adolescents themselves.

These were the qualities that the Beatles—or, rather, the boys who became the Beatles—had first loved about rock 'n' roll. And these were the musical qualities—the immediacy, intensity, and urgency—that they had first learned to generate during their apprenticeship in the clubs of Hamburg and that had earned them, upon their return, the status of local heroes on Merseyside. And yet, had the Beatles chosen to remain fixated on generating this singular effect, it is hard to imagine that they ever would have achieved success or recognition beyond the cellar clubs and dance halls of Liverpool and Hamburg. The process by which they shifted their orientation from the past to the present and the future was not entirely a commercially determined one; instead, it was an outgrowth of their own musical curiosity, their gradual improvement as singers and instrumentalists, and their desire to distinguish themselves from the many other groups in their musical milieu who were performing the same material as they were. Like other young white musicians of their generation, they were inspired and instructed in this transition by the fortuitous fact that the Dark Age of Rock corresponded with the dawn of a Golden Age of Rhythm and Blues: a period when, for the first time in the history of the music business, black artists, black producers, and black-owned record companies began to address themselves, confidently and indiscriminately, to black and white audiences alike. The social revolution that began in 1954, the year of "Rock Around the Clock" and *Brown v. Board of Education,* had arrived on the pop charts.

Leading the way was a trio of brilliant singers and songwriters consisting of Ray Charles, Sam Cooke, and Ben E. King (first as a member of the Drifters and later as a solo artist), who between 1959 and 1963 would account for more than two dozen pop hits, turning the "crossover" success of black artists into such a routine occurrence that *Billboard* magazine in 1963 decided to do away with its separate chart listings for pop and R&B. More important, by drawing on a cultural background they shared with millions of other black Americans, these three singers imbued popular music with a new style of gospel-based emotionality that was providentially in tune with the style of gospel-based moral authority that was being expounded during the early 1960s by civil rights leaders like the Reverend Martin Luther King Jr. Within a few years this passionate, aspirational, and commercially potent style of rhythm and blues would become known, simply, as soul music.

The Beatles' engagement with this new style of R&B was considerably more cautious than their engagement with 1950s rock 'n' roll had been. On a practical level, their guitar-based instrumentation was not particularly well suited to the sound of gospel-blues, which tended to rely on piano, horns, and even, in the case of the Drifters, strings. But there was a deeper and more interesting reason for this reticence as well. While other British singers of their generation would go on to imitate Ray Charles and Sam Cooke as brazenly as their forebears had imitated Frank Sinatra or Elvis Presley, the Beatles felt a self-consciousness about imitating black American dialect in their singing that would mark them throughout their careers. Not that they didn't or couldn't do it. Both John Lennon and Paul McCartney were excellent musical mimics, as demonstrated by their letter-perfect impersonations of Larry Williams and Little Richard. But as they developed their own abilities as singers, both Lennon and McCartney began to shy away from the impersonation of black artists, particularly those as technically accomplished and emotionally expressive as Ray Charles, Sam Cooke, and Ben E. King. The Beatles did perform some of their songs, including "What I'd Say," which Tony Sheridan had made obligatory in the clubs of Hamburg, Sam Cooke's "Bring It on Home to Me," and the Drifters' big hit from 1961, "Save the Last Dance for Me." But they felt much more comfortable emulating the work of less intimidating black singers like Arthur Alexander, whose recordings of "Anna (Go to Him)" and "Soldier of Love" echoed the rueful sound of the Drifters, or the Isley Brothers, who had hitched a ride on Chubby Checker's bandwagon with a sequel to their 1959 gospel-blues hit "Shout" called "Twist & Shout." Another new favorite was the Miracles, a Detroit-based vocal group whose young lead singer, Smokey Robinson, was an ardent admirer of Sam Cooke. The Miracles' 1960 recording of "Shop Around" marked the first major success for a new black-owned label, Tamla-Motown, whose founder, a part-time songwriter named Berry Gordy, had co-written an earlier R&B hit the Beatles liked to perform, Barrett Strong's version of "Money (That's What I Want)."

John Lennon handled the lead singing on most of this more recent rhythm and blues, leaving Paul McCartney to divide his attention between his extensive collection of 1950s ravers and a new cache of lighter, jazzier ballads by singers like Dinah Washington and Peggy Lee. Apart from their renditions of songs by the Coasters, group vocals had not figured heavily in the Beatles' repertoire of 1950s rock, not least because the makeshift sound systems they worked with made it almost impossible for them to harmonize over the din of the band. That John and Paul played their guitars right- and left-handed respectively made it easier for the two of them to share a microphone, which was often the only way they could hope to hear each other sing on stage. But one of the amenities of the Top Ten Club was the presence of a decent sound system, and this encouraged the Beatles during their second trip in Hamburg to devote more attention to singing together as a group. Their models were the simple backup harmonies and call-and-response patterns they heard on records by the so-called "girl groups" that characterized yet another offshoot of the musical marriage between pop and rhythm and blues.

The girl groups embodied some of the best and worst elements of early-1960s pop. With the notable exception of the Beatles' favorite, the Shirelles, most of them were composed of rank amateurs who were signed straight out of inner-city high schools by record producers seeking to capitalize on the fact that a wildly disproportionate share of the popular records sold in America (more than *half,* according to *Seventeen* magazine) were purchased by the nation's 11 million teenage girls. The marketing strategy employed by these would-be pop moguls was simple. Teenagers, they believed, wanted a beat they could dance to and performers they could identify with. The girl groups were designed to satisfy these simple needs by turning the basic unit of adolescent social structure—the high school clique—into a subgenre of pop. Yet, despite the patronizing nature of the whole enterprise, the best of the girl group records had a piquancy and poignancy not found in any other music of the time. Some of this owed to the sheer callowness of the singing, which came across on record as the voices of authentic teenagers, and conveyed an authentically adolescent sense of vulnerability, solidarity, and longing. And some of it was due to the skill of a group of prolific young songwriters who operated out of offices in the Brill Building, home to dozens of New York's small-time music publishing firms.

Styling themselves as the successors to the great Broadway composers and lyricists (in homage to whom they revived the old device of a recitative opening verse), the Brill Building songwriters set out to corner the market in ready-made teenage pop. They included such 1950s veterans as Jerry Leiber, Mike Stoller, Doc Pomus, and Mort Shuman. Among the newcomers, the cream of the crop was a pair of young newlyweds, Gerry Goffin and Carole King, whose hits included "Chains" by the

Cookies, "One Fine Day" by the Chiffons, and the song that set the style for the entire girl-group genre, "Will You Love Me Tomorrow" by the Shirelles.

In addition to providing the Beatles with current hits to cover, the Brill Building composers (and the young team of Goffin/King in particular) were instrumental in emboldening John Lennon and Paul McCartney to introduce some of their own tentative efforts at songwriting into their act. By the end of 1961, the Beatles were performing perhaps a half-dozen original songs on a regular basis. Some, like "Hold Me Tight" and "The One After 909," would eventually surface on Beatles albums; others, like "Love of the Loved" and the Buddy Hollyish "I'll Be on My Way" would eventually be recorded by other artists; still others, with titles like "Thinking of Linking," were wisely consigned to the dustbin of musical history. But none of these songs, it is fair to say, gave any significant indication of the effusion of musical talent and imagination that would become synonymous with the words "Lennon-McCartney" in the years ahead.

10

This was the real thing. Here they were, first five and then four human dynamos generating a beat which was irresistible. Turning back the rock clock. Pounding out items from Chuck Berry, Little Richard, Carl Perkins, The Coasters, and the other great etceteras of the era.

—Bob Wooler, *Mersey Beat*

The Beatles returned to Liverpool from Hamburg in July of 1961 and wasted little time in reclaiming their position as one of the city's leading bands. During the week they resumed their regular lunch-hour and evening sessions at the Cavern Club; on the weekends they played a circuit of suburban dance halls in Aintree, Litherland, Huyton, Tuebrook, and Knotty Ash. Another frequent venue was Mona Best's Casbah Club. With Allan Williams out of the picture (after a dispute over whether he was entitled to take a commission on the Beatles' Hamburg dates), Pete Best and his mother began to handle the bookings for the band. Best also persuaded a friend named Neil Aspinall, who had also been a classmate of Paul McCartney's at the Liverpool Institute, to buy a secondhand van and serve as the equipment manager for the group.

If, as George Harrison once said, "our original intention was just to be in a band as opposed to having a job," the Beatles by the summer of 1961 had attained this modest goal. The four of them were now earning something in the neighborhood of ten pounds each per week, which was slightly more than the pay of the average young laborer, shop clerk, or factory worker. All four of them continued to live at home, John Lennon having moved backed in with his aunt Mimi after his return from Hamburg the previous fall. Now, following the Beatles' second trip to Hamburg, John's girlfriend, Cynthia Powell, began to rent one of the extra bedrooms at Mendips. Having set her sights on becoming an art teacher, Cynthia was in the middle of a two-year certification program at the Art College.

For the next year, from the summer of 1961 through the summer of

1962, the Cavern would serve as their base. The club was located on Mathew Street, several blocks up from the dockland, in the cellar of an old fruit-and-vegetable warehouse. The stone floor, brick walls, and low, vaulted ceilings made it the most resonant of rooms, with the only acoustic dampening coming from the sodden bodies of the hundreds of teenage patrons who typically lined the walls and clustered in front of the low wooden stage. Between its opening in 1957 and its purchase in 1960 by an accountant named Ray McFall, the Cavern had served as one of Liverpool's principal jazz clubs, with a music policy (as the Quarry Men learned in their one appearance there) prohibiting rock 'n' roll. McFall, however, was more of a businessman than a jazz buff. Impatient with the poor attendance at the Cavern's weekly "Modern Jazz Night," he substituted an evening of rock; the response was so enthusiastic that he decided to run the place as a rock club on weekdays, a jazz club on weekends. The Beatles played there, on average, two lunch-hour and two evening sessions a week. The lunch-hour sessions they treated as paid rehearsals, while the evening sessions were longer but only slightly more formalized. Day or night, the Beatles' performances were marked by their willful disregard for the niceties of a polished presentation. Because musicians spend so much of their time performing in unfamiliar surroundings, the psychology of residency can exert a strong influence on how they approach their work. With its low, cramped stage, its near-absence of backstage facilities (the "dressing room" was a coat closet), and its general air of squalor, the Cavern encouraged an unaffected attitude in which the distinctions between the performers and the patrons were held to a minimum.

An added attraction of the Cavern for both the Beatles and their fans was the club's dulcet-voiced disc jockey and master of ceremonies, Bob Wooler, a twenty-seven-year-old record aficionado who had recently quit his job as a railway clerk to become a self-styled "rhythm-and-blues consultant." Wooler bore much of the responsibility for educating the musical taste of the Beatles and the many other groups that regularly performed at the Cavern. He was also a tireless booster of the whole phenomenon of beat music in Liverpool. According to his estimate, by the summer of 1961, no fewer than 250 beat groups were active on Merseyside, competing for recognition at scores of venues that included music clubs, social clubs, dance halls, church halls, coffee bars, cinemas, bowling alleys, and municipal swimming pools. They played under names that advertised both their native wit and their lack of serious professional ambitions—names like the Drone Tones, Ahab and His Lot, Wump and His Werbles, the Kommotions, Johnny Autumn and the Fall Guys, Foo Foo and His Flashing Falcons, and the Live Jive Five.

In years to come, a great deal of attention would be paid to the question of why Liverpool, of all places, should have spawned the most vital and proudly indigenous pop music scene in Britain. By 1961, lunch-hour record hops had become a staple of teenage entertainment in many British towns, while most cities of any size supported a number of clubs and dance halls that presented local bands. But nowhere else in Britain, not even in London, did the extent of local music-making approach the scale of the scene in Liverpool. When called upon to account for this phenomenon, Liverpudlians pointed first, as always, to their city's diverse population, citing the large numbers of Welsh and Irish—ethnic groups who were believed to have a God-given gift of song—living on Merseyside. Some local sages offered a musical variation on the theme of the "Cunard Yank," suggesting that the traffic of the port provided a conduit for American records that were otherwise unobtainable in Britain. Speaking in his capacity as Lord Mayor of the city, the Honorable Louis Caplan preferred to attribute the beat boom to Liverpool's exceptional love for and indulgence of its children. That there was something atypically English about the status of children in the city, many people agreed. "Liverpool children are the noisiest and most ebullient I have ever come across," wrote the journalist Graham Turner. "Many of their antics have become legendary to an adult population which seems both dazed by their exploits and at the same time, proud of them." One expression of this ebullience was found in the city's tradition of teenage gangs, each identified with a particular street or park or neighborhood landmark. No less an authority than Bob Wooler believed that Liverpool's gang culture was central to the growth of its beat culture, and Wooler's opinion was subsequently affirmed by an article that appeared in the journal *New Society,* written by a sociology student at Liverpool University named Colin Fletcher, who recounted how a street gang he had joined in the late 1950s was transformed from a band of brawlers and vandals into a fan club and support network for five of its members who formed a beat group.

The main problem with most of these popular explanations for the proliferation of beat groups on Merseyside was that none of them had much bearing on the Beatles, or on Gerry & The Pacemakers, Rory Storm

& The Hurricanes, the Remo Four, and the city's other leading bands. (John Lennon's Woolton Outlaws hardly qualified as the sort of urban street gang that Colin Fletcher was writing about.) A more convincing cause for the beat boom in Liverpool involved the distinctive tension between provincial and cosmopolitan attitudes that had shaped the cultural life of the city for more than a hundred years. Energy and innovation in popular music have often thrived in places geographically or socially insulated from the tyranny of prevailing taste. In the United States this tendency was spectacularly illustrated during the first half of the twentieth century by the growth of indigenous styles of jazz and blues in such provincial centers as New Orleans, Memphis, and Kansas City. In Britain, the brass-band movement of the nineteenth century had a similarly provincial origin, arising in factory, mill, and mining towns across the industrial North. But with the advent of records and radio, and the resulting popularity of imported American styles, the influence of London on the music business in Britain became all but absolute. Here especially, the contrast with the United States was striking. By 1960, every major American city was serviced by its own radio stations, recording studios, and, in most cases, independent record labels on the lookout for local talent. Liverpool possessed none of these musical amenities. For musicians growing up there, it remained a foregone conclusion that any professional ambitions would have to be pursued in London. And still, Liverpudlians had always believed their city to be unique, and this fierce tradition of local patriotism had always encouraged them to make the most of their collective enthusiasms. When Liverpudlians of the 1960s touted their city's reputation as the "Nashville of Britain," they were partaking of a spirit of local boosterism that reached back to such nineteenth-century conceits as the "Florence of the North."

In the case of the beat boom, however, such claims were qualified by a factor that was easy to ignore in the collective excitement of the time. For Liverpool in the early 1960s was the site of a great effusion of musical enthusiasm, but not of musical talent. While more than a dozen local groups or solo singers eventually went on to enjoy some degree of national and even international success as recording artists, the records they made attest to the fact that the *only* first-rate talent to emerge from the city during this period was vested in the Beatles themselves. For if the beat scene in Liverpool had no equivalent in the rest of Britain, the Beatles had no equivalent in Liverpool. No other local group sounded like them, looked like them, or behaved like them. In a proletarian city where any form of singularity was inherently suspect, there was a natural tendency for Liverpudlians to see the Beatles as the proud product of the beat scene on Merseyside. But by the fall of 1961, the inverse was equally true. By then it was the singular presence of a group as talented, stylish, and ambitious as the Beatles that made the difference between the beat boom in Liverpool and the much less vital music scenes in other provincial cities and towns.

Another critical component in the promotion of the local music scene—and a symbol of the Beatles' preeminence in it—was the fortnightly newspaper *Mersey Beat,* which was founded in the summer of 1961 by John Lennon's friend from the Art College, Bill Harry. Harry's original intention was to cover the full spectrum of musical activity on Merseyside, from beat and trad to country and folk and everything in between. But from the beginning he was most interested in promoting his friends the Beatles. The debut issue of the paper contained John Lennon's mythological fancy "A Short Diversion on the Dubious Origins of Beatles." The cover of the second issue featured one of Astrid Kirchherr's portraits of the group beneath a banner headline announcing the Beatles' "recording contract" with Polydor. Other early issues included further installments of whimsy from Lennon and a column by Bob Wooler that can scarcely be improved upon as an assessment of the Beatles' appeal in Liverpool. "Why do you think the Beatles are so popular?" Wooler asked. "Many people many times have asked me this question since that fantastic night at the Litherland Town Hall. . . .

> I think the Beatles are No. 1 because they resurrected original style rock 'n' roll. . . . They hit the scene when it had been emasculated by figures like Cliff Richard and sounds like those electronic wonders, The Shadows and their many imitators. Gone was the drive that inflamed the emotions. The Beatles, therefore, exploded on a jaded scene. And to those people on the verge of quitting teendom—those who had experienced during their most impressionable years the impact of rhythm & blues music (raw rock 'n' roll)—this was an experience, a process of regaining and reliving a style of sounds and associated feelings identifiable with their era. Here again, in the Beatles, was the stuff that screams are made of. Here was the excitement—both physical and aural—that symbolized the

rebellion of youth in the ennuied mid-1950s. . . . Rugged yet romantic, appealing to both sexes. With calculated naiveté and an ingenious, throw-away approach to their music. Affecting indifference to audience response yet always saying "Thank you." Reviving interest in, and commanding enthusiasm for, numbers which descended the charts way back.

In addition to providing the Beatles with a good deal of free publicity, *Mersey Beat* was also the medium that brought the group to the attention of a local businessman by the name of Brian Epstein. Twenty-seven years old in 1961, Epstein was the firstborn son of one of Liverpool's most prominent Jewish families. His grandfather Isaac had emigrated from Lithuania around the turn of the century and opened a furniture store in the Liverpool suburb of Walton. Brian's father, Harry, had expanded the business and established himself as a pillar of the Jewish community; Brian's mother, Malka, known to all as Queenie, had grown up in Sheffield, where her family owned a major furniture manufacturing firm. A woman of graceful bearing and refined taste, she retained an edge of snobbery toward Liverpool, which she expressed by doting protectively on Brian and his younger brother, Clive. By 1961, Clive Epstein had married and started a family of his own. But Brian still lived with his parents in their large house on Queen's Drive in the affluent suburb of Childwell.

As a boy, Brian Epstein had attended an almost yearly succession of private day and boarding schools, eventually winding up at Wrekin College in Shropshire, a "minor" public school. By his own description he was a sensitive, solitary child who did poorly at his studies and worse at sports. "Throughout my schooldays I was one of those out-of-sorts boys who never quite fit. Who are ragged, nagged, and bullied," Epstein recalled in his 1964 autobiography, *A Cellarful of Noise*. His only successes came in the extracurricular areas of art and drama club. Yet, however much he languished at each of his many schools, Brian's education did succeed at one of its primary goals. By the time he was done at Wrekin, he had acquired the polish—the accent, the argot, and the genteel demeanor—of an English public-school boy.

Upon leaving school at the age of fifteen without any academic certification, Brian informed his parents of his ambition to become either a stage actor or a fashion designer. His father had other ideas, and put him to work as a salesclerk in one of the family furniture stores. There, for the first time, Brian excelled at something that mattered in Harry Epstein's eyes. As a salesman, Brian discovered that he enjoyed what he described as "procuring people's confidence." He also took it upon himself to modernize the fusty manner in which I. Epstein & Sons displayed its merchandise.

In November 1952, shortly after his nineteenth birthday, Epstein was called up for National Service. He was trained as an army document clerk, posted to a barracks in Regents Park, London, and promptly discharged a few months later after a psychiatric examination determined that he was unsuited to military life. He returned home in March 1954 and rejoined the family firm, assisting his father in the expansion of a subsidiary called North End Music Stores—NEMS for short—that sold pianos, radios, and record players. In his spare time, Brian became a patron of the Liverpool Playhouse (then regarded as the best repertory theater in Britain) and began to socialize with members of the company. "There was a sort of wistfulness about him," recalled the actress Helen Lindsey. "He wanted to belong to what he perceived as a charmed circle. He was obviously bored to death with the furniture business and he thought we were terribly lucky people, that we inhabited a magic world, which he wanted to become a part of."

Suitably stage-struck, Epstein applied, with his parents' blessing, to the Royal Academy of Dramatic Arts in London. Helen Lindsey helped him with his audition piece; to her surprise, he was admitted to RADA in the fall of 1956. By his second term at the school, he had begun to impress his instructors as "a really promising student." But in the spring of 1957, expressing disillusionment with his prospects as an actor, Epstein abruptly resigned from RADA and again returned to Liverpool, this time to oversee the establishment of a new downtown branch of NEMS, specializing in phonograph records. Diligently managed by Brian and his brother Clive, the new store was an immediate success. In 1959 they opened at a second location, on Whitechapel Street in the center of Liverpool. By 1961 the Epstein brothers had built NEMS into one of the largest record retailers in the North of England, with nine stores on Merseyside. But for Brian, the idea of belonging to a charmed circle retained its grip on his imagination. "I fancy Rome," he wrote in his journal around this time. "I want to live in luxury, learn the language, live Italian, and just add myself to that very attractive, utterly ridiculous little group that calls itself the International Set."

When Bill Harry began to publish *Mersey Beat,* the NEMS shops were an obvious outlet for the paper, and Epstein, impressed at how quickly the early issues sold out, became both an advertiser and a contributor, writing a column in which he previewed new record releases. Since the paper was filled with news and photographs of the Beatles, this was his introduction to the group. Early in November 1961, he went to see them perform at one of their lunch-hour sessions at the Cavern, which was just around the corner from his Whitechapel store. At first he was taken aback. "I had never seen anything like the Beatles on *any* stage," he later said. "They smoked as they played and they talked and pretended to hit one another. They turned their backs on the audience and shouted at them and laughed at private jokes." He found them to be uncouth and "ill-clad," but he was also struck by how funny and appealing they were. A few weeks later, after a couple of return visits to the Cavern, he met with the group and expressed an interest in managing them. They were flattered by the attentions of this well-known merchant, but wary of him as well. They explained that their goal was to get a recording contract in Britain. Eager to demonstrate his good faith, Brian offered to see what he could do on their behalf.

There are two main theories about what first attracted Brian Epstein to the Beatles, and both of them are true. The authorized version, as told by Epstein in his (ghostwritten) autobiography and elaborated in numerous interviews and press accounts, is the story of a shy, sensitive young man growing restless and bored in the provinces, vacillating between his sense of duty to his family and his desire for a more exciting life, who toys at different points with the idea of becoming a designer or an actor, and then serendipitously finds in the Beatles the perfect vehicle for all of his unformed and unrealized creative aspirations. "Everything about the Beatles was right for me," Brian said in a 1964 interview. "Their kind of attitude toward life, and their humor, and their own personal way of behaving—it was all just what I wanted. They represented the direct, unselfconscious, good-natured, uninhibited human relationships which I hadn't found and had wanted and felt deprived of. And my own sense of inferiority evaporated with the Beatles because I knew I could help them, and that they wanted me to help them, and trusted me to help them."

The second theory about Brian Epstein and the Beatles turns on the one important piece of information that was omitted from the authorized version of his life. According to his ghostwriter, Derek Taylor, Brian had known he was homosexual since his early teenage years. Given his family's intensely proprietous nature, it was probably inevitable that this should serve as a source of shame, and like most homosexuals in Britain during the 1950s, living under laws unchanged since Oscar Wilde's time, he led a double life. By the time he met the Beatles, this dual existence had become a matter of preference as well as self-protection. Drawn to the extremes of highlife and lowlife—to any kind of life, it seems, besides the "atmosphere of middle-class commercialism" in which he was brought up—Epstein had reached an accommodation with his homosexuality that was common among middle-class gay men in the days before gay pride: he sought to segregate his sex life from the rest of his life by centering his interest on so-called rough trade, engaging in casual, usually anonymous, sometimes violent sex with ostensibly straight, working-class men with whom he would otherwise rarely come into social contact. To this end, while living with his parents in Childwell, he also kept a flat on Falkner Street in the heart of Liverpool 8.

Over the years, the truth about Epstein's sex life (which only became public knowledge after his death) has come to serve a kind of object lesson in the revisionary power of suppressed information. On the one hand, no realistic characterization of him is possible without reference to his homosexuality. His own descriptions of being "ragged, nagged, and bullied" at school, of his attraction to the worlds of fashion and the theater, and of his unfulfilled emotional life are all brought into sharper focus by the knowledge that he was gay. Though he professed to have taken no interest in the pop scene prior to meeting the Beatles, Epstein may still have known that homosexuality was virtually the norm among British pop managers of the period, and his interest in this field, like his earlier interests in fashion and acting, may have been informed by the hope that he would feel less closeted in the music business than in other lines of work. Moreover, if we are to believe Pete Best and John Lennon, both of whom said that they were shyly propositioned by Epstein (Best in the spring of 1962, Lennon in the spring of 1963), it is clear that sexual desire played at least some part in his attraction to the Beatles.

On the other hand, the posthumous revelations about Brian Epstein's sex life have threatened to overshadow all other aspects of his personality and sensibility, and they have contributed to an impression that sexual attraction was indeed the prime motivation behind his relationship with the group. (This reductionism found its fullest expression in Albert

Goldman's fanatically revisionist 1988 biography of John Lennon, which posited a long-term sexual relationship between Lennon and Epstein, and then presented this fictive bond as a homoerotic subtext of the entire Beatles saga.) But unless one subscribes to the belief that sexuality is destiny, any one-dimensional view of Epstein's motivation misses the mark, for the larger truth about him at the time he met the Beatles involves how deeply conflicted he was in *every* aspect of his life. To characterize his sudden interest in managing a pop group as narrowly sexual, emotional, or entrepreneurial is to oversimplify. Epstein's attraction to the Beatles was all of these things combined, and it was precisely their ability to provide him with an all-purpose outlet for his energy and creativity that led him to state that truly "everything" about the Beatles was right for him. To the extent that sexual desire came into it, his subsequent career as their manager must be seen as a triumph of sublimation. Long after any hope of a sexual liaison with one or another of the Beatles had been conclusively laid to rest, Epstein would perfect on their behalf a devotional style of management that bore no resemblance to the predations of gay pop moguls like Larry Parnes.

In December 1961, however, all the Beatles knew about Brian Epstein was that he came from a prominent Jewish family, that he was known to be honorable in his business dealings (so said Bob Wooler, whose opinion they solicited), and that he had offered to help them land a British recording deal. Epstein approached this task with the disarming mixture of confidence and naïveté that would become his trademark as a manager. He and his brother ran one of the largest record retail operations in the North of England. So Brian telephoned the sales managers of Britain's two major record companies, Decca and EMI—men with whom NEMS did an enormous amount of business—and asked them if they would be so kind as to inform their A&R departments about this exciting new group from Liverpool. Anxious to avoid displeasing a client of Epstein's worth, the sales managers passed on the materials Brian gave them—photographs of the Beatles and copies of their Polydor tape—to the recording managers of their respective labels. No one at EMI showed any interest, but Decca sent a man to Liverpool to hear the group perform. On his recommendation, the Beatles were invited to a recording test at Decca's London studios on January 1, 1962.

The Decca audition was a fiasco. Whether they were intimidated by their first encounter with the environment of a real recording studio, or simply unnerved by the arrival of a moment they had dreamed about for years, the Beatles collectively choked. In a misguided effort to show off their versatility, they ran through old standbys like the Coasters' "Searchin'," current hits like Bobby Vee's "Take Good Care of My Baby," a healthy sampling of their Carl Perkins/Buddy Holly/Chuck Berry repertoire, a dance song from John (Barrett Strong's "Money"), a torch song from Paul ("Till There Was You"), a pair of Lennon-McCartney originals, and George Harrison's inexplicable rendition of "The Sheik of Araby." The effect of this hour-long musical miscellany was confusing to say the least. The crowning touch was provided by John Lennon, who eventually exploded in frustration at Brian Epstein, calling him "a Jewish git" after Epstein, sitting in the control room with the Decca A&R man, ventured a suggestion over the studio intercom.

Faced with an oddly named, oddly dressed, and openly quarrelsome four-piece group playing a grab-bag of outdated material, none of it too well, Decca did what any other well-run record label would have done: after a polite interval, it turned the Beatles down. Brian Epstein later claimed that Dick Rowe, the company's head of A&R, told him flatly that "groups of guitarists are on the way out"—thereby earning the unfortunate Rowe (who vehemently denied ever having made the statement) a place in the Third Edition of *The Oxford Dictionary of Famous Quotations.* But even if the quote was accurate, Rowe was merely letting Epstein down gently. The same month that it rejected the Beatles, Decca signed another, significantly more polished guitar group called Brian Poole & the Tremeloes.

Unaware as yet that they had failed the recording test, the Beatles (despite John Lennon's outburst) came away from their Decca audition properly impressed with Brian Epstein, who in less than a month had gotten them in the door of a London studio. Brian had his family's solicitor prepare a simple contract (which he then didn't bother to sign), and in January 1962 he officially became the Beatles' manager. He began by adding the appurtenances of a business—or better yet, a firm—to their rudimentary operation. From now on, at the start of each week, the group was provided with a carefully typed memo listing their coming engagements, stressing the importance of particular venues, and beseeching them to be on time. Their finances were similarly regularized, with the band members receiving a weekly accounting of income and expenses. What little there was to do was suddenly done with a new precision and flair.

On a more practical level, Epstein moved to cover the cost of his commission—at this point, a standard agent's fee of 15 percent—by raising the Beatles' asking price from fifteen to twenty pounds a night. He also succeeded in drawing Peter Eckhorn of the Top Ten Club into a bidding war with a rival Hamburg club owner named Manfred Weissleder for the chance to present the Beatles in the spring. Weissleder, who was in the process of opening a vast new Grosse Freiheit venue called the Star-Club, eventually bested Eckhorn with an offer equivalent to £165 ($460) a week. In the meantime, Epstein began looking for opportunities to present the Beatles beyond the immediate area of Merseyside. In February they played their first club date in Manchester. In March they made their first radio broadcast, also from Manchester, singing songs by Chuck Berry, Roy Orbison, and the Shirelles on the regional BBC program *Teenager's Turn*.

IN APRIL 1962 the Beatles flew to Hamburg to begin a seven-week engagement at the Star-Club, their mode of travel reflecting their manager's success at raising their rates of pay. They were met at the airport by the solitary figure of Astrid Kirchherr, bearing the horrifying news that Stuart Sutcliffe had collapsed and died of a brain hemorrhage the day before. Stuart, Astrid told them, had been suffering excruciating headaches since the previous fall. The doctors he consulted were unable to find a cause, which led Astrid to attribute these seizure-like episodes to the intensity with which Stuart had thrown himself into his art studies. By the winter of 1962 the symptoms had grown so severe that Stuart was forced to stop attending classes, but six weeks of prescribed bed rest had brought him no relief. His autopsy X rays later revealed the presence of a small tumor on the right side of his brain.

The Star-Club, filling the ground floor of a converted cinema, was the largest and best-run nightclub the Beatles had ever played. The owner, Manfred Weissleder, was an enterprising St. Pauli promoter and pornographer who meant to turn the place into a showcase for the big-name rock-'n'-roll acts that came to Germany on tours of American military bases. In April the Beatles initiated the Star-Club's perpetual "Rock 'n' Twist Parade," topping a bill of five singers and groups. In May, Tony Sheridan took over as headliner, with the Beatles and their fellow Liverpudlians Gerry & The Pacemakers as supporting acts. In June, Weissleder presented his first big name when he succeeded in booking Gene Vincent, with Sheridan, the Beatles, and the Pacemakers filling out the bill.

With the Beatles in Hamburg, Brian Epstein returned to London to renew his efforts at securing a record deal. Faced with mounting pressure from his father, who regarded his new avocation as a pop manager to be yet another distraction from the family firm, Brian was running out of options. His hopes now rested on the Decca audition tape, but the recording managers at Pye and Phillips confirmed Decca's diagnosis, and a personal visit to the offices of EMI's main pop labels, Columbia and HMV, proved no more productive than his earlier indirect approach. At a loss for his next move, Epstein decided to have the songs on the Decca tape transferred onto disc, on the theory that this would make for a more polished presentation. An HMV record store on Oxford Street offered such a service, and the technician who supervised the dubbing commented favorably on the tape. Having no one else to deliver his pitch to, Brian started in, and the technician offered to put him in touch with a man he knew at Ardmore & Beechwood, the music publishing subsidiary of EMI. Within the hour, Brian was telling Sydney Coleman of Ardmore & Beechwood about his efforts to get the Beatles a recording contract. Coleman expressed a vague interest in the group's original material and offered to introduce Brian to one of the few recording managers in London he had not yet spoken with, George Martin at Parlophone Records, which was still another subsidiary of EMI. The next day, Epstein met with Martin at the EMI studios in St. John's Wood. Martin listened to the Decca recordings and was not overly impressed. He felt the Beatles' original songs were mediocre and their cover songs obsolete. Yet he also heard what he would later describe as "an unusual quality of sound, a certain roughness" that he found sufficiently intriguing to offer the group a recording test.

At the time he met Brian Epstein, George Martin had served as the head of Parlophone Records for seven years. A tall, slim man in his mid-thirties, blessed with what the press would one day describe as "Prince Philip good looks," Martin's manner, speech, and bearing belied his working-class origins in the North London district of Drayton Park. His father, a carpenter by trade, had been reduced to selling newspapers during the Depression, but George, at age eleven, had won a scholarship to a Jesuit grammar school. Despite their strapped condition, his family owned a piano, which attracted Martin's interest at an early age. As a teenager he took lessons on the instrument, played in a pickup dance band, and fantasized (he later wrote) about becoming the next Rachmaninoff. In 1943, at the age of seventeen, he enlisted in the Fleet Air Arm. After flight training in Trinidad and radar training in Lancashire, Martin, newly commissioned as a junior officer, was about to be posted to a torpedo squadron when the war ended in 1945. While still in the service he initiated a correspondence with a professor at London's Guildhall School of Music named Sidney Harrison, to whom he sent a number of "Debussy-like" pieces he had composed. After his demobilization in 1947, Martin received a grant to attend the school, where he spent the next three years studying piano and composition. Reasoning that piano players were a dime a dozen, he also took up the oboe, with which he tried to earn a living after he completed his studies in 1950. When his skills as an oboist proved less than marketable (the instrument, he recalled, felt "like a live eel in my hands"), Martin, thanks again to Sidney Harrison, found a job as an assistant to Oscar Preuss, who was the head of Parlophone.

Parlophone's parent company, EMI (which stood for Electrical & Musical Industries), was the world's largest record company, with recording, manufacturing, and distribution facilities in nineteen countries, and a dominant share of the market in Europe and the British Commonwealth. Like its American counterpart, RCA, EMI was a technological as well as a commercial leader; the company was a pioneer in the development of television and radar, and the first patent for stereo recording was granted to one of its engineers. By the early 1950s, however, size and success had generated a sense of complacency throughout the corporation. While the American giants Columbia and RCA Victor vied with one another over which new microgroove format, LP or 45, would become the industry standard, EMI initially decided that *neither* was worth adopting, and vowed to stick with 78s. At a time when American-produced records accounted for more than two-thirds of EMI's sales, this shortsightedness contributed to the loss of lucrative licensing deals with Columbia and RCA. Under a new, more aggressive management team headed by Joseph (later Sir Joseph) Lockwood, EMI moved to restore its access to American music and the American market by purchasing Capitol Records, a major label based in Hollywood.

Parlophone, as George Martin liked to think of it, was the "poor relation" in the corporate family of EMI. Martin's former boss, Oscar Preuss, had built up a roster consisting mostly of novelty and light classical acts; he had also signed the jazz trumpeter Humphrey Lyttelton and the accordionist Jimmy Shand. Martin succeeded Preuss in 1955 and wasted no time in flirting with the Dick Rowe kind of immortality by passing up a chance to sign Tommy Steele. In 1956, Martin produced his first hit record with a jazz parody of "Three Blind Mice" by the Johnny Dankworth Band. In 1957 he recorded the comic songwriters Flanders and Swann in their popular West End revue, *At the Drop of a Hat*. The following year he produced an album with Peter Sellers that marked the beginning of his association with the Goons. Making records with Sellers and Spike Milligan was a formative experience for Martin, since both these artists were natural improvisers who knew a great deal about working with tape and sound effects from their radio show. Martin's success with the Goons and Flanders and Swann earned him a reputation as a producer of comedy records. In 1961 he recorded the cast album of *Beyond the Fringe* and signed the Temperance Seven, whose recording of "You're Driving Me Crazy" was his first number-one hit. Yet the one type of music with which George Martin had virtually no experience was rock 'n' roll. Parlophone had the pop singer Adam Faith under contract, but he was handled by an EMI staff producer named John Burgess. Otherwise the label's occasional forays into rock (e.g., Shane Fenton's 1961 single "I'm a Moody Guy") were produced by Martin's assistant, Ron Richards.

The Beatles were still in Hamburg when Brian Epstein informed them of George Martin's offer of a recording test. They returned to Britain in June of 1962 determined to take a more professional approach with their Parlophone audition than they had brought to the debacle at Decca. They arrived at EMI's Abbey Road Studios in London only to learn that George Martin had assigned his assistant Ron Richards to supervise. After rehearsing for several hours, they put four songs on tape: three original compositions and an old Latin-American number called "Besamo Mucho" (or "Kiss Me Much") that the Beatles knew from a Coasters record and performed as a parody of pop arias like "It's Now Or Never." Their choice of material reflected their newfound desire to emphasize their songwriting over the cover tunes that formed the bulk of their repertoire. It was during an original called "Love Me Do" that Richards called Martin in. Hearing the group in the studio confirmed many of the impressions Martin had formed from the Decca tape. He remained doubtful about their songwriting and their instrumental skills, with Pete Best's drumming in particular striking him as weak. (On the tape that survives from this audition, Best's playing goes completely to pieces behind the solo in "Love Me Do.") But their singing was stronger than he had expected, and when he invited the group to join him in the control room, Martin was completely won over by their humor and repartee, which reminded him, unsurprisingly, of the Goons. Entranced by their personalities, Martin decided that none of his reservations about the Beatles' music was a major impediment. Nobody expected pop singers in 1962 to write their own material, and it was routine to compensate for the instrumental shortcomings of prospective teen idols with hired hands in the studio. Martin mentioned to Brian Epstein that *if* he were to sign the Beatles, he would want to use a session drummer when it came time to record.

It was more than a month before a firm offer was forthcoming from Parlophone. The terms of the contract were typical for 1962, which is to say that they were stacked completely in favor of the record label. The contract ran for one year, during which Parlophone agreed to record four singles. It promised the Beatles a royalty of precisely one penny per double-sided single sold (approximately one percent of the retail cost), and it contained three one-year options to renew, with a rise in the royalty of one farthing (one-quarter penny) for each of the option years.

That the contract was typical did not make it any less inequitable. For years record companies in Britain and America had sought to justify the minuscule royalty rates they paid to all but their most successful artists by pointing to their substantial investment in the means of production, distribution, and promotion of records. But these costs were routinely overstated, especially in Britain, where the record market was dominated by two exceedingly well-capitalized corporations, and where the break-even point on a pop single was less than five thousand copies in 1962.

Still, it remained that Brian Epstein and the Beatles were in no position to press for a better deal. They had been turned down, not once but twice in some cases, by every other British label. So Epstein and the Beatles jumped at Parlophone's offer, for they cared little and knew less about royalty rates and option clauses. For them, as it had been for so many aspiring musicians before them, the chance to make records completely obscured the question of what, if anything, might happen if their records actually sold.

11

I was the new boy. It was like joining a new class at school
where everybody knows everybody else but me.

—Ringo Starr

Although the financial implications of the contract would only become apparent over time, there was one immediate and momentous repercussion of the Beatles' record deal. In the course of reviewing the terms of the agreement, George Martin reminded Brian Epstein of his intention to use a session drummer when it came time to record. Epstein relayed this information to Lennon, McCartney, and Harrison. Never ones to stand on sentiment, the three founding members of the Beatles decided to mark this turning point in their careers by inviting their old acquaintance Ringo Starr to replace Pete Best on drums. Brian Epstein was assigned the task of breaking the news to Best; Lennon, McCartney, and Harrison never so much as spoke with their former drummer again.

Across Liverpool, fans were thunderstruck by the simultaneous announcement that the Beatles had signed with Parlophone and that Pete Best had been summarily replaced by Ringo Starr. ("Pete forever! Ringo never!" proclaimed the graffiti outside the Cavern, echoing the old sectarian slogan "Orange forever! Popery never!") To the extent that the Beatles were beloved on Merseyside as a throwback to the glory days of rock 'n' roll, their statuesque, uncommunicative, lushly pompadoured drummer had served for many as the focal point of the band. Best conformed to the prevailing visual image of a rock musician as none of the others did, and there is no doubt that he was viewed with some jealousy by his bandmates on account of his popularity with the Beatles' female fans. And yet, from the perspective of Lennon, McCartney, and Harrison, Best had never been fully included in their circle of friendship and aspiration. As far as they were concerned, he had come in late, on the eve of their first trip to Hamburg, and they had taken him on out of sheer necessity, as the only drummer they could find. He had shared in their music mainly as a sideman, in their humor mainly as a straight man, and while he was hardly unintelligent, his intelligence had no edge.

Ringo Starr, whose real name was Richard Starkey, was something else again. Born in Liverpool in July 1940, he was three months older (and, at five feet seven inches, three inches shorter) than John Lennon. His parents, Richard and Elsie Starkey, had met and married as co-workers at a bakery in 1936. Like their parents before them—"just ordinary poor working-class on both sides of the family," in Ringo's estimate—they lived in a notoriously run-down, crime-ridden section of Liverpool 8 called the Dingle ("where they play tag with hatchets," according to local lore). When "Little Richie" was three, his parents divorced, and though he remained in close contact with his paternal grandparents, he rarely saw his father again.

From the age of six, Richard's childhood was overshadowed, and his education compromised, by a series of protracted medical crises. In his first year at St. Silas, a Church of England primary school, a burst appendix put him into a coma for several weeks and required that he be hospitalized for nearly a year. The trauma of this experience was compounded by a policy, common in Britain at the time, that discouraged parents from visiting their children in the hospital. When he finally returned to school, Richard's health remained poor and he was hopelessly behind in his studies. As a result, what little formal education he received came mainly from a neighbor's daughter who taught him to read and write. His absences from school made it hard for him to sustain friendships, and much of his time was spent in the care of his grandparents, for his mother had taken a job as a barmaid after her marriage broke up. In 1951, barely literate, Richard passed directly from St. Silas to the Dingle Vale secondary modern high school without bothering to take the eleven-plus. There, for the next two years, he occupied the "C" stream in one of Liverpool's worst inner-city schools. ("A quiet, thoughtful type . . . helpful and willing," one of his masters wrote.) Just past his thirteenth birthday, Richard was again hospitalized, this time with a bout of pleurisy and tuberculosis that lasted for nearly two years and ended his schooling for good.

It was during this second hospitalization that Elsie Starkey, with her son's blessing, married a transplanted Londoner named Harry Graves, who worked as a painter and plasterer for the Liverpool Corporation. Harry and Richard got on exceedingly well. Discharged from the hospital in 1955, Richard worked briefly as a messenger and then as a waiter until his stepfather found him a position as an apprentice pipe fitter with a

Liverpool firm called Hunt's. In 1957 he joined with some friends from work to form a skiffle group, graduating from the washboard to the drums after his grandfather bought him a set. Within two years he had improved sufficiently to be offered a spot with Allen Caldwell's Raging Texans, which soon metamorphosed into Rory Storm & The Hurricanes and emerged as one of the most popular bands on Merseyside. In the summer of 1960 the Hurricanes landed a steady gig at a Butlin's holiday camp, and Richard, now known as Ringo Starr, was able to quit his job at Hunt's. At Butlin's, he became a featured performer with the Hurricanes, fronting the group during a portion of its set called "Starr Time." Later that year he met the Beatles at the Kaiserkeller in Hamburg, where he also became friendly with Tony Sheridan, who rated him highly as a drummer. In January 1962, Ringo left the Hurricanes and moved to Hamburg to play in Sheridan's band. But by the summer he was back with Rory Storm at Butlin's, which was where Brian Epstein contacted him in August with a guarantee of twenty-five pounds a week.

Though their handling of the matter was utterly callous, the Beatles' decision to replace the strapping Pete Best with this diminutive product of the Dingle was based on sound musical considerations. Lennon, McCartney, and Harrison had been hearing about their drummer's shortcomings for more than a year from Tony Sheridan, whose musical judgment they respected. George Martin's comment to Brian Epstein had seconded Sheridan's opinion with the force of a voice from on high. Though Martin had no way of knowing it, the Beatles had never thought of themselves as anything but a self-sufficient musical unit; the idea of having to rely on a session drummer (or, conversely, on a live drummer who wasn't considered good enough to play on records) was an insult to their sense of autonomy. Like Best, Starr possessed no more than a rudimentary technique on the drums. He had never been one to practice, much less study, the instrument, but what distinguished him from Pete Best was the authority and feeling with which he applied his rudimentary skills. Ringo's playing was much punchier and more syncopated than that of his predecessor, and his fills—the accented interjections by which a drummer annotates the structure of a song—were more varied and propulsive. Like all beat drummers in Liverpool, Starr played loud and hard. But whereas Pete Best tended to keep time with pounding quarter-notes on his bass drum, Ringo had learned to distribute the weight of his playing among his cymbals, bass, and snare. However much an element of personal jealousy may have figured in the Beatles' decision to change drummers, there was no question as to who was the better player of the two.

What was true of Ringo's drumming was true of his personality as well. Though his face retained the melancholy countenance of a sickly child, his disposition was generally agreeable and upbeat, while his long hospitalizations and his many comings and goings from school had made him something of an expert at fitting in. At first he was scarcely more outspoken than Pete Best. "It's how I'm built," he explained. "Some people gab all day and some people play it smogo. I haven't got a smiling face or a talking mouth." But where Best was bland, Starr had a decided flair. He knew how to pick his moments, and he was a master of the quizzical Liverpudlian deadpan, the slow Liverpudlian double-take, and the curt Liverpudlian retort. In some ways, his personality was everything the other three Beatles were not: stoic, unassuming, and unpretentious, with the only inauthentic thing about him being a stage name so preposterous that no one could be expected to take it seriously. On account of his impoverished background and his lack of formal education, the other three Beatles looked down on him at first, for Ringo was truly a slum kid, utterly lacking in the glib confidence of suburban grammar-school boys. Yet this also made him a source of fascination to them. As John Lennon put it, "To be so aware with so little education is rather unnerving to someone who's been to school since he was fucking two onwards."

There is little question that the invitation to join the Beatles was the single luckiest thing that ever happened to Ringo Starr. But Ringo's acceptance of that invitation was also one of the luckiest things that ever happened to the Beatles. It is hard to imagine that these three headstrong, self-satisfied young men could have anticipated how perfectly Starr's looks and personality would complement their own, or how central the presence of this little comic drummer would be to the iconography that would develop around their group in the years ahead. In any case, from the moment he joined, the Beatles became almost unimaginable without him. As the author of the change from John-Paul-George-and-Pete to John-Paul-George-and-Ringo, he brought the ring of poetry to their common Christian names. Moreover, at precisely the point where events were unfolding that would separate the Beatles forever from the city of their birth, they had added to their ranks an authentic souvenir of Liverpool. Ringo's presence ensured that, however far they ventured, they would always carry with them an unmistakable piece of home.

THE OFFER TO join the Beatles came with several strings attached. Unlike Pete Best, Starr would be expected to adopt the band's distinctive hairstyle; he would also be expected to change his mode of dress. Gone were the pastel stage suits he had worn at Butlin's with Rory Storm. But gone as well were the leather Rocker outfits the Beatles were known for in Liverpool. In their place, "the new boy" was issued a wardrobe consisting of the sharply tailored mohair suits, narrow knit ties, and ankle-high, Cuban-heeled boots that had become the focus of Brian Epstein's efforts during the spring and summer of 1962 to remake the Beatles' image as a group. In John Lennon's famous phrase, Brian had "cleaned them up." Paul McCartney seems to have been Epstein's principal ally in this makeover; George Harrison initially wanted no part of it. (An early photograph of the Beatles in suits shows their normally stylish and self-possessed guitarist sitting churlishly on his hands, looking precisely like a Liverpool electrician's mate dressed up in his "bezzies.") At first the Beatles went along with their manager's taste because they were learning to trust his judgment in matters of presentation. In time they would discover that they liked the way they looked. In any case, it wasn't as if Brian Epstein meant to fit them out as a collection of singing stockbrokers. He was a fashion-conscious, boy-conscious observer who had been spending a lot of his time in London of late. While making the rounds of the record companies in the winter of 1962, Brian had glimpsed the future, and seen that it was Mod.

After a decade of baroque exaggeration, the image of the Teddy boy had lost its last vestige of appeal for British youth by the early 1960s. Enclaves of aging Teds still lingered in Liverpool and other provincial cities, but as a fashion-cum-social statement, Edwardianism had long since been defeated by the ease with which its original irony reverted to futility. What began as a working-class burlesque of upper-class dandyism was now perceived as a caricature of lower-class loutishness. Withdrawn inside their irreconcilable nostalgias of chip-shop tribalism and Hollywood Western individualism, the Teds were seen as proud losers, but losers all the same.

The Mods sought not a retreat into the past, but a symbolic alliance with the future. At first glance they seemed to be exactly what the optimists had hoped would emerge from the new towns and the new schools and the new consumer-based economy of Britain's newfound Age of Affluence. Alone among the succession of fashion subcultures that would be taken up by British teenagers in the decades after World War II, Mod carried a suggestion of compliance with the expectations of the adult world. What happened after that suggestion was made, however, was anybody's guess.

The progress of the style followed the pattern set by the Teds. There was the same extended gestation among working-class youth in London; the same gradual fusion of fashion, music, and social self-consciousness; the same slow dissemination of the style throughout the country; and, ultimately, the same conversion of an individualistic impulse into a uniform of subcultural and generational identity. It began among a small group of London teenagers and centered on the Italian-designed clothes that were becoming available at the time. This new "Continental" look was a streamlined variation on conventional men's tailoring. It included closely fitted suit jackets with slim lapels; narrow, cuffless trousers; pin- and tab-collared shirts, trilby hats with "stingy" brims; laceless footwear in supple leathers; and an overall preference for smooth, lustrous fabrics. To this raw stock, the original contingent of Mod "individualists" added an obsession with the smallest details of cut and cloth, the nuances of which lent an almost psychiatric intimacy to the relationship they maintained with their tailors. The look was sleek, subtle, obsessively neat, and self-consciously modern.

One tenet of their modernity was that Mods aspired to cosmopolitan attitudes. The Continental look had already caught on among black American jazz and rhythm-and-blues musicians, whose taste was emulated by some of the young West Indians then settling in the working-class districts of London. "Subconsciously we knew that blacks had no real power in the States, any more than we did, but their clothes made them look in control, on top, not to be messed with," recalled the Mod impresario Chris Stamp. Teddy boys had been singularly unconcerned with the cultural contradictions of dancing to Little Richard records one night and dancing on the heads of British subjects from Jamaica or St. Lucia the next; Teds had been in the vanguard of violent reaction to black immigration.

Mods felt differently. They viewed the immigrant blacks less as a

threat to their jobs and their neighborhoods than as a fascinating exception to the drab homogeneity of English life. Actual contact between the
races remained a wary affair, but the Mods treated the more public
aspects of black culture—music, dance, and dress—as a trove of stylistic
expertise. At first their music of choice was modern jazz. The very term
Mod began as a contraction of *Modernist,* and the early adherents of the
style defined themselves against the reactionary taste and unstylish
bohemianism of the trad jazz fans. But the enthusiasm for modern jazz
was limited by its unsuitability for dancing, and by 1962 the Mods had
switched their allegiance to contemporary rhythm and blues—particularly the more polished "uptown" style of R&B heard on American labels
like Atlantic and Tamla-Motown.

The fascination with black taste in music and dress shaded easily into
a fascination with the demeanor of exaggerated detachment and imperturbability represented by the ironic mask of "cool"—another version of
which could be found on the Continent, in the world-weary sensibility of
European university students. The Beatles had encountered this stance
firsthand among their "exi" friends in Hamburg. The Mods encountered
it mainly through the medium of French films, which were popular in
any event on account of their sexiness. French stars like Jean-Paul Bel-
mondo, Jean-Claude Brialy, Anna Karina, and Jeanne Moreau portrayed
images of disaffected Youth that seemed more sophisticated and enigmatic than the stereotypic Hollywood outsiders on which their characters were often based. Theirs was a mode of stylish self-dramatization
that traveled surprisingly well, and working-class kids in Britain who had
barely heard of Sartre or Genet began adopting emblems of European
student life, including the "French-cut" or *pilzenkopf* hairstyle, which the
Mods renamed a "college boy."

Primarily, Mod was a fashion statement for teenagers. But, even more
than Edwardianism, Mod was construed as a social statement as well.
From Ted to Rocker to Mod to Skinhead to the many permutations of
Punk, each of the distinctive fashion-and-music subcultures adopted by
successive subgenerations of postwar British youth has elicited the same
hermeneutic question: Given the wide range of possibilities presented by
popular culture and everyday life, why should *this* style, shaped by *these*
influences, captivate the adolescent imagination at *this* particular time?
Mod civilization flourished along the fault line between the "never had it

so good" consumer ideology and the "secondary modern" social reality that marked the Macmillan years. By the early 1960s the Mods had evolved into a kind of living parody of the expectations and aspirations of postwar British life. Finding jobs in shops and offices, they adopted a mode of dress that satisfied the white-collar requirement to "make a good impression" with a vehemence that turned the markers of class identity upside down. Away from the workplace, they cultivated a demeanor as preoccupied and self-important as that of any City financier. Not for them the idle streetcorner turf of the Teds. Mods had destinations, rounds, and appointments to keep. Restlessness was a creed with them, and what they lacked in social mobility, they made up for by being mobile in the literal sense of the word. Their leisure lives centered on an urban network of music clubs, clothes boutiques, record shops, and coffee bars, and they brought to their pursuit of pleasure the dedication that a scholarship boy might have brought to the chance to attend a university. Structuring their lives around the period between the end of one workday and the start of the next, they made the most of those precious hours with the help of the essential Mod drug, amphetamine, which kept the embers of immediacy glowing long and bright.

The special privilege of parody—social or otherwise—is that it allows its authors to participate in the very set of conventions they mean to debunk or transcend. Mods *were* eager, well-dressed, young men on the go. (And in its formative stage, it was primarily a male fashion.) That they weren't really going anywhere, most of them—that there wasn't anywhere in Britain for them to go—was rendered momentarily insignificant by the satisfaction of suggesting that success was merely a function of *style* to begin with. Working-class people had long nursed the suspicion that middle-class status was as superficial as stepping into the right suit of clothes and believing that it meant something. Now that Britain had succeeded in providing its young people with alternatives to manual labor, a widening familiarity with the world beyond their homes, and a market in goods and services that catered to their needs, working-class teenagers could move beyond simply noting the ironies of their station in society. Some were responding by becoming self-styled virtuosos of superficiality, their world defined by the cut of their clothes and the brand of their cigarettes and the obscurity of their taste in music—into which fine distinctions they packed all the significance they could, as if to invent a new code by which social relations might be governed more nearly in their favor.

In this the Mods defied not only the expectations of the Establishment but those of the working class as well. For only a die-hard Marxist could ignore the fact that chief among the social codes the Mods sought to transcend was the code of class itself. Britain's traditional working-class culture had been governed by a thoroughgoing preference for well-defined boundaries—between the classes, between the sexes, and between a range of categories that succumbed to the satisfying logic of Us and Them. Beginning with their dandified rejection of an aggressively masculine style, and continuing with their openness to the influence of such unlikely objects of working-class toleration as blacks, foreigners, and homosexuals (who were seen as fashion leaders), the early Mods were a striking exception to this rule. In time these attitudes would draw them into a celebrated rivalry with the loutish and retrograde Rockers. But the most important result of the Mods' connoisseurship and cosmopolitanism involved the way that their cool, chic style appealed to middle-class youth as well. In the early 1960s this allowed the Mod subculture to serve as a bridge across which middle-class and working-class talent and ambition could commune. "The new arty-crafties are different," Ray Gosling wrote of a group of London grammar-school students in 1961. "They're still the same terribly conscious lot . . . still looking and listening and talking and laughing in all the right places, but you want to see the way they dress. They've got all tight in all the right places and their hair's all sharp and well-razored, and they're as much involved in things as the secondary-modern kids."

Ultimately the common sense of identity that underlay the links between the Mods, the blacks, and the students was that of Youth itself. The demographic phenomenon of the "baby boom" has served as a facile explanation for nearly every aspect of youthful behavior in the decades after World War II. Yet the phenomenon was real, and the leading edge of the generation it created entered adolescence with a great shudder of social self-consciousness in the early 1960s. Young people were a growing presence on the streets of every British town, and though young people had always been fascinated by their peers, they had never been afforded the degree of access to representations of one another that was now routinely provided as the media of mass entertainment began to cater expressly to their needs. Spurred by records, radio, films, television, and mass-market advertising, this newfound sense of connection with "people like me who like what I like" encouraged the young to gravitate toward Youth as a primary focus of identity. In this sense the cosmopolitanism of the Mods was more than a search for new sources of stylistic inspiration; it also represented an attempt to substitute for traditional forms of identity like class, job, family, and neighborhood, the feeling of membership in a growing community of like-minded young people.

The strange truth is that, over time, the influence of Mod style would be most strongly felt in this, its most diffuse and evangelical form. It would be an overstatement to suggest that a majority of British teenagers in the 1960s subscribed to a Mod identity in the sense of describing themselves as such. Yet through an inexorable process of popularization and commercialization, Mod style went on to transform the image of British youth in the eyes of the world. Carried to America on the coattails of British pop, and spread from there by the dynamo of American mass culture, Mod established a standard of adolescent dandyism that would endure for decades to come. Long after it shed all subtlety and swelled to supernova proportions in the celebrated "Swinging London" scene of the mid-1960s, Mod style and some faint echo of the attitude it expressed toward status and materialism could be seen on the streets, not only of New York, Amsterdam, Toronto, and Tokyo, but of Mexico City, Jakarta, São Paulo, and Tehran—the streets, that is, of every major city where there existed a mass of young people, their lives suspended between the old world and the new, who sought to wrap themselves in the potent illusion that modernity itself was somehow on their side.

As for the Beatles, who would be instrumental in sending Mod style on its way around the world, they were already a little old, by 1962, to qualify as Mods per se. Yet for several years they had been assimilating many of the same influences and cultivating many of the same fine distinctions of taste. Though they had convinced their fans in Liverpool and Hamburg with their swaggering impersonation of Rocker nihilism, under the leather, under the skin, the Beatles were quintessential Mods: young men who had rejected the sanctioned avenues of advancement as too narrow, too compromised, and simply too boring to pursue. Their idea of success was an all-or-nothing affair. But until they met up with Brian Epstein, the Beatles hadn't a clue of how to get from here to there. Of all the contributions Epstein would make, none was more critical than his insistence on dusting the last residue of anachronism and provincialism from their shoulders and putting the Beatles in suits. For the change in dress corresponded to a change in outlook and attitude. It allowed the Beatles to see themselves in a new light, suddenly looking like young men on the verge of adulthood whose lives were just beginning, not just beginning to close in.

This new sense of possibility had a special importance for John Lennon in August 1962. A week before the upheaval that brought Ringo Starr into the band, John had learned that his girlfriend, Cynthia Powell, was pregnant. The two of them had been together now for more than three years, and apart from John's promiscuous adventures in Hamburg, their relationship had remained remarkably stable. Even so, Cynthia was surprised by John's reaction to the news of her pregnancy: he announced that the only course was for the two of them to get married immediately. This they did, in a sparsely attended civil ceremony on August 23. Cynthia's mother was absent, as she was visiting with relatives in Canada; John's aunt Mimi and the rest of his family did not attend the affair. After a brief celebration at a local pub, the newlyweds accepted Brian Epstein's gracious offer and took up residence in his flat on Falkner Street.

Two weeks after the Lennon nuptials, with their new drummer in tow, the Beatles flew from Liverpool to London to make their first record for Parlophone. They arrived at EMI's Abbey Road studios with a bone to pick. In preparation for the session, George Martin had sent them a demo of a song called "How Do You Do It," which Martin considered an ideal choice for their first single. Written by a comparative unknown named Mitch Murray (who went on to become one of the great hack songwriters of the 1960s, with hits ranging from "I'm Telling You Now" by Freddie & The Dreamers to "The Night Chicago Died" by Paper Lace), "How Do You Do It" was typical teen-market pap, with a mindless lyric and a pointless octave leap in its opening bar. The Beatles hated the song, and though they had dutifully worked up an arrangement for it, they made their feelings known to George Martin when they arrived at Abbey Road. Martin noted their objection and had them record it anyway, along with "Love Me Do," which he and Ron Richards considered the best of the three original songs the Beatles had performed at their recording test in June.

What happened next isn't entirely clear (memories of those early sessions have tended to run together over the years). But one way or another, the Beatles managed to persuade George Martin to designate "Love Me Do" as the A-side of the single, whereupon Martin, reluctant to waste "How Do You Do It" as a B-side, decided that the song should either be held in reserve for the Beatles or else offered to someone else. The tape of "How Do You Do It" was interred in the EMI archives. And the Beatles were spared the indignity of beginning their professional recording careers with John Lennon singing the lines, "You give me a feeling in my heart (oo-la-la) / Like an arrow, passing through it."

Not that "Love Me Do" was anyone's idea of a pop classic. Written in the days of the Quarry Men and revived by the Beatles during their last trip to Hamburg with an arrangement based loosely on Roy Orbison's "Candy Man," it consisted of one verse, two voices, and three chords. Stylistically the song was an anomaly for the Beatles, for its two-beat rhythm, harmonica accompaniment, and acoustic rhythm guitar brought it closer to the feeling of a country blues than anything else in their repertoire. "It was probably the first bluesy thing we tried to [write]," Paul McCartney recalled. "It came out whiter because it always does." The performance, too, was uncharacteristic in its restraint, as Paul's cool delivery of the coy lyric ("so please . . . love me *do*") combined with John Lennon's raucous harmonica to make the track sound like a collaboration between Noël Coward and Sonny Boy Williamson.

George Martin's willingness to release "Love Me Do" as the A-side of the single was all the more significant because, on further reflection, Martin decided that he wasn't happy with the track. The news that the Beatles had acquired a new drummer since their recording test in June had caused him to hold off on his original intention to hire a session man. But Ringo Starr impressed Martin as only a slight improvement on Pete Best. New to the group, and even newer to the studio than were his bandmates, Starr's playing on "Love Me Do" sounded timid, and the tone of his drums was awful. The decision to shelve "How Do You Do It" required that the Beatles return to the studio to record another song to go on the B-side of the single; for this second session, which took place one week after the first, Martin hired an experienced studio drummer named Andy White. The session began with White playing drums and Ringo playing maracas on the prospective B-side, an earnest, medium-tempo ballad by Lennon and McCartney called "P.S. I Love You." When an acceptable take of the new song had been obtained, White remained on the drums for another attempt at "Love Me Do." This remade version was rhythmically superior to the earlier recording. White's playing was stronger, steadier, and, thanks to the crisp sound of his drums, much more present than Starr's—so much so that John Lennon, whose harmonica solo was the high point of the original version, had trouble keeping up. Whether because of the inferior solo, or out of a belated concern for the Beatles' morale, Martin eventually decided to release the earlier version of "Love Me Do"—the one with Ringo on drums.

"Tact is the *sine qua non* of being a record producer," George Martin would later say. "One has to tread a fine line between, on the one hand, submitting to an artist's every whim, and, on the other, throwing one's own weight around." In these, the opening moves of a relationship that would blossom into one of the most inspired and influential collaborations in the history of popular music on record, both parties sent strong signals to each other. By recording "How Do You Do It," the Beatles demonstrated that they were willing to try almost anything in the studio; by then disclaiming the song, they showed their insistence on upholding their own standards of musical taste. By acquiescing to "Love Me Do," George Martin demonstrated his willingness to respect the Beatles' taste; at the same time, by hiring Andy White, he showed them that he, too, was insistent on upholding his own standards of musical craft. Whether or not Ringo Starr was, as they claimed, the best beat drummer in Liverpool, Andy White was Martin's way of letting the Beatles know that the level of musicianship that prevailed in the provinces was not going to be good enough for his purposes. Martin later regretted that Starr should have to bear the brunt of this opening exchange, for his sudden demotion to the role of incidental percussionist came as a harsh blow to his pride. But in the months ahead, as he settled into his new musical surroundings, Starr would respond to the memory of Andy White as a challenge, not a slight.

"Love Me Do" was released in October 1962. When George Martin made his pitch for the record at an EMI sales meeting, several of his colleagues were convinced that a beat group called the Beatles could only be a send-up by the Goons. ("It's another of your funny ones, isn't it, George?") Unsurprisingly, sales of the single were strongest in Liverpool, where it was rumored that Brian Epstein had ordered thousands of copies through NEMS in an effort to ensure that "Love Me Do" appeared on the pop charts. But considering that the Beatles were by far the most popular band on Merseyside, the NEMS stores would have been foolish *not* to have carried the record in quantity. (In fact, chart position was determined by a method that made it impossible for the sales in any one locality—outside of London—to make a song a hit. What the large NEMS order did ensure was that Parlophone made a profit on "Love Me Do.") The single appeared on the charts toward the end of October and lingered in the middle latitudes of the Top Fifty throughout the fall, rubbing shoulders with recent releases by Elvis Presley, Cliff Richard, Frank Ifield, and a crop of twangy guitar instrumentals that included the theme from the first James Bond film. Commercially, "Love Me Do" was a modest, respectable debut in a business where modesty and respectability have never counted for much.

A week before the release of the record, Brian Epstein and the Beatles signed a five-year management contract, in which Brian agreed to represent the group in return for 25 percent of their earnings. How exactly they arrived at this figure, no one seems to know, but 25 percent was the same share that Elvis Presley paid to Colonel Tom Parker to manage his career. (By comparison, Larry Parnes took 40 percent off the top from his stable of stars.) Epstein signed this contract on behalf of an entity called NEMS Enterprises, the newly incorporated managerial and promotional branch of his family's business.

With a single on the charts, Epstein turned his attention to booking the Beatles into bigger and better venues in an expanding radius around Liverpool—places like the huge Tower Ballroom in the Wirral resort of New Brighton. During the summer of 1962, Epstein and Bob Wooler had promoted several shows at the Tower that were designed to build up the Beatles' prestige by presenting them with established acts like Joe Brown & His Bruvvers. Now, in October, Epstein booked the Beatles into the Tower as the supporting act to none other than Little Richard, who had recently ended his self-imposed exile from the secular side of the music business on the strength of a lucrative offer from the British promoter Don Arden. (Richard later claimed that Arden had lured him to Britain on the pretext of a gospel tour, only to insist that he perform his greatest hits.) The Beatles were naturally thrilled to share the stage with one of their original musical idols, and Richard, for his part, returned to the States a few months later raving about a band he had heard in Britain who could "imitate anybody"—beginning, of course, with himself.

One of Brian Epstein's boldest moves during this period was a phone call he placed to the home of the pop promoter Arthur Howes, who ran a lucrative business in provincial package tours. Howes offered the Beatles a date in Peterborough as a supporting act to Frank Ifield, the Australian country-western singer, whose yodeling version of the Johnny Mercer song "I Remember You" was the top-selling British single of 1962. The Beatles fell flat in their one appearance with Ifield, but after hearing them play, Howes agreed to include the group on a package tour he was organizing for February 1963. In itself, Epstein's success in calling Howes at home and keeping him on the line long enough to interest him in the Beatles was a testament to the effectiveness of Brian's sales pitch, which he delivered in a voice that was impossible for most people in the music business to connect with the term "pop manager." Employing all the little hedges and dodges of genteel English speech ("I rather think . . . I don't suppose . . . not to bore you, but . . ."), Brian was perfecting the ability to say the most outlandish things in the most understated manner. "I really must confess that I think these boys are going to be bigger than Elvis Presley," he would say.

The Beatles, meanwhile, were engaged in some linguistic refinement of their own. Two weeks after the release of "Love Me Do," they performed for the first time on television, traveling to the Granada studios in Manchester to appear on the regional program "People and Places." Watching the live broadcast in a Liverpool pub, Michael McCartney was delighted with the band's performance, but taken aback at the broad Scouse accents John and Paul affected in their brief exchange with the host. "Why did you *talk* like that on the TV?" Michael teased his brother. "It sounded like George gone wrong."

In fact, John and Paul had been exaggerating the Scouse inflections in their speech since the time of their first trip to Hamburg. Many Liverpudlians liked to play up the local dialect, especially in the presence of non-Liverpudlians, and speaking in a Scouse accent provided the Beatles with an effective way of obscuring their grammar-school backgrounds in the proletarian milieu of rock 'n' roll. They now discovered that adopting the stereotype of a salty Scouser was also an effective way of sounding witty and self-possessed when being interviewed. Though his residence in Speke and his defiance of grammar school had left George Harrison with a more robust version of the local dialect, John or Paul could easily have chosen to purge their speech of its Liverpudlian identity. But this would have been perceived by their fans as a betrayal of their roots, and the Beatles were not about to jeopardize their status as local heroes on

Merseyside. So they chose instead to stop "talking fine" (as D. H. Lawrence's Oliver Mellors had put it) and "went back to speaking broad."

They were emboldened in this choice by the chorus of provincial accents that could now be heard in British films, plays, and television shows, a prominent example of which was the popular new BBC crime series *Z-Cars,* whose setting was directly modeled on Kirkby, a vast council-house estate on the eastern outskirts of Liverpool. Its hard-bitten cast of characters spoke in authentic Liverpudlian accents and expressed authentic Liverpudlian attitudes. By the end of its first season, 14 million Britons were watching it every week.

THE BEATLES SPENT the autumn of 1962 shuttling between their usual bookings on Merseyside, occasional dates in the Midlands, and a pair of two-week engagements at the Star-Club in Hamburg that had been scheduled months before. (Though Hamburg had lost all of its allure for them by now, Brian Epstein felt obliged to honor the contracts he had signed with Manfred Weissleder.) In the interval between these Hamburg dates, the Beatles returned to London to record their second single for Parlophone. Heartened by the steady sales of "Love Me Do" and increasingly convinced of the group's potential, George Martin had high hopes for a song the Beatles had played for him at their first recording session in September. John Lennon had written "Please Please Me" as a melodramatic ballad in the style of Roy Orbison. On first hearing, Martin had pronounced it "dreary" and suggested that they liven it up as best they could. By the time they returned to Abbey Road the following week to remake "Love Me Do," the Beatles had already devised a more energetic arrangement for "Please Please Me," which they recorded for future reference (with Andy White on drums). Upping the tempo completely transformed the song, and Martin, reviewing the demo tape, believed it had the potential to become a hit. All that remained was to refine the arrangement by adjusting the vocal harmonies and adding a harmonica part to achieve a sense of instrumental continuity with "Love Me Do." "The whole session was a joy," Martin recalled. Genuinely excited by the Beatles' music for the first time, this normally reserved man heard himself issuing a wild prophecy over the studio intercom: "Gentlemen," he announced to the startled musicians on the other side of the glass, "you've just made your first number-one record."

With George Martin, EMI Studios, London, January 1963

12

Sexual intercourse began / in nineteen sixty-three

(Which was rather late for me)

Between the end of the Chatterley ban /

And the Beatles' first LP

—Philip Larkin, "Annus Mirabilis"

I t lasts less than two minutes and it sounds like one long exclamation delivered in a single breath. Brimming with tension and exertion, "Please Please Me" plunges forward, held together by its momentum alone. Like the Beatles' previous single, the track begins with a harmonica introduction, though the tone is shriller and more haunting this time. The voices enter brightly, with John singing the descending melody, "Last night I said these words to *my* girl," against Paul's high harmony that hangs on one note, pulling against his lead. At the end of the first line, the melody is kicked back up the scale by a jerky guitar and drum fill that sets up the second half of the verse. An abrupt stop, followed by a rising call-and-response that culminates in the refrain, "Please *please* me, whoa yeah, like I please you." Following the second verse, the song races through a frenetic eight-bar middle where, on the last word of the last line, the melody leaps a startling full octave into the upper reaches of the singers' range. In the squealy falsetto enthusiasm with which the Beatles reach for these seemingly unreachable notes, "Please Please Me" seems to laugh off all its pretense as a little tale of woe and offer up its own rhythmic and melodic energy as a remedy for the emotional and sexual complacency to which the lyrics allude. In the refrain of the final verse, the singers hit that same high note again, and brazenly hold it to end the song.

The ingredients of this little musical bombshell were easy enough to trace. The harmonica introduction echoed the introduction of Frank Ifield's hit, "I Remember You." The choppy, stirred-up rhythm was the same beat the Beatles had been imposing on nearly every up-tempo number in their repertoire since 1961. The lyric was partly inspired by a song

Bing Crosby had sung in a 1934 film called *The Big Broadcast* whose punning line, "Please lend your little ears to my pleas," had lodged in the back of John Lennon's mind. The call-and-response of the chorus was a fixture of R&B dance records, and the falsetto interjection was a signature of Little Richard, who had recently given the Beatles a refresher course in his frenzied style. Yet the combination of these ingredients had resulted in something new, for the record sounded like nothing the Beatles had written or played before. As the first new song they had composed since they signed their contract with Parlophone, and the first new arrangement they had recorded since Ringo Starr joined the band, "Please Please Me" orchestrated a moment of musical self-realization that was analogous to the moment Elvis Presley had first experienced on the night in 1954 when he recorded "That's All Right." Originally conceived as a pop aria, the song had been wrenched from its intended context by George Martin's suggestion that they raise the tempo, and then transformed by the Beatles' muscular playing and their distinctive ensemble singing into a musical template for all they would accomplish in the miraculous year ahead.

Paired with a breezy, incessantly melismatic Lennon-McCartney ballad called "Ask Me Why," "Please Please Me" was released in the middle of January 1963. It entered the Top Fifty a week later and began a rapid ascent, reaching number twenty by the first of February. Its progress was spurred by the professional enthusiasm of a music publisher named Dick James, whom George Martin had recommended to Brian Epstein after Epstein complained about the inattention EMI's publishing subsidiary, Ardmore & Beechwood, had given to "Love Me Do." Dick James, whose real name was Richard Vapnick, was a former big-band singer who had recorded for Parlophone in the 1950s, when he scored a minor hit with the theme song to the British-made television series *Robin Hood*. His eponymous publishing company was less than two years old, but George Martin recommended him because he knew James to be both honest and hungry for work. (James was also the publisher of "How Do You Do It," and Martin may have felt a pang of guilt about the Beatles rejecting the song.) At their first meeting, James did his best to impress Epstein by placing a call to the producer of the pop television program *Thank Your Lucky Stars* and securing the Beatles an appearance on the show. On the strength of that one phone call, Dick James would never go hungry for work again.

. . . .

THE WINTER OF 1962–63 was the coldest and snowiest to hit the British Isles in modern memory. The freakish, frigid weather gripped the country in mid-December and held fast until the end of March, when the snows gave way to torrential rains. Though no region was spared, the economic effects of the weather were worst in the North of England, where docks and shipyards were shut down, rail and road transport ground to a halt, factories ran on reduced hours to cope with the shortages of coal, and hundreds of thousands of workers were laid off. As a transportation center, Liverpool was especially hard hit, with close to forty thousand people out of work.

The disproportionate economic impact of the winter weather fueled a fresh round of commentary in the press about the widening "prosperity gap" between the North and South of England. But concern for the plight of Britain's aging industrial heartland was only one strain in a rising chorus of journalistic angst decrying the state of the nation and its declining position in the world. Much of the impetus for this grim exercise in soul-searching came from abroad. The Cuban Missile Crisis of October 1962 had revealed in the starkest possible terms the extent to which Britain was now a mere bystander in the escalating superpower confrontation between the United States and the Soviet Union. In December 1962, as if to underline this point, the distinguished American diplomat Dean Acheson delivered a speech on the topic of European security in which he dared to say what had been tacitly apparent since the Suez crisis of 1956. "Great Britain has lost an empire and has not yet found a role," Acheson famously declared. His remarks were denounced as "a stab in the back" by the tabloids and received as "a calculated insult" in official circles, not least by Prime Minister Macmillan, who publicly accused Acheson, in underestimating Britain, of making a mistake "which has been made by quite a lot of people over the last four hundred years, including Philip of Spain, Louis XIV, Napoleon, the Kaiser, and Hitler." "It is the nature of nations diminished in power to feel humiliated when that fact is called to their attention," *The Spectator* observed dryly.

The sense of humiliation only grew stronger in January 1963 when the French president Charles de Gaulle ended months of high-level negotiations by unilaterally vetoing Britain's bid to join the European Common Market, membership in which had become the centerpiece of the government's economic policy. In the wake of this diplomatic debacle, *Time* magazine (which enjoyed a wide English readership) published a cover story on "Britain's Troubled Mood" that examined the underside of the postwar Welfare State: the hidebound institutions, the bitter industrial relations, the half-baked educational reforms. Many of the points in the *Time* article were derived from a current best-seller by the journalist Anthony Sampson titled *The Anatomy of England*. "The old ethos was molded by the success of an invincible imperial machine," Sampson wrote in his concluding chapter. "Its style was to make big things small, exciting things boring, new things familiar; but in the unconfident context of today this bland deprecation—and the assumed superiority that goes with it—merely succeeds in dispelling enthusiasms, blunting curiosity, and dulling experiment."

During these same months, on a no less critical note, the Satire movement was following in the footsteps of its Angry predecessor by expanding from the theaters and nightclubs of London into the realm of mass entertainment. The satirical weekly *Private Eye* was on its way to becoming a fixture of metropolitan life, finding an avid readership among many of the Establishment types it most liked to ridicule. Woodfall Films, having exhausted the gray vistas of Northern Realism, was hard at work on an innovative, American-financed adaptation of Henry Fielding's ribald satire of *pre*-industrial England, *Tom Jones*. (The picture would be the overwhelming choice of critics and viewers as the best British film of the year.) The winter of 1963 also saw the television debut of *That Was the Week That Was*, a BBC series consisting of satiric sketches and sardonic commentary on current events. The cast of the show was led by David Frost; its staff of writers included such current and future luminaries as John Braine, Peter Shaffer, Christopher Booker, Dennis Potter, John Mortimer, John Cleese, and Bernard Levin. *TW3* brought the anarchic spirit of the *Goon Show* back to the BBC, and when the time came to make an album of the program's best bits, it was a foregone conclusion that the record would be produced by George Martin and released on Parlophone. Though the Beatles' busy schedule often conflicted with the program's Saturday-night broadcasts, their affection for *TW3* can be deduced from the fact that several of John Lennon's more memorable press conference witticisms (e.g., "Women should be obscene and not heard") had their origin there.

. . . .

THE BEATLES SPENT the frigid winter of 1963 huddled in vans and tour buses, traveling to engagements farther and farther afield of Liverpool. During the blizzards of January they played a week of one-nighters in Scotland and taped television and radio appearances in Birmingham (*Thank Your Lucky Stars*) and London (the BBC's *Saturday Club*, Radio Luxembourg's *Friday Spectacular*). In the first week of February, with "Please Please Me" now at number nine on the charts, they joined the package tour that Brian Epstein had booked with Arthur Howes the previous fall. The headliner was Helen Shapiro, a petite teenager from the East End of London with an unaccountably big voice, five hit singles, and a top-selling album to her name. Though the Beatles had originally been signed as an opening act, the success of "Please Please Me" earned them a place as featured performers on this month-long expedition, which covered more than two thousand miles on an itinerary that ran the length and breadth of England. Intensive travel of this sort was a new experience for the Beatles, as was the promoter's requirement that they confine their nightly performances to a single thirty-minute set structured around their current hit record.

Despite the Beatles' growing popularity outside of Liverpool, coverage of the group in the press had thus far been confined to *Mersey Beat* and occasional items in other local publications like the Liverpool *Echo*. The entertainment reporters of Britain's national newspapers, to the extent they even noticed, treated the Beatles and the beat scene in Liverpool as a story of purely regional interest. The first break in this indifference came in February 1963 when the London *Evening Standard* printed a "Disc Date" column by a young feature writer named Maureen Cleave. Titled "Why the Beatles Create All That Frenzy," this short piece set the mold for all subsequent coverage of the group in the British press. Dubbing them "the darlings of Merseyside," Cleave attributed the Beatles' popularity to their novel appearance and their confident demeanor. Employing a standard journalistic contrivance, she called upon "my friend, a Liverpool housewife" to say of the group, "Their physical appearance inspires frenzy. They look beat-up and depraved in the nicest possible way." The article went on to sketch the stereotypes that would come to identify and eventually haunt these four young men for many years to come: John, witty; Paul, charming; George, handsome; Ringo, "ugly but cute." "They are considered intelligent," Cleave reported in reference to the Beatles' grammar-school backgrounds. She then illustrated this point with a quote from John Lennon talking about how he would "rather be thick and rich than bright and otherwise." Lennon also described how the Beatles were grooming themselves for success by practicing what they called "grinnings-at-nothings." "One-two-three and we all grin at nothing," he said. By the time Cleave's column appeared, "Please Please Me" was selling at a rate of fifty thousand copies a week.

In the third week of February, during a brief lull in the Helen Shapiro tour, the Beatles returned to Liverpool and played the Cavern Club. That evening a telegram arrived from the offices of the *New Musical Express* announcing the fulfillment of George Martin's prophecy: "Please Please Me" would appear at number one in the paper's next weekly listing of the best-selling pop singles. At the start of the Beatles' set, an excited Bob Wooler relayed this news to the crowd—which fell dead silent in response. As one Cavern Club regular recalled, "It was awful, because the reaction was the opposite of what they expected. Everyone was stunned. That was the end of it as far as we were concerned."

EVEN BEFORE IT reached number one, the robust sales of "Please Please Me" had led George Martin to accelerate his plans to record an album of the Beatles' work. This was not as obvious a decision in 1963 as it would be in years to come. When long-playing records first became widely available in Britain during the mid-1950s, they were viewed as a godsend by fans of classical music, opera, jazz, and musicals, who in the first half-century of sound recording had been required to listen to extended performances in a series of truncated five-minute segments, interrupted by intervals of clicking and fumbling as the records were flipped or changed. The impact of the LP on the rest of the record market was initially less pronounced. Not only was their long-playing capacity irrelevant to the format of most popular songs, radio programming, and the jukeboxes that had become a vital source of record promotion and sales, but LPs were also significantly more expensive than 78-rpm records, and they required the purchase of more-sophisticated phonographic equipment. (As late as 1965, less than a third of all British households owned such equipment.) This promised to limit the appeal of the LP among the less affluent segments of the record-buying public who formed the core audiences for pop, rock 'n' roll, country and western, and rhythm and blues, all of which embraced the microgroove replacement for the 78, the 45-rpm single.

Ultimately, the attribute that sealed the success of the LP in the popular market had little to do with its expanded capacity or its improved sound quality. Designated "packaged product" by the recording industry, LPs were the first records to be sold in foot-square cardboard jackets faced with glossy cover art, which served as an alluring advertisement for the music within. This allowed them to be prominently displayed in racks or bins in virtually any kind of store; it also allowed them to be advertised as recognizable products in newspapers and magazines. (Singles, by contrast, were still packaged in plain paper sleeves and sold mainly in record shops.) The LP cover became a companion piece to the listening experience: a contemplative object that functioned like a fan magazine by providing photographs, biographical information, and promotional copy. On the most basic level, it put a face to the sound of a singer's voice.

George Martin's background in classical music and comedy predisposed him to the production of albums, so it didn't take much for him to decide that the success of "Please Please Me" warranted the release of an LP. Martin's initial impulse was to record the Beatles live at the Cavern Club, and in the winter of 1963 he took a trip to Liverpool to explore this possibility. But one look at the Cavern banished any thought of trying to make a record in a room that had the acoustic ambience of an oil tank. Instead, Martin proposed to capture the excitement of the Beatles onstage by recording them "live" in the studio, performing a typical set of their material with a minimum of sound enhancement or production effects. Commercial considerations dictated that the album would include the four tracks that had already been released on the Beatles' two singles. In addition, Lennon and McCartney had completed four new original songs, which Martin encouraged them to supplement with some of the group's more current cover tunes. In a single marathon session at Abbey Road in February 1963, the Beatles recorded usable versions of ten songs, which were combined with the four previously recorded originals, and released, toward the end of March, on an album titled *Please Please Me*.

Each of the two sides of the Beatles' first LP is structured like a suspension bridge, with firm footings at the ends supporting a thinning span toward the middle. The strongest tracks consist of "I Saw Her Standing There," the Lennon-McCartney original that starts the album; "Please Please Me" and "Love Me Do," which end the first side and begin the second; and "Twist and Shout," the Isley Brothers song that brings the record to a close. The ten tracks in between are a mixture of beat music and ballads. They include an unaccountably cheerful Lennon-McCartney original called "Misery," which features an a cappella opening with a roundly Scouse inflection and a stagy lyric ("The wo-o-rld is treating me ba-a-ad: MISERY!") reminiscent of a music-hall song; the Buddy Hollyish "Do You Want to Know a Secret," written by John Lennon and sung with rich, salivatory intimacy by George Harrison, and Paul McCartney's nod to Northern Realism, the theme from the Woodfall film *A Taste of Honey,* whose nautically flavored vocal arrangement (the male lead was a seaman) has John and George chanting the phrase "ta-do'n'doo" like a pair of contented galley slaves. The most peculiar of the original songs is an awkward-sounding rewrite of "Please Please Me" called "There's a Place," whose title alludes to the great Bernstein-Sondheim ballad "Somewhere" and whose dreadful lyrics ("There's a place / Where I can go / When I feel low / When I feel blue / And it's my mind") have been generously described by some listeners as the first telltale sign of an introspective strain in the Beatles' music.

The non-original songs include Arthur Alexander's mournful R&B ballad "Anna (Go to Him)" and a trio of girl-group numbers: "Chains" by the Cookies (written by Goffin-King) and two songs by the Shirelles, one of which, "Baby It's You," was a recent hit, the other of which, "Boys," had entered the Beatles' repertoire as a vehicle for Pete Best and was then inherited by Ringo Starr, who can be heard drumming and singing himself into a good-natured lather on it. The Beatles' performance of these cover tunes was competent if uninspired, but the material was a far cry from the hard-edged rock that Bob Wooler had extolled in the pages of *Mersey Beat* a year and a half before.

The tracks that open and close the album are the ones that best convey the sort of excitement the Beatles were capable of generating onstage. "I Saw Her Standing There" kicks off with a theatrical "one-two-three-FOUR!" and is peppered with shouts, hand-claps, and other "live effects" that make it, paradoxically, one of the album's more carefully produced tracks. Hoarsely sung by Paul, the lyric recounts an encounter on the dance floor with a girl who was "just seventeen, if you know what I mean." It's an innuendo worthy of Chuck Berry, whose spirit leers over the song. The relentless instrumental accompaniment can be heard as a distillation of everything the Beatles had learned from three years of hard labor in the clubs of Hamburg and Liverpool: each 4/4 bar of "I Saw Her Standing There" contains eight eighth-notes, and the Beatles make the most of this fact by playing nearly every one of them as loudly as possible.

As for "Twist and Shout," if ever the term "orgasmic" could be applied to a popular song, it applies to the Beatles' rendition of this Twist-craze record by the Isley Brothers. How far can dancing be taken as a metaphor for sex? The Beatles' answer to this question involves a string of half-coherent inducements to shake it up and work it out, exuberantly delivered over a droning three-chord harmony that repeats in every bar, the sameness broken only by a climactic vocal crescendo, built on the tonic chord, which sounds, in the Beatles' version, like a barbershop quartet taking collective leave of its senses. "Twist and Shout" is less a song in the conventional sense than an opportunity for the expression of carnal personality, to which John Lennon rises like a shark to bait. Singing in a voice conditioned by years of shouting over countless repetitions of this same beat and these same chords, Lennon does on "Twist and Shout" what every aspiring white rock-'n'-roll singer since Elvis Presley has had to do as a rite of musical passage: he takes a song that was originally recorded by a black artist and so surpasses the original that, henceforth, the song is his to sing.

The cover of *Please Please Me* was shot by a well-known theatrical photographer named Angus McBean, and it marks the psychic distance the Beatles had traveled in the two and a half years since Astrid Kirchherr first pictured them as scruffy, sullen proletarians amid the grunge of Hamburg's Reeperbahn. Shot from below and rotated diagonally on its axis, McBean's color photograph shows the Beatles nattily dressed in brown suits, pink shirts, and black ties, leaning with studied nonchalance over the railing of an interior stairwell, with only their heads, arms, and shoulders in view. The four of them are all smiling broadly, and with the upper landings of the stairwell receding behind them in vertiginous perspective, they seem to be pausing in the midst of their ascent to some great penthouse of success. The photograph looks like something that might have been dreamed up by the Board of Trade and Tourism: the sun is out, the architecture is up to date, the natives are well dressed and friendly. These four beaming lads posed along the railing of what might be taken as a spanking new apartment block (it was actually EMI's corporate headquarters, on Manchester Square in London) were a vignette of the New Britain, the very model of an advertising stereotype the sociologist Richard Hoggart had previously characterized as "a minor mythology imported from America . . . the teenage 'gang,' fond of jive and boogie-woogie but still healthy and open-faced . . . full of gaiety and drive, the reverse of everything dusty and drab."

Released toward the end of March, the Beatles' first album duplicated the progress of its namesake single in taking about six weeks to rise to number one. Unlike the single, however, the album would remain in that position from May until December of 1963. Except for the soundtrack to the film *South Pacific,* which topped the British LP charts from their inception in the fall of 1958 until the spring of 1960, no album before or since has approached the thirty consecutive weeks *Please Please Me* spent at number one. For the British recording industry, this was an incontrovertible sign that something extraordinary was happening. Previously the only pop singers to achieve the velocity of sales needed to reach the top of the albums charts in Britain had been Elvis Presley and Cliff Richard. The sustained popularity of the Beatles' first LP confirmed that it was the group itself, and not some fortuitous combination of chords and lyrics, to which their fans were responding. Initial sales of the album were spurred by George Martin's decision to adopt a bold and unusual marketing strategy that involved releasing the Beatles' third single, "From Me to You," just two weeks after the release of the LP. An artful reworking of the instrumental textures of "Please Please Me," "From Me to You" had a bluesy, syncopated melody that pitted the guttural tones in John's voice ("If there's *anything* that you want") against Paul's emphatic falsetto ("anything *I can do*") on a lyric so ingratiating that it sounded like a musical thank-you card. The synergy between the new single and the new album was such that both records arrived at the top of their respective charts during the same week in May.

Though George Martin's visit to the Cavern Club during the winter of 1963 had failed to result in a live Beatle album, it did give Martin a chance to see for himself the intensity of the beat music scene in Liverpool. He responded by signing the city's *second* most popular band, Gerry & The Pacemakers, whom Brian Epstein had started to manage the summer before. The Pacemakers were a quartet dominated by the impish charm of their lead singer, Gerry Marsden, and like most beat groups on

Merseyside besides the Beatles, they were performers, not songwriters. For their first single, Martin presented them with the irrepressible "How Do You Do It," which affirmed his professional judgment by rising to the top of the pop charts in April 1963. For the newly formed troika of Martin, Epstein, and Dick James, this marked the start of a remarkable run of success. All told, Liverpool bands produced by George Martin, managed by Brian Epstein, singing songs published by Dick James, would hold the number-one position on the pop charts for more than thirty weeks during the spring, summer, and fall of 1963.

In April the Beatles joined with Gerry & The Pacemakers and Billy J. Kramer and the Dakotas, another of Epstein's new signings, for a series of NEMS-produced "Mersey Beat Showcase" dates. That same month in Liverpool, Cynthia Lennon gave birth to a son, who was named Julian in memory of John's mother. The Beatles' hectic schedule ensured that it was a full week before John could find the time to see his wife and son. In May the group toured as co-headliners with one of their current American favorites, Roy Orbison, whose frozen stage persona—he would stand stock-still at the microphone, shrouded in black from his boots to his ever-present sunglasses—provided a keen contrast to the bedlam of the Beatles' show.

The Beatles also performed with increasing frequency on BBC radio during the spring of 1963. Secure in its monopoly of the airwaves and constrained by its long-standing agreements with the British musicians union, the BBC Light Programme (as it was then known) continued to resist the simple expedient of playing popular records on the air. What the Corporation did instead was use its own studios to make its own recordings of popular singers and groups, which were then broadcast on any of a half-dozen teen-oriented shows. Over the first half of 1963, the Beatles made numerous prerecorded appearances on programs like *Here We Go, Side By Side,* and *Saturday Club.* In addition to plugging their latest records, they used these shows to highlight their enormous repertoire of rock 'n' roll and rhythm and blues, providing their many new fans with a sense of their musical range and roots that was not necessarily apparent from the short sets they performed on their package tours.

In the middle of April the Beatles received a frantic reception when they performed at a BBC-sponsored concert of pop and jazz acts that was broadcast live from London's Royal Albert Hall. A week later, on April 21, the group played their first club date in London, at the Pigalle Club in

Piccadilly, which was fast becoming a rendezvous of the city's Mod underground. As one former Mod recalled, the Beatles' effect on this hip London audience "was amazing, like a Hollywood movie. Dancing stopped. Everyone watched and listened. As each number finished the audience went wild. The applause and cheers were deafening."

What the audience at the Pigalle Club saw that night was an archetype-in-the-making, the symmetry and simplicity of which would influence the presentation of popular music for decades to come. The Beatles onstage presented a line of three singer-guitarists standing toward the front, with the drummer sitting behind and above them on a small platform flanked by guitar amplifiers. They would be dressed in matching gray, black, or brown suits, their tight-fitting jackets and trousers trimmed with velvet or, in the case of one collarless Cardin-inspired design, outlined in dark piping. Their haircuts had been regularized into shiny, bowl-shaped helmets that framed their faces and enlarged their heads, giving them an almost childlike silhouette. They were dressed identically, coiffed identically, and the three in front were all of equal height. Yet their uniformity of appearance was offset by an almost complete lack of uniformity in their individual styles of performance. On the right side of the stage stood John Lennon, facing the audience squarely, his feet planted widely apart, his body flexing up and down at the knees in a motion that suggested Elvis Presley idling in neutral. Half-blind as he was without the glasses he refused to wear onstage, John's naturally petulant expression was compounded by an air of obliviousness as he sang, his head tilted back, squinting down his nose at the blur of lights and shapes that swam before his eyes. Across the stage from his songwriting partner, Paul McCartney bounced and hopped and twisted as if his movements were being controlled by an apprentice puppeteer, the neck of his violin-shaped bass guitar alternately jerking up and down or sweeping across the stage as he turned to face his bandmates. In contrast to John, Paul seemed to take in *everything* that was happening around him onstage, as reflected on his face by a constant flow of smiles, frowns of concentration, surprised laughter, and histrionic double-takes—one moment the picture of crooning sincerity with his head bowed and his eyes raised, the next moment actually shaking from head to toe with the excitement of the music. A more sober form of concentration could be seen on the face of George Harrison as he stood in the middle of the band, his guitar held perfectly level and worn high on his body. George onstage was a collection of small, poised gestures: now stepping forward to take a solo, now leaning over to share a microphone with Paul or John on the chorus harmonies. Behind the others sat Ringo, surrounded by his new American-made drum set, the front head of his bass drum displaying the name of the band in stark black lettering. Raising his sticks high, fanning his hi-hat cymbals with his arm drawn across his body, Ringo seemed to vie with the audience for the attention of the three guitarists in front of him, at times actually lifting out of his seat with the enthusiasm of his playing. And on his face, mixed in with the sidelong glances and knowing grins that linked the Beatles to one another onstage, could be glimpsed a look of absolute astonishment that the others, if they did nothing else, managed to suppress.

IN THE SPRING of 1963, as the bitter winter weather gave way to torrents of rain and mud, factories, mines, and dockyards reopened and life returned to normal across the Industrial North. Down in London, however, the spring thaw had a very different effect, giving rise to a flood of salacious rumor that first began coursing through the press rooms of Fleet Street and the cloakrooms of Parliament in the middle of March. Had it been concocted by an opportunistic novelist seeking to fuse the Lawrentian themes of class and sex with the current vogue for Satire and the hot new literary genre of Cold War espionage, the Profumo Affair might have been dismissed by discerning readers as outlandishly contrived. As it was, the whole thing unfolded like a thickly plotted thriller.

Back in December 1962, a young Jamaican immigrant named John Edgecombe had been arrested on charges stemming from an incident in which he had fired several gunshots into the front door of a London residence belonging to a well-known osteopath and portrait artist named Stephen Ward. Ward's house was occupied at the time by a pair of young women, one of whom, a former nightclub dancer named Christine Keeler, was the object of Edgecombe's (as it turned out) jealous rage. The incident was reported in the press, but apart from the fact that Edgecombe was black and Keeler was white, it attracted little notice until Keeler, ostensibly concerned about what the police might discover when they looked into the nature of her relationships with Edgecombe and Ward, began to share her concerns with a widening circle of people that included a Member of Parliament and a reporter from the *Sunday Mirror,* which paid her £1,000 for the rights to her story. The most newsworthy part of Christine Keeler's story had nothing to do with John Edgecombe. Rather it involved her claim that in 1961 she had had an affair with John Profumo, a rising star in the Conservative Party who currently served in the Macmillan Cabinet as the Secretary of State for War. Two aspects of this alleged affair were of special interest. The first was that Profumo was prominently married to a former film star named Valerie Hobson. The second and more incendiary piece of information was that during the same period when Keeler claimed to have been sleeping with Britain's War Minister, she also claimed to have been sleeping with a Russian naval officer named Evgeny Ivanov, who was attached to the Soviet Embassy in London and was almost certainly a spy.

Though the *Mirror* was legally constrained from printing any of this juicy gossip, the link between Profumo, Keeler, and Ivanov was real, and it turned on Stephen Ward. Ward's medical patients included such celebrated figures as Sir Winston Churchill and Danny Kaye; his portrait subjects included members of the Royal Family; and his friends included Lord Astor, on whose Cliveden estate Ward rented a cottage where, on a summer evening in 1961, like characters in a bedroom farce, Profumo, Keeler, and Ivanov had first met. For all his talents as a doctor, artist, and bon vivant, Stephen Ward's chief entrée into the upper reaches of English society came from his ability to provide his wealthy friends with introductions to a carefully selected group of attractive young working-class women who together constituted the toniest call-girl ring in London.

Christine Keeler first became a public figure *in absentia* in March of 1963 (as Philip Larkin's poem suggested, right around the release of the Beatles' first LP), when she failed to appear at the trial of John Edgecombe, where she was scheduled to testify as the principal witness for the prosecution. Reporters eventually found her vacationing in Spain, which whetted their suspicions that she had fled the country to avoid giving testimony that might have revealed her links to Profumo and Ivanov. In the meantime, having privately assured both Prime Minister Macmillan and the head of the Security Services that there had been "no impropriety whatsoever" in his acknowledged, but supposedly platonic, relationship with Keeler, Profumo sought to lay the matter to rest by repeating his denial on the floor of the House of Commons and threatening a slander suit against anyone who claimed otherwise. This did nothing to quash the rumors, but it did serve notice on the press.

It was shortly after Profumo issued his public denial that Stephen Ward, who had dutifully corroborated the War Minister's account of his platonic relationship with Keeler, learned that he was the subject of a police investigation. Stunned by this development, Ward attempted to blackmail the government into calling off the police by quietly informing the Prime Minister's private secretary that Profumo had in fact lied about his relationship with Keeler. When this failed to produce the desired result, Ward repeated his charge against Profumo, first in a letter to the Home Secretary, and then in a letter to the new head of the Labour Party, Harold Wilson. Under mounting pressure in Parliament, Prime Minister Macmillan finally decided in June 1963 that an official inquiry was warranted. Before this step could be announced, however, John Profumo bowed to the inevitable, publicly admitted his deceit, and resigned from the House of Commons. Three days later, Stephen Ward was arrested and charged with living off the earnings of prostitution.

Profumo's confession and resignation released the newspapers from the legal constraints that had kept them from publishing a story they had been piecing together for months. Fleet Street responded with all of its pent-up powers of moral indignation. The mood of the popular papers was epitomized by the *Daily Mirror,* which demanded in a full-page tabloid headline, WHAT THE HELL IS GOING ON IN THIS COUNTRY? The staid *Times* attempted to answer this same question in a series of uncharacteristically harsh editorials that attributed the current climate of decadence to the steady rise of affluence, declaring that "eleven years of Conservative rule have brought the nation psychologically and spiritually to a low ebb." Britain's most popular paper, *The News of the World,* rewarded its readers by taking a different tack: having outbid its competitors for the rights to Christine Keeler's "Confessions," it heralded their publication with a stunning nude photograph of the author, artfully straddling a chair whose curved back preserved whatever remained of her modesty.

From June onward, fantastic rumors of depravity and debauchery at the highest levels of public life proliferated as fast as tongues could wag. Whole panels of High Court judges were said to have participated in orgies; a Cabinet minister was said to have performed as a masked "sex slave" at elegant Mayfair dinner parties; yet another Cabinet minister was said to be the naked man lying next to the naked duchess in a defaced photograph that had been introduced as evidence at the Duke of Argyll's recent divorce proceedings; unnamed members of the Royal Family were said to have consorted openly with prostitutes. The press was inflamed. The public was enthralled. Britain's frigid winter of discontent had given way to a lewd summer of scandal. "A great shock has been given to Parliament and indeed to the whole country," admitted Prime Minister Macmillan, whose performance in the House of Commons (where the debate centered on his willingness to take Profumo at his gentlemanly word) was described by the staunchly Tory *Daily Telegraph* as that of "a broken man." Though Macmillan narrowly survived a vote of no confidence, it was widely assumed that his days in office were numbered. A senior judge, Lord Denning, was appointed to conduct an inquiry into all aspects of what the *Times* described as "this grave, sordid, almost incomprehensible affair." And then the spotlight of public attention turned to the trial of Stephen Ward.

If there was any doubt that the Profumo scandal marked the second act of a national morality play that began with the earlier adulterous *cause célèbre* of *Lady Chatterley,* the link between the two was made plain by the trial of Stephen Ward, which generated the same sort of lurid public fascination, took place in the same Old Bailey courtroom, and was once again dominated, in a perfect stroke of casting, by the prosecutorial presence of Mervyn Griffith-Jones. This time, by branding the defendant "a thoroughly filthy fellow" and eliciting damning testimony from Christine Keeler and several of Ward's other girls (who retaliated by naming Lord Astor, in open court, as one of their best clients), the prosecution prevailed. Before the jury could deliver its verdict, however, Stephen Ward had also bowed to the inevitable, and lay dying from a self-prescribed overdose of sleeping pills. His death in the first week of August fulfilled the classic role of a scapegoat, freeing the press and the public to divert their attention from the postimperial decadence of Britain's ruling classes to a fresh source of outrage: the so-called Great Train Robbery, touted in the tabloids as the "crime of the century," in which a gang of thieves working with commando-like precision highjacked £2.5 million from a London-bound mail train and vanished into the night.

IT WAS AGAINST the tragicomic backdrop of the Profumo scandal, whose screaming headlines threatened to bring down a Conservative government and validate the darkest fears of "Britain's Troubled Mood," that the Beatles came to the attention of teenagers throughout the British Isles during the summer of 1963. While their songs cavorted atop the pop charts like a pack of playful seals, the Beatles spent the months of June, July, and August crisscrossing England, performing in ballrooms and cinemas in the seaside resorts of Southport and Blackpool in the North, Margate and Bournemouth in the South. Increasingly, these shows were selling out days in advance. Increasingly, the young girls in the audiences were showing their appreciation by emitting high-pitched shrieks in addition to clapping, shouting, and singing along with the music. For the Beatles, these screams, like the constant requests for their autographs and the experience of being gaped at by young strangers in the street, were yet another token of life at a peak-popularity point. This was stardom as they had always imagined it, and they were determined to take it in stride.

In July, George Martin brought the group into the studio to record their fourth single, fulfilling the terms of a one-year contract that EMI unhesitatingly renewed. In the intoxicating atmosphere of the summer's success, Lennon and McCartney had begun to write new songs at a prolific rate. The first of this crop to be recorded was "She Loves You."

Often described as the "quintessential" early Beatles song, "She Loves You" was a turbocharged realization of the musical possibilities first sketched by "Please Please Me." Equipped with a chord progression of some complexity, the song featured an arrangement that had it begin, not with the usual verse, but with the explosive exuberance of its refrain. The effect of this reversal was to make the tonal center of the music ambiguous (the song is played in G, but the refrain begins on E minor); in the ear of the listener, this created the feeling of plunging into the middle of a boisterous musical party that seemed to have been going on for some time. The juxtaposition of verse and refrain was often used by pop arrangers as a simple way of providing an instrumental introduction. But at George Martin's suggestion, the Beatles took it a step further by starting with the singing as well, orchestrating a giddy jolt of excitement that hurled them headlong into the song.

It was as pure *sound* that "She Loves You" was first experienced—as a jumble of tones, voices, pulsations, and noise blasting out of transistor radios, jukeboxes, and phonographs—and it is as sound that its impact should be addressed. George Martin once noted that his main goal when he began recording the Beatles consisted of "getting a really loud rhythm sound." This priority owed something to technical considerations, but it was also a result of Martin's uncomplicated, if slightly patronizing, notion of rock 'n' roll as dance music with a big beat that teenagers liked to lose themselves in. On the Beatles' fourth single, Martin achieved his first fully successful version of "a really loud rhythm sound." "She Loves You" is a record that will make cups dance in their saucers. From the opening rumble of drums, the music is marked by a booming resonance in the bass tones, the weight of which is only enhanced by the contrasting presence of a lot of high-pitched noise: a stratosphere of cymbal wash and stray harmonics from the guitars.

Over the thud of the downbeats and the clang of the rhythm guitars floats the sound of the Beatles' singing, resounding like a voice from the sky. John and Paul sing most of "She Loves You" in *unison,* not harmony, with George joining in on the refrain. They sing it the way a group of friends or fans might sing it, and the effect, on a record, is unique. Thanks to the recent advent of multitrack recording, it had become a common practice by 1963 to "double" a singer's voice in the studio—that is, to record two separate versions of the vocal part and combine them on tape in order to "fatten" the sound. Two singers singing in unison achieved all the fattening effect of doubling, along with an added dimension that came from the consensus of two voices expressing different nuances of tone and personality while singing the same notes and words at the same time. On "She Loves You," this resulted in a kind of common voice that was expressive of the Beatles' own collective persona: the musical equivalent of an editorial *we.*

The "yeah, yeah, yeahs" in the refrain of "She Loves You" were soon to become a catchphrase of the Beatles: blazoned in headlines, imprinted on promotional merchandise, and widely evoked in the press to illustrate either the innocent exuberance or the numbskulled inanity of the band. Yet all of the attention paid to these shouts of affirmation obscured an otherwise ambitious song lyric that sets up a potential love triangle only to dismantle it in the first verse. The song invites us into a conversation between two boys about a girl in which the singer is acting as a go-between, doing what he can to repair a breach of trust. "You think you've lost your love?" he asks, "Well I saw her yesterday . . ." Like the explosive refrain that starts the record, this opening line plunges the listener into the middle of a familiar scenario at a point where who is speaking is initially unclear. Having already reassured the girl of her boyfriend's good intentions, the singer now proceeds to tell her prideful, hurtful lover that it's up to him to apologize. In a one-dimensional pop universe where the quest for personal happiness is commonly seen as life's sole preoccupation, this singer is an uncommonly generous character, who surely wants the same for himself but is committed here and now to seeing it fulfilled in a friend. "She Loves You" celebrates the socially vicarious dimension of romantic love, and its chorus provides a commentary in the Sophoclean sense: "With a love like that," the Beatles sing, "you know you should be glad."

Released in late August, the single sold three-quarters of a million copies in less than four weeks, which made it the fastest-selling record of any kind that had ever been released in Britain. Sensing that popular enthusiasm for the Beatles was entering a new phase, Brian Epstein chose this moment to end their careers as nightclub and dance-hall musicians; henceforth, NEMS announced, the group would perform exclusively in theaters. (The Beatles had already played their unheralded last engagement at the Cavern Club in the middle of August.) By the middle of September, when the four of them traveled abroad on a two-week vacation—John and Cynthia to Paris, Paul and Ringo to Greece, George and his brother Peter to St. Louis, Missouri, to visit their sister Louise—the record-breaking sales of "She Loves You" and the growing pandemonium surrounding the Beatles' concerts had begun to earn them attention in the national press (FOUR FRENZIED FAUNTLEROYS WHO ARE EARNING £5000 A WEEK! announced a headline in the *Daily Mirror*). The Beatles also began to catch the eye of powerful people in the world of British show business who knew how to read sales figures, and recognized a show business phenomenon when the sales figures showed one to be occurring: people like the theatrical impresario Bernard Delfont, who invited the group to appear at the annual Royal Variety Performance in November, and the producer Val Parnell, who in October presented the Beatles on his top-rated television variety show, *Sunday Night at the London Palladium*, which broadcast the extinct ambience of the English music hall into the homes of some 15 million viewers across the land.

On the day after the live October 13 broadcast, most of the London tabloids ran photographs and articles that focused on the riotous goings-on outside the Palladium before, during, and after the Beatles' appearance. Beatles fans, the papers reported, had besieged the theater and engaged the police in maneuvers throughout the afternoon and evening. Estimates varied as to the numbers involved—one thousand fans versus sixty police; five hundred fans versus twenty police—but the gist of the story was that enthusiasm for the Beatles had driven their adolescent admirers well beyond the limits of civil behavior. The mounting chaos of the group's recent concerts in the provinces had finally arrived full force in London, a cab ride away from the newspaper offices on Fleet Street. Now, every sentient being in Britain was going to read all about it. Beatlemania had begun.

13

Within the last century, and especially since about 1900,
we seem to have discovered the processes by which fame
is manufactured.

—Daniel Boorstin

I n the spring of 1962, barely a year before the Beatles began to intrude upon the collective consciousness of Britain, the American historian and social critic Daniel J. Boorstin published a book called *The Image* in which he contended that the modern media of mass communications, by supplanting the rationality of the written word with a dazzling array of graphic and electronic imagery, were compromising the values, expectations, and fundamental worldview of the vast audiences they served. "We risk being the first people in history," Boorstin warned, who "have been able to make their illusions so vivid, so persuasive, so 'realistic' that they can live in them." An enduring feature of *The Image* was its identification of a new type of public event that is staged or otherwise brought about for the express purpose of being disseminated by the mass media to a mass audience. Boorstin characterized these contrived occurrences as "pseudo-events," and he saw them as signs of a rising tide of banality and unreality in the realms of politics, commerce, and culture. The prime protagonists of this burgeoning pseudoreality, Boorstin wrote, were celebrities, a new species of "manufactured" public figures who were tautologically "known for being well-known." Drawing a comparison with previous eras when fame was considered a consequence of "greatness" in word or deed, Boorstin suggested that the essential appeal of celebrities lies precisely in their ability to personify and glamorize the commonplace, thereby making it easy for ordinary people to identify with them.

What the British press dubbed "Beatlemania" (employing a coinage that dated back to such bygone cultural crazes as "Lisztomania" and "Pinaforemania") was initially perceived by newspaper readers and television viewers as a prototypical "pseudo-event": a concerted effort by the news and entertainment media to convert the fresh faces of four young

Liverpudlian pop musicians into a commercial bonanza of newspaper headlines, advertising revenue, ticket receipts, and record sales. Even as significant numbers of readers, viewers, and listeners found themselves drawn to unexpectedly appealing qualities in the Beatles' music and their public personalities, they assumed that somewhere, somehow, the group's fame was being expertly manufactured, and that their principal talent lay not in their ability as musicians and performers, but rather in their ability as celebrities to command the attention of the press and the public. This explains why, from the moment it began, the question that dogged the Beatles and their phenomenon was the question that applies to all hoaxes, spells, and popular delusions: How long will it last?

If anyone was presumed to be hard at work manufacturing fame for the Beatles, it was Brian Epstein, who emerged as a figure of fascination in his own right, anointed by the press as the new Svengali of pop. Epstein's instant reputation rested not only on his success with the Beatles, but also on his management of the "Merseybeat" groups Gerry & The Pacemakers and Billy J. Kramer and the Dakotas, whose string of Top Ten hits during the spring and summer of 1963 contributed to the impression that this unaccountably genteel, soft-spoken Northern businessman was leading a provincial insurgency in the British music business. ("Brian had more fans than we did," Gerry Marsden recalled.) Yet unlike the *old* Svengali, the self-aggrandizing Larry Parnes, Epstein went out of his way to qualify his role in the Beatles' success. "The Beatles are famous because they are good, but they are a cult because they are lucky," he told a reporter in November 1963. "It was not my managerial cunning, not my tutelage at all, that has brought about this Beatlemania. It is simply a kind of mass pathology; they have an extraordinary ability to satisfy a certain hunger in the country." However much the failed actor in him may have pined for the limelight, Brian preferred to cast himself in the role of an indispensable functionary—diligent, devoted, and utterly different from what anyone in or out of the music business expected from the manager of a pop group. He lent the Beatles' whole operation an air of brisk, upper-middle-class self-confidence that conveyed the impression that *he* certainly would not be wasting his time with *this* if the Beatles were not something very special indeed. In a way that would earn him a certain amount of criticism, Epstein's sense of personal discretion and decorum carried over into his business dealings as well—the stereotype of the "pushy" Jewish businessman was anathema to him—and he was occasionally taken advantage of as a result. Yet he remained willing and able to pay the price for appearing graceful in his work. Asked by a reporter, "Does it irk you when some people say they think you aren't a very good agent?" Epstein replied, "I'm an amateur as an agent. I don't pretend to be a good one."

As a pop impresario, Epstein's principal insight into the teenage market was that most of what was offered there was patronizingly shoddy and second-rate. His ambition, he said, was to make the Beatles "the biggest *theatrical* attraction in the world," and he pursued this goal by applying the more refined promotional and aesthetic standards of the legitimate theater to the pop scene. Epstein's management style was also notable for some of the things he did *not* do. He has often been portrayed as a somewhat nannyish figure—not least by the Beatles themselves. But by comparison with most pop managers of the period, he did not attempt to mold or rein in the Beatles' public personalities in any appreciable way. Instead, having dressed the group in a style that conveyed an aura of chic respectability, Brian allowed the tension generated by the contrast between how they looked and how they spoke and behaved to play itself out on a grand scale.

Still, what people found hard to believe about Brian Epstein was that, as he insisted, very little managerial cunning contributed to the Beatles' success. Once they had records to sell, the trio of Epstein, George Martin, and Dick James had gone about trying to sell them in a thoroughly conventional manner, relying on the same routine of television appearances, radio broadcasts, and provincial tours that had been used by scores of would-be pop stars since the 1950s.

As for the press, it needed no help from Epstein. Having feasted for months on the daily outrages of the Profumo Affair and the Great Train Robbery, the tabloid papers were quite capable of manipulating themselves into a paroxysm of press coverage. The big national newspapers helped inadvertently by taking as long as they did to find the story, so that instead of coming to the attention of the general public in a steady dribble of entertainment reporting over the course of 1963, the Beatles seemed to explode into national prominence as front-page news during a single week in October. But this fashioning of the group into the promotional equivalent of a shaped charge was not the work of Epstein and his publicist Tony Barrow, who had been trying and, for the most part, failing to interest the press in the Beatles since the release of "Love Me Do."

Instead, skyrocketing record sales and crowds of shrieking teenagers succeeded where press agentry had not. Within days of the Palladium show broadcast, Epstein and the staff of NEMS Enterprises were forced to make a transition from kindling a promotional fire to accommodating the crowds of reporters who were now lining up to throw newsprint onto the flames:

> Screaming like an animal, and wearing almost as much leather as one, the young girl writhed and shook in some private ecstasy.

So wrote the *Daily Mail*.

> A horde of screaming Beatle fans—estimated at 10,000—went wild in a fantastic stampede yesterday.

So wrote the *Daily Mirror*.

> Most of the 5,000 hysterical youngsters were schoolgirls. But it took fifty policemen, four on horseback with sixteen other mounted officers in reserve, to control them outside a cinema. Some of the children had queued since Thursday night, sleeping on the pavement. Frantic parents searched among the crowds for their children.

So wrote the *Sunday Times*.

And so wrote nearly every major newspaper in Britain from the middle of October 1963 onward, as the Beatles, variously described as the Fab Four, the Mop Tops, or the Mersey Wonders, joined a diverse cast of characters drawn from the increasingly convergent worlds of politics, show business, high society, criminality, and sports who together formed the purview of the popular press. The sense of convergence was especially strong in the Beatles' case, because the group's appearance on *Sunday Night at the London Palladium* had come during a week of high political drama. A few days before the broadcast, as the Conservative party prepared to convene for its annual conference at Blackpool, Prime Minister Macmillan fell ill with a prostate condition. Macmillan's power, along with his party's reelection prospects, had been seriously eroded by the Profumo scandal, which had returned to the headlines in September with the issuance of the report by Lord Denning, whose well-meaning efforts to clear the air had caused him to recount, in lurid detail, nearly every unfounded—and, in some cases, previously unreported—rumor of sexual misconduct that had been leveled at members of the government. (As a result, the report sold more than 100,000 copies on the first day of its publication.) Now, in October, Macmillan's sudden illness plunged the Blackpool conference into a struggle for the party's leadership in which rivalries that had been building during more than a decade of Tory rule flared angrily into view. Four days after the Beatles' Palladium show broadcast, Macmillan resigned in favor of an improbable compromise candidate, Alec Douglas-Home. Officially, Macmillan's resignation was attributed to his ill health. Unofficially, it was seen as the inevitable outcome of the Profumo Affair.

The 1960s would prove to be a fertile ground for conspiracy theories. Many of the decade's dramatic events would be seen by skeptics and cynics as the work of invisible hands, and the outbreak of Beatlemania was no exception. That the sudden discovery of the Beatles by the national press should coincide with the resignation of the Prime Minister in the wake of a sensationalistic sex scandal gave rise to a theory that the press lords of Fleet Street, whether out of concern for the morale of the nation, or perhaps even from remorse at the results of their own sensationalism, had seized on the Beatles as a lighthearted and reassuring antidote to the patricidal political fallout of the Profumo Affair. There is no question that the summer of scandal, with its revelations of deceit and decadence among members of the ruling classes, provided a perfect contrast to the unpretentious charm and exuberance of a working-class pop group from the stolid North of England. But the problem with the notion of the Beatles as a manufactured antidote to Britain's "troubled mood"—some versions of which went so far as to claim that there were in fact no screaming fans outside the Palladium theater, and that the newspapers had invented the entire episode—is that the initial coverage of the group was anything but reassuring. Instead, the newspaper reports of stampeding teenagers, frantic parents, and overburdened police made the frenzy of Beatlemania seem like the latest loose strand in what many Britons saw as the unraveling social fabric of the nation. Nor did the coverage of the Beatles serve to push the political situation out of the minds of the most avid newspaper readership in the world. Instead the Fab Four were served up, somewhat lower on the page, as the latest installment in the enthralling saga of Youth. Youth had become one of the favorite motifs of

British journalism in the twenty years since the war, for it was a topic that could be sensationalized to everyone's satisfaction in a nation that viewed its burgeoning numbers of young people, with no small amount of jealousy, as the "affluent" beneficiaries of a new era of social reform. And Beatlemania promised to play on all angles of the Youth story. "This hysteria presumably fills heads and hearts otherwise empty," cautioned an editorial in the staunchly Conservative *Daily Telegraph*. "Is there not something a bit frightening in whole masses of young people, all apparently so suggestible, so volatile and rudderless? What material here for a maniac's shaping. Hitler would have disapproved, but he could have seen what in other circumstances might be made of it."

In a matter of days, however, the story took an unexpected turn. Alongside the accounts of crazed fans and the dizzy tabulations of tickets and records sold, the newspapers began to feature quotes and quips from the Beatles themselves. What escaped from their mouths—and from John Lennon's mouth in particular—would have impressed any seasoned press agent of the time as a public relations nightmare:

REPORTER: Is it true that Decca turned you down?

PAUL: A guy from Decca turned us down.

REPORTER: He must be kicking himself now.

JOHN: I hope he kicks himself to death.

RINGO: People call them bloody animals. They slave away in factories and things and then they let off a bit of steam. There's nothing sexy in that shaking. There's nothing unhealthy or unpleasant about it.

GEORGE: The fans have a right to scream the place down if they want to. If that's their way of enjoying themselves, good luck to them.

PAUL: Cliff and the Shadows invited us to this great kind of party. I mean all I could say was, "Oh, wait till I tell the girls back home." Mind you, I knew it was a soft thing to say.

JOHN: Yeah, you're supposed to make things up, like, uh, "What a great job you're doing in the industry . . ."

PAUL: Because we've never been fans of Cliff's . . .

JOHN: We've always *hated* him. He was everything we *hated* in pop. But when we met him we didn't mind him at all. He was very nice. We still *hate* his records, but he's really very nice.

GEORGE: I wouldn't do all this if I didn't like it. I wouldn't do anything I didn't want to do, would I?

REPORTER: Why do you wear all those rings on your fingers?

RINGO: Because I can't get them through my nose.

JOHN: What I like about this is the money and being famous. I mean, having a fellow putting Reserved on the carriage door and everybody doing everything for you. I'm dead lazy.

That millions of newspaper readers preferred to take this insouciant repartee as an amusing daydream may have owed something to G. K. Chesterton's observation that "nothing is more English than the fact that a group of comrades is comic in their incongruity. They differ and do not quarrel; or they quarrel and do not part." Speaking in accents that unmistakably advertised their Northern working-class origins, yet possessed of a quick-wittedness that reflected their grammar-school backgrounds and a confident eccentricity that could seem vaguely aristocratic at times, the Beatles were received by the press and the public as a comic composite of the English national character, cast in a newly flattering light. In the parlance of the time, they were "classless." Yet the Beatles' version of classlessness suggested a merging of traditional class identities rather than the dissipation of all identity that many feared would come from a blurring of class lines. And their style of insouiance could find no better sounding board than the British tabloid press. Then as now, the reporting style of the tabloids relied heavily on the technique of "personalization," in which news was translated into "human interest" and rendered with a tone of familiarity and mateyness that editors conceived as the voice of the Common Man. This meant that the Beatles were presented on a daily basis with questions designed to elicit the sort of minor details and anecdotal information that reporters needed to "personalize" their stories. Since the banality of these questions made it obvious that the newspapers were interested in them solely because news of them sold papers, the Beatles responded by treating their interviewers as fellow travelers in the world of show business. This lack of deference, in turn, disarmed many reporters, for it played directly on their own misgivings about their work. When John Lennon began criticizing the press during a radio interview with a reporter named Dibbs Mather, Mather complained, "This is going wrong. I want to get a nice 'personality' bit." "I haven't *got* a nice personality," Lennon replied. On a daily basis, their wit was rarely that sharp, but the group functioned as an ensemble both on and off the stage. Instead of a single Beatle being questioned by a crowd of reporters, their interviews generally consisted of a single reporter being harassed by a crowd of Beatles. This allowed them to appear unusually poised in print, as the quips and qualities of each were attributed to them all.

In the first week of November, the sympathies of the press and much of the public were conclusively captured by the Beatles' triumphant appearance at the Royal Variety Show, an annual charity gala that had served since the reign of George V as a royal benediction of the world of British show business. At the 1963 Variety show, the Beatles played for an audience that included the Queen Mother and Princess Margaret, topping a bill that featured Marlene Dietrich, Harry Secombe, Flanders and Swann, and Tommy Steele. Prior to serenading this shimmering sea of gowns and tails with the strains of "Twist and Shout," John Lennon remarked quietly into his microphone, "For our last number, I'd like to ask your help. Will the people in the cheaper seats clap your hands? And the rest of you, if you'll just rattle your jewelry." The line, which had been perfected in advance, got a tremendous laugh, and turned the evening into a set piece for the press: a vignette of the Queen Mother and Princess Margaret gamely digging these four cheeky lads from the far end of society, who in turn knew exactly how, and how much, to razz the Royal Family. "In seven successive Royal shows I have never heard anything approaching the reception given to them by the predominantly middle-aged, middle-class audience," wrote the theater critic of the *Daily Telegraph*. "How refreshing to see these rumbustious young Beatles take a middle-aged Royal Variety performance by the scruff of their necks and have them beatling like teenagers," added the *Daily Mirror*. Thus was the embodiment of happy modern Youth as pictured on the cover of *Please Please Me* conflated with the nostalgic mirage of a world in which class distinctions had served as a source of social confidence ("you knew where you stood") instead of resentment and frustration. The approval of the Queen Mum, who was pictured in the newspapers chatting amiably with the Beatles after the show, exerted a powerful influence over a multitude of English Mums. Having charmed the press and charmed the Royals and charmed a sizable portion of the public to which these two formidable institutions played, the Beatles laid claim to a place in the popular imagination.

In the aftermath of the Royal Variety Show there was no holding back by the press. Whereas previously the coverage had been confined mainly to the tabloids, now the quality papers weighed in. The *Sunday Times* took a psychoanalytic approach in a piece titled the "Anatomy of Beatle-mania." The *Observer* illustrated its article on "The Roots of Beatlemania" with a photograph of a pre-Hellenic fertility symbol (courtesy of the British Museum) that resembled a modern guitar. Britons of all ages, classes, and educational backgrounds, it seemed, shared a tendency to regard the Beatles as heartening specimens of Youth. "I think I'll invite them down for the weekend just to see what kind of fellas they are," Viscount Bernard Montgomery, the retired general and war hero, told a reporter. The historian Eric Hobsbawm (who, as "Francis Newton," reviewed jazz records for *The New Statesman*) spoke for many when he wrote: "The Beatles are an agreeable bunch of kids, quite unsinister (unlike some of the American teenage comets), with that charming combination of flamboyance and a certain hip self-mickey-taking [i.e., put-on] which is the ideal of their age group."

The self-sufficiency of a group of young musicians, barely out of their teens, who wrote, played, and sang their own songs confounded the accepted view of the pop scene as a fleecing of adolescent lambs by rapacious adult wolves. This in turn freed many of the same people who had complained for decades about the effects of "Americanization" on British popular culture to swell with pride at the prospect of a native strain of rock 'n' roll rendered in identifiably Liverpudlian accents. And even among those who didn't feel strongly one way or another, there were a good many rather stuffy people who welcomed the Beatles as an amusing opportunity to show their families and friends that they really weren't so stuffy after all. A decade of Goonery and Satire had conditioned a sizable portion of the British public to be more easily embarrassed by Colonel Blimp or Lord Astor than by Ringo Starr. The antics of the Beatles and the ardor of their fans made for good reading and lively conversation. Beyond that, few people over the age of eighteen would have doubted Eric Hobsbawn's confident prediction that "in twenty years' time, nothing of them will survive."

14

Anarchy is too strong a word, but the quality of confidence that the boys exuded! Confidence that they could dress as they liked, speak as they liked, talk to the Queen as they liked. . . . They said if you want to do something, do it. Forget all this talk about talent or ability or money or speech. Just do it. And this has been their great strength.

—Richard Lester

That such a broad cross-section of the British public should respond with interest, much less enthusiasm, to the advent of a pop group from Liverpool was unprecedented; but by October 1963 it was also somewhat beside the point. For it was *teenagers* who bought the Beatles' records and attended their concerts: boys and girls between the ages of twelve and twenty, including a hard core, consisting mostly of girls, who camped on sidewalks, jostled police outside of theaters, and, once inside, screamed like banshees, swooned like damsels, and otherwise carried on. Many of the things that adults found appealing about the Beatles, teenagers found appealing as well. But the kids' response was on an entirely different level of interest, intensity, and, above all, identification.

If there was one perception that bridged the gap between teenage and adult appreciation of the Beatles, it concerned the detachment and amusement ("that certain hip self-mickey-taking") the group exhibited toward the subject of their own success. The impression that the Beatles didn't take their sudden celebrity too seriously was no mere conceit— although, with the exception of Ringo Starr, neither was it the result of any innate humility on their part. As might be expected of any four young men who had set their sights on fame, they loved to read about themselves in the newspapers, hear their songs on the radio, and see themselves on TV. (The film producer Walter Shenson recalled a London cab ride with the Beatles during which they kept hopping out at stoplights to scan the corner newsstands for headlines about themselves.) For years they had followed the careers of other pop performers in the press and on TV; now they set about experiencing their own success in the same way. But their scrutiny of the public behavior of stars like Elvis Presley and Cliff Richard had also left them with a strong self-consciousness about the machinery of public relations and the opportunities for self-promotion that were offered by the press. Now those same opportunities were being offered to them, accompanied by the expectation that they, too, would affect the broad smile, exaggerated sincerity, and false modesty of the grateful entertainer who only wants to say how happy and honored, fortunate and flattered he feels.

"I mean, we don't believe in our fame the way Zsa Zsa Gabor believes in hers," Paul McCartney told a reporter. "We're kidding everyone, you see," John Lennon added. "We're kidding you and we're kidding ourselves. We just don't take anything seriously." Rather than strive to affirm their sincerity, the Beatles surprised nearly everyone by cultivating a cheerful public relationship with the hoax element in their success. In their daily contacts with reporters, John and Paul in particular developed a routine in which each set out to puncture the other's pretensions, which consisted mainly of Paul's evident concern and John's evident unconcern for what was expected of them as public figures. As products of a provincial working-class culture in which any form of big-headedness or "getting above yourself" was considered a cardinal social sin, they now relieved their mutual embarrassment at having arrived at the absolute center of national attention by engaging in a form of reflexive self-deflation. When it was announced in November 1963 that they had signed a film contract, the Beatles assured reporters, "We won't do a rags-to-riches story, or the one about the record being smuggled into the studio and put on by mistake. We've *seen* that one." When Paul McCartney began musing in public on the contradictions of fame ("I mean, I don't feel like I imagine an idol to feel, [though] anyone who gets this amount of publicity is in ordinary people's eyes a fantastic being"), the others dubbed him "The Star" and began answering questions about whether the band rehearsed by explaining, "Paul does; the rest of us don't."

Underlying their self-mockery was the simple fact that the Beatles' collective self-esteem was largely invested elsewhere, in the idea of themselves as musicians and performers, not show-business celebrities. They strongly resented the tendency of the press to treat their music as a sidelight of their appeal. "Don't forget that music is a part of our lives," John Lennon told a reporter from *Melody Maker*. "We played it because we loved doing it." This attitude led them to draw a distinction between Beatlemania, which they saw in much the same way that Daniel Boorstin might have seen it, as a pseudo-event of immense proportions manufactured by the press, and the Beatles, which they saw as the collective expression of their own identity, ambition, and talent. Implicit in their debunking of their phenomenon was the assertion that it was indeed their talent, and not the publicity, which lay at the root of their appeal. Yet what nobody could fully understand at the time was that the more cavalier the Beatles became about the four "fantastic beings" at the center of Beatlemania, the more fantastic they became in the eyes of their teenaged fans. At some point during the fall of 1963, the four of them slipped their moorings in the safe harbor of show business and drifted out onto the murky, uncharted waters where they would remain for the next seven years. Though no reference to the true nature of their phenomenon could be found amid the growing sociological and psychological commentary in the press, a statement John Lennon made to Michael Braun suggests that he, at least, had some sense of what was going on. "This isn't show business," Lennon announced to Braun. "This is something else. This is different from anything that anybody imagines. You don't go on from this. You do this and then you finish."

> It is devotion to the extraordinary and unheard-of, to what is strange to all rule and tradition . . . a devotion born of distress and enthusiasm.
>
> —Max Weber

In March 1961, *Vogue* magazine's venerable guide to the latest trends, "People Are Talking About," included a brief and mangled reference to "the overdeveloped and curious use by literary critics of the word *charism* [*sic*], which means special divine or spiritual gift." Within a few years the term *charisma* would emerge as a cliché of first resort, an all-purpose synonym for "presence," "aura," or "magnetism," favored by journalists, press agents, and pop biographers for the luster a little Greek can add to a person's reputation. From its origins in Christian theology, where it referred to miraculous powers of healing or prophecy, the term first passed into secular usage in the early-twentieth-century writings of the

German sociologist Max Weber, who elevated the concept of "charismatic authority" to the level of general principle in his work. Societies, according to Weber, have an inherently conservative drift: they favor the development of "institutions of daily routine," beginning with the family and extending to priesthoods, professions, bureaucracies, and other hierarchical groups that seek to ensure the stability and continuity of social life by upholding the rule of custom, convention, and law. During periods of significant "psychic, physical, economic, ethical, religious, or political distress," however, the adequacy and authority of these stabilizing institutions may be called into question. It is in such conditions that groups of people, whether in small sects or in large social movements, may turn to a seemingly autonomous figure who eschews all claim to traditional or institutional authority and instead gains and maintains power or influence "solely by proving his strength in life." The historical archetypes of charisma are military heroes, revolutionary leaders, and religious prophets. But Weber considered the dynamic tension between institutionalized routine and charismatic innovation to exist "universally" throughout culture, and he personally applied the concept to such sociologically offbeat subjects as the role of maestros and virtuosi in the development of European art music. In essence, Weber assigned charisma a role in social and cultural life akin to that of mutation in evolutionary theory. He saw it as the embodiment of an irrational yet potentially creative force that challenged the existing order and ran counter to the increasing rationalization and bureaucratization of modern industrial societies. Over time, through a process he termed "routinization," the innovations wrought by charismatic leadership may become the basis of a new institutional order.

Max Weber's death in 1920 made him seem more like a prophet than a sociologist. Bolshevism in Russia, Fascism in Italy, Nazism in Germany, and Maoism in China were all textbook charismatic movements, arising in conditions of severe societal distress, led by self-dramatizing outsiders who seized power and maintained it in a series of spectacular (and often murderous) demonstrations of their "strength in life." Yet these cataclysmic manifestations of Weber's theory also served to narrow his concept of charisma by branding it as an inherently demagogic phenomenon. Not until the 1950s, when Weber's writings on the subject became widely disseminated in translation, did the broader applications of his theory begin to be recognized—on the eve, that is, of a decade in which charismatic challenges to institutional authority would be played out in virtually every theater of politics, culture, and society.

Political charisma has almost always involved the application of stagecraft to the realm of statecraft, and the creation of modern political personality cults has relied on the same media of mass communications that serve the entertainment industry. It should come as no surprise, then, that show business has always exemplified some of the principles that Weber identified. Performers, after all, are self-dramatizers by profession, perceived with each successful performance to "prove their strength" in life. The allure of the outsider has always been part of the romance of show business, as evidenced by the high proportion of entertainers in countries like Britain and America who have hailed from the social and geographic margins of society. The very mythos of "Hollywood" as the world capital of entertainment is based on the carefully cultivated image of an entire community of seemingly autonomous figures who are perceived to exist, as Weber wrote, outside the ties of the world, outside routine occupations ("there's no business like show business"), and outside the routine obligations of family life. The principal embodiment of charisma in the world of entertainment is found, of course, in the concept of the *star*—the performer who stands out from other performers on the strength of some special, ineffable quality that transcends mere beauty, talent, or ambition to suggest, in the eye of the beholder, a state of grace.

Rarely, however, does the star power of an entertainer translate into anything that could be convincingly described as charismatic authority. For one thing, few performers have any inclination, much less opportunity, to play anything but the most superficially charismatic roles. For another thing, the entertainment industry has come to embrace a paradox that would have interested Weber no end: as epitomized by the "star system" that dominated Hollywood in the 1930s and 1940s, it has evolved into an institution, marked by the conservatism of all institutions, that trades on a continual promise of novelty and innovation. In return for their status as movie stars, Hollywood's leading men and women were once expected to inhabit the personas that were created for them, play the parts that were written for them, and generally do as they were told. To behave otherwise was to invite professional ruin. It was the very rigidity of this system that enabled a later generation of film stars, beginning with such 1950s "antiheroes" as Marlon Brando and James Dean, to affirm their authenticity and enhance their popularity by openly chafing against the conventions and expectations of Hollywood. In an industry devoted to the manufacture of fame, true charisma attached to those who demonstrated their autonomy from the means of production. In the early 1960s, however, this principle, which has become thoroughly routinized in contemporary popular culture, was still only dimly understood.

Apart from his insight that charismatic personalities inspire "a devotion born of distress and enthusiasm," Weber did not speculate on the psychology of the phenomenon. Where he left off, however, Sigmund Freud stepped in. What Weber called "distress and enthusiasm," Freud called "ambivalence," the term he used to describe the simultaneous presence of powerfully conflicting emotions such as love and hate, hope and fear, attraction and aversion. Ambivalence, in Freud's view, was the essence of the human condition and the trigger for a wide range of unconscious psychic "defenses" by which the mind seeks to manage the anxiety that arises from strong emotional conflict. The list of available defense mechanisms is long and varied, and it includes such now-familiar concepts as repression and denial. But the defense that Freud associated most closely with the response of groups to leaders was that of idealization, in which a state of ambivalence is resolved by attributing all of one's positive feelings of love, hope, or attraction to a suitable person (or "object" in Freudian parlance) while either repressing one's negative feelings or else projecting them onto another suitable object.

On a one-to-one basis, idealization figures heavily in the Freudian conception of what it means to fall in love, which helps to explain why a distinguishing feature of charismatic involvement is a level of passionate devotion that is commonly compared by participants and observers alike to the all-encompassing rapture of romantic love. In charismatic groups, these romantic idealizations are further organized and intensified by the process Freud called "identification," in which a person selects another more powerful or prominent figure as a role model or "ego ideal." Freud regarded identification as central to the formation of many types of groups: having chosen a suitable leader, the members of a group seek to share in the resulting aura of power by patterning their personalities on the idealized qualities of that leader. But Freud also acknowledged a second form of identification that reaches a special intensity in charismatic groups. This is the identification of the group members with one another, which causes each member to feel personally enhanced, rather than threatened, by the existence of others who feel the same way toward the object of his or her affections. Freud's own example of this (written in 1921) could hardly be more apt:

> We have only to think of the troop of women and girls, all of them in love in an enthusiastically sentimental way, who crowd round a singer or pianist after his performance. It would certainly be easy for each of them to be jealous of the rest; but, in the face of their numbers and the consequent impossibility of their reaching the aim of their love, they renounce it, and, instead of pulling out one another's hair, they act as a united group, do homage to the hero of the occasion with their common actions, and would probably be glad to have a share of *his* flowing locks. Originally rivals, they have succeeded in identifying themselves with one another by means of a similar love for the same object.

Freud regarded the identification of a group with its idealized leader as a form of regressive behavior: a pining for the sort of protection and direction a child seeks from a parent. And in those cases where the chosen leader is affiliated with and empowered by the governing institutions of society, he may assume the role of a proverbial "father-figure." But another possibility exists, in which instead of identifying with a figure who promises to preserve the existing order, groups made anxious by uncertainty and ambivalence may seek to relieve their anxiety by idealizing and identifying with a figure who suggests a sense of autonomy from the institutions and conventions that uphold the status quo—a figure who appears both to represent and resolve in himself the ambiguity, alienation, and ambivalence of the situation. This, too, can be seen as a form of regression—not to a childlike state of dependency, but to a characteristically adolescent state of rebellion in which the idealized parents of childhood are rejected in favor of freshly idealized figures drawn from the outside world. Adolescents are primed to identify with autonomous outsiders who give the impression of living by their own rules. And in modern industrialized societies, where adolescence has come to be seen as an increasingly distinct, protracted, and institutionalized stage of life, the role of charismatic response has grown accordingly.

Weber acknowledged a link between charismatic response and adolescent psychology when he wrote that "charisma is contrary to all patriarchal domination." Yet the most provocative insight into this relationship is found in one of the most controversial chapters of Freud's work: his attempt to link his ideas about social psychology to his theory of the "primal horde." This was Freud's belief, based on the "armchair anthropology" of his day, that human beings originally lived in small patriarchal hordes, each of which was ruled by a single dominant male who expelled his male offspring as soon as they posed a threat to his dominance. At some point in the depths of prehistory, Freud theorized, a group of these outcast sons joined together in a primordial "band of brothers" who murdered their despotic father and then sought to assuage their guilt and grief at this act of patricide by projecting those feelings outward in the form of veneration for a sacred totem animal, which then became the symbol of their fraternal clan. From an anthropological perspective, the theory of the primal horde has little credibility. But as a cultural myth it exerts great imaginative force, for it suggests how, down through the ages, fraternal solidarity has posed the principal challenge to patriarchal power in many spheres of life.

A totemic band of brothers. A troop of women and girls. An idealized devotion born of psychic distress and shared enthusiasm. Taken together, the theories of Weber and Freud provide the sociological and psychological background for a serious understanding of how and why the Beatles phenomenon first took hold in Britain in 1963, spread to America the following year, and then went on to serve as the personification of a spirit of social and cultural upheaval that reached throughout the industrialized world during the second half of the 1960s.

The specific iconography of charisma is a cultural construct that varies widely in time and place. But the ability of charismatic figures to resolve and relieve the ambivalence and alienation of their followers begins with their ability to embody those feelings in themselves. Over and above the self-evident fact that the Beatles, like other successful entertainers, were capable of generating great excitement and emotional intensity in their music, and the equally self-evident fact that their success had lent them an aura of economic autonomy as well, their qualifications as charismatic heroes in Britain really began with their origins in Liverpool, whose Northern geography, ethnic diversity, and proletarian identity confirmed their status as social outsiders and heightened the drama of their rapid ascent from provincial obscurity to national celebrity. Their unconventionality was proclaimed by their distinctive clothes and hairstyle, which (in the beginning, at any rate) set them apart from everyone else, and also added an element of sexual ambiguity—as much childlike as feminine—to a group of young men whose uniformity of appearance made them look like a band of brothers, and who gave the impression, while young women literally hurled themselves at their feet, of reserving their primary loyalty for one another.

Still, it is questionable whether these attributes by themselves would have caused the Beatles to generate such a powerful charismatic response among British, and later American, teenagers, were it not for the critical twist they brought to their newfound fame: their insistence on skewing the very conventions of show business self-presentation that would normally have restricted their appeal, however formidable, to the relative insignificance of show business. For the true measure of the Beatles' autonomy in the eyes of their teenage fans lay in their willingness to turn the entire "process by which fame is manufactured" into grist for their mill. By mocking the pretension of their celebrity and inviting their fans to share with them in the happy joke of their success, these four fantastic figures seemed to pass *back* into real life. Their own personal improvisation on charisma involved less a direct challenge to the social order (as Richard Lester said, "anarchy" *was* too strong a word for it) than a challenge to the artificial, allegorical world of show business that had come to reflect the social order in such a narrow, predictable, and patronizing manner.

Central to that challenge was their identity as a group. Though the Beatles cannot be said to have *invented* the rock group, they did embody the sovereign identity and solidarity of a group with a clarity that had rarely been seen before in the era of mass entertainment. For, as Freud suggested, the image of a teenage gang, dismissed by Richard Hoggart as "a minor mythology imported from America," had its roots in a major mythology imported from antiquity. The solidarity of young men has always held a special place in the human imagination, serving the arts and literature as a staging ground for the themes of heroic adventure and romantic love. Yet, prior to the 1960s, the portrayal of groups in the context of mass entertainment was compromised by a basic incompatibility between the concept of a group and the concept of a star—the principal protagonist of mass entertainment, who does nothing if not stand out from the crowd.

To their fans, the Beatles appeared to have reconciled the adverse identities of the group and the star. They were understood to be a "band" in both senses of the word: as musicians, of course, but also, on a more elemental level, as a group of young men who shared a sense of loyalty and purpose. This enabled teenagers in general and working-class teenagers in particular to see John-Paul-George-and-Ringo as the apotheosis of every group of "mates" in Britain. Male solidarity in itself was nothing new. What was new was the working-class ethic of male solidarity cured of its "chippy" defensiveness, imbued instead with a confident good humor and an aura of triumphant success. By reconciling the adverse images of the group and the star, the Beatles appeared to reconcile the adverse ideologies of working-class solidarity and middle-class ambition that had shaped the English class system since the nineteenth century. Just as they assuaged the anxieties of many adults about the young, the Beatles relieved the apprehensions of many young people about what adulthood held in store. They seemed to demonstrate that you could have the best of Us *and* Them. You could make a success of yourself in the world, yet retain your loyalty to your friends.

A large number of young people, nearly all of them male, responded to this vision in the most direct manner possible—by joining with their mates in forming pop groups of their own. Sales of musical instruments skyrocketed in Britain during the second half of 1963, as the adolescent population of every industrial town, inspired by the sudden celebrity of Liverpool, pounded away at the creation of a distinctive local "sound." Most other major cities had already spawned nascent pop scenes; these now bloomed with foursomes and fivesomes got up in modish uniforms and Beatleish haircuts. The success of some of these groups—beginning with Freddie & The Dreamers and the Hollies (both from Manchester), and continuing with the Dave Clark Five and the Rolling Stones (both from the suburbs of London)—only seemed to confirm that whatever magic the Beatles possessed lay dormant in the soul of every English boy.

For most male adolescents, however, the Beatles' success remained a vicarious pleasure. They listened and danced to the group's records, followed their exploits in the newspapers, and emulated their dress, speech, and attitudes. In this they were inspired by one consideration that had little to do with the nuances of social symbolism—the simple fact that the Beatles drove an extraordinary number of teenage *girls* absolutely wild.

In truth, no one knew what to make of the girls. By the dozens, they stood watch outside the London lodgings of the Beatles and the Liverpool homes of their families; by the hundreds, outside the theaters and television studios where the group performed. Great shrilling crowds of them brought the functioning of airports and train stations to a standstill. And the scene inside the theaters, during the concerts, was safely beyond description.

In the press, the operative word was *hysteria*. How else to account for whole crowds of young women leaping, weeping, falling over theater seats and one another, literally rolling in the aisles, their bodies compressed into fetal positions, their hands grasping and fluttering around their heads, now covering their eyes, their ears, their mouths, all the while shrieking with such intensity that they overwhelmed the sound of the music, turning the Beatles' performance into a surreal pantomime? During the summer of 1963, when the screaming began in earnest, it functioned as a form of high-pitched applause that greeted the band when it came onstage, filled the gaps between numbers, or erupted in those moments, outside a hotel or theater, when a Beatle would dash into view. By the fall of that year, the screaming at the concerts was such that it simply never stopped, swelling to truly deafening levels when a Beatle onstage did anything as remarkable as grin or shake his head. Outside the theaters, the mere opening of a door or the arrival of a vehicle became enough to set it off.

It was noted that girls had gone crazy over entertainers before. In America they had screamed for Valentino, Sinatra, and Presley. In Britain there had been *squealing*, at least, for Cliff Richard and Tommy Steele. The obvious comparisons were drawn between the behavior of Beatle fans and that of expressive crowds at sporting events and political rallies. (Nor were these parallels lost on the band itself. Appearing at a window or on a balcony before a throng of *Beatlejungend,* John Lennon liked to amuse his bandmates at the expense of the *Daily Telegraph* by snapping his heels together and saluting the crowd with his right arm stiffly raised.) It was a crowd of such single-minded enthusiasm that it posed some danger to itself. Girls fainted, some fell underfoot, and in a few instances people were pushed through plate-glass windows and doors. The Beatles were outspokenly tolerant and appreciative of this multitude, but they were also privately unnerved by their exposure to its leading edge of flailing arms, grasping hands, and screaming mouths. For the girls' behavior had an unhinged intensity that had *not* been seen before— not in such numbers, least of all in Britain. And yet, despite the chaos and the incidental violence, there was something about the whole thing that was hard to take seriously. The reporter Michael Braun watched on more than one occasion as an entire audience of girls, having reached a peak of frenzy at the close of the Beatles' performance, fell dead silent for the playing of the national anthem, only to resume at gale force on the final note of "God Save the Queen."

The newspapers consulted psychiatrists, who returned the favor by basing their diagnoses on what they read in the newspapers. "You don't have to be a genius," a London clinician informed the *Sunday Times,* "to see parallels between sexual excitement and the mounting crescendo of delighted screams through a stimulating number like 'Twist and Shout.'" Asking a psychiatrist in 1963 about hysterical females was a bit like asking a Newtonian physicist why apples fall from trees, hysteria being the syndrome on which Freud cut his analytic teeth. In the psychoanalytic sense, the word describes the involuntary "conversion" of psychological stress into symbolic symptoms or behavior. Since the really dedicated screamers consisted of girls aged twelve to seventeen—the years between the onset of puberty and the beginning of active sexual experience—and since hysterical symptoms are thought to symbolize specific frustrated impulses, you certainly didn't have to be a genius to see that the frenzy of the girls at Beatle concerts suggested a simulation of orgasm. Though suspicions to the contrary added mightily to the fascination of the general public with whatever was going on, the Beatles did not preside over mass masturbatory orgies. And yet, as the feminist author Barbara Ehrenreich has written,

> For the girls who participated in Beatlemania, sex was an obvious part of the excitement. . . . It was rebellious (especially for the very young fans) to lay claim to sexual feelings. It was even more rebellious to lay claim to the active, desiring side of a sexual attraction: the Beatles were objects; the girls were their pursuers. . . . To assert an active, powerful sexuality by the tens of thousands and to do so in a way calculated to attract maximum attention was more than rebellious. It was, in its own unformulated, dizzy way, revolutionary. . . . At the same time, the attraction of the Beatles bypassed sex and went straight to the issue of power.

To grasp what the Beatles meant to the hard core of teenage girls who worshiped them so enthusiastically, one might begin by noting that prior to the summer of 1963, girls had served as silent partners in the youth culture of postwar Britain. British society was hardly unique in holding its young men and women to a double standard of social conduct. Though they represented a major share of the teenage market in entertainment and consumer goods, most girls were precluded from the forthright expression of group identity practiced by Teddy boys, Mods, Rockers, and their legion of informal imitators. Working-class solidarity itself was considered a male ethic, with its roots in the common experience of the workplace, not the home. And, much as they might look forward to a few years of holding a job and leading a life of their own, the ultimate career of the vast majority of British girls in 1963, as it had been in 1863, was assumed to be marriage and motherhood. In anticipation of this, they were subject to greater domestic responsibilities and stricter parental controls. While working-class boys were expected to live out their social lives on the streets, the social lives of girls were more centered in their homes, where small groups of friends could gather to play records, model clothes and makeup, read fan magazines, gossip, joke, and generally pass the time. This was especially true of girls in their early teens, all of whom still lived at home, and few of whom had any emotional involvement with boys of the nonfictional variety.

The male pop idol, whether in the guise of a singer or an actor, was a fixture of this female "bedroom culture" long before the Beatles had ever struck a chord, and his presence in the home was an indication of how the wishful thinking of adolescent girls differs from that of boys. A neat economy of the teenage market involves the fact that girls start to develop an appetite for idealizations of the opposite sex at an age when boys are still chiefly enthralled by idealizations of their own sex: cool guys, tough guys, and bad guys. At the same time, their orientation toward marriage and motherhood has generally encouraged girls to situate their feelings and fantasies about sex, from the beginning, in the context of enduring emotional relationships. To a much greater extent than boys, teenage girls translate "sex" into "romance," and a major branch of the entertainment industry stands ready to assist them in doing so.

Prior to the advent of videocassettes and DVDs, the pop recording star had an important tactical advantage over his rivals on the screen. A film star could enter the homes of his admirers only through the media of print and photography. To see him in his dramatic element required a trip to the local cinema. The expressive medium of the recording star, on the other hand, was made to be heard in the home. Records had the added advantage of being programmed by the listener herself, which meant that, once she owned his record, a fan could commune with her favorite singer at will. (She also had the satisfaction of possessing a physical object, covered with a photographic portrait, that symbolized her connection to him.) This gave record-listening a potential for intimacy that was perfectly suited to the intimate, confidential tone of many popular love songs. When enjoyed in solitude, records encouraged a fantasy that you were the only one listening: the only one for him.

By the early 1960s the recording industry in Britain and America had begun to cater with a new awareness to the use of records by teenagers, and especially teenage girls. The advent of actual girl groups was one example of this. But the surest avenue to the market in teen romance remained the great warhorse of pop, the romantic ballad, transformed by the technology of the modern recording studio into the booming strains of *opera d'adolescentia*: the sound of an enormous voice, recorded loud and close, silhouetted against a backdrop of booming echo. This new type of pop ballad orchestrated a heightened form of synthetic solitude, aimed directly at female listeners. For many girls, their most intense experience of popular music had become one that was best enjoyed alone, accompanied by the face and quivering voice of a singer who himself sounded marooned on some distant, reverberative shore.

It was into this cloistered community of prematurely lost souls and lonely hearts that the Beatles burst, dispensing a fantasy that was made to be shared, turning the languid, self-pitying world of teenage romance inside out. Here, for the first time, was a group of lively, attractive boys, each with his own distinctive attributes, among whom a group of girls could choose and, by their choices, define themselves—not only in relation to the Beatles, but in relation to one another as well. The scenario corresponded closely to the reality of teenage social life, where boys and girls tended to meet in groups and pair off, keeping one eye on their partners and the other on their friends. All across Britain in the summer and fall of 1963, cliques and friendships were realigned and redefined as each of perhaps a million girls picked the Beatle who most caught her fancy. For the adventurous, John; for the conventionally romantic, Paul; for the motherly, Ringo; and for those who couldn't quite make up their minds, perhaps George, who couldn't quite make up his. The sharp-tongued, intimidating one, the pretty, personable one, the unassuming, homely-but-cute one, the vague, handsome one—around and around it went. By themselves, the Beatles described a tiny universe of associative and disassociative choice (she who "loved" Paul might profess to "hate" George). Within any group of friends, there would be competition for favorites, but underlying any competition was the comforting awareness that in this fantasy there was a boy for every girl, with no one left out in the cold. The Beatles suggested that you could fall in love, and have your friends fall in love alongside you, and together share in the special world these four boys appeared to share with one another: their happiness, their success, their fun.

What the British nation witnessed with growing amazement during the fall of 1963 was the expressive world of its adolescent girls, which had formerly been confined to the privacy of small groups and the solitude of individual imaginations, spilling out into the spaces of public life. "Bedroom culture" had embraced an active principle and taken noisily to the streets. Having reached critical mass, the response to the Beatles and their music provided a socially and emotionally secure environment for the expression of female assertiveness, female aggression, female sexuality, and female solidarity. Because the initial sense of connection was indeed mediated by records, radio, television, and the press, it became vitally important for the serious fan to experience the Beatles firsthand. ("I've never seen them alive before!" a teenage girl exclaimed outside a theater in Cambridge.) By this time the band's appearances scarcely qualified as "concerts" at all, consisting instead of large-scale public demonstrations of affection and affiliation. Though the same could be said of many gatherings of the opera or the symphony, the Beatles' actual contribution to these concerts was musically and even theatrically perfunctory. Half the time, they could barely hear a thing they were playing. And yet, while nothing that could be projected from the stage of the Rialto in York or the Adelphi in Slough could compare with the sound of "She Loves You" thundering out of a jukebox or a radio, this mattered little, for the girls were engaged primarily in an act of ritualistic confirmation. They had come to see for themselves that this really was happening: here in York, here in Slough, in Bristol and Glasgow and Stoke-on-Trent. Here in *Britain*, of all places!

The screams that first arose spontaneously when a few girls were undone by their proximity to these chimerical heroes soon became

CAN'T BUY ME LOVE   185

established as a signature of the fans, turning the girls into active participants in the phenomenon of Beatlemania. Screaming set a lofty standard of participation. It was emphatic. It was physically and emotionally
cathartic. And it soon dawned on these girls that there was no effective
way for anyone to stop it. The police reacted with confusion and embarrassment. These were schoolgirls, after all, and the implication that
there was indeed "something sexual" at the root of their behavior turned
the authorities into captives of their own official reticence; there weren't
enough police *matrons* in the entire country to deal with such an outrageous possibility. The girls had stumbled onto a brilliant tactical gambit.
There, inside a frenetic, shrieking mass of Beatlemaniacs, the voice of
adult authority was utterly still.

The thrill of uninhibited participation was made possible by a sense
of permission that came from the Beatles themselves, who possessed the
only form of authority that was capable of penetrating the din. George
Harrison's assertion that "the fans have a right to scream the place down
if they want to" represented a form of license so alien to the everyday
experience of adolescents at home or at school that it had to be tested
before it could be accepted as real. Screaming and mobbing, which
among other things constituted misbehavior of the boldest sort, was a
way of testing it. Pushing the idea of vicarious romance past the honeymoon stage, the girls were gauging the depth of the Beatles' affection and
the strength of the Beatles' protection by giving expression to every ounce
of distress and enthusiasm they could muster. And the Beatles passed
this test by granting their fans a share of the autonomy they had taken for
themselves. Their public posture toward the girls' behavior was sympathetic but distanced, tolerant but unpatronizing, and perpetually amused.
("They, who are causing the storm, are its calm eye," gushed the *Daily
Mail*.) To the press, they defended the fans' "right" to scream. But neither
did they hesitate to tell their audiences in as many words to "shut up"—
shrugging it off when the girls only roared louder at their apparent refusal
to pander. Almost never did the group engage in the show-business catechism of "if not for the fans." They made light of any debt they might owe
their public in the same way that people their age made light of all debts
and dependencies. They presumed to do exactly as they pleased, and
they extended the same privilege to the fans. Something about the girls'
behavior was hard to take seriously because, as a case of people being

swept away by some involuntary force, it wasn't entirely serious. The girls came to scream. Bursting with anticipation, they led one another up to and over the brink of self-control. The real secret wasn't sexual; the real secret was that they could turn it on and off at will. They were free to lose themselves, regain themselves, and lose themselves again. In the benevolent presence of the Beatles, the border between chaos and composure lay wide open for them.

15

The outstanding English composers of 1963 must seem to have been John Lennon and Paul McCartney, the talented young musicians from Liverpool whose songs have been sweeping the country since last Christmas.

—William Mann, *The Times* of London

In the third week of November 1963, as the Beatlemania craze in Britain reached an early, dizzy height, Parlophone Records released the group's second LP. Innocuously titled *With the Beatles,* the new album took two weeks to end the seven-month reign of the group's first album at number one; it would go on to extend the Beatles' unprecedented residency at the top of the British LP charts for another five months. Replicating the format of the first album, *With the Beatles* contained eight original tunes, five songs previously recorded by black American artists, and one Tin Pan Alley–style ballad. Eight of the tracks (including all six of the cover tunes) had been recorded in the comparative calm of July 1963, prior to the release of "She Loves You." The six additional tracks were completed during a hectic two-day session in September. Despite the fact that many of the hastily written original songs were underdeveloped and underrehearsed at the time they recorded, the album as a whole was an altogether more polished piece of work than its deliberately primitive predecessor. With a couple of notable exceptions, the Beatles' singing and playing sounded markedly more confident, and increased use was made of studio techniques like voice-doubling and instrumental overdubbing (mainly of piano and organ) to enrich and enlarge the sound. Still, *With the Beatles* contained no jewel as bright as "Please Please Me" or as rough as "Twist and Shout," thanks mainly to a decision by George Martin and Brian Epstein to omit the group's new single, "I Want to Hold Your Hand," which was scheduled for release one week after the LP. The enormous popularity of the Beatles had inverted the standard practice by which a hit single was used to promote an album; in this case, "I Want to Hold Your Hand" was withheld from *With the Beatles* so that sales of the LP would not detract from sales of the single.

The trio of Lennon-McCartney songs that begin the album are by far the best of the originals. Lyrically, they are three variations on a theme. Each presents a sketchy romantic narrative of separation, anticipation, and return; taken together, they reflect the psychic distances the Beatles had traveled over the course of 1963 by referring, all three, to "home." "It Won't Be Long" is a clever reworking of the usual bag of tricks. It begins with a muscular call-and-response in which "yeah, yeah, yeahs" recycled from "She Loves You" are bandied about between the lead and backup singers with an arresting urgency. John comes at the song in the manner of "Please Please Me," his self-pitying pose in the verse yielding to a punning refrain that turns on the line "It won't be long, till I belong to you." An insistent instrumental commentary is provided by George Harrison's prominent lead guitar, which answers each of John's lamentations with the same sardonic run, until the line "Every night, the tears come down from my eyes" is punctuated by a jeering cascade of notes that sound more like brickbats than teardrops hitting the floor.

The next two tracks, "All I've Got to Do" and "All My Loving," are the first in a long series of Lennon-McCartney companion pieces: jointly credited, musically related, and often similarly titled compositions on which John and Paul would seek to establish more-individualized identities as singers and songwriters. John's "All I've Got to Do" is a medium-tempo "beat ballad" in the wistful "uptown" style of Sam Cooke and Ben E. King. It grows in strength from its tentative, harmonically ambiguous opening into an ostensibly affirmational love song whose lyrics reprise the "call on me" theme of complete emotional availability the Beatles first sounded in "From Me to You." But the texture of John's singing, with its long, plaintive melismas on the words "I" and "do," combines with Ringo's quirky, off-balance drumming (adapted from Arthur Alexander's "Anna") to generate an underlying anxiety so strong as to suggest that the entire song may well be a wishful fantasy. Paul follows with "All My Loving," a corny "letter song" whose superficial resemblance to his earlier "P.S. I Love You" is obliterated by a surging, swinging rhythm of walking bass, splashy cymbals, and crazed triplets from the rhythm guitar that puts a charge of sexual urgency behind his dutiful pledge to "write home every day / and send all my loving to you." Capped by George Harrison's ringing homage to Carl Perkins in his eight-bar solo break, this instrumental accompaniment marked a great leap forward for the Beatles, who had been incapable of generating any appreciable swing until Ringo joined the band.

With its smoothly streaming melody and its devotional sentiment, "All My Loving" became a showcase for Paul and a great favorite among Beatle fans. (It is the one original song on the album that became a staple of the group's concert repertoire.) For the most part, however, McCartney plays a supporting role on *With the Beatles* to John Lennon, whose singing completely dominates half of the fourteen tracks, including those like "Little Child"—a raucous, harmonica-heavy dance tune with an Everly Brothers lilt—on which John and Paul ostensibly share the lead vocal. Of the songs that are Paul's to sing, "Hold Me Tight" (a rerecorded reject from the *Please Please Me* sessions) devolves from a strong beginning into a morass of mannered lyrics and meandering chords, while "Till There Was You," a ballad from the Broadway show *The Music Man* (1957), comes close to an outright gaffe. The Beatles knew this song from an album by the jazz singer Peggy Lee, whose Latin-tinged arrangement they adapted to their own use. Conventionally tuneful and conventionally romantic, with a lyric based on the sort of pastoral conceit (the bridge speaks of "sweet fragrant meadows of dawn and dew") that characterized postwar Broadway songwriting at its most poetically pretentious, "Till There Was You" was what some music-business insiders in 1963 still referred to as a "legitimate" popular song. Its fans included Brian Epstein, who urged the Beatles to feature it in their television appearances as an appeal to mainstream taste. (Epstein also saw to it that the track was given an inordinate amount of attention in the liner notes his publicist Tony Barrow contributed to the back of the album cover.) The Beatles had had their fun with schmaltz like this before, most notably in their satiric bar-band versions of "Besamo Mucho" and "A Taste of Honey." But their rendition of "Till There Was You" tries so hard to downplay the inherent sentimentality of the song that it comes off as a rare joke at their expense. While his bandmates noodle away on claves, bongos, and Spanish guitars, generating the sort of musical ambience one might expect to hear in the lounge of a Majorca tourist hotel, Paul delivers the lyric in a voice so constrained and misconstrued that his performance sounds like a proud act of memorization by a singer who doesn't otherwise speak a word of English.

Some of the space left vacant by McCartney on *With the Beatles* is filled by George Harrison, who sings or shares the lead on four of the tracks. These include a capable rendering of Chuck Berry's first great anthem to the rise of rock, "Roll Over Beethoven" (which provided the recently paroled Berry with some welcome publishing royalties), and an oddly affecting performance of "Devil in Her Heart," the original version of which, "Devil in *His* Heart," was recorded by the Donays, an American girl group so obscure that they never placed a record on the charts. As written, "Devil in His Heart" is a classic girl-group melodrama in which a helplessly love-struck lead singer struggles to refute her girl-friends' words of warning about her boyfriend's bad intentions, insisting instead that she has fallen under the spell of "an angel sent to me." Unlike the songs by the Shirelles and the Cookies that the Beatles covered on *Please Please Me,* both of which refer to a gender-neutral "baby," their rendition of "Devil in Her Heart" required a change of pronoun in both the title and the lyric. This transformed a song about a stereotypical Bad Boy into a song about a much less typical Bad Girl, inverting the sexual double standard of early-1960s pop in a way that caused this otherwise mediocre track to have a powerful resonance for many female Beatles fans.

George Harrison's most significant contribution to *With the Beatles* was his first self-written song, a defiantly gloomy number called "Don't Bother Me." Prior to the summer of 1963, in his five years as a Quarry Man and a Beatle, Harrison had shown no apparent interest in songwriting. (His one credited co-composition, the 1961 instrumental "Cry for a Shadow," was merely a guitar duet that he and John Lennon had devised.) The very existence of "Don't Bother Me" was thus a reflection of the revolutionary influence that the success of Lennon and McCartney was exerting on a whole generation of young musicians in Britain, at a time when the concept of a pop singer-songwriter was much less common there than it was in the United States. George's decision to try his hand at songwriting also opened a new (and, in the long run, contentious) chapter in the politics of the Beatles as a group, for despite the collaborative model on which they worked for years, neither John nor Paul seems to have given any consideration to the possibility that they might collaborate with George as well. Instead, with its prickly title, minor-key harmony, and bleakly desolate mood, "Don't Bother Me" could scarcely offer a more pointed contrast to the exuberant musicality and upbeat emotionality that had marked the work of Lennon and

McCartney over the course of 1963. Just past his twentieth birthday, Harrison retained a strong streak of adolescent antipathy in the face he showed the world. It was therefore fitting that he should have been the Beatle whose recommendation to the president of Decca Records, Dick Rowe, had helped Rowe to rehabilitate his reputation as "The Man Who Turned the Beatles Down" by signing the Rolling Stones, a quintet of rhythm-and-blues aficionados from the suburbs of London who had begun to attract attention during the summer of 1963 as a studiously scruffy and willfully uncharming alternative to the darlings of Merseyside.

John Lennon and Paul McCartney had also done their bit for the Stones by endowing them with a song, "I Wanna Be Your Man," which became their second Decca single and their first real British hit. The Stones' manager, Andrew Oldham, had worked briefly as a publicist for Brian Epstein during the spring of 1963, and it was Oldham who invited Lennon and McCartney to attend a Stones rehearsal, where the two Beatles wowed their future friends and rivals by offering them an unfinished snippet of twelve-bar rhythm and blues and then composing a middle section for it, right before their eyes. Like virtually every other property they leased out to the trade, John and Paul considered "I Wanna Be Your Man" to be beneath their dignity as singers. But this did not prevent the song from showing up on *With the Beatles* as a vehicle for Ringo Starr. From the beginning, the Beatles, Brian Epstein, and George Martin agreed that Ringo, despite his drastically limited vocal range, should have a go at singing on the albums, if only to affirm his status as a full-fledged member of the group. To judge by "Boys" and "I Wanna Be Your Man," the initial idea was to present him as a kind of elemental Northern bloke, rough and ready, making the most of his moment in the spotlight by bashing his drums and bawling out his songs. This characterization was something of an in-joke as well, for a year of daily exposure to Ringo's earthy, unassuming personality had left the other Beatles quick to find signs of a noble savage in their midst.

That all three of the cover songs John Lennon sings on *With the Beatles* were linked to the Tamla-Motown label gives a fair idea of the source from which the Beatles were drawing their musical inspiration during the latter half of 1963, at a time when the upstart black-owned company was coming into its own, colonizing the airwaves (and selling more singles than any of its competitors besides the industry giants Columbia and RCA) with its distinctive brand of kinetic, gospel-based pop. It so happened that each of the three Motown-derived songs on *With the Beatles* represented a landmark in the rise of the label. "Money (That's What I Want)" was the 1959 R&B hit whose royalties had provided Motown's founder Berry Gordy with the seed capital for his new company. The Beatles' version of the song was a particular favorite with their fans at the Cavern Club, and John Lennon's raving, raw-voiced vocal rivals "Twist and Shout" as an example of a cover that surpasses the original. Yet the Beatles' accompaniment to John's exceptional performance is a muddled, leaden mess. Poorly played and poorly recorded, the track is an inadvertent throwback to the amateurish, ham-fisted style of the beat-music scene on Merseyside.

A similar lack of finesse applies to the Beatles' rendition of "You Really Got a Hold on Me" by Smokey Robinson and the Miracles, which features an unusual pairing of John and George singing lead, with Paul joining in on the refrain. "I think he's got the most perfect voice," Lennon would later say of Robinson, who served as Motown's *beau ideal* of singing, songwriting, and personal style. Rising high on the American charts in the winter of 1963, "You Really Got a Hold on Me" was Motown's first million-selling single. It was also, uncoincidentally, Smokey Robinson's first unequivocally great record, on which he revealed the gift for romantic irony that became his trademark as a lyricist and sang in a manner that fully conveyed the mixture of emotional sophistication and vulnerability that John Lennon so admired. But this same admiration may help to explain why the Beatles had so little to add to the song. Though reasonably well sung and well played (Ringo inserts a brilliant double-time fill at the start of the second release), their rendition comes across as an act of simple homage, spurred by the hope that, through a process of musical osmosis, some of its inspiration might rub off.

Happily, the Beatles took a much less reverential approach to the third volume of their Motown trilogy, "Please Mr. Postman," the original version of which was recorded in 1961 by the Marvelettes, a gaggle of Detroit teenagers whose records served the production staff at Motown as a proving ground for their subsequent work with the be-all and end-all of girl groups, the Vandellas and the Supremes. "Postman," too, was a commercial milestone at Motown: the label's first number-one pop hit. Strongly influenced by the Shirelles, the Marvelettes' recording strived for a tone of helpless, heartbroken sincerity, the effect of which was only enhanced by lead singer Gladys Horton's stilted, talent-show diction. The Beatles, by contrast, perform the song as if it were somehow supposed to be funny, reveling in its contrivance and mocking its anxious plea of "Mr. Postman, look and see / Is there a letter, a letter for me?" John Lennon's double-tracked vocal overpowers the slender premise of the lyric; his performance is enough to send the average postman fleeing down the street. Behind him the band set up a thick, sensuous rhythm that seemed to explode off the record in the opening verse of the song. Simultaneously impassioned, exciting, and absurd, this marvelous throwaway performance is the one cover tune on *With the Beatles* that approaches the level of "Twist and Shout," and it epitomizes all that is best about the Beatles' second album: the overwhelming authority of John Lennon's singing, the growing instrumental power and confidence of the band, and the emergence in the Beatles' music of a playful pop irony based on the tension between songs whose lyrics still trade, for the most part, in conventional romantic sentiments, and performances of those songs that qualify or undermine the stated intent of the words.

FAR MORE DRAMATIC than any of the music on *With the Beatles* was the stunning black-and-white portrait of the group that served as the cover of the LP. The picture was taken by Robert Freeman, a twenty-seven-year-old Cambridge-educated photographer and graphic designer. A former staffer at London's Institute for Contemporary Art, Freeman's circle of friends, associates, and camera subjects included many of the young artists and critics affiliated with Britain's emerging Pop Art movement, and his involvement with the Beatles marked one of the first points of direct contact between the worlds of pop and Pop. The cover photograph for *With the Beatles* was taken in a hotel ballroom in Bournemouth, where the Beatles were performing at the time. They were dressed in matching black polo-necked sweaters, and Freeman shot them face-on against a dark backdrop, their heads and shoulders brightly lit from the side. John, George, and Paul form a receding row of heads running from left to right across the top of the picture, with Ringo to the right and below. The uniformity of their clothes and haircuts merges with the black background, accentuating the differences in their faces, while the angle of light and the graininess of the print gives the image a soft, pointillistic glow.

That the cover was photographed in black and white was highly unusual in 1963, when glossy, "kissable" color was the medium of choice for popular LPs in both Britain and the United States. George Martin and Brian Epstein (whose understated vision of the Beatles this portrait captured best) had to browbeat the art department at EMI into accepting an image they considered much too formal, somber, and reserved for the cover of an album by a phenomenally successful pop group. And it is the austerity and impassivity of the expressions on the Beatles' faces as they loom out of the dark background that gives the photograph its haunting, mysterious power. Nine months after they posed for the cover of *Please Please Me* as a quartet of happy-go-lucky lads, clambering up the staircase of show-business success, these Beatles are no longer smiling. Instead, bathed in shadow, they stare back levelly and warily at the camera, and at a world which seems to have gone mad around them. Their year of "grinnings-at-nothings" had come and gone.

16

New York can destroy an individual, or fulfill him, depending a good deal on luck. No one should come to New
York . . . unless he is willing to be lucky.

—E. B. White

Early in November 1963, two days after the Royal Variety Show
and two weeks before the release of *With the Beatles,* Brian Epstein flew
to New York. Though his trip had been planned for more than a month,
its timing could not have been better, for at that very moment, John
Lennon's "rattle your jewelry" remark was proving as irresistible to the
London bureaus of the American news magazines *Time* and *Newsweek* as
it had to the British press. "The Queen Mother beamed," *Time* reported
the following week in an article titled "The New Madness," which represented the first mention of the Beatles in a mainstream American publication. Until this point, however, the United States had been the prime
source of frustration for Brian Epstein and George Martin in an otherwise miraculous year. Like many inhabitants of the Old World, Martin's
Parlophone label had a rich relation in the States—Capitol Records, the
third-largest record company in America and, since its acquisition in
1955, a subsidiary of EMI. In February 1963, when "Please Please Me"
began to ascend the British charts, the single had been routinely offered
to Capitol for sale in the United States. And Capitol—in the person of
Dave Dexter, a crew-cut jazz-and-blues aficionado who had been with
the company since the 1940s and currently served as its head of international A&R—had declined. This same ritual of corporate protocol had
been repeated with each subsequent Beatle release of 1963. As George
Martin would later point out, EMI had the power to "instruct" Capitol to
release the records, but such was the extent of British deference to
American expertise in the field of popular music that this was never seriously considered by the parent company. Instead, the first Beatle records
in the United States were released under a licensing agreement with Vee-
Jay, a black-owned, Chicago-based independent label whose fortunes
had recently soared with the release of its first million-selling record,

Gene Chandler's "Duke of Earl," and its signing of the Four Seasons, a white doo-wop group from New Jersey whose first three singles went to number one. Vee-Jay's receptivity to the Beatles may have owed something to its success with another EMI offering that Dave Dexter had rejected, Frank Ifield's rendition of "I Remember You," which had risen into the American Top Ten in 1962. By the spring of 1963, however, Vee-Jay was putting all of its promotional energy into the Four Seasons, and after two Beatles singles and an album seemed to sail off the edge of the earth, EMI licensed the next single, "She Loves You," to Swan Records, a Philadelphia-based label that was partially owned by the teen television host Dick Clark and known mainly for its success with novelty records. But Swan could not do for "She Loves You" what it had done for recent hits like Freddy Cannon's "Palisades Park."

Brian Epstein's business in New York, then, was to persuade Capitol Records to put its corporate weight behind the Beatles, and to persuade the television impresario Ed Sullivan to present the group on his network variety show. Thanks to the fortuitous intervention of several thousand frenzied Beatle fans, Epstein had spoken with Sullivan only the week before, after Sullivan had happened to pass through London's Heathrow Airport on the day when the Beatles were returning from a series of concert dates in Sweden. The place was a madhouse, and Sullivan, who prided himself on showcasing international talent, was sufficiently impressed to invite Epstein to look him up in New York. One week later, there was Brian, who knew enough about Ed Sullivan to recognize that his show was the precise American equivalent of *Sunday Night at the London Palladium*—same night of the week, same variety format, same vast national audience.

In his negotiations with Sullivan and his producer Bob Precht, Epstein drove his version of a hard bargain. He didn't press for any money to speak of, but he insisted on "top billing"—an obscure concept in the world of television, which mainly ensured that the Beatles would be featured in the network advertising for the show. Though they were puzzled by Epstein's priorities, Sullivan and Precht agreed to his terms, and signed the Beatles for a total of three appearances—two live, one taped—on successive Sundays in February 1964. Sullivan's eagerness to present the Beatles undoubtedly owed something to the crow he had eaten on behalf of Elvis Presley eight years before. After publicly announcing that Presley's style of performance was too vulgar for his show, Sullivan had wound up paying the singer $50,000 for three appearances. The Beatles' price, by contrast, consisted of their transatlantic airfare and a nominal fee of $4,000 for each of their two live performances.

With his television contract in hand, Epstein next turned his attention to Brown Meggs, the urbane, thirty-two-year-old director of Eastern Operations for Capitol Records. At a meeting with Meggs at the label's midtown offices, Brian waved his press clippings, recited his sales figures, and played his demo pressings of the Beatles' forthcoming single and album. He also informed Meggs that, under the terms of a film contract the Beatles had just signed with the British division of United Artists, the rights to release the soundtrack for the film in America were assigned to United Artists Records. Yet not even the prospect of another major label releasing a Beatles album in America could induce Brown Meggs to commit his company to the group, for the simple reason that Meggs, whose specialty was classical music, lacked the authority to make such a decision. He could only agree to forward the materials Epstein gave him to Capitol's headquarters in Hollywood.

Several factors had contributed to Capitol Records' year-long indifference to the Beatles. The first was the conventional wisdom in the record business that the Atlantic trade in popular music ran almost exclusively one way. Though novelty and instrumental records made in Britain had occasionally sold well in the United States, for Americans of the early 1960s, the very idea of a British pop singer belonged in a category of cultural curiosities that included Japanese outfielders and Soviet beauty queens.

A second factor in Capitol's indifference involved the label's institutionalized distaste for rock 'n' roll. Founded in Los Angeles in 1942 by the songwriter Johnny Mercer and a local record store owner named Glenn Wallichs, Capitol Records was the youngest of the four corporatized major labels (the others being RCA, Columbia, and Decca) that had dominated the American record market since the end of World War II. As the first major label to be based in Los Angeles, it symbolized the growing alliance between Tin Pan Alley and Hollywood. By 1955, when EMI purchased the company to make up for the loss of its long-standing affiliation with Columbia, Capitol boasted a formidable roster of popular talent headed by Frank Sinatra and Nat "King" Cole, a growing catalog of film soundtracks and original cast recordings, a distinguished classical music subsidiary (at a time when classical LPs accounted for nearly 20 percent of the record market), and a strong country-and-western division based in Nashville. What happened next was rock 'n' roll, which shattered the hold of the major labels on the popular singles market. As Dave Dexter complained in a 1956 memo to his new bosses at EMI, "We are in a most discouraging revolution in the pop singles field. A great majority of singles are bought not by college students but by mere children, youngsters as young as eleven, twelve, and thirteen years old. They buy strictly for the beat and, as you can tell from the recent Elvis Presley and Guy Mitchell releases over here, the lyrics are juvenile and maddeningly repetitive."

Considering that RCA had Elvis Presley under contract, and Decca had Bill Haley and Buddy Holly, the biggest losers in this "discouraging revolution" were Columbia and Capitol. Unlike Columbia, whose A&R chief, Mitch Miller, took to the circuit of parents' groups and civic associations denouncing rock 'n' roll as "musical baby food," Capitol tested the waters by signing Gene Vincent as its answer to Elvis. But Vincent's career soon fizzled, and Capitol spent the second half of the 1950s ignoring the cutthroat competition in the pop singles market in favor of albums by jazz- and folk-inflected vocal groups like the Four Freshmen and the Four Preps, whose music appealed to a more mature and affluent audience of college students and young adults. This strategy paid off brilliantly in the fall of 1958 when the Kingston Trio's recording of an old Appalachian murder ballad called "Tom Dooley" received so much unsolicited radio airplay that Capitol released it as a single and saw it rise to number one, transforming the "folk revival" movement of the 1950s from a subcultural sideline into a commercial bonanza. Over the next five years the Kingston Trio rewarded Capitol with more than a dozen Top Ten albums, whose sales far outstripped those of every rock-oriented artist of the period with the inevitable exception of Elvis Presley.

The Four Preps, the Four Freshmen, and the Kingston Trio provided some of the musical inspiration for the third and final reason for Capitol's indifference to the distant strains of Beatlemania in 1963. A year before, the label had signed a five-man group from the suburbs of Los Angeles who had recently changed their name from the Pendletones to the Beach Boys. After a respectable debut with a record called "Surfin' Safari," the group's second single, "Surfin' U.S.A.," became a Top Ten hit in the spring of 1963, establishing a new subgenre of pop called "surf music." Within a few months there were "surf bands" performing in places like Topeka, Kansas, seven hundred miles from the nearest breaking wave.

The Beach Boys' early records were commercials for the California Dream. Brimming with West Coast place-names and peer-group consciousness, their songs extolled the joys of surfing, hotrodding, girl-watching, and high school. Their music was a synthesis of recent pop styles, combining the glee-club harmony and doo-wop counterpoint of vocal groups like the Four Preps and the Four Seasons with a backing of guitar-group rock. The band had little visual style to speak of, and their playing was barely competent, but all five of them could sing. They sang with a deadpan bass on the bottom, a whooping falsetto on top, and, in between, a kind of epic Californian nasality, so calmly enthusiastic that they sounded like the sons of NASA personnel.

What made the Beach Boys especially attractive to Capitol was that they represented not only a synthesis of pop styles, but also a synthesis of approaches to the teenage market that had eluded the label since the advent of rock 'n' roll. The group's music contained enough raw energy to inspire a dance called "The Surf," which was promoted with a Twist-like fervor over the course of 1963. That three of them were actual brothers combined with their clean-cut good looks to suggest characters out of a family television show—a musical "My Three Sons." Best of all, surf music could be tied to the preexisting craze for surfing itself, which had become popular among California teenagers during the 1950s, and to a preexisting genre of Hollywood films—"bikini Westerns," as they were known to the trade—in which hordes of half-nude ingenues were shown at play in a blindingly bright Technicolor environment of sun and sand, skin and teeth. What the Beatles were to the adolescent beat culture of Merseyside, the Beach Boys were to the adolescent beach culture of Southern California, and with two hit singles and albums to their credit in 1963 alone, they were enough to convince the A&R staff of Capitol Records in Hollywood that the label had already discovered the Next Big Thing in teenage pop, right in its own backyard.

THE AMERICAN TELEVISION and record executives who dealt with Brian Epstein during his visit to New York in the fall of 1963 were by turns amused and irritated by this well-spoken young Englishman and his obsessive concern for detail. (The most "particular" pop manager he had ever met, said one; "absolutely inflexible" complained another.) Epstein in New York behaved like a man who knew exactly what he was doing—

a performance that was all the more impressive given his lack of any practical knowledge of how the music business in America worked. His plan for breaking in the Beatles in the United States amounted to a kind of haiku version of what they had just achieved in Britain. He would dispense with the provincial preliminaries, release a single on a major label, present the band on national television, and hope that everyone for some reason went nuts over them. Here, as in Britain, Brian's inexperience would prove a peculiar source of strength. Not knowing how to operate like a typical pop manager was no handicap for him in New York because, unlike nearly everyone he was dealing with, he viewed the Beatles not as a potential pop craze but as a legitimate *theatrical* phenomenon. This had been his singular vision of them from the start, and his every move in New York was designed to lend an aura of theatrical legitimacy to the group. Legitimacy was the reason he demanded "top billing" on *The Ed Sullivan Show.* Legitimacy was the reason he arranged for the Beatles to stay during their February visit at the most theatrically grand of New York's grand hotels, the Plaza. And legitimacy was the subtext of the one interview he gave during his visit, to a reporter from *The New Yorker* (delivered, the magazine noted, "with an air that we associated more with an English drawing room than with Tin Pan Alley"), in which Brian explained that the Beatles were different from "the other big English rock-'n'-rollers in that they are not phony. They have none of that mean hardness about them. They are genuine."

Epstein's singular vision of the Beatles did more than insulate him from the indifference of people like Brown Meggs and his associates at Capitol Records. It also allowed him to feel increasingly hopeful about the Beatles' prospects in America as he went about his business in midtown Manhattan. For New York City in the fall of 1963 abounded with signs of a new strain of Anglophilic sentiment whose growing influence on popular entertainment in the United States was in many ways a cultural reflection of the historic changes in the Anglo-American relationship that dated from World War II. The war had profoundly transformed the image of Britain in the minds of most Americans. Long seen as an arrogant, aristocratic, and imperialistic rival (a characterization rooted in the patriotic mythology of America's Revolutionary past), Britain was abruptly recast in the dark days of 1940, first as a plucky little democracy, vulnerable and defiant on the edge of fascist Europe, and then as a staunch ally in the victory that set the stage for America's emergence as the most powerful nation on earth. Out of this sudden crystallization of roles that had been quietly reversing for decades came a newly liberalized view of Britain and its people that was informed by the experience of millions of American servicemen and relieved of its reactionary associations by the election of a Labour government in 1945. Throughout the 1950s, as the taste for "I Love Lucy" and Elvis Presley flooded into British society from the bottom up, a growing fascination with things English filtered into American society from the top down. Now that the Lion had been detoothed and declawed, ordinary Americans could discover how much they enjoyed watching the creature preen and clown and roar.

In the realm of popular culture, the great watershed of the new American Anglophilia was the hugely successful 1956 production of *My Fair Lady,* in which Alan J. Lerner and his collaborator Frederick Loewe transformed George Bernard Shaw's play *Pygmalion* into a shining example of what many people regarded as America's greatest popular art form, the Broadway musical. The London audiences that flocked to *Pygmalion* when it opened in the West End in 1912 had enjoyed a Fabian socialist satire on the nature and nurture of class distinctions. The American audiences that flocked to *My Fair Lady* on Broadway (in the year of Elvis Presley and *Look Back in Anger*) were treated to much the same story with one significant twist: in the musical version, Eliza Doolittle and Professor Henry Higgens get each other in the end. The sentimentality of this outcome would have appalled George Bernard Shaw, but it served a different audience and a different purpose, for Lerner had turned the story into an allegorical romance between Britain and America. To an extent that would have mystified their Edwardian forebears, American audiences identified with the character of Eliza Doolittle from beginning to end. From their perspective, the story of Eliza's transformation from an uncouth streetcorner wastrel into a woman of the world mirrored the story of their country's own ascendancy, while the descent of Henry Higgins from a state of haughty indifference to a grudging acknowledgment of his need for Eliza mirrored the story of Britain's new dependency as seen through American eyes.

The success of *My Fair Lady,* which ran for seven years on Broadway and sold more than 5 million copies of its original cast recording, combined with the success of the Oscar-winning films *Around the World in Eighty Days* (1956) and *The Bridge on the River Kwai* (1957) to create an open market for British theatrical talent in the United States. At the same time, a cult audience was growing for imported British films, beginning with Alec Guinness's quirky Ealing comedies in the early 1950s and continuing with the Northern Realist dramas of the late 1950s, which were revered by American critics and art-house audiences as taut, understated alternatives to the grandiosity of Hollywood. (*Room at the Top* was nominated for ten Oscars, including Best Picture, in 1960.) By the early 1960s, the popularity of British films in the United States led several Hollywood studios, beginning with United Artists, to open their own production offices in London. Among the most successful pictures that were made in Britain with American money for release in the American market were *The Mouse That Roared* (1960), which established Peter Sellers as an international star, and *Dr. No* (1962), which launched the film career of Sean Connery as James Bond.

In the fall of 1963, five of the eleven successful Broadway productions that opened that year were imported from the West End. A pair of British musicals, Anthony Newley's *Stop the World I Want to Get Off* and Lionel Bart's *Oliver!* (featuring a cast of mop-topped Dickensian street urchins) were enjoying extended runs. Despite a disastrously timed opening during the week of the Cuban Missile Crisis in October 1962, *Beyond the Fringe* had earned rave reviews from the New York critics and set off a boomlet on Broadway for English satirical revue. In the big Times Square movie theaters, audiences flocked to see young British stars like Peter O'Toole in *Lawrence of Arabia,* Albert Finney in *Tom Jones,* and Sean Connery in *From Russia With Love.* (Several months before, the tabloid fascination with the Anglo-American romance of Elizabeth Taylor and her co-star Richard Burton had generated an unprecedented advance ticket sale of $20 million for the sword-and-sandal epic *Cleopatra.*) The fascination with things English extended to fashion as well. As Tom Wolfe would soon report in the *New York Herald Tribune,* growing numbers of the city's young bankers, lawyers, and media executives were adopting the "secret vice" of bespoke English tailoring; tweedy British woolens were a staple of the "Ivy League" style preferred by Eastern college students; and the youthful fashions of the English designer Mary Quant were being touted by American fashion magazines and marketed by the J.C. Penney chain in its stores from coast to coast.

Such was the panorama of British cultural influence that Brian Epstein observed during his visit to New York. And because Epstein (and at this point, Epstein alone) understood that the Beatles were cut from the same cloth as the Angry playwrights and the Northern Realist actors and the Oxbridge satirists, he had every reason to believe that Americans would respond to four sexy, witty, ostensibly "classless" Liverpudlians in the same way they were responding to all of these other liberalized manifestations of contemporary British culture. Especially now that America, beginning with Ed Sullivan, was finally showing signs of meeting the Beatles halfway.

Shortly after his return to Britain, Epstein received a transatlantic phone call from a New York theatrical agent named Sid Bernstein, who had been monitoring the outbreak of Beatlemania in the weekly airmail edition of the *Manchester Guardian*. Having just seen a notice in *Variety* announcing the dates of the Beatles' upcoming appearances on *The Ed Sullivan Show*, Bernstein was calling to see about promoting a concert in conjunction with their February visit. Epstein remained cool to the idea until Bernstein mentioned Carnegie Hall. Steeped in the legitimacy that Epstein craved, Carnegie Hall was the most prestigious performance space in New York. Along with its reputation as a shrine of classical music, it had also served as the site of several historic concerts by jazz and popular artists—most notably that of the Benny Goodman Band in 1938. Epstein leaped at the chance to have the Beatles perform there. For his part, Sid Bernstein contributed some shrewd promotional instincts of his own. Just old enough to remember the tens of thousands of schoolgirls who brought Times Square to a standstill when Frank Sinatra performed at the Paramount Theater on Columbus Day in 1944, Bernstein booked the hall for two shows on the evening of February 12, Lincoln's Birthday, three days after the Beatles' debut on *The Ed Sullivan Show* and a school holiday in New York. When the Carnegie Hall management balked at the idea of presenting a British rock group, Bernstein won them over by suggesting that the concert would help to promote "international understanding."

17

In the modern world, we Americans are the old
inhabitants.

—Paul Goodman (1960)

"International understanding" was a watchword in New York in the fall of
1963, as the city prepared to host a great World's Fair, due to open in the
spring of the following year. A garish, sprawling monument to the commercial and cultural power of New York, the 1964 fair had taken shape in
the mind of its creator, the redoubtable Robert Moses, as a twentieth-
century equivalent of the great international expositions with which
London and Paris had proclaimed themselves the centers of the
nineteenth-century world. The official theme of the fair was "Peace
Through Understanding." Its official symbol was a skeletal steel structure
called the Unisphere, which depicted the great globe of Earth, ringed by
the orbits of communications satellites. The Unisphere was an apt symbol of New York City as well, for communications was the one industry
upon which the growth of all other American industries in the postwar
era was predicated, and communications defined the role of New York as
the commercial and cultural capital of the United States.

The city was the center of American broadcasting, publishing, advertising, mass marketing, and public relations. For a foreign businessman
like Brian Epstein, New York offered the solution to the most daunting
problem posed by the United States. The country had a population three
and a half times that of Britain, spread over thirty-five times the geographic area. Its entertainment industry was divided between two coasts,
its broadcasting industry served by thousands of independent radio and
television stations, its record business diversified among scores of labels
and distributors. But in New York there were people whose livelihood
depended on making commercial sense of this vast country: people like
Eugene Gilbert, whose discovery of the teenage market in the years after
World War II had made him a folk hero to American business, and whose
company, Gilbert Youth Research, functioned as a "vast seismograph for
picking up the tremors of teenage intentions in every corner of the

nation." Marketing experts like Gilbert possessed the power and knowledge to get word of a person or a product into the living rooms of homes
across America. They had to be persuaded to do this, of course, and the
easiest way to persuade them, Brian Epstein surmised, was to create a
sensation right there in New York.

THE NEWEST AND brightest jewel in the crown of America's communications empire was television, which in the twenty years since World War II
had grown from a technological novelty into the most popular entertainment medium in the country. By 1963 the three commercial networks
had largely abandoned the format of live comedy, variety, and drama that
had characterized broadcast television's brief "golden age" in favor of a
strict weekly regimen of filmed entertainment shows. As seen on TV, the
American day was devoted to the romantic intrigue of soap operas and
the crazed consumerism of game shows. The American night, in turn,
was divided between domestic comedies set in the affluent suburban
milieu of the day and violent, moralistic dramas, consisting mainly of
Westerns and crime shows, set in any conceivable modern or historical
context *except* the affluent suburban milieu of the day. The picture was
rounded out by live coverage of sports, prime-time and late-night variety
shows, and daytime programming aimed specifically at children and
teenagers. But the standard fare, along with the commercials that made
the whole thing possible, was soap operas, game shows, sitcoms, and
shoot-outs. "The dream of violence and the fact of security," wrote the
critic Leslie Fiedler. "The dream of failure and the fact of success—here
is the center of our new comedy." In the fall of 1963, one year after a
best-seller by Michael Harrington called *The Other America* exposed the
plight of 30 million Americans who had lived in rural poverty for generations on end, the top-rated television show in America was *The Beverly
Hillbillies,* a sitcom depicting the antics of a dirt-poor family from
Appalachia who had struck it rich and gone to live among the mansions
and movie stars of Beverly Hills.

While the American public communed on a nightly basis with the
heroes and villains of the Old Frontier, their country was being led by a
preternaturally telegenic young president who had campaigned for office
on the promise of a New Frontier. John F. Kennedy was the first American president to be born in the twentieth century, the first to grow up in

thrall to the movies, radio, and the glossy idealizations of magazine advertising—the first American president to have his sensibility molded in the
crucible of modern mass culture. In the young politician who emerged
from this background, long-standing affinities between the political man
and the theatrical man were combined to dazzling effect.

It was Kennedy's good fortune to grow up in the age of film and radio
and then run for the presidency at precisely the moment when television,
combining the spectacle of the one medium with the intimacy of the
other, was emerging as the new stage of public life in America. Poised yet
never flamboyant, Kennedy personified the celebrated "coolness" of the
television medium; like a "regular," he projected the air of a man going
about his (vitally important) business, neither playing to the cameras nor
pretending to ignore their presence. In the crisis-filled atmosphere of his
first two years in office, he turned the televised presidential address into
a theatrical tour de force, the televised presidential press conference
into a vehicle for his personality. On television, as President, Kennedy
exuded a quick intelligence and a wit that was teasing, ironic, and skillfully preemptive. Deeply fascinated by his own reflection in the media,
his apparent candor and confidence in his ability to control the apparatus
of publicity disarmed and enthralled the press. As a result, the President,
his beautiful wife, their young children, his brothers and sisters, and his
whole extended family became the great American feature story of the
early 1960s in mass-circulation magazines like *Life, Look,* and *The Saturday Evening Post.* Kennedy further inhabited the world of popular culture
as the hero of a movie based on his war exploits, *PT-109,* and as the inspiration for a hit comedy album, *The First Family,* which in the fall of 1962
became the fastest-selling record ever released in the United States.

To a Kennedy acolyte like Norman Mailer, JFK exuded a charisma
that would have made Max Weber blush. "It was a hero America needed,"
Mailer wrote, "a hero central to his time, a man whose personality might
suggest contradictions and mysteries which could reach into the alienated circuits of the underground, because only a hero can capture the
secret imagination of a people . . . the subterranean river of untapped,
ferocious, lonely and romantic desires, that concentration of ecstasy and
violence which is the dream life of the nation."

Of the young president's effect on America's population of college
students, teenagers, and schoolchildren, swollen to unprecedented proportions by the postwar "baby boom," there was no doubting Mailer's

word. Young children were drawn into the relentlessly publicized world of his family, which seemed so large and close, and into a sense of identification with *his* young children, who were shown bursting into the Oval Office as they might burst into their father's den at home. College students could see him as a kind of gloriously attractive and dynamic older brother, a paragon of wit and poise and Ivy League style whose rhetoric of action and sacrifice showed them the potential of politics as an outlet for energy and altruism. And for American teenagers, who were old enough to have tasted the drama of the 1960 election and the ensuing Cold War crises in Berlin and Cuba, Kennedy was an idealization of unparalleled versatility, a man who himself seemed to move at will between the worlds of youth and maturity. It was an idealization brought to them, moreover, in the format they knew best, for John F. Kennedy was nothing less than the preeminent leading man of television in his day. On television, as President, he brought the charismatic aura of stardom to politics. It was an august and unprecedented merger, not of "poetry and power" as Robert Frost had envisioned in the poem he wrote to honor Kennedy's inauguration, but of power and popular culture.

THE RISE OF television had a revolutionary effect on the entire American entertainment industry—weekly attendance at movie theaters declined from a peak of 90 million in 1948 to 25 million in 1961—but its most traumatic impact was on radio broadcasting. In 1948 the United States had approximately a thousand independent radio stations grossing $57 million a year; by 1961, though the number of stations had more than tripled, their gross revenue had declined to $51 million a year. Having lost its national audience to television, commercial radio in the 1950s set out to reinvent itself as a local and regional entertainment medium. It did this in large part by adopting formats that consisted of playing recorded music over the air.

Music radio was inexpensive to produce and especially attractive to local advertisers, who recognized that they could target specific portions of the public based on the style of music they sponsored. If a car dealership in Columbus, Ohio, wanted to sell more Buicks to the black steelworkers who had settled in that part of the state, it could advertise on the nearest rhythm-and-blues station and be confident of reaching the people it wanted to reach. And in the car-crazed suburban culture of the

1950s, the radio market was enhanced by the fact that, for the first time, nearly every car sold had an AM receiver lodged in its dashboard. As a result, while television was busy establishing itself as the country's new favorite form of home entertainment, radio was on its way to becoming America's new favorite form of away-from-home entertainment. Radio penetrated into the fantasy spaces of American life. It forged a link—for whites, to the world of blacks; for suburbanites, to the energy of the city; for teenagers, to the wild party that was happening somewhere else.

Records provided the radio business with unlimited cheap programming; radio provided the record business with unlimited cheap advertising. It was a marriage made in heaven, but not on Tin Pan Alley. Among the biggest losers in the rock-'n'-roll revolution of the 1950s were the major song publishing houses, whose control over the music business in America had once been absolute. Particularly frustrating for the music publishers was the way the rapid expansion of the record business and its alliance with music radio had shattered the orderly system by which songs had once been promoted. The obvious culprits in this regard were the new arbiters of taste, disc jockeys, who commanded loyal followings of their own and were beholden only to their ratings. During the 1950s, deejays chose which pop singles to play (out of nearly a hundred released each week) according to a variety of criteria. Some relied on their personal taste; some on their intuition of what their listeners would want; and some on the easy availability of "consulting fees" to focus their attention on particular records and the offerings of particular labels. This last was a type of petty bribery endemic to commercial situations in which supply outstrips demand, but broadcasting was a public trust, and "payola," as the newspapers called it, resonated with broader American anxieties about the corruption of the young by the mass media. In 1959, at a broadcasting convention in Miami Beach, the levels of consulting among disc jockeys reached truly saturnalian proportions, as reported by *Time* magazine in a story titled "Booze, Broads, and Payola." Capitalizing on the sudden aura of scandal, the American Society of Composers, Authors, and Publishers appealed to the courts and lobbied Congress to bring honor and decency back to the music business. In response, a congressional committee that was already making headlines with its investigation into television's high-stakes, prime-time game shows opened hearings and summoned witnesses. Editorialists across America came to the triumphant conclusion that rock music was such patent garbage that they had to *pay* people to play it on the air, and legislation was eventually passed that was designed to curb the peddling of influence in the broadcasting business. By that time, however, most music radio stations had already taken steps to clean up their act.

Many of the larger stations responded by adopting a format called Top Forty radio, which had been pioneered in the 1950s by a chain of stations in the South. The Top Forty format took responsibility for what went out over the air away from a station's disc jockeys and placed it in the hands of a technocratic-sounding figure called a "program director." Playlists became increasingly restricted and systematized. The essence of the Top Forty concept (which had existed in principle since the advent of the Hit Parade in the 1940s) was a demonstrable link between the amount of airplay a record received and its position on the national sales charts tabulated each week by the trade magazines *Billboard* and *Cashbox*. Based on surveys of selected record stores and radio stations, the charts reflected how well a record was selling, and how much airplay it was receiving, relative to other records; no actual numbers were involved, and there remained considerable room for speculation as to which records were gaining or losing strength. The new system was clearly less responsive to the influence of a record company sales representative with a roll of fifty-dollar bills. But thanks to the circular relationship between airplay and record sales, it remained open to distortions and manipulations of a more subtle sort. The charts favored records that did well in big urban markets where the promotional budgets and efficient distribution systems of the major record labels could have a pronounced effect. Moreover, because every Top Forty station in the country was ostensibly basing its playlist on the same criteria, program directors across America found themselves relying on the actual playlists of successful Top Forty stations in major markets, whose program directors, with millions of dollars in advertising revenue at stake, were presumably more adept at gauging the winds of public taste. The biggest radio market of them all was New York City.

The rise of Top Forty radio set off a ratings war in the New York metropolitan area, with three of the city's big AM stations—WMCA, WINS, and WABC—competing for the largest listening audience in the country. Since all three stations were playing essentially the same music, the competition centered on promotions, personalities, and packaging: the frenetic ambience of banter, sound effects, and raving nonsense that resulted from the efforts of adults to compete for the attention of teenagers. As the "flagship station" of one of America's vestigial radio net-works, WABC was the most closely watched of the three combatants, especially once it began winning the ratings war, its powerful signal pulling in listeners from Boston to the Carolinas. WABC's success was all the more dramatic because it had performed so poorly during the 1950s by sticking with an outdated format of live music and variety shows. It converted to Top Forty in the fall of 1960, and within two years had turned itself into the most profitable station in the country. When the three hundred affiliates of the ABC radio network saw this turnaround, many of them became converts to the Top Forty format as well, basing their playlists on the flagship station in New York. By the end of 1963, it could be said that if a record made it on WABC, it had made it in America. As yet, however, nobody knew what this marketing mechanism could do for a record that excited listeners the way "Heartbreak Hotel" had excited them in 1956. In other words, a record that didn't just catch their attention, but stopped them in their tracks.

18

So this is America. They all seem out of their minds.

—Ringo Starr

On December 1, 1963, three weeks after his inconclusive meeting with Brian Epstein, Brown Meggs opened his copy of the Sunday *New York Times Magazine* to find an article by Frederick Lewis titled "Britons Succumb to Beatlemania." Illustrated with black-and-white photographs of the Beatles chatting with Princess Margaret and of their fans battling with police, this article, while neither long nor prominently featured, was still an extraordinary piece of publicity in an era when newspapers like the *Times* rarely reported on the vagaries of popular music for teenagers. Even so, the impact of the *Times* piece on Meggs and his colleagues at Capitol Records paled before that of an article that appeared a few days later on the front page of the show-business weekly *Variety* announcing that the Beatles' latest single, "I Want to Hold Your Hand," had just become the first record ever issued in Britain to sell a million copies (based on wholesale orders) *prior to its release*—a feat that had previously been accomplished only once in the American market, by Elvis Presley in 1957 with his double-sided hit "Hound Dog" b/w "Don't Be Cruel." *Variety* went on to report that sales of the Beatles' previous single, "She Loves You," had also passed the one-million mark, and that their second British album had sold a half-million copies in the first week of its release. This meant that in a market one-third the size of the United States, the Beatles had released as many million-selling singles in 1963 as the entire American recording industry. It also meant that "I Want to Hold Your Hand" was arguably the fastest-selling single ever released in any market, anywhere, and now, with a kind of idiot's delight, it dawned on the men who ran Capitol Records that the rights to sell it in the United States were theirs for the asking.

Thus in a matter of days was Capitol consumed by a spirit of born-again Beatlemania. The company's president, Alan J. Livingston, contacted Brian Epstein in London and explained that his A&R staff had indeed discerned something in "I Want to Hold Your Hand" that had been lacking in the group's previous offerings. Capitol wanted to release the song as a single in the middle of January 1964, followed by an album whose arrival in stores would be timed to coincide with the group's appearance on *The Ed Sullivan Show* in the first week of February. As a sign of his company's commitment, Livingston agreed to budget $40,000 for a publicity campaign that would start with the placement of full-page ads in the trade journals *Billboard* and *Cash Box* around the first of the year. This campaign, which was to be concentrated in the New York metropolitan area, would eventually include the distribution of a half-million stickers reading "The Beatles Are Coming!" (an allusion to Paul Revere) and large quantities of a mock-newspaper called the *National Record News,* whose one and only edition would carry the headline BEATLEMANIA SWEEPS U.S. Capitol also informed its sales staff that, come January, they would be issued Beatle wigs that they would be expected to wear throughout the business day. ("You'll find you're help-ing to start the Beatle Hair-Do Craze that should be sweeping the coun-try soon," read a memo to the company's regional sales managers.) Finally, an extensive press kit was prepared for distribution to radio sta-tions across the country.

As the sales and publicity departments of Capitol Records marshaled their promotional resources, however, interest in the Beatles in America was gaining a momentum of its own. On December 10, the *CBS Evening News* aired a film clip of the group performing in Britain amid scenes of fan hysteria. Alerted by the broadcast, a disc jockey at a Top Forty station in Washington, D.C., obtained a Parlophone pressing of "I Want to Hold Your Hand" from an obliging airline stewardess and began to play it over the air, generating an immediate listener response. Tapes of this renegade copy were soon being broadcast by other Top Forty stations in Chicago and St. Louis. Reports of this groundswell prompted Capitol Records to accelerate the release date of "I Want to Hold Your Hand" from the mid-dle of January to the day after Christmas and to distribute advance copies of the single to radio stations across the country. Capitol also made arrangements to manufacture the single in huge quantities if the demand warranted.

"Extraordinary how potent cheap music is," Noël Coward famously wrote in *Private Lives.* Even more than "Please Please Me" or "She Loves You" in Britain, it was a single song, "I Want to Hold Your Hand," that catalyzed the Beatles' success in the United States. By the first week of

January, when the television host Jack Paar trumped his rival Ed Sullivan by showing a British film clip of the Beatles performing "She Loves You" on his Friday-evening variety show, the single, though still uncharted, was being played on radio stations across the country. It entered the charts the following week and began a precipitous climb that threw the whole Top Forty system into overdrive. Two weeks later, having already sold nearly a million copies, it stood at number one. ("Heartbreak Hotel," by comparison, had taken almost three months to rise to number one.) As the orders poured in, Capitol began to subcontract the manufacture of the single to its rivals' pressing plants so as to devote its full production capacity to the rush-release of a half-million copies of an album called *Meet the Beatles,* its cover and some of its content taken from the group's second Parlophone LP, which reached stores in the third week of January. By that time, both Vee-Jay and Swan were scrambling to rerelease "Please Please Me," "She Loves You," and the other Beatles recordings that had fallen on deaf ears in 1963.

As a wider selection of the Beatles' music became available, radio stations in New York and other major markets, inspired by unprecedented levels of listener response in the form of letters and telephone calls, began to adapt their formats to the promotion of the group. They played "I Want to Hold Your Hand" with the regularity of a news bulletin or a weather report. They sponsored Beatle-related contests and giveaways and incorporated the band's name into their station identification blurbs ("WA-Beatle-C"). They also made imaginative use of a prerecorded interview record, furnished by Capitol, which enabled disc jockeys to act as if they were conversing with the Beatles on the air, thereby providing American teenagers with their first exposure to the "sweet-sour" sound (as *Vogue* described it) of the group's Scouse accents. With the big Top Forty stations functioning as 50,000-watt fan clubs, WABC alone estimated that it was receiving three thousand Beatles-related letters a day. By the first of February, with the Beatles' materialization on American soil still a week away, "I Want to Hold Your Hand" had sold a million and a half copies nationwide, half a million in the New York metropolitan area alone. Never before had the capacity of radio to provide publicity for a record worked to such dramatic effect. The enthusiasm for the single had spread so quickly that it eluded the seismographic attention of teen marketing specialists like Gilbert Youth Research, whose founder would later express concern at "having missed the Beatle thing."

The little song at the center of it all had the same choppy beat, double lead vocal, and requisite falsetto gesture as all the other eager offspring of "Please Please Me." In his initial effort to persuade Capitol to release the record, Brian Epstein had claimed it was written with "the American market" in mind. If there was any truth to this, Epstein may have been referring to its use of a twelve-bar verse-refrain structure that was modeled on some recent Motown hits. But the more novel and compelling feature of "I Want to Hold Your Hand" was its incorporation of a harmonized release, which, for the first time on a Beatles single, supplied a strong musical and emotional contrast to the overall exuberance of the song. It begins with a rapid buildup of harshly syncopated accents over a grinding rhythm guitar—once, twice, three times—as if the song itself were shuddering to life on a cold January morning. On the third try the music seems to catch and take hold, the band humming with efficiency as John and Paul, singing in unison, enter on the line, "Yeah . . . well . . . I'll . . . tell you something, I think you'll understand." The rich melodic texture of their singing sounds almost wasted on a lyric that seems to revel in its own inexpressiveness, consisting mainly of liberal reiterations of the title line. But then, after two verses, the driving rhythm evaporates, the harmony shifts to D minor, and a stillness overtakes the song. "And when I touch you I feel happy—inside," the Beatles sing with an air of utter conviction. "It's such a feeling that my love, I can't hide, I can't *hide*, I can't hide!" The vocal harmony widens from a third to fifth as this last phrase crescendoes into a shout over the syncopated accents of the song's introduction. Then the whole progression repeats, verse and middle and verse again, to end on a string of slow, quarter-note triplets, triumphant and playfully grand.

Every pop generation reserves the right to disparage the musical taste of its offspring. When Frank Sinatra libeled rock 'n' roll as the music of "every sideburned delinquent on the face of the earth," he was only echoing the sort of condemnation that had been directed at his own singing and personal appearance a decade before. The Beatles' music, like that of Sinatra and Presley before them, was similarly dismissed and ridiculed. "High-pitched, loud beyond reason, and stupefyingly repetitive," was *Newsweek*'s initial assessment. "The pretext of a connection with the world of music was perfunctorily sustained," added the *New York Times*. A great many adult Americans in 1964—white or black, hip or square—

drew the line at rock 'n' roll, the sound of which was sufficiently divorced from prevailing notions of what was musically pleasing that even those with no particular cultural ax to grind often had trouble making sense of what they were hearing. A common source of incomprehension involved what Capitol Records' own Dave Dexter had described as the "juvenile and repetitive" nature of rock lyrics, most of which bore little resemblance to the style of romantic sophistication associated with Cole Porter, Ira Gershwin, and the other Tin Pan Alley masters of the 1930s and 1940s. With its tongue-tied verses and its repetitive refrain, the lyrics to "I Want to Hold Your Hand" were simplistic even by the Beatles' standards, and the song was roundly mocked for its apparent intention to reduce the rapture of romantic love to a childish matter of holding hands.

For teenagers who had come of age to the sound of backbeat drumming and electric guitars, however, the statement the Beatles were making on "I Want to Hold Your Hand" was loud and clear. All of the musical attributes that contributed to the success of their previous hit singles in Britain applied to "I Want to Hold Your Hand." In this case, however, the explosive energy of their playing and collective exuberance of their singing were harnessed to a single image that distilled physical contact between two people down to its simplest, most elemental form. The lyrics to "I Want to Hold Your Hand" conveyed both the awkwardness and exhilaration of the first moments of physical intimacy. It was a theme perfectly suited to the song's intended role as a calling card for the Beatles in America. And by not putting too fine a point on it, the artless lyric left itself open to a wider range of meanings—to implications of comfort, reassurance, and even consolation that drew on the image of holding hands as a common denominator of human connection between friends and lovers alike.

It is easy to recognize in retrospect that "I Want to Hold Your Hand," despite its limitations, was an exceptionally powerful pop record. Yet its musical attributes alone do not account for its astonishing popular success. For it was not the Beatles' music that had changed so dramatically in the six weeks that elapsed between Brian Epstein's visit to New York in the middle of November and the surge of popular enthusiasm for the group that erupted around the first of the year. It was rather the very tenor of life in America that had changed, with an almost unimaginable suddenness, on the afternoon of November 22, 1963.

•   •   •   •   •

"WE FEEL AS if the heart has been cut out of us," Lady Bird Johnson, the wife of the new President, told Rose Kennedy, the mother of the murdered President, on the evening of that day. "He was *so* living, and then 'poof,' he's dead," a junior high school student wrote in a class essay two months later. Some of the stunning impact of the assassination of John F. Kennedy on the American people stemmed from the way the news from Dallas resonated with an inchoate sense of vulnerability and apocalyptic dread that had been building steadily during the first fifteen years of the Cold War. Some of it had to do with the way Kennedy's princely aura of youth and good looks and vitality had come to personify for many Americans their country's most hopeful and flattering vision of itself. And some of it stemmed from the fact that never before in history had the means existed by which the people of an entire country could simultaneously bear witness to an event such as this. From the moment the CBS News anchorman Walter Cronkite broke into the noonday broadcast of the soap opera *As the World Turns* with the first reports of "shots fired" in Dallas, the unprecedented sense of interruption generated by the assassination and its immediate aftermath was amplified beyond all measure by its presentation on television—the medium whose very sameness and predictability had caused it to become, over the preceding decade, a prime source of continuity in so many American lives. Through countless nightly punch-outs and shoot-outs, television had ensured with absolute certainty that Good prevailed over Evil in the end, and that control, in the form of the ubiquitous "word from our sponsor," was reasserted with a strict and comforting regularity. Now, in a flash, for the first time ever, the commercials stopped. Under the strain of that afternoon in Dallas, the electronic window on the world cracked, flooding the living rooms of America with a tableau of unmediated shock and grief. For upward of eight and ten and twelve hours a day, men and women, boys and girls, watched the little screen as they had never watched anything before.

In the fragile climate of official reassurance that followed this deathly spectacle, attention was paid to the effect of what was described as a "television wake." The theory was that television's three full days of unblinking coverage had provided a form of therapy equal to the grief, enabling the stunned nation to get back quickly on its feet. As seen on TV, the return to normality was only slightly less sudden than the news of the assassination itself, and within a week, a concerted national effort was under way to accentuate the positive. The news media busied themselves with stories about the new president and the many challenges he faced. The commercials jabbered on as before. And, to judge by the results of numerous public-opinion surveys that were published after the fact, although Americans of all ages, races, classes, and political persuasions described themselves as more affected by the assassination than by any other public (or, said half of those in one survey, private) event they could name, the recovery from these feelings of shock and grief was far more rapid than would be expected in instances of actual personal loss. The principal exception to this pattern of rapid recovery, however, was among teenagers.

> I just didn't want to believe it. . . . At first I thought it was a prank of some radio station. Then it became real because every station was giving the news. . . . I was feeling the whole world is about to collapse on me. . . . I never felt so empty in my life. . . . I wanted to talk to somebody to see how they felt about it, and to see if other kids were as concerned about it as I was. . . . As I watched television and saw over and over the scenes of the assassination and the highlights of President Kennedy's career, I realized more and more what a horrible thing had happened. . . . I can remember how all the people around me felt, the same as I. . . . All the happiness of his family was gone in a few horrible minutes. . . . Things like that don't happen in this day and age in this country. . . . Please Lord, tell me this was a publicity stunt.

These words are drawn from essays written by students aged twelve to fourteen at a suburban New York junior high school in January 1964— just as the first wave of Beatlemania was breaking on American shores. Collected in a study titled *Children and the Death of a President* (1965), the essays, together with interviews and clinical observations, provided the source material for a chapter in which the noted child psychologist Martha Wolfenstein addressed the effects of the assassination on American adolescents. What most impressed Wolfenstein about the reaction of her teenage subjects to John F. Kennedy's death was, first, the sheer intensity of their response, which conformed to the standard psychological profile of deeply personalized grief; and, second, the fact that these intense feelings of grief did not appear to diminish or resolve nearly as quickly as those of the other Americans surveyed. The obvious explanation was that these teenagers had formed a deeper affective bond with the figure of President Kennedy, felt the impact of his murder more strongly, and took longer to recover from his death. Wolfenstein accepted the validity of this explanation. But as an experienced child psychologist, she was surprised by the intensity with which these feelings were expressed in the essays and interviews, since adolescents are known for the marked inhibition of their response to loss and grief. To account for the uncharacteristic demonstrativeness of her subjects, Wolfenstein suggested that the assassination presented an opportunity for what she termed "mourning at a distance." For young adolescents immersed in the psychological work of separating from their parents, she wrote, "the sudden death of the President provided an occasion for experiencing in an exceptionally dramatic and concentrated way some of the feelings of loss, and of having to give up elders to whom they have been attached, that usually go on in a diffuse, muddled, chronic, and episodic way over many years." Her point seems especially well taken in view of Kennedy's carefully crafted public image as an idealized parent as well as a figure of ultimate political authority.

Something else that impressed Wolfenstein about the reactions of her teenage subjects was the persistence of their disbelief, reiterated months after the event in their essays and interviews. In contrast to the reactions of the other Americans surveyed (including younger children), something seemed to be drawing the adolescents in her study back into their initial sense of shock and incredulity. Wolfenstein attributed this to their emotional immaturity, but here her insight may have been limited by her focus on Kennedy as a father figure and her failure to recognize the full extent of the idealization he had represented for many American teenagers. For this particular President was not only a figure of ultimate political and parental authority but also a charismatic star: a role model, ego ideal, and symbolic champion of personal autonomy whose sudden, violent death had the power to force a confrontation not only with the loss of a parent but also, on a level that could not be acknowledged directly, with one's own mortality as well. "If he wasn't safe, no one was," recalled the journalist Jeff Greenfield, who was fifteen years old at the time, and while the statement makes little sense given the long history of presidential assassination in America, it conveys the feeling of personal vulnerability that many young people experienced.

Compounding the response of teenagers to Kennedy's death were feelings of a wholly different nature, arising from the sheer *excitement* of the assassination and its aftermath: the unprecedented sense of interruption, the feeling of witnessing history in the making, and the thrill of experiencing a connection, through the medium of television, to vast numbers of people who felt, as one of Wolfenstein's subjects wrote, "the same as I." Added to this was the lurid fascination with the forensic details of Kennedy's murder and that of his alleged assassin—this last an astonishing aftershock that mocked the efforts of local and national authorities to reassert control. Thus was the formulation that Leslie Fiedler had characterized as America's "new comedy: the dream of violence and the fact of security . . . the dream of failure and the fact of success," abruptly turned on its head. The violence of the American past had invaded the American present, confronting a generation of "television babies" with the first experience of real-life, real-time tragedy they had ever known. The august merger of politics and popular culture that John F. Kennedy had effected had now ended in the atavistic murder of the chief of state. For the millions of young people who had joined in the idealization of Kennedy and identified strongly with the aura of power and glamour he exuded, his sudden violent death generated a maelstrom of ambivalent "distress and enthusiasm" that no improvised ritual of a "television wake" could possibly resolve.

FOR AMERICAN TEENAGERS, the Beatles first appeared as shadowy figures on the periphery of this riveting national drama. Some would have seen the brief articles about the group's performance at the Royal Variety Show that ran in *Time* and *Newsweek* in the middle of November, a week before Kennedy's death. Some in the New York metropolitan area would have seen the article in *The New York Times Magazine* a week after the assassination—had their attention called to it by amused parents, even ("will you look at all that *hair!*")—or read the short pieces in *Vogue, Life,* and *The New Yorker* that appeared during the month of December. Most American teenagers would have seen none of this, however. Their first inkling of the Beatles came in the vacation week between Christmas and

New Year's when radio stations across the country began playing "I Want to Hold Your Hand." After the first of the year, as students returned from their Christmas break, the sound of the song on the radio was accompanied by the arrival of the record in stores, and word of the Beatles began to spread through the high schools and middle schools of America.

At the same time, as the American news media was busy recapping the events of 1963 with a fresh round of elegiac tributes to John F. Kennedy, Jack Paar's broadcast of a film clip of the Beatles singing "She Loves You" gave large numbers of young people their clearest glimpse to date, not only of the band performing, but also of their frenzied, screaming fans. This was followed in the middle of the month by Capitol's rush-release of the LP *Meet the Beatles.* From then until the group's arrival in February, this album would serve as the focal point of Beatlemania in America. By buying it, as more than half a million people did during its first week of release, fans felt that they were affirming their participation in the Beatles phenomenon as well. On its cover, Robert Freeman's somber black-and-white photograph was providentially in tune with the contemporary American mood. ("Laughing in public, if you can, instead of worrying or crying alone is 'in,' " *Seventeen* magazine lamely advised its readers in its January issue.) Volumes could be read into the shadowy half-light of that album cover: shades of empathy, sensitivity, and, above all, an uncanny feeling of mystery. The liner notes that Capitol Records added to the back of the album cover described the Beatles as "the biggest, hottest property in the history of English show business." Musicians enjoying that kind of success really ought to be smiling, and a smaller photograph on the back of the album cover showed the Beatles doing just that. But it was the picture on the front cover that captivated its young viewers with its implication that there was another side to this music and the success that came with it. Who were these people? Where did they come from? And why should they come to us now?

THE TELEGRAM CONFIRMING that "I Want to Hold Your Hand" had risen to number one on the American pop charts reached the Beatles in the third week of January at their hotel in Paris, where they were spending the second half of the month performing an extended engagement at the venerable Olympia Theatre. Immune to the Beatles' verbal charm and chauvinistically unimpressed by their success in Britain, the French press had given the group a rough reception. "Their ye-ye is the worst we have heard," declared *France-Soir,* while *Le Monde* compared the sound of their music to that of an elevated train (this from a paper whose music critic had recently praised the American teen idol Paul Anka as "the Mozart of rock 'n' roll"). Any damage to the Beatles' pride, however, was amply offset by the news from the United States, which was soon substantiated by the arrival of a pack of American reporters and photographers, dispatched by their New York editors to collect quotations, pictures, and background material for the feature stories that were now being prepared in anticipation of the group's upcoming visit. By the time they left London for New York on the morning of February 7, 1964, the Beatles' success in America was a *fait accompli.* Yet the utter unreality of the situation as seen from their point of view—the idea that, in the span of a month, they had come to dominate the popular record market in the country that had served since 1956 as their musical land of dreams—caused them to be understandably nervous on their flight to New York. "They've got their own groups," said Paul McCartney. "What are we going to give them that they don't already have?" Two nights later, 70 million Americans tuned in to *The Ed Sullivan Show* in order to answer this question for themselves. It was the largest viewing audience in the history of commercial television, surpassed only by the audience that had gathered in November on the weekend when the commercials had stopped. Now, as Paul stepped up to the microphone and sang the words, "Close your eyes and I'll kiss you," the spell of fear and unreality was finally broken for America's 21 million teenagers. Eleven weeks after it began, the television wake was over, and the party had just begun.

The Ed Sullivan Show, *New York, February 1964*

19

Britain is in a revolutionary situation without any revolutionary grievances—a generation of Iagos are tempting each other with violence while we Othellos sit at home by the telly with Desdemona, fascinated and amazed. . . . The Affluent Decade has returned to the habits of earlier centuries when the lusty rogues, the masterless men, the idle apprentices, the unemployed artisans and the City mob regularly terrorized the respectable.

—Alan Brien

"England exploded, didn't it? I don't know when . . ." Paul McCartney remarked in an interview with the magazine *London Life* in 1965. Paul's haziness as to the exact timing of the explosion could be explained by his presence at what the *Daily Mail* had termed "the calm eye of the storm"—for most young people in Britain, the first flash of light and roar of sound had been the outbreak of Beatlemania in the fall of 1963. By revealing the international dimensions of the country's pop boom, the Beatles' visit to New York in the winter of 1964 had counted as a second major explosion. A third shock came in the spring, when fighting broke out between rival groups of Mods and Rockers at the seaside resort of Clacton on the Easter weekend in March and continued at the Channel coast towns of Margate and Brighton in May.

At its height, the Mod-Rocker mayhem involved no more than a few hundred teenagers milling around the beaches and boardwalks on a cloudy holiday weekend, waiting for a little recreational "bother" to erupt. There were few serious injuries, and the lone fatality involved a hapless Mod who fell asleep drunk on the edge of a cliff at Margate and had the misfortune to roll over in the night. Yet the disturbances provoked a storm of indignation, as the press, local officials, members of Parliament, and a vocal segment of the general public reacted to this outbreak of hooliganism with a vengeance that took the whole country by surprise.

An editorial in the local Brighton paper described the occurrences there as "without parallel in British history." An editorial in the *Daily Telegraph* characterized the antagonists as "grubby hordes of louts and sluts." An editorial in the *Evening Standard* decried the participants' "innumerable boring emotional complexes, their vicious thuggishness which is not cunning but a more bovine stupidity, their ape-like reactions to the world around them." The *Daily Mail* blanketed newsstands with an aerial photograph of the rioting on the beaches beneath a banner headline that read GOTHS BY THE SEA. The police were lionized for their efforts to stem the tide of barbarism, and a local magistrate in Margate, Dr. George Simpson, was hailed as a hero for the harsh sentences and even harsher rhetoric he handed down from the bench. In the course of fining one young man who had just pled guilty to the charge of engaging in "threatening behavior," Dr. Simpson, in his most famous statement, was moved to say, "It is not likely that the air of this town has ever been polluted by the hordes of hooligans, male and female, such as we have seen this weekend and of whom you are an example. These long-haired, mentally unstable, petty little hoodlums, these sawdust Caesars who can only find courage like rats, in hunting in packs, came to Margate with the avowed intent of interfering with the life and liberty of its inhabitants."

As starkly as the Mod-Rocker fighting dramatized the socially aggressive tendencies of Britain's working-class youth—tendencies that were already well known to several generations of dance-hall patrons and football fans—it exposed what the conservative pundit Henry Fairlie, writing in *The Spectator,* termed the "savagery" of adult reactions to the young. What disturbed Fairlie was the way the Mod-Rocker violence served segments of the adult population as an "excuse for rage" at the social assertiveness and simple youthfulness of the young. Some of this rage was a predictable backlash at the recent orgy of enthusiasm for the Beatles, who had been painted by the press as such an idealized picture of British youth. And some of it was attributable to the attitude expressed by Alan Brien, among many others, that *these* young people, unlike the strikers and dissidents and have-nots of earlier decades, had nothing much to complain about or to revolt against. On the contrary, their problem was widely understood to be one of too much discretionary income and too much idle time. Products of Harold Macmillan's Age of Affluence, these ungrateful teenagers, in the view of many adult Britons, had had it altogether *too* good.

The animosity between the Mods and the Rockers was real enough—a tribal conflict between the Cro-Magnons and Neanderthals of working-class youth culture. Yet the outraged responses of public officials and editorial writers helped to transform an outbreak of internecine warfare into a more archetypal confrontation between Youth and Age. For the Mods particularly (and Mods were by far the larger and more ascendant faction), these seminal seashore battles took on a kind of Homeric aspect in the year ahead, as the glare of media attention provided Britain's working-class modernists with the sense of grievance they had previously lacked. Intoxicated by the publicity, the Mods began to fancy themselves not only as dedicated followers of fashion and music but as an ad-hoc social "movement" as well. In years to come, thousands of British Mods would recount their presence on the sands of Clacton with the same fraudulent awe as the thousands of Irish patriots who claimed to have been barricaded inside the Dublin Post Office during a previous Easter uprising, half a century before.

On the same March weekend that the Mod-Rocker fighting first erupted at Clacton, Radio Caroline began broadcasting—to the tune of "Can't Buy Me Love"—from a ship anchored in the North Sea, just outside the British territorial limit. In contrast to the ad-hoc nature of the Mod-Rocker affront to authority, Radio Caroline was a calculated challenge to the most esteemed of British cultural institutions, the BBC. The station and the whole "pirate radio" phenomenon it initiated was a response to the government's decision in the 1950s to maintain its monopoly over radio broadcasting, notwithstanding the introduction of independent commercial TV. Named after the daughter of the late President Kennedy, Radio Caroline was conceived by a well-connected young Irishman named Ronan O'Rahilly, who had previously worked as the manager of a Mod nightclub called The Scene, and who was backed by a group of investors that included Jocelyn Stevens, editor of the fashion and society magazine *Queen*. Unconstrained by any restrictions on the amount of recorded or imported music it could play, Radio Caroline began by broadcasting an eclectic mix of pop, jazz, ballads, and show tunes that attracted a daily listenership of 7 million people in a matter of weeks. It was soon joined by a flotilla of imitators, including a more professional, high-powered, and pop-oriented station, Radio London, which barraged the South of England with an Americanized Top Forty format. By the end of 1964 a half-dozen pirate stations were in operation, bobbing up and down off the coast of Britain, playing whatever they pleased.

Still another manifestation of the newly assertive style of British pop culture was the television program *Ready, Steady, Go!,* which began its run on the commercial channel in August 1963. The original concept of *RSG* was to update the usual dance-party format of teen television with some of the quasi-Brechtian production values associated with *That Was the Week That Was.* As it happened, however, the debut of the program was perfectly synchronized with the start of the pop boom signaled by the release of "She Loves You," and by the spring of 1964 it had been appropriated by the Mods, who garrisoned its studio audience every Friday evening with a regiment of the sharpest-dressing, best-dancing teenagers in London—kids who saw pop television as a more suitable way of attracting attention than getting tossed into a police van in Margate and winding up on the front page of the *Daily Mirror.* Their dances, poses, and preferences in music and fashion were relayed instantly across Britain in a format catalyzed by the winning personality of the show's host, a coltish nineteen-year-old named Cathy McGowen. Giggly in manner and gangly in stance, McGowen became a representative figure; to the kids in the *RSG* audience, she was clearly one of their own. She was also, self-evidently, a *girl,* at a time when—apart from the mute, somnambulistic corps of celebrity fashion models—there were very few living, breathing, individualized girls to be found in a milieu of pop culture that was now more than ever dominated by the cult of the postadolescent male. By the way she gushed and giggled and generally interacted with the guests and fans on her show, McGowen came to exert a formative influence on a generation of British girls.

All told, 1964 constituted the populist phase of the sociocultural phenomenon *Time* magazine, two years hence, would immortalize as Swinging London. It was the year that youth culture in Britain conclusively shed its modesty, its camouflage, its subversive note of compliance with the expectations of the adult world. From the headlines of the tabloids, from the blaring of the pirate radio stations, from the weekly broadcasts of *Ready, Steady, Go!* and the proliferation of new clothing boutiques and dance clubs, came an impression shared by young and old that London was suddenly filling up with dandified boys in provocatively long hair and gamine girls in provocatively short skirts.

Metropolitan London actually *was* filling up, its resident population of nearly 2 million young people in their teens and twenties swelled by the arrival of tens of thousands more, many of them just out of school, a high proportion of them girls, who were streaming into the capital from provincial cities and towns. These newcomers found work in shops and offices and gradually assimilated into a thriving bedsitter culture that, for the girls especially, was like an outgrowth of the bedroom culture of 1963: Beatlemania on a residential scale. The concerted presence of Youth was conspicuous to say the least, and to walk among the boutiques in Carnaby Street or Kings Road, Chelsea, or to see the Mods crowding around the entrances to their cellar clubs in Soho, was to be struck by the feeling that a social or cultural revolution of *some* kind was under way.

The sense of social and cultural ferment in the city reached well beyond its population of teenagers. London during the spring and summer of 1964 was flush with the possibility that the recent explosion of interest in pop music and fashion would prove to be an outcropping of a still larger and more diverse vein of working-class aspiration and ability. There was excitement in the visual arts, as British Pop painters like David Hockney, Bridget Riley, and Peter Blake achieved the status of media celebrities. There was excitement in the film industry, spurred by ever-increasing levels of American investment and the international success of British actors and British films. And there was a particular excitement in the London theater, centering on a series of radical productions by the Royal Shakespeare Company and the outrageous debut of the playwright Joe Orton, whose sexual farce *Entertaining Mr. Sloan* elicited nothing but strong opinions when it opened in the West End in May. ("I feel as if snakes had been writhing round my feet," wrote the critic for the *Daily Telegraph;* "A disgusting piece of filth," added the playwright himself, pseudonymously, in a letter to the same paper.)

The celebration of "classlessness" reached its height around this time. Classlessness could refer to the merger of ambitious lower-middle-class talent and upper-class bohemianism represented by the partnership of the fashion designer Mary Quant and her entrepreneurial husband, Alexander Plunkett Greene. It could describe the alliance of puckish Northern charm and fresh-faced Southern gentility represented by the liaison of Paul McCartney and his actress girlfriend Jane Asher, the daughter of a prominent London psychiatrist. It could even apply, at the most rarefied level, to the Royal marriage of Princess Margaret and Lord Snowden, the former Anthony Armstrong-Jones, a fashion photographer and art director of *Queen*. In theory, classlessness was supposed to describe a new indifference to the long-standing British obsession with social origins. In practice, it often came down to a simple inversion of the traditional social and geographic hierarchies. "I'm very conscious of it, because it makes me seem all the brighter and cleverer and more 'super' to have come from the muck of the North," explained Margaret Foster, author of the best-selling novel *Georgy Girl*. "I'm received in some places as the Duke of Cockney," said the film actor Michael Caine. In accordance with this new system of peerage, the Beatles reigned as the Royal Scouse Family of pop.

20

On that first day I met the Beatles, they had just gotten
back from Sweden and I asked John, "Did you like Sweden?" And he said, "Yes, very much. It was a car and a
room and a room and a car and we had cheese sand-
wiches sent up to the hotel."

—Richard Lester

The offer to make a feature film had come to the Beatles and Brian
Epstein in October 1963 from a major American studio, United Artists,
which was interested in making a low-budget movie musical that would
give the company's record division a chance to market a Beatles soundtrack album in the United States. That an American film studio would be
sanguine about the commercial prospects of the Beatles in America at a
time when Capitol Records couldn't have cared less was largely a function of UA's intensive involvement in the British entertainment industry
since 1961, when it opened a production office in London, headed by an
American named George Ornstein. In 1962, Ornstein delivered the first
of the James Bond films, *Dr. No.* In 1963 he delivered a second, even
more successful Bond picture, along with the Woodfall production of
Tom Jones, which went on to win the Academy Award for Best Picture in
the United States. When the Beatles became a sensation in Britain in the
fall of 1963, Ornstein was on the ground in London, watching it happen,
and he wasted no time in authorizing an independent producer named
Walter Shenson to approach Brian Epstein with a proposal for the Beatles to star in a black-and-white film to be made on a shoestring budget of
half a million dollars.

Shenson, like Ornstein, was an American living in London. A former
publicist for Columbia Pictures, he had gone to Britain in 1959 to produce *The Mouse That Roared,* starring Peter Sellers, the success of which
earned Shenson a reputation as a man who knew how to market British-
made films to American audiences. In 1962, Shenson produced a sequel
called *The Mouse on the Moon,* this time without Sellers, and without

success. But the sequel was directed by a young American named Richard Lester, and when Ornstein approached Shenson with the idea of a Beatles film, Shenson thought of Lester to direct.

Born and raised in Philadelphia, Richard Lester had worked at a local television station before moving to London in 1955. Within a year he gravitated into the orbit of the Goons, with whom he made two short-lived television series (*Idiot's Weekly* and *A Show Called Fred*) and a sur-realistic home movie, set in an empty field, called *The Running Jumping and Standing Still Film,* which went on to earn a cult following in the United States and an Academy Award nomination for Best Short Feature in 1959. In 1962 he directed his first feature film, *It's Trad, Dad!,* a low-budget musical starring Helen Shapiro and such leading lights of the trad boom as Acker Bilk, Chris Barber, and the Temperance Seven. *It's Trad, Dad!* had all the makings of a typical teen exploitation film, yet, thanks to Lester, the filming of the musical sequences was very cleverly done, and the movie contained unexpected touches of satire and surrealism (includ-ing the use of a narrator to lend the picture a tone of journalistic exposé). Later that year, on Peter Sellers's recommendation, Lester was hired to direct *The Mouse on the Moon.* By demonstrating his knack for the pre-sentation of both pop music and comedy, these two films convinced Wal-ter Shenson that Lester was the man to direct the Beatles on the screen. As had happened with George Martin before him, Lester's record of ser-vice with the Goons convinced the Beatles of the same thing.

Thus did a thirty-two-year-old expatriate American join the small cir-cle of skilled facilitators whose talents would prove instrumental to the Beatles' success. Like Brian Epstein, George Martin, and Robert Free-man, Dick Lester was sincere and unpatronizing in his appreciation of the group. He identified with them, delighted in them, and took an anar-chic pleasure from his involvement with them. He resembled Epstein in his desire to distance himself from the hacks of his trade ("Directing films is really a job for a dilettante," he once said). He resembled Martin in having gained from his experience with the Goons a fluid, improvisa-tional approach to his work. And, much like Robert Freeman, Lester was brimming with the sensibility of a new generation of Anglo-American artists and intellectuals who were rebelling against the high seriousness of modernism and turning with an amused and ironic eye to the world of popular culture as a suitable arena for their talents. Richard Lester was one of the people, in 1964, who were helping to turn pop into Pop.

The name of Alun Owen as a possible screenwriter for the film was mentioned by Brian Epstein and seconded by the Beatles at their first meeting with Walter Shenson in October 1963. Owen was a playwright in his mid-thirties who was best known for a series of Northern Realist television dramas that were set on Merseyside and filled with local color. Though John Lennon once described him as "a professional Liverpudlian" (like Lennon himself at the time), Owen's feeling for life in the city was more complex and less sentimental than that designation might imply. The Beatles' endorsement of Owen as their screenwriter said something about their own state of mind during a time when they, too, were leaving the city behind. His involvement ensured that the film, whatever else it was about, would present them as four sons of Liverpool.

Although the Beatles had neither the time nor the inclination to exert much direct influence on the content of their film, they had made it clear to Walter Shenson that they had no intention of making fools of themselves on the screen. They had no claim to being actors, but they did want their film to avoid what they saw as the embarrassing contrivance of movie musicals in general and of the Elvis films in particular. Dick Lester had already made use of mock-documentary effects in *It's Trad, Dad!* Now, Shenson, Owen, and Lester came up with the idea of having the Beatles portray themselves in a mock-documentary about life at the center of their pop phenomenon. Alun Owen was dispatched to observe the phenomenon firsthand during a weekend of concerts in Dublin, and came back sufficiently impressed by the claustrophobic "room and a car" nature of their existence to introduce the more serious notion of the Beatles as "prisoners of their success." During the winter of 1964, while the Beatles were performing in France and America, Shenson and Lester assembled a cast and crew. Wilfred Brambell, the crusty star of the popular BBC-TV series *Steptoe & Son,* was hired to play the part of Paul McCartney's fictitious grandfather. Norman Rossington was cast as the group's road manager, Victor Spinetti as a neurotic television director, and Kenneth Haigh as the producer of a teen television program modeled on *Ready, Steady, Go!* Gilbert Taylor, who had just finished filming Stanley Kubrick's *Dr. Strangelove,* was taken on as cinematographer. Meanwhile, at United Artists' offices in London and New York, George Ornstein and his colleagues were rubbing their hands in glee at the thought of what the Beatles' success in America would mean for the fortunes of the picture and the sales of its soundtrack LP.

Filming began at the beginning of March and continued for six weeks, shifting back and forth between the comparative calm of Twickenham Studios and the chaos of numerous locations around London. The location work was complicated by the fact that wherever the cameras were on a given day became the momentary epicenter of Beatlemania. But Richard Lester seemed to thrive on the circus atmosphere. ("It was like being at the center of the universe," he recalled.) He enjoyed working with the Beatles, not least because he had no expectation that they would perform like professional actors. Instead, as he described it, "the structure of the script had to be a series of one-liners. This enabled me, in many of the scenes, to turn a camera on them and say a line to them and they would say it back to me. If it didn't work out terribly well, I would say it another way and they would say it back another way."

THE SIX WEEKS the Beatles spent working on their film marked their longest uninterrupted stay in London since they had first begun coming to the city on a regular basis two years before. By this time the four of them had abandoned the hotel rooms they had occupied during their constant comings and goings over the course of 1963 in favor of slightly more permanent lodgings. John and Cynthia Lennon and their infant son, Julian, were living in a third-floor walk-up apartment in Kensington. Paul McCartney had more or less moved in with Jane Asher, who lived with her family in the West End. George Harrison and Ringo Starr shared a flat in Knightsbridge, in the same modern building as Brian Epstein, who was also in the process of relocating NEMS Enterprises from Liverpool to a suite of offices in the West End, directly next door to the Palladium Theater. In addition to the Beatles, NEMS was now representing a half-dozen acts, and its staff had grown to twenty-five employees.

In the middle of March, Beatlemania branched off in a new and still more unlikely direction with the simultaneous publication in Britain and America of a small book of whimsical prose and verse titled *John Lennon In His Own Write*. *In His Own Write*—the title and a brief introduction were supplied by Paul McCartney—was a collection of some thirty short pieces, each a page or two in length, with accompanying line drawings by the author. They were the sort of things Lennon had been turning out for his own amusement and that of his friends since his early teens, including several items drawn directly from his occasional column in *Mersey*

Beat. The style was one of incessant wordplay and inspired misspelling applied to the exploits of what one reviewer described as "a literal menagerie of creatures born on the blackboard during a break." Streams of punning and portmanteau words ran through the work, as well as an abundance of fashionable 1960s "sick" humor ("not even his wife's battered face could raise a smile on poor Frank's head," John wrote in "No Flies on Frank"). There was a story about a bucolic English village called Squirmly-on-the-Slug, a fan letter to a Reeperbahn-inspired rock group called Berneese und zee Rippers, and a passing reference to the Beatles' Royal patron, HRH Priceless Margarine.

The book sold hundreds of thousands of copies and received enthusiastic reviews in mainstream literary publications on both sides of the Atlantic. References were made to Lewis Carroll and Edward Lear, James Thurber and S. J. Perelman. Too much was said, on account of the puns, about James Joyce, and not nearly enough about Spike Milligan, whose *Goon Show* scripts had been Lennon's closest brush with the style of *Finnegans Wake,* and whose 1959 book, *Silly Verse for Kids,* was the direct antecedent to *In His Own Write.* In a bizarre sidelight, literary criticism of Lennon's book spilled over into the House of Commons, where an MP named Charles Curran recited several stanzas of a poem called "Deaf Ted, Danoota, and Me" during a debate on education policy. While explaining that he had personally "never seen or heard the Beatles," Curran read the poem to support his view that John Lennon, despite his obvious "feeling for words," had been consigned to "a state of pathetic near-literacy" by his defective education in Liverpool.

Basking in his new identity as the "literary Beatle," Lennon was discussing his book with Dick Lester on the set of the Beatles' film, which, for lack of a better idea, had a working title of *Beatlemania.* John was explaining to Lester that much of his wordplay and skewed syntax were derived from the way that ordinary people spoke in Liverpool; Ringo, for example, was often coming out with odd expressions and turns of phrase, or "Ringoisms" as the other Beatles called them. John pointed to one he had used in the book, in a story about "Sad Michael," who woke up sad one morning after "a hard day's night."

FROM THE PERSPECTIVE of United Artists, the Beatles' most important contribution to the film was the six original songs that would determine the musical structure of the picture and provide the company's record label with the soundtrack album that had inspired the project in the first place. Because the Beatles would have no time for recording once filming began in March, all six of those tracks, together with "Can't Buy Me Love" (which was added to the soundtrack) and "You Can't Do That," had to be completed in the week following the group's return from America in February 1964. The productivity of these sessions was enhanced by the recent installation of four-track recording equipment at EMI's Abbey Road studios. This new technology would ultimately revolutionize the Beatles' approach to making records. At this early stage, however, its main function was to reduce the margin of error by allowing for greater flexibility in the recording and mixing of the vocal and instrumental tracks.

In keeping with the lighthearted spirit of the film, most of the songs Lennon and McCartney wrote for the soundtrack were emotionally upbeat—no matter what they professed to be about. "Tell Me Why" is a mock-lament in the style of "Please Please Me" that toys halfheartedly with a theme of betrayal before yielding to a definitive moment of Beatle self-parody in the bridge, where John, Paul, and George answer the line "If you'll only listen to my pleas" by launching into giggling, girlish falsettos, their voices orbiting unintelligibly, up in the range of their fans. "I'm Happy Just to Dance With You" was written by John and Paul for George to sing in the film; it serves up its utilitarian sentiment with a hard beat and a crackling rhythm guitar part that sounds like somebody fiddling with an old radio dial on a stormy summer night. "I Should Have Known Better" is a supercharged variation on "Love Me Do," complete with a coy lyric, a wailing harmonica, and a double-tracked vocal from John on which he asserts his presence by sustaining the pronoun "I" for six full beats at the start of every verse.

Rounding out the soundtrack songs were a pair of romantic ballads that were designed to serve as musical set pieces for John and Paul in the film. John's "If I Fell" was a songwriting breakthrough for him: his first forthright expression of the soft core of emotional vulnerability that he otherwise sought to mask with bravado, insouciance, and wit. The song begins in a state of harmonic limbo, with an old-fashioned recitative introductory verse in which John's solo vocal is unaccompanied but for a series of diaphanous guitar chords that descend chromatically, leaving the key of the music obscure. The uncertainty in the harmony is beautifully matched to the uncertainty in a lyric that asks, "If I fell in love with you, would you promise to be true? And help *me*"—John's voice jumps an octave on this word, and nearly cracks—"understand / 'Cause I've been in love before, and I found that love is more / Than just holding hands." The allusion to "I Want to Hold Your Hand" was unmistakable to Beatle fans; it enlists the celebrated innocence of that earlier song to stand for an earlier, painfully naïve conception of love. Even more strikingly, it is on those words that the harmony of "If I Fell" finds its footing in the key of D major, as the bass and drums come in at surprisingly strong tempo, and John and Paul embark on the subtly harmonized duet that constitutes the body of the song. From the moment Paul's voice joins John's on the stately, rising melody, the whole tenor of the track changes. Their two parts do not move in simple parallel motion (like a couple holding hands); instead their voices perform an intricate courtship dance, ranging from a sixth to a third apart, alternately closing and widening the distance between them. "If I Fell" is a love song that seeks to move beyond the shaky ground of infatuation—beyond the very idea of *falling* (like the chords in the introduction) in love. By the last verse, the music sounds like a hymn, the singing an exchange of vows.

Paul's "And I Love Her" is a far more conventional love song than "If I Fell," if "conventional" is a strong enough word to describe a lyric so thoroughly steeped in the postulates of pop romance. (The song was a godsend to mainstream pop and jazz singers who wanted to update their repertoires with a Beatles tune.) In its Latin-flavored accompaniment of claves, bongos, and acoustic guitars, "And I Love Her" sounds like a homegrown version of "Till There Was You." The prettiness of the melody is balanced by the dryness of Paul's vocal delivery, while the banality of the lyric is offset by a lovely release in which the standard declaration of romantic immortality ("A love like ours could never die") is gently qualified by an acknowledgment of the need for physical proximity ("As long as I have you near me").

An added virtue of "And I Love Her" is George Harrison's understated solo, which is cued by a half-step key change and played with a pronounced rubato inflection on a classical (i.e., nylon-stringed) guitar. Beginning with "Can't Buy Me Love," George Martin had decided to make Harrison's soloing on record one of his pet projects in the year ahead. Rock-'n'-roll lead guitar playing was still in its infancy in 1964. The now-familiar techniques of sustaining, trilling, and bending notes that were developed by jazz and blues masters like Charlie Christian and

B.B. King were still a mystery to most young white guitarists of the time, and George, like all but a handful of his contemporaries, did not possess a great deal of melodic facility on the instrument. Previously, when he performed an extended solo—as opposed to the runs, licks, ostinatos, and other embellishments that formed his principal contribution to the Beatles' arrangements—his playing had tended to have more to do with the mechanics of the guitar than the particulars of the song. Now, in the studio, Martin began encouraging him to rely more on his ear than on his hands by keying off the melody and focusing his attention on the phrasing and timbre of his lines. Harrison proved an eager student. Over the course of 1964, he would add a bold new palette of tone colors to the Beatles' music, employing a variety of newly acquired electric guitars. The most distinctive-sounding of these was the Rickenbacker twelve-string electric, a recently invented instrument (a prototype of which had been given to George by the manufacturer) whose piercing "attack" and dense, piano-like overtones would provide Harrison's lead playing with a powerful new presence on record.

The sound of the Rickenbacker twelve-string figured prominently in a song that was added to the soundtrack of *A Hard Day's Night* almost as an afterthought. In April, shortly after Richard Lester and Walter Shenson had adopted Ringo's phrase as the title for the film, Shenson asked Lennon and McCartney to compose a title track, to be played over the credits at the beginning and end of the picture. To Shenson's amazement, in a matter of days the Beatles wrote and recorded an overture of soul-stirring intensity. Perhaps, after six long weeks of being told what to say and what to do on a daily basis, they saw this assignment as an opportunity to make their mark on the film, working in their own area of expertise. Whatever the source of their inspiration, the four of them had never spoken so eloquently on record before.

"A Hard Day's Night" unfolds like a pop-Freudian discourse on the themes of Work and Love, commuting between the economic world of the day and the emotional world of the night. It begins with a musical wake-up call: the harsh clang of a solitary guitar chord that hangs in the air for an elongated moment, its densely packed notes swimming into focus like eyes adjusting to the light. (Though the song is in the key of G, this opening chord is a D minor 11th, as if a C-major triad were being played over a D-minor triad.) Two bars later, reality rushes in, as John's vocal pickup ("It's been a . . .") is swept up and carried along by a swift current of guitars, bass, drums, rippling bongos, and cowbell. It's the rhythm from "Hitch-Hike" yet again, with the tempo turned up a notch, leaping off the record in a musical caricature of life in the fast lane. Against this unyielding rhythm, the verses unfold across twelve bars, like a blues. Each word of the repeated phrase "hard day's night" is seconded by the hard *thwop!* of Ringo's snare, while the narrow, conversational melody rises up and over the flatted seventh chord that sounds under "I've been work*ing*," before falling back resignedly, "like a dog." Paul adds a high harmony on the line beginning, "But when I get home to you," and then the pattern repeats. The second verse restates the transactional model of the first in even starker terms: he works all day for money to buy her things, while she, in turn, is going to give him "everything." But now a fresh voice—Paul's—bursts in, singing the praises of home and brimming with excitement at the prospect of "feeling you holding me tight, *tight,* yeah!" Through it all, Ringo labors below, his cymbals awash, his bass and snare lopping off great slabs of the beat. The momentum builds through another verse until, with a shout, the singers seem to leap out of the path of George Harrison's twelve-string electric guitar and George Martin's piano as they combine on a deep, bluesy run that resolves in a delighted little jig-step of sixteenth notes. The singing returns, the middle repeats, and finally, a full three minutes after it began, the song heads wearily for home, the band slowing imperceptibly, until the rhythm falls out and George's twelve-string explodes into the chord that opened the song—arpeggiated this time, its notes distinct and shimmering like stars against the sky.

21

"Are you a Mod or a Rocker?"

"No, I'm a Mocker."

—Ringo Starr, *A Hard Day's Night*

Between the completion of their work on *A Hard Day's Night* at the end of April and the release of the picture in July, the Beatles took a month-long vacation before embarking on the first leg of the regimen of international touring that would occupy their summers for several years to come. They began with concerts in Holland and Denmark, then flew to Hong Kong (still a Crown Colony at the time) as a prelude to two weeks of engagements in Australia and New Zealand. This "Far Eastern Tour" served as a striking demonstration of the international dimensions of the Beatlemania phenomenon. Of all the tumultuous public receptions the group would experience, nothing before or after, in terms of scale, would compare with what awaited them in Australia. As their newly hired press agent, Derek Taylor, observed, Australia turned out for the Beatles the way a Latin American country might turn out for the Pope. In each of the five cities they visited, they encountered vast crowds of teenagers, children, and adults. In Adelaide, a city of nearly a half-million inhabitants that was not initially included on the tour's itinerary, 80,000 signatures were collected on petitions imploring the Beatles to play there, and more than 250,000 people lined the route of their motorcade from the airport to the center of town. In Brisbane, 200,000 turned out. In Sydney, where a line of teenagers ringed the perimeter of the airport, the Beatles' plane landed moments ahead of a driving, typhoonlike rainstorm. Not wanting to disappoint their fans (and probably having little choice in the matter to begin with), the group allowed themselves to be trundled along the tarmac on the back of a flatbed truck: four tiny, black-clad figures clustered atop a movable stage, racked by the wind and drenched to the skin, waving to the crowd with one hand while clutching the shredded remains of their umbrellas in the other. It was a scene truer to the spirit of classic slapstick comedy than anything Richard Lester could devise, and it made a perfect prologue to the Beatles' ensuing three years on the road.

. . . .

A HARD DAY'S NIGHT opened in London at the beginning of July, in Liverpool a few days later, in America three weeks after that. The London premiere was like a reprise of the Royal Variety Show, with Princess Margaret in attendance and Piccadilly Circus festooned with gigantic Beatle heads affixed to the theater's facade. The Liverpool premiere was a homecoming of nearly Australian proportions, as more than a hundred thousand people lined the route from the airport at Speke and jammed the streets around the Town Hall, where the Beatles were received by the Lord Mayor and the city's police band playing "Can't Buy Me Love." In the United States, no such formalities were observed. *A Hard Day's Night* went into simultaneous release in seven hundred theaters across the country, became the top-grossing picture in America that summer, and went on to set a film industry record for "return on investment" that stood for years to come. Business was hampered only by the desire of fans to stay glued to their seats at the end, intent on seeing the picture over and over again.

What they saw on the screen was a thinly fictionalized account of two days in the life of the Beatles, who are never actually referred to as the Beatles, just John, Paul, George, and Ringo, on the entirely reasonable assumption that everyone in the film (with a few contrived exceptions) and everyone watching the film knows precisely who They are. To the breathless accompaniment of the title song, the picture begins with scenes of the group racing through the narrow streets of an English town, barely ahead of a pack of their lunging, squealing fans. They are chased around corners and down alleyways, into a railroad station and onto a departing train, where they meet up with their two harried road managers—a Mersey Mutt and Jeff—and Paul's irascible "Grandfather," a wily Liverpool Irishman with a devilish, twisted leer. After various incidents en route—including a performance of "I Should Have Known Better" by the prisoners of success in the cage of the train's baggage car—the group arrives in London to another mad crowd scene. They proceed to their hotel, then out for an evening of dancing to their own records at a Soho discothèque. The scenes of them communing happily with one another are juxtaposed with shots of Grandfather, who has absconded with an invitation addressed to Ringo and a tuxedo loaned by an obliging room-service waiter and gone to one of London's decadent new gambling clubs, posing as an Irish peer.

The story resumes the next day at a television studio, where the Beatles are scheduled to tape a performance before a live audience later in the afternoon. They deadpan their way through a press reception, rehearse their songs, and while away the hours backstage, idly feeding the anxieties of their managers and the paranoia of the television director. Grandfather, testy and bored, occupies himself by forging the Beatles' signatures on publicity photos and subverting the fragile self-esteem of Ringo, whom he eventually convinces to strike out on his own. Ringo slips out of the theater, assumes a scruffy disguise, and sets out in search of the life he's been missing. Unrecognized—"Get lost, shorty," says the first teenage girl he meets on the street—he's treated with indifference by passersby and suspicion by the police. Nothing goes right for him until he meets up with a ten-year-old boy, a self-styled "deserter" from school. "I'm a deserter, too," says Ringo, and the two of them trudge along in melancholy empathy until the boy runs off to join three of his mates playing happily on the banks of an industrial canal. Ringo takes the hint, but on his way back to the theater he's arrested as a public nuisance. This necessitates his rescue by the other Beatles, who have been trying to track him down. After a long slapstick chase—the bobbies after the Beatles, the Beatles after the bobbies—everyone arrives back at the television studio just moments before the band is due to go onstage before a crowd of frenzied fans. The last fifteen minutes of the film consist of this performance, with excerpts from a half-dozen songs, after which the Beatles and their entourage rush out the back door of the theater and board a waiting helicopter. The last shot has them ascending skyward into the rays of the setting sun, as a cloud of Grandfather's forged publicity photos flutters down from on high.

The prime convention of the teen-market movie is elegantly simple: a collection of carefree young heroes in a world of anxious old fools. It is a classic—arguably *the* classic—comic situation, and Alun Owen's script did not shrink from it in the least. As expected, Owen's principal contribution to the film was to provide it with a Liverpudlian ambience. He wrote lines for the Beatles that suited the singsong rhythms of their speech and laced their dialogue with a glossary of Scouse slang. But Owen's screenplay also went beyond the language of Liverpool to touch upon the defiant identity of the place. "The things I wanted to say were about the way people behave to each other," he later wrote, "and *A Hard Day's Night* is largely about how the Beatles behave to each other and everyone else." His script set up a series of neat parallels between the Us-and-Them mentality of teen-market entertainment and the analogous mentality of life in the Industrial North. Virtually "everyone else" in *A Hard Day's Night* is doubly cursed, not only as an anxious adult but as a Londoner, and the film unfolds as a series of confrontational encounters based on the overlapping themes of North and South, Youth and Age. Some of these episodes come off as smug paeans to the Beatles' cool. Others find a vein of real comedy in the collisions of class, geography, and generation.

A scene that Owen wrote as a set piece for George Harrison combined these themes with a sharp satire of the pop-culture industry itself. It begins backstage at the theater when George wanders into the production offices of a teen television show, where he is greeted by a flirtatious secretary and ushered into the presence of her boss. (The casting of Kenneth Haigh as the boss was a terrific inside joke, since Haigh was known in Britain as the actor who first played Jimmy Porter on the stage. The original Angry Young Man of the 1950s was thus portrayed as the calculating teen-market mogul of the 1960s.) Thinking that he is interviewing a prospective "guest teenager" for the show, the producer tosses some shirts in George's lap:

PRODUCER: Now . . . you'll like these. You'll really *dig* them. They're *fab* and all the other pimply hyperboles.

GEORGE: I wouldn't be caught dead in *them*. They're dead grotty.

PRODUCER: Grotty?

GEORGE: Yeah, grotesque.

PRODUCER: [*to an assistant*]: Make a note of that word and give it to Susan. It's rather touching, really. Here's this kid, trying to give me his utterly valueless opinion and I know for a *fact* that within four weeks he'll be suffering from a violent inferiority complex and loss of status if he's not wearing one of these nasty shirts. [*To George*] Of course they're "grotty," you wretched nit! That's the way they were designed and *that's what you'll want!* Besides, you won't get to meet our Susan if you don't cooperate . . .

GEORGE: And who's this Susan when she's home?

PRODUCER: Only Susan Campy, our resident teenager. You'll have to love her. She's your symbol.

GEORGE: You mean that posh bird who gets everything wrong?

PRODUCER: I beg your pardon?

GEORGE: Oh yeah. The lads sit round the television and watch her for a giggle.

PRODUCER: She's a trendsetter. It's her profession.

GEORGE: She's a drag! A well-known drag! We turn the sound down on her and say rude things . . .

The directorial style Richard Lester contributed to *A Hard Day's Night* was a bubbling mixture of Goonish whimsy and New Wave verve. The Goonery was evident in the movie's flippant, self-delighted manner, in the touches of surrealism and non sequitur, in the Pirendellian atmosphere of the backstage scenes, and in the incessant running gags. The New Wave influence was evident in the look and feel and rapid pace of the picture, which employed the characteristic *verité* effects of high-contrast cinematography, free-hand camerawork, and overlapping sound. Lester's *Cahiers du Cinema* sensibility was also reflected in the compulsive subtext he provided of references to other films. "Why don't we do the show right here?" John Lennon shouts at the start of a rehearsal, mouthing the oldest and tritest cliché of the Hollywood musical, exposing the world of difference between the Beatles and *Babes in Arms*. Ringo mugs like Groucho in one scene, dresses like Harpo in another, and shambles like Chaplin in a third. There are allusions to the work of Eisenstein and Fellini, Busby Berkeley and Mack Sennett.

Given these numerous references to other films, Lester could take pride in the fact that the single most acclaimed scene from *A Hard Day's Night* was an allusion to his own work. At one point during their long, idle afternoon, the Beatles burst out the back door of the television studio, clamber down a fire escape, and occupy an adjoining field. There, for the next three minutes, they enact a variation on *The Running, Jumping and Standing Still Film* to the exhilarating rhythm of "Can't Buy Me Love." Dashing, clowning, leaping, and dancing, their acrobatics and pratfalls are filmed with kaleidoscopic virtuosity as the camera peers up from the turf one moment, races beside them the next, and swirls omnisciently over the field a moment after that. The film itself is made to speed up and slow down in places, and the action seems to pulsate visually, musically, and conceptually in every direction at once. The idea, in a film otherwise confined to the claustrophobic interiors of rooms and cars, train compartments and backstage corridors, was to show the Beatles momentarily released from the job of being Beatles, on the lam from the prison of success. The scene accomplished this and more. It provided the picture with its most fully realized moment, the place where the talents and sensibilities of the stars and the director reached their point of closest accord. The Beatles are shown to invade this barren field with the same elemental joy and vitality with which they had just invaded the barren field of British popular music. On the screen are four young men, and *any* four young men they could be, while their music on the soundtrack could be mistaken for no one else.

Somewhat less successful were the concert scenes at the end. Lester described this fifteen-minute sequence as "the meat of the piece": an opportunity to experience the Beatles in concert for the millions of fans who had not yet had a chance to take part in the real thing. To this end the filmmakers rented a London theater, fitted it with cameras, and filled it with fans. Oddly, the depiction of Beatlemania under these laboratory conditions could not have been much tamer had a real laboratory been used. On the screen, an audience of weeping, hysterical girls can be seen screeching and swooning, screaming the names of their favorites and shouting in the ears of their friends. But the pandemonium seems to be taking place behind a thick pane of glass. It was as if some cinematic uncertainty principle were in effect, that to observe the Beatlemania phenomenon this closely was necessarily to alter its nature. To be sure, the kids in the movie were not only fans but paid extras, screaming when they were told to scream, and the Beatles were not really playing, only lip-synching to recordings of their songs. Yet the cinematographer Gilbert Taylor professed to be so disturbed by some of the hysterical behavior he witnessed during the filming of these scenes that he refused to work with the Beatles again, and a number of newspaper accounts that came out during the shooting of the film corroborate his impression of the event. Rather, it is the eye of the camera itself—elsewhere so intrusively *verité*—that seems to shrink from the action by constantly panning and jumping and searching out odd angles that effectively distract from what is really going on. Comparing *A Hard Day's Night* to a documentary by the Maysles brothers about the Beatles' first visit to America that came out around the same time, some reviewers questioned whether the concert scenes had been deliberately "sanitized." But the problem had more to do with the way that, in these last scenes, *A Hard Day's Night* becomes caught up in the contradictions of its mock-documentary format. Previously, though the whole film has turned on the distinction between the Beatles and Everyone Else, it has shown little about the nature of the relationship between the Beatles and their fans, thereby preserving the fiction of a special, ineffable bond. In the final fifteen minutes, however, the anxious, hysterical teenagers in the audience join company with the anxious, neurotic adults in the rest of the film. And by carrying its depiction of the Beatles' insularity through to the very end, *A Hard Day's Night* touched on a deeper, more unsettling truth. The film shows the screams and adulation of their fans washing over the Beatles onstage like the torrents of rain on the tarmac in Sydney. And it shows the group, enclosed within the walls of what Paul McCartney had recently likened to a bell factory, mouthing the words to their songs and grinning back coldly at the crowd.

> The legitimacy of the Beatles phenomenon is finally inescapable. With all the ill-will in the world, one sits there, watching and listening—and feels one's intelligence dissolving in a pool of approbation and participation.
>
> —*Newsweek*

Almost without exception, the reviews of *A Hard Day's Night* in the British and American press were profusely and apologetically enthusiastic. This was supposed to be the Beatles' awful movie—the point in their meteoric careers where whatever actual talent they possessed became hopelessly overextended. That the results proved otherwise made for a dramatic demonstration of the power of diminished expectations. The reviews conformed to a pattern as predictable as the questions at the group's press conferences. Each began with an expression of astonishment ("This is going to surprise you—it may knock you right out of your chair," wrote Bosley Crowther in the *New York Times*) followed by paragraphs of praise for the wit and grit of Alun Owen's script and the stylish sophistication of Dick Lester's direction. In a phrase that captured Lester's pretensions precisely, Andrew Sarris of the *Village Voice* (after confessing, "So help me, I resisted the Beatles as long as I could") called the picture "the *Citizen Kane* of juke-box musicals." Arthur Schlesinger Jr., moonlighting as a movie reviewer for *Show* magazine, described the film as a "conspiracy of delinquency against pomposity" and found it "exhilarating in its audacity and modernity." Critics delighted in picking out the cinematic allusions with which Lester had baited the hook. Ringo Starr was compared by some with Harpo (virtually every American review mentioned the Marx Brothers), by others with Chaplin, and by still others with his mournful Liverpudlian double, the actress Rita Tushingham.

The reviews of *A Hard Day's Night* also provided an occasion for some of the first good writing about the Beatles by people with a background in writing well about popular art. In her review for *The Observer,* Penelope Gilliatt suggested that they treat one another with "the stoicism of clowns [and] the kind of unbothered rudeness that is usually possible only between brothers and sisters." Comparing the look of the group to "a litter of perfectly groomed jaguars," Isabel Quigley in *The Spectator* was similarly impressed by "their whole style, not just of singing, but of behaving, of sitting, of relaxing and becoming alert, of raising one eyebrow higher into the hair, of taking things quizzically and giving as good as they get." Perhaps the most insightful review of the film was a piece by Elizabeth Sutherland in *The New Republic.* Sutherland found the Beatles neither wildly funny nor particularly outrageous, and she admitted that their music left her cold. Instead, she credited them with integrity, complexity, and an "astonishing" level of charm: "Here are four successful young men who suggest a nostalgia for their own youth; who are obvious professionals and have made the most anti-professional of films. They poke fun at their own myth and move with deep self-respect. Their eyes can be hard and Mod-like, then newborn, and both images are true." Commenting on their fans, Sutherland wrote, "There is one sub-teenage girl in the audience of their final performance who weeps quietly, and it seems to be more from an appreciation of their hidden effort to please, from a sense of shared tenuousness, than from the relief of some pseudo-orgasm." "The Beatles stand for a style based on not pushing," Sutherland suggested. "In an age when our comedy has become hysterical, our surrealism too surreal, they will not try too hard to be funny or angry or poetic."

For the teenagers who formed the principal audience for the film, *A Hard Day's Night* simply concentrated all the pertinent aspects of the group's appeal—their music, their looks, their style, and their humor—into a format that could be revisited time and again. This made it, in effect, a training film for Beatlemaniacs. Many fans screamed in their seats during the musical numbers (which added to the realism of the concert scenes at the end). But during the rest of the movie, they watched and listened and learned their lessons well. Here, too, the overall impact was stronger in the United States than in Britain, if only because the Beatles had remained a somewhat chimerical presence in the States between their February visit and their return in August for a national tour. Though American teenagers could have little feeling for the social significance of the Beatles' success in Britain, this did not shut them out of the picture, because Americans, as a group, viewed the English, as a group, to be as stereotypically pretentious as Liverpudlians considered Londoners to be. Alun Owen's efforts to root the Beatles in the rude specificity of Liverpool merely lent an exotic tinge to the film's portrayal of generational conflict, while Dick Lester's efforts to present the Beatles as comedic and cinematic archetypes gave the picture a universality that easily bridged any problems of cultural translation.

ALTHOUGH *A HARD DAY'S NIGHT* wound up making millions for United Artists at the box office, it had originally been conceived as an excuse to sell records, and its release was accompanied by the release of a profusion of singles and albums. In Britain, Parlophone combined the songs from the soundtrack with six additional Lennon-McCartney compositions on an LP called *A Hard Day's Night;* simultaneously, the title song from the movie was released as the Beatles' second single of 1964. In the United States, thanks to the competing contractual claims of United Artists and Capitol, the songs from the film became the latest addition to the feeding frenzy that had surrounded the release of Beatles records since January. UA released its soundtrack album in June, a month before the picture opened in the United States. This LP consisted of the seven songs from the film interspersed with instrumental arrangements of some of the same material performed by a group called "George Martin & His Orchestra." The presence of these sonorous interludes made the soundtrack album a frustrating experience for many fans, who tended to hover near their turntables, ready to guide the stylus over the offending tracks. (The inclusion of this material served a useful purpose, however, since Martin's translation of Beatle melodies into the instrumental vernacular of mainstream adult pop paved the way for cover versions of the group's songs by non-rock artists. In addition, Martin's credits as a performer and arranger on this album earned him the first real remuneration he would receive from his work with the Beatles, since EMI, whose profits had risen by 80 percent during the first half of 1964, continued to pay him his salary as the head of Parlophone and not a penny more.)

Capitol Records launched its counteroffensive in the middle of July. While United Artists owned the rights to the soundtrack, Capitol owned the rights to the same music in any format *but* a soundtrack. So Capitol began to release the songs from the film as singles—"A Hard Day's Night" one week, "And I Love Her" the next—until finally there came an album called *Something New*—a cunning title considering that five of its tracks had already been released *twice* in the American market, once by United Artists and once, as singles, by Capitol. As an added curiosity, the album also included the German-language version of the Beatles' breakthrough hit, "Komm, Gib Mir Deine Hand."

In terms of sheer volume, the presence of thirteen original songs on the Parlophone version of *A Hard Day's Night* represented a tour de force of songwriting on the part of Lennon and McCartney. Yet the non-soundtrack side of the album contains its share of unmemorable tracks. "Any Time at All" is yet another variation on the theme of emotional availability that began with "From Me to You"; "When I Get Home" is yet another variation on the Marvin Gaye–inspired vocal and rhythm of "You Can't Do That." The gulping, rockabilly-styled "I'll Cry Instead" was originally intended to provide the accompaniment to the open-field sequence in the film, but Richard Lester disliked the track, and wisely replaced it with "Can't Buy Me Love." The musical highlights of the album's second side are a pair of Lennon-McCartney companion pieces that share similar harmonic schemes, similar acoustic instrumentation, and a similar desire to introduce a new level of emotional maturity into the Beatles' work. Paul's "Things We Said Today" is a darkly beautiful love song that runs on an alternating current of major and minor tonality. The verses are set in A minor and sung in the second person, with the lyrics projecting into the future: "You say you will love me, if I have to go." The release is set in A major and sung in the first person, with the lyrics in the present tense, proclaiming that "love is here to stay." The two sections shift seamlessly back and forth, the transitions marked only by the change in the harmony and a pair of rasping flourishes on an acoustic guitar. Paul sings the simple, folklike melody in a quiet, measured voice, holding out the ends of his lines as if trying to prolong the happiness of the present moment. A mixture of wonder and apprehension fills his voice, which sounds haunted by the knowledge that promises like these have been made in so many songs before.

John Lennon's "I'll Be Back" begins with a pair of acoustic guitars strumming brightly on a chord of A major before veering suddenly to A minor just as the singing—John and Paul, with John's double-tracked voice predominant—comes in. The chords beneath the opening line— "You know, if you break my heart I'll go"—move in a dirgelike progression down the scale before reentering the major key under the words "But I'll be back again." Each line of the three verses enacts a similarly fleeting return toward that bright moment of A major, a harmonic scheme that, along with the title and lyric, endows the song with a deeply nostalgic cast. "I'll Be Back" was preceded on the second side of *A Hard Day's Night* by "You Can't Do That," which orchestrated a juxtaposition of John at his most domineering with John at his most contrite. Taken together, the two songs could be heard as chapters in an episodic romantic narrative that ran through the Beatles' early songwriting. For the singer of "I'll Be Back" sounds a lot like the boy from "She Loves You," swallowing his pride on the advice of his friend, and asking the girl for a second chance: "This time / I will try to show that I'm / Not trying to pretend." There are thirteen tracks on *A Hard Day's Night,* and John Lennon's voice dominates the sound of nine of them, but only on "I Should Have Known Better" did John venture to sing alone, sharing all or part of the vocals with Paul on the rest. When the two of them sang together in this way, no matter what they were singing about, they always sounded something like the characters in "She Loves You": John the boy, Paul the friend, the passion of the one balanced by the compassion of the other. In the summer of 1964, at a time when their individual personalities as singers and song-writers were growing more distinct, the close and uncompromised coexistence of their voices on record remained the moral of their music to their fans around the world.

22

Go ahead and let yourselves go. It's not our place anyway.

—John Lennon

In the middle of August the Beatles returned to North America, to reap what they had sown the winter before. Their month-long tour consisted of thirty concerts in twenty-three cities, beginning in San Francisco and ending in New York. In every town the frenzied routine of airport arrivals, besieged hotels, and clandestine getaways was the same, all of it centered on an increasingly perfunctory and almost inaudible thirty-minute performance before a crowd of ten to twenty thousand cicada-like teenagers who had been waiting to hatch into this moment for seven months. The tour was a concerted moneymaking operation on a scale that no recording artist had ever attempted before. Playing in large municipal arenas, the Beatles received a minimum of $50,000 a night (roughly equivalent to $250,000 in current dollars), which netted them well over a million dollars in ticket sales alone. Beyond that, the enthusiasm generated by their concerts was reflected in record sales, film receipts, and the merchandising of a vast array of Beatles-related paraphernalia—posters, magazines, trading cards, stationery, book covers, handbags, hats, dresses, suits, scarves, sweatshirts, pajamas, boots, sneakers, jewelry, cosmetics, buttons, dolls, plastic model kits, games, jigsaw puzzles, cameras, guitars, harmonicas, phonographs, record cabinets, wallpaper, pillows, bedspreads, dinner plates, glassware, flatware, serving trays, and lunchboxes—totaling millions of dollars more.

In every city they visited, the local press treated their presence as a major news event, and to review those almost interchangeable front-page stories from August and September 1964 is to encounter in the adjoining headlines a tableau of the political and social themes that would be played out in a spirit of compounding tragedy in the tumultuous years ahead. The tour began in San Francisco at the same Cow Palace arena where the Republican Party had recently bestowed its presidential nomination on Barry Goldwater, harbinger of a new era of American conservatism, who began his campaign with a ringing endorsement of "extremism in the defense of liberty" and a threat to reverse the growing Communist insurgency in South Vietnam through the use of nuclear weapons. The Beatles performed at the Atlantic City Convention Center just days after the Democratic Party had gathered there to nominate Lyndon Johnson, the self-styled "peace candidate," whose own, more Machiavellian solution to the Vietnam crisis involved exploiting a minor naval skirmish in the Tonkin Gulf as a pretext for direct American entry into the war. (Brian Epstein had politely declined a request from the White House press office that the Beatles be photographed with the President in Washington, laying a wreath on John F. Kennedy's grave.) The Beatles toured the American South, performing in Jacksonville, New Orleans, and Dallas at the end of a second "Freedom Summer" in which segregationist violence had culminated in the murder of three young civil rights activists by the Ku Klux Klan in Meridian, Mississippi. The group performed in New York shortly after the shooting of a black teenager by an off-duty police detective had touched off the first full-scale urban race riot of the 1960s. In September, as their tour leapfrogged around the country, the incidents that gave birth to the Free Speech Movement at the University of California at Berkeley were taking place, leading to the first student "takeover" of an American college campus. And one week after the Beatles returned to Britain, the Warren Commission issued its report on the assassination of President Kennedy, a vast document whose omissions and inconsistencies would draw millions of distressed and skeptical Americans into a labyrinth of doubt concerning the identity and motivation of the person or persons responsible for this epic crime.

Apart from a proliferation of RINGO FOR PRESIDENT buttons, there was little perceived connection between these portentous events and the sound of pop music in the summer of 1964; in the United States, the notion that Beatlemania might have social or cultural implications that reached beyond the ephemera of a teen craze remained far from most people's minds. After entirely dominating the record and radio market from January through April, the Beatles had been joined by the second wave of what would be termed a British Invasion. The Dave Clark Five were the first British band to be successfully promoted in the wake of the Beatles' February visit. Next came a pair of NEMS artists, Billy J. Kramer and Gerry & The Pacemakers. The vocal duo Peter & Gordon reached number one in June with a Lennon-McCartney castoff called "World Without Love." The Animals followed in August with an electrified version of the folk-blues standard "House of the Rising Sun." Fall would bring the first American hits by the Kinks, the Rolling Stones, Herman's Hermits, and Manfred Mann. After decades of commercial irrelevance, British singers and groups would account for nearly a third of the Top Ten singles released in the United States over the course of 1964.

For the Beatles themselves, a high point of their American tour was an encounter so laden with retroactive cultural significance as to seem mythologically contrived. So far as they could remember, they had first heard the music of Bob Dylan during their three-week engagement at the Olympia Theater in Paris in January 1964, when Paul McCartney acquired a copy of Dylan's second album and installed it on the group's hotel-room phonograph. So far as he could remember, Bob Dylan first heard the Beatles that same month, when "I Want to Hold Your Hand" became a ubiquitous presence on American radio. Though he kept it to himself, he was immediately intrigued. "They were doing things nobody was doing," he later said. "Their chords were outrageous, just outrageous, and their harmonies made it all valid." Three months later, while driving cross-country at the moment when the Beatles' records occupied the first five positions on the American pop charts, Dylan was struck by the extraordinary confluence of commercial and cultural power they were beginning to represent. "It seemed that a definite line was being drawn," he told his biographer Anthony Scaduto in 1971. "This was something that had never happened before."

Nineteen-sixty-three had been as much of a breakthrough year for Bob Dylan in the United States as it had been for the Beatles in Britain. After arriving in New York from Minnesota in 1961 and earning a reputation as a rising young topical folksinger in the Greenwich Village coffeehouse scene, Dylan had exploded to national attention in the spring of 1963 when Columbia Records released his second album and folk stars like Peter, Paul and Mary and Joan Baez began to champion his songs. In June, Peter, Paul and Mary released their recording of Dylan's "Blowing in the Wind," which simultaneously became a Top Ten hit and an anthem of the civil rights movement at a moment when thousands of white college students were heading south to participate in the first "Freedom Summer" initiative of voter registration drives. In July, Dylan gave a mesmerizing performance at the Newport Folk Festival. A month later he shared the stage with the Reverend Martin Luther King, Jr., at the mass demonstration in Washington where King delivered his famous

"I Have a Dream" speech. Written up in *Time* and *Newsweek* as the very model of the modern American troubadour, Dylan was acclaimed as the conscience of his generation and the leader of what was now described as the "folk protest" movement.

In May 1964, four months after the Beatles first came to America, Dylan performed a series of concerts in Britain, culminating in an enthusiastically received performance at London's Royal Albert Hall. Columbia had recently released his third album, *The Times They Are A-Changin'*, with its stirring title track, and his renown as a protest singer was reaching new heights on both sides of the Atlantic. But Dylan himself was bristling with resentment at what he had come to regard as the self-seriousness and self-satisfaction of the folk movement. New songs were pouring out of him, but they were mainly songs about his personal life and his painfully awkward reaction to the mixture of approbation and scrutiny that success had brought his way. (Columbia would release a collection of these new songs later that year under the explanatory, almost apologetic title *Another Side of Bob Dylan*.) A firsthand glimpse of the excitement that had overtaken the British pop scene since he had last visited the country as an unknown folksinger in January 1963 further piqued his interest in the Beatles and their phenomenon. But while Dylan was performing in London, the Beatles were vacationing abroad, catching their breath before their summer of international touring.

Their meeting, when it finally did occur, was arranged by Al Aronowitz, a New York–based journalist whose sympathetic reporting on the Beat writers of San Francisco and the Greenwich Village folk scene had earned him a wide circle of contacts in America's bicoastal bohemia. Two years before, while working on an article for *The Saturday Evening Post*, Aronowitz had interviewed and befriended Dylan. In February 1964, Aronowitz was assigned by the *Post* to cover the Beatles' visit to New York. Since then, Aronowitz had come to see Dylan and the Beatles as the charismatic leaders of two flourishing musical subcultures, folk and pop, and he seems to have taken it as his mission to effect a meeting of their minds. Yet the pertinent fact about Dylan and the Beatles in the summer of 1964 was that their respective musical constituencies were indeed perceived as inhabiting two separate subcultural worlds. Dylan's core audience was comprised of young people emerging from adolescence—college kids with artistic or intellectual leanings, a dawning political and social idealism, and a mildly bohemian style. His music appealed to their maturity, their sensitivity, their morality, and their verbal sophistication. The Beatles' core audience, by contrast, was comprised of veritable "teenyboppers"—kids in high school or grade school whose lives were totally wrapped up in the commercialized popular culture of television, radio, pop records, fan magazines, and teen fashion. They were seen as idolaters, not idealists.

Within six months of their meeting in August 1964, John Lennon would be making records on which he openly imitated Dylan's nasal drone, brittle strum, and introspective vocal persona. Within one year of their meeting, Bob Dylan would walk out on the stage of the 1965 Newport Folk Festival dressed in the height of Mod fashion and proceed, with the help of a five-piece group and a Fender Stratocaster electric guitar, to shake the monkey of folk authenticity permanently off his back. ("Where's Ringo?" disdainful voices would shout from the crowd.) By then the distinctions between the folk and rock audiences would have nearly evaporated. The Beatles' audience, in keeping with the way of the world, would be showing signs of growing up. But far more surprising would be the apparent readiness of Dylan's audience, in effect, to grow *down,* as hundreds of thousands of folkies in their late teens and early twenties, entranced by the allure of a newly energized and autonomous pop culture, would redirect some central tenet of their attitudinal allegiance back toward the ethos of their adolescent years.

Such was the cultural significance of their meeting in hindsight. The actual event began as a nervous encounter between a paradigmatic individualist and a paradigmatic group. As ever with Dylan, there was posturing. According to Al Aronowitz's published account, Dylan arrived at the Beatles' suite in the Delmonico Hotel, was introduced all around, and requested some "cheap wine." Ever the gracious host, Brian Epstein offered his apologies for the absence of cheap wine in the Beatles' suite that day, whereupon Dylan accepted a higher-priced alternative and the gathering settled down. What did they do? At Dylan's suggestion, they got *stoned* is what they did, the Beatles for the very first time.

"When you're with another tea smoker it makes you feel a special sense of kinship," Louis Armstrong once remarked. The wonder of it was that the Beatles had never experienced that sense of kinship before. Their innocence was not due to their nationality. Though the traffic in cannabis was criminalized in Britain in 1928 (ten years before it was banned in the United States), the laws against it were rarely enforced,

and by the early 1960s, its use was quite prevalent among British entertainers (especially jazz musicians), merchant seamen, West Indian immigrants, and Mayfair decadents. (Christine Keeler's fateful liaison with
John Edgecombe had begun with her efforts to buy some pot on behalf of
Stephen Ward.) Since the Beatles had had considerable contact with
three of these four groups during their years in Liverpool and Hamburg,
it is surprising that they had never sampled the stuff properly—especially
since they were hardly babes in the woods when it came to using drugs.
Ever since their introduction to Preludin in Hamburg, they had come to
rely on several varieties of amphetamine to maintain the whirlwind pace
of their professional commitments.

Still, marijuana was different from any drug they had known before,
and to a man, the Beatles were completely taken with the difference.
Though its physical effects were relatively mild compared with pills or
alcohol, its social and psychological effects were uniquely suited to the
lives of four individuals for whom contact with some of the more absurd
and outlandish manifestations of human behavior had become part of
their daily routine. Pot magnified the Beatles' already formidable tendency to operate on their own private wavelength as a group. Whereas
amphetamines helped them to keep up with the frantic pace of their professional lives, marijuana seemed to slow the pace down to the point
where experiences could be selectively sampled and savored. Moreover,
as several generations of jazz and blues musicians had already discovered,
the drug, when used in moderation, was uniquely suited to both the performance and the appreciation of music. For the Beatles, as it would be
for millions of other young people in the United States and Britain who
were introduced to it over the next few years, pot would serve as the key
to a secret garden. It divided up the world the way their movie did, the
way their fans did, the way every aspect of youth culture did: between
those who knew what was happening, and those who hadn't a clue.

23

You could call our new one a "Beatles country-and-western LP."

—John Lennon

The Beatles ended 1964 with a month-long tour of Britain, another bluesy new single, and a glossy Christmas present of an album called *Beatles for Sale*. The album was packaged in a gatefold sleeve and faced with a color portrait by Robert Freeman that pictured the Beatles outdoors against a swimmingly out-of-focus background, their pale, gaunt faces framed by long scarves, turned-up collars, and an abundance of windblown hair. Their exhausted, unsmiling expressions in the photograph went well beyond the reserve they had shown on the cover of *With the Beatles* to suggest an even more pointed defiance of show-business convention, while the increasingly iconic nature of their public image was emphasized by the near absence of the word "Beatles" anywhere on the album cover (it does appear, in small print, beside the Parlophone trademark). In keeping with Capitol Records' indifference to the new aesthetic standards that Robert Freeman's work with the Beatles had brought to the pop scene in Britain, the American label elected not to use this handsome portrait on its version of the LP. Instead, beneath a banner of thick block letters reading BEATLES '65, Capitol's art department selected several inane images of the group posed as stereotypically "eccentric" Englishmen amid a surrealist grab-bag of coil springs, open umbrellas, and other photographer's props. The difference between the British and American product was further accentuated by the difference in the liner notes. The elegantly laid out jacket copy of *Beatles for Sale* was written in a style of breezy understatement by Derek Taylor, who described the record as "quite the best of its kind in the world." The notes on *Beatles '65*, by contrast, went straight for the psychological jugular, reminding readers, "Some said it couldn't really be happening . . . But you, the Beatles' fans, knew all along. And it's simply because you like them (and they like you) that this fantastic success story has happened."

The weary expressions on the Beatles' faces in the cover photograph betrayed the effort it took to record the album within. *Beatles for Sale* marked the point where the intense commercial pressures generated by the magnitude of the Beatles' success began to conflict with the group's creative aspirations in a serious way. The fourteen tracks on the album were recorded in eight sessions at Abbey Road over the summer and fall of 1964. Two of these sessions, yielding two finished tracks ("I'm a Loser" and "Baby's in Black"), preceded the group's American tour. The remaining six sessions took place between their return to Britain at the end of September and a late-October deadline that was mandated by the desire of EMI and Capitol to release both a new single and a new album in time for the Christmas market. Adding to the pressure was the fact that the grueling pace of international touring had left Lennon and McCartney with little time or energy to write over the course of the summer. "Material's becoming a hell of a problem," John complained to a reporter from *Melody Maker*—not least because, after filling both sides of *A Hard Day's Night* with original songs, he and Paul had nearly exhausted the backlog of old songs and song fragments they had relied on for ideas and inspiration over the previous two years. As it was, by the time they began their tour of Britain in the second week of October, the Beatles had recorded a total of seven tracks, all of them original songs. Because this was half the number they would need for an LP, a decision was made to revert to the mixture of original and cover tunes that had characterized the albums they made in 1963. In a long session on October 18, the Beatles recorded five covers, all of them first or second takes, most of them drawn from their old Cavern Club repertoire. Somehow they also found the time during this session to rehearse and record two more original songs, one of which, a jammy number called "I Feel Fine," became the A-side of their next single. A week later they completed the album by recording one more cover and one more original song.

The result of this process was an album with a split personality. On almost every level of singing, playing, songwriting, and arrangement, the eight new Lennon-McCartney songs on *Beatles for Sale*—"No Reply," "I'm a Loser," "Baby's in Black," "I'll Follow the Sun," "Eight Days a Week," "Every Little Thing," "I Don't Want to Spoil the Party," and "What You're Doing"—far surpass any collection of album tracks the Beatles had recorded to date. The improvement in the quality of the arranging was particularly noticeable. Effects that were novel on previous Beatles recordings, such as the insertion of stops and starts for dramatic impact, or the use of strong dynamic and instrumental contrasts to distinguish the different sections of a song—were employed routinely on track after track. Though the Beatles' approach to lyric writing remained simplistic and formulaic, the emotional range of their songwriting had widened over the course of 1964. Six of the eight Lennon-McCartney songs (including all four on the first side of the album) were expressions of romantic loss, disappointment, or discontent, and with the exception of "Baby's in Black," a waltzing lament that sounds like a cross between a sea shanty and a drinking song (with George Harrison's guitar playing the part of a drunken sailor), these themes were addressed with a new seriousness.

What gives *Beatles for Sale* its split personality is the fact that the cover songs on the album are of such a different provenance from the contemporary rhythm and blues the Beatles had used to fill out their earlier LPs, consisting instead of a catalog of the group's earliest musical influences. Elizabeth Sutherland had remarked on the Beatles' nostalgia for their youth; here they put it on record. On the first side of the album, John belts out a blistering version of Chuck Berry's "Rock 'n' Roll Music," and Paul sings a medley that segues from the Leiber-Stoller warhorse "Kansas City" into the minimalist rock of Little Richard's "Hey Hey Hey Hey." On side two, John and Paul combine on a letter-perfect rendition of Buddy Holly's "Words of Love," on which their breathy, Everly Brothers–style harmony—almost a parody of Holly's dreaminess—is offset by George's stingingly bright guitar; Ringo bluffs his way through Carl Perkins's "Honey Don't," sounding like the average fan singing along with the track; and George ends the album with an echoey, lackluster performance of yet another Carl Perkins song, "Everybody's Trying to Be My Baby." Rounding out the cover tunes is "Mr. Moonlight," an obscure relic of early-1960s rhythm and blues with an over-the-top vocal by John that falls completely flat.

Neither the Beatles nor George Martin ever suggested that there was a conscious artistic motive behind the decision to include these 1950s cover tunes on *Beatles for Sale*. Most likely, the songs were picked because they were the quickest and easiest way for the Beatles to come up with the half-dozen tracks they needed to complete the LP. But their inclusion has the interesting effect of drawing the music on the album forward and backward in time, setting up a kind of dialogue between the Beatles' musical present and their musical past. This is particularly true because the sound and feel of the older music carries over into some of the new songs on the album. Both "I'm a Loser" and "I Don't Want to Spoil the Party" have a jolting rockabilly rhythm reminiscent of Carl Perkins and Chuck Berry; "Eight Days a Week" takes its loose-jointed shuffle from "Kansas City"; and "Every Little Thing" has a devotional quality that is strongly reminiscent of Buddy Holly. This reversion to their roots in blues and rockabilly was the culmination of a year-long trend in the Beatles' music; it also reflected the growing influence of Bob Dylan, whose folk-based style of acoustic guitar accompaniment the Beatles tended to associate with country music in a general sort of way.

It is the strumming of acoustic guitars that sets the stage for "No Reply," which opens *Beatles for Sale* with a romantic melodrama that seems to pick up unhappily where "I'll Be Back" left off—acoustic guitars and bossa-nova accents from the drums that dart through the song's finely crafted opening verse like the singer's eyes, playing anxiously on the darkened façade of his girlfriend's house: "This happened once before, when I came to your door: no reply." The song turns on its voyeuristic setting and the sense of indignant accusation in John's voice, which rises to a shout on the literal and figurative revelation, "I saw the light!" in response to the image of the girl, peeking through her window to see who's at the door. The narrative of jealousy and betrayal resumes in the second verse, where the singer's worst suspicions are confirmed by the sight of his girlfriend coming home with another man.

According to John Lennon, the music publisher Dick James praised "No Reply" as the first song the Beatles had ever written that "resolved" itself. If so, James had it exactly wrong, for this was the first lyric the Beatles ever wrote that set up a painful emotional situation and then offered no way out of it in the end. "No reply!" the singers cry out in the coda, as the indignation turns to anguish over the same harshly syncopated chords that accompanied the lines "I saw the light" and "I nearly died"; then for good measure, they sing the words again.

"I'm a Loser" addresses the disappointments of love from a more theatrical angle, beginning with a stagey a cappella introduction that harkens back to "Misery" on the Beatles' first LP. Singing over a thunderous rockabilly accompaniment topped by his own braying harmonica, John assumes the role of the fool-hearted narrator endemic in country-and-western songs, the man who has played at love and lost, riding the melody of the verse into a morass of self-pity that eventually bottoms out on a low G more than an octave below its starting point. "Although I laugh and I act like a clown," he sings, "Beneath this mask I am wearing a *frown*." Despite the joke's-on-me tone of his performance, there is a note of conviction in the singing that hints at the autobiographical significance John would later ascribe to this song. Lennon's second rockabilly-flavored original on *Beatles for Sale,* "I Don't Want to Spoil the Party," reprises this theme of emotional masquerade. The song's high point is a superb twelve-bar middle section where John and Paul, harmonizing in parallel fifths, fall all over each other in their eagerness to forgive the girl for whom they've "waited far too long," before breaking into a sing-song of sustained whole notes on the phrase "I . . . still . . . *love* . . . her."

Shortly after the release of *Beatles for Sale,* John Lennon told *Melody Maker* that both "I'm a Loser" and "I Don't Want to Spoil the Party" reflected the growing influence of Bob Dylan on the Beatles' songwriting. At this point, John was presumably referring more to the general tone of Dylan's music than to his words, since neither the content nor the style of the lyrics to either song, apart from their vaguely introspective cast, bear much resemblance to anything specific in Dylan's work. Although Paul McCartney's "I'll Follow the Sun" was an old song, an unfinished version of which dated back to 1961, its revival on *Beatles for Sale* may well have reflected Dylan's influence as well. In keeping with his vagabond persona, one of Dylan's favorite song-forms on his early albums was a type of rueful fare-thee-well patterned on the many traditional blues and folk ballads that address the vicissitudes of "rambling" and the inevitability of moving on. "Don't Think Twice, It's All Right," from Dylan's second album, was a prime example of such a song. So was "I'll Follow the Sun," whose only verse consists of Paul's prediction that "One day, you'll look, to see I've gone / For tomorrow may rain so—I'll follow the sun." With its symmetrical melody and acoustic instrumentation, the track has the simplicity of an old folk song, combining a spirit of musical innocence with a pessimistic view of human relations that is almost perverse by the standards of pop romance.

Given the uniformly unrequited romantic mood of the four original songs on the first side of *Beatles for Sale,* the second side of the album is marked by a pair of wholly appreciative love songs (both of them initiated by Paul, with lead vocals by John) that strive to make a virtue out of their lack of emotional complication. "Eight Days a Week" is the most exuberant track on the album and, indeed, one of the most exuberantly forthright love songs the Beatles would ever record. Conceived as a possible single (and released as one by Capitol in the United States, where it went to number one), it has an intriguing, made-for-radio introduction that fades *in* the way that most pop songs fade out, beginning as a tiny speck on the sonic horizon that grows larger and louder, guitar chords chiming, until it arrives in the musical foreground as a loping shuffle demarked by handclaps, Ringo's sloshy cymbals, and Paul's purposeful bass. The utterly formulaic lyric restates the I-love-you-so-please-love-me-too motif of "Love Me Do." With its evenly phrased melody, shuffle rhythm, and brassy major chords, "Eight Days a Week" serves up the idea of love as if it were a big dish of vanilla ice cream. "Every Little Thing" turns this same theme of romantic contentment into an expression of gratitude so heartfelt as to be almost heartbreaking. True to its title, the track is a mere slip of a song that draws its unexpected emotional power from a series of deft musical touches—"little things" that demonstrate the Beatles' growing sensitivity to the expressive nuances of arrangement. These include a pining lead guitar motif that sounds once at the beginning, returns to echo the title line in chorus, and then opens out into a luminous solo break; a complex bass line in which Paul's over-dubbed piano performs a contrapuntal duet with his bass guitar; and a rhapsodic moment in the chorus where the vocal harmony widens from a third to a fourth to a fifth as Ringo divides the line "Every little thing she does / She does for me" with a pair of portentous timpani accents whose depth of tone somehow translates directly in a depth of feeling.

Several of the tracks on *Beatles for Sale* were considered for release as the Beatles' third and final Parlophone single of 1964, including "No Reply," "I'm a Loser," and "Eight Days a Week." In the end, the group wound up finishing the year in much the same way they began it, with a matched pair of Lennon-McCartney songs on which they renounced all traces of romantic woe and existential weariness, and chose instead to pour every ounce of musical energy they could muster into their own private synthesis of pop music and the blues. The decision to forgo "No Reply" and "I'm a Loser" may well have reflected a lingering caution on the part of George Martin, Brian Epstein, and the Beatles about whether the group's fans would respond to a single that was something other than emotionally upbeat. At the same time, from a rhythmic perspective, "I Feel Fine" b/w "She's a Woman" was the Beatles' hippest single to date. Both tracks were written and recorded on extremely short notice, and they share a similar unpremeditated simplicity and fiercely kinetic drive. Paul McCartney composed the bluesy melody and third-person lyric ("My love don't give me presents / I know that she's no *peasant*") of "She's a Woman" on his way to the studio one day. Upon his arrival, the Beatles added the purest distillation of a backbeat, an unvarying succession of snare hits and guitar chops whose only lateral linkage is supplied by Paul's brilliantly strained lead vocal (which is doubled on piano in the later verses) and his enormously loud and mobile bass guitar. Its companion, "I Feel Fine," was composed *in* the studio, immediately after the Beatles had finished recording their ill-fated version of "Mr. Moonlight." This makes it easy to imagine how the song came together, with John fingering a two-bar guitar riff he knew from another 1961 R&B record called "Watch Your Step," George doubling the riff, and Ringo responding in an almost Pavlovian manner to the sound of their Latin-inflected off-beats by breaking into the inverted mambo pattern he and every other drummer of his generation knew from Ray Charles's "What'd I Say." Both the flat, bluesy melody and the exultant, banal lyric sound similarly improvised, with John's interjections of "you know" providing him with the split-second pause he needed to think of the next line: "Baby's good to me, you know, she's happy as can be, you know, she said so. . . ." As prefigured by the palate-clearing wash of guitar feedback that was added to the track as a radio-friendly introduction, the sheer power of the performance obscures the fact that there is almost nothing but spirit and energy to the song, and when Paul and George add their high harmony to the refrain, "I'm in love with her and I feel fine," the joy that radiates from the blend of their voices sounds like another installment of their gift of grace to the world.

24

Most nights, this new aristocracy used to hang out at the
Ad Lib Club, getting stoned on whiskey and coke, and
they'd wait intently for the Beatles to show. They'd slump
around in the half-dark and not move until it got light outside. After a few hours, they'd go into a stupefied dream
and they'd sit there blind, not looking and not hearing,
just steadily boozing and nodding their heads. Through
everything, music played incredibly loudly.

—Nik Cohn

If 1964 marked the populist phase of the great surge of social and cultural aspiration and enthusiasm that, as Paul McCartney said, "exploded"
across Britain in the wake of Beatlemania, by the beginning of 1965, the
focus of press and public attention had begun to narrow perceptibly,
homing in on a few ranks of individual faces that stood in the forefront of
pop London's burgeoning In-crowd. "Face," in fact, became a new term
of Mod argot that described a new, rather perversely refined form of
celebrity: not a talent, necessarily, or a persona, exactly, so much as an
aloof, narcissistic essence that was best expressed in the mutely frozen
format of a photograph. A face was an instant photographic icon, and in a
milieu of pop society that communed with itself and the rest of the
world, to a large extent, visually, photographers, conferrers of facehood,
came to play a role as social arbiters analogous to that of portrait painters
in eras past. When the Italian director Michelangelo Antonioni arrived in
London in 1965 with the intention of capturing the contemporary mood
of the city on film, it was a fashion photographer he chose as his protagonist—and the confusion between reality and illusion he developed as his
theme. The character played by David Hemmings in *Blow-Up* was modeled on a type established by David Bailey, mentor of the model Jean
Shrimpton and, from 1964 onward, house photographer to the Rolling
Stones. In 1965 Bailey published his *Box of Pinups,* an LP-sized folio of

photographs that presumed to single out the thirty-six most important "faces" in London—people who were celebrated in Francis Wyndham's introduction for having "gone all out for the immediate rewards of success: quick money, quick fame, quick sex—a brave thing to do." The cast of characters was evenly divided between faces from the world of fashion (models, designers, hairdressers, boutique owners, and photographers, including Bailey himself, photographed by Mick Jagger) and the world of entertainment (actors, club owners, impresarios, and pop stars, including—in a pointed gesture of Southern chauvinism—only Lennon and McCartney, but all five Rolling Stones). By the time this social register of the Swinging London scene was published toward the end of 1965, the chatter about classlessness had all but run its course. Palpably bored with populism, it was the "New Aristocracy" that the press was singing the praises of now. Less than eighteen months after the first bright flash of Britain's pop revolution, the English obsession with social hierarchy was bringing a reassuring new sense of order to the scene.

Over the fervent swinging and smashing presided the Beatles, or so it seemed to their fans in Britain and around the world, and so it had seemed to the four of them as well. "We were like kings of the jungle, then," John Lennon recalled of their first year of living in London, when they spent what little free time they had dashing around the city, communing with other meteoric pop personalities at chic new discothèques. Most of the time the Beatles had been in a state of perpetual motion, touring and filming and recording, living out of hotel rooms and half-furnished London flats—all except Paul McCartney, who had become a permanent guest at the home of Jane Asher and her progressive-minded parents. But as the year wore on and the level of fan worship became only more intrusive, the pressure to get out of London grew only more intense. The first to leave was John Lennon, who moved his family into an elaborately renovated mock-Tudor mansion in Weybridge, thirty miles southwest of the city in an upscale swath of suburban Surrey known as London's "stockbroker belt." Shortly thereafter, George Harrison bought a house in neighboring Esher, a few miles closer in. In February 1965, Ringo Starr married his steady girlfriend, Maureen Cox, who was two months pregnant at the time; a month later, Ringo purchased a mock-Tudor mansion of his own, just down the hill from John's house in Weybridge. Only Paul McCartney remained in London. The Beatles continued to spend much of their time together, at work and at play, dropping in on one another's houses, meeting up at nightclubs like the Ad Lib and the Scotch of St. James, whose reputations depended on their patronage. But their increasingly peripheral living arrangements reflected a new accommodation with the Swinging London scene.

For one thing, if Swinging London was to some extent the pop spirit of Beatlemania writ large, the Beatles had grown desperately tired of Beatlemania by now. Their remarkably poised performance as public figures had earned them an aura of invulnerability that would linger on for years, but they had long since run out of cheerful tolerance and snappy ripostes and shared amazement at the absurdity of it all. (Any treasury of their public wit would be heavily weighted toward the first year of their success.) The worst of it for them was touring, where they felt themselves to be totally constrained by the fans, the police, and the press. But in London, too, there was an enormous logistical complication to anything they wanted to do. That the NEMS office made all the necessary arrangements on their behalf with brisk efficiency was small compensation for the fact that they could barely venture out in public during the daylight hours without causing a scene. Their state of luxurious isolation was often compared by reporters to that of royalty, but, unlike real aristocrats, they had never been bred for this life.

Facile though it was, the very notion of the New Aristocracy epitomized the way that pop society was evolving into a none-too-subtle reassertion of the South of England sensibility against which the Beatles had originally defined themselves. On the music scene, with the exception of the Beatles, the Hollies, and the Spencer Davis Group, most of the bands that would thrive during the Swinging London years of the mid-1960s came from London and its suburbs. The same was true of film stars like Michael Caine and Terence Stamp, art stars like Bridget Riley and Peter Blake, and fashion stars like David Bailey, Jean Shrimpton, Mary Quant, and Vidal Sassoon. Though many of these people shared with the Beatles a working-class background, it remained that they were Londoners nevertheless, and in their presence, even worldfamous Liverpudlians were apt to feel ill at ease. And so it was that over the course of 1965 the Beatles began to withdraw from the public eye into the privacy of their suburban homes and the company of a small circle of old friends they had imported from Liverpool and those few new friends from London with whom they felt they could let down their guard. Hoisted as they were sky-high on the petard of pop celebrity, their enormous success had served to disassociate them from the world of ordinary experience. As successful popular artists *par excellence,* they were now faced with the difficult task of translating this sense of disassociation into successful popular art.

THE CRITICAL AND commercial success of *A Hard Day's Night* ensured that the Beatles' second film would be a more elaborate and expensive production than the first. United Artists approved a budget of $2 million for the picture, which would again be produced by Walter Shenson and directed by Richard Lester. Given free rein over the picture, Lester decided to dispense with the lingering residue of social realism a writer like Alun Owen would provide, and relied instead on a far more fantastical script by Charles Wood, who had written the screenplay for *The Knack,* a seminal Swinging London film that Lester had made during the second half of 1964. David Watkin, who had also worked on *The Knack,* was hired as cinematographer. The cast included the Australian character actor Leo McKern and the comedienne Eleanor Bron in supporting roles. Sparing no expense, Lester slated sections of the film to be shot on location in the Bahamas and the Austrian Alps. Filming was scheduled to start in Nassau in the last week of February and extend through the middle of May.

Prior to leaving for the Caribbean, the Beatles spent a week at Abbey Road, recording the songs for the film's soundtrack. The sessions began with a powerful track that was quickly designated for release as a single in the spring. After the gaiety of "I Feel Fine," "Ticket to Ride" seemed to mark a shift in the wind. Like its predecessor, the new song was written around a distinctive guitar riff that served as an introduction and recurrent instrumental motif; yet unlike the sinuous mambo that snakes through "I Feel Fine," the ostinato riff in "Ticket to Ride" is harmonically rooted in place, a bright arpeggiation of the tonic chord that throws the song back on its heels. Ringing out unaccompanied in the introduction, the notes glisten as if caught by the rays of the sun, but this bright opening is a mirage, shattered after two bars by a throbbing drone of bass and an acutely syncopated drum rhythm that seems to rise shakily and stagger unsteadily through each bar of the song. It is an altogether more ominous version of awakening than that offered by the jarring introductory chord of "A Hard Day's Night." Here the music stirs angrily as Lennon's voice comes in; "Ticket to Ride" pulsates with a threatening energy, thickly bottled up: "I think I'm gonna be sad, I think it's today . . . yeah! / The girl that's driving me mad, is going away . . . yeah!" The song transpires in the interval between expecting the worst and having it come to pass. John edges into the first line of each verse in a half-whisper, like a person talking to himself, his voice filling with incredulity as he builds up to an indignant shout of "yeah!" He is deep inside the role he burlesqued in "I'm a Loser"—the domineering lover who's finally met his match in a girl who has the temerity to do as she likes. In the release, Paul joins in over a suddenly steady backbeat and together they urge this carefree lover to "think twice" and "do right." Yet the force of this sentiment is so feeble that the verse, returning by way of an anguished guitar fill, seems to swallow it up. The song's sympathies are firmly with the girl—it's her need to be free of him, not his loss of her, that is driving the music ahead. In the last verse the beat shakes free of its stagger, and in the coda, amid piping falsetto voices that declare the girl's unconcern, the rhythm shifts into double-time, and she's not his baby anymore.

The February sessions that began with "Ticket to Ride" yielded a total of nine finished tracks, six of which were selected by Richard Lester for the film soundtrack; the remainder were set aside for the group's next Parlophone LP. In addition to "Ticket to Ride," the soundtrack songs included a ballad by John called "You've Got to Hide Your Love Away," a rocker by Paul called "The Night Before," a pair of matching Lennon-McCartney tunes titled "Another Girl" and "You're Going to Lose That Girl," and George Harrison's "I Need You," his first self-written song since "Don't Bother Me" on the Beatles' second LP. Although each of these tracks has its moments of interest, the collection as a whole was uninspired. George's "I Need You" is a modest, mild love song that sounds a lot like the efforts of other contemporary songwriters to write in the style of Lennon and McCartney. (The same applies to "You Like Me Too Much," another new Harrison original that was recorded during these sessions.) Paul's "The Night Before" puts a tremendous charge of musical energy behind a lyric based on the age-old pop theme (e.g., "After the Ball") of an overnight change of heart. The vocal arrangement highlights the increasingly complex and conversational relationship between lead and backup singing that would figure heavily in the Beatles' music in the years ahead. (It was as if the group had decided to transplant their repartee from their press conferences into their songs.) In this case, the colloquy casts Paul as the straight man, asking, "Were you telling lies? Was I so unwise?" while John and George respond with overblown sympathy, exclaiming after each line, "Ah! The night before!" More than anything that Richard Lester dreamed up in *A Hard Day's Night,* it has the feeling of a Marx Brothers routine.

The first of the matching "girl" tunes, McCartney's "Another Girl" is an exercise in emotional pragmatism that uses its pounding country backbeat to hammer another nail into the coffin of "only you." "I don't want to say that I've been . . . unhappy with you / But as from today well I've got . . . somebody that's new," Paul sings, inserting pregnant pauses at all the ticklish spots. (Later, in the bridge, the song changes key as it happily changes girl.) Lennon's response, "You're Going to Lose That Girl," is a more substantial effort with a distinct Motown flavor in the rhythm and backup singing. John's powerful lead vocal moves between an air of threat and anticipation, culminating in a little falsetto victory dance that packs a half-dozen syllables into the word "lose." The lyric revisits the romantic triangle of "She Loves You," and in the release, having exhausted every other variation on the theme, the Beatles finally come around to embracing the very sentiment the earlier song disavowed: "I'll make a point of taking her away from you / The way you treat her, what else can I do?"

One of the Beatles' favorite songs on *Another Side of Bob Dylan* was a ballad of romantic frustration called "I Don't Believe You (She Acts Like We Never Have Met)," which begins with the lines "I can't understand / She let go of my hand / And left me here facing the wall." John Lennon wrote "You've Got to Hide Your Love Away" as an undisguised homage to Dylan and his song: "Here I stand, head in hand, turn my face to the wall." In some ways the overtness of the imitation ("practically a Dylan impression," Paul McCartney would say) only serves to underscore the differences in the emotional sensibilities of the two singer-songwriters.

As Dylan matured as a lyricist, his approach to romantic drama became intensely subjective and personalized. In the case of "I Don't Believe You," though the lyric is couched in the third person, the song (as the title suggests) is implicitly addressed to the girl. In reworking this material, Lennon replaced the sense of incredulity that Dylan sustained over five long narrative verses with two short stanzas that expressed his own acute sense of self-consciousness—shifting the emphasis, as ever with John, from his pain to his pride. He sings the refrain in a harsh, jeering voice, repeating the phrase "Hey! You've got to hide your love away" with an angry intensity that startles the ear after his muted delivery of the verse. The litany of self-pity resumes in the second stanza until John interrupts himself with a sudden unguarded thought. "How could she say to me: 'Love will find a way'?" he asks, referring to the girl he's barely mentioned until now, and his voice grows wide with hurt at the thought of this careless platitude. Everything about this quick side trip into the specific feels right, and it snaps the song out of its head-holding pose. The refrain is sung more tenderly the second time around, and it is answered by an instrumental passage unlike anything to be heard on a Beatles record (or, for that matter, on any pop record) to date. At exactly the point in the song where Dylan's wheezing harmonica could be expected to make its entrance, the melody of "Hide Your Love Away" is turned over to a pair of *flutes,* matched in octaves, playing soft and low. The serenity of their tone would seem a joke on Dylan's shrillness, except that, skimming the surface of the song like a pair of swallows, their gentle tandem motion sounds so inexpressibly sad.

HAVING RECORDED MORE than enough songs for the soundtrack of the still-untitled sequel to *A Hard Day's Night,* the Beatles spent the next three months working almost exclusively as film actors, bemoaning the need to appear bright and early on the set each weekday morning, but otherwise enjoying the novel experience of having their evenings and weekends free to do as they liked. By the beginning of April, filming in the Bahamas and the Austrian Alps had been completed, and the production was alternating between Twickenham Studios, on the outskirts of London, and various locations in the English countryside. Several titles for the film had been considered and rejected, including the ungainly *Eight Arms to Hold You.* Now, in keeping with the film's Pop Art pretensions, someone (though no one seems to remember who) came up with idea of calling the picture *Help!,* as the word might appear in a bubble of comic-strip dialogue, and the Beatles were once again asked to compose a title song. However flippantly the title was intended, they took it more seriously in the song, which John Lennon came to regard as one of his personal favorites. "I *meant* it," John recalled. "It was me singing 'help' and I meant it. . . . You see the movie: He—I—is very fat, very insecure, and he's completely lost himself." The track certainly begins like he means it—bursting to life with Paul and George gasping the word *"Help!"* over a charging rockabilly beat, and John interjecting, "I need somebody!" Again: *"Help! . . . Not just anybody! . . . Help! . . . You know I need someone! . . . He-e-elp!"* Harrison's guitar percolates into the space after this final exclamation, and the song tumbles into the verse, where John mourns the loss of the brazen self-assurance of his younger days. The flat, bluesy melody is embellished with contrapuntal backup vocals that anticipate some of his lines and echo others, like thoughts circling around in his head. The driving energy of the singing and the playing recalls the sonic overload of early Beatles hits like "She Loves You," but after the opening flourish of excitement, the song is carried by its words. It was the lyric, certainly, that made John Lennon proud—so much so that when the first verse repeats near the end of the song, the beat drops out and John sings it unaccompanied, as if to emphasize that the words are coming from *him*. A year before, Lennon would have been embarrassed to use a term like "self-assured" in a song lyric, or to craft an image like that in the second verse, where his "independence seems to vanish in the haze." Still, what makes "Help!" compelling is not that it's so eloquent, but rather that it is written and sung in a more overtly *authorial* voice than any of the Beatles had attempted thus far. It's a slippery distinction—the point at which the *I* in a popular song ceases to refer to a singer who is playing the part of a musical actor, and starts to refer to the singer "himself." But the slipperiness of this distinction takes on special significance in the case of a singer who is also a songwriter. Nothing about the way John sings "Help!" is any more intimate or personal than his singing on "I'll Be Back" or "If I Fell." Yet there is an emotional authority in "Help!" that is absent from those earlier songs, in part because "Help!" is not a love song in the conventional sense. Instead, the neediness and nostalgia it expresses seem to play off the ideal of Autonomy that the Beatles had come to represent in the minds of their fans. The drama of John's performance depends upon the fact that it is a Beatle who is singing it, a Beatle who is saying that his life has changed in so many ways, a Beatle who is asking his listeners to help him "get my feet back on the ground." In this sense, "Help!" initiated a new and adventurous stage in John Lennon's career as a songwriter, in which he would begin to draw, with conscious intent, on the power of his own celebrity.

25

Jesus El Pifco was a foreigner and he knew it. He had imigrateful from his little white slum in Barcelover a good thirsty year ago having first secured the handy job as a coachman in Scotland. The job was with the Laird of McAnus, a canny old tin who have a castle in the Highlads. . . . One could see Jesus almost every day, grooming his masters horses, brushing their manebits and hammering their teeth, whistling a quaint Spanish refrain dreaming of his loved wombs back home in their little white fascist bastard huts.

—John Lennon

The single "Ticket to Ride" was released in April 1965 and went immediately to number one in Britain. In the United States, however, sales were somewhat sluggish by comparison with previous Beatles singles, and the song took more than a month to rise to number one, where it remained for a single week. The Beatles completed their work on *Help!* in the middle of May and went on vacation until the middle of June, when they returned to Abbey Road studios to record the half-dozen tracks they needed to fill out the non-soundtrack side of their next Parlophone LP.

That same month, John Lennon published his second book of fiction, whimsy, and verse, *A Spaniard in the Works*. The cast of characters (Silly Norman, Mr. Boris Morris) and the format of poems, satiric sketches, short-short stories, and line drawings was the same as *In His Own Write*. Overall, the language was less inhibited than in the first book, the stories less concise (some of them ran a full five or six pages), and the parodies more forced, sending up "Snore Wife and Some Several Dwarts," "Shamrock Wolmbs," and Lewis Carroll yet again in a poem called "The Wumberlog." *In His Own Write* had been compiled over a period of years, with parts of it dating back to the *Mersey Beat* columns Lennon had written in

1961. *A Spaniard in the Works* was written almost entirely over the course of 1964, and the overall standard of the writing is not up to that of its predecessor. But the punning, as ever, was inspired, nowhere more so than Lennon's commentary on the recent political trends:

> Azue orl gnome, Harrassed Wilsod won the General Erection, with a very small marjorie over the Torchies. Thus pudding the Laboring Partly back into powell after a large abcess. . . . Sir Alice Doubtless Whom was—quote—"bitherly dithapointed" but managed to keep smirking on his 500,000 acre estate in Scotland with a bit of fishing and that. The Torchies (now in apperition) have still the capable qualities of such disable men as Rabbit Bunloaf and the very late Harrods McMillion. What, you arsk, happened to Answerme Enos (ex Prim Minicar) after that Suez pudding, peaple are saying. Well I don't know.

The election to which Lennon referred had been held in October 1964 and had brought a Labour government to power for the first time in fourteen years—a political upheaval that counted as another big rumble in the populist "explosion" of Britain that year. Harold Wilson, the new Prime Minister, stood in sharp contrast to his blue-blooded Conservative opponent, Alec Douglas-Home. Of lower-middle-class background, Wilson was a former scholarship boy from the Yorkshire town of Huddersfield. He had attended Oxford, worked briefly in the civil service, and then stood for election to a parliamentary seat from Huyton, just west of Liverpool. As a politician, he played the part of the pragmatic Northerner to the hilt, and he could speak in the blunt tones of Huddersfield when the occasion demanded. Labour's narrow victory in 1964 was largely dependent on its strong showing in the North, and it is therefore not entirely facetious to suggest that Wilson's election represented some final stage of the infatuation with Merseyside—*Z Cars*, the Beatles, and Harold Wilson—that had gripped the British imagination with such intensity of late. Nor was it at all facetious to suggest (as did many commentators at the time) that Wilson's popularity marked the wholesale importation into British politics of America's Kennedy cult.

While the new Prime Minister's public image was in no way as glamorous as Kennedy's had been, he was nevertheless perceived as young and dynamic by the standards of his recent predecessors (the youngest

Prime Minister since Disraeli, it was noted), and he made no bones whatsoever about imitating Kennedy in the rhetoric of his campaign. Once elected, Wilson's emulation of the Kennedy style included a desire to associate himself and his government with the lively arts, and with the unprecedented popularity of certain lively artists, which was where the Beatles entered in. The group had been courted by politicians before. Sir Alec Douglas-Home once described them enigmatically as his "secret weapon." Edward Heath, who would soon assume the leadership of the "Torchies," had credited the Beatles with keeping the world safe for British corduroy during his days as president of the Board of Trade. But with his Merseyside constituency and his hands on the levers of power, Wilson was in a position to make a far more dramatic gesture. In June of 1965, the Prime Minister's office announced that the names Lennon, McCartney, Harrison, and Starkey would henceforth be embellished by the initials MBE.

Outside of Britain, there was great merriment about the Beatles and the MBE; fans in America reacted as if the Fab Four had been invited to join King Arthur at the Round Table. In Britain, however, the awarding of MBEs, CBEs, KBEs, and GBEs (not to mention KCMGs, GCVOs, and the occasional OM) was a semiannual affair, with the names of the honorees consuming nearly two pages of exceedingly fine print in the *Times* every January and June. The Beatles' designation, MBE, which stood for Member of the Order of the British Empire, was the lowest rank in the least ancient of the "orders of chivalry" that constitute the British system of Royal Honors. The order was established by George V as a gesture of Commonwealth unity during World War I and had since provided a fitting climax to thousands of military and civil-service careers. The order was also used to acknowledge contributions to the nation in the fields of commerce and the arts. Over time, a countertradition had developed among artists and writers of turning their Honors down—so much so that a discreet mechanism for refusal was built into the notification process. Although John Lennon would later claim otherwise, the Beatles never seriously considered refusing their Honors. In any case, they were cited for their contribution to commerce, not the arts—specifically for adding their weight to Britain's precarious balance of trade. "MBE," explained George Harrison, "really stands for 'Mr. Brian Epstein.'"

Although exact sales figures in the record industry have always been hard to come by, *Variety* reported in August 1965 that the Beatles had sold in excess of 150 million records worldwide. (By the end of the year this estimate would rise to 200 million, surpassing Elvis Presley's total since the start of his career.) In addition to these unprecedented record sales, there was the revenue from *A Hard Day's Night,* which had grossed approximately $10 million in its first year of release, the revenue from their tours, publishing royalties from their own recordings and the hundreds of versions of Lennon-McCartney songs that had been recorded by other artists, and the royalties from Beatle-related merchandising operations around the world. By 1965 the group's combined efforts were thought to be grossing something on the order of a hundred million dollars a year. And this counted only the commerce generated directly by the Beatles themselves. Even more significant for the British economy was the fact that the group had single-handedly created an export market in popular music where *none* had existed before. Moreover, by fanning the flames of pop Anglophilia in the United States, Europe, and parts of Asia, they had contributed significantly to the growth of Britain's fashion, entertainment, and tourism industries.

The Beatles' fellow MBEs in 1965 included J. S. Buller, for his services as a cricket umpire, J. Y. Couts, secretary of the Scottish Amateur Swimming Association, and C. J. Stripley, deputy chief driving examiner at the Department of Transportation. Their inclusion in this august company would seem a comparatively uncontroversial act on the part of Her Majesty's Government. Yet the whole point of the Royal Honors lay in their symbolism, and it was to the symbolic legitimization of the Beatles that some people took offense. The controversy began when a number of MBEs contacted the newspapers and announced their intention to return their medals in protest. A group of Labour MPs countered with a motion in the House of Commons expressing support for the government's decision to honor the darlings of Merseyside. A flurry of letters was received by the Prime Minister's office, some of them sent by fans of rival pop groups who claimed that a gross injustice had been done. The *Times* ran a story citing the remarks of two well-named critics of the award, a Colonel Wagg from Dover and a Councilor Drudge from Poole. When a Canadian Member of Parliament joined the ranks of those renouncing their Honors, Ringo Starr could take no more. "I don't care if Mr. Dupuis eats his medal," he said.

I said in a more fatuous moment recently that it's Wilkie
Collins's *The Moonstone* as drawn by Jasper Johns.

—Richard Lester

The Beatles' position as figureheads of Harold Wilson's New Britain was in fact the central comic premise of *Help!*, which premiered in London—with Princess Margaret and ten thousand fans again in attendance—in July. Audiences in Britain and America found a second cinematic installment of the Beatles' music and drollery to be highly entertaining, and the film matched the commercial success of *A Hard Day's Night*. Yet this time around, the consensus among the critics was that *Help!* was a bit of a mess—for all its brilliant color and high spirits, a pale sequel to Richard Lester's pop masterpiece of 1964. The Beatles shared this view. "We enjoyed making *Help!* more than *A Hard Day's Night* but looking back on the two I think *A Hard Day's Night* was the better film," Paul McCartney recalled. "*Help!* was great but it wasn't our film—we were sort of guest stars. It was fun, but basically, as an idea for a film, it was a bit wrong."

In light of the Beatles' subsequent enthusiasms, the screenplay that Richard Lester and Charles Wood concocted had a certain prescience. Inspired by a subgenre of English popular fiction that includes Wilkie Collins's *The Moonstone* and Arthur Conan Doyle's *The Sign of the Four*, the plot of *Help!* centers on the efforts of a sinister Indian swami (played by Leo McKern) and the members of his sect to capture and sacrifice Ringo, who has come to possess a sacred jeweled ring that was stolen from the sect's temple in India and sent to him by a fan. Once he realizes the fix he is in, Ringo wants no part of the ring, but it refuses to come off his finger. This leaves him and his fellow Beatles with no choice but to flee for their lives. The pursuit begins in London, crosses to the Alps for a snowy reprise of the open-field sequence in *A Hard Day's Night*, returns to Britain for a tour of national landmarks that includes Stonehenge, Scotland Yard, and Buckingham Palace (where the Beatles are sequestered for their own protection), and ends with a melee on the beach in Nassau that pits the swami's henchmen against a squad of Richard Lester's Kolonial Kops.

The idea of Ringo beset by a band of fanatics who crave something that has been given to him, yet now cannot be separated from him, over which he has no control; the portrayal of the Beatles as a national treasure, put up in Buckingham Palace, defended by the army, and protected by Scotland Yard—these were clever conceits, and *Help!* had the makings of sharp satire on the relationship of the Beatles to their fans and the cooptive power of the British Establishment. But Richard Lester had lost the patience for satire by 1965. Instead, *Help!* conformed to the slapdash style of film comedy that became known in the 1960s as *spoof,* and like many of the genre spoofs of the period, it tries to turn its own facetiousness into the biggest joke of them all. Up on the screen, the picture will not stop winking and mugging at its viewers; for all of its aura of hipness, it is as relentless as a music-hall clown. Even the reviewers who most admired the film were reduced to contorted praise like that of Philip French, who wrote that "its innovatory character lies precisely in its apparent lack of originality, its depth in the consistency of its two-dimensionality, its complexity in its simplicity." Other critics found it hard to bend over backward quite that far. "It's commercially safer to be deliberately foolish than to attempt something and be thought foolish," Pauline Kael noted in her *Atlantic Monthly* review.

The problem with the second Beatles movie—and the way in which it differed from the first—is most apparent in the handling of the allusions and visual quotations that figured so prominently in both. It made sense to provide *A Hard Day's Night* with a subtext of parodic references to the clichés of Hollywood musicals, precisely because the movie itself was so unlike the sort of banal movie musical that its viewers had every reason to expect. In *A Hard Day's Night,* moreover, this parodic dimension remains a subtext, a subsidiary pleasure of the film. But *Help!* tries to enlarge so strenuously on the success of its predecessor that it turns referentiality into a style: nearly every frame of the picture is explicitly derived from some other genre of film. There are bits from adventure movies, war movies, heist movies, travelogue movies, horror movies, sci-fi movies, and silent movies. Most of all, there are countless references to United Artists' *other* big Anglo-American venture, the James Bond movies. It was all very well for Richard Lester to cite Wilkie Collins and Jasper Johns as his inspirations; the fact remains that, from its jet-set itinerary to its corpulent villain, its malfunctioning gadgetry to the 007 theme music that is played during some of the chase scenes, *Help!* is mainly a relentless spoof of Bond. And the problem with making Bond the butt of the joke was that by the time of *Goldfinger,* the 007 pictures were taking on their own protective coating of irony and self-parody. This put *Help!* in the uncomfortable position of trying to spoof a spoof.

That the second Beatles film should reserve its most sustained parody for the spy genre was inadvertantly appropriate, however, because behind its "innovatively unoriginal" façade, *Help!* is struggling to hide its conformity with one of the most contrived film genres of them all: namely, it is the *sequel* to a fresh, distinctive, and commercially successful film. ("The chief problem with the second film," noted Stanley Kauffman in *The New Republic,* "is that the first one has been made.") And try as it might, *Help!* cannot parody this contrivance away. Once again, Richard Lester was content to establish the Beatles as the droll center of gravity, and to send the film racing crazily in circles around them. But the fanaticism that is supposed to serve as a foil for the Beatles in *Help!* is so calculated that their nonchalance—the cool, dignified indifference with which they appraised the hysteria surrounding them in *A Hard Day's Night*—seems calculated as well. This turns their native wit into a kind of Liverpudlian schtick. The second Beatles movie does the very thing that the first Beatles movie, to the credit of its makers and the delight of its audiences, didn't do—what *nobody* had succeeded in doing until now. Guest stars in their own film, the Beatles wound up being patronized by the picture.

THE PREMIERE OF *Help!* was accompanied by the release of the film's title track as the Beatles' second British single of 1965, and a few weeks later by the release of soundtrack albums on Parlophone and Capitol. The British and American versions of the soundtrack were patterned with exactitude on those of *A Hard Day's Night.* The Parlophone album again contained seven original songs from the film on its first side; the non-soundtrack side held five more originals bracketed by a pair of cover tunes. EMI released this collection with a whimsical cover photograph by Robert Freeman that showed the Beatles in the vaguely Victorian ski wear (leather hats, cloth capes, and boots) they wore in a scene from the film, silhouetted against a snow-white background. With their arms outstretched, they appear to be semaphoring the letters H-E-L-P, though their gestures spell nothing at all. The American soundtrack album was released by Capitol, not United Artists, this time; but it was once again marketed purely as an adjunct to the film, or "a very special soundtrack souvenir," as the liner notes maintained. The record interspersed the seven songs from the movie with brassy orchestrations of Beatles tunes and other incidental music from the film performed by George Martin and His Orchestra. "Is that all there is?" remarked Capitol's president Alan Livingston after he first heard the record. Many American Beatles fans felt the same way. As if to make up for the paucity of songs, Capitol packaged the album in an elaborate gatefold sleeve adorned with color stills from the film.

John Lennon's contribution to the soundtrack of *Help!* marked the furthest extension of his musical domination of the Beatles as a group. Of the seven songs in the film, John was the lead singer and principal songwriter on four of them, including both of the singles, "Help!" and "Ticket to Ride." (By contrast, on the soundtrack to the Beatles' first film, Paul McCartney sang "Can't Buy Me Love," shared the lead on "A Hard Day's Night" and "If I Fell," and sang the featured ballad "And I Love Her.") The second side of the Parlophone album restored some measure of balance. It opens with "Act Naturally," a 1963 hit by the country singer Buck Owens, which provides Ringo Starr with a perfect opportunity to poke fun at himself and the praise he earned for his part in the Beatles' films, singing, "We'll make a film about a man that's sad and lonely / And all I got to do is . . . act naturally." (When Paul adds a high harmony in the last verse, he sounds like the good singer who lives inside the head of every bad singer.) Next comes "It's Only Love," a halfhearted effort that John Lennon would later disown on account of a pretentious lyric that includes such inane lines as "When you sigh my mind's eye just flies, butterflies." George Harrison follows with "You Like Me Too Much," another pleasant, inconsequential original, which sets the stage for three songs in a row by Paul McCartney. In the first, Paul and John infuse the verses of "Tell Me What You See" with a breathy intimacy reminiscent of their cover version of Buddy Holly's "Words of Love." From its chivalrous beginning, "If you let me take your heart, I will prove to you," the song goes on to explore the vicissitudes of eye contact, as Paul enjoins his prospective lover to "look into these eyes now, tell me what you see." In the bridge the singers repeat the title line in octave harmony, and the music jolts to a stop, as if demanding an answer from the girl. What they get instead is a coy little flicker of musical equivocation (a hemming and hawing of parallel thirds, played on an electric piano) that provokes an exasperated reentry from the band.

The next track, "I've Just Seen a Face," has the feverish tempo and acoustic accompaniment (four guitars and brush-beat drumming) of a world-class skiffle song. The twelve-bar verses seem to pour out of Paul without a pause for breath or punctuation: "I've just seen a face I can't forget the time or place where we just met she's just the girl for me and I want all the world to see we've met . . . hmm, hmm, hmm, huh-hmm, hmmm!" The adrenaline rush of love at first sight is complemented by a gently syncopated refrain of "Falling, yes I am falling, and she keeps calling me back again" that Paul sings in double-tracked harmony with himself. In the solo, where the two-beat skiffle rhythm flattens into a jazzier 4/4 pulse, George Harrison's Djangoish tendencies surface, and the Beatles sound for a few fleeting bars like Le Hot Club of St. John's Wood.

Third in the McCartney trilogy is the ballad "Yesterday," a song so widely praised (as well as reviled for many of the same reasons it was praised) that it is useful to mention a few things that "Yesterday" was *not*. It was obviously not the first romantic ballad the Beatles ever recorded; McCartney had made a subspecialty of this genre from "A Taste of Honey" on. Neither was "Yesterday" even remotely the first pop record to make prominent use of strings—although it was the first Beatles recording to do so. There were violins in popular music long before there were electric guitars, and "sweetened," string-heavy pop arrangements had become a musical status symbol during the decade before the Beatles, called upon to add a touch of class to Elvis Presley's arias, the Drifters' uptown rhythm and blues, and the stylizations of singers as diverse as Connie Francis and Ray Charles. Finally, for all its musical integrity and tunefulness (the musicologist Wilfred Mellers characterized the song as a "small miracle"), "Yesterday" did not represent some sort of a compositional quantum leap on the part of the Beatles; it was rather that the more traditional sound of strings allowed for a fresh appreciation of their talent as composers by listeners who were otherwise allergic to the din of drums and electric guitars.

Its novelty thus qualified, "Yesterday" remains a marvel (if not quite a miracle) for the manner in which it combines Paul McCartney's dry naturalistic vocal with an accompaniment of violins, viola, and cello, scored by George Martin in the style of a classical string quartet. To his credit, Martin didn't burden the arrangement with an attempt to be overly clever or correct. It was rather an approximation of chamber music he provided—a musical metaphor uniquely appropriate to a song that otherwise shows such an acute concern for "classical" considerations of clarity, form, and restraint. For "Yesterday" is an act of compositional sleight-of-hand. It drapes verses of apparent symmetry—each one ending on the same word and chord with which it began—over an eccentric seven-bar structure that is so well matched to the phrasing of the lyric that the "missing" bar goes all but unnoticed. This utterly empirical construction—a seven-bar verse is about as common as a seventeen-hole golf course—supports a fragile arch of melody that droops dispiritedly over the word "yesterday" in the opening measure before pausing with a kind of dramatic inertia for a span of four full beats. The tune then rises steeply from the second beat of the second measure ("All my troubles seemed . . ."), slipping briefly out of the key of the song, as if to emphasize the uncertainty of "seemed," and reaches its furthest melodic extension in the third bar ("so *far* away . . ."). The line then retraces the path of its ascent, falling steeply through bars four and five ("Now it looks as though they're here to stay"), sliding across another patch of harmonic ambiguity in the sixth measure ("Oh I *believe* . . ."), and coming to rest on a gentle upturn (". . . in yesterday").

It is at this point that the conventionally minded composer or arranger would have inserted an instrumental measure, most likely echoing the last melodic strain, so as to create a conforming eight-bar verse (the way that Harold Arlen did in "Stormy Weather," the melody of which also transpires over seven bars). McCartney didn't bother, and the "missing bar" turns into a subtle joke on itself when the next verse arrives—four beats too soon, by the rules—on the line "*Suddenly,* I'm not half the man I used to be." (There had always been humor associated with "Yesterday," which was initially conceived with one of the more ludicrous "dummy" lyrics in the annals of popular song. The first time George Martin recalled hearing Paul sing it, accompanying himself on a room-service piano in the Beatles' Paris hotel suite in January 1964, it began with the words "Scrambled eggs," dramatic pause and all.)

The compositional ingenuity of "Yesterday" would have meant nothing without Paul McCartney's exquisitely restrained performance of the song. "No vibrato" was McCartney's one stipulation when George Martin first suggested that they record the song with strings, and "no vibrato" it is for him as well. He sings with an air of slight distraction, his tone and phrasing completely unadorned. And he sings alone—in the first verse, before the strings join in, *really* alone, just him and an acoustic guitar. The other Beatles neither play nor sing on the track (this was a first for the group), and their very absence contributes to the mood of abandonment and despair. In certain parts of "Yesterday," Paul sings as if he can barely bring himself to sing, with an eerie hollowness in his voice. It was precisely this restraint that, along with its inherent tunefulness, attracted so many other singers to the song; they had the feeling that "Yesterday" had yet to be done up right. But the original version is by far the nakedest, and thousands of impassioned interpretations later, it remains unique and unsurpassed.

McCartney's three songs on the second side of *Help!* amounted to a great burst of self-assertion on his part—particularly "Yesterday," which Capitol Records went on to release as a single in America, where it became, along with "I Feel Fine," "Eight Days a Week," "Ticket to Ride," and "Help!", the Beatles' fifth number-one record of 1965. The last word on *Help!*, however, belonged to John Lennon. The Larry Williams tune "Dizzy Miss Lizzy" is as raw and lewd an example of the primordial spirit of rock 'n' roll as the Beatles would ever record, and it comes across as an act of musical restitution after the sound of a string quartet. Into the hushed aftermath of McCartney's ballad comes the stinging, hornetlike whine of George Harrison's lead guitar, playing a riff from the Williams record that George proceeds to repeat, note for note, without variation, for the entire two and a half minutes of the track, adjusting for local harmonic conditions (the song is a twelve-bar blues) as they present themselves. Thirty, forty, fifty times he plays it, with the self-absorption of a child perfecting his signature, and each repetition seems to affirm some deeply held belief that *these* eight notes, in *this* configuration, represent the only conceivable accompaniment to the song. While his lead guitarist pumps new meaning into the concept of *ostinato*, John Lennon simply howls the nonsensical lyric ("You make me dizzy, Miss Lizzy, the way you rock 'n' roll"), once again turning Abbey Road Studios into an annex of the Cavern Club. John's performance—or, more accurately, his *behavior*, for he finishes some of the verses by simply throwing back his head and *shrieking* at the top of his lungs—harkens back to the monumental version of "Twist and Shout" he sang at the end of *Please Please Me* in 1963. That track had been the Beatles' first great recording of a non-original song. "Dizzy Miss Lizzy" would be their last.

26

I asked about Beatlemania and George remarked: "You're a bit behind the times, aren't you? A year or two ago, that was Beatlemania. Now it's just fan worship."

—Alan Levy

The Beatles began their working summer at the end of June 1965 with a two-week tour of France, Italy, and Spain. Consisting of fifteen shows in eight cities, this tour proved to be an ill-conceived and ill-promoted affair. In Genoa and Milan the group performed in blazing afternoon heat at outdoor arenas that were less than a quarter filled with fans, while their four shows at the cinema-sized Teatro Adriano in Rome were played to half-full houses. They returned to London in July to attend the premiere of *Help!,* then flew to the United States in the middle of August to fulfill an itinerary of ten dates—half as many concerts as the year before, held in venues twice as large. The tour opened with the biggest live concert they would ever play, a performance in front of 55,000 high-decibel New York teenagers filling all four decks of the newly built Shea Stadium, to which the Beatles were delivered by means of an armored car. The spectacle of this and their subsequent appearances at Atlanta County Stadium and Chicago's Comiskey Park was unprecedented in pop terms—rock 'n' roll had arrived in the major leagues. But as *The Saturday Review* pointed out with a certain relief in its report on the concert at Shea, more than seventy thousand listeners had recently turned out to hear the New York Philharmonic perform Beethoven's Ninth Symphony in Central Park.

The Beatles' sets at these enormous open-air concerts were short, inflexible, thirty-minute affairs that began with an abbreviated overture of "Twist and Shout" followed by a succession of their hits—"I Feel Fine," "She's a Woman," "Ticket to Ride," "Can't Buy Me Love," "A Hard Day's Night," and "Help!", rounded out by a song from George, "Everybody's Trying to Be My Baby," and a song from Ringo, "Act Naturally." Between songs, they bantered with the audience, Lennon wittily, McCartney earnestly: "Yes." [SCREECH] "Well." [SCREEECH] "We

England 1965

hope you like this next number . . ." [SCREEEECH]. Some idea of the music itself can be found on a set of recordings that were made at the Hollywood Bowl in Los Angeles in the summers of 1964 and 1965 and released years later by Capitol. These concerts were somewhat atypical, since the Hollywood Bowl had famously good acoustics and a public address system that was less inadequate than most. Yet the sound quality on the recordings is uniformly dreadful, with only a rough outline of the singing and playing filtered through the jet-noise roar of the crowd. The 1964 recordings, in which the band sounds consistently out of tune and out of time, support the Beatles' own contention that the quality of their live performances went steadily downhill after the onset of Beatlemania. The performances from 1965 tell a somewhat different story, however.

In keeping with their desire to experience the United States in a more civilized manner this time, the Beatles spent a full week toward the end of their 1965 tour ensconced in a house in Benedict Canyon, on the out-skirts of Los Angeles, communing with a carefully vetted selection of visiting celebrities. At the end of this week-long retreat, they came down from their mountaintop to perform at the Hollywood Bowl, and with all of hip Hollywood in attendance, they felt they had something to prove. Their singing is remarkably strong and expressive under the circumstances, their playing spare, weighty, and pistol-hot, as if they were trying to push the music through the dense curtain of screams to some imaginary discerning audience that was listening on the other side. Paul sings a definitive version of "She's a Woman." John bellows "Dizzy Miss Lizzy" like some great rock-'n'-roll dragon, writhing in carnal delight. Then they combine on a world-weary rendition of "A Hard Day's Night" that makes the original, good as it is, sound like a demonstration track.

Their 1964 American tour had ended with the marijuana summit with Dylan in New York. The 1965 tour ended with an encounter of similar symbolic magnitude: an audience with Elvis Presley. Toward the end of their week-long stay in Los Angeles, at the point where the media coverage generated by their presence in the city had reached its absolute peak, Brian Epstein received a call from Colonel Tom Parker, inviting the Beatles to visit with Presley at his home in Beverly Hills. Parker had been trying to arrange this meeting (on his own terms) for more than a year, but he had been unable to get Elvis to agree, because Elvis, who hadn't placed a record in the Top Ten since 1963, had taken the Beatles' success *very* personally. In the spring of 1965, however, RCA released a recording that Presley had made in 1960 of a gospel song called "Crying in the Chapel." "Crying in the Chapel" rose to number three in the United States; even better, it became Presley's first number-one record in Britain since the Beatles came on the scene. This reassertion of his commercial prowess seems to have emboldened the King to meet the Pretenders in the flesh.

For Colonel Parker, the visit was all business, and while the Beatles took pains to arrive as unobtrusively as possible, the Colonel saw to it that there were reporters, television crews, and hundreds of fans waiting at the gates of Presley's home. The particulars of what went on inside are lost in a cloud of apocrypha. Most accounts agree that Brian Epstein and Tom Parker played roulette together, that Ringo Starr shot pool with members of Presley's "Memphis Mafia," that George Harrison shared a joint and discussed Hindu philosophy with Elvis's hairdresser and spiritual adviser Larry Geller, that John Lennon amused his host with his imitations of Peter Sellers, and that Elvis himself spent much of the evening lounging on a sofa with an electric bass in his hands. "Coming along quite promising on the bass, Elvis," Paul McCartney is supposed to have said. The encounter was apparently marked by considerable electricity but little warmth, for Presley subsequently declined the Beatles' invitation to visit them at their house in Benedict Canyon, and the ultimate rock group and the ultimate rock star never crossed paths again. We do know that one member of Elvis's entourage, Alan Fortas, unable to tell the guests apart, addressed them generically: "Hey! Beatle!"

THE SUMMER OF 1965—when, in the larger scheme of things, the United States began its precipitous escalation of the war in Vietnam, and the riots in the Watts district of Los Angeles conclusively shifted the focus of the civil rights movement from the towns of the South to the cities of the North and the West—marked another riveting season of popular music on American Top Forty radio. From the Motown studios in Detroit came Top Ten hits without end: "Back in My Arms Again" by the Supremes (their fifth number-one song in a row), "Nowhere to Run" by Martha and the Vandellas, "I Can't Help Myself" by the Four Tops, and Smokey Robinson and the Miracles with the ballad "The Tracks of My Tears." From the Stax/Volt studios in Memphis came the first hit records by a pair of premier soul singers, Wilson Pickett ("In the Midnight

Hour") and Otis Redding ("I've Been Loving You Too Long"). And from James Brown, who had been a dominant presence on the rhythm-and-blues charts since the 1950s, came his first pop hit, aptly entitled "Papa's Got a Brand New Bag."

The British Invasion continued apace in the States. Though most of the Merseybeat groups (with the exception of the Beatles) fell by the wayside during 1965, bands like the Kinks ("Tired of Waiting") and the Dave Clark Five ("I Like It Like That") built upon their success of the year before. There came a sudden influx of groups from Manchester, led by Herman's Hermits, whose campy revival of the Edwardian music-hall standard "I'm Henry VIII, I Am" was irresistible to American teenagers (though the record didn't even make the charts in Britain). The Anglophilic trend in pop had broadened sufficiently for American listeners to embrace such mainstream British singers as Tom Jones and Petula Clark, as well as Shirley Bassey belting out the theme from the James Bond film *Goldfinger* (on a record produced by George Martin). But the most significant musical development from Britain concerned the fortunes of the Rolling Stones, who had achieved only limited success in the American record market in 1964. Now, recording in Los Angeles under the tutelage of the engineer Dave Hassinger, the Stones managed to translate the full force of their menacing public image into music, and produced an extraordinary record. "(I Can't Get No) Satisfaction" was their "She Loves You," an anthem of adolescent alienation that topped the charts in America for most of the month of July.

Yet for all this rich mixture of Motown, Southern Soul, and British Invasion bands, the driving force in American popular music in the summer of 1965 was suddenly a figure who, until this point, had never been recognized as a pop singer, much less as a pop star. In March, Bob Dylan had released his fifth Columbia album, which he pointedly titled *Bringing It All Back Home*. The phantasmagoric cover photograph showed a wild-haired, sallow-faced, and modly-dressed Dylan, cradling a Siamese kitten, seated on a chaise beside a classic Lady in Red. She looked like something out of *Vogue;* he looked like something the kitten dragged in. The back cover of the album showed snapshots of the poet Allen Ginsberg, the folksinger Joan Baez (with whom Dylan had recently concluded a much-publicized affair), and Dylan himself in a top hat, beaming like the Mad Hatter or a cousin of Harpo Marx. On the opening track of *Bringing It All Back Home,* Dylan splashed across the Rubicon of pop, singing with complete confidence over a stomping, wailing backbeat of drums and electric guitars. "Subterranean Homesick Blues" updated the themes of youthful disaffection and paranoia that Chuck Berry had sounded in songs like "School Days" and "Too Much Monkey Business" a decade before. "Ah get born, keep warm, short pants, romance, learn to dance, get dressed, get blessed, try to be a *suc*-cess," Dylan sang, spinning out a line of erudite jive as verbally compelling as the groove of a good dance record. Columbia released the song as a bona fide pop single, and it catapulted Dylan into the biblical Top Forty for the first time in his career.

The first side of *Bringing It All Back Home* contained six more songs with electric band accompaniment. On the second side, Dylan reverted to his usual format of voice, harmonica, and acoustic guitar. Among these acoustic numbers was a tuneful ballad he had been performing in concert for nearly a year. "Hey, Mr. Tambourine Man, play a song for me," it began, "I'm not sleepy and there is no place I'm going to." "Mr. Tambourine Man" came on the radio in the spring of 1965 and by the start of the summer had risen to number one—but not with Bob Dylan singing it. Instead, the song achieved its great success in a rendition by the Byrds, a Los Angeles–based group led by a former folk guitarist, Jim McGuinn. An accomplished instrumentalist who had performed and recorded with commercial folk groups like the Limeliters during the early 1960s, McGuinn was not the only young person in America whose life was changed by what he had witnessed on *The Ed Sullivan Show* on February 9, 1964, but his response went a good deal further than most. Within weeks he was growing his hair and performing a set of solo "Beatle Impressions" in Greenwich Village clubs. Six months later he was in Los Angeles when *A Hard Day's Night* came out, precipitating his second epiphany of 1964. Although McGuinn had been smitten with the Beatles' music since February, it was not until he saw the depiction of their camaraderie in *A Hard Day's Night* that he got it in his head to form a pop group of his own.

After acquiring a twelve-string Rickenbacker electric guitar like the one George Harrison played in the film, McGuinn hooked up with some itinerant Los Angeles folkies and an old acquaintance from prep school who happened to be in town. (According to his bassist Chris Hillman, all that the five members of the group had in common was "a love of pot and the Beatles.") They called themselves the Jet Set at first, and what happened to them over the next six months gives some idea of the turmoil in the American record business at the time. In a matter of weeks the Jet Set signed with Elektra Records, changed their name to the Beefeaters, released an unsuccessful single, were dropped by Elektra, then signed by Columbia, and renamed yet again, in the manner of the Beatles-with-an-*a*, the Byrds-with-a-*y*. Somewhere in the midst of this metamorphosis, they acquired as their publicist none other than Derek Taylor, who had resigned his position as the Beatles' press officer in the fall of 1964 and moved to California to live the life of a Hollywood Brit. Next, in January 1965, having heard "Mr. Tambourine Man" on a Dylan demo tape that was making the rounds at Columbia, the Byrds, backed by a group of Los Angeles studio musicians, recorded the song in a dreamily harmonized version dominated by the chiming of McGuinn's twelve-string (he was the only Byrd to play on the track). The effect was quite different from the weary transcendence of Dylan's acoustic version; as the Byrds performed it, "Mr. Tambourine Man" sounded like surf music for the mind. The publicity department at Columbia dubbed it "folk-rock" (so eager was the label, still, to avoid the taint of rock 'n' roll), a term that meant Dylanesque lyrics combined with rock rhythm and Beatlesque harmonies.

Dylan heard the Byrds' version of his song before it was released and liked it; but he liked the *idea* of it even more. In May 1965, as "Mr. Tambourine Man" entered the charts, he left on a month-long tour of Britain, where he again performed at the Royal Albert Hall, this time before an audience that included all four Beatles. (He also visited with John Lennon, who was by all accounts *obsessed* with *Bringing It All Back Home*.) Dylan's popularity in Britain had always been strong, but on this visit he was received as a full-blown pop star, attracting a level of frenzied attention from fans and the press that exceeded anything he had experienced in the States. He returned from this exposure to the fast lane of pop resolved to continue recording with a band, and ready to start performing with one as well. In August he bid farewell to the folk movement by turning his annual appearance at Newport into a cacophonous rock concert that was received with confusion and at least some hostility by the same crowd whose adulation had helped to make him a national celebrity in 1963. That same month Columbia released Dylan's second pop single. It was one of the songs he performed at Newport, a watershed recording called "Like a Rolling Stone."

Notwithstanding that it broke a cardinal rule of Top Forty radio by running nearly five minutes, "Like a Rolling Stone" earned Dylan the hit single he had quietly dreamed about since high school. It rose through the charts in August to a peak at number two, shut out of the number-one spot only by the imperious presence of "Help!", and its success propelled its author into the most extraordinary stage of his career. No longer the conscientious voice of social protest, Dylan now embodied a literate and idiosyncratic style of cultural radicalism that harkened back to his bohemian forebears in San Francisco in the 1950s and Greenwich Village in the 1920s, to the Surrealists and the Symbolist poets with whom new friends like Allen Ginsberg had begun to familiarize (and compare) him. Shakespeare in overalls was thus reborn as Rimbaud in polka dots: the first true artist-provocateur of pop. The esotericism and frequent rancor of this enterprise was mitigated by the brilliance of Dylan's wit and the raw vitality of the musical accompaniment, most of it played in a style of roadhouse blues as static and straightforward as the lyrics were shifting and complex. Dylan's intensity was also mitigated by the fact that much of what he had to say went straight past his new pop audience, just as the nuance of his social protest had gone straight past the ideologues in the folk revival movement. To most of his young listeners, "Like a Rolling Stone" was in no sense a cautionary tale; it wasn't *them* that Dylan was addressing when he berated his fallen debutante. Instead, they heard the refrain of "How does it feel? To be on your own?" as an expression of their own yearnings for freedom and adventure—an invitation, not a warning. Dylan would continue to be misunderstood by his fans and simply ignored by a large segment of the pop audience for whom his voice would always be too tuneless, his lyrics too obscure, and his persona too enigmatic. But in terms of artistic influence, if not commercial impact, his conversion to rock in the summer of 1965 set the world of popular music as sharply on its ear as the Beatles had done the year before.

Coming into the studio was a refuge for them. It was the
time and place when nobody could get at them. The
strange hours for their sessions were really necessary
because of the frenetic life they were forced into. . . .
Recording was important but it had to be squeezed in
between everything else.

—George Martin

In August 1965, George Martin resigned the post he had held for ten years as the head of EMI's Parlophone label. Martin had been contemplating the move for some time, ever since the management of EMI made it clear that the company intended to continue to pay him his annual salary of £3,000 and not a penny more—this despite the fact that, in two years, Martin's work with the Beatles and his other artists had been responsible for more than doubling the profits of EMI's record division as a whole. In the summer of 1965, after one last effort to persuade the company to compensate him for his success, Martin made good on his promise to leave, setting up his own independent record production company and taking several of his fellow EMI staff producers along with him. It would seem that EMI had simply failed to recognize that the man who had been running their "comedy and novelty" label since 1955 had become the most sought-after record producer in the world. EMI further failed to recognize that the Beatles would insist that Martin be retained as an independent producer on their records—on Martin's terms, this time.

Any doubts that this would be so had been laid to rest by "Yesterday." Until the shift in their relationship symbolized by that recording, Martin's contribution to the Beatles' music had been largely supervisory. He had begun by suggesting simple improvements to their simple arrangements, telling them when they were singing or playing out of tune, selecting the songs to be released as singles, sequencing the tracks on the albums, and generally taking overall responsibility for the recording, mastering, and

pressing of the finished product. (Martin himself possessed little technical knowledge of the recording process, and he relied extensively on the
skill of his engineer Norman Smith to achieve the effects he desired.)
Toward the end of 1963, as Lennon and McCartney became progressively more ambitious in their songwriting, Martin began to function as
an informal music teacher to them as well. He even learned how to play
the guitar in a rudimentary manner in order to facilitate communication,
since, as he liked to point out, the Beatles identified chords not so much
by their notes as by the *shapes* their fingers made on the fretboard. "Oh,
that's my D shape," John Lennon would say.

With "Yesterday" the relationship entered a new phase. It was Martin
who suggested the string quartet accompaniment, and the Beatles who
were skeptical until they heard the result. Their appreciation of the track
opened up a new world of musical possibilities for them. "Yesterday"
made them realize that they could draw on Martin's conventional skills as
an arranger and orchestrator without having to put up with the intimidating formalities that usually went with the services of arrangers, orchestra-
tors, and the studio musicians who performed their work. Having access
to Martin's musical sensibility, they would find, was like having access to
a wondrous musical synthesizer capable of reproducing not only pitch
and timbre but also style and genre—a synthesizer that came with a
built-in sense of musical humor as well. If they wanted to hear "something baroque" on a song, and didn't care to narrow it any further, they
could ask Martin for "something baroque" and see what he produced.
Usually, it was the right thing, and if it wasn't, he would change it without fuss. Though he liked to characterize himself as the hapless victim of
the Beatles' whims—"I've changed from being a gaffer for four Herberts
from Liverpool to what I am now, clinging to the last vestiges of recording
power," he told an interviewer in 1967—the truth is that Martin thrived
on the challenge presented and the freedom afforded by the Herberts'
requests.

Though Martin's new creative relationship with the Beatles would
evolve steadily over the next two years, there were several immediate
changes in October 1965 when the group returned to the studio for the
first time since Martin had left EMI. Until now they had been working
for him; from this point forward he was working for them. For as long as
Martin had served as the head of Parlophone, he had an obligation to run
a tight ship at Abbey Road. Though he was by nature highly disciplined in

the way he approached his work, this became much less of a concern after he left EMI.

In 1965, big commercial recording studios in Britain and America adhered to a set of policies that were designed to reflect the fact that the recording industry was a business, and needed to function in a businesslike manner. One of the most influential of these policies was that of booking studio time in three-hour blocks. At Abbey Road, sessions typically ran from 10:00 a.m. until lunch at 1:00 p.m., then from 2:30 until 5:30 in the afternoon, and from 7:00 p.m. until 10:00 p.m. It was a well-regulated system, and it did more than determine the procedure by which popular records were made. Together with the informal three-minute time limit for singles, the standard of the three-hour recording session also determined, to a considerable extent, what a pop record *was,* since it institutionalized the assumption that three hours was more than enough time to make a record—the two sides of a single, at a minimum, and preferably more than that. This assumption was central to the recording industry as a whole; it secured the livelihoods of a multitude of producers, engineers, arrangers, and studio musicians who specialized not only in the ability to get things done, but in the ability to do them *fast.* ("A lot of my learning experience had to do with the speed with which you did a date," recalled the senior American engineer and producer Phil Ramone. "Then, the big thing was to do three or four songs on a session.")

Having been transformed in the 1950s by the development of magnetic tape, the technology of sound recording was again transformed in the 1960s by the development of multitrack recorders, which were installed at Abbey Road in the fall of 1963, just in time for the recording of "I Want to Hold Your Hand." (Nearly all of the records the Beatles made from then until 1968 were made on these four-track decks.) The initial hope for multitrack technology was that it would make the recording process more efficient by making it possible to record more cleanly and balance more precisely, to isolate individual instruments and voices, and to edit more selectively and discreetly. But like most technological advances, multitrack recording had unanticipated effects. It made the process so much more flexible, in fact, that record-making began to take on a dynamic very different from the dynamic of live performance that had determined the nature of musicianship since musicianship began. From its inception, sound recording had revolutionized performance practice by providing performers with the ability to listen to themselves from "outside" the music—to listen the way an audience listens, as opposed to the way a performer listens, from deep within the music, where he is busy generating sound. Now, with the advent of multitrack equipment, studios began to develop and employ sophisticated methods not only of listening, but of shaping, coloring, editing, and augmenting a performance from the "outside," after the fact. Instead of simply capturing the sound of a live performance, the new technology could be used to hold that performance in a state of flux, its component parts broken down and stored on four (and later eight) separate tracks, any one of which could be rerecorded, embellished, or treated with special effects without necessarily altering the sound of the other three. This far-reaching elaboration of the process brought a new level of self-reflection to record-making. And, combined with self-sufficiency, self-reflexiveness ate up time.

The Beatles adhered nominally to the format of three-hour sessions during their first year at Abbey Road, but the sheer velocity of their success led them to wreak havoc with the routine there in 1963. With "Please Please Me" racing up the charts, their first album was recorded in a mad rush—ten tracks in twelve hours. Their second album consumed about forty hours of studio time, which averaged out to a little less than three hours a track. *Hard Day's Night* took slightly longer, owing to the increased use of overdubbing and the greater diversity of the songs, many of which were freshly written and virtually unrehearsed. The Beatles' fourth Parlophone album, *Beatles for Sale,* required about the same amount of studio time as its predecessor, while *Help!,* with its elaborately overdubbed backup vocals and its use of flutes and strings, took a bit longer, but not much longer, for the Beatles could not have spent more time making their records if they'd wanted to—not if they intended to make movies, tour the world, and release two albums a year on the assumption that they had to make the most of their popularity while it lasted. But as their popularity lasted over the course of 1965, the Beatles grew less concerned with squeezing every last penny out of what was proving to be an extended turn in the limelight. If the velocity of their success required them to bend the rules at Abbey Road, it was the durability of their success that emboldened them to shatter the routine there for good. Scaling back their tour of Britain in the fall, the group left themselves a full, uninterrupted month in which to write and record their next album. They requested—and EMI agreed—that they be allowed to use the studios whenever they liked, for as long as they liked. Probably the only person with enough influence to have dissuaded them was George Martin, and he didn't work there anymore. The group responded by spending more than a hundred hours at Abbey Road in the fall of 1965. They spent so much time on some of the songs that they found themselves confronted by a mid-November deadline for Christmastime release, which forced them to record three final tracks the old-fashioned way, in a single marathon session that began at six in the evening and ended at seven in the morning of the following day.

One established policy the Beatles did observe in the fall of 1965 was that of withholding the tracks they released as a single from their album, and as in previous years, it diluted the quality of the LP. "We Can Work It Out" and "Day Tripper" represented such a formidable pair of songs that both were designated A-sides of the single and sent out into the world to compete with each other for the affections of radio programmers and record buyers. "Day Tripper" was a straightforward sequel to "Ticket to Ride," in which the recycled railroad metaphor was hitched to a druggy double entendre, the whole thing pulled along by a recurrent motif on guitar. Derivative though it is, the song has interesting qualities, beginning with its exhilarating introduction—a growling, angular riff on one guitar echoed by the same riff on another, joined by a shimmy of tambourine and then the sound of Ringo, rumbling down a steep grade into a hard, head-snapping beat. The result is as fine an example of utilitarian dance music as the Beatles would ever record.

The winner of the Beatles' A-side sweepstakes would prove to be "We Can Work It Out," and no wonder, for it is an exceptionally powerful record, in which Paul and John, as they did in "A Hard Day's Night," divide the lead singing between the verse and the bridge of the tune. The track starts in mid-conversation at a measured, urgent tempo—a march almost—paced by a jangle of tambourine and the swells and moans of a harmonium imitating the sound of a Parisian street organ. "Try to see it my way," sings Paul, over a suspended tonic chord that seems to suspend the entire song in a state of doubt. "Only time will tell if I am right or I am wrong." The harmonium part is a musical cliché of melancholy, but, used in a knowing manner, it suggests that this stereotype of sadness is what lies in store for these two lovers should they fail to reach some accord. Paul ends the verse with a promise: "We can work it out." Then

John slides in over the song's only minor chord, singing about the futility of "fussing and fighting" as the music lurches into a reeling circus waltz that offers an exaggerated contrast to the marchlike meter of the verse. The effect is one of time out of joint. John sings another six bars in this fashion, and then Paul sweeps him aside, as if impatient with these generalizations, resuming the crisis diplomacy of the verse. To listen to "We Can Work Out" is to be pleaded with by a pair of experts. The song completes a year-long emotional trajectory that began at a high point with the single "I Feel Fine," and descended through the foreboding of "Ticket to Ride" in the spring and the confessions of "Help!" in the summer, to arrive in this anxious place.

28

We've got some comedy songs on our new LP. There's one called "Norwegian Wood." It's something new for us. It's just we're a bit sick so we thought we'd write something funny.

—Paul McCartney

The title *Rubber Soul* was suggested by Paul McCartney and meant as a self-deprecating pun on the relationship between white musicians and black music, 1965 being the year when the term "soul music" came into general usage as a description of gospel-based rhythm and blues. But the title also carried an implication that it was not just the Beatles' lives but their very souls that had been bent out of shape by the stresses and strains of success. Certainly this was the impression created by Robert Freeman's woozily distorted cover photograph, in which the Beatles' pale, grave faces are shown looming out of the deep green foliage behind them. George, Ringo, and Paul are all gazing off to the side like figures communing with Destiny in a classic Romantic tableau. Only John peers down his long nose into the lens, his expression exquisitely dandified, his mocking eyes ringed in red. Swirling across their foreheads, over their ears and down their necks, the Beatles' hair in the photograph is not only full but *long*—as long as the hair in storybook illustrations of the Middle Ages. They no longer looked like pageboys, but more like full-fledged knights, and in the fourteen songs on the album, they showed every intention of leaving all vestiges of storybook romance behind. The music on *Rubber Soul* is well advertised by this cover: it is the Beatles as before, but twisted on their axis, looking in different directions, arrayed against a background of darker, more somber hues.

From the beginning of its association with the Beatles, Capitol Records had reserved the right to release the tracks supplied by Parlophone in any format it chose, and at times it seemed that all the promotional energy the American label had once withheld from the Beatles was now being channeled into devising new ways to repackage and exploit their music. Unsatisfied with the group's prodigious Parlophone output of three singles and two LPs a year, Capitol maximized its profits by issuing album tracks as supplementary singles and by withholding three or four tracks from each of the Parlophone albums, thereby generating enough of a backlog over the course of a year to squeeze out another LP. The Beatles' American releases in 1965 therefore included "Eight Days a Week" as a single in February; an album in March called *The Early Beatles* (a reissue of the original Vee-Jay LP, to which Capitol had gained the rights); "Ticket to Ride" in April; an album called *Beatles VI* in June (consisting of a half-dozen tracks from *Beatles for Sale* that had been left off *Beatles '65,* plus a few songs from Parlophone's *Help!*); the single of "Help!" in July, followed by the soundtrack album in August; then "Yesterday" as a single in September, "We Can Work It Out" in November, and finally *Rubber Soul,* which happened to be the first Beatles album since *Meet the Beatles* to be released with the same cover in both Britain and the United States. The uniformity of the packaging obscured the differences in the product, for Capitol had dispensed with four of the songs on the Parlophone album (including several of the strongest cuts) and replaced them with a pair of tamer tracks, as yet unreleased in America, that were remaindered from the British *Help!*

Paul McCartney's "I've Just Seen a Face" thus led off side one of the American *Rubber Soul,* while John Lennon's embarrassment, "It's Only Love," led off side two. The intent was to capitalize on the growing enthusiasm for folk-rock in the United States, but the altered format turned the album title into an even more obscure joke, since the Capitol version showed less of a soul or rhythm-and-blues influence than any collection of songs the Beatles had released to date. The American *Rubber Soul* has an almost pastoral mood. While this gave a misleading idea of where the group's music was heading, Capitol could not be faulted from a commercial standpoint, because this denatured *Rubber Soul* proved to be extraordinarily popular in the States. It sold a million copies in its first week of release, and it would prove to be the instrument by which legions of folk-music enthusiasts were coaxed into the camp of pop. Over the years, many Beatles fans have come to consider this record a culmination of sorts. The Beatles felt no sense of culmination, however; both Lennon and McCartney expressed the feeling that it was "just another album" to them.

· · · ·

THE GENUINE ARTICLE, on Parlophone, begins with an acerbic fanfare of lead guitar that hangs in the air like a taunt until it is snatched up by the pounding pulse of a soul song called "Drive My Car." Gruffly sung by Paul and John, who shout the monotonal melody in a dissonant two-part harmony, "Drive My Car" is the first of the so-called "comedy songs" on *Rubber Soul*. The lyric applies the classic blues metaphor of Memphis Minnie's "Me and My Chauffeur" to a quasi-romantic encounter between an eager boy with good prospects and an ambitious girl who wants to be a famous movie star. "Baby, you can drive my car," she promises him in the chorus, the offer accompanied by a suggestive little shimmy of quarter-note triplets on piano, "and maybe I'll love you." Gears grinding and tires squealing in anticipatory delight, the boy's fantasies of gainful employment are played out by Paul's slide guitar in a lewd solo that delivers the song to its final verse, where the job interview ends with the girl's confession, "I've got no car and it's breaking my heart / But I've got a driver and that's a start." With that she exits the song, escorted by a cordon of Beatle voices chirping, "Beep-beep! beep-beep! yeah!"

The first of John Lennon's three jewel-like ballads on *Rubber Soul,* the cumbersomely titled "Norwegian Wood (This Bird Has Flown)" describes an equally fraught and inconclusive encounter, this one set on a higher plane of pop society than "Drive My Car." "I was trying to be sophisticated in writing about an affair," Lennon recalled, "but in such a smokescreen way that you couldn't tell." Whatever its basis in fact or fiction, "Norwegian Wood" is implicitly the story of a Girl and a Beatle as opposed to a Girl and a Boy. A traditional-sounding narrative ballad with a lilting modal melody in 12/8 time, sung to the strum of an acoustic guitar, the homage to Dylan is clear from the opening line. Yet, once again, in contrast to Dylan's verbosity, Lennon's lyric wastes not a word. The entire physical setting and social dynamic is evoked in the opening stanza, whose first line parodies the start of a hundred traditional ballads. "I once had a girl," it begins, "Or should I say, she once had me." The solemn melody traverses the scale in a series of spidery arpeggiations, and John sings it with an air of deep resignation. Yet the song itself is an emotional black comedy about a dance of seduction between a pair of prospective lovers with different agendas in mind.

Although the phrase "Norwegian Wood" would be taken by some

listeners as a reference to pot or hashish, the words refer to nothing more or less intoxicating than the Scandinavian-style teak furniture with which this young career girl has sought to transform her tiny bed-sitter into a showcase of cool sensuality and Sunday-supplement design. The image of this smooth, dark-grained teak works as an extended metaphor in the song. It symbolizes the girl's pretensions, as well as the minimalist agenda of seduction (wine, talk, bed) she seems to have in mind, and it carries over into the music, where George Harrison plays the melody at the start of each verse on a (teak-bodied) Indian sitar that provides the track with an instrumental effect as calculatedly exotic as her come-on. They're a perfect match: the sitar, with its bright, metallic, zitherlike notes sounding against a background of darker overtones, and the girl, who exists in an analogous state of sympathetic vibration with her surroundings, sounding her catch-phrase: "Isn't it good?"

Except of course that it *isn't* good—that much has been certain from the start. While it's not entirely clear which of them demurs, the night hardly ends as the Beatle, biding his time, had hoped. And the end of the song is even more of a puzzle, a conclusion as cryptic as the opening was concise. Waking in the morning to find the girl gone, John sings, "So I lit a fire: Isn't it good? Norwegian wood." Whether the words describe a spiteful, teak-fed blaze in the hearth to take the chill off a night in the tub, or perhaps (as McCartney later suggested) a more general conflagration, "Norwegian Wood" ends with a multiple act of revenge, directed at both the girl and the very idea of a denouement. When all other attempts at resolution fail, the song seems to say, why not just burn the place down?

After the claustrophobic intrigue of this darkly funny vignette, "You Won't See Me" seems to enter from another dimension, its syncopated introduction of guitar chords and cymbal crashes arriving like a blow to the head. "When I call you up, your line's engaged," Paul sings, inaugurating the third track in a row on a theme of miscommunication. Once past the introduction, the song settles down into a typical Beatles comedy of contrast between the lead and the backing vocals, embellished by rumbles and flourishes on the drums and a hyperactive Motown-style bass line that surges so far in front of the beat that the tempo seems to drag. While Paul states his case—he's losing his mind because his ex-girlfriend refuses to answer his calls—John and George respond with the same blasé verdict to each point of his well-reasoned appeal. "Woo-ooo-la-la-la!" they sing, embodying the girl's indifference, transforming their voices into a pair of deaf ears.

"Nowhere Man" opens with a barrage of sibilant Liverpudlian sarcasm, the a cappella voices stacked in double-tracked three-part harmony: "He's a *real* nowhere man / Sitting in his nowhere land." But the mockery recedes as the instruments join in and the song wheels on its axis toward a more compassionate stance. In the release, while the backup singers *ooh* and *aah,* John attempts to coax this lost soul out of his shell by enjoining him to listen, tempting him with the thought of what he might be missing, and finally exhorting him with the possibility that the very world is at his command. The guitar solo that follows is formed of notes so loud and bright, they could be played with bell-hammers on the strings of some celestial lyre. This stirring approximation of "the world at your command" (George Harrison's best solo on record since "A Hard Day's Night") lifts the song onto a new emotional plane before winding down to a single, wondrously delicate high harmonic that shines through the surging background of cymbal wash like a glint of enlightenment. When the singers return with the verse, it is as a great confederacy of Nowhere Men that they sing, and all trace of satiric distance has given way to the musical contradiction of these three enormous voices in close and sympathetic harmony, crowding into the existential predicament of a single solitary fool.

If George Harrison's songs on *Help!* sounded like imitations of Lennon and McCartney, "Think for Yourself," the first of his two contributions to *Rubber Soul,* reflected its author's admiration for Bob Dylan and the Rolling Stones. From the Stones' hit "Satisfaction," "Think for Yourself" borrowed an electronic effect called "fuzz-tone" that added a ragged edge of distortion to any notes that were fed through its primitive circuitry. Intended for use with electric guitars, the fuzz-tone on "Think for Yourself" sounds all the more extreme for being applied to the thick signal of Paul McCartney's bass, playing a grossly syncopated pattern of quarter-note triplets that answer each line of the verse like the snarls of an enraged schnauzer, snapping and straining at its lead. This effect, combined with the inert melody and the minor-chord harmony, gives the track a sourness of tone that is well suited to a lyric in which George aspires to Dylanesque heights of accusation: "I've got a word or two to say about the things that you do," he jeers. "You're telling all those lies about the good things that we can have if we close our eyes."

Harrison seems to have intended this song as a form of social commentary. "[It] must be about somebody from the sound of it . . . probably the Government," he later wrote. But it's doubtful that many of his listeners heard it that way in 1965. Then as now, popular songs were assumed to address romantic situations until proven otherwise. And the assumption that its lyric was indeed addressed to a girl placed "Think for Yourself" into a new genre of "anti-love" songs that was pioneered by Bob Dylan (with "It Ain't Me Babe" in 1964) and subsequently refined by the Rolling Stones. The overtly misogynistic attitudes that figured prominently in mid-1960s pop could be traced back ten years to the bullish infusion of the blues into the china shop of pop romance. But the sexual politics of the blues, with its endless array of capricious, mendacious, unfaithful, and hard-hearted women, had focused mainly on the sexual and emotional *power* that women exerted over men (and vice versa). The novel component in mid-1960s pop was a willingness to ridicule the sensitivities and vulnerabilities of women as avidly as their strengths, and to reserve a special scorn for the efforts of women to uphold the ideals of romantic love ("the good things that we can have if we close our eyes"). In some ways this was Jimmy Porter all over again: angry at the world, taking it out on his wife.

The first side of *Rubber Soul* concludes with a pair of tracks that present nearly as strong a musical contrast as the pairing of "Yesterday" and "Dizzy Miss Lizzy" at the end of *Help!* "The Word" is fundamentalist mid-1960s soul music. The verse features a simple bluesy melody (sung by John and Paul, with John dominating) set to a rolling heartbeat of bass, drums, piano, and syncopated squawks on guitar. Later, in the solo break, the shrill whine of George Martin's harmonium joins the song, sounding like a church organ in the throes of a crisis of faith. The lyrics can be heard as an affectionate parody of the marriage of sacred and secular that lay at the heart of soul music: "Say the Word and you'll be free / Say the Word and be like me." (In light of the levels of fan worship the Beatles had experienced, this first chapter of the gospel according to John and Paul has an edge of self-parody as well.) But the cumulative effect isn't comic. The repetition of the phrase "say the word" at the start of every line becomes an incantation over the course of the song, and the lyric in the release, "It's so fine, it's sunshine / It's the word Love," is sung straight, to the accompaniment of bright major triads that sound very much like "sunshine" after the flatted seventh chord harmony of the verse. Had John Lennon never assumed another oracular stance in a song, "The Word" could be heard as an appreciative send-up of soul music and left at that. But Lennon was becoming more interested in the dispensation of wisdom than anyone might have guessed.

The commercial success of "Yesterday" and the stampede of mainstream singers to cover the song naturally inspired Paul McCartney to come up with more conventionally romantic, conventionally melodic material—"the Big Ballad," as John Lennon liked to call it. The first such effort was "Michelle," which ends side one of *Rubber Soul*. In strictly musical terms, "Michelle" is a precocious piece of work. Reviving a breezy melody Paul had written some years before, he and John threaded the tune through a smooth sequence of minor, relative major, diminished, augmented, and major seventh chords—any one of which would have represented a proud compositional event in their music a year or two before. Far more conspicuous than its harmonic ingenuity, however, is that "Michelle" is performed in the sentimental style of a French cabaret song, with portions of the lyric actually sung in French. "Michelle, *ma belle,* these are words that go together well," the verse begins, *"sont des mots qui vont tres bien ensemble."* (The translation was provided by Jill Vaughn, a French teacher and the wife of Paul's old schoolmate Ivan Vaughn.)

Though the sound of Paul McCartney singing in French was heard by some pop fans as proof that the Beatles were putting on cultural airs, "Michelle" does have a plausibly Gallic premise. The song presents the sovereign nations of Boy and Girl, Masculine and Feminine, reaching out to one another across the gulf of language. As if conscious of the need to hold the pretension in check, McCartney brings off the vocal by understating everything. The actual words "I love you" are notoriously hard to sing in a love song. The phrase occurs twice in "Michelle." The first time, in the release, Paul's undulating "I love you I love you I lo-o-ove you" comes off sounding forced. The second time occurs at the beginning of George Harrison's brief guitar solo, where Paul tosses the words out one by one with rising inflection, the whole phrase hanging from the bluest note in the melody, in a manner that expresses the tenuousness of connection better than anything else in the song. This ghostly love call is the most spontaneous moment in "Michelle," and it's crazily enhanced by the arrival of Harrison's guitar, which comes sauntering into the music just then like one of Jean-Paul Sartre's existentialist café waiters, self-consciously playing the part of the guitar in a French pop song. By briefly diverting onto itself all of the affectation of the track, George's solo releases "Michelle" from the conventions of the genre. Under this reprieve, Paul sings another verse before shambling off into the misty Parisian night.

The second side of *Rubber Soul* begins with "What Goes On," a country-and-western song of almost callous mediocrity that dated from John Lennon's days with the Quarry Men. With John singing the lead vocal, the Beatles had tried to record it in 1963 and wisely given up. During the sessions for *Rubber Soul*, it was fitted out with some new lyrics and tossed like a bone to Ringo, who gnaws on it dutifully for two and a half minutes before yielding the floor to John, singing a sensuous ballad called "Girl." With its vampish rhythm and minor-key harmony vaguely reminiscent of the composer Kurt Weill, "Girl" is a companion piece to "Michelle"; it substitutes a German cabaret ambience for McCartney's Gallic mood. The title is both generic and intimate, while the lyric extends the emotional ambivalence of "Norwegian Wood" from a one-night stand into the context of an ongoing relationship. John sings it with the same tone of resignation he used in the earlier song ("And she promises the earth to me and I believe her / After all this time I don't know why"). The ambivalence is crystallized in a marvelously simple refrain in which John half-purrs and half-growls the phrase "ah, girl" as a wavering exhalation, followed by a sharp intake of breath that somehow splits the difference between a sigh of enchantment with a groan of exasperation. Later, in the coda, the relationship between these two lovers is enacted instrumentally as a dialogue between an acoustic guitar, tittering away in eighth notes, and a crash cymbal in half notes, its blows choked off with the hand.

"Tell Me What You See," "I've Just Seen a Face," "You Won't See Me," "We Can Work It Out"—the titles alone attest to the many songs Paul McCartney wrote over the course of 1965 that were based on the scenario of a face-to-face (if not necessarily eye-to-eye) encounter between lovers. "I'm Looking Through You" is like a disillusioned sequel to them all. The track begins haltingly, with a strum of acoustic guitar (a false start, actually, as if Paul couldn't quite work himself into the right frame of mind on the first try). It picks up a peculiar, ticking percussion part under an opening verse that describes his sense of incomprehension at the girl he thought he knew (the ticking sounds like his patience, getting ready to explode), and then opens up on the line, "I'm looking through you—you're not the same," which is answered by a series of harsh, almost shrewish interjections on an electric guitar. Once the song gets going, it's gone—the soft acoustic strumminess of the opening verse is given over to the brisk energy and sentiment of up-tempo rhythm and blues. "Love has a nasty habit of disappearing overnight," warns the Beatle who claimed to believe in "Yesterday," only this time it's the ever-willing, ever-amorous Paul who has finally had enough.

There follows a third ballad from John, "In My Life," written and sung with Paul in a devotional manner reminiscent of "If I Fell." With its dreamy guitar introduction and its surprisingly forceful beat (it is a *punctuated* ballad), the song owed a conscious debt to Smokey Robinson's recent hit, "The Tracks of My Tears," which made it the most recent installment in the lively cultural exchange between Motown's Hitsville Studios and EMI's Abbey Road. Given Lennon's profound respect for Robinson, it must have given him special satisfaction in 1965 when the man he had been emulating for several years began to show signs of emulating *him* by conflating the themes of emotional masquerade that characterize two of John's songs on *Beatles for Sale,* "I Don't Want to Spoil the Party" and "I'm a Loser," into one of the most eloquent soul ballads ever written. On *Rubber Soul,* Lennon returned the compliment gracefully. It was mainly the vocal delivery and instrumental texture of "In My Life" that was influenced by "Tracks of My Tears"; the melody bore no resemblance, and the lyrics were more directly personal than anything Lennon had written before. Earlier drafts of the opening verse were filled with Liverpool place-names, and though these were gradually weeded out of the finished version, the emotional charge they provided lingers in this wise and affecting song. Paced by Ringo's drumming, a clever combination of bumps and clicks and thwacks that mark the passage of time like some battered mantelpiece clock, and graced by an elegant, active melody, enclosed within a neat octave of musical space that straddles the keynote of the song, the lyric strikes a delicate balance between a sense of longing and a sense of fulfillment. In the first verse John looks back over his life with nostalgia for the places he remembers and the people ("lovers and friends") they bring to mind, evoking the dead and the living, and affirming his love for them all. In the second verse he brings this sense of nostalgia to bear on his life in the present, allowing that none of these friends and lovers "compares with you / And these memories lose their meaning, when I think of love as something new."

John Lennon liked to speak about resolution when he spoke about writing songs. Whether on account of the compliment Dick James paid him for "No Reply," or on account of Dylan, whose last verses sometimes really did sound like last chapters, Lennon put a lot of stock in the idea that good lyrics were supposed to resolve, to wrap themselves up in the end. In practice, tidy endings can often seem trite in pop songs, but "In My Life" sets up a pair of emotions and achieves a genuine resolution of them, to end on a convincingly affirmational note. (It is the only song on *Rubber Soul* that sounds the Beatles' original ground theme of happiness-in-relationship.) The second verse is followed by a piano solo, played by George Martin in an ornamental baroque style. (Unable to articulate the notes at tempo, Martin ingeniously recorded his part at half-speed, an octave below, and then sped up the tape, a technique that lent the piano a harpsichord-like tone.) Martin's baroque stylization, while thoroughly satisfying in its own right, gently parodies the song's nostalgic leanings; like Ringo's clockwork drumming, it helps to hold the sentimentality in check. The solo is followed by a repeat of the second half of the verse, and the song ends with the sweetest surprise of all, as the music stops beneath the last line, and John, in a nod to Smokey Robinson, lifts into a reedy falsetto to sing the phrase "In my-y life" before dropping back down into his normal range for "I love you more." It's as if the first half of the line were ruled by his head, the second half by his heart.

The remainder of *Rubber Soul* is somewhat anticlimactic in the wake of this brilliant track. "Wait" is an obvious throwback. Another addition to the Beatles' expansive catalog of "coming home" songs, it was originally recorded and rejected for the soundtrack of *Help!* and then revived at the last minute to fill out *Rubber Soul*. It features a ferocious percussion part of maracas and tambourine, a gasping chorus of "Wait!" (in a straightforward imitation of "Help!"), and a guilty concession from Paul, who sings, "I feel as though, you ought to know, that I've been good—as good as I can be." George Harrison's rueful rain check of a love song, "If I Needed Someone," is a more substantial effort that reflected the Beatles' reciprocal admiration for the Byrds, whom they had met during their recent stay in Los Angeles. The instrumental track is dominated by the rich, ringing timbres of the twelve-string electric guitar that Harrison introduced on the *Hard Day's Night* LP and that Jim McGuinn subsequently adopted as the instrumental signature of his band. Sung in parallel, Byrds-like, three-part harmony, the song is an exercise in hypothetical romance. "If I needed someone to love," George begins, "you're the one that I'd be thinking of." This theme of the right person at the wrong time is cleverly mirrored in the music, where the entire melody is phrased on the off-beats. Combined with McCartney's drastically arpeggiated bass line, this disjointed motion helps to create an illusion of the music rising ever upward in the verse, building up an atmospheric pressure that is then released in a chorus of lush "ahhhs" (with Paul singing a third above and John singing a droning *tenth* below George's lead) that descend like a force of nature. After all the emotional intrigue in the songs on *Rubber Soul,* this track serves as a pleasant reminder of the pure kinetic energy of the Beatles' earlier work.

The final track on the album, John Lennon's "Run for Your Life," is another attempt at homage, but this one gone awry. The salient feature of "Run for Your Life" is that its lyric includes a direct quotation from a song that Elvis Presley recorded at the outset of his career. Released in 1955, "Baby Let's Play House" was Presley's fourth single on Sun Records, and it stands as an obscure monument to the social and musical cross-currents that created rock 'n' roll. The song was written and originally recorded by a third-rate Nashville-based blues singer named Arthur Gunter, who intended it as an "answer record" to a recent country-and-western hit by Eddy Arnold called "I Want to Play House With You." That is: "Baby Let's Play House" was an attempt by a black blues singer to cap-italize on the success of a white country singer, which was then recorded by the young white country singer whom Sam Phillips had been encour-aging to sing like a black blues singer. Because Gunter's performance of the song was about as tame as a blues can be, Elvis's transformation of it was far more extreme than his earlier transformations of "That's All Right, Mama" and "Good Rockin' Tonight." Drawing on every vocal man-nerism and affectation in his repertoire, he began by milking the infan-tilized sexual metaphor of the song title for all it was worth, and ended with a murderous vow of jealousy that seemed to come out of nowhere in the final verse.

By the end of 1965 the Beatles had paid their respects on record to every one of their principal musical influences with the exception of Elvis Presley. Though they had performed any number of his songs in the clubs of Liverpool and Hamburg, they had scrupulously avoided any direct imitation of Elvis when they began to make records of their own—almost as if he were indeed the reigning deity and they a group of novitiates, proscribed from speaking his name. But now they had met the man himself, and had a chance to judge for themselves whether the course of his career since those early, world-beating recordings had been the colossal put-on they so dearly would have wanted it to be. They surely grasped the fact that Elvis resented them, and it seems that, having satisfied their curiosity, they now felt ready to settle their accounts.

"Run for Your Life" was meant to be a reminder of what Presley's music had once been all about—an act not only of homage but also of connoisseurship in its reference to a record that only a die-hard fan would know. And it would have been stirring if the Beatles had risen to the challenge of honoring their original inspiration. But gratitude was never their strong suit, and "Run for Your Life" comes across as an uninspired, rockabilly-inflected remake of "You Can't Do That." "I catch you with another man—that's the end," sings John, who later went out of his way to express his dislike of the song, claiming that he wrote it to please George Harrison, whose lead guitar supplies its only spark. "Run for Your Life" is mainly notable for the way it manages to deflate the impact of the record it celebrates. The genuinely chilling effect of "Baby Let's Play House" derived from the almost psychopathic indirection Presley brought to the song, waiting until the very last line to make the depth of his feelings known. In "Run for Your Life," however, Lennon *starts* where Presley ended up, singing the fateful words "Well I'd rather see you dead little girl than to be with another man" as the *first* line of the song—as if it were just about the most ordinary thing a person could say. And that, perhaps, was the inadvertent point. Revolutionary though it sounded a decade before when Elvis Presley first embraced the role, by the end of 1965 the whole business of white boys striking fierce poses in pop songs was becoming the operative cliché.

The difference between the way Lennon and McCartney behave with the people around them is incredible. What Lennon does is he sits down, immediately acknowledges the fact that he's John Lennon and that everything for the rest of the night is going to revolve around him. [He] just dribbles little jokes, little rubbish like he's got, *In His Own Write* and little things. Of course everybody gets into his thing and also has a generally good time.

—Pete Townshend

On successive Fridays in March 1966, the London *Evening Standard* published a series of full-page profiles of John Lennon, Ringo Starr, George Harrison, and Paul McCartney, run beneath the heading, HOW DOES A BEATLE *LIVE?* The articles were written by Maureen Cleave, the newspaper's young pop columnist, whose piece on "the darlings of Merseyside" three years before had provided the Beatles with their first coverage in the British national press and set the tone for much of the subsequent reporting on the group. Cleave's inaugural column had earned her a spot in the Beatles' hearts; she was as close to the group as a journalist could be, and her *Evening Standard* series represented the most candid and comprehensive portraits of them as individuals yet to appear in print. Though her focus was on "lifestyle," in the course of presenting a detailed accounting of their houses, cars, toys, and personal tastes, she encouraged them to speak their minds.

A notable feature of the series was the individualized format itself. While the sheer demand for press coverage during the Beatlemania period had occasioned brief interviews with individual members of the group, the band's public image had been built entirely on the strength of their ensemble performances in press conferences and group interviews—so much so that the Beatles routinely employed a collective *we* in their contacts with the press, and reporters reciprocated by placing the words of each into the mouth of the collective whole: "The Beatles feel . . ." Cleave's series was conceived as an attempt to break through this united front and present the members of the group as distinct individuals. She found her subjects all too willing to oblige.

The first two installments of "How Does a Beatle *Live?*" focused on what Cleave called "the Weybridge community" of John Lennon and Ringo Starr, elders of the group at the age of twenty-five. "Their existence is secluded and curiously timeless," Cleave wrote. " 'What day is it?' John Lennon asks with interest when you ring him up with news from outside." Still, she assured her readers, "[John] is much the same as he was before. He looks more like Henry VIII than ever now that his face has filled out. He is just as imperious, just as unpredictable, indolent, disorganized, childish, vague, charming, and quick-witted." Though the comparison to King Henry was not one that would have occurred to many Beatles fans, or to anyone else who still pictured Lennon as the angular, astringent Mod of 1964, his face in the accompanying photograph and his demeanor in the interview seemed to bear it out. Throughout, John spoke with the regal self-regard of one who has grown accustomed to being considered a great wit. "Famous and loaded as I am, I *still* have to meet soft people," he confessed to Cleave. "It often comes to my mind that I'm not really rich. There *are* really rich people, but I don't know where they are." Of an invitation to lunch in London, he asked: "Do you know how long lunch lasts? I've never been to lunch before."

Lennon spirited Cleave through the many expensively decorated rooms of his "Hansel and Gretel house," whose points of interest included a suit of medieval armor, a life-size crucifix, and a gorilla costume ("the only suit that fits me"). There was an attic full of model racing cars ("a hobby I had for a week") and a parlor full of randomly blinking light-boxes that John had bought as Christmas presents and forgotten to give away. "One feels that his possessions—to which he adds daily— have got the upper hand," Cleave noted. Daily life at "Kenwood" was centered on a small room at the back of the house, adjoining the kitchen and the garden, where the family ate its meals, and where John spent long hours of the day and night curled like a cat on a settee, simultaneously reading, listening to records, and watching television. "He is probably the laziest man in England," Cleave wrote. "*Physically* lazy," Lennon added. "I don't mind writing or reading or watching or speaking, but sex is the only physical thing I can be bothered with any more."

Lennon's otherwise facetious performance did include a few glimmers of his more serious, or at least strong-minded, nature. Cleave reported that his house contained a well-organized library, citing works by Swift, Tennyson, Huxley, Orwell, and Wilde among the titles on the shelves. ("I've read millions of books," John boasted. "That's why I seem to know things.") She wrote that he was currently "reading extensively about religion," and illustrated this with a quote. "Christianity will go," John told her. "It will vanish and shrink. I needn't argue about that; I'm right and I'll be proved right. We're more popular than Jesus now; I don't know which will go first—rock 'n' roll or Christianity. Jesus was all right but his disciples were thick and ordinary. It's them twisting it that ruins it for me." It was exactly the sort of pretentious remark that would have elicited hoots of derision from the other Beatles had Lennon come out with it in the context of a group interview. (They might have called him King Henry, in fact). But reported here, interspersed with Cleave's account of him shopping "in lightning swoops" on London specialty stores, John's commentary on Christianity failed to elicit a word of response in any of the established forums of Beatle controversy.

DOWN THE HILL at "Sunny Heights," Ringo Starr stood ready to confirm the impression of jaunty, pixilated commonality the public had intuitively grasped. "A family man, as it were," was how Ringo described himself now. He was "Richie" to his nineteen-year-old wife Maureen; she was "Mo" to him. ("I own her, of course," joked Ringo.) At the time of their marriage in February 1965, Maureen had been two months pregnant with their son Zak, whose name, like his father's stage name, was taken from a cowboy on TV. "I get all my knowledge from TV," Ringo explained. Cleave found him to be "less complicated and more mature than the others, which makes him restful company and a charming host." His tour of the premises was accompanied by Zak in his pram. It began in the garden, passed through the garage (where Cleave noted the presence of a Facel Vega, an Italian sports car that Ringo liked to say he could drive but couldn't spell), and wound up in the basement of the house, which contained a full-scale working replica of a typical English pub, complete with a name, "The Flying Cow," and sporting prints on the walls ("I've always wanted a bar, from the movies I think"). Asked what he felt strongly about, Ringo expressed optimism at the recent improvement in the

British upper classes ("Don't you think so? Much less piggy and inter-bred") and annoyance at the decline of British patriotic pride ("It drives me mad"). "He used to have a four-minute plan for when he was Prime Minister," Cleave reported, "but all he can remember now is that he wanted everybody's house joined to the houses of friends by underground tubes." As for his three and a half years with John, Paul, and George, Ringo said that it was not until 1964 that the feeling of being the "new boy" entirely left him. "It took about two years to get each other sorted out, but from then on I had the feeling there was four of us in it. I sup-pose we get on together because we're the only four people like us; we're the only ones who really know what it's like. When there was all that Beatlemania we were pushed into a corner, just the four of us. A sort of trap, really. We were like Siamese quads, eating out of the same bowl."

IN ITS THIRD week the series turned to George Harrison, who was por-trayed by Cleave as a satellite in synchronous orbit around the Weybridge community, his relationship with the older Beatles resembling that of any other well-adjusted twenty-two-year-old who has successfully left the nest but retains a set of close ties to the home. Belying his reputation as "the quiet Beatle," Harrison approached the interview with a mixture of earnestness and humor, savoring the opportunity to vent some of the strong opinions he had once been too shy to express ("Good old George, plodding along—a mere morsel," was the way he now pictured himself in the early days of the Beatles' success). He spoke out sharply to Cleave against the war in Vietnam, and against war in general, complaining that the vast sums the Beatles paid the British government in taxes were used to buy bombs and planes. "Taking all the money and then moaning about deficits here, deficits there," he said of his patron Harold Wilson, whom he likened to the Sheriff of Nottingham. Harrison seconded Lennon's remarks on the hypocrisy of religion: "All this love they neighbor and none of them are doing it. If Christianity's as good as they say it is, it should stand up to a bit of discussion." And he was blunt on the subject of fame and the fans: "I can't understand some of them being so aggressively bad-mannered. I suppose they feel belittled wanting something from four scruffy louts like us. OK, we're the famous Beatles. So what? There are other things apart from being famous Beatles. It's not the living end."

As Cleave described it, George's life in the spring of 1966 revolved around a pair of passionate enthusiasms. The first was his new bride, Pattie Boyd, the twenty-two-year-old model from Bristol whom he had lived with for more than a year and married some two months before. (The couple had met on the set of *A Hard Day's Night*, in which Pattie played the part of a starstruck schoolgirl. Prior to that, she had appeared in television commercials as the Smith's Potato Crisps Girl.) "I married her because I loved her and because I was fed up not being married," George announced. "Twenty-two is the normal age for people to get married. That's when a petrol pump attendant gets married, though he hasn't got all these people looking at him." Unlike the proverbial petrol pump attendant, however, George went out of his way to emphasize the equality of their relationship—an attitude that contrasted sharply with the seeming indifference of Lennon, who barely mentioned his wife, and the cheerful chauvinism of Starr. "The natural thing when you get money is that you acquire taste," George explained. "I've got a lot of my taste off Pattie. You get taste in food as well. Instead of eggs and beans and steak you branch out into the avocado scene. I never dreamt I would like avocado pears. I thought it was like eating bits of wax—fake pears out of a bowl—when I saw people shoving it down."

George first encountered his other current passion, the sitar, as a prop on the set of *Help!* Intrigued by the exotic appearance and timbre of the instrument, George explained, he had purchased a sitar at a local emporium called Indiacraft and set out to teach himself to play, gleaning what technical knowledge he could from the liner notes on albums by the Indian virtuoso Ravi Shankar and from his contacts with London's Asian Music Circle, a group of amateur performers and enthusiasts. His use of the sitar on "Norwegian Wood" had started a minor trend in pop and stirred a new wave of interest in Indian music itself. A few weeks before his interview with Cleave, George had attended his first concert by Ravi Shankar at London's Festival Hall. The experience filled him with awe: "It was just like everything you have ever thought of as great coming out all at once." His appreciation of Shankar's mastery made him sheepishly modest when discussing his own ability on the sitar. Recounting his effort to learn how to hold the cumbersome instrument in the prescribed manner, George told Cleave that his "legs went to sleep and when he stood up he fell over." "I wish I could sit on the floor like Ravi," he said.

But Paul McCartney worries. He wants a genuine conversation, a genuine relationship, starting off from square one.
And he's starting to tell me that he digs me and that we're
on an even par so that we can begin the conversation—
which completely makes me an even bigger fan. That's all
it serves to do. The conversation comes to no purpose and
all he serves to do is to confuse himself.

—Pete Townshend

Along with its individualized format, Cleave's *Evening Standard* series
was also notable for the order in which it presented the group. John, Paul,
George, and Ringo it had usually been until then, for reasons that went
beyond the rhythms of their names to reflect the internal hierarchy of the
group. Cleave's revised order was based on geography, not hierarchy, and
the geography suggested how the internal dynamic of the Beatles was
changing, the axis elongating, with John in Weybridge, Paul in London,
and Ringo and George in between. "I thought maybe we should all be
grown up together, and then I thought, I don't want to live in Weybridge.
I love the *look* of London," McCartney explained, speaking like the cos-
mopolite he was striving to become. By far the most telling feature of
Cleave's series was the contrast between John and Paul. As avidly as John
flaunted his celebrity ("famous and loaded as I am"), Paul belittled his
fame: "Fame in the end is getting off your parking ticket because he wants
your autograph, and fame is being interrupted when you're eating by a
fifty-year-old American woman with a ponytail." "I'm thinking of getting
myself a *bicycle* with black windows," he joked, referring to John's recent
purchase of a Rolls-Royce limousine. Having characterized John as
"imperious, unpredictable, indolent, and disorganized," Cleave described
Paul as "neatly dressed and well organized . . . self-conscious, restless,
nervy, and on the go." "He is half-Beatle," she decided, "and half-not."

Unlike John, George, and Ringo, who satisfied the public's curiosity
by inviting Cleave into their homes, Paul met her for lunch at a restaurant, in the manner of a man-about-town. Appearances aside, there was a
practical side to this arrangement, for though he had recently purchased
a house of his own, right around the corner from the EMI studios in St.
John's Wood, the place was undergoing extensive renovations, and
McCartney's principal London lodging in the winter of 1966 remained a
room on the top floor of the West End residence where Dr. and Mrs.

Richard Asher lived with their nineteen-year-old daughter, Jane. Even without a Beatle, this was some household. Richard Asher was a rather eccentric figure who ran the psychiatric clinic at London's West Middlesex Hospital and appeared from time to time as a guest commentator on BBC-TV. His wife, Margaret, was a music teacher whose former students included George Martin during his days at the Guildhall School. Their son, Peter, was one half of the pop duo Peter & Gordon, whom Lennon and McCartney had staked to success in 1964 with the million-selling "World Without Love." Their younger daughter, Claire, was a part-time television actress. And Jane Asher, their elder daughter, was a former child star of the stage and screen who was currently regarded in British theatrical circles as a young actress of real ability. She had begun her career in show business at an age when her future Beatle boyfriend was still in short pants, and a major source of contention in their relationship was her determination to pursue her own career. Strong-willed and self-possessed, Jane Asher was a bird of an altogether different feather from the other three Beatles' wives, and the *haute* bohemian atmosphere of her household had exposed Paul to a set of social and cultural influences unlike anything he had known on Merseyside.

The evidence of this fairly leaped out of McCartney in his interview with Maureen Cleave. "I don't want to sound like Jonathan Miller going on," he told her, "but I'm trying to cram everything in, all the things I've missed. People are saying things and painting things and writing things and composing things that are great, and I must know what people are doing. . . . I vaguely mind people knowing anything I don't know." Paul voiced enthusiasm for the work of the electronic composers Karlheinz Stockhausen and Luciano Berio and the absurdist drama of Alfred Jarry. He allowed that he wouldn't mind growing old like Bertrand Russell, and he championed the cultural programming on the BBC ("whether you want to listen to it or not, it's there"). He expressed annoyance with the attitude that "if a navvy or a workie is seen coming out of an art gallery, it's a joke," adding, with supreme self-consciousness, "if this workie tried to find out about strip clubs in Hamburg, then his mates would have thought that was all right." He mentioned that he was taking music lessons from a colleague of Margaret Asher's whom he described as "by no means thick." And in response to Cleave's standing invitation to say something suitably outspoken, Paul turned his sights on the United States, decrying the state of its race relations ("it's a lousy country to be in where anyone who is black is made to seem a dirty nigger") and the narrow-mindedness of its people in general. "There they were in America, all getting house-trained for adulthood with their indisputable principle of life: short hair equals men; long hair equals women. Well, we got rid of that little convention for them."

THE ENTHUSIASM PAUL McCartney expressed for living in London and his interest in "people [who] are saying things and painting things and writing things and composing things that are great" were a direct reflection of his role as the one member of the Beatles who was personally involved in the formative stages of the countercultural movement that would soon become known in Britain as the Underground. The birth of the Underground could be traced back to June of 1965, when a group of poets including Allen Ginsberg, Lawrence Ferlinghetti, Gregory Corso, and Christopher Logue gave a reading at the Royal Albert Hall that attracted an overflow crowd of more than seven thousand people, most of whom had never imagined that there were so many other kindred spirits living in London at the time. (The sponsors of the reading had been worried about selling the five hundred tickets they needed to pay for the rental of the hall.) Among the many paths that crossed that evening were those of John Dunbar, a former public-school boy turned Cambridge hipster and art critic, and Barry Miles, a former art student turned Beat poet and bookstore manager who was serving as Ginsberg's London host. Several months later, Dunbar and Miles decided to pool their interests by opening a combination bookshop and gallery called the Indica, in a building off St. James Square. (The name of the establishment was derived from *Cannabis indica,* a botanical term for marijuana.) The seed capital for this enterprise came from Jane Asher's brother, Peter, who was an old schoolmate of Dunbar's. The Indica opened its doors in January 1966. Paul McCartney helped the proprietors stock the shelves and paint the walls; he also personally designed the shop's wrapping paper.

McCartney had known John Dunbar through the Ashers since 1964—the same year that Dunbar had taken up with an arrestingly beautiful seventeen-year-old schoolgirl named Marianne Faithfull, who promptly embarked on a whirlwind career as a pop singer under the tutelage of the Rolling Stones' manager, Andrew Oldham. (Dunbar and Faithfull had since married, had a child, and drifted apart.) In his capacity as a gallery manager, Dunbar did his best to cultivate the Beatles' patronage by inviting them to openings and introducing them to his contacts in the London art world. But it was Paul McCartney's friendship with Barry Miles that formed the most important and influential link between the Beatles and the avant-garde cultural ferment that was occurring beneath the brightly swinging surface of London life.

A studious-looking twenty-four-year-old whose mild manner and horn-rimmed glasses led one of his friends to characterize him as "the Clark Kent of the Underground," Miles had been making the scene in London since the late 1950s. He had marched with the Committee for Nuclear Disarmament, smoked pot with the Rastafarians in Notting Hill, published a succession of little poetry magazines, and worked as a manager at Better Books, London's principal alternative bookstore, literary hangout, and avant-garde performance space. Over the years he had developed at least a nodding acquaintance with every scuffling poet, writer, artist, filmmaker, and avant-gardist in the city. Miles had first met the Beatles around the time of the Albert Hall poetry reading in 1965, when his houseguest Allen Ginsberg asked him to invite the group to a birthday party for Ginsberg. As it turned out, the meeting was very brief. John Lennon and George Harrison accepted the invitation and arrived at the party with their wives—only to beat a hasty retreat when they were greeted effusively by Ginsberg, who was naked except for a "No Waiting" sign that was hanging by a string from his genitals.

"Miles was a great catalyst," Paul McCartney recalled. "He was a literature buff. . . . He had the books. We had a great interest, but we didn't have the books." From the time the Indica opened, in January 1966, Miles began to serve as a kind of staff intellectual and librarian to McCartney and his fellow Beatles. The books he provided them ran the gamut from Jung and Huxley to Aleister Crowley, the Tolkien trilogy, and Martin Gardner's *Annotated Alice*. It was Miles who introduced Paul to the work of electronic composers like Karlheinz Stockhausen and Luciano Berio; Miles who escorted Paul to various happenings, openings, and screenings; Miles who helped Paul shed the last of his provincial self-consciousness and expand his circle of friends and acquaintances. However awkward and futile it may have seemed to another pop star like Pete Townshend, McCartney's desire for "a genuine conversation, a genuine relationship" made him open to meeting new people and interested in new ideas in a way that the other Beatles were not.

30

> "This is how one ought to see," I kept repeating as I looked down at my trousers, or glanced at the jeweled books in the shelves, at the legs of my infinitely more than Van-Goghian chair. "This is how one ought to see, how things really are." And yet there were reservations. For if one always saw like this, one would never want to do anything else. Just looking, just being the divine Not-self of flower, of book, of chair, of flannel. That would be enough. But in that case what about other people? What about human relations? In the recording of that morning's conversations I find the question constantly repeated, "What about human relations?
>
> —Aldous Huxley, *The Doors of Perception*

John Lennon's affected behavior in his *Evening Standard* interview was more than a mood of the moment, encouraged by his flirtatious relationship with Maureen Cleave. Instead, the air of passivity and detachment John exhibited reflected real changes that had been taking place in his personality over the course of 1965—changes that John and the people around him attributed to his deepening involvement with LSD. Along with George Harrison, Lennon had first taken "acid" in the spring of 1965, at a time when it was still essentially unknown in British pop circles. Their initiation came at a dinner party given by their dentist, who surreptitiously placed the drug in their coffee, apparently intending it as some kind of mega-*digestif*. This left the guests—John and Cynthia, George and Pattie—convinced they were losing their minds. "We were cackling in the streets," Lennon recalled of the bizarre evening that followed. "It was just terrifying, but it was fantastic. I was pretty stunned for a month or two." At the time the experience reminded him of passages he had read in Thomas De Quincey's *Confessions of an English Opium-Eater*, a classic work of

Victorian drug literature that was enjoying a revival among cannabis-conscious Londoners in 1965.

Together with Ringo and several members of the Byrds, John and George next took LSD—intentionally this time—during the frenetic week the Beatles spent in Los Angeles near the end of their 1965 tour. In the months that followed, they began dropping acid regularly—though rarely in one another's company, despite what their fans might assume. In fact, a salient point about LSD as far as the Beatles were concerned was that it was the first recreational drug they encountered that they did *not* engage in as a group. Ringo, after trying it in Los Angeles, took it rarely, if ever, again. Paul McCartney would wait until the fall of 1966, a year and a half after the others' initiation, before taking his first dose of the drug. And John Lennon, for all the times he took it, took it mainly on his own.

LSD impressed its legion of enthusiasts during the 1960s as an entirely new kind of drug. Compared with mere intoxicants like pills or pot or alcohol, acid engendered a departure from normal waking consciousness so preternaturally extreme that its users felt themselves to be communing with "another world" in something more than a figurative sense. Whether or not individuals were permanently transformed by their experiences on the drug, the point, at the time, was that they fully believed that they were. For hundreds of thousands, possibly millions, of young people during the second half of the 1960s, LSD would serve as a rite of passage into an esoteric community of blown minds and kindred souls who were linked by a sense of shared astonishment and revelation.

Though all four of the Beatles would eventually acknowledge having taken LSD, George Harrison was the only member of the group who ever discussed his experiences in public with any degree of insight. "It was like opening the door, really, and before, you didn't even know there was a door there," he later said. "It just opened up this whole other consciousness, even if it was down to, like Aldous Huxley said, the wonderful folds in his gray flannel trousers. It was like gaining hundreds of years of experience within twelve hours. It changed me, and there was no way back to what I was before. It wasn't all good, because it left a lot of questions as well. And we still had to continue being fab, you know. Now with *that* added perspective." John Lennon's pronouncements on the subject, by contrast, ranged from wild exaggerations (like his claim of having taken "a thousand trips") to vague understatements ("It was more of a visual thing, and a therapy, that looking at yourself bit"). What John did make clear was that he took a great deal of acid over the course of 1966—as often as twice a week when his work schedule allowed—and that his expectations of the drug and his attitudes toward it were strongly influenced by his reading of a trio of books by Aldous Huxley, Timothy Leary, and Carl Jung.

Beginning with his essay *The Doors of Perception* (1954), the English author Aldous Huxley was the first and by far the most eloquent mainstream writer to address the psychedelic or "mind-manifesting" properties of drugs like mescaline, psilocybin, and LSD. In essays, articles, and finally a novel, *Island,* published in 1962, Huxley ranged over the subject with intelligence and imagination, providing much of the vocabulary and metaphorical imagery with which the inexpressibly subjective nature of these experiences would henceforth be expressed. A lifelong orientalist, Huxley was also responsible for promoting a set of influential analogies with Eastern mysticism that would inspire the belief—central to the ideology of the psychedelic movement during its heyday in the 1960s—that these drugs had the power to bring about a revolution in Western consciousness. Among the Eastern sources he cited was a Tibetan Buddhist book of "last rites" that describes the experiences awaiting the human spirit in its passage from death to rebirth. First translated into English in 1927 by the Oxford orientalist W. Y. Evans-Wentz, the *Bardo Thödol,* or *Tibetan Book of the Dead,* had been reprinted in 1955 with a preface of psychological commentary by the eminent Swiss psychologist Carl Jung.

It was Huxley who first brought *The Tibetan Book of The Dead* to the attention of Timothy Leary, a flamboyant clinical psychologist who began conducting psilocybin research at Harvard in 1961. Huxley saw Leary's affiliation with America's most prestigious university as a powerful marketing tool, and Leary responded by ushering a widening circle of artists, writers, academics, and even socialites into the psychedelic fold. In the spring of 1963 these activities precipitated a scandal that resulted in the dismissal of Leary and two of his colleagues from the Harvard faculty. The debacle at Harvard had serious consequences, in that it prompted the first calls for criminalization and poisoned the future of legitimate research into these remarkable drugs. But its most immediate effect was to launch the post-academic career of Timothy Leary, who would be to LSD what Barnum had been to humbug.

Leary's penchant for colorful phraseology had already led him to construe the effect of LSD in stripping away psychic defenses as a form of "ego-death." He therefore did not require much encouragement from people like Huxley or Jung to find parallels between the stages of physical death and rebirth described in *The Tibetan Book of The Dead* and the stages of psychological "death" and "rebirth" he had identified in the course of his Harvard research. This insight led him to collaborate with his two defrocked Harvard colleagues on a book called *The Psychedelic Experience*. Dedicated to the memory of Huxley (who died in 1963) and prefaced with a tribute to Jung (who died in 1961), *The Psychedelic Experience* was devoted to the revelation of "the pre-mortem death-rebirth experience, a mystery that has been handed down for over 2,500 years." Part One of the book consisted of a perfectly ludicrous retranslation of the Evans-Wentz text into Leary's own brand of psycho-jargon. Part Two was written as a user's manual for an acid trip, based on a series of guidelines that emphasized the importance of a person's predisposition and environment—which Leary termed "set and setting"—to the quality of the experience at hand. In 1966, already in its fourth printing, this New Testament of the psychedelic movement became an integral part of the set and setting of the Beatles' own incipient program of freelance research. Or, as John Lennon later said, "You see, I got the message on acid that I should destroy my ego and I did, you know. I was reading that stupid book of Leary's."

More than any of the other Beatles, John Lennon's involvement with LSD over the course of 1966 had the aura of personal quest. He said as much at the time, in his vague way, brooding to Maureen Cleave about how "there's something else I'm going to do, something I must do—only I don't know what it is. That's why I go round painting and taping and drawing and writing and that, because it may be one of them. All I know is, this isn't *it* for me." In its very vagueness, this theme of "something else" mirrored the language found in another mainstay of Lennon's psychedelic reading list, Carl Jung's *Man and His Symbols*. The book itself made no direct reference to psychedelic drugs. But to the initiated the relevance was plain as day. At the heart of *Man and His Symbols* was a long chapter describing Jung's theory of personality growth, which can be understood as an attempt to integrate the Western view of the ego or conscious mind as the purposeful center of the psyche with the Eastern view of the ego as an encumbrance that serves to mire a person in worldly illusion and blind him to the existence of higher forms of consciousness. Jung believed that the development of a strong ego-identity is the principal psychological goal of childhood and adolescence. But he considered this to be only a first step, resulting in the creation of a mask-like, socially adaptive personality for which he coined the term *persona.* True psychological maturity, he maintained, was the product of a longer and more subtle process of "creative self-realization" in which the ego is gradually induced to relax its hold on the psyche, so as to allow for the emergence of an innate "nucleus" of deeper, more universal conscious-ness. "One must surrender consciously to the power of the unconscious," *Man and His Symbols* advised its readers. "Give in to this almost imper-ceptible, yet powerfully dominating, impulse." Jung believed that the path to true self-knowledge and fulfillment lay across years of close, introspective attention paid to the hints and messages of the uncon-scious as revealed in fantasies and dreams. Only in this way, he felt, could an individual come to a true understanding of what life held in store. "One sometimes feels that the unconscious is leading the way in accordance with a secret design," read the passage in *Man and His Sym-bols* that closely mirrored Lennon's musings to Maureen Cleave. "It is as if something is looking at me, something that I do not see but that sees me. . . . One is seeking something that is impossible to find or about which nothing is known."

The name Jung gave to this process was "individuation," and its rele-vance to the psychedelic experience was hard for turned-on readers of *Man and His Symbols* to miss. Psychedelics short-circuited the function-ing of the ego or conscious mind more effectively than anything short of psychosis itself. As such, the drugs seemed to provide a form of direct access to the unconscious—the wellspring of creativity, the domain of the universal Self. From this, it was a short step to the assumption that the hard-earned Jungian wisdom of a lifetime—or, in the still more labo-rious Eastern conception, of multiple lifetimes—could be radically com-pressed: "hundreds of years of experience within twelve hours," in George Harrison's estimate. Never mind that Jung had characterized individuation as an inherently "slow, imperceptible process." Or that direct access to the unconscious was hardly synonymous with developing a meaningful understanding of what one might find there. Distinctions like these mattered little in the analogy-crazed world of acid ideology. As popularized by Timothy Leary and further diluted by word of mouth, this little seed of Jungian theory went a long way toward providing the psy-chedelic experience with a psychological rationale.

The relevance of individuation to John Lennon's state of mind in the spring of 1966 was hard for *him* to miss, beginning with the obvious point that Lennon and his fellow Beatles had come to inhabit one of the most celebrated personae on earth. It was apparent by now to all of the Beatles that their collective identity had become, in Ringo's words, "a trap." Yet John's relationship to this identity was more complex than that of the others, because the persona of the group, from its inception, had been so strongly shaped by his own psychological needs. He had always been, of the four of them, both the boldest and the most insecure; many people who knew him commented on the strength of this dichotomy in him. ("He seemed to oscillate between extremes of frivolity and shyness, arrogance and humility," wrote the photographer Robert Freeman.) John's personal dialectic of aggressiveness and vulnerability, assertiveness and doubt, had helped to make his artistic temperament distinct. But it also ensured that he would be more affected than the others by any movement toward individuation by the group, because Lennon had the greatest emotional investment in the Beatle status quo. "I have to see the others to see myself," he explained in an interview. "I realize then there is someone else like me, and it's satisfying and reassuring. It's frightening, really, when it gets too bad. I have to see them to establish contact with myself."

In 1966, as the Beatles began to rebel against the increasingly tiresome identity of being Beatles, it was John who lagged behind. Having emboldened these three mates of his, by his own assertive example, to think and do as they liked, he was now put in an oddly passive position as they applied the lessons they'd learned—Ringo with his family and his proud suburban home, George with his new bride and his developing passion for the sitar, Paul with his expanding cultural horizons and his busy urban life. Sharing no equivalently compelling interest outside of himself, John turned his attention inward with the help of LSD, in the hope that this drastic form of introspection might wean him from his dependence on the persona of Beatle John. It was under the influence of this Jungian self-diagnosis that he withdrew into his little room off the kitchen in Weybridge to spend long hours in diffuse contemplation, wandering the corridors of his mind. By far the most revealing thing he ever said about his experiences with LSD was a comment he made in 1970 on the subject of his very first trip. "I did some drawings at the time," he recalled. "I've got them somewhere—of four faces saying, 'We all agree with you.'"

The changes in the internal dynamic of the Beatles arising from their shared need to assert separate identities would have important repercussions over time. For the moment, however, the experience of being Beatles continued to outweigh their individual variations on the theme. They still considered themselves to be more like one another than they were like anyone else, and apart from the strains caused by Paul McCartney's reluctance to take LSD, there were few signs of disaffection within the group. On the creative level, moreover, the widening polarity between John and Paul only seemed to enhance the competitive tensions on which their relationship as songwriters thrived. Both of them, over the course of 1965, had begun to chafe at the shopworn conventions of pop romance. Where once it had seemed enough to inject some small twist of wit, realism, or expressive honesty into the timeless saga of Boy Meets Girl, now, under the influence of Dylan and the impetus of their own maturing talents, Lennon and McCartney were aspiring to a higher and more personalized standard of artistic truth.

At the same time, the logistics of their creative partnership was undergoing a change. The vitality of that partnership had always depended on a great deal of pure proximity. Since they began writing in earnest in 1962, the Beatles' relentless schedule of touring, filmmaking, and recording had ensured that Lennon and McCartney were constantly together in hotel rooms, dressing rooms, and waiting rooms, where they tended to work on their songs as a way of passing the time. At the beginning of 1966, however, the Beatles entered a three-month period when their professional commitments were sharply curtailed. McCartney, ever eager, did his best to take up the slack, driving out to Weybridge at regular intervals. But to an unusual extent, each was left to his own creative devices during this period.

For Paul McCartney, these months would mark an artistic coming of age: a rapid ascent to a high plateau of creativity that would lead, over the next few years, to the loftiest peaks of his musical career. Throughout this transition, Paul retained his focus on romantic themes—the difference being that his love songs were now addressed to the relations of men and women, not the yearnings of boys and girls. He also retained the essentially fictional approach to songwriting that he and John had always used—the difference being that Paul's songs were now tending more toward satire, parody, and vignette. "I don't know whether poets think they have to experience things to write about them, but I can tell you that our songs are nearly all imagination," Paul told Maureen Cleave. Inspiration seems not to have been a major issue for him. Words and music came freely, and he was comfortable starting with modest or half-formed ideas and gradually building them up. Like most great popular songwriters, he remained a consummate thief, quick to seize on anything he heard that struck his fancy and adapt it to his needs. Here, too, the change in his approach was mainly one of degree. Instead of confining his scavenging to the current trends in pop, Paul was now ranging more widely, into other styles of music, for ideas to appropriate.

For his part, John Lennon meant to move in an entirely new direction, away from the conventions of pop romance, toward a form of self-expression that placed the emphasis firmly on the "self." The two songs John had written in 1965 of which he felt most proud, "Help!" and "In My Life," both reflected his desire to write as directly and subjectively as possible about his own emotions and concerns. His published books of short fiction and verse notwithstanding, Lennon harbored a narrow and surprisingly unsophisticated attitude toward the concept of fictional art. He was inclined to feel that there was something inherently dishonest about it. "I like first-person music," he would later say. "The only true songs I ever wrote were the ones I really wrote from experience and not [by] projecting myself into a situation and writing a nice story about it, which I always found phony." This austere standard of authenticity was derived from his study of Bob Dylan, whose influence John took so personally, and who by 1966 was intimidating all of his contemporaries with the intense subjectivity of his songs. Yet what Lennon failed to appreciate was that Dylan was, if anything, the most overtly fictional of popular songwriters: a master at projecting himself into a situation and writing a story about it, and a consummate musical actor who had never let the limits of his own experience inhibit what he wanted to say.

In his efforts to conform to this austerely autobiographical standard of "first-person music," however, Lennon came up against the very limitations that fiction was designed to overcome. Autobiographical writing places inordinate demands on the quality of a writer's experience. And while the cult of celebrity may be based on the premise that fame itself is an exaltation, exposing its beneficiaries to realms of experience and awareness of which ordinary people can only dream, the reality for John Lennon (no less than for other celebrities) had settled into something more mundane. John's increasingly insular existence in Weybridge did not abound in the sort of rich, evocative experiences that cried out to be turned into songs. Nor was his nature especially introspective. Since childhood he had masked his sensitivities from himself and others behind an aggressive front, projecting the force of his personality ever outward onto an appreciative audience that began with his friends and fellow Beatles and had now grown to include his fans, the press, and the public. Much of the expressive power of John's singing on the Beatles' early records came from the way the slightest acknowledgment of sensitivity or vulnerability seemed like such an enormous *concession* coming from him; in songs like "If I Fell" or "I'll Be Back," one could actually hear the tenderness fighting its way through the hard shell of his pride. This inner conflict lay at the core of his personality as a performer. Yet as a songwriter, the "looking at yourself bit" came hard.

Until he took acid, that is. Whatever else it did, LSD undermined the distinctions between subject and object until they collapsed of their own accord, revealing unseen convergences between images, emotions, and ideas. Acid imbued observations with the depth of insights, and insights with the lucidity of visions. The drug brought an interesting duality between introspection and grandiosity into Lennon's creative life. On the one hand, it encouraged the sort of frank self-examination he associated with "true" autobiographical art. At the same time, acid enlivened John's insular existence by generating just the sort of heightened, symbolically charged experiences that the Romantic tradition had always extolled as the proper subject of art. "I was suddenly struck by great visions when I first took acid," Lennon recalled. From the winter of 1966 onward, much of his creative energy would be devoted to capturing those "visions" in the words and music of his songs. LSD supplied Lennon with a trove of intuitions and inspirations that promised to turn his inner life into something worthy of his fans' expectations—to substantiate, in effect, the charisma that others attributed to him.

A potential problem, of course, was that acid had the capacity to imbue almost *anything* with an aura of visionary significance: "Eternity in a flower, Infinity in four chair legs, and the Absolute in the fold of a pair of flannel trousers!" in Aldous Huxley's words. "Real life in Cinemascope," as John himself would say. For many musicians, artists, and writers, the psychedelic muse would serve as an invitation to self-indulgence on a suitably cosmic scale. Though Lennon was not immune to this type of excess, as a Beatle he was able to avoid the worst pitfalls of psychedelic art. His own ethic of professionalism was such that he never considered performing or recording while under the influence of the drug. But an even more important constraint was the fact that his every creative whim remained dependent on the help of the other Beatles and George Martin for its realization. If anything, this was truer now than ever before, since the textures and timbres John sought in his acid-influenced songs were derived from visual and verbal imagery whose translation into music placed extraordinary demands on the creative resources of his producer and his accompanists. George Martin especially would assume the responsibility for bringing John's musical visions to life, and the two of them, the stoned-out musician and his stone-sober facilitator, would make an odd yet brilliantly complementary couple at Abbey Road in the year ahead.

THE FIRST SIGN of the metamorphosis that was under way in the Beatles' music came on the group's first single of 1966, "Paperback Writer" b/w "Rain," a record that recalled "Can't Buy Me Love" b/w "You Can't Do That" in its pairing of songs that matched sharp distinctions of style with close similarities of form. Paul McCartney's "Paperback Writer" was a satire of pop ambition in the style of "Drive My Car," set like its predecessor in a musical context of relentless simplicity. Instead of a melody that clamors on one note, the song has a harmony that clamors on one chord, confining itself to long stretches on the tonic relieved by brief forays to the subdominant. This going-nowhere chord progression suggests a harmonic metaphor for unfulfillment that jibes with the lyrics of the song.

Like its budding author-narrator, "Paperback Writer" tries to make the most of its meager resources by heaping an elaborate arrangement on its simple harmonic frame. In the introduction, the song title is triplicated in an a cappella chorale that has Paul, John, and George staggering their entrances like children singing rounds. Their voices invert in a cascade of "writer, writer, writer" as the singers complete their lines, whereupon Ringo comes bolting out of the gate with a beat of almost comic intensity behind a driving, harshly distorted figure on guitar. "Son of Day Tripper" was how Lennon described the song, but the lyric is much wittier than that of the earlier single. There's a wealth of satiric nuance in the formality of the author's query on behalf of his "dirty story" with its thinly fictionalized plot and its obsessive dimensions ("a thousand pages give or take a few"). The mangled reference to "a novel by a man named Lear" sounds like a dig at Lennon, whose own paperback writings had drawn comparisons with Edward Lear. But the butt of the joke rests firmly with McCartney himself. He, after all, was the one who wrote the query letters back in the days of the Quarry Men and the Silver Beatles, soliciting work for the band in his most affected grammar-school prose. And the tight fit between the singer and his character helps to drain the condescension from the song. When Paul exclaims the words "Paperback Writer" at the end of every verse, he brings a starry-eyed reverence to this dubious occupational title that almost stands up to the punning counterpoint of "Pay-per-back-er" (sung to the tune of "Frère Jacques") that John and George provide.

If the words and music of "Paperback Writer" could be said to capture some of the spirit of London in 1966, enlivened by people from all stations of society on the move and on the make, then John Lennon's "Rain" on the flip side of the single captured the dreamy private languor that formed the flip side of the city's "swinging" scene. The two tracks are similar in the simplicity of their chord progressions and the fullness of their sound, but the rhythm of "Rain" feels enervated, and the accompaniment eschews the clipped, Mod-like precision of "Paperback Writer" for a more impressionistic wash. Where the one track is a line drawing, the other is a blurry pastel.

In keeping with the allusion to Edward Lear on McCartney's side of the single, the *they* who run and hide from the weather in Lennon's song, the *they* who "might as well be dead," resemble the *they* of Lear's limericks: "the realists, the practical men, the sober citizens in bowler hats who are always anxious to stop you doing anything worth doing," as George Orwell once described Them. "Rain" is a postcard from Weybridge, a subversive salutation from the heart of the stockbroker belt. The lyric is more overtly imagistic than in any previous Beatles song, with "rain" and "shine" juxtaposed as mere "states of mind" in a meteorological yin and yang. The accompaniment is more imagistic as well, dominated by droning guitars, long rolls from the drums that rattle through the verses, and lush choral singing in the bridge that fills the air with melismatic sheets of sound: "Ra-a-a-a-a-a-a-a-a-ain—I don't mind! Shi-i-i-i-i-i-i-ine—the weather's fine!" Another novel element is the treatment of Lennon's voice, lispy with treble and thickly double-tracked, which seems to be strained through the soup of drums and guitars. "Can you hear me?" John asks in the song's last intelligible line, introducing a coda in which the drumrolls and the choral voices mingle with an audio hallucination created by rerecording the vocal track *backwards*. The result is a stream of apparent gibberish that retains the form of speech but reverses the shape of its acoustic "envelope" in a way that suggests another dimension in which time and meaning have turned around.

31

There's a lot of random in our songs. By the time we've taken it through the writing stage, thinking of it, playing it to the others and letting them think of bits, recording it once and deciding it's not quite right and do it again and find, "Oh, that's it, the solo comes here and that goes there," and bang, you have the jigsaw puzzle.

—Paul McCartney

Having spent the previous year reforming the politics at Abbey Road, the Beatles began to work there in the spring of 1966 as if they owned the place. The sessions that produced "Paperback Writer," "Rain," and the fourteen other tracks that would constitute the group's sharply reduced recorded output for 1966 began in the first week of April and ran through the middle of June, consuming some three hundred hours of studio time, or three times what it took to make *Rubber Soul*. The added expenditure of time and effort reflected several changes in the Beatles' working method. They now preferred to record in long, relaxed sessions that usually began in midafternoon and lasted well into the night. Where previously John and Paul had tried to complete each song before presenting it to George Martin and the rest of the group, they were now increasingly apt to come in with more of a sketch—a verse or two, and perhaps a release—which was enough to permit the recording of a basic track, to which additional verses, solos, and distinctive instrumentation could be fleshed out and added on. It became their habit around this time to take home rough mixes at the end of each session—tape "dubs" analogous to the "rushes" viewed at the end of a day's shooting on a film. According to John Lennon, this was how he hit on the backwards vocal in "Rain"— returning one night from the studio ("stoned out of my head") with a dub of the track, he mistakenly reversed the reels on his home tape deck, then sat back to marvel at the result.

One result of this newly flexible and open-ended approach to recording was a much greater emphasis on the possibilities of arrangement and production, which led the Beatles to engage in hours of hit-or-miss experimentation with new sounds and effects. Freed from his responsibilities as a cost-conscious employee of EMI, George Martin encouraged them in this experimentation, as did the presence of a precocious young engineer named Geoff Emerick, who was assigned to the Beatles after their previous engineer, Norman Smith, succeeded Martin as a staff producer at EMI. A mere twenty years old in 1966, Emerick was filled with innovative ideas about how to record and manipulate sound on tape. He exemplified the upside of the white-coated atmosphere at Abbey Road—the slightly outdated manner in which the place still functioned as an audio laboratory as well as a commercial recording facility. Among the most influential of the studio's innovations were new methods of "close-miking" instruments (thereby emphasizing presence and "attack" over timbre and ambient sound) and a soon-to-be-ubiquitous technique called automatic double-tracking (ADT), which was devised expressly for the Beatles, who loved to double-track. ADT was a method of electronically simulating the effect of voice doubling without requiring the singer to duplicate his performance. Its greatest exponent became John Lennon, who dubbed it "flanging" (after Fred Flange, a pseudonym George Martin had used on a Peter Sellers LP) and relied on it so heavily that it soon became as much a signature of John's voice on record as Sam Phillips's wobbly echo had been a signature of Elvis at Sun. With the Beatles' encouragement, Martin and Emerick immediately began to exaggerate this new effect, using it to add a woozy edge to John's singing that was particularly well suited to druggy songs like "Rain."

The Beatles wound up spending so much time recording at Abbey Road in the spring of 1966 that Capitol Records became concerned that the group would not have a new album ready for release by August, in time for their planned American tour. In May, as a hedge against this possibility, Capitol asked EMI to provide it with three of the tracks that *had* been completed—*any* three tracks would do. Capitol wanted to capitalize on the success of the single "Yesterday" in the United States by releasing an album called *Yesterday and Today*, utilizing the backlog of tracks it had saved from its abridged versions of *Help!* and *Rubber Soul*. The Beatles had always resented Capitol's practice of repackaging their albums in America, and some of this resentment may have influenced the photograph they submitted for the cover of *Yesterday and Today*. Drawing on a macabre side of their humor that had rarely been seen in public outside of John Lennon's books, they provided Capitol with a photograph that showed the four of them dressed in blood-smeared butchers' smocks, leering into the camera, their laps and shoulders strewn with hunks of raw meat and the dismembered bodies of dolls. Whether or not it was intended as a commentary on Capitol's "butchery" of their albums, the image was utterly grotesque. But Capitol, after two years of presuming to tell the Beatles how to market their music in America, chose *now* to stop arguing with success. The cover was duly printed up and the album mass-released. The first expressions of outrage came from disc jockeys and record distributors, and their reactions were so strong that Capitol frantically reversed field, recalled hundreds of thousands of copies from its distribution network, and replaced the offending image with an innocuous photograph of the Beatles grouped around a steamer trunk, looking stoned and unrepentant.

SPURRED BY THE release of the landmark albums *Rubber Soul* and *Highway 61 Revisited* (Bob Dylan's all-electric successor to *Bringing It All Back Home*), the pop music scene in Britain and America entered a period of unprecedented creative ferment in 1966. Prior to the mid-1960s, most popular recording stars had been content to think of themselves as entertainers and to compete with one another on a predominantly commercial level, in terms of records sold. Popularity, after all, was the essential creed of pop: what people liked, they bought, and what they bought, was good. Creative rivalries of the sort that were common among jazz and classical musicians were rare in the popular field—not least because a lack of artistic pretensions was felt to be part of pop's appeal. Those few recording stars who professed an autonomous commitment to their art—Frank Sinatra from the early 1950s onward being the prime example—were the exceptions that proved the rule.

This situation began to change with the arrival of the Beatles, who sought to justify the implausible dimensions of their commercial success by linking their ambition to sell more records to their ambition to write better songs. Their effect on popular music in the 1960s can be compared to that of Charlie Chaplin on filmmaking in the 1920s, since, like Chaplin, they possessed not only the commercial clout, but also the self-sufficiency as songwriters, performers, and public personalities to exercise complete control over the artistic direction of their careers. Yet for the first few years of their success, the Beatles, much as they were embarrassed by the pretensions of show business, were also embarrassed by the pretensions of art. Theirs was a heightened pop aesthetic—a Mod aesthetic, really—based on searching out new ideas and styles and adapting them to their needs, guided by the principle that it's *boring* to repeat oneself. Their success made these attitudes contagious, and other British groups like the Rolling Stones, the Kinks, and the Who, whose members had never conceived of themselves as anything but performers, began to write their own songs and exert much greater influence over the sound of their own recordings. Dylan's conversion to electric music in 1965, along with the advent of the Byrds, the Lovin' Spoonful, and other folk-rock groups, brought a more forthright ideology of self-expression to pop. Most of the new American bands consisted of middle-class kids with conventionally romantic and bohemian attitudes about the nature of artistic work, and they saw pop as a wide-open and potentially lucrative field in which to play the role of the artist for an audience of their peers. To the extent that they became commercially successful, many of them, like the Beatles, felt a need to validate their success by experimenting with songwriting and record-making in ways that would have seemed unimaginable only a few years before. Intense creative rivalries developed. (The Beach Boys went so far as to hold prayer meetings in the studio, at which they asked the Creator to give them the inspiration to make a better album than *Rubber Soul*.) Though commercial considerations remained paramount, by 1966 a growing segment of the pop world was doing its best to live up to John Lennon's dictum: "This isn't show business. This is something else."

In the minds of most pop fans, the Beatles' principal rivals were unquestionably the Rolling Stones. In Britain the popularity of the two groups was nearly comparable, especially among fans with a strong ideological investment in pop, who loved the Stones for their ability to inspire the antipathy of parents, teachers, and other authority figures. Elsewhere, in America and around the world, the Beatles' audience was much larger, but the Stones possessed a vivid musical, visual, and attitudinal presence that distinguished them from all the other British and American groups. By 1966, most serious pop fans revered both bands, and had begun to incorporate them into a kind of formal dialectic: the Beatles a bright Apollonian sun, the Stones a pale Dionysian moon. The Beatles themselves remained on friendly terms with the Stones, and they regarded them as commercial competitors as a result of the formidable string of hit singles the group had released since their breakthrough with "Satisfaction" in 1965. But the unevenness of the Stones' songwriting and their slipshod approach to recording ensured that the Beatles never took them quite so seriously as rivals in a musical sense. Instead, as had been the case since 1956, it was music emanating from America that turned the Beatles' heads.

For John Lennon especially, the emanation that still mattered the most came from Bob Dylan, who had nearly stolen the Beatles' thunder in 1965. Following the international success of "Like a Rolling Stone," Dylan had hired a backup band and set out on a grand tour of North America, Australia, and Western Europe. Arriving in Britain in May 1966, he visited with Lennon at his home. (Dylan's unreleased film *Eat the Document* documented these two pop princes engaged in a testy verbal sparring match in which Lennon, enjoying the home-field advantage, gained the upper hand.) A few days later, Dylan and his band performed a raucous concert at the Royal Albert Hall, where he previewed many of the songs that were about to be released on an unprecedented double album called *Blonde on Blonde*. These tangled emotional allegories presented Dylan's poetics at their most surreal, discursive, and dense, while his adverbial song titles ("Absolutely Sweet Marie," "Obviously Five Believers") and his sardonic vocal delivery added a flavor of put-on to the material that Lennon, who attended the concert along with George Harrison, found very intimidating. Among the songs Dylan performed that night was a ballad called "4th Time Around," which Lennon understood to consist of Dylan parodying Lennon parodying Dylan in "Norwegian Wood." John later admitted that the song had left him feeling "very paranoid."

As a pop lyricist, Lennon (along with virtually all of his contemporaries) would continue to live in Dylan's shadow for years to come. But the active rivalry between them was effectively put on hold in July 1966 when Dylan was hurt in a motorcycle accident near his home in upstate New York. Though the nature and extent of his injuries would remain a matter of considerable speculation, the consensus among Dylan's friends was that the accident, once he survived it, may have ultimately *saved* his life, such was the murderous pace he had maintained in the preceding year. He used his convalescence as an opportunity to cancel all commitments and withdraw from the public eye. It would be a full eighteen months before he was heard from on record again.

If Dylan's writing on *Blonde on Blonde* epitomized the infusion of literary values that was revolutionizing the lyric content of popular music in 1966, the studio wizardry of Brian Wilson, the American musician with whom Paul McCartney felt the keenest sense of artistic rivalry, epitomized the infusion of production values that was transforming the sound of the music itself. Wilson accounted for one-fifth of the personnel and nine-tenths of the talent in Capitol Records' *other* big group, the Beach Boys. As a public personality, the breezy, self-deprecating McCartney had little in common with the neurotic, self-aggrandizing Wilson, who was capable of describing a record like "California Girls" as "a hymn to youth." But their musical proclivities were alike in many ways. Both were gifted melodists, instinctive pop arrangers, and precocious electric bassists. Wilson was not in McCartney's league as a singer or a lyricist, but in the recording studio, where he doubled as the producer on the Beach Boys' records, he was unsurpassed.

Worn out by the strain of constant touring, Wilson had suffered a nervous breakdown in the fall of 1965. While the Beach Boys soldiered on without him, he returned to Los Angeles, pulled himself together, and set out to paint his masterpiece. The result was the album *Pet Sounds*, which was released in the spring of 1966. The other four members of the Beach Boys sang on the record, supported by an elite ensemble of Hollywood session men. But every note and nuance of *Pet Sounds* was written, produced, and directed by Brian Wilson, who presided over its creation with the tyrannical determination of a successful popular artist making his bid to be Taken Seriously.

As one of the first pure products of the age of multitrack recording, *Pet Sounds* was well named, for it was indeed a collection of sounds more than songs. Brian Wilson's musical mentor was Phil Spector, the original boy genius of the Los Angeles studio scene, and the music on *Pet Sounds* was built on the Wagnerian principles of arrangement that Spector had brought to pop. Conspicuously absent from most of the tracks was the stiff spine of backbeat and the blustery strum of electric guitar that had characterized most post-Beatles rock. Instead, Wilson achieved his effects with bold juxtapositions of mood, abrupt shifts in meter, and motifs derived from all kinds of music, including film scores and television themes. He then crowned his meticulously layered arrangements with the ethereal doo-wop harmonies and madrigal vocal counterpoint in which the Beach Boys specialized—performed, as ever, with the precision of a high school pep squad.

Brian Wilson's feats of pop production were all the more protean in light of the cloying sentimentality of his songs. On the Beach Boys' previous records, the lyrics had come mainly from lead singer Mike Love, whose hangdog voice and goofball personality brought a certain authenticity to the band's efforts to chronicle the life and times of the California teenager. By 1966, however, paeans to surf and sand, jalopies and bikinis had begun to sound like the echoes of a distant age amid the emerging psychedelia of hip Los Angeles, and Mike Love was, in any event, out on the road with the band. In his place, Wilson enlisted the aid of a local freelance writer named Tony Asher, and Asher, playing Werther to Wilson's Wagner, supplied him with a collection of anxious, painfully self-conscious reflections on adolescent identity and love. At a time when pop songwriters were striving to bring a new emotional realism to their work, *Pet Sounds* sounded like a song cycle on the theme of Arrested Development. It began with the twenty-five-year-old Brian Wilson singing the part of a guy pining for the day when he and his girl could consummate their love. "Wouldn't it be nice if we were older and we wouldn't have to wait so long?" he asked, setting the tone (jejeune) and the tense (conditional) for the album as a whole.

The puerility of Tony Asher's lyrics contributed to the disappointing sales of *Pet Sounds* in the United States, as did the failure of Brian Wilson's complex arrangements to satisfy the utilitarian needs of the Beach Boys' original dance-party constituency. Yet the disjunction between the innocence of the lyrics and the sophistication of the music seemed to have just the opposite effect in Britain, where *Pet Sounds* went on to become one of the top-selling albums of 1966, and the Beach Boys became a craze. The enthusiasm for the group was shared by many British musicians, who responded to *Pet Sounds* in a way that had no parallel among their American peers. Over the course of 1966, the techniques of production, arranging, and group singing showcased on the album rivaled the innovations of the Beatles in their effect on British pop. *Pet Sounds* even got the Rolling Stones singing in counterpoint—although the first song they tried this on, their 1967 single "Let's Spend the Night Together," was enough to make Brian Wilson blush.

Among the Beatles, John Lennon damned the Beach Boys with faint praise by claiming to envy their ability to sing on key. George Harrison considered himself a fan, but George was channeling more and more of his musical energy into the sitar by now. That left Paul McCartney, whose taste had always been more catholic than that of the others, to be "simply amazed" by the ambition and invention of *Pet Sounds*. Undeterred by the sentimentality of the songs, Paul dissected the album with the ear of an accomplished musical magpie, scavenging ideas for production, orchestration, and arrangement. Beyond the specifics, the single most inspiring feature of Brian Wilson's work was his refusal to be bound by the very conventions of guitar-group rock that the Beatles had brought to a peak of refinement in the songs on *Rubber Soul*. *Pet Sounds* opened Paul's eyes to a world of eclectic musical possibilities, and it was against what he termed the "standard" of this record that he would measure his own remarkable work in the year ahead.

32

We were just sort of going on there, leaping about making
a noise, and they were making a noise back, and then
we'd fly off to some other place and make a noise, but it
wasn't a show or anything, it was ridiculous.

—George Harrison

Had it been entirely up to them, the Beatles would never have left
Britain in 1966 for their third straight summer of touring the world. Concerts before crowds of unhinged adolescents had become a travesty of
music-making to them, and the money they stood to make from live performances was beginning to seem like more trouble than it was worth.
Brian Epstein had to plead the existence of prior commitments to persuade them to tour again—prior commitments reinforced by his own
worries about the effect an end to touring might have on the group's popularity. On this score the Beatles were far more confident than their manager, who remained haunted by the sense of not really knowing what it
was he and they had done three years before that had been so extraordinarily *right*. In 1965, Epstein had sought to duplicate the Beatles' successes of the previous year by carefully retracing their steps—the film,
the albums, the tours. This had worked beautifully, which caused Brian
to want to repeat the procedure again. But the Beatles were becoming
less inclined to do what their manager asked.

Concern about their longevity was not entirely misplaced. Conventional wisdom in the music business held that pop recording stars needed
to maintain a physical presence in the minds of their fans in order to sustain their careers, and even then could figure on no more than three years
at a peak of popularity. While the Beatles had already shown themselves
to be something much more potent than a typical pop craze, to a cautious
man like Epstein, it seemed rash to start bucking the conventional wisdom just as the three-year limit approached. Compounding Brian's anxiety were signs that the whole pop scene in Britain was going soft. *Time*
magazine's belated discovery of Swinging London notwithstanding, 1966

was shaping up as a year of looming economic crisis in Britain, in which the boom mentality that had carried the country through the first half of the 1960s finally began to deflate. An early casualty was the pop boom, as sales of popular records declined by 25 percent after a decade of general prosperity and three years of unprecedented growth. Despite its number-one status, "Paperback Writer" had sold fewer copies in Britain than any Beatle single since "Love Me Do." With the economy stalling and credit tightening, nightclubs and discothèques began closing in London and many provincial towns. (The most telling of these was that of Liverpool's Cavern, which shut its doors in February, only to reopen under new management in the summer, with Prime Minister Wilson in attendance, as Britain's grubbiest national shrine.) Those clubs that managed to stay afloat found themselves increasingly reliant, like the fashion boutiques in Carnaby Street and Kings Road, on a steady stream of young visitors from America and the Continent. Swinging London held its value on the export market for some time after its force was spent at home, as the write-ups in the international press combined with the novelty of cheap jet airfare and the undiminished cachet of British music, fashion, and film to inspire a tourist boom. But in "the world's most exciting city" itself, posters could now be seen in shop windows asking cynically: "Have You Helped to Keep London *Swinging* Today?"

What this meant for the music business was that British bands that wanted to maintain their standard of living would henceforth be more dependent than ever on success in the United States, where the boom in popular music had only just begun. (In 1966, American record sales registered their sharpest one-year increase since 1956.) Yet the United States was no longer the open market for British pop it had been since 1964. Newer British bands were encountering stiff competition from the many American groups that had been patiently growing their hair, affecting names like the Buckinghams, the Beau Brummels, and the Sir Douglas Quintet, and placing their records on the charts. This was the legitimate source of Brian Epstein's concern about the Beatles' reluctance to tour. Epstein could take some comfort in the knowledge that Elvis Presley had retired from live performances at an analogous peak in his career. But Elvis had retired to Hollywood, to enrich himself and appease his fans by releasing two or three films a year. In light of the Beatles' refusal to make any more movies like *Help!*, it was unclear how they would maintain a presence in the critical North American market if not with regular tours.

Epstein had worries of a more personal nature as well, based on his concern that he was losing his influence over the group. Though this is an old story in show business, it seems to have been more a loss of purpose than of power that Epstein feared. Touring involved travel and travel involved logistics, and Brian was never happier than when he was looking out for the Beatles' needs. None of his subsidiary ventures—his car dealership, his purchase of the music paper *Disc and Music Echo,* his management of an English bullfighter by the name of Henry Higgins, not even his acquisition of a lease on London's Savile Theatre, where he planned to present both pop concerts and legitimate plays—had proven sufficiently successful or satisfying for him. His personal life, meanwhile, was in a state of disarray. He had emerged from the frenzy of the Beatlemania years with a roller-coaster addiction to prescription sedatives and stimulants that made him prone to sudden mood swings, while his sybaritic existence as a wealthy and well-connected London homosexual had brought him little in the way of emotional fulfillment. An interview Epstein gave to Maureen Cleave as a postscript to her Beatle series rivaled John Lennon's in its level of pose ("I don't feel tycoonish today," she quoted him as telling an aide). But it did reveal the extent to which he remained completely identified with the Beatles, whom he described to Cleave as his closest friends.

In June 1966, then, on the strength of their manager's prior commitments, the Beatles left Britain for what they fully intended to be their final summer on the road. The tour began with several dates in West Germany, the third of which returned them to Hamburg for the first time since 1962 and allowed them a brief reunion with some of their old friends and acquaintances. Astrid Kirchherr was now married to a drummer from Liverpool and working as a waitress in a Reeperbahn lesbian bar. Bert Kaempfert, their Polydor producer, was riding high after getting a song he had co-written recorded by Frank Sinatra. "Strangers in the Night" had already reached number one in Britain, and was nipping at the heels of "Paperback Writer" at number two on the American charts. The Beatles greeted Kaempfert's arrival in their dressing room with howlingly off-key choruses of his melancholy hit.

From Germany they flew to Tokyo for five performances at the Nippon Budokan, a spanking new martial arts arena built for the 1964 Olympic Games. Next came the Philippines. DON'T MISS THE WORLD'S BEST! proclaimed the posters for the Beatles' one-night stand in Manila, where, in a manner reminiscent of Australia in 1964, their presence took on the character of proud national event, symbolic of full Filipino participation in the cultural affairs of the West. In the days leading up to the group's arrival, the local media devoted much attention to the Beatlemania brewing in the household of the country's dynamic new president, Ferdinand Marcos, a former war hero who had been promoting himself and his wife Imelda as the Jack and Jackie Kennedy of the Far Pacific Rim. All of Manila knew that the Beatles would be attending a pre-concert reception with the Marcos family at the presidential palace—all but the Beatles, who were only informed of the reception at the last minute, and then declined to attend. Instead they went about their business, performing shows in the afternoon and evening before a total of 80,000 fans. They awoke the next morning to a headline in the *Manila Times,* IMELDA STOOD UP: FIRST FAMILY WAITS IN VAIN FOR MOPHEADS. The accompanying photograph showed the forlorn First Lady, her children, and a few of their four hundred disappointed guests. Imelda Marcos's loss of face triggered an ugly chain of events. That morning, as the Beatles prepared to depart, they found themselves in a scene out of a spy thriller: the lobby of their hotel empty, the street outside deserted, with no porters, policemen, or limousines anywhere in sight. Unescorted, trundling their own bags and instruments, the group and its tiny entourage were met at the airport by a volatile mixture of angry Marcos partisans and shrilling teenage Beatlemaniacs. In the ensuing chaos, one of the Beatles' road managers was roughed up, and their plane was detained on the runway while Brian Epstein haggled with the authorities over the requisite liens and bribes. Manila added up to the single most frightening episode the Beatles had ever experienced on tour. They took it as a sign that after three years of seemingly charmed contact with large, emotional crowds, their luck was running thin.

The group returned to Britain for the remainder of July. "We're going to have a few weeks to recuperate before we go and get beat up by the Americans," George Harrison told the press. In the interim, *The New York Times Magazine* published an article by Maureen Cleave titled "Old Beatles—A Study in Paradox." This was mainly a rewrite of her *Evening Standard* series, updated with some amusing speculation on what the Beatles had taken to calling their "Downfall." For the *Times,* Cleave omitted Paul McCartney's views on the "house-training" of Americans, condensed George Harrison's reflections on the avocado pear, and retained

John Lennon's views on the future of Christianity. This provoked no more response from *Times* readers in July than it had from *Evening Standard* readers in March. But when Lennon's words were yet again reprinted in the August issue of the American teen magazine *Datebook,* Judgment Day was at hand.

Emblazoned on the cover of *Datebook,* Lennon's remarks about Christianity raised a storm of indignation from fundamentalist Christians throughout the American South. (Interestingly, although Paul McCartney's remark that America treated its black people as "dirty niggers" was also quoted on the cover, it prompted no response.) The furor began when a pair of radio stations in Alabama and Texas announced their intention to ban the Beatles from their playlists. "We just felt it was so absurd and sacrilegious that something ought to be done to show them that they can't get away with this sort of thing," deejay Tommy Charles of WAQY in Birmingham told the Associated Press. The radio boycott was eventually joined by some two dozen broadcasters—many of them country music stations that hadn't played the Beatles to begin with. Several stations in the South took their protests a step further by organizing demonstrations at which crowds of repentant teenagers hurled Beatles records and memorabilia onto bonfires with an enthusiasm their forebears had once reserved for high school biology texts. In Memphis, the city council voted to cancel the Beatles' upcoming concert in August, lest "municipal facilities be used as a forum to ridicule anyone's religion." In South Carolina, a Grand Dragon of the Ku Klux Klan was photographed nailing a Beatles album to the base of a wooden cross.

In a matter of days the controversy spread beyond the United States, as anti-Beatles demonstrations broke out in Mexico City and several nations, including Spain and South Africa, banned the group from their national radio stations. Yet by the time the Vatican newspaper *L'Osservatore Romano* weighed in with a reminder to its readers that "some subjects must not be dealt with profanely, even in the world of beatniks," a counterpoint of commentary was rising on the Beatniks' behalf. One radio station in Fort Knox, Kentucky, announced that it would *start* playing Beatle records as a gesture of "contempt for hypocrisy personified"; another station in Atlanta, while acknowledging the "extreme bad taste" of Lennon's remarks, maintained that "a man should have a right to make a fool of himself, even if he is a Beatle." An editorial in the Jesuit journal *America* allowed that "Lennon was simply stating what many a

Christian educator would readily admit." Back in Britain, the columnist Robert Pitman wrote in the *Daily Express,* "It seems a nerve for Americans to hold up shocked hands, when week in, week out, America is exporting to us a subculture that makes the Beatles seem like four stern old churchwardens."

The roots of this "Jesus Controversy" (as it came to be called) reached back several years. Show-business argot has always favored the theological—terms like "fan worship" and "matinee idol" come quickly to mind—and from the start of the Beatle phenomenon, the press had harped on the analogy between the zeal of Beatlemaniacs and that of religious devotees. "They are a band of evangelists, and their gospel is fun," *Newsweek* proclaimed in 1964. "Lo! Beatles Descend From the Sky for Apotheosis in Frisco," *Variety* quipped at the end of their first American tour. Reporting from London for *The Partisan Review* in the summer of 1964, Jonathan Miller took the metaphor for a ride:

> They have become a religion in fact. The days of their ministry on earth seem to be over—they don't seem to perform so much—and they have been taken up into heaven preferring to conserve the holy mystery of the Holy Quaternity in a delicious incommunicado. All over the place though there are icons, devotional photos and illuminated missals which keep the tiny earthbound fans in touch with the provocatively absconded deities.

It was that same summer, in Australia, that the messianic aura of their phenomenon fully dawned on the Beatles themselves; news photographs show John Lennon adding an open-armed papal benediction to his repertoire of balcony gestures there. In Australia, the Beatles' press agent Derek Taylor told Al Aronowitz of *The Saturday Evening Post,* "Cripples threw away their sticks [and] sick people rushed up to the car. . . . It was as if some savior had arrived and all these people were happy and relieved." "They're completely anti-Christ," Taylor continued, giving a fair idea of why he didn't last long at NEMS. "I mean, I'm anti-Christ as well, but they're so anti-Christ they shock *me,* which isn't an easy thing." One *Post* reader who took Taylor's hyperbole to heart was the Rev. David Noebel, a Baptist minister affiliated with the Oklahoma-based Christian Crusade. Noebel drew heavily on Taylor's words in a pamphlet he wrote called "Communism, Hypnotism, and the Beatles," which circulated widely among fundamentalist congregations in 1965. "We are in the fight of our lives and the lives of our children," Noebel warned in this bizarre document, its fifteen pages of text annotated with 140 footnotes citing sources from Plato to Pavlov. "Action taken now by concerned Christians and patriotic Americans is of the utmost importance. Let's make sure four mop-headed anti-Christ beatniks don't destroy our children's emotional and mental stability and ultimately destroy our nation." The next time anyone connected with the Beatles had something to say about Jesus, at least one group of concerned Christians and patriotic Americans was primed to respond.

Obviously there was a world of difference between having a "religioso" aura ascribed to one by the editors of *Variety* and appearing, however flippantly, to ascribe such an aura to oneself. The tone of Lennon's remarks to Maureen Cleave ("I'm right and I'll be proved right," etc.) was indeed boastful and self-important. But John's real mistake had been to speak as a mere Englishman, an inhabitant of the one nominally Christian nation on earth where his remarks may well have been literally true. In Britain, plummeting levels of church attendance had made the decline of Christianity a staple topic of public discourse since the end of World War I. Only recently, in 1963, the Anglican Bishop of Woolwich had sold three million copies of a controversial book called *Honest to God* in which he urged Christians to dispense with their outmoded belief in an "Old Man in the Sky" and reject the proscriptive morality of traditional church teachings in favor of a universal ethic of Love. The Satire comedians had had a field day with the increasingly desperate attempts of the Church to make itself seem more relevant ("Don't call me vicar, call me *Dick* . . ."), while the Beatles themselves had experienced the ministrations of the Rev. Ronald Gibbons, who told reporters at the height of Beatlemania that a Fab Four version of "O Come All Ye Faithful" might provide the Church of England with "the very shot in the arm it needs."

Outside of Britain, however, the decline of Christianity was by no means a foregone conclusion or the butt of satiric jokes. On the contrary, the future of the faith was the crux of theological controversy of historical proportions that was reaching a kind of climax in 1966. The Second Vatican Council had just adjourned in Rome after initiating the most extensive reappraisal of church doctrine since the Counter-Reformation. Among mainstream Protestants in the United States and Europe, a heated debate was under way over the tenets of "secular Christianity" associated with the maverick theologians Paul Tillich and Dietrich Bonhoeffer. In the United States especially, the leading role played by the clergy in the civil rights movement had revived the dispute over "social gospel" that had bitterly divided the Protestant denominations a half-century before, while evangelical Christian fundamentalism, convoked by the "media ministries" of charismatic preachers like Oral Roberts and Billy Graham, was beginning the resurgence that would transform American politics and society in the decades ahead. In the spring of 1966, *Time* magazine had created a sensation by advertising its report on "The New Theology" with a cover that asked, IS GOD DEAD? Conservative Christians were beside themselves—merely to pose the question was a blasphemy to them—and the magazine was deluged with irate letters that it published for weeks on end.

To a certain extent, the Jesus Controversy could be regarded as the international equivalent of the flap over the MBE—a convenient opportunity for people outside of Britain who were fed up with the Beatles and everything they stood for to make their feelings known. But in the United States it was significant that John Lennon's remarks had failed to elicit any response until they were brought to the attention of that segment of the Christian community whose concept of religion was most strongly rooted in charismatic response. These were Christians whose faith was founded on the concept of a personal relationship with Jesus, to which a notion like "popularity" could apply. They were also, in many cases, Christians who were accustomed to finding their religion on radio and television, in a format permeated with entertainment values. The irony, of course, was that it was this same Bible Belt subculture that, a decade before, had contributed its own style of charismatic theatricality to popular music in the person of Elvis Presley. And Elvis had gone on to play the part of a sanctified Southern hero to the hilt, turning his home in Memphis into a veritable theme park of charisma called Graceland.

For the Beatles, the furor in America came as a revelation—"the first time we started to see the power that could turn against us," Paul McCartney recalled—and what was revealed in the broadest sense went well beyond the issue of John Lennon's insouciance or sacrilege. The seriousness with which some Americans were prepared to respond to the theological musings of a British pop star was an indication of the extent to which the Beatles were becoming identified by admirers and detractors alike with a growing political and cultural movement in the United States. Not until 1968 would the term "counterculture" be coined to describe the confluence of psychedelic bohemianism and New Left radicalism that would sweep through American society in the years ahead. In the summer of 1966, all that anyone could be sure of was that *something* dramatic was happening to what was then called "youth culture" in America, and that the prime catalyst for this change appeared to be the country's rapidly escalating involvement in the war in Vietnam.

At a time when public opinion polls showed a large majority of Americans strongly supporting the war, Vietnam recast the abstract notion of a "generation gap" in the most personal and potentially dire terms. It was over the issue of the war that the dissident spirit that had first surfaced at Berkeley in 1964 ("the Bastille of the student revolution," wrote the historian William O'Neill) spread to colleges and universities across the United States. Antiwar sentiment was neither confined to American college students nor universal among them, but it was on and around the college campuses that the political activism of the New Left communed with a more generalized spirit of rebellion against America's social mores and modes of authority in *all* their institutionalized forms. The cultural component of this anti-authoritarian movement was centered on issues of personal freedom, expression, and pleasure, and its prime catalyst was the Prohibition-like situation that was developing around the use of recreational drugs, the enthusiasm for which was infecting growing numbers of disaffected young people with the old American ethos of living righteously outside the law. On a characteristically grand scale, American youth was entering into its version of a "Mod moment." Instead of working-class teenagers enacting an ironic social fantasy of being "college boys," the counterculture in America would consist of large numbers of actual college boys and college girls embracing a romantic social fantasy of identification with their nation's real and mythic population of outsiders, outcasts, and outlaws.

For all their reflexive sympathy with the cause of disaffected youth, the Beatles had had very little personal contact with student dissidents, and they were still only dimly aware of the strength of these gathering trends. Yet for millions of young people in America—a great many of whom (if asked) would have dated the current crisis of authority from the moment of John F. Kennedy's death—the Beatles were pivotal figures in the creation myth of the counterculture. Their transformation of popular music since their arrival in America in 1964 was widely recognized as the foremost expression of the cultural power of youth, an influence so pervasive that the progression of their records had begun to mark the passage of time in their listeners' lives. (As Charles Perry wrote of the scene in San Francisco's Haight-Ashbury district in the fall of 1965, "You could party hop all night and hear nothing but *Rubber Soul*.")

Equally potent was their transformation of male fashion in America, beginning with their affront to the "indisputable principle that short hair equals men, long hair equals women." Two and a half years since the Beatles' arrival first popularized the style in America, long hair on men had begun to provide a generation of cultural rebels with a banner of their rebellion that struck an especially raw (and therefore satisfying) nerve among several generations of older Americans who had been conditioned by the sharply polarized ideals of gender that had prevailed since World War II. Still another powerful influence the Beatles exerted stemmed from their identity and solidarity as a group. In their loyalty to one another and their autonomy from everyone else, the Beatles had come to personify an ethic of *collective* nonconformity that took the loneliness out of rebellion and linked the activist and hedonist wings of the emerging counterculture as few things could.

For a succinct illustration of the niche that the Beatles had come to occupy in the pantheon of America's dissident youth, one could do no better than to cite an incident that occurred on the Berkeley campus during a student strike in the fall of 1966, when a crowd of approximately a thousand demonstrators segued spontaneously from a desultory rendition of the "Internationale" (to which few of them knew the words) into a rousing sing-along of the Beatles' current single, "Yellow Submarine." Lest it be lost on anyone, the symbolism of the moment was explained by an activist named Michael Rossman (one of the founding members of the Free Speech Movement) on a flyer that blanketed campus bulletin boards the following day. "The Yellow Submarine was first proposed by the Beatles," the flyer read, "who taught us a new kind of song. . . . Last night we celebrated the growing fusion of head, heart and hands; of hippies and activists; and our joy and confidence in our ability to care for and take care of ourselves and what is ours. And so we made a resolution which broke into song, and we adopt for today this unexpected symbol of our trust in the future, and of our longing for a place fit for all of us to live in. Please post, especially where prohibited. We love you."

Coming as it did on the eve of the Beatles' departure for the States, the news of boycotts, bonfires, and cross-burnings threw Brian Epstein and his staff at NEMS into a panic; there was talk of canceling the tour. The concern on the part of Epstein and the Beatles was not with bad publicity as such. The concern, given the perception of the people who took offense and the tenor of their response, was that somebody would try to *kill* them. (It did nothing to calm anyone's nerves that, just days before the *Datebook* story appeared, a young man named Charles Whitman had commandeered a clock tower at the University of Texas and staged one of the most horrifying mass murders in recent American history, killing thirteen people and wounding thirty-one, for no motive that could be discerned.) Brian Epstein flew to New York and held a press conference at which he took *Datebook* to task for reprinting Lennon's words "out of context," and expressed the Beatles' regret "that people with certain religious beliefs should have been offended in any way." But Epstein's charge that the journalistic practices of a teen gossip magazine left something to be desired did little to stem the controversy. With time growing short, a decision was reached to proceed with the tour and have John Lennon issue some sort of apology or explanation when the group arrived in Chicago for their first set of dates. "If I had said television was more popular than Jesus, I might have got away with it," he told reporters in Chicago. "I used the word 'Beatles' as a remote thing, not as what I think as Beatles—as those other Beatles, like other people see us. . . . But I'm not saying that we're greater or better or comparing us with Jesus as a person, or God as a thing, or whatever it is." Echoing the Bishop of Woolwich, John affirmed his belief in the Almighty, "but not as an old man in the sky. I believe that what people call God is something in all of us." Pressed by reporters, he concluded by saying, "If you want me to apologize, if that will make you happy, then okay, I'm sorry."

At the Beatles' subsequent public appearances, however, their mood was less contrite. In New York—where their news conference began with a press aide announcing (for the benefit of photographers), "The Beatles are about to enter. I'd like to ask you people in front to kneel," and the room exploding in laughter at the unintended joke—Lennon dismissed further questions about the controversy by noting philosophically, "There are more people in America so there are more bigots." "We don't care about those who don't like us because of that statement," Paul McCartney added.

Compared with their previous visits, which for all the chaos had been triumphant affairs, the 1966 tour was plagued by mishaps, rain-outs, and an undercurrent of fear. The Beatles' concerts in Washington, D.C., were picketed by members of the Maryland Ku Klux Klan. Their show in Memphis took place after all, but telephone threats were received, and the performance was momentarily interrupted when a firecracker thrown from the audience convinced all four Beatles that someone was shooting at them. Elsewhere, at some of the big ballparks—including Shea Stadium in New York—there were rows of empty seats.

Whereas each of the Beatles' previous tours of America had ended in symbolic encounters, their 1966 tour ended with a geographic epilogue. At the last of their fourteen concerts, near the close of their half-hour set, Ringo hopped out from behind his drums to join the others in posing for a photograph, taken from behind the stage. The Beatles then reassumed their places, belted out a final version of Little Richard's "Long Tall Sally" ("have some fun to-ni-i-i-ight!"), and with that were gone for good. The venue was Candlestick Park in San Francisco, where five months later, in January 1967, some twenty thousand young people would converge on Golden Gate Park for an event billed as the "First Human Be-In: A Gathering of the Tribes." Inspired by the call of Michael Rossman and others for a "fusion" of hippies and activists, the Be-In was conceived as a coming-out party for a local bohemian scene that had been coalescing over the past year around a series of neo-tribal dance concerts combining the pleasures of rock music, kinetic lighting, and psychedelic drugs. Among the earliest sponsors of these dances was a collective of hip entrepreneurs who called themselves the Family Dog and whose stated intention was to transform the city of San Francisco into "America's Liverpool." Thus was the torch passed—between continents, within a generation. Having watched their luck run thin in the Philippines and their charm run out in the States, the real Liverpudlians, after more than 1,400 live performances, were withdrawing from the field.

33

Let me tell you how it will be . . .

—George Harrison, "Taxman"

They left behind them the album *Revolver,* released in the first week of August 1966, and there had never been a record like it, for the simple reason that there had never been a recording group like the Beatles in this, their newly individuated form. During its three months of development at Abbey Road, the album had evolved into a conscious effort to reconstitute the celebrated whole as the sum of its celebrated parts. After considering titles like *Abracadabra* and *Magic Circles,* the group had settled on *Revolver* as a kind of McLuhanesque pun—revolve is what records *do*—that also described the way the focus of attention on the album turned evenly from one Beatle to the next. Woven with motifs of circularity, reversal, and inversion, *Revolver* was the first record on which the Beatles consciously made the interplay of their individual personalities a theme of the music itself.

Every aspect of the new album was designed to signal a break with the past. Its cover, for example, consisted for the first time of something besides a flattering photograph of the group. Here instead was a stark, arty, black-and-white collage that caricatured the Beatles in a pen-and-ink style beholden to Aubrey Beardsley, whose *Yellow Book* illustrations were the subject of a major retrospective at London's Victoria and Albert Museum in the summer of 1966. The collage was made by the Beatles' old "exi" friend from Hamburg, Klaus Voorman (who in the intervening years had taken up Stuart Sutcliffe's old instrument, the bass guitar, moved to London, and joined the pop group Manfred Mann). Voorman assigned each Beatle to a quadrant of the record sleeve and tied their four heads together with a great common field of hair, its tousled surface swarming with elfin Beatle caricatures and tiny Beatle likenesses taken from old album covers and publicity shots, crawling around in the Beatles' hair like the ideas crawling around in their heads.

On the back of the album jacket, above a dimly lit photograph of the Beatles all wearing sunglasses—Ringo is sporting a particularly ludicrous, bug-eyed pair—the list of song titles is paralleled by a list of names designating the "Lead Singer" on each track. Liner notes on previous Beatle albums had identified who sang on which songs, but on *Revolver* the matter of lead voice and authorship was emphasized as never before. Whereas no fewer than half the songs on *Rubber Soul* and its predecessors were listed as jointly sung, each song on *Revolver* was linked to the name of a single Beatle. These designations were repeated on the record label itself, and even in the advertisements EMI placed in the trade papers to announce the album's release. (This emphasis on authorship was one of the reasons the Beatles responded so angrily to Capitol's requisition of three tracks for *Yesterday and Today,* since all three of those tracks happened to be John Lennon's songs. Their subsequent omission from the American version of *Revolver* skewed the whole concept of the album, leaving John as lead singer on only two of the remaining tracks. The result was the most seriously compromised version of the Parlophone product that Capitol would ever release.)

The first surprise is that the album should begin with a song by George Harrison; the second surprise is that it should be such a witty song, its humor compounded by the irony that George should finally realize his ambition to write caustic social commentary in the style of Bob Dylan with a song protesting the soak-the-rich policies of the British Welfare State. Harrison had never been one to make light of the burdens of success; "Taxman" is his reminder that even millionaires get the blues. It begins with a grim, miserly voice, slowly intoning, "One, two, three, four, one, two," against a background of exaggerated tape hum. Sounding like a half-speed version of the brisk shout of "one-two-three-*four!*" that kicked off the Beatles' *first* LP, this opening is an elaborate conceptual joke: in place of that earlier "live effect," a deliberate "tape effect" that broaches the idea of the Beatles beginning anew in the studio and hints with subtle self-mockery at how the focus of their lives had shifted in the three years since *Please Please Me* from the dance floor to the counting house.

"Let me tell you how it will be . . ." George sings the verses of "Taxman" with an authoritarian air, phrasing on the offbeats against a stiff soul riff from the band. "Should five percent appear too small [a tambourine sloshes like a pocketful of change], be thankful I don't take it all [joined by the tock of a cowbell, as hollow as a beggar's cup]." In the bridge, the backup chorus (John and Paul) comes to the foreground, feeding their lines to George, who answers them as implacably as if he were checking off boxes on a form. There's a flavor of comic opera in their exchange, which ends with a shriek of *"Taxman!"* that alludes to the theme of the popular 1966 television series *Batman*. The awestruck manner in which the Beatles announce the name of this civil service superhero is the song's true inspiration, a terrific musical joke, and it is answered by an eruption of lead guitar (played by Paul) that knifes into the body of the song like a sinister peal of funhouse laughter. The guitar subsides into a squawking accompaniment to another bullying verse in which John and Paul provide breathy interjections of "A-ahh, Mr. Wilson!" and "A-ahh, Mr. Heath!" cooing the names of the two party leaders like a pair of Profumo-era chorus girls. Then the song merges the certainties of death and taxes in a macabre parting shot, advising even the dead to declare the pennies on their eyes. The extortionary lead guitar sounds again and the music—coins jangling, cup rattling—fades away.

"Ahhh—look at *all* the lonely people!" The Beatles' voices surge into the grousing aftermath of "Taxman" on a bright rush of melody and urgency—their most arresting beginning since "Can't Buy Me Love." "Eleanor Rigby" is a neoclassical tour de force, sung to the accompaniment of an eight-piece string ensemble that knits fretfully behind this opening chorus before settling under the verse into a pattern so taut and staccato it sounds like the baroque equivalent of a backbeat. The use of strings in popular music is not called "sweetening" for nothing, but the violins, violas, and cellos in George Martin's arrangement are grating, insistent, and bleak. Nor are they given much in the way of harmonic material to work with, since the whole song—chorus, verse, and refrain—transpires over two chords, a minor tonic and a major sixth, that are distinguished by a solitary note of difference. Though the movement between them is accomplished with considerable finesse, these two chords exert so little pull on each other that they barely describe a progression at all. They function instead as another of Paul McCartney's minimalist harmonic metaphors, mirroring, in their similarity and stasis, the characters in the song.

Much was made at the time of the poetic quality of the lyric, the first two verses of which were written by McCartney, the third with Lennon's help. The critic Karl Miller included a transcription of "Eleanor Rigby" in his 1968 anthology, *Writing in England Today*. The poet Thom Gunn, writing in *The Listener,* compared the lyric favorably to an Auden ballad from the 1930s, "Miss Gee," about another old maid who lives for the church, dreams of the vicar, and dies an anonymous death. In 1967, Allen Ginsberg made a point of playing the song during an audience with Ezra Pound (who was reported to have "smiled lightly" at the end). "I don't think there's ever been a better song written," the lyricist Jerry Leiber would say of "Eleanor Rigby," and George Melly, hearing it for the first time, felt that "pop had come of age."

The lyric is both vivid and remarkably concise. The phantom relationship between the lonely spinster and the threadbare priest is evoked with great nuance—with nothing *but* nuance, really, since, like the two chords that constitute the harmony, their relationship is based on little more than the fact that they're the *only* two characters in the song. The verses are haunted by the furtive, ghostly image of the woman, waiting (like some aging Juliet) at a window, "wearing a face" that she's never let anyone see. Eleanor Rigby is a classic type, familiar from novels and films, but the surreal and colloquial touches in the lyric dispel the sense of cliché. McCartney liked to point out that she was a younger girl named "Daisy Hawkins" in the original version ("a bit like Annabel Lee"), and that the priest was named "Father McCartney," which was changed to MacKenzie because Paul considered it "a bit of a hang-up for my dad, being in this lonely song." His account suggests that he wrote the first two verses without knowing how the song would end, and that the lyric became progressively less sentimental with Lennon's help, until, in the final version, the song's compassion is tempered by its insistence on holding these sad characters responsible for the quiet desperation of their lives. "Eleanor Rigby" draws on some of the hardness a lapsed Catholic like McCartney can feel for the Church and the vision of life it promotes; there is a chilling hint of callous satisfaction in the description of the priest "wiping the dirt from his hands" at the end.

But the lyric, as ever, sounds even better than it reads. Each section of the song—chorus, verse, and refrain—is written, performed, and recorded so as to present a different form of commentary. There's a sense of real anguish in the opening chorus, where the melody is fluid and the harmonized voices full. In the verse the focus narrows, and Paul's solo voice is tinged with resignation. (The movement of the melody under the woman's name—three half-steps up on "Eleanor," two whole steps back on "Rigby"—is like the story of her life.) Extreme stereo imaging in this section places the singing on one side, the strings on the other, with an eerie emptiness in between. The song's refrain ("All the lonely people") is a thing of somber beauty. Here, Paul's voice softens as it floods both sides of the track, but the melody is marked by leaps of an octave ("where *do* they all come from?") and a tenth ("where *do* they all belong?") that bring a new dimension of distance and detachment to the song. More than anything else, it is this hint of ambivalence, signaled by those leaps, that gives "Eleanor Rigby" the unsettling emotional complexity that impressed many listeners as something new to pop. The questions the song poses aren't rhetorical; they're unanswerable. They're the sort of questions people ask when they don't know what else to say, and by raising them as he does, Paul calls attention to the inadequacy of his own response. In the last eight bars, his mixed feelings are the subject of an extraordinary double-tracked duet in which the urgency of the chorus is played off contrapuntally against the detachment of the refrain. The effect is truly provocative: having already stretched its listeners' powers of identification by addressing the familiar theme of unrequited love using characters and a context completely divorced from the world of pop romance, the song leaves off with a concise and starkly honest statement about the limits of empathy.

IT'S EASY TO generalize about the difference between the songs by Lennon and those by McCartney on *Revolver*. Paul's songs, without exception, address the importance of human relations. John's songs mainly express a desire to be left alone. The first of these, "I'm Only Sleeping," is another missive from the back room at Weybridge. "When I wake up early in the morning, lift my head, I'm still yawning," John sings over a sensuous, swinging accompaniment that moves in dream time, forward through the verses and backward through sinuous interludes of George Harrison's tape-reversed guitar. "I'm Only Sleeping" can be heard as the testimonial of a devoted Jungian, so hooked into the dreamworld of his unconscious that he can't bear to leave his bed. It can also be heard as an answer to the question that was posed by Maureen Cleave. How does a Beatle *live*? John Lennon lived like this.

The musical accompaniment to this reverie is filled with mimetic effects, beginning with the melody, which opens on a drowsy plateau, stirs slightly under the phrase "lift my head," and then gapes upward a sixth on "I'm still *yaw*ning." The rhythm is dotted with quirky anticipa-tions and retards, including moments when the whole band seems to nod off for an instant and then hastily regain its place. Paul's bass nudges into the otherwise empty space between the verse and the bridge with the muffled insistence of sounds impinging on sleep; John later fills this same spot with a histrionically unstifled yawn. Best of all is George's mewing, backward guitar solo, which draws on the capacity of music to suspend the laws of time and motion to simulate the half-coherence of the state between wakefulness and sleep, extending the analogy between dreams and drugs that underlies the song. John himself handles this innuendo in the same way that music-hall comedians handled sexual double entendre—by simply defying his listeners not to take him at his word. "Please don't spoil my day, I'm miles away," he pleads in a voice of wistful innocence—the voice of a tired child. "And after all, I'm *only* sleeping."

Of George Harrison's second incarnation on *Revolver, Melody Maker* said it best, crediting the Beatles on "Love You To" with "going the whole Indian hog." From its first cascading arabesque of shimmery, bejeweled notes, the track unfolds like a musicological expedition East of Suez, as the first in a series of quixotic attempts to translate the formal elements of Indian raga into the format of Western pop. Though Paul adds a spot of harmony and Ringo a tambourine, the track is a one-Beatle show, spotlighting George alone, singing and playing the sitar to the rather shaky accompaniment of a tabla drummer, recruited from the Asia Music Circle, by the name of Anil Bhagwat. The track begins with an unaccompanied sitar prelude that corresponds to the ruminative, intro-ductory movement of a raga known by the term *alap*. Filled with croak-ing drones, pregnant pauses, and softly elasticized notes, the effect is both a stereotypic evocation of the Mysterious East and a total surprise (in its very presence on a pop album). Eventually the sitar settles on a ceremonious eight-note riff that serves the song as a hook, the tabla come bounding in, and the song itself begins. Lyrically, "Love You To" is the pop equivalent of a *carpe diem* poem. It means to counterpoise an ecstatic and presumably Eastern sensibility ("Make love all day long! Make love singing songs!") against a repressive and presumably Western one (the second verse refers darkly to "people standing round, who'll screw you in the ground"). But the tone of George's vocal is so priggish and judgmental that it's hard to know which side he's on. "Love You To" plays at metaphysics the way that other bad pop lyrics play at romance; it trades in puppy wisdom in place of puppy love.

And still, despite its shortcomings, the presence of this little outpost of internationalism on *Revolver* was a signal pop event. By inspiring other musicians to take up Indian instruments, or to simulate Indian tonality using electric guitars, it loosed upon the music scene a torrent of "raga-rock." And as one of the most brazenly exotic acts of stylistic experimentation ever heard on a popular LP, the track represented a bold declaration of artistic autonomy on the Beatles' part. It showed the extent to which recording stars who could afford to do so would henceforth do as they liked on their records, regardless of whether the results had any redeeming commercial value, or conformed in the least to the current stylistic parameters of pop. And for George Harrison himself, the track was the first overt manifestation of the Orientalist bent that would provide him with the sharply defined identity, as a musician and as a public personality, that had eluded him thus far.

The ascending triads at the start of "Here, There, and Everywhere" come as a vigorous reassertion of Western harmony after the modality of "Love You To," but Paul McCartney's willowy ballad represents a form of musical adventurism in its own right. How high, ask these opening bars, can a song soar on a passing gust of schmaltz and still return safely to earth? Soar it does, on a current of "ooohs" that, for once, carry no double edge, and a stilted, Hallmark-style sentiment that sounds like an item on the agenda of self-improvement Paul discussed with Maureen Cleave: "To lead a better life," he sings with the virtue of a Victorian tenor, "I need my love to be here." That said, the song alights on a stately progression of chords that carries it forward with an air of predestination through three exquisite verses and an equally exquisite bridge. As an example of song-writing craft—of superior melody, subtle harmony, and lyrical rhythm and rhyme—"Here, There, and Everywhere" is one of the few pop ballads from the 1960s that compare with the work of Tin Pan Alley masters like the Gershwins and Rogers and Hart. The song is laid out on a formal plan. Its verses begin, respectively, with the words "here," "there," and "everywhere"; its first two stanzas conform to different rhyme schemes, which are then combined in the third; and the title of the song is not sung in its entirety until the very end, where it functions as a deferred refrain. Yet the overall effect is one of intoxication, not organization, for the music is drunk with love.

Paul sings against a demure background of muffled drums and oddly acerbic plinks on an electric guitar, moving effortlessly into and out of falsetto with a lilt that disarms the dissonant notes that dot the melody and charms them into agreement with the key. It's hard to believe that this is the same singer who once made such a suave hash of "Till There Was You." Here his performance is enriched by the unique prerogative available to a singer-songwriter, for he sings with what amounts to a composer's faith in the unembellished perfection of the song. And "Here, There, and Everywhere" is filled with moments that warrant such faith, like the minor seventh chord that accompanies the line "Changing my life with a wave of her hand" with a harmonic gesture as capricious as her wave, or the understated arrival at "everywhere" at the start of the last verse, where the word flows effortlessly off the end of the bridge, escorted by a droll chromatic guitar run; or the utter conviction of the last line, where Paul sings, "I need her here, there, and everywhere" while the harmony lifts from the tonic to the subdominant, then falls back to the tonic in the hymnal cadence of "Amen."

From its height of romantic rapture, *Revolver* next descends to the allegorical depths of the sea. Written by Paul, with help from John, expressly for Ringo to sing, "Yellow Submarine" is by all rights a children's song, with simple words, simple chords, and a numbingly simple refrain. It is performed in a sing-along manner removed from the context of contemporary pop, sounding more like a throwback to an earlier era of participatory music-making that atrophied—among adults, at any rate—in the era of records and radio. Yet its simplicity and childishness are deceptive, for nothing the Beatles had recorded to date was more dependent on technological sleight-of-hand. "Yellow Submarine" is a simple song transformed by the wonders of multitrack technology into a sophisticated sonic pastiche. In 1966 it stood as a cockeyed monument to the whole self-sufficient and self-absorbed existence the Beatles were creating for themselves at Abbey Road. Sung by anyone else above the age of thirteen, it would have smacked of deliberate camp. But Ringo lacked the vocal resources to be anything but guileless, and he brought to the song the same deadpan quality he brought to the Beatles' films. In his hands the Yellow Submarine became a satirically updated version of the improbable craft in which Edward Lear put his characters to sea—the Owl and the Pussycat's pea-green boat, the Jumblies' unsinkable sieve.

Like "Norwegian Wood," the song begins by subverting the narrative cliché. "In the town where I was born, lived a man who sailed to sea," Ringo drones over the strum of an acoustic guitar, "And he told us of his life, in the land of submarines." Like all good nonsense, the lyrics to the world's first *undersea* shanty are based on a single incongruity, taken to its logical extreme: men have been sailing to sea in songs like this for centuries, but not in submarines. The second verse is accompanied by the frothing of the ocean, closing in overhead, while the third competes with a hubbub of conversation, clinking glassware, and jovial bonhomie: "And our friends are all aboard, many more of them live next door / And the band begins to play. . . ." Whereupon a full brass band does just that, shattering the calm of this polite gathering with two bars of booming oompah, which is just enough to conjure the image of tubas in a submarine. Between verses, Ringo stands at the head of a sailors' chorus, chanting the refrain. There's also a solo, of sorts, composed entirely of sound effects drawn from the collective unconscious of a generation of schoolboys raised on films about the War Beneath the Seas. Valves squeak, pipes hiss, bells sound, hatches slam, and crisply garbled voices relay terse commands, until the song's last verse is discharged from this Goonish concerto with the *whoosh* of a torpedo exiting its tube. Here Ringo is joined by John, who echoes each line in the strained, sardonic voice of an old vaudevillian with the crowd in the palm of his hand. John signs off with a maniacal laugh and the ship's company falls in for the final refrain, which has taken on an aura of daffy sincerity like some old patriotic number, sung to the tramp-tramp-tramp of marching feet.

EMI accompanied the release of *Revolver* by pairing "Yellow Submarine" with "Eleanor Rigby" on a single designed to advertise the expanding dimensions of the Beatles' musical world. The one was a song of childhood, extolling the joys of togetherness; the other was a song of old age, expressing the pain of loneliness; and neither track bore the slightest resemblance to what was thought of as rock 'n' roll. "Eleanor Rigby" received most of the airplay and attention in Britain, where it became the top-selling single of 1966. In America, however, Capitol Records was leery of promoting a song with religious connotations in the midst of a Jesus Controversy. So Capitol put its promotional weight behind the seemingly innocuous "Yellow Submarine," which rewarded the label's caution by becoming the first "designated" Beatles single since 1963 to fail to reach number one, and then, amazingly, by generating some controversy of its own.

As it turned out, the sheer childishness of the record strained the credulity of many Beatle fans. Seeking deeper significance, some fans responded by associating the image of a Yellow Submarine with the yellow capsules in which the barbiturate Nembutal was sold. Others decided that the title referred to the resin-stained hull of a marijuana cigarette. For some it was enough that the song described a trip of any kind; by the summer of 1966, searching for drug references in popular songs was becoming a new kind of parlor game. Yet the childishness of "Yellow Submarine" was simply an expression of Paul McCartney's feeling, expressed around this time, that "we've all of us grown up in a way that hasn't turned into a manly way. It's a childish way." And to focus on drug innuendo is to ignore the affectionate form of self-parody that this little song provides. Like the Beatles themselves, "Yellow Submarine" takes a potentially threatening image and renders it festive and benign. It then goes on with a kind of offhand genius to touch on the controlling irony of their lives: the way that they had set out from Liverpool like generations of young, seafaring men before them, only to become so deeply immersed in the frenzy of fame as to be shut off from normal forms of contact with any of the places they had been, and thrown back, the farther they traveled, on the pleasure and solitude of their own company. In his commentary on the original submarine adventure story, Jules Verne's *Twenty Thousand Leagues Under the Sea*, Roland Barthes describes the underwater world as a "self-sufficient cosmology" with "its own time, its own place, space, fulfillment, and even existential principle. This principle, it seems to me, is the ceaseless action of secluding oneself. To enclose oneself and to settle, such is the existential dream of childhood." And who better to express the Beatles' version of that dream than the one whose half-forgotten plan for the country involved having everyone's house joined to the houses of friends by underground tubes?

THE ABSURDITY OF the controversy surrounding "Yellow Submarine" was indirectly emphasized by the track that followed it on *Revolver,* "She Said She Said," which owed its inspiration to an incident that occurred during the acid trip John Lennon took in Los Angeles during the Beatles' 1965 American tour. As Lennon recounted it, he took the drug during a party

the Beatles were hosting at their house in the Hollywood Hills, only to
find himself bedeviled by one of the guests, the actor Peter Fonda, who
was intent on sharing with a Beatle the story of his own "pre-mortem
death-rebirth experience." "This guy who I didn't really know kept coming over, wearing shades, saying, 'I know what it's like to be dead.' " In his
acute condition, John found the unsolicited offer of Fonda's experience
to be more than he could stand, and out of the ensuing collapse of
human relations came "She Said She Said." As an example of the way
that one man's ego-death was the next man's ego trip, the incident had
the makings of a sharp satire of psychedelic grandiosity. But John had
already written a song for *Revolver* that overtly satirized the drug culture
("Dr. Robert" on side two). So he chose instead to turn the encounter
into a romantic black comedy by recasting Peter Fonda as a self-satisfied
girl like the one in "Norwegian Wood." "She said, 'I know what it's like to
be dead,' " John sings in the opening verse, "And she's making me feel
like I've never been born."

"She Said She Said" was the last track recorded for *Revolver,* slapped
together at the last minute to give John another song to sing. The lyric, as
a result, is sketchy, but the song succeeds on the strength of John's performance and an instrumental accompaniment that shows the Beatles at
their absolute peak. The track opens with the shrilly electrified, *Bride of
Frankenstein* whine of George Harrison's lead guitar, wringing the neck of
a G-major chord as it caterwauls up the scale—smack into the leaden
crash of a downbeat and a series of evasive maneuvers from the drums. In
the three minutes of pandemonium that follows, George with his aggressive, repetitive runs seems to be playing the part of the girl; Ringo, twisting and thrashing like a man possessed, embodies the part of the boy. The
anguished emphasis of the performance turns poignant in the bridge,
where the music slides into waltz time over Paul's calliope bass, and John
recalls that things were right in his younger days, as if to convince himself. But the memory emboldens him enough to come back at the girl in
the verse, if only to tell her that he's ready to leave. His escape is played
out in the coda, where voices echo spookily, Paul's bass rises oppressively,
and Ringo breaks into double-time, in a headlong rush for the door.

"I NEED TO laugh, and when the sun is out, I've got something I can
laugh about. I feel good, in a special way—I'm in love and it's a sunny

day. Good day sunshine! Good day sunshine!" So sings Paul, kicking off the second side of *Revolver* with a gentle riposte to "Rain"—all else being equal, he'll take a sunny day. "Good Day Sunshine" gathers up the romantic rapture of "Here, There, and Everywhere" and puts it on parade. Aspects of the song, including the chords and the weather, were borrowed from "Daydream," a recent hit by the Lovin' Spoonful. But the music itself is a testament to Paul's growing proficiency as a piano player, since it's the sound and feel of the instrument, played in a rolling, barrelhouse style, that dominates the track. Previously, when Lennon or McCartney composed on the piano, they used the keyboard mainly as a convenient way of voicing chords, which they would then transpose to guitar when it came time to record. "Good Day Sunshine," by contrast, is written *for* piano; much of its charm (and it is mainly a charming song) comes from the way its rhythmic and harmonic complexities are masked by the proud mannerisms of the accomplished amateur pianist—hammy chromatic runs in Paul's left hand under the verse; hot-footed tremors in George Martin's right hand during his overdubbed solo break. The height of this artful innocence occurs in the final refrain, where Paul's jubilant, three-against-four exultations of "Good day sunshine!" stride smoothly through alternating bars in 4/4 and 3/4 time, followed by a change of key (from B to F) that lifts the roof right off the tune. The whole thing is carried off with such aplomb that the intricacies of the arrangement are perplexing only to people with trained ears. The song works hard at being unassuming, and the work pays off handsomely.

"And Your Bird Can Sing" sounds like the second act of "She Said She Said"—another song about personal pretension, sung by John to the accompaniment of George's crazed, cacophonous guitar. "Tell me that you've got everything you want, and your bird can *sing*, but you don't get me," John taunts his anonymous adversary in the opening verse. Listeners tended to assume that the "bird" in question was British slang for "girl," and the song works well on that assumption. But Lennon was stalking bigger game in "And Your Bird Can Sing." The song was inspired by a profile of Frank Sinatra by Gay Talese that appeared in the April 1966 issue of *Esquire*. "Bird," Talese wrote, "is a favorite Sinatra word. He often inquires of his cronies, 'How's your bird?'; and when he nearly drowned in Hawaii, he later explained, 'Just a little water on my bird'; and under a large photograph of him holding a whiskey bottle that hangs in the home of an actor friend named Dick Bakalyan, the inscription reads,

'Drink, Dickie! It's good for your bird.' " What brought the article to
Lennon's attention in the first place was not its revelations about Sinatra's private vocabulary, but rather its description of his attitude toward
an upcoming network television special with which he hoped to reassert
himself as a force in contemporary pop:

> Sinatra had been very excited about this show; he saw here an oppor-
> tunity to appeal not only to those nostalgic, but also to communicate
> his talent to some rock-and-rollers—in a sense, he was battling The
> Beatles. The press releases being prepared by Mahoney's office
> stressed this, reading: "If you happen to be tired of kid singers wear-
> ing mops of hair thick enough to hide a crate of melons . . ."

After the crack about mops and melons, John Lennon could take
some satisfaction in reading about "an inconspicuous little grey-haired
lady" on Sinatra's staff whose sole responsibility was to care for the
singer's collection of *sixty* "remarkably convincing" toupees. But Talese's
fawning description of Sinatra's charisma ("the embodiment of the fully
emancipated male, perhaps the only one in America, the man who can do
anything he wants") and Sinatra's wealth ("his film company, his record
company, his private airline, his missile-parts firm, his real-estate holdings across the nation, his personal staff of seventy-five") was more than
enough to inflame John's sense of professional jealousy. Insult had been
added to injury around the time the article appeared with the announcement of the Grammy Awards for 1965. In the year of *Highway 61* and
Rubber Soul, the American record industry turned its back on the youthful trends in pop by honoring Sinatra in the categories of best male vocalist and best album for a world-weary collection called *September of My
Years.* "Tell me that you've heard every sound there is," crooned the
world's greatest kid singer in his enigmatic reply, "and your bird can
swing. But you can't hear me. You can't hear *me.*"

In the context of *Revolver,* the ballad "For No One" is a dark sister to
"Here, There, and Everywhere." In the context of Paul McCartney's
career, this carefully crafted song, with its neoclassical instrumentation
and its theme of love gone wrong, was the true heir to "Yesterday." Yet for
all its expressive power, nobody rushed to record it, or hailed it as a musical coup, and it was destined to languish in relative obscurity on
Revolver's second side. What made "Yesterday" an instant standard was

neither its subtle structure nor its use of a string quartet, but rather the way that structure and those strings created a novel setting for the song's conventional brand of nostalgia and its strong melodic line. The brooding emotional impact of "For No One" derives from the way it violates these genre conventions by treating the very idea of melodic energy as an expression of futile hope.

Paul sings it alone, to the spindly accompaniment of a harpsichord comping evenly on the beat. The melody hammers dully on one note over the first and third lines of each stanza, rising and falling in between along a shallow arc whose limpid motion is overmatched by the incessantly downward movement of the harpsichord's gravelly bass. "For No One" runs on a reality principle—a steady sinking feeling, deep in the gut of the song. Paul's voice is recorded unusually loud, which together with the flatness of the melody and the second-person form of address gives his singing a deeply internalized feel. He sounds like he's talking to himself, and we seem to be hearing not his words but his thoughts as they well up inside his head. In the release a piano takes over, its notes spinning anxiously, and the melody spirals upward in a sudden show of strength that's mocked by the negation of the words: "And in her eyes, you see nothing, no sign of love behind the tears, cried for no one." The verse that follows is almost clinical in its detachment—"You want her, you need her, and yet you don't believe her"—and it sets up a wondrous interlude in which the singer's false hopes are literally played out in a French horn solo, performed by Alan Civil of the London Philharmonica Orchestra. As the most magisterial and fragile of instruments, the choice of the horn is a masterstroke of arrangement. The beauty of Civil's playing lifts the sullen weight of the song, but the reverie he provides has a hollowness at its core, and at the end of his allotted eight bars, he's simply brushed aside by Paul, returning to the nightmare at hand. When he repeats the opening verse, with its gaunt image of the day breaking and his mind aching, Paul's voice is shadowed by a wistful reprise of the horn. "You find that all the things she said will fill your head: you won't forget her," sings the Beatle who claimed to "believe in yesterday." Yet here there's no comfort in the prospect of memory, and the words sound more like a curse.

JOHN LENNON HAD no shortage of real-life characters upon whom to base "Dr. Robert," his satiric sketch of a psychedelic medicine man. They included the unnamed London dentist who dosed him with LSD, the world-famous Dr. Timothy Leary, and the merely notorious Dr. Charles Roberts, a New York physician whose practice consisted of administering amphetamine-based hypodermic "cocktails" to well-connected people who wanted the kick of hard drugs but lacked the nerve to shoot themselves up. By 1966, access to Dr. Roberts had become a status symbol at certain strata of New York's high society and demimonde. "Often people got introduced to Dr. Roberts as a present," recalled Cherry Vanilla, the Andy Warhol "superstar." "If you really loved someone, you took him to Dr. Roberts as a gift and let him feel the feeling." While there's nothing to suggest that the Beatles ever had any personal contact with this man, they surely knew people who did.

Then there was Dr. Robert MacPhail—or "Dr. Robert," as he's called in Aldous Huxley's psychedelic novel *Island*. Huxley's Dr. Robert is an elderly Scot with a saintly demeanor and a shock of silver hair. As a member of the ruling oligarchy of the island kingdom of Pala, his duties include dispensing a drug called *moksha*-medicine, which provides the Palanesians with "a succession of beatific glimpses, an hour or two, every now and then, of enlightening and liberating grace." Lennon's song owed its existence to the sparks generated in his imagination by this unseemly coincidence of fiction and fact, ideal and reality—Huxley's Schweitzer-like patriarch and Cherry Vanilla's Park Avenue pill doctor. Set to a taciturn rockabilly accompaniment of drums and gulping guitars, "Dr. Robert" is a reminder that John's skepticism was not totally blunted by the effects of LSD. The verses vacillate between the paranoid protocols of the drug scene ("Ring my friend, I said you'd call") and ironically inflected expressions of Huxley's fondest hopes ("You're a *new* and better man"). The tension between malevolence and benevolence is brought to a head in the bridge, where the beat drops out, an organ chord rises, and a chorus of Beatles proclaims, "Well well well, you're feeling fine!" while a lone guitar drones in the background like a set of freshly stupefied nerve endings.

Though it would have been a standout on any previous Beatle album, George Harrison's "I Want to Tell You" gets lost in the shuffle of Lennon and McCartney tunes on side two of *Revolver*. Fading in like "Eight Days a Week" on a riff like "Ticket to Ride," the song has a great introduction, a powerful backing of hypnotic piano and bone-crushing fills on the drums, and a highly serviceable lyric on which Harrison manages to turn his own inarticulateness into a theme. "I want to *tell* you," he sings in a glottal Liverpudlian drawl. "My head is filled with things to say / When you're here, all those words they seem to slip away." Throughout, John and Paul embellish George's lead vocal with incandescent bursts of harmony, and in the coda, the three singers join on a lovely a cappella chorale, their voices ululating on the line "I've got time" like a trio of Mersey muezzins.

The protagonist of Paul McCartney's "Got to Get You Into My Life" has got anything but time; his sense of expectation can barely be contained. The track begins with a great fanfare of horns over a stamping, teasingly inert rhythm that comes alive with the simultaneous arrival of Paul's voice and his bass guitar. "I was alone, I took a ride, I didn't know what I would find *there*," he sings over crescendoing trumpets and saxophones, lifting his voice an octave between "find" and "there." The words suggest a spirit of psychic adventure more commonly associated with John, but this being Paul who's singing, what he finds down the road is a girl: "Ooooh, then I suddenly see you! Ooooh, did I tell you I need you?" The nervous energy, those giddy "ooohs," the loping bass and boxy drums—all bear the stamp of a Holland-Dozier-Holland production, and Lennon would later characterize the track as the Beatles "doing our Tamla-Motown bit." But as an act of homage, "Got to Get You Into My Life" falls flat. *Revolver* abounds in songs that were brought to life in the studio; this one was nearly done to death there, by a horn arrangement that lured George Martin out of his musical depth. The track's windy assemblage of too much trumpet and not enough sax (stiffly played by a NEMS group called Sounds Incorporated) overshoots the idiom of soul music entirely, landing closer to the sophistication of big-band jazz at its blandest. And the problem is further compounded by an unfortunate decision to omit (or, more likely, delete) the guitar or piano that would normally anchor the band, leaving these hapless horns to carry the full musical weight of the song. Even so, this rare lapse in production is substantially offset by the ferocious exaltation of McCartney's singing, which salvages the excitement of the track. Each of Paul's four previous lead vocals on *Revolver* was, in its way, a model of restraint; here he cuts so totally loose that the instruments can't keep up. In timbre and presence, *he's* the real horn on "Got to Get You Into My Life," and it is not until the end, when an electric guitar playing the fanfare from the introduction comes barging into the mix, that any feature of the accompaniment measures up to the strength of his voice, turning the last few bars into a fleeting glimpse of the track this might have been.

Revolver ends with "Tomorrow Never Knows," on which the Beatles, as *Melody Maker* might have put it, go the whole hallucinogenic hog. Originally entitled "Mark I" (as if it were some kind of experimental prototype), this was the first track the Beatles recorded at Abbey Road in the spring of 1966, and it seems likely that the whole album was made on the assumption that this was where it would end. John Lennon eventually renamed it with a Ringoism that the Beatles had been meaning to use. (On account of its Bond-like ring, "Tomorrow Never Knows" was briefly considered as a title for their second film.) Although John once said that the new name was chosen to relieve the song of its "heavy philosophical edge," there's a case to be made that Ringo's fractured catchphrase is a good deal weightier, philosophically speaking, than the lyrics John supplied. It seems to mark the point where Scouse stoicism shades over into Zen.

More than any other track on *Revolver*—even "Yellow Submarine"— "Tomorrow Never Knows" was a figment of the recording studio. Previous Beatle recordings had employed production techniques or combinations of instruments that would have been hard for the band to reproduce live. Yet however much the strings may have added to "Eleanor Rigby," it is not hard to imagine Paul McCartney singing the song to the accompaniment of a piano or a guitar. The same cannot be said of "Tomorrow Never Knows"—unless one cares to imagine John Lennon singing it in the shower with both taps opened wide. Its melody sounds like a bugle call; its harmony consists of two chords. It does without the niceties of a chorus, release, or refrain. The song is nothing without its arrangement, and its arrangement, apart from bass and drums, consists entirely of electronic effects. As written, the song is simply a stripped-down vehicle for John Lennon's vocal personality, which makes it oddly reminiscent of "Twist and Shout," the final track on the Beatles' *first* LP. What that song was to beat music, this was to acid rock.

It makes a spectacular entrance, riding in on a drone of sitar that whines like an incoming shell, bursting on impact into an up-tempo vamp of astonishing power: the bass an enveloping, shadowy hum, the drums a cannonade of downbeats, upbeats, and a pair of stuttered offbeats that are played with such force that the rhythmic vacuum created in their wake sucks the music dizzily ahead. Behind the beat come gales of banshee-like cries and whoops that spill into the music and then scatter before John's voice. "Turn off your mind, relax and float downstream," he intones. "It is not dying." The words are an incantation, sung with a sepulchral air, and beneath the word "dying" there sounds a brooding G minor seventh chord, played on an organ, that rises over this roiling musical landscape with the spectral presence of an eclipsed sun. The lyric presents the spectacle of John Lennon skating blithely across the surface of Timothy Leary's gloss on *The Tibetan Book of the Dead,* and it brings a certain symmetry to the album, since it was this same bombast about ego-death that sent John fleeing back to his childhood in "She Said She Said" at the end of side one. The quotation of Leary continues: "Lay down all thought surrender to the Void," John proclaims, having seen the light. The banshees spill back into the gaps in his singing, their whoops and wails joined by odd sparkings and snatches of backward sound that gradually coalesce into a sonic headwind over the opening stanzas of the song, until, as John invokes the "meaning of within," there's a palpable shift in the balance, a tilt from forward to back, and the music unravels crazily into a swirling vortex of sound. Reeling across the stereo spectrum, whole inverted orchestras are heard to approach and rocket past, playing in alien keys, bowing at impossible speeds. They are chased by the berserkly backward emissions of a tape-reversed guitar, each phrase unwinding to a vanishing point at a sudden, vertiginous blip.

The method behind this madness was a species of *musique concrète*—music created by the manipulation and selection of sounds on tape—and George Martin, Geoff Emerick, and the Beatles turned the EMI Studios upside down in pursuit of these otherworldly effects. Martin and Emerick began by wiring together every tape deck they could find—a total of eight machines, scattered throughout the building, connected by cables, snaking down hallways and stairs. Each deck was then set up with a continuous loop of tape and manned by either a Beatle or an engineer, each of whom was equipped with a pencil with which to randomly vary the tension and speed of the tape. This whole jury-rigged, hydra-headed organism was then thrown into synchronous motion while Martin and Emerick sat at their mixing board, panning and sifting and sampling as the streams of raw data flowed in.

When the singing returns, John's voice, which in the early going possessed its usual double-tracked strength, seems now to be tethered by a thread to the body of the song. His request in "Tomorrow Never Knows" was surely unique in the annals of record production; he merely asked George Martin to make him sound "like the Dalai Lama," beaming out onto the astral plane from the windswept peaks of Tibet. With his usual canny wit, Martin engineered a rite of technological sanctification in pursuit of this Lama Effect. He fed John's vocal through a mechanically rotated device called a Leslie speaker that was designed to make electronic theater organs sound more like acoustic church organs by simulating the natural vibrato caused by air pushing on the reeds of the pipes. The strained and disembodied howl produced by this contraption came about as close as modern science could to the Himalayan epiphany Lennon had in mind. As the singing fades up and away, the bass hums, the drums stutter, and the banshees wail. "Or play the game Existence to the end—of the beginning . . . of the beginning . . . of the beginning," John repeats, over and over, like a proverbial broken record, or a skip in the Wheel of Rebirth, ending *Revolver* with a conceptual joke as elaborate as the one with which it began. "The end of the beginning" completes the album's motif of circularity and declares the Beatles' intent to initiate a new phase of their career. But the phrase, as John Winston Lennon knew, comes from Churchill, not Leary, in a famous wartime address. "Of the beginning . . . of the beginning . . ." intones the Dalai Beatle over the *apocalypso* rhythm of the band, dispensing crumbs of Buddhist wisdom, Learyite prattle, and Churchillian rhetoric, all balled into One. On this last allusive laugh, the track decomposes in a cloud of musical debris—a Mighty Wurlitzer glissando from the organ, a tack piano jazzing into the afterglow—and *Revolver* thunders to a close. It was three years to the month since the release of "She Loves You." The 1960s were in high season.

34

We sort of half hope for the Downfall—a nice Downfall. We've been Beatles as best we'll ever be. Those four jolly lads. But we're not those people anymore. We've got to find something else to do. Paul says it's like leaving school and finding a job. It's just like school, really, because you have the group to lean on, and then suddenly you find you're on your own. What we've got to do is find something we can put the same energy into as we did into being Beatles.

—John Lennon

The Beatles returned to Britain in September 1966 from the ordeal of their American tour and began what amounted to a trial separation— three months set aside for the express purpose of pursuing their individual aims. John Lennon accepted an offer from the director Richard Lester to play a part in his latest film and left for eight weeks on location in Germany and Spain. Paul McCartney accepted an offer from the producer John Boulting to work with George Martin on the soundtrack for a film called *The Family Way*. George and Pattie Harrison departed for a six-week visit to India as Ravi Shankar's guests. And Ringo Starr repaired to Weybridge, "a family man as it were."

Lennon's was the most publicized of these independent ventures. On the basis of a phone call from Lester, he had agreed to play the part of a British soldier named Private Gripweed in a United Artists production called *How I Won the War*. The film was ostensibly adapted from Patrick Ryan's jocular World War II novel of the same name, but Lester and his screenwriter Charles Wood had acquired the rights to Ryan's book with the intention of curing it of its jocularity and recasting it as a bitter farce. Wood's screenplay drew heavily on a stage play he had written called *Dingo*, which was described by the London *Times* as "a savage anti-militaristic cartoon which sets out to deflate the heroic myth." The same applied in spades to his script for *How I Won the War*. The ideological slant of the picture and the rather unsavory character of Private Gripweed made it an adventurous part for Lennon to play. A sidelight of the role, and a promotional boon for the film, was the requirement that he cut his hair. Photographs of John's initiation into the rude fellowship of short-back-and-sides ran in newspapers and magazines worldwide, recalling the photographs taken of Elvis Presley at the time of his induction into the (actual) American army some eight years before. Lennon was also issued a pair of round, wire-framed spectacles that gave him an owlish look.

While his fellow Beatle slogged across the plains of Spain in camou-flage battle dress, Paul McCartney settled into the music room of his newly renovated house in St. John's Wood to write a soundtrack for *The Family Way*. The film was an "adult comedy" starring Hayley Mills and Hywel Bennett as a pair of newlyweds struggling to consummate their love in the close confines of the bride's parents' council house. (The script was by Bill Naughton, fresh from his triumph with *Alfie*.) Much of the responsibility for the soundtrack fell to George Martin, who, as the film's musical director, was charged with arranging and orchestrating the handful of appealing, rather conventional motifs McCartney supplied. "He's the interpreter," Paul told the *Sunday Times*. "I play themes and chords on piano or guitar. He gets it down on paper. I talk about the idea I have for instrumentation. Then he works out the arrangement." Because the film was set in the Lancashire mill town of Bolton, McCart-ney indulged his taste for the robust style of brass-band music performed by uniformed "works bands" and "district bands" throughout the Indus-trial North. (The Beatles had already sampled this sound on "Yellow Sub-marine.") In November, having completed his work on the soundtrack, McCartney adopted his preferred disguise of horn-rimmed glasses and slicked-back hair and spent a couple of weeks in anonymity, driving around the French countryside with a notebook and a movie camera.

Because he was the Beatle who had always been least tolerant of the trappings of Beatledom, it was no surprise that George Harrison's sabbati-cal from the group should turn out to be the most personally fulfilling. In the summer of 1966, Harrison had overcome his embarrassment at the inordinate amount of attention that was being paid to his modest accom-plishments on the sitar and allowed a mutual friend to introduce him to Ravi Shankar. Shankar had spent the spring performing in Europe and was curious to meet the British pop star whose well-publicized enthusiasm for

Indian music had caused such a dramatic increase in the attendance at his concerts of late. ("The great sitar explosion began early in 1966—at least that's when I became aware of it, when I went to Britain," Shankar wrote in his autobiography, *My Music My Life.*) Despite the differences in their ages and backgrounds, they took to each other at once.

Shankar, born in 1920, was the son of a government minister and a product of India's Bengali Brahmin intelligentsia. After spending his adolescence living in Paris and touring the world as a dancer in his brother Uday's Indian ballet troupe, he had renounced "the sparkle and easy fame of my artist's life in Europe," returned to India, and devoted the next seven years to the study of the sitar under the fierce tutelage of Ustad Allauddin Khan, the great Muslim patriarch of North Indian classical music, who treated his precocious Hindu pupil like a second son. Shankar emerged from this apprenticeship just as World War II was ending and, amid the chaos of India's emergence as an independent state, quickly earned a reputation as a young virtuoso of the sitar. In 1948 he accepted a position as the musical director of All India Radio, the international arm of the government broadcasting service. In 1956, after supervising the formation of a National Orchestra, he resigned this government post and took up the mantle of cultural ambassador full-time, performing frequently at concerts and music festivals in Europe and the United States. So it went until 1966, when his career was abruptly transformed by the strains of "Norwegian Wood."

At their first meeting, Shankar was sufficiently impressed by Harrison's humility ("very charming and polite, not at all what I expected") and intrigued by Harrison's celebrity to offer his young admirer some basic instruction on the sitar. He also invited George and his wife to visit him in India in the fall, both to see something of the country and to attend classes at a conservatory that Shankar had recently founded in Bombay.

Prior to this trip, George Harrison's interest in India had been largely confined to its music, supplemented by a smattering of Eastern philosophy he had gleaned from the psychedelic scribes. In the course of his visit with Ravi Shankar, a deeper fascination took hold. On the most rudimentary level, instruction in the sitar with a teacher of Shankar's stature involved an immersion in Indian culture, for the instrument was taught in a highly personalized manner that was based on the traditional relationship between a guru and a disciple. "I am trying not only to teach the music of India, but also to emphasize the many aspects of our culture and customs that are so closely associated with the music," Shankar wrote in *My Music My Life*. Although Harrison never became a disciple in the formal sense of the term, it appears that he did at least flirt with the idea of renouncing the "sparkle and easy fame" of *his* artist's life in the way that Shankar had. In India, Harrison established a routine of practicing the sitar for several hours a day with a formal dedication he had never applied to the guitar, taking a special delight in the densely codified musical heritage to which the instrument belonged. This attitude carried over into George's growing interest in Indian religion as well. Like a long line of disaffected Europeans before him, his attraction to India involved a fascination with its orthodoxy that overrode his own anti-authoritarian reflexes and allowed him to introduce a new kind of discipline into his life. The sitar led him to yoga (for his aching legs), yoga led him to meditation, and meditation would lead him, over time, to a sincere if inevitably awkward engagement with the Hindu religion itself. In Bombay, Harrison told a BBC correspondent that he already felt more comfortable with the form of religion he encountered in India than with the Catholicism of his youth: "The difference over here is that their religion is every second and every minute of their lives—how they act and how they conduct themselves and how they think."

> LONDON, Nov. 25 (AP)—The Beatles ended three months of separation last night and got together to make a new record. When asked what it felt like to be working as a group again, John Lennon replied: "Just lovely." Since returning from an American tour at the end of August, the four singers had been following different lines of work and play. Reports that they were breaking up have been denied.

The Beatles reunited in London toward the end of November amid a flurry of speculation on their future, or lack thereof. Because no official announcement had been made of their decision to forgo all live performances, the abrupt cancellation of a fall tour of Britain that had been scheduled earlier in the year had inflamed the suspicions of the press. "Last week, it emerged that the Beatle phenomenon was ending," the *Sunday Times* announced in a full-page article titled "The Beatle Break: Insight on the Dissatisfied Monarchs of Show Business." Remarks to reporters by the Beatles themselves did nothing to dispel the impression that some sort of an Abdication, if not necessarily a Downfall, was at hand. "We'll work together only if we miss each other," Paul McCartney told the *Sunday Times,* adding, in reference to the mustache he had grown, "It's part of breaking up the Beatles. I no longer believe in the image." Despite the fact that they had *all* grown mustaches by then, McCartney's comment inspired a front-page headline in *Variety:* BEATLES BREAKING UP. Interviewed on the set of *How I Won the War,* John Lennon had sounded similarly uncertain about the future of the group. Yet what neither Beatle was prepared to say publicly was that their trial separation had been a failure. McCartney, for all his brave talk about going it alone, had grown restless and bored during their time apart. Lennon had an even stronger reaction. "I did try to go my own way after we stopped touring," he later said. "I had a few good laughs and games of monopoly on my film, but it didn't work. I didn't meet anyone else I liked. I was never so glad to see the others. Seeing them made me feel normal again."

Concerning their next move, an album was the obvious choice. The Beatles had not set foot in the studio since the *Revolver* sessions ended in June, and 1966 would be the first year since they became successful that they would release no new music in the fall. (EMI filled this gap with a collection of their greatest hits.) At the same time, having proclaimed *Revolver* to be nothing less than "the end of the beginning," the group felt a need make a dramatic gesture of some sort. One idea that had been kicking around for a while was that of an autobiographical album, based on Liverpudlian themes. John Lennon had returned from Spain with a wistful new ballad called "Strawberry Fields Forever," whose title was taken from the name of a Salvation Army orphanage near his Menlove Avenue home. For the first time, the Beatles were consciously searching for a new conceptual frame in which to work, and autobiography, the first resort of the self-conscious artist, seemed a natural choice. When they reunited at Abbey Road in November, it was to see what they could make of this idea.

SPURRED BY THE Beatles' decision to stop touring, Brian Epstein was faced with pressing business on all fronts during the fall of 1966. A considerable portion of the Beatles' earnings since 1963 had come from live performances; as a result, Epstein's most immediate concern was to make up for the loss of this income by negotiating a new recording deal for the group, whose contract with EMI was due to expire in June of 1967. For its part, EMI was anxious to sign a new contract before the old one expired, lest the company be drawn into a bidding war over its single most profitable asset. In an effort to test the market, Epstein quietly contacted the heads of several major American labels in the hope that one or more of them might make the Beatles a truly revolutionary offer. But the American record industry was still about six months away from recognizing how thoroughly the economics of its business had changed in the era of album-oriented rock, and none of these labels was willing to substantially raise the ante on EMI. (Goddard Lieberson, the president of Columbia Records, reportedly told Epstein that he thought the Beatles had peaked.) In the absence of a much better offer, Epstein and the Beatles were quite content to stay with EMI; they regarded the world's biggest record company as a suitable home for the world's biggest recording act. But in recognition of the importance of the American market, Epstein wisely chose to negotiate separate contracts with Capitol and EMI. By the middle of January 1967, both of these deals were done. Effective immediately, the Beatles would receive a royalty of 7.5 percent on the retail price of all newly issued records in Britain. In the United States, Capitol agreed to a royalty of just under 9 percent and paid the Beatles a $2-million signing bonus. (Upon learning of the bonus, EMI's chairman, Sir Joseph Lockwood, told Capitol's president, Alan Livingston, that he was out of his mind. Having learned his lesson in 1963, Livingston assured Lockwood—correctly, as it turned out—that he would recoup the bonus on the Beatles' next LP.) Both contracts ran for the unusually long term of nine years, but instead of committing the Beatles to releasing a specific number of records, they merely required them to deliver a total of sixty-five master tracks. Since this was barely half the number of tracks a successful group would expect to release over a nine-year period, the deal contained an implicit provision for renegotiation once this quota was filled. The terms of the contract also stipulated that all future LPs would be released with standardized covers and content in Britain and the United States, thereby ending Capitol's practice of repackaging the Beatles' work.

In years to come, Brian Epstein would be criticized by rival managers, disgruntled associates, and several of the Beatles themselves for his handling of these record deals. There is no question that he exhibited his usual reluctance to appear pushy or petty in his negotiations with Sir Joseph Lockwood and Alan Livingston. But, like most major labels at the time, EMI and Capitol had an established policy of offering their top-selling artists a maximum royalty of 5 percent on the retail price of their records. (In 1960, Capitol had allowed Frank Sinatra to leave the label rather than pay him more.) Though royalty rates would rise dramatically over the next few years, this ceiling had barely begun to crumble in 1966, and the rates paid to the Beatles under the terms of their new contracts were the highest that either of these labels had ever offered an artist at the time.

In addition, Epstein's negotiating position was not as strong as it might have seemed. *Revolver* had sold as well as any previous Beatles album, but the eclectic single of "Yellow Submarine" and "Eleanor Rigby" had only risen as high as number two on the American charts, raising concerns that, as their music became more sophisticated, the Beatles might be at risk of leaving their fans behind. Epstein was also contending with the advent of the Monkees, a brazenly synthetic, flagrantly successful pop group–television show package, based on the antic style of the Beatles in *A Hard Day's Night,* whose first single, a cunning variation on the theme of "Day Tripper" called "Last Train to Clarksville," had raced to number one on American charts. Nor was Epstein's negotiating position strengthened by the Beatles' own extraordinarily ill-timed comments in the press about the prospect of their breaking up.

The Beatles' decision to stop touring forced Epstein to reassess his own role as a pop manager as well. During the same period when he was working to secure the Beatles' financial future, Brian was also seeking to rid himself of the headache of running NEMS Enterprises. In the five years since its formation, the entertainment division of the Epstein family business had grown into a multifaceted management, booking, travel, public relations, and concert promotion agency with scores of employees and a roster of twenty-five acts. Overseeing its operations had become a full-time administrative job that had little to do with Brian's interests or talents. His plan to relieve himself of this burden involved offering a partnership interest in NEMS to a flamboyant, Australian-born pop tycoon named Robert Stigwood.

On the face of it, this was a strange alliance, for Stigwood was precisely the sort of flashy show-business operator that Epstein had always shunned. His freebooting style as a businessman had earned him the animosity of powerful figures in the British entertainment industry, and had forced him into bankruptcy in 1965. But Stigwood was also recognized as one of the most innovative pop managers in Britain—a pioneer of leasetaping and a founder of Reaction Records, one of the country's few viable independent record labels. His current clients included two up-and-coming groups, Cream and the Bee Gees, both of whom would make strong additions to NEMS's roster. The deal Epstein worked out with Stigwood was a potential boon for them both. Stigwood would join NEMS as a "joint managing director" and gradually assume responsibility for the day-to-day operations of the company. NEMS would provide Stigwood with the stable, solvent base of operations he needed to restore his reputation and pursue his management schemes. This would leave Epstein free to devote his full attention to the Beatles.

There was one further provision of the deal between Epstein and Stigwood. This was an option that gave Stigwood the opportunity to purchase a *controlling* interest in NEMS for the sum of £500,000, provided he could raise the money by October 1967. Considering that Epstein had previously rejected offers of nearly four times that amount, his asking price to Stigwood seemed inexplicably low—except for the fact that the firm's principal client, the Beatles, was not included in the deal. Instead, the option offer to Stigwood was predicated on the expiration of Epstein's own five-year management contract with the Beatles in October 1967. After that, Epstein and the Beatles planned to form a new jointly held company, independent of NEMS, that would collect the group's royalties and manage their affairs. NEMS would continue under Stigwood's aggressive stewardship while Epstein, in addition to collecting a half-million pounds, would retain a substantial minority interest in everything Stigwood produced.

For the moment, however, with the recording contracts signed, Stigwood on board at NEMS, and the Beatles sequestered in the studio, Epstein was left to ponder the question of how best to keep the group in touch with their fans in light of their unwillingness to tour. The same question had been weighing on Walter Shenson's mind for more than a year. Ever since *Help!,* Shenson had been shopping around for the right combination of script and director that would entice the Beatles into making the third film called for in their contract with United Artists. This was no simple matter. The Beatles had been expert at playing themselves in *A Hard Day's Night* and *Help!,* but neither film had convinced anyone who knew anything about acting that they could carry a picture in which they were called upon to play characters *other* than themselves. At one point Shenson had tried to persuade them to appear as a quartet of cowpokes in a film based on Richard Condon's satiric Western novel, *A Talent for Loving.* At another point he had proposed casting them in a remake of *The Three Musketeers* (with Ringo as D'Artagnan). In January 1967, in keeping with the current climate of communion between pop and the avant-garde, Shenson commissioned the playwright Joe Orton to revise a script called *Shades of a Personality,* to which the Beatles had optioned the rights. Orton took it upon himself to rewrite the script from beginning to end, but the result, retitled *Up Against It,* impressed Shenson as totally unsuitable for the Beatles.

Ultimately, Shenson's efforts to make a third Beatles film were preempted by an offer from an American television producer named Al Brodax, whose company, the Hearst-owned King Features Syndicate, was responsible for an animated children's cartoon series called "Beatletoons" that had been running for several years on ABC-TV. Early in 1967, Brodax contacted Brian Epstein with a proposal to make a feature-length animated film based on the single "Yellow Submarine." All that King Features wanted from the Beatles was their endorsement of the project and permission to use their songs. But Epstein insisted on approval of both the film's visual content and script, in return for which he was willing to commit the Beatles to providing four new songs for the soundtrack. On this basis, Brodax went to work on the film, and Epstein went to work on Brodax. By the time the project was publicly announced in June, Brian had prodded King Features into hiring a production team that included some of the best young animators in the world.

Still another offer that came to the Beatles early in 1967 was a proposal by Hunter Davies, a columnist for the *Sunday Times* and the author of a best-selling coming-of-age novel called *Here We Go Round the Mulberry Bush,* to write an "authorized" biography of the group. As the product of a provincial, working-class, grammar-school background, Davies typified the younger breed of British journalist who identified strongly with the Beatles. He first broached his idea for a "big, definitive, serious book" about the group to Paul McCartney, whom he interviewed for his *Sunday Times* column in the fall of 1966. In January 1967, with McCartney's blessing, Davies pitched his proposal in a letter to Brian Epstein. "As Truman Capote put together a murder, I'm sure there's a need for a full anatomy of the Beatle phenomenon," he wrote. Unfazed by the odd reference to the current best-seller *In Cold Blood,* Epstein liked the idea, and a contract was signed whereby the Beatles and their manager, in return for one-third of the author's proceeds, agreed to welcome Hunter Davies into their lives.

35

Personally, I don't think any of these groups will produce a song that is about Liverpool. They don't see anything romantic here. Harry Warren and Mack Gordon could see their way to writing about Kalamazoo, Michigan, but these Liverpool boys are really embarrassed by their hometown.... Unless John Lennon and Paul McCartney can sort of forget the American influence for a while, nothing new will happen. They are the only two with enough talent to do something new.

—Bob Wooler, 1963

Of the many ambitious pop singles released during the fall of 1966, none had a stronger influence on the Beatles than the Beach Boys' "Good Vibrations," on which Brian Wilson rounded up a whole herd of his pet sounds to create what he described as a "pocket symphony." In a remarkable feat of studio production, "Good Vibrations" compressed a half-dozen sea changes of harmony, rhythm, texture, and timbre into the standard three-minute format of an AM radio song. Each of these miniature movements was built around a distinctive instrumental motif—the sci-fi oscillation ("ooo-*weee*-ooo") of a theremin in one, a brace of turgid cellos in another, a wedding-chapel organ in a third—all of which returned to sound simultaneously beneath a delirious chorus of "good, good, *good,* good vibrations!" on which the record faded away. Musicians and fans alike marveled at the complexity of Wilson's self-confessed masterpiece, and one of the things that made it easy for them to marvel was the way the saga of this record's creation was reported in the music press, thanks to the efforts of Derek Taylor, who had recently added the Beach Boys to his West Coast clientele. Taylor saw to it that by the time "Good Vibrations" came on the radio in the fall of 1966, nearly everyone who followed the pop scene on either side of the Atlantic was aware that this one single had consumed a full six months of Brian Wilson's life; that it had cost nearly three times what it cost most groups to make an entire LP; that it had been recorded at no less than four different Los Angeles studios, each of which was chosen for its specific acoustic ambience; and that on several occasions, with the recording ostensibly finished, Wilson had stunned his fellow Beach Boys by declaring the need, on further reflection, to restart the production again. In the hands of Derek Taylor, "Good Vibrations" came across as the *Gone With the Wind* of pop singles. And since, like *Gone With the Wind* (and unlike *Pet Sounds*), this herculean effort was rewarded with immediate commercial success, topping the charts in America and Britain, "Good Vibrations" set a new standard of extravagance in the field of record production. For the Beatles, who sold more records than anyone else, there was now no cause for constraint. If EMI's American subsidiary could underwrite this sort of perfectionism in the name of popular art, so could EMI.

By the middle of January 1967, the recording sessions that began at Abbey Road in late November had consumed 125 hours of studio time and yielded three finished tracks. Two of these, "Strawberry Fields Forever" and "Penny Lane," were songs about Liverpool; the third, "When I'm Sixty-Four," was an updated version of a song that Paul McCartney had originally written *in* Liverpool some ten years before. Though the work was proceeding slowly, the Beatles' plans for an autobiographical album seemed to be on track. But it had now been almost five months since the release of their last records, "Yellow Submarine" and *Revolver*. Having just signed the group to a new recording contract, EMI and Capitol were anxious for some fresh Beatle product to sell, while Brian Epstein, with one eye on the Monkees, was eager to restore the Beatles' slightly dented aura of commercial supremacy. This led to a decision to release "Penny Lane" and "Strawberry Fields Forever" as a double-A-sided single in February 1967.

Packaged in a slip-jacket showing snapshots of the Beatles as children, the new single generated the usual advance sales of more than a million copies in the United States, where both sides of the record placed in the Top Ten ("Penny Lane" at number one, "Strawberry Fields" at number eight). British sales were also strong, but not strong enough to displace a billowy pop ballad called "Release Me" by a former 1950s crooner named Gerry Dorsey, now recording under the campy stage name Engelbert Humperdinck. The popularity of "Release Me" made "Penny Lane" the first Beatle single since "Love Me Do" that failed to reach number one in Britain.

Situated on the main route into the city center of Liverpool from the suburbs of Allerton, Woolton, and Speke, Penny Lane was the name of the shopping and residential district where John Lennon had lived with his mother and grandfather before he moved in with the Smiths. Later, in the days of the Quarry Men, it was the place where the paths of John, Paul, and George had crossed on their daily commute to the Art College and the Liverpool Institute. The Beatles' tribute to this old stomping ground incorporated all the distinctive features of Paul McCartney's recent work—the concise poetics of "Eleanor Rigby," the metaphorical meteorology of "Good Day Sunshine," the solo horn of "For No One," the sound effects and childish spirit of "Yellow Submarine." "Penny Lane" melds these elements into a bright façade of verbal and musical imagery that led the London *Times,* in an appreciative and unprecedented editorial, to credit the song with satisfying "a youthful appetite for simplicity, naturalness, and the ordinary." Yet such a description barely scratches the surface of a record whose words and music are pitted with strange incongruities, behind which a shadow-world of sadness and longing may be glimpsed. "Penny Lane" is something much more complex than a pleasant expression of musical nostalgia; its real subject is the distinction between a place as it exists in the glow of memory and a place as it really exists.

"In Penny Lane there is a barber showing photographs. . . ." In a manner suggestive of "Good Vibrations," the record just starts right in with the sound of Paul's voice ringing out on the downbeat over the plinks of his piano and the nudging line of his bass. The unspoken point, perhaps, is that Penny Lane needs no introduction; with its doubly diminutive name, it sounds like a place out of everyone's childhood, populated by the sort of archetypal adults—the Barber, the Banker, the Fireman—one finds in the pages of picture books. The key of the tune is B major (the same as "Good Day Sunshine") and the gently strolling melody rises and falls in long, unbroken lines—up to the point in the middle of the verse where a B *minor* chord intrudes, casting a sudden shadow over the inherent comedy of a barber in a Beatle song, and holding the music in a state of mild suspense until the harmony reverts to B major once the passersby "say hello." This melodramatic minor chord is almost a joke in the opening verse of the song. But with each successive stanza, its import seems to grow, sounding next behind the banker's back as he and the local children enact a rainy variation on the tale of the Emperor's New Clothes. "Very strange," Paul allows, as the harmony modulates from B to A major for the bright, unequivocal refrain: "Penny Lane is in my ears and in my eyes / *There* beneath the *blue* suburban skies. . . ."

The third verse begins with the image of the fireman and his hour-glass. Faintly surreal, faintly anachronistic, the reference to the hourglass evokes "the sands of time," and when the minor tonic chord sounds beneath this line, embellished by a pair of drooping flutes, something about this fireman seems inexpressibly sad. But then the fireman rings his bell as if to dispel the gloom, and the sound of a piccolo trumpet, impossibly high and bright, comes rippling over the chords of the verse in a neo-Baroque pastiche of every fanfare ever blown. (The solo was played to Paul McCartney's specifications by David Mason of the London Philharmonia Orchestra.) In the refrain that follows this magical interlude, the Beatles test the strength of its spell by substituting a pair of Liverpudlian indelicacies, "four of fish and finger pies," for the "blue suburban skies."

A fictional character who ponders the way that life seems to imitate art, the Pirandellian nurse in the fourth verse is one of the Beatles' most remarkable creations. Young and pretty and smartly dressed (in just the sort of uniform McCartney's mother wore), she enters the song laden with historical baggage, holding a tray of the red-paper poppies that mark the annual observance of Britain's Remembrance Day. Yet she carries this burden with an air of girlish distraction that makes the barber, the banker, and the fireman seem frozen in their roles. Compared with them, she's so modern in her self-consciousness, imagining herself as an actress in the theater-of-the-roundabout at Penny Lane. Which only adds to the startling impact of Paul's pronouncement that "she is anyway." (In *his* play, that would be.) There is a world of sensibility wrapped up in that line, which is left to hover between perfect wisdom and perfect whimsy as the action returns to the barbershop for the tiny anticlimax—the barber working, the banker waiting, the fireman rushing in—that passes for a denouement in the diminutive world of the song. Leading Paul to reaffirm that the scene is "Very strange!"

What's truly strange, of course, is the *weather* in this song: pouring rain in the verses, blue skies in the refrain. Nostalgia by definition improves upon the past, but it isn't just the singer who's got the forecast wrong. The banker is so oblivious to the elements that he doesn't bother to wear an overcoat. And the fireman reacts to the downpour as if the sky were falling down. Add to them the image of the pretty nurse and her poppies, and the blue skies of Penny Lane remembered begin to conform to twentieth-century Britain's most poignant meteorological cliché. They are drawn from the same inexhaustible Edwardian high-pressure system that supplied the perfect weather for a nostalgic vision of the past that, memorialized by the carnage of the Great War, retained its hold on the country's historical imagination for generations to come. "In those days it seemed the sun would always shine," recalls one of the characters in Alan Bennett's elegiac stage play *Forty Years On*. "Then in 1914 it begins to rain and all through the war and after it never stops. . . . The war and everything that comes after: grey and wet and misty and nasty."

In an intuitive act of genius that could never have been conceptualized, the Beatles conjured an entire world of meaning in this ostensibly simple, carefree song. The barber, the banker, and the fireman of "Penny Lane" are figures in a dream—an orderly, imperial dream of sunny skies and clean machines and well-trimmed heads that generations of oblivious Englishmen had once pursued to the very ends of the earth, back in a time when poppies were simply flowers, not symbols of national mourning. In Penny Lane it's the grown-ups who are living a fiction, just as the nurse suspects, and it's only the little children, laughing behind the banker's back, who see that the rain is pouring down. Yet the consummate honesty of the song lies with Paul McCartney's unwillingness to exempt himself from any of this. While the satirist in him is capable of seeing the dream for what it is and skewering it mercilessly ("four of fish and finger pies"), the sentimentalist in him continues to believe in the stately vision of those blue suburban skies. Like the pretty nurse, *he* is, anyway. "Penny Lane is in my ears and in my eyes," he calls out near the end, as an ominous peal of thunder sounds behind the pickup "meanwhile back." As he sings this phrase, the key of the refrain modulates from A to B major—*back* to the key of the verse. The effect is magical, like that of a person stepping into a photograph. With the flutes piping like penny whistles and the taut lines of David Mason's virtuoso toy trumpet snapping like brightly colored pennants in the wind, Paul sends the words reeling back over the years: "Penny Lane!" The music compresses into a shrill whine of distortion, and the memory dissolves.

. . . .

"STRAWBERRY FIELDS FOREVER" took its name from another Liverpudlian landmark: a massive Victorian-era mansion near John Lennon's
house in Woolton that had been donated to the Salvation Army during
the 1930s and converted into an orphanage. With its wrought-iron
gates and its forbidding array of turrets and dormers and chimney
stacks, the building looked like something out of a Charles Addams
cartoon. As a small child, John was taken to Strawberry Fields by his
aunt Mimi for an annual summer fête. As he grew older, he and his
gang of Outlaws claimed the mansion's parklike grounds as part of their
neighborhood turf.

"We always had fun at Strawberry Fields," Lennon recalled in a 1980
interview. The song, he went on to explain, "had nothing to do with the
Salvation Army. I just took the name as an image: Strawberry Fields Forever." That said, John launched into a rambling fifteen-minute mono-
logue in which he ranged over his whole childhood. "This image of me
being the orphan is garbage because I was well protected by my auntie
and my uncle and they looked after me very well," he insisted. "My childhood was *not* all suffering . . . I was always *well* dressed, *well* fed, *well*
schooled, and brought up to be a nice lower-middle-class English boy,
you know?" That this impassioned autobiographical outburst should be
triggered by a question about a song he had written more than a decade
before (in the midst of his longest separation from his fellow Beatles in
many years) attests to the Proustian importance Lennon attributed to the
image of Strawberry Fields. But it also belies his contention that the significance of the place "had nothing to do with the Salvation Army." That
Strawberry Fields was the name of an orphanage would seem to have
everything to do with the song. Behind the pastoral image in the title and
refrain lies the shadow of abandonment that hung over John Lennon's
childhood years.

Another indication of the song's intensely personal significance was
the extraordinary effort that went into getting it down on tape. John had
written the song in Spain on an acoustic guitar, and the first time he
played it for George Martin, it had the ballad-like simplicity of a folk
tune. Martin liked it simple, but John had other ideas, so the Beatles
began by recording it with their standard instrumentation of bass, drums,
and electric guitars, supplemented by a recently invented keyboard

synthesizer called a Mellotron, which used prerecorded tapes to reproduce the timbres of acoustic instruments. This electrified version was all but finished when John pronounced it lacking in character, and asked Martin to score the song for brass and strings. Embellished with overdubs of piano, percussion, Mellotron, guitar, and Indian table harp, the new arrangement was recorded at a faster tempo and in a different key. Next, after reviewing the tapes at home, Lennon informed Martin that he liked sections of *both* the versions they had recorded—the beginning of one and the end of the other, to be precise. He proposed that they simply join the two versions together at some convenient point. When a bemused Martin broached the problem of the different tempos and keys, John told him, with affecting faith, "You can fix it, George."

As always, George fixed it. It happened that the two recorded versions were set in neighboring keys. By carefully increasing the tape speed of the first and decreasing the speed of the second, Martin found a point where the tempos and pitches more or less aligned. From there it was a fairly simple matter of splicing the two versions together at the end of the song's first verse.

The record begins with a brief introduction of Mellotron-synthesized flutes: a quiet, pining wind song that resolves in the moan of the tonic chord. Shadowed by Ringo's drums, which totter and tumble and land with a thunk, like Alice down the rabbit hole, John's voice descends on this sylvan setting with an air of dreamy languor. "Let me take you down, 'cause I'm going to . . ." he sings in this opening refrain, pausing a moment before lapsing into lazy triplets that lag behind the beat: "Strawberry fields . . . Nothing is real." Sharing a rhythm and a rhyme, these two phrases—the image and the ethos—are fused in meaning for the duration of the song. "And nothing to get hung about," John adds over rising major chords, mixing reassurance with a rather grisly pun, "*Straw*berry *Fi*-elds for*ev*er."

Sung to the strains of the mutant flutes that introduced the track, this first verse is a far cry from the joyous cosmology that the Beatles expounded in "Tomorrow Never Knows." Instead, "Strawberry Fields Forever" is informed by an awareness that surrendering to the power of the unconscious mind can be difficult, even dangerous, work. John sings the words "living is easy with eyes closed" in a voice drawn from the same well of sadness with which he mourned the loss of his independence in

"Help!" and his innocence in "She Said She Said." However much it doesn't matter, however much things work out, his singing suggests there is still plenty to get "hung about" in a place where nothing is real. Like its companion piece "Penny Lane," "Strawberry Fields Forever" is filled with longing for a state of blissful ignorance that preceded the mind's awakening to the painful complexities of life.

The second refrain seems to plunge the song to a deeper level of consciousness, for this is the point where the Beatles' original guitar-based version yields to the richer, darker hues of George Martin's trumpets and cellos. The timbres of these orchestral instruments sound weighty and almost venerable compared with the sound of electric guitars, and their infusion into "Strawberry Fields" has the subtle effect of drawing the music back in time. In support of a lyric that draws its imagery from John's life before rock 'n' roll, the music, too, seems to reach back, *through* the sound of an electric band, to the instrumental textures of an earlier era. (This makes John's suggestion that George Martin just join the two versions of the song together seem more like a stroke of a genius than a flighty musical whim.)

The two verses that follow this shift in the instrumentation are swept by glissandos from George Harrison's table harp and paced by the anxious palpitations of a backward cymbal track; while the trumpets voice the chords, the cellos maneuver below. Against this mysterious musical backdrop, John's singing simulates the mounting derangement of the mind on LSD. The second verse is couched in a metaphor suggestive of child's play. The third verse dissolves into a babble of equivocation, contradiction, and self-negation that is equally funny and sad.

John concludes the final refrain by singing the line "Strawberry fields forever" three times, inflecting it differently each time, as if weighing for himself the shades of meaning the image could hold. Next, to a patter of footsteps, the song continues its descent into a musical catacomb of spasmodic guitar, scattershot drumming, groaning cellos, flinty notes from the table harp that leap around the scale, and tiny half-heard voices that are buried in the mix. Slowly, in the manner of most pop singles, this coda fades away. Then, in the manner of no pop single, the coda comes roaring back, this time led by the Mellotron madly spewing its notes, chased by the drums and the trumpets blowing a fractured call to hounds. After one last circuit of this murky sonic landscape, the instruments fade for good, while from deep within the frightening montage of sound, a small, slurry voice utters a phrase that some listeners hear as "cran . . . berry . . . sauce" and others as "I'm . . . very . . . bored."

WITH THE RELEASE of this astonishing "Liverpool single," rumors that the Beatles might be breaking up were immediately replaced by rumors that they were immersed in a recording project so ambitious that it would change the face of rock. From the group's perspective, however, their plans for a "Liverpool album" had been seriously compromised. While continuing to search for an organizing principle or theme that might serve to set their next album apart from their previous work, Lennon and McCartney fell back on their current inventory of bits and pieces and half-written songs, some of which retained a tinge of autobiographical reference, others of which did not. (At this point, George Harrison was still so preoccupied by the musical and spiritual consequences of his trip to India that he was hardly writing anything at all.) The first song the Beatles took up after the completion of "Penny Lane" was a combination of two unfinished pieces—the verses by John, the middle by Paul— joined for the time being by twenty-four bars' worth of blank tape. Lennon called it "A Day in the Life Of" and it promised to be a big production, of the sort that might end an LP. Having roughed out a possible destination, the Beatles' next task was to find a place to begin. Early in February, McCartney came into the studio with a catchy, rather contrived number called "Sgt. Pepper's Lonely Hearts Club Band," and any thought of an overtly autobiographical album went out the window for good.

36

Man is least himself when he talks in his own person. Give
him a mask, and he will tell you the truth.

—Oscar Wilde

"Sgt. Pepper's Lonely Hearts Club Band" was a rudimentary rock-
'n'-roll song with a heavy beat, loud guitars, and a lyric satirizing a live
performance by an imaginary, eponymous group. McCartney first conceived of the Pepper Band as a cross between the uniformed brass bands
of Lancashire he had used on the soundtrack of *The Family Way* and the
ornately named acid-rock groups from California that were making their
first inroads on the pop scene in the fall of 1966. His jokey inspiration of
a bandleader named Sgt. Pepper drew on the stereotype of a truculent
NCO that several generations of compulsory military service—and service comedies—had etched on the popular mind; it also spoofed the
vogue in Britain for military fashions and the recent success in America
of "The Ballad of the Green Berets," a jingoistic tearjerker performed by
an earnest Vietnam vet who billed himself as Staff Sgt. Barry Sadler. But
the true inspiration of this whimsical conceit involved its possibilities as
a parody of the Beatles themselves. By the time the song was recorded
and set aside, the group, at Paul's urging, had consciously started to think
of themselves as Sergeant Pepper's Band.

"I thought it would be nice to lose our identities, to submerge ourselves in the persona of a fake group," McCartney recalled. "I remember
hitting on this idea and saying, 'For this one album we won't be the Beatles. This is going to be our safety valve. We're going to think of a new
name for ourselves, a new way of being, a new way of recording, everything fresh. . . .' And we agreed that we weren't the Beatles anymore,
[that] it wasn't 'John' singing on this track or that. It was anyone John
wanted to be." Instead of a collection of Liverpool songs, this album
would purport to be a concert by Sgt. Pepper's Band—a transparent hoax
that contained a rich potential for interplay between the Beatles' unmistakable musical identities and the characters they "wanted to be." The
contrivance of the Pepper Band allowed them to revive their original

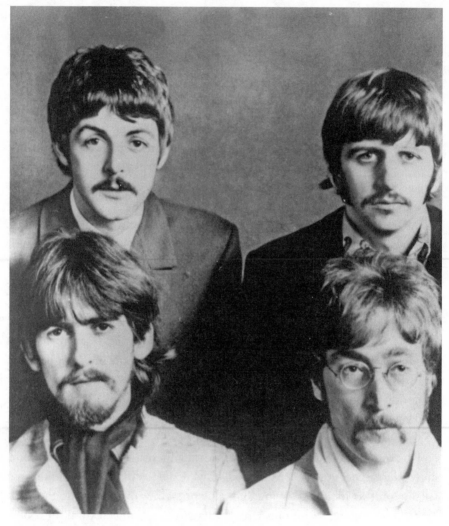

London, February 1967

foil—show business—with the transcendent distinction that, this time around, they meant to include their own phenomenon in the meaning of that term. As an experiment in role-playing and shape-shifting, the Beatles' impersonation of the Pepper Band was utterly in tune with the spirit of a time when hundreds of thousands of young people in America and Britain were adopting fanciful new identities and allying themselves with fanciful new communities that were founded on a belief in the transformational power of mind-expanding drugs. "Not only a self-portrait," George Melly would write, "but a microcosm of a period that could produce and sustain a phenomenon like the Beatles."

Contrary to the popular impression, *Sgt. Pepper* did not take the Beatles all that much longer than *Revolver* did to record; according to the logs at Abbey Road, the oft-cited estimate that it required seven hundred hours of studio time was roughly twice the truth. It was rather the tone of the sessions that was different: more deliberate and ambitious, yet also more capricious and impulsive at times. The Beatles' sense of the studio as a sanctuary from the fishbowl of fame reached its apex during these months, and in this insular environment, the experimentalism of *Revolver* became the established rule. "The Beatles insisted that everything on *Sgt. Pepper* had to be different," recalled their engineer Geoff Emerick. "We had microphones right down in the bells of brass instruments and headphones turned into microphones attached to violins. We plastered vast amounts of echo onto vocals. We used giant primitive oscillators to vary the speed of instruments and vocals and we had tapes chopped to pieces and stuck together upside down and the wrong way around." Many hours of studio time were spent toying with special effects. Yet despite this air of indulgence, the songs themselves are marked by an unusual economy; rarely is a verse repeated, or an instrument employed for gratuitous effect, and several of the arrangements sound stripped down rather than built up. Many additional hours of studio time were devoted to the laborious process of mixing and consolidating tracks that had already been recorded so as to free up space on EMI's overburdened four-track tape decks for further overdubs. To offset this drudgery, the Beatles promoted a festive spirit whenever possible. When it came time to record George Harrison's Indian-influenced track, they softened the institutional ambience of Abbey Road with imported paisley carpets and a haze of smoldering incense. When it was determined that nothing less than a forty-piece orchestra was needed to fill the twenty-four-bar gaps in

"A Day in the Life," they turned the session into a gala affair: inviting friends, providing tables of food and drink, and asking the musicians (drawn mainly from the London Symphony and the Royal Philharmonic) to appear in formal dress. When all was in readiness, the Beatles distributed party hats, clown noses, fright wigs, and gorilla paws for the orchestra members to wear. A bubble-making machine was turned on, and everyone got down to work.

There is no denying the influence of drugs on the artistic sensibility that produced the Pepper project. Marijuana had been a staple of the Beatles' creative method since 1965, and its effect on their approach to songwriting and recording was so pervasive as to be taken for granted by now. The very concept of the Pepper Band was itself a kind of extended pipe dream, sustained by the capacity of pot to inspire flights of collective fancy among close-knit groups of friends. Similarly, some of the Brechtian "alienation effect" inherent in the transparent premise of the Beatles impersonating another group came not from any conscious aesthetic sense (though Brecht was an icon of the London avant-garde) but rather from the tendency of marijuana to expose the element of playacting in all sorts of social situations.

Contributing to the collective consciousness that made the Pepper project possible was Paul McCartney's decision in November 1966 to take his first dose of LSD. For more than a year, Paul's unwillingness to participate in this rite of passage had fostered a significant sense of division within the group. According to George Harrison, "After having had the experience, we wanted the others to know about it because suddenly there seemed to be a big space between us and the other two." Ringo had been at least willing to try the drug. But Paul's resistance was seen by John and George not only as a sign of his stubbornness, but also as a failure of nerve. The aura of psychic risk associated with LSD led many acidheads to think of the uninitiated as people who were afraid of confronting the truth about themselves. In the context of a group whose members had shown an almost compulsive desire to share in one another's interests and experiences, Paul's abstinence had come to seem like an affront to the Beatles' solidarity. "It was peer pressure of the highest variety," McCartney recalled. "They were saying, 'What's wrong with him?' "

McCartney's change of mind had a decided effect on the internal dynamics of the group. Though his involvement with LSD was much more measured than that of John and George, it filled him, as it had filled them, with an expansive new sense of possibility. And it was this aura of newborn experience ("a new name . . . a new way of being . . . everything fresh") that gave the Pepper project its distinctive character. Paul's initiation, moreover, came at a time when both John and George were reaching the point of diminishing returns in their far-flung hopes for the drug. George's response was to follow the chimera of transcendence into the realm of Indian music and spirituality. For John, however, it was the chance to play the role of psychedelic guide to Paul that helped him to sustain his own belief in the transformational power of LSD. On the strength of this new bond, Lennon and McCartney began to work together in the winter of 1967 with an intensity reminiscent of their earlier years. The closeness of their collaboration was further enhanced by Jane Asher's departure in January 1967 on an extended tour of America with the Bristol Old Vic repertory troupe. Her absence made the Pepper project seem like an extended boys' night out. "When I came back after five months," Asher told Hunter Davies, "Paul had changed so much. . . . All he could talk about were the spiritual experiences he'd had with John."

Having all but abandoned romantic themes as a subject of his song-writing in 1966, John Lennon continued to derive most of the inspiration for the songs he initiated on *Sgt. Pepper* from the books and newspapers and television programs that provided him with his principal link to the world beyond his insular life in Weybridge. The refrain to one of his songs ("Good Morning Good Morning") was inspired by a television commercial. The lyrics to another ("Being for the Benefit of Mr. Kite!") were taken from an old circus poster he owned. The title of "A Day in the Life" referred to a popular journalistic genre of the 1960s, while the opening verse of the song was based on a newspaper story about the death in a car crash of a prominent New Aristocrat named Tara Browne, an heir to the Guinness fortune and an acquaintance of the Beatles. Yet another of John's songs, "Lucy in the Sky With Diamonds," drew its hallucinatory imagery from a chapter in Lewis Carroll's *Through the Looking Glass*—a lifelong fascination of John's that had recently been refreshed by Jonathan Miller's darkly psychological production of *Alice in Wonderland* for BBC-TV. Paul McCartney also drew inspiration from the BBC, basing his ballad "She's Leaving Home" on Jeremy Sandford's muckraking docudrama "Cathy Come Home," a disturbing account of a suburban girl who runs away from home, takes up with a truck driver she meets on the way to London, and falls through the cracks of the Welfare State into pregnancy, poverty, and despair. (The program generated what one critic called "the most clamorous 'morning after' furor in British television history.")

This motif of "mediated" experience was not confined to the lyrics; it carried over into the music on *Sgt. Pepper* as well. An intriguing aspect of this record that would be heralded as a landmark of innovation in popular music was that so many of its songs seemed to have a foot in the past. The album is filled with the strains of brass bands, dance bands, and pit bands. In a spirit of affectionate parody, echoes of Tin Pan Alley, Denmark Street, and Broadway drift from track to track, exploiting the same sorts of incongruity between style, form, and content that characterized "Penny Lane."

Gradually, as the sessions continued over the course of February and March, the Pepper project assumed the form that would cause it to be recognized—somewhat erroneously—as pop's first "concept" album. The initial working "concept" consisted of little more than an intention to begin with the "Sgt. Pepper" theme song and end with "A Day in the Life." Over time, a sense of formal unity was created by the addition of a stagy number called "A Little Help From My Friends," which flowed seamlessly out of the "Sgt. Pepper" theme, by Lennon's circus song, which wound up at the end of side one, and by a spirited reprise of the opening theme that was inserted before the final track, thereby providing the Pepper Show with a beginning, a middle, and an ending, to which "A Day in the Life" was appended as a kind of epilogue. In the final stages of production, the feeling of continuity was enhanced by a decision to minimize (and in some cases eliminate) the usual intervals of silence between the individual tracks. What happened within the framework of the Pepper Show, however—the interrelation of the individual songs, and the arrangement of those individual songs into something that impressed many listeners as a coherent whole—was more the result of an inspired form of intuition and indirection than of any master plan. Still, the overall theatricality and eclecticism of the songs combined with the anachronistic image of the Pepper Band to give the album the feeling of a traditional "variety" show, with the dozen individual tracks resembling the dozen individual turns that made up a typical music-hall bill. Thus did a record that would be justly praised as a landmark of *phonography*—that is, music made expressly for record—wind up paying tribute to the last great genre of popular entertainment to predate the phonograph.

> We realized for the first time that someday someone
> would actually be holding a thing they'd call "the Beatles'
> new LP" and that normally it would just be a collection of
> songs with a nice picture on the cover, nothing more. So
> the idea was to do a complete thing that you could make
> of what you liked—just a little magic presentation.
>
> —Paul McCartney

The idea of putting something more than "a nice picture" on the cover of *Sgt. Pepper* originated with an art dealer named Robert Fraser, a flamboyant member of London's pop aristocracy whom Paul McCartney had befriended in 1966. After hearing about the Pepper project from McCartney, Fraser suggested that the Beatles commission one of his artists to design the album cover. (As Andy Warhol's London dealer, he probably knew that the artist had recently been commissioned to do the cover for the Velvet Underground's first LP.) When McCartney responded with interest, Fraser suggested Peter Blake.

A rumpled, wispy-bearded man in his mid-thirties, Peter Blake was then at the height of his reputation as a "pioneer" of Pop Art in Britain— a mantle that had been bestowed upon him in 1962 by the critic John Russell in the London *Sunday Times*. An accomplished figurative painter, Blake was best known for his meticulous portraits of pinup girls, professional wrestlers, circus performers, burlesque queens, and pop stars— including one of the Beatles circa 1963—which he embellished with badges, buttons, trinkets, trophies, and other three-dimensional objects drawn from a vast personal collection of kitsch. Despite their assuredly Pop content, Blake's paintings exuded an affectionate and openly nostalgic attitude toward the past that set them apart from the more modernistic and futuristic work of his contemporaries and made him an obvious choice for the Pepper project.

By the time of Blake's recruitment in March of 1967, the Beatles were fully immersed in the operational fantasy of the Pepper Band, and the gaudy bandsmen's uniforms they planned to wear on the album cover had already been designed. "Paul explained that it was like a band you might see in the park," Blake recalled. "So the cover shot could be a photograph as if they were a town band finishing a concert in the park, playing in a bandstand with a municipal flowerbed next to it, and a crowd of people around them. I think my main contribution was to decide that if we made the crowd a certain way the people in it could be anybody." Consciously emulating the Beatles' collaborative style, Blake asked the four of them to draw up lists of the people they would like to see in the audience at a concert by the Pepper Band—anyone, he suggested, who "meant something" to them. File photographs of the nominees were then obtained, enlarged to life size, pasted on hardboard backings, and mounted on a horizontal scaffolding in the photographer Michael Cooper's studio to form a great assemblage of heads. On the day of the photo session, Blake asked everyone involved with the project to bring along a few props or possessions that held some special significance for them. McCartney arrived with a vanload of brass-band instruments. Lennon brought his favorite TV. Blake's wife, the artist Jill Haworth, contributed a debauched-looking doll in a sweatshirt inscribed WELCOME THE ROLLING STONES. Reveling in the influence that came with working on behalf of a national institution, Blake had requisitioned a number of waxworks from Madame Tussaud's London Museum to stand in front and flesh out the crowd.

"All legends, all mythologies and all myths . . . await their exposed resurrection, and the heroes crowd one another at the gate." So wrote the French director Abel Gance in a 1927 essay on the epic potential of film—anticipating by forty years the conclave of cult heroes on the cover of the Beatles' eighth LP. At first glance the image recalls one of the elaborately posed commemorative portraits of wedding parties, fraternal orders, or imperial general staffs that date from the early decades of commercial photography. In the near foreground, surrounded by a border of leafy plants and a number of wreathlike floral arrangements in the shape of a star, a crown, and a guitar, the word BEATLES is rendered in large block letters composed of red hyacinths. At the center of the picture, flanked by a pair of potted palms and an array of prized possessions that includes a hookah, a tuba, and John's TV, sits a big bass drum, its front head emblazoned with the words SERGEANT PEPPER'S around the top, LONELY HEARTS across the middle, and CLUB BAND around the bottom, the lettering outlined circus-style and embellished with fleurs-de-lis. Behind the drum stand John, Paul, George, and Ringo in their dazzling uniforms of puce, magenta, turquoise, and scarlet satin. All four of them are holding band instruments and their expressions, enhanced by their drooping mustaches and sideburns, are sober, intent, and composed. To their left, on loan from Madame Tussaud's, stand the Fab Four as they looked in 1963. Neat as a pin in their dark suits and ties, these waxworks look like schoolboys compared with the Beatles of the present day.

Drawn up behind them in four loose ranks are gathered some sixty soul mates, forebears, and assorted friends-of-friends, some in black and white, some in color, some crudely "colorized." At the far left of the picture stands the scowling wax colossus of the prizefighter Sonny Liston; at the far right stands the comely wax vision of the film star Diana Dors ("Diana Dors has no drawers / Will you kindly lend her yours?" schoolchildren of the Beatles' generation had sung in Liverpool). Between these pillars of strength and beauty lies an unclassifiable collection of instantly, faintly, and unrecognizable faces. They include the comedians Laurel and Hardy, W. C. Fields, and Tommy Handley, the writers Lewis Carroll, Aldous Huxley, and Oscar Wilde, and the poets Dylan Thomas and Edgar Allan Poe. Bob Dylan, Aubrey Beardsley, Karlheinz Stockhausen, and the occultist Aleister Crowley are faces in the crowd. There is a quartet of Hindu yogis at George Harrison's request, and leading men of all persuasions, paragons of camp (Tom Mix), sophistication (Fred Astaire), and hip (Marlon Brando). A trio of blond bombshells consisting of Mae West, Marlene Dietrich, and Marilyn Monroe vie for attention with a bevy of anonymous pinup girls. There are the intellectual heavyweights Karl Marx and Carl Jung, and the imperial adventurers T. E. Lawrence and Dr. David Livingstone. At the far left of the photograph, the doomstruck face of Stuart Sutcliffe stares palely out of the crowd.

As with any great gathering of notables, the question of who is *not* present is nearly as intriguing as the question of who *is*. Since this is the Beatles' affair, the most conspicuous absences are those of their musical heroes like Elvis Presley, Chuck Berry, and Little Richard. (Besides Dylan, the only other pop singer present is Dion of the doo-wop group Dion & The Belmonts, chosen by Peter Blake.) Mahatma Gandhi was included in the original photograph, only to be airbrushed out at the insistence of EMI's chairman Sir Joseph Lockwood, who was concerned about the sensitivities of the label's Indian subsidiary. Another famous figure who failed to make the final cut was the ever-popular Adolf Hitler, a guest of John Lennon's, whose spot was taken—at the last minute, after heated discussion—by a more acceptable *Übermensch*, the film actor Johnny Weissmuller.

The diverse cast of characters made it inevitable that the *Sgt. Pepper* cover would lend itself to associations and interpretations its creators had not planned. But one unintended meaning outweighed all the rest. While Peter Blake may have conceived of the floral arrangement in the foreground of the picture as a "municipal flowerbed," many viewers would see that rectangular plot of freshly turned earth as a grave. This had the effect of transforming the cover into a portrait of the Downfall, depicting the Beatles as mourners at their own funeral—or, rather, at the funeral of their former selves, the Moptops, dressed for eternity in their dark suits, their faces aglow with the embalmed look of wax effigies, standing to the side while their alter egos in the Pepper Band command the center of the photograph, resplendent and reborn.

The two inner panels of the album's gatefold sleeve were filled with a photographic close-up of the Beatles that showed off the details of their uniforms and the deep pools of dilation in their eyes. The change in their appearance since their last "official" photographs from the summer of 1966 was striking—particularly the change in John Lennon, whose new mustache and wire-rimmed spectacles made him look both wizened and quizzical. Enclosed in the album jacket was a cardboard sheet of "Sergeant Pepper Cut-Outs," designed by Blake and Haworth to look like something one might find on the back of a cereal box. Inscribed on the sheet were a set of sergeant's stripes, a clip-on mustache, a pair of lapel badges, and a picture-postcard portrait of the Sergeant himself. As a final innovation, the back of the album jacket was printed with the lyrics to all the songs, laid out newspaper-style in columns of small-point type—a libretto-like amenity that had never before been offered on a popular LP.

All record covers (even in the miniaturized format of CDs) serve as visual adjuncts to the experience of record listening. Yet very few record covers have managed to reflect so closely or cleverly both the form and the content of the records they are designed to advertise as the *Sgt. Pepper* sleeve. By drawing on such a wide range of mixed media, combining elements of photography, collage, costume, waxwork, illustration, printed word, souvenir, and *objet trouvé,* Peter Blake created a visual analog to the diverse techniques of conception, composition, arrangement, production, and performance with which the Beatles and George Martin were striving to revolutionize the art of sound recording. Perhaps the most striking example of this involved the use of what Peter Blake described as a "life-size collage." Most people looking at the front cover of *Sgt. Pepper* would assume that the image reproduced there was created by means of a standard photographic collage, with the foreground of flowers, bass drum, and Beatles superimposed on a background of cut-out, pasted-up heads. That this familiar graphic effect was instead achieved through the use of blown-up, propped-up, life-size hardboard figures (of the sort used by novelty photographers at fairgrounds and tourist sites) was itself a bit of commentary on the two-dimensionality of popular icons, for it is literally the façades of Poe and Jung and Brando that we see in the photograph. Yet the main reason for creating the image in this cumbersome manner was to create a sense of *occasion*: to imbue this historically impossible gathering of famous people with the semblance of an actual event, at which the real-life Beatles would appear and be photographed. And because a sense of occasion is precisely the artistic conceit behind the music on *Sgt. Pepper*, Blake's work functions as a true visual prelude to the album. The cover purports to be a conclave of cult heroes in the same way that the record purports to be a concert by Sgt. Pepper's Band; the one parodies and manipulates the conventions of live portraiture in the same way that the other parodies and manipulates the conventions of live performance. Nothing remotely like it had ever been tried before.

By May of 1967, with ten months having elapsed since the release of *Revolver* and three since "Strawberry Fields Forever" and "Penny Lane," the level of anticipation among Beatle fans was running at an all-time high. The upcoming album was awaited with an almost millennial sense of expectation. "New music from the Beatles is one of the biggest events we have," wrote the pop critic Greil Marcus. "Rumors fly for months and weeks ahead of time, rumors that reverse themselves and double up, canceling each other out, continuing up to the great day itself." In London, Brian Epstein added to the sense of occasion by devising a new kind of promotional rite: a "listening party" at which a select group of journalists were invited to hear the album for the first time. A few days before the release date, the BBC provided the record with some additional, superfluous cachet by banning both "A Day in the Life" and "Lucy in the Sky With Diamonds" from its playlist on the grounds that the lyrics promoted the use of illegal drugs. Britain's pirate stations, it goes without saying, were immune to such squeamishness.

Sgt. Pepper's Lonely Hearts Club Band was released on June 1, 1967, to the most momentous public reception that had ever been given to a popular recording. On the basis of its stunning initial impact and its subsequent influence, the debut of the album bears comparison with such earlier celebrated landmarks of twentieth-century popular music as the 1943 opening of the Rodgers and Hammerstein musical *Oklahoma!* and the 1927 premiere of George Gershwin's Jazz Age icon, "Rhapsody in Blue." In the sense that all three of these works reflected the ambition of their authors to create a popular masterpiece, and were recognized as such by audiences who felt thrilled to be hearing music that seemed to express some essential spirit of what it meant, at that moment, to be alive, the comparisons are apt. An important distinction, however, involved the matter of scale, for while the first performances of those earlier works astonished a few thousand well-to-do New Yorkers who had the luck or foresight to attend their public debuts, *Sgt. Pepper* was heard on record or radio by many millions of listeners on the first day of its release. The extent of the airplay it received was unprecedented even by the Beatles' standards, for in the absence of a designated single, many stations simply played the entire album with the frequency of a Top Ten hit. The record had an advance sale of more than a million copies in the United States, where it remained at the top of the album charts for fifteen consecutive weeks and sold two and a half million copies by the end of 1967. In Britain it topped the charts for twenty-three consecutive weeks and became the first LP since *Beatles for Sale* to sell more than a million copies. "The summer of 1967 was spent listening to *Sgt. Pepper*," wrote Paul Williams, editor of the new rock journal *Crawdaddy.* "It was unavoidable, inevitable, more constant and universal than the climate or any other aspect of the season."

37

From the moment when the conductor, in his elaborately luxurious and irredeemably faulty dress suit, addresses his first and infinitely disabused bow to the audience . . . the main thing is the band, the harsh, rapid band, that never stops, that plays anything. . . . From it gush patriotism, comedy, or sentiment, and all three burst forth with their full headline value. There is no tickling of big drums; when the drum is banged you know it; nor is there measure in the sigh of the oboe, for the music-hall paints not in wash-greens and grays; scarlet, black, white and electric-blue are its gamut.

—W. L. George, *London Mosaic* (1921)

Sgt. Pepper's Lonely Hearts Club Band opens with the expectant murmur of a theater audience and the muted cacophony of an orchestra tuning up. After a few seconds the band eases into a lethargic rock-'n'-roll vamp, the rhythm demarked by piercing squawks on the offbeats from a strident lead guitar. There comes a rest, then a leaden drum fill, whereupon Paul McCartney bursts in with the excited, occupationally breathless voice of a master of ceremonies, introducing "the act you've known for all these years," setting the scene for the crowd in the theater and everyone listening at home: "It was twenty years ago today, Sgt. Pepper taught the band to play."

Whoops, whistles, and applause fill the house as a jovial chorus of horns huffs up and down the scale, their progress interrupted by a sudden swell of laughter in response to some visual cue—some bit of stage business, most likely, between the emcee and the band. We have no way of knowing, of course, those of us unable to be present at this special twentieth-anniversary concert. Twenty years into the *future*—that's the premise of the Pepper Band and the creaky brand of rock 'n' roll with which they start the show. They are a projection of something very much like the Beatles twenty years down the road, as if the group had simply carried on, touring the world on an annual basis reprising their greatest hits, decades after their legion of hysterical admirers had grown up and settled down. The album begins with the specter of rock 'n' roll settling into middle age, becoming as steeped in the cant and corn of show business as every other brash style of popular music that has enjoyed a spell of wild popularity before yielding to something new. John Lennon makes his entrance at the head of a chorus, singing, "We're Sgt. Pepper's Lonely Hearts Club Band, we hope you will enjoy the show." The bandleader's name is Pepper, after all, and John's voice, with its acrid edge, is properly the mouthpiece of the group. Thrilled at the rousing reception, he starts to get carried away, telling the audience that they're all so very "lovely," he'd like to take them home. The crowd erupts in furious applause at this unbelievably ingratiating sentiment (from a group that has spent the last four years performing in front of some of the most hysterically *un*lovely, inhospitable audiences imaginable). Paul dashes back to the microphone, lest anyone have a chance to reflect on his partner's sincerity, and starts to introduce the evening's featured vocalist. The crowd emits a Beatlemaniacal shriek of recognition (it's the real thing, taken from a tape of their 1964 concert at the Hollywood Bowl) and the band sets up a rolling chant of *"Bil . . . ly . . . Shears."* Then, like a little leaf spinning dolefully to the ground, a lone guitar picks out the opening notes of "A Little Help From My Friends."

From the first bar, there is a sense that Ringo's entire career has been leading up to this moment. Paul McCartney, who created the character, once described Billy Shears as the sort of name that an "old schoolmate" might have. But the name itself—combined with that shriek from the crowd—suggests that a more specific antecedent may well have been Tommy Steele. At the very least, it's easy to picture Shears, back in some dubious prime, as one of the original contingent of Anglo Elvises whose collective appeal lay almost entirely in their *representativeness*—the quality that made every one of them seem like an old schoolmate under the gloss. Billy Shears is the rock-'n'-roll equivalent of an aging music-hall star: the singer who can't really sing, selling himself as a sentimental favorite with carefully crafted material like "A Little Help From My Friends."

He begins on a note of pure preemption: "What would you think if I sang out of tune?" he warbles. "Would you stand up and walk out on me?"

Paul's bass, like a dancing bear, turns pirouettes under his voice, and Ringo adds a backbeat to embolden his alter ego as he prepares to ascend the refrain. *"Oh,* I get by with a little help from my friends," Shears drones with a wave at his highest note. There's a stop, then a jewel of a drum fill—two bars of booming asymmetry, impossibly round and deep—that brings on the second verse, where Shears engages his friends in the Pepper Band in a stagy Socratic dialogue on the state of his emotional health.

Previously, when Ringo sang on a record, the other Beatles had tended to downplay the unflattering contrast between their voices and his, either by laying out altogether or confining themselves, as on "Yellow Submarine," to chanting along with the refrain. Here, where the singer's tunelessness is the premise of his song, the others are free to play up the contrast shamelessly. Does he need anybody? they ask in a rainbow arch of melody that seems to soar high over Shears's head. Only somebody to love, he growls from down below, sowing a seed of pathos that grows in the final verse, after he voices his too-firm belief in the idea of a love at first sight. "What do you see when you turn out the light?" the backup chorus teases. "I can't tell you but I know it's mine," Shears replies, unfazed by the innuendo, taking the joke in stride. In this last exchange, the song goes beyond singing the praises of friendship to show how friendship works, and it does so unsentimentally, by means of a bawdy joke. Together the singers recite the catechism of the bridge ("Do you need? . . . I need") and the litany of the refrain ("get by . . . get high . . . gonna try"). By now Shears has succeeded in making his needs seem modest. As he says, it's a *little* help he requires: a little indulgence from the fans, a little support from the band, a little *imagination,* is all. And never more so than on the great bawling finale ("frien-en-en-en-ends") with which he ends the song.

With its shimmery music-box introduction, the next track marks a critical transition: the point on the album where the overt spoofing of show business leaves off and the broader fictional possibilities suggested by the Beatles' decision to masquerade as the Pepper Band take over. "Lucy in the Sky With Diamonds" was a song like no other love song John Lennon had ever written, a chaste, ethereal fairy tale in which Boy meets Girl, Boy loses Girl, and then keeps on meeting her and losing her again. To the bare accompaniment of Paul's bass, descending one note to the bar, John sings the verse in his "sleepy child" voice, piped through a battery of filters that give it a piquant, almost sugary edge, as the melody ripples in waltz-time through the notes of the A major scale: "Picture yourself in a boat on a river, with tangerine trees, and marmalade skies / Somebody calls you, you answer quite slowly—a girl with kaleidoscope eyes." The bass line quickens to quarter-notes as the music seems to slip from the shallows and get caught by the current of the stream. Slowly receding into the middle distance, John's still-drowsy vocal is doubled by a dragonfly buzz of guitar, until the drums intrude with three enormous accents that seem to jolt both the singer and the song out of their waltzy trance and into the real world of common time. "Lucy in the sky with di-i-a-monds!" John exclaims in a full-voiced shout, his voice cascading through "diamonds" like a silvery shower of stars. He sings the song title twice by himself, then again with Paul joining in, and they end on a long, wordless exclamation of "Ahhhh" that brings the song back to the verse. The dreamy pursuit continues across a surreal landscape of gargantuan flowers, then on via "newspaper taxis" to a last verse set on a train in a station, and a final fleeting glimpse of the girl with kaleidoscope eyes. Cued by another trio of enormous wallops from the drums, the spell is once again broken by the onset of the refrain. As the guitars chime and the organ croaks, the song rides out on the singers' cries of wonder and their shouts of Lucy's name.

The brief interval of silence that follows the fade of "Lucy in the Sky" is broken by a series of strident plinks on guitar that introduce "Getting Better," the Beatles' hilariously ambivalent satire of 1950s Britain, an autobiographical fragment that seems to be set at the exact moment in the spring of 1957 when John and Paul first met and Harold Macmillan was reminding the British people that, notwithstanding the Angry Young Men, they had "never had it so good." A collaboration in every sense of the word, "Getting Better" pits Paul's optimism against John's sarcasm, Paul's penchant for self-improvement against John's reputation as a hard case. "It's getting better all the ti-i-ime," the two of them carol in the opening bars, the sentiment underscored by a steely tattoo on the snare. The official mood of optimism, though, is undercut by those plinks, whose stridency derives from the addition of a ninth to an otherwise innocuous F major chord, setting up a tinny dissonance that serves as a harmonic metaphor for the split personality of the song. Punctuated by an exasperated splash of cymbal, the opening verse looks back in anger at the joys of grammar school. While Paul provides the narration, John and

George add a running commentary on the straitlaced teachers and the endless succession of rules. "Fools!" trills the chorus, as the refrain comes marching back to the parade-ground plinks of guitar, with Paul declaring, "I've got to admit it's getting better," and the chorus countering with the suggestion that, in any case, things couldn't get much worse.

The second verse is couched in a form of baby talk (with "Me" taking the place of "I") that reduces the Angry ethos to its essential childishness. But the satire cuts the other way during the song's expansive bridge, with its brainwashed, lockstep chant of *"Get-ting-so-much-bet-ter-all-the-time."* In the instrumental break that precedes the final verse, the tension between adolescent antipathy and adult complacency is played out in a wonderful musical joke that sets the malevolent whine of a tamboura against the benevolent bounce of a conga drum. Over this wry opposition of East and West Indian sonorities, John and Paul revisit the misogynistic spirit of the Jimmy Porter years: "I used to be cruel to my woman / I beat her and kept her apart from the things that she loved." The refrain rings out for the last time and the song goes its merry way, secure in the knowledge that the love of a good (if slightly battered) woman can turn a man's world around.

The two bars of spindly harpsichord that introduce "Fixing a Hole" generate a languid swing reminiscent of "I'm Only Sleeping" and other Lennonesque paeans to the pleasures of solitude. But since it's McCartney who's singing, there's a difference in attitude. Instead of merely pleading with the world to leave him alone, Paul comes at the song with his toolbox in hand and proceeds to hammer out an analogy between mind expansion and home renovation: "I'm fixing a hole where the rain gets in / And stops my mind from wandering." The motion of the melody (in the key of F minor) is exquisitely matched to the words. After rising and falling from C to F and back to C on the opening line, Paul drops to the F an octave below on "stops my mind," climbs back to the C ("from wandering"), and then, on the phrase "where it will go," sails free of the octave that has thus far enclosed the tune in an exhilarating upward glide to a high falsetto A flat. This note is then caught by George Harrison's guitar, which descends through a series of biting inversions on the tonic chord, until the sequence repeats.

In the release the harmony shifts from minor to major, while the melody wraps itself tightly around a single declamatory note. The first two lines are backed by "ooohs" that parody Paul's unconcern about whether he's right or wrong; the second two lines by a peevish guitar that embodies his impatience with people who "disagree and never win."

The verse returns with Paul applying the first coats of paint to the walls, and then the song is given over to George's lead guitar in an astonishing eight-bar outburst that starts by rattling the walls of that colorful room with a series of jagged phrases and culminates in a two-octave, stair-stepping descent of raucous honks. The release and verse repeat, and then the song ambles off, with Ringo sloshing his hi-hat cymbals through the puddles of water on the floor.

THE THIRD IN a row from McCartney, "She's Leaving Home" was consciously conceived as a sequel to "Eleanor Rigby." ("It's a much younger girl," Paul allowed, "but the same sort of loneliness.") The arrangement again features strings, the refrain is again contrapuntal, and the lyric again consists of two verses expressing the different viewpoints of the two protagonists, followed by a third, abbreviated verse that serves as a denouement. Much as "Eleanor Rigby" was inspired by a rash of journalistic hand-wringing over the plight of the elderly in Britain, "She's Leaving Home" was inspired by the controversy surrounding the television program "Cathy Come Home." By the time *Sgt. Pepper* was released, the phenomenon of "teenage runaways" fleeing their suburban homes for the communal crash pads of the Haight-Ashbury and the East Village had become a subject of anxious attention in the American press as well.

The significant musical difference between "Eleanor Rigby" and "She's Leaving Home" involves the fact that whereas the earlier track was a true hybrid, conforming to no recognizable style or genre of song, "She's Leaving Home" is cast in the mold of a sentimental Victorian ballad, its words and music filled with the clichés of musical melodrama. It was not George Martin's work, this arrangement. McCartney had telephoned Martin during a break in the Pepper sessions to tell him about a newly completed song that he wanted to score for strings. When Martin turned out to have a prior commitment that day, McCartney, in his haste (and insensitivity), called up another arranger named Mike Leander and commissioned him to write a score. Leander was best known for his rather overwrought work with Marianne Faithfull and the Rolling Stones; though a capable pop arranger, he possessed none of George Martin's originality or restraint. Yet the Beatles could do no wrong in the spring of

1967; as it turned out, the clichéd sentimentality of Leander's arrangement provided the perfect foil for the track.

The song begins in waltz time with the biggest cliché of them all: the willowy flutter of harp strings (or is it heartstrings?), which conjure an immediate Victorian-era vignette of recitals in drawing rooms. What we get instead is the voice of Paul McCartney, weary with resignation in the chill gray light of the dawn: "Wednesday morning at *five* o'clock as the day begins . . ." The melody droops a fifth over the opening half of this line, leaps a seventh at *"five* o'clock," then starts back down again. Cellos enter gravely, tracing a shallow arc that prefigures the lines ahead, and tremors from the violins accompany the girl as she leaves a note for her parents and "goes downstairs to the *kit*chen clutching her handkerchief." The melody of this last line replicates that of the first, and the leap to the high note on "kitchen" is the first hint that "She's Leaving Home" might include a dimension that isn't wholly serious. After the girl makes good her escape, the song slides gracefully into a two-tiered refrain, sung in the style of the Beach Boys, in which Paul's sustained falsetto, singing the title line, is interwoven with John's counterpoint, reciting the parents' litany of sacrifice. "She's leaving home after living alone for so many years," Paul concludes, descending from falsetto, while John adds a punning tag of "bye-bye."

The second verse plunges deeper into the maw of domestic melodrama, with Father snoring blithely and Mother awakening anxiously to find the fateful note. The violins emit a telegraphic distress call that teeters on the brink of absurdity, but the somber narration keeps the song on an even keel. That she calls her husband "Daddy" reveals in a single word how desperately this mother is identified with her child. And though her initial reaction is phrased in a manner appropriate to the genteel trappings of her life, her second thought ("How could she do this to *me*?") might be the first unvarnished emotion she has allowed herself in years.

Up to this point, the sympathies of the song have seemed to rest firmly with the girl. But "She's Leaving Home" isn't finished with its characters yet. The final verse takes place two days later, and finds the girl meeting up with "a man from the motor trade." American listeners, unfamiliar with the English idiom, speculated darkly about the nature of this rendezvous. But this vestigial reference to the truck-driving boyfriend in "Cathy Come Home" is simply a reminder that it isn't necessarily Prince Charming for whom this girl has fled the stifling security of her home. In the final refrain, the good intentions of the parents and their daughter are sadly intertwined. As Paul affirms that the girl is having fun, John adds that "Fun is the one thing that money can't buy."

Fun? The line is phrased so smoothly that it sounds like an old saw— as if everyone who has ever listened to popular music doesn't know that *love* is the one thing that money can't buy; as if the Beatles themselves hadn't said as much in one of their biggest hits. Love, not fun, is the stuff of Victorian melodrama, where daughters clutch their handkerchiefs and mothers break down on the stairs. Fun, by comparison, seems so ephemeral. Yet this artfully mangled platitude is the song's transcendent twist, and the source of its considerable emotional wisdom. By framing the issue in terms of "fun," the last verse affirms that it is not the presence of love but rather its expression that was lacking in this girl's home. "Something inside that was always denied for so many years," Paul sings in an epitaph that applies as much to the parents as it does to their child.

At the close of side one, *Sgt. Pepper* returns to the realm of show business where it began—albeit to a form of show business far removed from the pop cult of personality that is satirized in the album's opening tracks. "Being for the Benefit of Mr. Kite!" evokes the nineteenth-century circuit of village fairs, pleasure gardens, and amusement parks. The words to the song were taken from an antique poster John Lennon had acquired advertising a performance by "Pablo Fanque's Circus Royal" in the Lancashire town of Rochdale on the fourteenth of February (St. Valentine's Day, no less) in 1843. Printed in a jumble of decorative typefaces, the poster promised the "Grandest Night of the Season!" and listed a bill of "Mr. Kite (late of Well's Circus)" on the tightrope, and "Mr. J. Henderson (The Celebrated Somerset Thrower)" on trampoline, with a special appearance by "Zanthus . . . One of the Best-broke horses in the world." With a few minor adjustments, the Beatles transformed this grandiloquent hype into a musical *objet trouvé*.

True to its historical period, "Being for the Benefit of Mr. Kite!" seems to run on a combination of horsepower, wind, and steam. The introduction sets a swirling organ and a wheezing harmonica to a galloping circus beat; the verse is sung to the pressure-valve hiss of a hi-hat and McCartney's tuba-like bass. Cued by a circus drumroll, the pitchman's voice comes in: "For the benefit of Mr. Kite, there will be a show tonight . . ." John sings these lines (over minor chords) with the jaded confidentiality of a carnival barker, his voice betraying an edge of aggression that dispels all traces of camp. The contrast with the pandering emcee of the Pepper Show could hardly be more pronounced. In place of flattery and false personalization, this is show business pervaded by an aura of danger and freakish sensation: a form of entertainment that is one step removed from a blood sport. Mr. Kite is a high-wire artist, and his every performance is enhanced by the possibility that it may well be his last. Where Billy Shears can afford to turn his ineptitude into charm, one mistake in Kite's line of work could easily cost him his life. As a result, his relationship with his audience is distanced and purely professional—a straightforward matter of giving the people their money's worth. "Messrs. K. and H. assure the public their production will be second to none," John sings in the second verse, adding, "And of course Henry the Horse dances the waltz!"

The instrumental accompaniment to Henry's waltz is the high point of the song—a stunning refinement of the audio dada techniques the Beatles and George Martin first employed in "Tomorrow Never Knows." This time, in lieu of the Dalai Lama, Lennon asked Martin for something akin to a "whirligig, fairground" effect. Martin began by recording an organ duet—in waltz time, naturally—consisting of John, on one instrument, playing the chords of the tune, and himself, on another instrument, playing rapid chromatic runs. (After determining that he couldn't execute these runs with sufficient manic intensity, Martin repeated his trick of recording the part in half-time, an octave below, and then doubling the speed of the tape.) Next, as he explained it: "I got dozens of old steam organ tapes, playing everything from Sousa marches to 'The Liberty Bell.' I cut the tapes into fifteen-inch lengths and told [his engineer Geoff Emerick] to throw them all up in the air. Then I told him to pick them all up and stick them together again. Finally, we reshuffled them a bit until we had a tape which had no musical shape and was nonsense. But it *was* the sound of a steam-organ . . . an unreal hotchpotch of sound." Softened with echo and grafted on top of the more coherent organ duet, this burbling, swooning concoction works like a musical scrim, behind which the eye of the listener can picture the entire lunatic scene: Kite on his tightrope, teetering over the ring, Henderson flinging himself through fiery hogsheads down below, and Henry (née Zanthus) the Wonder Horse, a "hoofer" in the original sense, plodding through the paces of his equestrian ballet. The interlude ends like a carousel ride, with the sound of a clanging bell, and the music grows eerily quiet for a final verse in which John concludes his pitch with the steely prediction that a splendid time is all but "guaranteed." His voice is then swept up and away by a whooshing and whinnying reprise of George Martin's Amazing Composite Calliope. Eight bars later, with a wrenching cadenza, the curtain comes down on side one.

THE BEATLES PRESENT so many new and varied vocal personalities on the first side of *Sgt. Pepper* that George Harrison's near absence from the proceedings could almost pass unnoticed. Yet apart from his role as a backup singer and his marvelous solo on "Fixing a Hole," George, whose presence on *Revolver* rivaled that of John and Paul, is hardly in evidence. "Within You Without You," which starts the second side, is his sole contribution as a songwriter, and it only serves to confirm his status as the odd man out. Placed anywhere else, the track would have seriously compromised the album's sense of continuity. Its position at the start of side two represents not so much the best spot as the only conceivable spot for it in the overall sequence of songs. Coming on the heels of "Mr. Kite," it could pass as a musical sideshow: "Ladies and gentlemen, a taste of the Mysterious East!" Its unequivocal pretensions to seriousness make it, in the context of the Pepper Show, the purest of novelties.

Singing and accompanying himself on the sitar, Harrison is again the only Beatle to appear on the track, which was recorded with an ensemble of musicians from the ranks of the Asia Music Circle. Though the level of the performance (especially the tabla drumming and the part played by a shrill, violin-like instrument called a *dilruba*) is much higher than on "Love You To," the intent remains the same: to replicate the raga form in miniature. "Within You Without You" begins with a loose, contemplative, *alap*-like introduction, coalesces around a sprightly pattern of tabla pings and gulps, then presses forward with George's vocal, which is variously doubled and echoed by the dilruba throughout the song. The verses are linked by lively instrumental passages, and later in the track the accompaniment is joined by a contingent of George Martin's strings, which make their way through the bustle and drone of the Indian instruments with the slightly shaky dignity of a procession of sahibs in sedan chairs.

Though George's vocal is stylized nearly to the point of self-parody in its murky, hooded tone, the melody of "Within You Without You" is the song's strong suit, especially in the bridge, where the gently undulating tune complements the circularity of the lines, "And the time will come when you see we're all one / And life flows on within you and without you." The three verses soften their philosophical edge by striking a conversational tone. But the conversation tends to be dominated by George's fondness for spiritual straw men. Here, instead of "Love You To's" "people standing round who'll screw you in the ground," the trouble lies with people hiding behind their illusions, who (with a nod to the Gospel of Matthew) gain the world only to lose their souls. "Are you one of them?" George asks, throwing down the gauntlet like a Vedic valedictorian. Freed by the artifice of the Pepper Band to be "anyone he wanted to be," Harrison chose to remain resolutely in character as an earnest pop star with pretensions to spirituality. His song concludes, somewhat inexplicably, with a dubbed-in burst of laughter from the audience that may qualify as the one false move on the album.

"Within You Without You" is succeeded by "When I'm Sixty-Four," on which the members of the Pepper Band return with an air of palpable relief to their native English turf. Both of the musical period pieces that Paul McCartney wrote for *Sgt. Pepper* are concerned with domestic themes. "She's Leaving Home" addresses the perils of leaving the nest; "When I'm Sixty-Four" addresses the perils of building the nest. It is an old-fashioned courting song, couched in the form of a marriage proposal, arranged in the milquetoast style of a 1920s British dance-hall band. The tune itself had been germinating for nearly a decade before the Beatles finally recorded it in December 1966; Paul recalled picking it out on the family piano when he was fifteen years old. This would make it one of the earliest known examples of his prodigious ability to sublimate strong emotion behind the smiling face of a song—fifteen for him being the year after his mother died, the year when his widowed father reached the age of *fifty*-four. Ten years later, in honor of Jim McCartney's sixty-fourth birthday, Paul added new words, a new release, and, with George Martin's capable assistance, a new arrangement that turned the song into an affectionate parody of the corniness and coyness of popular music in the days when his parents were young.

It begins with four bars of droll clarinet over the standard foxtrot beat. "When I get older, losing my hair," Paul begins, poking fun at himself and his generation before adding the qualifier "many years from now." Directing himself to his sweetheart, he then proceeds to question what the future of love may hold. Will she still need him? Or, at the very least, *feed* him, when he's sixty-four? "You'll be older too," Paul insinuates in the bridge, where the harmony darkens and the meter shifts from a spry two-beat to a more insistent four.

The tone of the song is overtly tongue-in-cheek, but like all expert parody, "When I'm Sixty-Four" takes an evident delight in the conventions it's sending up. The line "I could be handy, mending a fuse, when your lights have gone" has an innuendo worthy of the risqué comic postcards English vacationers liked to send home from the seaside. And when Paul looks forward to a lifetime of summers on the Isle of Wight "if it's not too dear," the backup singers strike a note of Churchillian resolve in their promise to scrimp and save.

Though the arrangement was clearly inspired by "old-timey" groups like the Temperance Seven and their more recent imitators, the New Vaudeville Band, what sets "When I'm Sixty-Four" apart from those simple spoofs is the restraint of Paul's performance. Another, less confident singer would have sought to remind listeners of his ironic distance from the material; but McCartney has written the irony directly into the song and feels no need to play it up. What he strikes instead is a generous balance: satirizing the coy inhibitions and modest expectations with which his parents' generation approached the subject of sex and love, while acknowledging, at the same time, that out of those inhibitions and expectations, people like his parents fashioned a fulfilling emotional life. At a moment when popular music was preoccupied as never before with the thrill of being young together, the Beatles took a moment to sing a song about the prospect of growing old together.

Each side of *Sgt. Pepper* is presided over by the spirit of a girl. There's John's ethereal Lucy on side one, and Paul's much earthier Rita on side two. "Lovely Rita" is the show-stopper in the Pepper Band's repertoire: a funny, sexy, extroverted song that comes closer to the spirit of rock 'n' roll than anything else on the album. It begins with a fierce strumming of acoustic guitars and a wordless cry of "Ahhhh" that, for an instant, makes the link to "Lucy" overt. Brawny, half-time drumming (Ringo recycles the same jewellike fill—note for note and drum for drum—he played in "A Little Help From My Friends") and a lewd, masturbatory bass line move the music ahead. "Love-ly Ri-ta Meet-ah Maid," the Beatles sing in evenly accented syllables that slide off the tips of their tongues, setting up a verse whose opening line mocks every metaphor that was ever applied to Love: "Lovely Rita, meter maid, nothing can come between us / When it gets dark I *tow* your heart away!"

According to McCartney, the song grew out of nothing more complicated than his delight at learning that female traffic wardens (in British parlance) were called "meter maids" in America. He then displaced this delight to the streets of Swinging London, ablaze with demobilized military fashions, where a meek (or perhaps merely myopic) young Mod could fall for a public servant whose uniform he mistakes for the very height of chic. One of the subtle pleasures of "Lovely Rita" involves the way the discreetly phrased invitation to "take some tea" that arises from this encounter could so easily have come from the singer of "When I'm Sixty-Four." Heard together, back to back, the two songs satirize the courtship styles of successive generations, with the shy, euphemistic past yielding in the wake of George Martin's exultant four-bar piano solo to the more explicit present, as the couple return from their first date and "nearly" make it, "sitting on a sofa with a sister or two." "Love-ly Ri-ta Meet-ah Maid," the Beatles repeat as the rhythm grows insistent and a chorus of panting and sighing leaves a strong impression that Rita and her suitor may have made it after all.

"Good Morning Good Morning" was a song John Lennon professed to dislike, describing it at various times as a "knock-off," a "throwaway," and an outright "piece of garbage." His low opinion of the track may have had something to do with his claim that it was inspired by a cornflakes commercial. ("I always had the TV on very low in the background when I was writing and it came over and then I wrote the song.") It starts like a breakfast from hell with the crowing of a cock, a chorus of gratingly ugly horns (they sound as though they've had cornflakes poured into their bells) and strident shouts of "Good Morning!" After four bars, the whole nerve-racking mess is evened out by a drumroll that shoves the song into the verse, where the horns abate and the rhythm pulls itself together into a stamping Motown beat. But the sense of order is fleeting as the vocal line negotiates a jumble of odd time signatures. "Nothing to do to save his life, call his wife in . . ." John sings, phrasing in groups of three over two bars of 5/4 time, with the extra (tenth) beat taken up by an enormous cymbal crash that heralds the arrival of the wife. "Nothing to say but what a day, how's your boy been?" the sequence repeats, except that this time, instead of the crash, two more beats are tacked on to allow for the reentry of the horns and more shouts of "Good Morning!" The complex-ity of the meter—the nine-bar verse (if anybody's counting) is composed of three bars of 5/4, a bar of 3/4, a bar of 4/4, a bar of 5/4, a bar of 4/4, then two bars of 3/4—is effectively disguised by the smooth phrasing of the vocal and the steady downbeats from the drums.

Ever since the publication of *In His Own Write,* people had been ask-ing Lennon when he was going to start writing song lyrics that resembled his short fiction and verse. "Good Morning Good Morning" came closer to the flavor of his published prose than any song he had written to date. The verses are set in the dispirited domestic milieu of "No Flies on Frank" and similar sketches, whose protagonists drag themselves through the day "crestfallen and defective." The song follows its narrator as he leaves for work, thinks better of it, wanders through the deserted down-town, and stops by his old school. After a raging, sputtering guitar solo (played by McCartney) that seems to sum up the song's inchoate yearn-ings, it's five in the afternoon and the streets are alive with people. Faced with the prospect of "time for tea and meet the wife" (here, in place of the spousal cymbal crash, there's an anguished shriek from the guitar), the singer opts for a more promising source of stimulation in flirting with girls on the street. "Good Morning! Good Morning! *Good!*" the Beatles repeat in the final refrain, as a bizarre counterpoint builds against this cynical chorus of affirmation. It begins (like the song itself) with the cry of a rooster, which is answered in quick succession by the tweeting of a bird, the meowing of a cat, the yelping of a dog, the neighing of a horse, the earth-shaking roar of a lion, the trumpeting bellow of an elephant, and then by the sound of a full hunting party whose hounds and hooves come thundering across the stereo spectrum as the sour notes of a bugle sound overhead. It's as if all the animals that ever graced the front of a cereal box were stampeding off the television screen and chasing one another up the food chain to arrive at the ultimate predator: the fox-hunting English aristocrat.

Having begun with the crowing of a cock, "Good Morning Good Morning" leaves off with the clucking of a hen, which, in a further feat of sonic legerdemain, becomes the clucking of a rhythm guitar. A brisk voice counts off the tempo, the drums lay down a jolting backbeat ("thum *bop!* thum-thum *bop!*"), a sardonic voice whispers "bye," and an avalanche of guitars descends. The sound is that of rock 'n' roll ordered up from central casting, the "two guitars, bass, and drums thing" in all its grinding glory. After the many musical styles that have been featured on the album, we have arrived at the Beatles' own version of Square One. The effect is exhilarating when the voices enter singing the theme from the opening track, reprised here in quickstep: "We're Sergeant Pepper's Lonely Hearts Club Band, we hope you have enjoyed the show . . ." The mood of the music is triumphant, and the intensity only increases as the singers repeat the truncated phrase "Sergeant Pepper's Lonely" until the words become a statement of fact. They pull out of this broken-record effect by means of a lovely internal rhyme ("Sergeant Pepper's *one and only Lonely* Hearts Club Band"), inform their listeners that the concert is nearing its end, and then close it out in a big way: ". . . *Hearts . . . Club . . . Band!*" Cued by the whoops of the singers as they pull away from their microphones, the crowd is on its feet. The Pepper Band, twenty years on, has returned from the oblivion of pop history to once again challenge the world. But the cheers and applause fade with an unexpected swiftness, and in the few seconds it takes to dash down the backstage corridor and shut the dressing room door, the appreciative roar of the crowd is replaced by the raspy strum of chords on an acoustic guitar.

HAD IT ENDED right there, *Sgt. Pepper's Lonely Hearts Club Band* would still have been a remarkable achievement. But the Beatles elected to save the best for last, an idea that went counter to the pop aesthetic, which, whether in fashion, music, or visual art, was more concerned with making a strong impression than with making that impression last. Within the context of the Pepper Show, it is possible to view "A Day in the Life" as an encore. (In that case, it would be the encore that the Beatles never performed when they were playing live.) Yet in many ways the track is antithetical to all that has come before. It is devoid of the satire and sentiment, devoid of period flavor as well. Instead the song exists outside the context of the Pepper Show, in a parallel or alternative reality.

In the outpouring of critical commentary that followed the release of *Sgt. Pepper,* admirers of the album sought to exalt the Beatles' accomplishment by comparing it to such high-art antecedents as T. S. Eliot's "The Wasteland" and the song cycles of Schubert, Schumann, and Mahler. Yet the most strikingly similar antecedent to *Sgt. Pepper* in the realm of high art was a more obscure work, the modernist ballet *Parade,* a collaboration of Jean Cocteau, who wrote the libretto, Pablo Picasso, who designed the costumes and sets, and Erik Satie, whose score Cocteau likened to the sound of "an inspired village band" (and which included parts for type-writers, sirens, gunshots, and the roar of a dynamo). First performed by the Ballet Russe in 1917, *Parade* takes place at a Sunday fair in Paris, where a traveling theater troupe is preparing to perform inside a tent. In keeping with the traditional practice of itinerant entertainers, the man-agers of the company seek to draw a crowd by presenting a "parade" of vaudeville-style acts, who perform for free outside the tent. But the crowd that gathers confuses the parade with the performance it is intended to advertise. The frustrated managers resort to cruder and cruder forms of hucksterism to lure people into the tent, but their efforts are in vain. "The chief theme of *Parade*," wrote Cocteau's biographer Francis Steegmuller, is "that any performance seen by an audience is as nothing compared with the invisibles the artists are up to within." So, too, in "A Day in the Life," the Beatles presumed to show their real-life audience what lay within. The result is such a powerful and evocative performance that it threatens to turn the entire Pepper show, for all its brilliance, into a prelude, raising the *Alice*-like possibility that everything that precedes it might be a collection of vivid dreams or fond memories in the mind of the detached, disassociated narrator of the album's final track.

The scratchy acoustic guitar that starts the song sounds emaciated after the rich palette of instruments and timbres that have filled the album thus far, but it is soon joined by an ascending flourish of piano chords that billows across the track. Then the piano subsides, and the first verse of "A Day in the Life" is sung to the spare strum of the guitar, the pulse of a pair of maracas, and Paul McCartney's bass, which starts off with a stream of notes but, finding nothing to push against, quickly grows subdued. The voice that floats in behind the instruments is John at his most languid, singing as if in a trance: "I read the news today—oh boy. . . ." Here, too, there is a sense of explicit contrast with the powerful presence and rich affect that has characterized the singing on all the pre-ceding tracks. This contrast is deepened by the vast amount of echo on the vocal, which creates the impression of an immensely broad depth of field, with the singer at its far end. The melody steps lightly up the scale under the words "I read the news today," then falls back on the phrase "oh boy," a corny cliché of enthusiasm that John transforms into a tour de force of deflation.

Though the opening verses of "A Day in the Life" were surely inspired by the death of the Guinness heir Tara Browne, to associate the song with Browne is to confuse the inspiration with the art, for it is only John's identification with this unfortunate figure that has any bearing on the song. Both were young, rich, and famous, and the laugh that John had to laugh is a laugh of recognition, an involuntary response to glancing through the newspaper and finding a familiar face. In John's case, of course, this was an everyday occurrence, although the face he most often encountered in this manner was his own.

In the second stanza, Ringo's tom-toms make a thunderous entrance, adding a counterpoint of percussive violence to the darkening imagery of the song, with its description of a car crash and its macabre play on the drug slang "blow your mind." The lyric is chillingly matter-of-fact in describing the momentary lapse of attention that caused the accident. And it is chillingly plausible in its account of the witnesses at the scene, whose attention is focused entirely on the question of whether or not the victim was famous—possibly even a lord. Their reaction parallels that of the singer himself: they're trying to connect the corpse in the wreckage to a name they might recognize while he's trying to connect the photograph in the newspaper to the face of his friend.

The theme of mediated experience plays a part in every song that Lennon wrote for *Sgt. Pepper,* but "A Day in the Life" compounds this theme in the third stanza of the verse, with its deflated reference to a film in which the English army has won the war. As with Tara Browne, so with *How I Won the War;* the point is not the allusion to Lennon's recent role in Richard Lester's movie, but the use he makes of it. The implication is that for members of the postwar generation, the stirring story of Britain's Finest Hour is just another media cliché. Only the singer bothers to pay attention—not out of any compelling interest, but rather out of a sense of curiosity concerning how closely the movie version coincides with the book he has read.

John's voice ends the verse on high falsetto G. He clings to that note at the start of the refrain, "I'd *love* to . . ." before descending a fifth to warble the second half of the line, ". . . turn you on," between a pair of adjoining notes. The effect is like the hum of a turbine revving up. The acoustic guitar and drums gradually melt away, leaving a faint pulse of bass and piano, while in some new sonic center, a swell begins to build. On it comes, this new sound, the volume increasing while the strings mirror the waver in John's voice. Then, after four bars, the pitch lifts off crazily as well. This new sound is emanating from the Beatles' Clown Nose & Gorilla Paw Orchestra, whose forty members, having been given a low note on which to begin, a high note on which to end, and twenty-four bars over which to complete the journey, are behaving the way any large group of highly trained musicians would behave if they were asked on the spur of the moment to do something that violated every principle of their performance practice *except* the basic tenet that they should do as they were told. *"Don't* try to stay together," George Martin instructed them. The ascending, accelerating, crescendoing glissando of sound they produce seems to skirt the edge of music and enter the realm of pure sonic sensation; it turns those twenty-four bars into a vertiginous eternity that sweeps away the preexisting musical landmarks, before ending, with electronically enhanced precision, in a sudden blip. What remains are the piano plinks—in a different key, to be sure, but otherwise quite like the plinks from which this eruption arose. An alarm clock rings. The drums sputter to life at twice the tempo of the earlier verse, followed by a voice—*Paul's* voice it is, phrasing briskly, without a trace of echo, the opposite in every respect of John's voice in the verse. He recounts a morning routine of waking up, getting out of bed, combing his hair (a piano fill intrudes over a foreshortened bar of 2/4 time, simulating the expert twists and turns of a teenager's comb), then heading downstairs for a cup of tea, glancing at the clock, and seeing that he's late. Carica-tured by a series of panting breaths that hark back to "Lovely Rita," the very concept of "late" seems far removed from the languid, timeless place where "A Day in the Life" began. Here, in its bridge, the song seems to have passed by means of that dizzying instrumental eruption into another dimension. As he grabs his coat and races to catch his bus, the singer is back in the workaday world of *un*mediated experience, and the use of Paul's brighter, keener voice to express this shift in time and place is a remarkable touch. But now, cued by the sound of "somebody" speaking, that other voice, John's voice, returns with an anguished, echoey cry that rises and falls across an eight-bar sequence of chords that search for a key before yielding to five huge notes, voiced in stacked octaves by the entire orchestra, descending E . . . D-C . . . D-G, which muscle the music back into G, the original key of the song. All that survives from the middle section is the tempo; "A Day in the Life" is racing at speed as it nears its end. Though he's phrasing in half-time, John can barely keep up with the band as he delivers his final news bulletin, this one referring to the presence of ten thousand holes in Blackburn, Lancashire, each of which had to be counted, thereby yielding the number of holes it would take to "fill the Albert Hall." Against chiming C major piano chords, John's voice goes up like a choirboy's on the last two notes of the line.

This choice morsel from the Beatles' ashcan school of lyric-writing inspired no end of speculation on the part of critics and fans. But the ten thousand holes in Lancashire are neither needle marks nor an allusion to Britain's grisly "Moors Murders" of 1966. They refer instead to *potholes* (no pun intended) as noted in a column called "Far & Near" that ran in the *Daily Mail*. It's not hard to see how John Lennon's sense of the absurd would have been piqued by the unintended Goonery of an item titled "The Holes in Our Roads," which read in its entirety:

> There are 4,000 holes in the road in Blackburn, Lancashire, or one twenty-sixth of a hole per person, according to a council survey. If Blackburn is typical there are two million holes in Britain's roads and 300,000 in London.

One can only marvel at the mind that thought to factor the number of potholes into the total population of Blackburn, and then went on to apply the same ratio to the whole of Britain as well. "The Holes in Our Roads" can scarcely be bettered as an example of rationality gone mad, and its incorporation into "A Day in the Life," by equating this trivia to the previous descriptions of a personal tragedy and a national triumph, is an implicit act of commentary on the earlier verses of the song. But the reference to the Albert Hall is something else again. One of the prime venues of British show business, the Albert Hall was the site of the Beatles' first London concert in 1963, and by applying the lunatic logic of "The Holes in Our Roads" to this great showplace, "A Day in the Life" revives the metaphor of performance that links the preceding twelve tracks on *Sgt. Pepper*. The question on which the song and the album ends may be rephrased to ask: How many holes—that is, how many lonely hearts and empty souls—does it take to fill the Albert Hall? Thus does the last line of the last verse reintegrate this astonishing last track into the concept of the album it ends. *Sgt. Pepper's Lonely Hearts Club Band* is an act of exquisite artifice: a recording posing as a live concert, performed by a world-famous group of musicians posing as a once-famous group of musicians. It is the concert that the real-life Beatles could never have given live. This was not only because the complex sounds on the record could never be reproduced onstage, but, more important, because the response the Beatles elicited from their audiences during the three years they toured the world was of such a magnitude as to make it impossible for them or their audience to hear the music they played—an all-but-unprecedented development that effectively placed them into the role of the spectators at their own concerts. In the epilogue that ends *Sgt. Pepper,* John Lennon's brilliantly disassociated performance presents us with the disquieting spectacle of the singer as a spectator in his own song, lost in a daze of imagery and information, constructing his world out of whatever it is that happens to pass in front of his eyes.

If the twelve songs that precede "A Day in the Life" may be likened to the dozen or so "turns" that made up an evening of music-hall entertainment, they may also be likened to the "somersets" in "Being for the Benefit of Mr. Kite!" For each of these carefully conceived tracks is a feat of artistic skill and daring that strikes its own balance between the poles of laughter and longing, satire and sentiment, that form the spectrum of popular art. "A Day in the Life" is literally another story. By breaking out of the theatrical frame, the song (wrote the critic Richard Poirier) "projects a degree of loneliness that cannot be managed within the conventions of *Sgt. Pepper's Lonely Hearts Club Band*"—nor, for that matter, within the conventions of popular music as they existed in 1967. "A Day in the Life" pushes the metaphor of variety entertainment beyond the stunts of the stolid Hendersons, performed "on solid ground." This incomparable final track, which is arguably not only the single greatest performance in the Beatles' canon, but in the history of recorded rock, raises the artistic ante to the level of the celebrated Mr. Kite himself, who performs his daredevil twists and turns in the air above the ring, to a crowd that thrills with fear and excitement at each improbable leap. It is the sound of that crowd that can be heard in the second, crescendoing rush of the orchestra that follows the final verse, rising again from a hum to a gasp to a shout to a roar, fusing at last into a deafening shriek (its similarity to the sound of the crowds at Beatle concerts is surely no accident), a surge of unmediated sensation that combines every form of response an audience has ever felt toward a performer—every shade of love, lust, awe, envy, laughter, suspense, and delight. The onrushing sound of the orchestra at the end of "A Day in the Life" has transcended more than the conventions of *Sgt. Pepper's Band.* It is the nightmare resolution of the Beatles' show within a show. It is the sound in the ears of the high-wire artist as the ground rushes up from below.

There is a blinding flash of silence, then the stunning impact of a tremendous E major piano chord that hangs in the empty air for a small eternity, slowly fading away, a forty-second meditation on finality that leaves each member of the audience listening with a new kind of attention and awareness to the sound of nothing at all.

38

It was the summer of 1967, the summer that went down as the Summer of Love... *Sergeant Pepper's Lonely Hearts Club Band* had just been released. It was the first aroma of summer, it wafted over the horizon like sweet incense, and its permeation was so complete that everyone who heard it lived it, breathed it, and spoke of little else. You would hear it from cars, drifting out of windows where you walked, in your friends' homes, and in your head, always. Its timing, the unequalled beauty of its contents, the pyrotechnical extravagance, the powerful release of inspiration, the awe and hope it projected, made it the opus of the movement.

—Ellen Sander

The overwhelming consensus was that the Beatles had created a popular masterpiece: a rich, sustained, and overflowing work of collaborative genius whose bold ambition and startling originality dramatically enlarged the possibilities and raised the expectations of what the experience of listening to popular music on record could be. On the basis of this perception, *Sgt. Pepper* became the catalyst for an explosion of mass enthusiasm for album-formatted rock that would revolutionize both the aesthetics and the economics of the record business in ways that far outstripped the earlier pop explosions triggered by the Elvis phenomenon of 1956 and the Beatlemania phenomenon of 1963.

Two weeks after the album's release, when the force of its impact was reaching an early peak, an event grandly billed as the First International Pop Festival was held at a fairgrounds in the California coastal resort of Monterey, 150 miles south of San Francisco. The festival was organized by a group of hip young Hollywood entrepreneurs that included Derek Taylor, and it was overseen by a tony-sounding "Board of Governors" that included Paul McCartney, Mick Jagger, Smokey Robinson, and Brian Wilson (none of whom attended or performed). Monterey Pop was conceived as a showcase of the new California music and the new California tribalism. Out of deference to the utopian sensibilities of the Haight-Ashbury, the festival was run on a nonprofit basis, with the performers waiving their fees. (Out of deference to the sensibilities of Hollywood, some three-quarters of a million dollars in gate receipts and film rights were never accounted for.) Over the course of three days, the festival presented some thirty acts and drew more than forty thousand fans. Also on hand were hundreds of journalists and a spendthrift contingent of record company executives whose presence turned the proceedings into an open-air music business trade fair. Monterey was instrumental in launching the recording careers of Janis Joplin, lead singer with Big Brother & the Holding Company, and a half-dozen other San Francisco bands. It featured the first American appearance by the Jimi Hendrix Experience (who were booked on the recommendation of Governor Paul McCartney), a climactic set by the soul singer Otis Redding, and the reintroduction to America (after an unsuccessful 1965 tour) of the Who. The festival crowd was festooned with *Sgt. Pepper* buttons and badges and alive with rumors that the Beatles were planning to perform—thanks in part to the savvy inclusion of a "Group With No Name" on the bill. "They *are* here," Derek Taylor teased reporters. "But they are disguised as hippies."

The hundreds of reporters who covered the Monterey Pop Festival were the vanguard of a new journalistic genre in the United States. In Britain a certain amount of attention had been paid to the musical attributes of rock 'n' roll since the 1950s, when the venerable jazz journal *Melody Maker* began to cover the pop scene, to be joined in 1961 by its purely pop-oriented rival *The New Musical Express*. With the advent of Beatlemania in 1963, musically literate critics like George Melly, William Mann, and the musicologist Wilfred Mellers began to comment regularly on pop recordings in the pages of *The Observer,* the London *Times,* and *The New Statesman,* while Nik Cohn's column in *Queen* pioneered a new style of lively, opinionated pop criticism from the perspective of a passionate fan. In the United States, however, the mainstream press had preferred to cover pop and rock as a commercial or sociological phenomenon, but not, for the most part, as a form of artistic expression. *Crawdaddy,* America's first journal of rock criticism, was founded by its seventeen-year-old editor, Paul Williams, in 1966. Around that same time, magazines like *Vogue* and *Playboy* began paying greater attention to rock in their monthly guides to the arts, and a few hardy souls like Ralph J. Gleason, jazz critic of the *San Francisco Chronicle,* began to write about rock the way they had previously written about jazz. But it was not until the confluence of *Sgt. Pepper* and the Monterey Pop Festival in the summer of 1967 that newspapers and magazines in the United States began to feature regular coverage of rock as one of the lively arts.

In keeping its status as the country's largest mass-circulation weekly, *Life* led the way with a cover story on "The New Far-Out Beatles" that offered a detailed account of the *Sgt. Pepper* recording sessions and a five-page spread of photographs showing the group at work at Abbey Road. The Beatles, *Life* speculated, were "stepping far ahead of their audience, recording music so complex and so unlike the music that made them successful that they could very likely lose the foundation of their support." (The article also contained a quote from Paul McCartney in which he mentioned, in passing, that he had taken LSD.) Both *Time* and *Newsweek* reviewed *Sgt. Pepper* immediately after its release. *Newsweek* proclaimed the album "a masterpiece" and compared its songs to literary works by Edith Sitwell, Harold Pinter, and T. S. Eliot. *Time* reported on George Martin's behind-the-scenes wizardry in an article titled "Mix-Master to the Beatles." "George Martin's new LP was out last week," it began. The two magazines squared off over the import of "A Day in the Life." *Newsweek* deemed it the Beatles' equivalent of "The Waste Land." *Time* described it as "a larky little ditty about a Mod's sally from pillow to pot." The following week, *The New Yorker* published a long "Talk of the Town" entry that focused on the sense of occasion in the city's record stores on the day of *Sgt. Pepper's* release. Most of the article was given over to the opinions of a "professorial-looking" customer called Lawrence LeFevre, who delivered a "little lecture" in which he described their new album as "a musical *event,* comparable to a notable new opera or symphonic work." "Lawrence LeFevre" was actually a pseudonym for *The New Yorker's* fifty-nine-year-old editor William Shawn, who ended the piece by suggesting that "the Beatles have done more to brighten up the world in recent years than almost anything else in the arts."

In the weeks and months that followed, scores of articles appeared in the American press about the Beatles and their work, ranging from brief reviews to extended essays in literary and scholarly journals. The

Christian Science Monitor offered an editorial "Salute to Sgt. Pepper."
The Saturday Review praised the album as a work of "literature and criticism." The jazz journal *Downbeat* announced that it would henceforth
cover the rock scene, as did its longtime rival, *Jazz*, which advertised its
new editorial policy by changing its name to *Jazz & Pop*. Then *Time*, as if
to atone for the larkiness of its earlier coverage, put the Beatles on its
cover in a group of striking papier-mâché caricatures by the English car-
toonist Gerald Scarfe. The accompanying article, portentously titled "The
Messengers," contained a solemn account of the band's artistic development since 1963 and testimonials to the Beatles' preeminence from such
well-known classical musicians as Leonard Bernstein, Luciano Berio,
and Ned Rorem. It was Rorem, a former protégé of Aaron Copeland and
a noted composer of classical "art songs," who told *Time* in a much-cited
remark that "She's Leaving Home" was "equal to any song that Shubert
ever wrote."

In the fall of 1967, Rorem expanded on this view in an essay about
the Beatles in *The New York Review of Books*. "I and my colleagues have
been happily torn from a long antiseptic nap by the energy of rock, prin-
cipally as embodied in the Beatles," he began. His essay sought to place
the Beatles' music within the "artful tradition of song" and to account for
their "superiority" in the field of contemporary pop. "The Beatles are
good even though everyone already knows that they're good," Rorem
wrote, alluding to the way the group's immense popularity confounded
the usual notions of discriminating taste. The excitement of their songs,
he suggested, owed to "their absolutely insolent—hence innocent—
unification of music's disparate components—that is, in using the most
conservative devices of harmony, counterpoint, rhythm, melody, and
orchestration, and making them blend with a contagious freshness." He
ended his essay by thanking the Beatles for having "removed the sterile
martyrdom from art."

Rorem's hope that the example of the Beatles might help to reinvigo-
rate the "antiseptic" world of contemporary art music was echoed by
other critics who shared his historical sense. "Who would have thought
that the pop music of the 1960s would develop into a force as vital as that
of the jongleur of old?" the musicologist Joan Peyser asked in the *Columbia University Forum*. Her essay, "The Beatles and the Beatless," compared the inverse trends in art music and rock—the one increasingly
nonrhythmic, nonverbal, impersonal, and abstract, the other increasingly

rhythmic, verbal, personal, and concrete. An article along the same lines by Frederick Grunfeld in the quarterly arts journal *Horizon* credited the Beatles with having "nearly succeeded in bringing the two mainstreams of music, serious and pop, Bach and barrelhouse, flowing back into the same broad channel—something that hasn't happened since the days when they were dancing bourrées in the streets."

After a point, the praise for *Sgt. Pepper* became so extravagant as to generate a backlash of sorts. In Britain this reaction was centered among critics like Nik Cohn who valued pop music, above all, as the expression of a uniquely adolescent sensibility. "*Sgt. Pepper* was genuinely a breakthrough," Cohn wrote of the album. "Added up, it came to something quite ambitious; it made strange images of isolation, and it sustained. . . . Only, it wasn't much like pop. It wasn't fast, flash, sexual, loud, vulgar, monstrous, or violent. . . . So alright, the Beatles make good music, they really do, but since when was pop anything to do with good music?" America's chief dissident wrote with a similarly canonical cast, but Richard Goldstein, reviewing *Sgt. Pepper* in the *New York Times,* found the album to be *insufficiently* ambitious and sustained. At the age of twenty-three, Goldstein was prepared to take what he termed the "discipline of rock criticism" very seriously. ("If being a critic were the same as being a listener, I could just enjoy *Sgt. Pepper,*" he wrote in a published response to the onslaught of irate letters inspired by his *Times* review.) Goldstein dismissed the record as an "album of special effects, dazzling but ultimately fraudulent." He distrusted the elaborate production ("it reeks of horns and harps") and found the uncertain mixture of satire and sentiment in songs like "She's Leaving Home" and "When I'm Sixty-Four" to be deeply unsettling. Only "A Day in the Life," whose lyric he, too, likened to T. S. Eliot, and whose music he likened to Wagner, received his unqualified praise. " 'A Day in the Life' is such a radical departure from the spirit of the album that it almost deserves its peninsular position," he wrote, coming perilously close to the point.

THE OUTPOURING OF published commentary that accompanied the release of *Sgt. Pepper* was only a sampling of the vast amount of informal, conversational commentary that the album inspired among listeners around the world. By 1967 the audience for rock had grown to include large numbers of college students and college graduates, many of whom had gained from their educations certain critical habits of mind. This more mature and erudite audience had begun to engage in a more refined form of fan worship, based on the desire to establish a more cerebral bond of intimacy with rock auteurs like the Beatles and Bob Dylan by pondering the "inner" meanings of their songs. Having begun with the consideration of such minor mysteries as the true significance of Norwegian Wood, Doctor Robert, or a Yellow Submarine, exegesis of the Beatles' lyrics went into overdrive in the face of songs as genuinely complex and in some cases mysterious as those on *Sgt. Pepper.* Within weeks of its release, the album had become the subject of a cultlike body of lore that was widely shared by Beatle fans. Did the celebrated "Mr. K" refer to Franz Kafka? Was the "lucky man" in a "A Day in the Life" a victim of suicide? Many of the more popular interpretations and associations found their way into the published commentary as well, where they were often treated by deferential adult writers as a form of received wisdom.

For the most part, the prevailing idea of hidden meaning in rock songs meant references to drugs. That several of the songs on *Sgt. Pepper* contained fairly explicit drug references, nobody, including the Beatles, made any attempt to deny. Like most popular songwriters, Lennon and McCartney wrote in the vernacular of the day, and drug slang figured heavily in the vernacular of 1967. But the interpretive zeal of some listeners went far beyond those obvious references to see the imaginative power of drugs as the subtext of the entire album. Encouraged by oracles like Timothy Leary, who described *Sgt. Pepper* as "a complete celebration of LSD," they found allusions to marijuana lurking in the "weeds" of "When I'm Sixty-Four" and the "tea" of "Lovely Rita," allusions to heroin in the title of "Fixing a Hole" and the waltz of Henry the Horse.

Paul McCartney addressed this question directly in an interview with the artist and writer Alan Aldridge in the fall of 1967. "It seems to me that your songs appeal to two entirely separate audiences," Aldridge noted, "the mass teeny-boppers who accept your work at a humming and dancing level, and the new semi-intellectual audience which analyzes and seeks hidden meanings behind the lyrics." "We write songs," Paul replied. "We know what we mean by them. But in a week someone else says something about it, and you can't deny it. . . . You put your own meaning at your own level to our songs and that's what's great about them."

McCartney's comfort with the idea of people ascribing their own meanings to the Beatles' songs was not shared by his partner John

Lennon. In particular, Lennon had a strong reaction to the interpretive controversy that developed after listeners—including the BBC censors—noticed that "Lucy in the Sky With Diamonds," shorn of its modifiers, forms an acronym for LSD. The acronym, John insisted at the time (and ever after), was a "pure coincidence."

Despite its overtly fictional nature, "Lucy in the Sky" was a deeply personal song for John, in which he had taken the title and image of his son Julian's drawing of his playmate Lucy and applied them to a set of lyrics that were inspired by one of John's own fictional playmates from childhood, Lewis Carroll's Alice. Years later, Lennon would describe Lucy as "the image of this female who would someday come [and] save me." His characterization bears a strong resemblance to the Jungian concept of an *anima* or female archetype, which inhabits the male unconscious and can assume the form of a mother, a mate, or a muse. Considering that "Lucy in the Sky" was the first song John ever wrote in which he referred to a girl by her name, this makes it hard to ignore the phonetic similarity between the elusive Lucy and the equally elusive and archetypal female whose comings and goings exerted such a profound influence on John's own childhood, his mother Julia.

This rich web of conscious and unconscious associations—with Alice, with Julia, and with a desire to link the imaginative world of his own childhood with that of his son Julian—caused John to react angrily to the implication that "Lucy in the Sky With Diamonds" was nothing more than a thinly veiled salute to the Beatles' psychedelic muse. During the summer of 1967 he channeled this anger in an ambitious new song called "I Am the Walrus," written over the course of many weeks, in which he revisited the relevant sections of *Through the Looking Glass*, and plotted his revenge on those who would impose their own narrow meanings on "Lucy in the Sky."

OF ALL THE critical commentary inspired by *Sgt. Pepper,* Richard Poirier's essay titled "Learning from the Beatles," in the fall 1967 edition of *The Partisan Review,* stood in a class by itself. Poirier's status as a literary critic and professor of English at Rutgers ensured that anything he wrote about the Beatles would be taken by cynics on both sides of the generation gap as proof that highbrow adulation of the group had gotten entirely out of hand. ("Insufferably pompous . . . a typical academic's reaction," scoffed the born-again *Jazz & Pop.*) Yet despite its occasional gaffes of fogeyism—Poirier was capable of confusing not only Lennon and McCartney, but also Martin and Epstein—"Learning from the Beatles" was no mere exercise in unwitting academic burlesque. If Poirier's tone was professorial, his approach was a lot less pedantic than that of Richard Goldstein or *Time.* Declaring that "the Beatles are now beyond patronization," his concern lay less with subjecting their songs to the techniques of contemporary critical analysis than with the challenge their work posed to the attitudes deemed appropriate to the appreciation of "serious" art. "People who listen to the Beatles love them—what about that?" he asked. Poirier noted that his students were listening to the group's music with a degree of engagement that he, as a teacher of literature, could only envy, and he drew an analogy between the current fascination with rock and the rise of the popular novel in the nineteenth century, suggesting that "people tend to listen to the Beatles the way families in the last century listened to readings of Dickens."

Poirier was especially taken with what he described as the "mixed allusiveness" of the Beatles' recent work. "It's unwise ever to assume that they're doing only one thing or expressing themselves in only one style," he wrote. Their recordings "remind the listener that one kind of feeling about a subject isn't enough, and that any single induced feeling must often exist within the context of seemingly contradictory alternatives." "Especially in the later songs," he continued, "one of the interwoven strands is likely to be an echo of some familiar, probably clichéd musical, verbal, or dramatic formula." Noting "the participatory tenderness and joy" with which they responded to outdated musical styles, Poirier suggested a parallel between the Beatles' use of parody in songs like "She's Leaving Home" and "When I'm Sixty-Four" and the technique of modernist writers like Joyce and Nabokov, who used parody to revitalize shopworn literary styles, genres, and conventions that had ceased to hold meaning for them. At its best, he suggested, the group's music helped to restore "to good standing the simplicities that have frightened us into irony and the search for irony; they locate the beauty and pathos of commonplace feelings even while they wreak havoc with fashionable and tiresome expressions of those feelings."

39

In London in 1967, every Friday night until dawn, shimmering flower children, splashed with Day-Glo, spotted with marcasite, clad in diaphanous revamped negligées, tarted-up Grenadier Guards jackets, in tat and glitter from the markets of Asia and Portobello Road, in anything as long as it was beautiful, tripped inside a monstrous basement or queued outside, bedazzling the passing traffic.

—Richard Neville

The qualities that Richard Poirier singled out for praise in the Beatles' music would never be more apparent than on the single the group released in July of 1967 as a kind of postscript to *Sgt. Pepper.* "All You Need Is Love" was destined to become one of the most rapidly disseminated musical recordings ever made, thanks to its debut on an international television special called "Our World," which aired on a Sunday evening in Britain toward the end of June. A joint production of the BBC and the European Broadcasting Union, "Our World" was a three-hour live broadcast designed to commemorate the recent completion of the first satellite network capable of sending a television signal around the world. When plans for the program were made public in the spring of 1967, the BBC announced that the Beatles had agreed not only to represent Britain, but also to write a song especially for the show. In deference to the worldwide audience, the group had reportedly agreed to limit itself to "basic English" in the lyrics of this song.

By the time the program aired, the global reach of "Our World" had been significantly compromised by the wholesale defection of the Soviet Bloc countries, who withdrew their participation in protest over the allegedly biased coverage of the recent Arab-Israeli war on British and American television. The total audience was further diminished by the program's limited availability in the United States, where it could only be seen on the nation's then-primitive patchwork of public television stations. As a result, only a fraction of the projected 600 million viewers ever saw or even knew about the show. And much of what they did see conformed to the soporific mode of "educational TV." Though the second half of "Our World" was devoted to artistic achievement and presented, in addition to the Beatles, scenes from a rehearsal of *Lohengrin* at Bayreuth and an interview with the artist Joan Miró, the entire first half of the program was devoted to the mind-numbing theme of world population growth, during which the international audience was subjected to live reports on soybean farming in Wisconsin and prawn fishing in Japan. "After a time it became almost fascinating to see just how much banality the cameras of five continents could root out of the teeming world," *The Observer* noted. "A vast exercise in electronic rhetoric," grumbled *The Spectator*'s Stuart Hood, who ended his review with the patriotic plug "Thank Heaven for the Beatles!"

Their six-minute segment, live from Abbey Road, looked like a reprise of the "Day in the Life" recording session, minus the party hats. It opened with a shot of the Beatles perched on stools in the studio, rehearsing the backup vocals to "All You Need Is Love." Seated at their feet was the cream of Britain's pop aristocracy, including delegates from the Stones, the Hollies, and the Who. "This is Steve Race in the Beatles' recording studio in London," the BBC announcer begins. The cameras cut to George Martin in the control room as the music comes to a stop. "Thank you, John," says Martin. "I think that will do for the vocal backing very nicely. We'll get the musicians in now." "The supervisor is George Martin," the narration continues, "the musical brain behind all the Beatles' records." A brief description of the technical process by which the earlier tracks have been prepared is followed by some terse commands from the control room, and then, as a fitting introduction to Britain's official entry into the first electronic congregation of the Global Village, the orchestra strikes up the national anthem. The only thing is, it's the *French* national anthem that they're playing, "La Marseillaise," booming out over a firing-squad drumroll in a colossal mock-mistake that demolishes any thought of the Beatles as dutiful cultural ambassadors. Then, in a seamless transition, the old anthem yields to the new. "Love . . . love . . . love," chants a choir of Mersey angels, as John comes in on the offbeat over the steady slog of the drums: "There's nothing you can do that can't be done / Nothing you can sing that can't be sung . . ."

While sticking with "basic English" for the sake of easy translation, the Beatles contrived a lyric that is a riddle in any tongue. "All You Need

Is Love" speaks in a series of Delphic double negations ("Nothing you can . . . that can't") that offer the listener a choice between accepting the words at face value or plunging into a doubtful effort to pin the meaning down. "It's easy!" John declares over alternating bars of 4/4 and 3/4 time, phrasing with such assurance that the irregularities of the meter are barely perceptible. The Beatles certainly make it *sound* easy. But, on closer inspection, the verses are a parody of wisdom: while they seem to express a sense of unlimited possibility, what they wind up saying is that there is nothing new under the sun. Then, from this morass of twisted meaning and shifting meter, comes the catchphrase of the refrain: "All you need is love," repeated three times, each time answered by a chorus of horns in a goosey chromatic run.

There is no better illustration of the Beatles' ability to be all things to all people than this powerfully ambiguous song. Many listeners, caught up in the millennial spirit of the summer of 1967, took the words to be saying that all things are made possible by Love. Others, more apprecia-tive of the Beatles as tricksters than as troubadours, noted the joke of "La Marseillaise" and the brain-teasing syntax of the verses and pronounced the song a spoof. Yet "All You Need Is Love" is no more conducive to a knowing interpretation than it is to a naïve embrace. It spreads a deadpan Liverpudlian irony over the most clichéd sentiment in all of popular music—not to debunk the sentiment, but rather to free the sentiment from its imprisonment in the cliché. This subtle design becomes clearer in the song's extended coda, where the orchestra resumes the motif of musical quotation that began with "La Marseillaise." Peppered by whoops and cheers and vaudevillian interjections ("All together now!") from the Beatles and their in-house cheering section, the brass instru-ments begin with a rippling fragment of Bach; the reeds answer with a syncopated riff from Glenn Miller's Swing Era theme "In the Mood"; the strings come back with "Greensleeves." Having touched on the genres of classical, jazz, and folk, all that remains is for Paul McCartney to apply the parodistic coup de grace by breaking into the chorus of "She Loves You"—a reference to the Beatles' own musical innocence that has the startling effect of imputing an innocence to all the other musical refer-ences in the song. In musicological terms, a medley of melodic quota-tions is called a *quodlibet*—a word that also refers, in philosophical discourse, to a proposition that is raised for the purposes of argument. And that, when all is said and done, describes the entire song. "All You

Need Is Love" doesn't mean to disabuse anyone of their belief in the power of Love. But neither does it propose Love as a cure for all the world's problems. Instead the song restates the need for Love as something independent of the doing and the saying, the singing and the playing. To paraphrase Ned Rorem: Love is all you need even though everybody already knows that Love is all you need—that is, even though musicians and poets have been singing its praises in every conceivable manner and style since music and poetry began.

A WEEK AFTER its broadcast on "One World," "All You Need Is Love" was released as a single in Britain and America, where it became an anthem for the season that had already been christened by the hippies in the Haight-Ashbury and advertised by the American news media as the Summer of Love. In London, the summer of 1967 was graced by the sort of sentimentally perfect weather the Beatles had satirized in "Penny Lane." Day after day of cloudless skies and balmy temperatures seemed to summon the city's neophyte "heads" and "freaks" and hippies out of their Underground haunts and into the streets and parks, where their increasingly visible presence and uninhibited behavior not only bedazzled the populace, but also drove the tabloid press into a frenzy of moral panic concerning what was now routinely described as an "epidemic" of illegal drugs.

In February 1967, Britain's most popular Sunday paper, *The News of the World,* had published a typically sensationalistic exposé called "Secrets of the Pop Stars' Hideaway" that named Mick Jagger of the Rolling Stones as a frequent guest at "LSD parties" hosted by an up-and-coming rock group called the Moody Blues. Jagger responded, in a televised interview, by denouncing the story and threatening a libel suit. (His indignation was unfeigned; the paper's source had confused him with his guitarist Brian Jones.) A week later, acting on what proved to be a tip from *The News of the World,* the police had raided a party at the Sussex home of the Stones' *other* guitarist, Keith Richards. (When George Harrison learned the details of this raid, he realized that the police had been considerate enough to wait for him to leave the party before they initiated their search.) Three months later, in the middle of May, charges were filed against Richards, Jagger, and the art dealer Robert Fraser. Richards was charged with the crime of permitting the use of cannabis in his home, Jagger with the possession of four amphetamine pills that had been purchased legally overseas, and Fraser with possession of two dozen heroin ampoules.

In June, while Parliament debated a bill that would authorize warrant-less searches of anyone the police "suspected" of possessing illegal drugs, it was the Beatles' turn to be vilified in the press, as the *Daily Mirror* jumped all over Paul McCartney's offhand "admission" in *Life* that he had taken LSD. I MIGHT TAKE LSD AGAIN, SAYS PAUL, the paper's headline read. "Paul told me that LSD has made him see God," wrote the *Mirror*'s James Wilson, who reassured his readers that McCartney nevertheless "remained a Beatle" throughout his epiphany. An editorial in the same issue of the paper accused McCartney of "behaving like an irresponsible idiot" and suggested that he consult both a psychiatrist and a lawyer. The Beatles responded by closing ranks, with Brian Epstein, John Lennon, and George Harrison all announcing that they, too, had taken the drug. In a neat reversal of the previous summer's controversy over the Beatles and Jesus Christ, McCartney's admission in *Life* elicited little reaction in the United States.

Two weeks later the ranks of the Underground closed even tighter when the Stones Case came to trial in a Sussex magistrates court. There, in consecutive proceedings against Jagger, Fraser, and Richards, a jury of rural Chichester residents wasted little time in finding each of the defen-dants guilty as charged. Up to this point the case had served mainly as a source of prurient delight for the British public, who thrilled to testimony that an unidentified female guest (correctly rumored to be Marianne Faithfull) had been clad in nothing but a fur rug when the police came on the scene. The Stones, after all, were resented and disliked by a great many people who took the group's carefully cultivated Visigoth image seriously. ("What one cannot and should not forget is that their wealth and fame has come to them almost entirely because everything in their songs and appearance was a protest against conventional society and its attitudes," wrote the columnist Monica Furlong in the *Daily Mail*.) But the liberal press and much of its readership responded with a different kind of outrage to the harshness of the sentences handed down: Jagger to three months, Fraser (who pled guilty) to six months, and Richards to a year in jail. "Who breaks a butterfly upon a wheel?" demanded a memo-rable lead editorial in the London *Times*, whose editor risked a contempt citation for commenting on a case under appeal. "The verdict of one generation on another," added *The Observer*.

The public response to the verdicts included demonstrations outside the offices of *The News of the World* (whose role in the case was revealed at the trial) and a well-attended "Legalize Pot" rally in Hyde Park. Toward the end of July, a petition calling for the reform of Britain's marijuana laws ran as a full-page advertisement in the *Times*. "The law against marijuana is immoral in principle and unworkable in practice," it began. The sixty-five signatories of the petition included one Nobel laureate, two Members of Parliament, a dozen prominent physicians and clergymen, numerous writers and artists, and the four celebrated MBEs who, along with their manager Brian Epstein, had put up the money for the ad. A week after its publication, an embarrassed Lord Chief Justice intervened to throw out the verdict against Richards and suspend the sentence against Jagger, who was whisked by helicopter from his court date to a televised symposium with the editor of the *Times* and the Bishop of Woolwich on the subject of "Youth and Drugs." (As the son of a Scottish peer, Robert Fraser was left to serve his time, a victim of noblesse oblige.) Together, a sensationalistic Sunday tabloid and a vengeful magistrate's court had performed the seemingly impossible task of generating a wave of public sympathy for the Rolling Stones.

AWAY FROM THE headlines, the Beatles spent the summer of 1967 basking in the glow of their artistic accomplishments and continuing their adjustment to the novelty of having free time on their hands. ("I get bored like everyone else, but instead of having three hours a night, I have all day to be bored in," Ringo told a reporter.) In July the whole group traveled to Greece to explore the Huxleyan possibility of buying a private island in the Aegean Sea. In August, George Harrison traveled to Los Angeles to hear Ravi Shankar perform at the Hollywood Bowl and to help Shankar publicize the opening of an American branch of his Indian music school. In the course of this trip, George and his wife, Pattie, chaperoned by their friend Derek Taylor and a reporter from *Melody Maker*, took a trip to San Francisco for a whirlwind inspection tour of the Haight-Ashbury. After dropping a tab of acid and donning a pair of heart-shaped, rose-colored glasses, George and his little entourage left their limousine and strolled through the heart of the district, attracting a crowd of several hundred startled, worshipful hippies in the space of several blocks. At the edge of Golden Gate Park, Harrison bantered with the people around him and obligingly strummed a guitar before retracing his steps along Haight Street, where a contingent of local dope dealers, sensing a once-in-a-lifetime promotional opportunity, pushed their way into the crowd. "I gotta turn George on," one of them shouted. "Let me get to him, man." An hour later Harrison was on board a private jet, flying back to Los Angeles.

Obscured by the rose-colored glasses and beaming vibes of this visit was a jarring collision of worlds. Harrison had gone to the Haight-Ashbury for the same reason tens of thousands of other young people had gone there over the course of 1967, drawn by its reputation as a psychedelic paradise. Expecting to find a community of "healthy wonderful enlightened people," George was appalled by the squalor of the street scene, with its collection of "drunks and down-and-outs and spotty little school kids" begging for spare change. It reminded him of the Bowery, he said, "Just 'hey man' for about an hour by all these horrible people." By August of 1967 the San Franciscan strain of urban hippie utopianism had proved a delicate flower indeed. After blooming spectacularly in the spring and sending its spore billowing eastward on gusts of media hype, the scene in the Haight had collapsed in a Malthusian crisis of homelessness, drug crime, and social disease at the height of the Summer of Love. Soon after Harrison's visit, a group of Haight-Ashbury residents would take their cue from the cover of *Sgt. Pepper* and stage a mock funeral marking the "Death of the Hippie" in hopes of reclaiming their vision of the community from what they saw as the corrupting attention of the mass media.

To some extent, George Harrison's reaction to the squalor of Haight Street was simply a reminder of how elevated the Beatles' own standards of comfort and taste had become during the five years they had lived in a celebrity world of suburban mansions, deluxe hotels, doting tailors, and chauffeured limousines. (Even the rock-'n'-roll elite of the Haight-Ashbury looked decidedly "spotty" compared to the dandies of British pop.) But the lesson that Harrison drew from his visit went much further than that. "This was the first thing that turned me off drugs, seeing the Haight-Ashbury," he recalled. "That's when I stopped taking acid and started trying to make up for all those hideous people we'd seen who'd somehow tripped themselves through us." Like other thoughtful people who regarded LSD as more of a spiritual pursuit than a recreational one, Harrison had taken about two years to move from the initial shock of mystical revelation into the advanced stages of psychedelic ennui. "I can't see in retrospect that anything was gained after the first couple of uses," said the beat poet Michael McClure, a founding father of the Haight-Ashbury. "To experience it over and over doesn't seem to lend anything. It's so beautiful, and it promises so much, but there isn't any more that way."

In the waning days of summer, the Beatles embarked on another well-publicized excursion, leaving London by train with their friend Mick Jagger and a herd of reporters in tow. Their destination was the university town of Bangor in northern Wales, where they planned to participate in a three-day retreat sponsored by the British chapter of the Spiritual Regeneration Movement. The SRM was an organization dedicated to promoting the teachings of the Maharishi Mahesh Yogi, a fifty-year-old Hindu swami whose gnomish face was known to millions of London commuters from its presence on posters that papered the (non-metaphorical) Underground. The trip to Bangor was an experiment in spontaneity. It marked the first time since they became famous that the Beatles had traveled anywhere as a group without the logistical support of NEMS, and the results were not encouraging. The journey began with Cynthia Lennon getting left behind on the station platform in a scene out of "Lucy in the Sky"; it ended over dinner at a Chinese restaurant in Bangor with the realization that none of the millionaires present had brought any cash to cover the check.

One of those millionaires, the Maharishi Mahesh Yogi, had come to the Beatles' attention by way of Pattie Harrison, who had taken a course in his technique of Transcendental Meditation a few months earlier. Inspired by Pattie's interest and reports that the Maharishi's visit to Britain in August would mark his final appearance in the West, John, Paul, and George—Ringo being preoccupied with the birth of his second son Jason—attended a lecture by "His Holiness" at the London Hilton Hotel. After the lecture they were introduced to the swami, who turned out to be a good deal wittier, wilier, and more effervescent than they had any reason to expect. The Maharishi, in fact, was a charmer. He spoke in a crisp, high-pitched giggle that sounded precisely like one of Peter Sellers's *Goon Show* Indians, and he showed a keen awareness of what the Beatles' patronage might mean to his Spiritual Regeneration Movement, which claimed to have chapters in thirty-five countries and more than 100,000 adherents. "I believe [the Beatles] will come out with a blowing trumpet of Transcendental Meditation," he told the *Daily Express*. In the private audience that followed his lecture, the Maharishi invited the Beatles to attend the retreat in Bangor as his personal guests, and that was how the four of them happened to be staying in a college dormitory in Wales on the holiday weekend in August when they received a telephone call informing them that Brian Epstein had been found dead in the bedroom of his London home.

"YOU'VE HAD AN immensely successful career, but has there ever been a period in your life when you were filled with despair?" Mike Hennessey of *Melody Maker* had asked Epstein in an interview conducted a month before his death. "There have been many instances throughout my successful, semi-successful, and failure periods," Brian replied with typical candor. "Has any period of despair ever been acute enough for you to contemplate suicide?" "Yes. But I think I've got over that period now." In September, a coroner's inquest, citing Epstein's habitual use of stimulants and sedatives, ruled his death an accident, the result of an "incautious self-overdosage" of sleeping pills, the effects of which were compounded by the presence of alcohol in his blood. By the time this determination was made, however, the circumstances of Epstein's death had been compounded by a different set of factors, including the open secret of his homosexuality and the lurid fascination of the press and the public with the hidden costs of success, to create a strong suspicion that the Beatles' manager had killed himself.

It was apparent to everyone around him that Brian's behavior had grown increasingly furtive and erratic over the course of 1967. One NEMS employee described Epstein's treatment of his staff as "monstrous" during this period; another recalled an endless round of abruptly canceled appointments and unreturned telephone calls. The root causes of this deterioration lay in the loneliness and insecurity that had dogged Epstein throughout his life. But his ability to cope with these chronic sources of unhappiness had been seriously eroded in the year before his death by his addictions to barbiturates and amphetamines, which added a new element of instability and paranoia to his already hypersensitive temperament. According to his assistant Peter Brown, Epstein took an intentional overdose of sleeping pills in the autumn of 1966 during an emotional crisis triggered by worry over the Beatles' decision to stop touring and a blackmail attempt by a young American actor with whom he had become infatuated. His recovery from this episode was facilitated by the enormous amount of Beatles-related business that required his attention during the fall of 1966. By the spring, however, the various deals were done, the Beatles were deeply immersed in the Pepper project, and the tensions with his new partner, Robert Stigwood, were mounting by the day. In May, Epstein consulted a psychiatrist, who diagnosed him as suffering from depression and insomnia and placed him in a sanitarium for several weeks, under heavy sedation, in an effort to cure him of his addiction to pills. Coming on the eve of the release of *Sgt. Pepper,* this breakdown symbolized Epstein's diminishing role in the conduct of the Beatles' affairs. Friends who visited him in the sanitarium were amazed to hear him express doubts about his future as the group's manager.

Revived by his rest cure and thrilled with the success of *Sgt. Pepper,* Epstein spent the summer of 1967 entertaining in style at a newly purchased country house and promoting concerts at the Savile Theatre, where his weekly shows anticipated the formula that Bill Graham would apply with great success at the Fillmore East in New York. It was during this period that Epstein and Paul McCartney began to discuss the formation of a Beatles-owned investment company that would consolidate the group's holdings and provide them with a more comprehensive solution to their tax liabilities. The idea of Apple Corps (as the company would be called) was entirely consistent with Epstein's plan to separate his interest in the Beatles from his interest in NEMS when his contract with the group expired in October 1967. But the subsequent creation of Apple would lead to speculation that the Beatles had been on the verge of disassociating themselves from Epstein at the time of his death—a prospect that, if true, would all but confirm the suspicions of suicide. There is no way of knowing for certain what would have happened had Epstein lived. Yet no one with any knowledge of the situation regarded Brian's occasional doubts about his future as the Beatles' manager to be anything but paranoia. By the time of his *Melody Maker* interview in August of 1967, he felt confident enough to state publicly, "I am certain that they would not agree to be managed by anyone else."

That same month, however, Brian's father, Harry, died suddenly of a heart attack at the age of sixty-three. Devastated by the loss, Queenie

Epstein came to stay with her son in London, while Brian, for her benefit, simulated the life of a conventional businessman: rising in the morning, working all day at the office, and retiring at a reasonable hour after spending the evening at home. To his associates, he seemed delighted with his ability to maintain this unfamiliar routine. Yet, given the extent of his addictions, Epstein would have required prodigious doses of sedatives and stimulants to maintain such regular hours—a consideration that lends credence to the coroner's determination that his death was an accident. He died on the weekend that followed his mother's return to Liverpool. In the summer of *Sgt. Pepper,* it was hard to ignore the parallel with the "lucky man" in "A Day in the Life" whose death was also assumed by many people to have been a suicide, instead of the fatal, banal lapse of attention that the words to the song describe.

"Brian Epstein was essentially a gentleman businessman," read his obituary in the London *Times.* "In all his dealings he was completely honest and trustworthy. By his presence and success in the pop world he not only transformed its power and stature, he made it more respectable." Though the *Times* was known for its generous eulogies, the vast majority of those who had professional dealings with Epstein confirmed these sentiments. "He never took advantage of any relationship that he had established with anyone," said Ron White, an EMI executive who went on to become managing director of the company. "His part in it all has tended to be put down," wrote George Martin, alluding to the posthumous criticism of Epstein concerning the deals he *might* have made. "He was incredibly honest and a little naïve, but he entered a world that was totally alien to him. I don't think the Beatles will ever acknowledge how lucky they were to meet up with a man who was devoted to them so completely and an honest man to boot." As might be expected of the shy impresario who single-handedly brought a sense of English understatement to the world of pop promotion, Epstein's own assessment of his part in the Beatles' success remained circumspect to the end. "Well, they are certainly not where they are today because of me, if that's what you are suggesting," he told Mike Hennessey. "But our good relationship has been a contributing factor. When people ask why the Beatles have been so tremendously successful they always expect one short answer. But there isn't one. There are hundreds of contributing factors."

For John, Paul, George, and Ringo, the death of their manager, mentor, and friend marked the moment when all the latent physical and psychic risk that had shadowed their lives during the preceding five years seemed to compress into a single irreversible event. Their initial reaction to the news came at an impromptu press conference in Bangor, where they emerged from an audience with the Maharishi to deliver a fresh bouquet of platitudes about the ultimate irrelevance of death. They all looked badly shaken, however, and within a few days their façade of cosmic composure had yielded to a more compassionate view. "We loved Brian. He was a generous man. We owe so much to him," Ringo Starr told reporters. To which John Lennon added simply, "He was one of us." Coupled with their grief was a sense of disorientation and fear. "I knew that we were in trouble," Lennon later said. "I didn't really have any misconceptions about our ability to do anything other than play music and I was scared."

40

In all the time he managed them, they never once made
fools of themselves. Since he died, they've done practically nothing else.

—Nik Cohn

On the first of September, four days after Brian Epstein's death,
the Beatles convened at Paul McCartney's house in London to assess
their situation and make some immediate plans. The theme of this meeting was self-reliance, and it emerged in several forms. On the question of
their management, the group agreed that it was futile to think about
finding a replacement for Brian. Instead they decided that they would
henceforth manage themselves, under the umbrella of NEMS for the
time being, but with the clear intention of forging ahead with the formation of Apple Corps. Control of NEMS was now in the hands of Brian's
younger brother, Clive, a stolid Northern businessman whom the Beatles
trusted to look out for their interests and to serve as a check against
Robert Stigwood. By now there was no love lost between Stigwood and
the Beatles. They viewed him as an interloper, and they made it clear to
Clive Epstein that they would not tolerate Stigwood's involvement in
their affairs. Within two months Epstein would negotiate Stigwood's
departure from NEMS.

On the question of what creative activities they should pursue in the
near future, Paul McCartney took the lead. During their weekend in
Bangor the Beatles had impulsively told the press that they would soon
be accompanying the Maharishi to his ashram in India to receive
advanced instruction in the technique of Transcendental Meditation.
McCartney now proposed that they postpone this trip to India and
devote their energies in the weeks ahead to a film project that he had
conceived during a trip to California he had taken the previous spring. In
the course of that visit, Paul had spent some time socializing with members of the Jefferson Airplane and the Grateful Dead, who introduced
him to the rich hippie folklore surrounding the exploits of Ken Kesey, the

Merry Pranksters, and the multicolored, multimedia school bus that had borne them on their epic stoned journey across America in 1964. After hearing the saga of Kesey and the Pranksters, McCartney got to thinking about what fun it would be if the Beatles were to hire a bus, fill it with a film crew and an assortment of zany characters, and set off for points unknown on a "Magical Mystery Tour." What he had in mind was a psychedelicized version of the coach-bus excursions to the seaside that were a popular holiday pastime in the North of England. As Paul conceived it, the Magical Mystery Tour would do for the quaint custom of "chara trips" what *Sgt. Pepper* had done for the hoary tradition of the music hall.

After returning to London in May, McCartney had written and the Beatles had recorded a theme song for this prospective Mystery Tour. Then, amid the excitement surrounding the release of *Sgt. Pepper,* the project was put on hold—until Paul revived it in the service of his belief that work, not meditation, was the best therapy for the Beatles in the wake of Brian Epstein's death. He proposed that they set their sights on producing an hour-long television film that would be ready for broadcast by Christmas. The Beatles would write the script and direct the picture themselves. Paul estimated that the project should take them about a month—two weeks of filming and two weeks of editing—from beginning to end. For music, they already had their theme song, along with "Your Mother Should Know," a campy, music-hall-style number they had recorded over the summer that would serve as a suitable finale for the film. John, Paul, and George would each contribute an additional song to the soundtrack. The rest of the Beatles agreed to postpone their trip to India and proceed with the Mystery Tour. Whatever misgivings John Lennon may have had about the group's ability to do anything besides play music, he kept them to himself.

A pervasive artistic conceit of the 1960s was the belief that anyone with a whit of creativity could make an interesting film. Where filmmaking had once been seen as a costly, complex, and technically forbidding medium, this perception had been transformed by the proliferation of home movie cameras and the vogue among young professional directors for cinema verité. All four of the Beatles owned home movie equipment; Paul McCartney had been so bold as to screen some of his films for Michelangelo Antonioni when the director was in London making *Blow-Up*. The Beatles' principal experience with filmmaking, of course, had come from working with Richard Lester, a director who masked his professionalism behind a deceptively offhanded and spontaneous style. Having proven themselves to be such instinctive masters of the recording process, it was easy for the Beatles to imagine that they might be instinctive filmmakers as well—especially because they were conscious by now of the parallels between working with tape and film. "Making films in sound," was the way George Martin liked to describe their current approach to recording. They expected that *Magical Mystery Tour* would be "just like making a record album," McCartney told the press. "A record is sound and a film is visual, that's the only difference."

The logistical complexity of the project made it a practical test of the Beatles' ability to function in the absence of Brian Epstein and his finicky head for detail. The NEMS office handled the preparations with typical dispatch. In a matter of days the Beatles had assembled a cast and hired a film crew and set out from London in a chartered motor coach emblazoned with the rainbow logo of the Magical Mystery Tour. From that point on, however, the gods of chaos ruled. Having made no effort to keep their trip a secret, the Mystery Tourists were escorted by a flotilla of taxis and private cars filled with reporters and fans, whose presence turned every stop along their route into an immediate traffic jam. Added to this were equipment problems, union problems, and morale problems caused by repeated foul-ups in the accommodations for the cast and the crew. After a week of tooling aimlessly around the countryside west of London, the Beatles decided to take their show off the road and onto a sound stage—only to discover, to their genuine surprise, that it was impossible to book time at a major London film studio on a few days' notice. They wound up shooting the rest of the picture in and around the hangar of an abandoned air base in Kent.

In October, while the Beatles were editing the footage and recording the soundtrack for *Magical Mystery Tour*, Richard Lester's new film *How I Won the War* had its world premiere in London. The picture was greeted with a barrage of bad reviews ("a disgusting example of the nastiness that has recently become part of the nihilism promoted by those films which are put together by Britain's Mod-monsters," raged the critic for *Films in Review*) and expressions of outrage from those who considered the British ordeal in World War II to be a singularly inappropriate subject for a pacifist polemic—especially one produced and directed by an expatriate American whose own wartime experience had consisted of living peacefully as a child in Philadelphia. In the press, Richard Lester and his screenwriter Charles Wood defended their work as an attempt to debunk the movie myth of World War II, citing as their inspiration Joseph Heller's best-selling novel *Catch-22*.

Apart from an occasional tendency to deliver his lines with the triumphant lilt of a Beatle press conference *bon mot,* John Lennon performed credibly in the part of Private Gripweed, a craven orderly who hopes to survive the war by ingratiating himself with his young, homicidally inept commanding officer, Lieutenant Goodbody (played by Michael Crawford). As intended, John's presence was a promotional boon for the film. The advertisements for *How I Won the War* showed the image of Lennon as Gripweed, crouched in a foxhole, his famous face staring grimly out from beneath a camouflage-netted helmet, an Enfield rifle in his hands. Reproduced on the cover of the first issue of *Rolling Stone* magazine and, in poster form, on countless bedroom and dormitory walls, this photograph became an instant icon in the United States, where the incongruous image of a Beatle in a foxhole symbolized the predicament of hundreds of thousands of much less famous young men who found themselves, no less incongruously, fighting for their lives in the jungles of Vietnam. In speaking with the press, Richard Lester made much of his star performer's commitment to the antiwar theme of the film. But Lennon himself refused all requests for interviews and generally steered clear of the controversy surrounding the picture. When Lester was asked to comment on the Beatles' current film project, he offered some prescient advice: "What the Beatles should do is make this glorious, world's most expensive home movie, at the end of which people will say, 'I don't know what the bloody hell it is, but it was quite interesting.'"

The editing of *Magical Mystery Tour* did not take the two weeks Paul McCartney predicted; eleven weeks was more like it, during which the Beatles learned about some of the critical *differences* between tape and film. The editing began as a group effort, but in the end it was Paul who was left to supervise. The musical soundtrack for the show was recorded on the days when the Beatles weren't otherwise engaged in shooting or editing the film. Since the opening and closing numbers had already been completed, the work centered on the three songs that were intended to showcase John, Paul, and George individually. The Beatles also recorded an instrumental called "Flying" (a bluesy nocturne for Mellotron, tape loop, and monks' chorus) and a stirring new song by Paul called "Hello Goodbye." In November, "Hello Goodbye" was paired with John's contribution to the soundtrack, his magnum opus "I Am the Walrus," and issued as the third installment in the trilogy of masterful singles the Beatles recorded in 1967.

The two sides of the new single conformed to the polarized pattern that had applied since "Paperback Writer" and "Rain," with "Hello Goodbye" striving for an almost childish simplicity and "I Am the Walrus" striving for a wizened obscurity. The sheer tunefulness of McCartney's song made it the obvious choice for the A-side, and it sounded good enough on the radio to become one of the Beatles' more durable hits in Britain, where it topped the charts for six weeks (in America for three). Like "Penny Lane," it starts with the sound of Paul's voice, ringing out on the downbeat over crescendoing piano chords and whole notes on the bass: "You say yes, I say no, you say stop, and I say go, go, go." The guitars emit a plaintive, piercing cry, to which Paul responds, "Oh no! You say goodbye, and I say hello." That's the extent of the lyric, but not the extent of the song, which is transformed by the exuberant energy of the Beatles' performance into something much more affecting than it has any reason to be. "Hello Goodbye" almost certainly started off as a potential "plain English" candidate for the Beatles' appearance on the "One World" television show. But in its finished form, with the dualistic lyric serving as a kind of naïve variation on "to be or not to be," and the eschatological question "Why?" echoing eerily through its bridge, the song suggests a response to Brian Epstein's death. The impression that something more is at stake than meets the ear is reinforced by the thunderous coda, a mantra-like chant based on the Polynesian salutation *aloha*. Used as both a greeting and a farewell, the word translates simply as "love."

> Well, they can take them apart. They can take anything apart. I mean I hit it on all levels, you know. I write lyrics that you don't realize what they mean till after. Especially some of the better songs or some of the more flowing ones, like "Walrus." The whole first verse was written without any knowledge.
>
> —John Lennon

The Mellotron introduction signals the link to "Strawberry Fields," but "I Am the Walrus" sounded more like John Lennon's *last* psychedelic will and testament—the song on which he took his quixotic attempt to translate altered states of mind into altered states of music as far as it could go. "The first line was written on one acid trip one weekend, the second line on another acid trip another weekend," John recalled. "I was writing obscurely, à la Dylan, never saying what you mean, but giving the *impression* of something. Where more *or* less can be read into it. It's a good game." The instrumental accompaniment to this game of wordplay consists of keyboard, bass, and drums, supplemented by George Martin's supremely confident arrangement for strings, horns, percussion, and a sixteen-voice chorus of professional jingle singers. John recites the song's three verses against a stringent, plodding backbeat and a monochromatic melody that alternates between a pair of adjoining notes. *"I am he as you are he as you are me and we are all together,"* it begins. The verses that follow present a succession of bizarre, disassociated images that are connected by rhyme, rhythm, and alliteration. At the midpoint of each verse, John interrupts his stream of consciousness to sing the phrase "I'm crying" in a lovely melodic aside. "I am the Eggman, they are the Eggmen, I am the Walrus—Goo goo g'joob!" he proclaims in the four-bar refrain, while the jingle singers shriek and swoon in perfect harmony. A release set in an English garden and a coda containing dubbed-in excerpts from the last act of a BBC radio production of *King Lear* ("Sit you down father, rest you . . .") completes an effect that is by turns ominous, obscure, and absurd.

"I Am the Walrus" was written and recorded at a time when a growing segment of the audience for popular music, having been conditioned by the effects of hallucinogenic drugs, was prepared to be entertained by the radical juxtaposition of words and images that is associated with the aesthetic of surrealism. Most of the pop surrealism of the late 1960s—as found in films, posters, and commercial advertising as well as acid rock—relied on an approach pioneered by painters like René Magritte and Salvador Dalí, who applied a high level of conscious craftsmanship to the representation of fantastic, incongruous, or otherwise dreamlike images. "I Am the Walrus" took the enterprise of pop surrealism a step further. While its musical accompaniment was indeed as carefully crafted as any Beatles recording, its lyrics suggest the technique of "pure psychic automatism" that the surrealist writer André Breton extolled as a way of giving direct expression to the workings of the unconscious mind. At the same time, "I Am the Walrus" was also the most overtly "literary" song the Beatles would ever record. This is not only because it includes dialogue from Shakespeare and a passing reference to Edgar Allan Poe, but more importantly because the key to the unconscious dimension of the song turns on a pair of literary allusions contained in its refrain. For readers of Lewis Carroll, the Walrus and the Eggman are unmistakable characters from the pages of *Through the Looking Glass*. Their incorporation into "I Am the Walrus" leaves little doubt that John Lennon wrote the song as a suitably obscure and fiendishly clever response to the interpretive controversy that had developed around the lyrics to "Lucy in the Sky."

An arch dissembler who preys upon the young by mystifying them with high-sounding rhetorical nonsense, Lewis Carroll's Walrus is one of the great con men in all of children's literature, and John Lennon's forthright identification with him turned this predatory creature into a potent symbol of John's contempt for the Beatles' idealized image as popular heroes of youth. Of course, like any good surrealist, Lennon disavowed all conscious intent. ("I never went into that bit about what [Lewis Carroll] really meant, like people are doing with the Beatles' work," he later said.) But the theme of the use and abuse of language becomes even more explicit in the case of the other Carrollian character with whom he identifies himself in the song. Alice encounters the Eggman, better known as Humpty-Dumpty, sitting alone in the forest, perched on his fateful wall. Their conversation centers directly on the relationship between words and their intended meanings. In Lewis Carroll's version, Humpty-Dumpty's fall is preceded by the pride he takes in his manipulation of language, which prompts him to treat every question as a riddle and every conversation as a game. "When I use a word," he announces, "it means just what I choose it to mean—neither more nor less." "The question is whether you *can* make words mean so many different things," Alice says. "The question is which is to be master—that's all," the Eggman replies. Alice then asks if he can tell her the meaning of the poem "Jabberwocky" that so befuddled her in the opening chapter of *Through the Looking Glass*. "I can explain all the poems that ever were invented," the Eggman boasts, "and a good many that haven't been invented just yet." The explanation that follows is a brilliant parody of literary exegesis, and it serves to demonstrate that Humpty-Dumpty can convince himself of virtually anything—including the safety of his precarious seat atop a wall. ("But if I *did* fall," he assures Alice, "the *king* has *promised* me . . .") Shortly after Alice bids him good-bye and continues on her way, the forest is shaken by the sound of a heavy crash, followed by a stampede of liveried men and horses.

I can't understand their interest in religion, though. That
was the last thing I would have expected.

—Pete Best

With varying degrees of diligence, all four of the Beatles kept up their practice of Transcendental Meditation during the fall of 1967, while their association with the Maharishi Mahesh Yogi became the latest demonstration of their effortless ability to command the attention of the press. From the Maharishi's standpoint, certainly, the effect of the Beatles' involvement on the fortunes of his Spiritual Regeneration Movement was nothing short of phenomenal. Previously, despite a decade of diligent self-promotion and the publication of his teachings in a book called *The Art of Living and the Science of Being,* the Maharishi's existence had gone largely unreported in the press. In the months following his first encounter with the Beatles, this impish, articulate swami became a ubiquitous media presence, first in Britain, then in America, and then throughout the West. As the religious historian Jacob Needleman wrote, "The appearance of this man and his teaching seemed more like the run of a Broadway show than the coming of a new spiritual dispensation."

In 1967 the popular interest in yoga, meditation, and other forms of Eastern spiritual practice was still in its infancy in the West—especially in Britain, which until recently had been much too busy imposing its own ideas of civilization on India to assimilate its culture in any meaningful way. Two centuries of colonial domination had left the English ruling classes with a taste for polo, paisley, and pajamas. It had also fixed the idea of India in the popular imagination as the quintessence of the Mysterious East. But a serious interest in Hindu religion or culture in Britain was largely confined to Oxbridge orientalists, literary intellectuals, and retired colonial officers who had "gone native" in the service of the Raj. During the 1940s, when Aldous Huxley and Christopher Isherwood became formal disciples of the Swami Prabhavananda in Los Angeles, their literary friends in England (who were familiar with Huxley's longstanding *intellectual* interest in mysticism) were openly amazed.

Some of this same amazement greeted the news of the Beatles' affiliation with the Maharishi, which the press in Britain seized on as the feature story of the day. "The much-discussed surrender of John, Paul, George, and Ringo to the soothing influence of the Maharishi Mahesh Yogi makes, in my view, depressing reading," John Mortimer wrote in *The New Statesman*, "not least because the talent of that remarkable quartet appears to be otherwise reaching a new and unexpected peak. . . . The unfortunate Beatles, like many of us, it seems, are in grave danger of coming into contact with the Spirit of Universal Truth, an unhelpful tipple which has in the past turned the great mind of Aldous Huxley to mystical blotting paper." *The Daily Telegraph* characterized the Maharishi's teachings as "preposterous" and "almost puerile." The BBC assigned its commentator Malcolm Muggeridge to debate the swami on the virtues of religious asceticism (Muggeridge was in favor, His Holiness against). The London tabloids reported on the Maharishi's comings and goings with the same incredulity they applied to all the other outlandish personalities and activities of the Underground. Yet, given the intensely xenophobic leanings of the tabloid press in Britain, the overall tone of the newspapers' disapproval was comparatively mild. Some of this reticence could be attributed to the Maharishi's disarming decision to start promoting his technique of Transcendental Meditation as a wholesome alternative and antidote to the current "epidemic" of psychedelic drugs.

The Maharishi himself took his sudden celebrity in stride. Though he dismissed all questions about his personal background as unimportant, a few basic facts were known. His given name was Mahesh Prasad Varma and he was the son of a civil servant, born and raised in the central Indian city of Jabalpur and educated in physics at the University of Allahabad. His spiritual awakening occurred in 1940, when he became a disciple of Swami Brahmananda Saraswati, a revered mystic and Hindu reformer who was known to his followers as Guru Dev. After the death of Guru Dev in 1953, Mahesh struck out on his own, assuming the title of Maharishi ("great sage"). Five years later, frustrated at the slow acceptance of his teachings in India, he formulated a ten-year plan for "the regeneration of the entire world through meditation." The following year he made his first journey to the West, where he established a meditation center in the fertile cultic soil of Los Angeles. Since then he had visited the United States and Europe on an annual basis—lecturing, training initiators, and forming an inner circle of adviser-disciples, several of whom were Westerners with backgrounds in advertising and sales. By 1967 the "practical guidance" of these consultants had helped to turn the Spiritual Regeneration Movement and its campus-based subsidiary, the Students International Meditation Society, into the best-organized and fastest-growing of the half-dozen evangelical Hindu sects that were active in the West.

A key to this success lay with the Maharishi's willingness to meet the West halfway. This began with his desire to "streamline" the ancient practice of meditation and detach it from any overt association with religious observance or faith. SRM literature repeatedly stressed that TM was "not a religion or a philosophy." Building on the teachings of his own Guru Dev, the Maharishi rejected the Hindu precept that the path to enlightenment required the renunciation of worldly ambitions and pleasures. Instead he promoted Transcendental Meditation as "a technique to live a spiritual life in the material world." Like many modern, educated Indians, the Maharishi blamed the Hindu doctrine of world-rejection for the economic and social backwardness of his country. He also downplayed the authoritarian nature of traditional guruism by performing his role with an abundance of *lila* ("playfulness"), dispensing with the usual devotions and austerities required of disciples, and rejecting the very concept of spiritual "surrender" itself.

The actual technique of Transcendental Meditation was described as simple, effortless, and foolproof. In return for a contribution of one week's wages or salary to the local chapter of the SRM, each initiate received a course of personalized instruction during which he or she was assigned a mantra—a phrase upon which to meditate twice a day for twenty minutes at a time. The purpose of this daily routine was to calm the mind to the point where all distraction fell away. TM instructors emphasized that no mental discipline or concentration was involved; on the contrary, the idea was to avoid all effort of any kind, for the underlying principle of the Maharishi's teaching was that "the natural state of man is joy" and that, freed of stress and left to its own devices, the mind would naturally gravitate toward a state of total happiness.

Though the TM technique was simple, the Maharishi's hopes for it were grand. A firm believer in the power of round numbers, his plan called for the establishment of one SRM center for every one million people on earth. Each center would in turn train a thousand initiators, each of whom would initiate a thousand people, thereby spreading

SRM's "one solution to end all suffering" the length and breadth of humankind. Given that every one of these initiates would presumably be contributing one week's salary or wages to their local SRM chapter, the spiritual arithmetic of the enterprise bore a striking similarity to a pyramid scheme, and it was this, combined with the Maharishi's admiration for the "material glories of life," that caused many people to regard him as a simple charlatan.

For their part, the Beatles embraced the Maharishi the way that people had once embraced the Beatles—as something new and strange, foreign yet familiar, provocative yet unthreatening. Reflecting their different temperaments, their involvement with meditation mirrored the pattern of their involvement with LSD. This is to say that George and John were avid converts, Ringo was game if uncommitted, and Paul, though he participated from the beginning this time, tended to hold back. Their respective feelings were reinforced by the women in their lives. As the first member of the Beatles' circle to take the TM training, Pattie Harrison was strongly supportive of George. Cynthia Lennon was similarly enthusiastic, not least because the Maharishi's opposition to drugs had curtailed John's use of LSD, which Cynthia had come to regard as a destructive influence on their marriage. (The Beatles seem to have interpreted the Maharishi's anti-drug stance as applying to psychedelics but not marijuana, which they continued to smoke at will.) Ringo's wife, Maureen, with a new baby on her hands, had little time for meditation, while Jane Asher was suspicious of the Maharishi from the start.

The most visible effect of the Beatles' involvement with the Maharishi was the way it thrust George Harrison into an unfamiliar role as a leader and a spokesman for the group. Ever since his trip to India with Ravi Shankar, Harrison had been looking for ways to extend his fascination with Indian music and culture into the realm of spirituality. Shankar had recommended Paramahansa Yogananda's classic text *The Autobiography of a Yogi,* which served George as an introduction to the basic concepts of Hinduism (and earned Yogananda, along with his guru, his guru's guru, and his guru's guru's guru, a place on the cover of *Sgt. Pepper*). *The Autobiography of a Yogi* is filled with accounts of serendipitous encounters in which spiritual seekers were brought together with their gurus. Harrison seems to have seen the Maharishi's arrival in London in August 1967 as the fulfillment of his and his fellow Beatles' karmically fated destiny. Now, defying his public reputation as the "Quiet Beatle," jealous of his privacy and suspicious of the press, Harrison consented to interview after interview in which he expounded with boundless enthusiasm on his new philosophy of life. As George announced to Michael Thomas of *Holiday,* "There's high, and there's *high,* and to get really high—I mean so high that you can walk on water, *that* high—that's where I'm going. The answer's not pot, but yoga and meditation and working and discipline, working out your karma."

Many of the people who admired the Beatles for the lack of pretension they had brought to their role as public figures found it hard to take these earnest, self-serious pronouncements from a pop star who suddenly seemed to be aspiring to a level of spirituality that verged on saintliness. But if there was something preachy and sanctimonious about Harrison's public embrace of Hinduism (a reminder, perhaps, of why novitiates are often held to vows of silence), there was something affecting about it as well. The sociologist Bernice Martin has suggested that one of the attractions of Eastern religion for "traumatically successful" celebrities like the Beatles "lay in the ability of the oriental monastic tradition to place positive value on their existential condition of anomie," helping them to make sense of "a world from which all limits had been magically removed." From this perspective, it is not hard to understand why a person in George Harrison's position might be drawn to the Hindu concept of *maya,* the belief that "this thing we call reality" is an illusion, or to the spiritual logic of karma, which holds, in essence, that everyone gets precisely what he deserves in his present life as a result of his actions in past lives.

Coming as it did on the heels of his visit to the Haight-Ashbury, Harrison's enthusiasm for Eastern religion also needs to be understood as a way of filling the void created by the psychedelic revelation that "nothing is real." LSD was unequaled for exposing the subjective nature of "everyday waking reality." Yet the drug itself was not a sacrament, and it remained utterly silent on the question of what awareness or wisdom might exist beyond the veil of illusion that could provide a new sense of purpose and meaning to a person's life. Eastern religion, on the other hand, had been wrestling with the concepts of maya and karma since antiquity. As the Indian author Gita Mehta wrote in *Karma Cola,* her wise and witty book on the commercialization of Hinduism in the West: "Alas, the mind can be expanded until it bursts, and when it does there stands an Indian parental type saying, 'Oh yes, this is a common mind-expanding problem, bursting. It has been going on in my country for more than a thousand years. Why not come to my ashram? I will heal your mind if you give me your soul.' "

THE BEATLES' AFFILIATION with the Maharishi came at a time of sharply rising anti-Asian sentiment in Britain, most of it directed at the tens of thousands of Indian and Pakistani immigrants who had entered the country during the 1960s and settled in traditional working-class strongholds like Brixton, Bradford, and Leeds. In the fall of 1967 this infusion of Hindus and Muslims (many of whom came from educated, middle-class families) became the focus of a campaign of thinly veiled racist rhetoric by the Conservative maverick Enoch Powell, who sought to further his political ambitions by drawing large numbers of disaffected working-class voters into the Tory fold. Though Powell was eventually disowned by his party's leadership, opinion polls showed that an over-whelming majority of the British public supported his opposition to racial integration and additional nonwhite immigration. Concurrent with the rise of "Powellism" was the emergence of a new youth subculture com-posed of working-class "skinheads" whose defiantly unfashionable uni-form of close-cropped hair, harnesslike suspenders, and thick-soled boots evoked, more or less consciously, the "proles" in George Orwell's *1984*. The "Paki-bashing" skinheads of the late 1960s were the lineal descen-dants of the Teds who had rioted against the West Indian presence in Notting Hill and Nottingham in 1958. In their current incarnation, how-ever, the skinheads observed a fine distinction between the young, black-skinned West Indians, whose "rude boy" style they emulated and whose ska, reggae, and rock-steady music they appropriated, and the brown-skinned Indians and Pakistanis, whose bourgeois social values and exotic cultural practices they despised. In addition to menacing the Asians who threatened the purity of their neighborhoods, the skinheads also vented their aggression on stray hippies and homosexuals, whose dandified style of dress affronted their standards of masculinity. Whatever else it signi-fied, the association of the Beatles with the Maharishi exposed a widen-ing cultural rift between Britain's most famous working-class youth heroes and a growing contingent of Britain's working-class youth.

42

The closest Western Civilization has come to unity since the Congress of Vienna was the week that Sgt. Pepper album was released. . . . At the time I happened to be driving across the country on Interstate 80. In each city where I stopped for gas or food—Laramie, Ogalalla, Moline, South Bend—the melodies wafted in from some far-off transistor radio or portable hi-fi. It was the most amazing thing I've ever heard. For a brief while the irreparably fragmented consciousness of the West was unified, at least in the minds of the young.

—Langdon Winner

Perhaps the only thing harder than creating a popular masterpiece is creating a successor to one. If nothing else, the rock critic Langdon Winner's world-beating entry into the Pepper Hyperbole Sweepstakes conveys a sense of the sort of millennial expectations that confronted the Beatles as 1967 drew to a close. Anxious to avoid comparisons with *Sgt. Pepper* (which was still ensconced atop the British album charts), the group wanted the soundtrack of *Magical Mystery Tour* to be marketed as just that, a film soundtrack, not "the next Beatle album." EMI obliged them by releasing the six songs from the film in the hybrid format of a double EP, its novelty affirmed by the inclusion of a twenty-four-page souvenir "programme" containing color stills and a storyboard synopsis of the film. In the United States, however, where EPs were an anomaly, Capitol Records received permission to package the soundtrack as a conventional LP, with the songs from the film on one side and the group's recent singles on the other. The front cover of both the EP and LP releases showed the Beatles dressed in animal costumes (Paul as a bull, George as a dog, Ringo as a rooster, and John as a walrus), clustered atop the rainbow logo of the Magical Mystery Tour. With the names of the songs in art-deco lettering amid a border of op-art clouds, the cover had the garish symmetry of a movie poster.

The inclusion of the Beatles' recent singles made Capitol's version of the soundtrack a much more substantial and satisfying product than EMI's. Still, the LP format did invite the very comparison the Beatles had hoped to avoid. With the "Magical Mystery Tour" theme as its fanciful beginning and "I Am the Walrus" as its weighty end, the first side of the album suggested a condensed version of *Sgt. Pepper*. "Roll up! Roll up for the Mystery Tour!" the Beatles announce in stratospheric harmony at the start of the opening track, which takes off to the sound of blaring horns, traffic roar, and lurching shifts in tempo that mimic the feel of a tour bus gearing up and down hills. Conceived as a musical "trailer" for the film, this theme song was a formidable pop production. Yet the satiric theatricality of the singing ("Step right this way!" snaps Paul; "Satisfaction guaranteed!" barks John) generated a strong sense of musical déjà vu. Once again the Beatles were starting a record by spoofing the conventions of "entertainment"—as if "A Day in the Life" hadn't already shaken those conventions to the roots. The feeling of *Pepper* redux was reinforced by the presence of "The Fool on the Hill," another cool, contemplative ballad by Paul that was reminiscent of "Fixing a Hole"; another droning epic by George that recalled "Within You Without You"; and another archaic number called "Your Mother Should Know" that clung to the apron strings of "When I'm Sixty-Four."

"The Fool on the Hill" was the most conventionally appealing of the new tracks. A variation on the theme of "Nowhere Man," the song presents a sympathetic portrait of a Holy Fool who spends his days in a motionless trance, oblivious to the derision and apprehension he inspires in the people around him. Though the words were widely assumed to refer to the Maharishi—a "man of a thousand voices talking perfectly loud" if ever there was one—the song predated the Beatles' involvement with the guru by several months. The track has the standard virtues of a McCartney ballad: a simple and evocative harmonic scheme (the verses are built on a D^6 chord that conveys a Disneyfied sense of wonder, reverting to D minor for the somber, reflective refrain), and a distinctive arrangement in which flutes and harmonicas provide a wistful counterpoint to the shapely, rising melody. Later in the song, a recorder solo answers the line "And the eyes in his head see the world spinning round," lending its shrill voice to the Fool's inner vision.

George Harrison's "Blue Jay Way" is a darkly funny song that inflates a minor social miscue into something that starts to sound like a metaphysical crisis. "There's a fog upon L.A.," George intones over the drone of a Hammond organ, awaiting the arrival of friends who seem to have lost their way. That's the full extent of the situation, but as the song unfolds, its musical textures grow increasingly ominous (George Martin gave it the full "Strawberry Fields" treatment of groaning cellos, moaning voices, and backward tape effects) until the production assumes an overblown, horror-movie quality that is comically out of proportion with the words. In the coda, the phrase "don't be long" is repeated with a shifting emphasis that turns it into a plea for nonattachment—"don't belong"—reviving a play on words that the Beatles had used on the opening track of their second LP.

The production number "Your Mother Should Know," is a halfhearted attempt at satiric nostalgia in the style of "When I'm Sixty-Four." "Let's all get up and dance to a song that was a hit before your mother was born," Paul sings over bittersweet minor chords and a jaunty foxtrot rhythm that shows off Ringo's talent as the leading vaudeville drummer in rock. The premise of the song is that the hit parade has a history that reaches back through the years and across the generations. But this appealing idea was left completely undeveloped in the rush to finish the soundtrack for *Magical Mystery Tour*. The original version, recorded in August, was little more than a demo, with a sketchy lyric consisting of slight variations on the opening line and countless repetitions of the phrase "Your mother should know." In September, after a failed attempt to remake the song as a military march, the Beatles tried to salvage the original version by overdubbing a lush current of backup harmonies and an ecclesiastical organ part that fills the space where a bridge might normally go. While this was sufficient as the accompaniment for the Beatles' song-and-dance number in the film, the song sounds lackluster as an album track.

THE TELEVISION PREMIERE of *Magical Mystery Tour* was scheduled for the evening of Boxing Day in Britain, December 26. In the weeks leading up to the broadcast, the Beatles unveiled the first tangible sign of their new, post-Epstein business plan with the opening of the Apple Boutique on London's Baker Street. The design of the shop and most of its merchandise were the work of The Fool, a trio of Dutch designers who had endeared themselves to the Beatles and a host of other hip Londoners for their flamboyantly multicultural fashion sense. The management of the shop was entrusted to Pete Shotton, John Lennon's old friend from Liverpool, who had spent the past few years running a supermarket that he had purchased with John's help in the Channel coast town of Hayling Island. The upper floors of the boutique contained a suite of offices where Neil Aspinall, the Beatles' former road manager, was charged with laying the groundwork for the creation of Apple Corps.

That same month, it was announced that George Harrison had agreed to write the soundtrack for a film called *Wonderwall,* and Ringo Starr spent a week in Rome, playing a cameo part as a lecherous Mexican gardener in a film based on the Terry Southern–Mason Hoffenberg novel *Candy,* a ribald spoof of *Candide.* Paul McCartney and Jane Asher spent the month of December vacationing at a secluded farm that Paul had recently purchased on the western coast of Scotland. Over Christmas dinner at Jim McCartney's house on the outskirts of Liverpool, Paul and Jane announced their formal engagement. The following day, Paul returned to London to watch the premiere of *Magical Mystery Tour.* By the time of the broadcast, the release of the soundtrack EP had ensured that the songs from the film, the outline of its story, and the script of its narration were already familiar to many of the estimated 20 million viewers who tuned in. This meant that for most Beatle fans the only remaining mystery lay in the visual content of the film. Yet the visual content was severely compromised by one of the many contingencies that the Beatles, in their ignorance, had failed to take into account. At considerable expense, they had shot the film in color, somehow ignoring the fact that color television was still a complete novelty in Britain, where few households owned color sets, and where the only channel equipped to broadcast in color was BBC-2. Since the premiere of *Magical Mystery Tour* was broadcast on BBC-1, what viewers saw was a muted, black-and-white version of a vividly colored film in which many of the more imaginative visual effects were rendered almost indecipherable. A second, color broadcast was scheduled for BBC-2 in January, but by then the verdict was in on *Magical Mystery Tour.*

The *Mirror* called it "chaotic," the *Mail* "a colossal conceit." "I cannot ever remember seeing such blatant rubbish," fumed John Rowland of the *Express,* for whom "the whole boring saga confirmed a long-held suspicion that the Beatles are four rather pleasant young men who have made so much money that they can apparently afford to be contemptuous of the public." "A sort of well-meaning, good-humored anarchy prevails," wrote the *Times*'s Henry Raynor, who added, "I was unfortunate—I lacked the necessary key." The judgment of the critics was all but unanimous, the prime exception being Keith Dewhurst of the *Guardian,* who managed to see the film as "a kind of fantasy morality play about the grossness and warmth and stupidity of the audience whose adoration has set the Beatles free."

Though it conformed to no known category of popular entertainment in existence at the time, *Magical Mystery Tour* is essentially a primitive fifty-minute music video in which mimed performances of songs are interspersed with comic skits, dream sequences, narrative interludes, and a great deal of raw footage showing a group of people getting on, getting off, and riding in a bus. Fifteen years before the advent of MTV, the song sequences serve mainly to demonstrate the trivializing, fish-out-of-water effect of showing rock performers pretending to perform their songs in a non-performance setting. "The Fool on the Hill" is illustrated with over-lush footage of Paul on a hill at sunset, playing the Fool as if the Fool were a model in a fashion ad. "I Am the Walrus" is subjected to a similarly literal treatment, complete with a conga line of shower-capped Eggmen and *Help!*-like shots of the Beatles performing in an open field, with John at a white piano, dressed in his walrus suit. "Blue Jay Way" benefits from some clever trick photography that yields prismatic projections of George yogically floating on air. But the sequence, like the song itself, goes nowhere. "Your Mother Should Know" is staged as a full-dress Busby Berkeley extravaganza, with the Beatles in white tie and tails, descending a celestial stairway into a maelstrom of pirouetting ballroom dancers and crisscrossing ranks of female Air Cadets. The best of the musical numbers involves the Beatles only as spectators: set in a strip joint, it features Neil Innes of the Bonzo Dog Doo-Dah Band (Britain's answer to the Mothers of Invention) as an unctuous Elvis imitator performing a brilliant spoof of rock-'n'-roll necrophilia called "Death Cab for Cutie."

"The criticisms of *Magical Mystery Tour* were as bitter, ignorant, and demented as any I have ever seen," wrote Jonathan Cott, London correspondent for *Rolling Stone.* Fans outside of Britain were quick to attribute the bad reviews to a churlish generational blindness that had nothing to do with the film. Yet even Cott, whose editors dictated a policy of mandatory approval where the Beatles were concerned, was forced to concede that "quite simply, there are too few lovely or magical moments." Like many avowedly "experimental" or "underground" films from the 1960s, *Magical Mystery Tour* was bad in a way that defied critical analysis—so naïvely and amateurishly bad that professional critics took it as an affront to their professionalism and reacted accordingly. One of the most damning insights into the production's avant-garde pretensions came from the critic with the strongest avant-garde credentials, the director Charles Marowitz, who reviewed the film from London for the New York *Village Voice*. "The unconscious 'magical' concept in the picture," Marowitz wrote, "was the Beatles' magical belief that anything they did was bound to come off, because they were the Beatles and, in some magical way, all the usual criteria for artistic achievement would be temporarily in abeyance. If one complains about the film (and one does) it is not because one expected plot, characters, and situation, but because it didn't realize its own surreal potentialities."

Paul McCartney was stunned by the bad reviews of *Magical Mystery Tour*. The project had been his brainchild, and he took its critical rejection as a personal rebuke. ("You're the first person I've talked with who didn't like it," he told a reporter who called him on the morning after the broadcast, betraying the climate of sycophancy in which the film was made.) The night after the broadcast, Paul appeared on *The David Frost Programme*, where he responded to the criticism that the plot of the film was "thin" by assuring Frost that the plot to any future Beatle film would be "very thick" indeed. Otherwise, Paul seemed uncharacteristically defensive, asking, "Was it really so bad compared with the rest of the Christmas TV?" Still, having failed for the first time to exceed the expectations of his audience, it didn't take him long to put that failure in perspective. "We knew we weren't taking time or doing things properly," he told Hunter Davies a few weeks later. "But when you've spent a long time on something, even when it's not good enough, you begin to feel perhaps it's better than you know it is. I'm glad now it was badly received. It would have been bad to have got away with all that." The problem, noted Neil Aspinall, was that "there was nobody to make the artistic and career judgment as to whether it was good or bad, or to decide whether we should go with it or not. I'm sure Brian would have been quite capable of saying, 'Oh, so we blew twenty thousand quid. So what?' "

43

> The hippies were there in great number, perambulating
> down the hill, some were gotten up like Arab sheiks, or in
> Park Avenue doormen's greatcoats, others like Rogers and
> Clark of the West, Wyatt Earp, Kit Carson, Daniel Boone in
> buckskin . . . hippies dressed like Turkish shepherds and
> Roman senators, gurus, and samurai in dirty smocks . . .
> the aesthetic at last was in the politics—the dress ball was
> going into battle.
>
> —Norman Mailer, *Armies of the Night*

On October 21, 1967, while the Beatles were recording "The Fool on the Hill" in the early-morning hours at Abbey Road, fifty thousand protesters were converging on Washington, D.C., to stage a mass demonstration outside the Pentagon, command center of the American military campaign in Vietnam. The events of that day were widely understood to mark a turning point in the course of the antiwar movement in America. At the Pentagon, for the first time at a major peace demonstration, organized groups of protesters sought to breach police lines and actively resist the efforts of federal marshals and military police to arrest them. At the Pentagon, the flags of the National Liberation Front—the Viet Cong—could be seen fluttering over the crowd, symbolizing the growing identification of antiwar activists with Marxist revolutionary movements throughout the world. And at the Pentagon, for the *only* time at a major peace demonstration, a solemn assemblage of poets, musicians, witches, and hippies sought to exorcise the evil spirits from the heart of America's military-industrial complex by chanting incantations designed to lift the five-sided, multimillion-ton structure three hundred feet into the air.

The March on the Pentagon was the high point of the "fusion of hippies and activists" that Michael Rossman had proclaimed in his Yellow

Submarine Manifesto of August 1966. During the winter, spring, and summer of 1967, the two great "tribes" of the counterculture had gathered, intermingled, and communed. From the activists, the hippies gained a sense of social vision that led them to imagine their "psychedelic city states" as models for the way that future generations of chemically enlightened humanity might live. From the hippies, the activists derived a penchant for magical thinking and a hedonistic creed of sex, drugs, and rock 'n' roll that some of them began to construe as a "politics of consciousness." By the fall, however, each of these factions was confronting its own specter of disillusionment. Among the hippies, the quality of life in their fledgling communities was being threatened by the combined forces of drug enforcement and drug crime, while the integrity of their newfound utopian visions was being compromised by the co-optive power of an American consumer economy that had the capacity to turn almost anything, even psychedelic bohemianism, into a mass market phenomenon.

Among the activists, the sense of disillusionment was even more pronounced. The Summer of Love had been nothing of the kind for the residents of Detroit and Newark, cities devastated by the worst race riots in modern American history. The violence in the ghettos gave new impetus to the Black Power movement, whose revolutionary stance and incendiary rhetoric many white activists began to emulate. In the meantime, the leadership of the antiwar movement was faced with the realization that three years of sober, orderly, and largely symbolic protest against the war and the military draft that sustained it had had no tangible effect on American foreign policy. This gave rise to a new spirit of militancy among the more radical factions in the antiwar coalition. Emblemized by the slogan "From Protest to Resistance," the increasingly confrontational attitude of the Students for a Democratic Society and other New Left groups was based on the desperate belief that the only way to stop the war in Vietnam was to disturb the peace at home.

"The plain and obvious fact," wrote the British author Jeff Nuttall in the preface to his book *Bomb Culture,* "is that between the autumn of 1967 . . . and the summer of 1968 . . . young people, under various pretexts, made war on their elders, and their elders made war on them." The rise of an insurrectionary spirit among college-aged and college-educated youth was not confined to the United States. Violent student protest would turn 1968 into a "year of the barricades" in Europe, Latin America, and parts of Asia as well. In Britain and Western Europe, though the Vietnam War was a source of moral outrage, it was never more than a pretext for student revolt. Elsewhere, including Mexico and Czechoslovakia, where student protest movements were most brutally repressed, Vietnam was not a factor. Instead, noted *The Atlantic Monthly*, "The youth of the world almost on signal have found local causes—economic, social, political, academic—to fit an apparently general need to rebel."

In the United States, the outbreak of generational warfare was only one theater of operations in a vortex of turmoil and violence that began with the shock of the Tet Offensive in January 1968 and continued into the spring with the campaigns of two antiwar Senators, Eugene McCarthy and Robert F. Kennedy, for the Democratic presidential nomination, the stunning announcement in March of President Lyndon Johnson's withdrawal from the race, and the assassination in April of the Reverend Martin Luther King Jr., which ignited another convulsion of rioting and arson in cities from coast to coast. Two weeks after the King assassination, a thousand students and their sympathizers occupied several buildings at Columbia University in New York, ransacking offices and establishing "revolutionary communes" to protest the university's ties to the defense industry and its indifference to the needs of the neighboring black community of Harlem. After a week-long siege, the campus was retaken in a nighttime assault by a regiment of riot police. More than seven hundred arrests were made, and more than a hundred protesters were injured. Columbia was only the most spectacular of the scores of demonstrations, strikes, and takeovers that occurred at campuses across America.

These shocks to the American system were felt in Britain as well. With the exception of the London School of Economics, a hotbed of Marxist ideologies that experienced frequent teach-ins and sit-ins from 1965 onward, British universities had remained relatively quiet until 1967, when significant numbers of students (inspired in part by the activism of American exchange students) began to view the Labour government's wholesale support for American foreign policy as a form of British complicity in the Vietnam War. On the day of the Pentagon March in October 1967, members of a group called the Vietnam Solidarity Committee had clashed with police while attempting to deliver an antiwar petition to the American embassy in Grosvenor Square. Six months later, in March 1968, the VSC staged a second demonstration outside the embassy that drew more than 20,000 people, some of whom came with the intent of provoking a confrontation with the police, and a full-scale melee ensued. More than three hundred arrests were made; scores of protesters and police were injured.

The Vietnam Solidarity Committee was a coalition of highly ideological groups, with distinct Maoist, Trotskyite, Anarchist, and Socialist factions, and the party-line nature of their organization ran counter to the laissez-faire sensibility of the Underground. Lacking any personal stake in the Vietnam War, most would-be British radicals extolled the politics of consciousness over the politics of confrontation. The *International Times* responded to the second Grosvenor Square demonstration by publishing an editorial "open letter" accusing the VSC leader Tariq Ali of "playing with fire" by leading young people "into direct confrontation with forces they are not equipped to defend themselves against. . . . It is just insane to pit a band of potentially violent but helpless people against the organized army of the State—the police." And still, for the students who participated in the VSC demonstrations, the drama and shared danger of "direct action" afforded a visceral sense of solidarity and an adrenaline rush of sensation that, for many budding street fighters, resembled the thrill of drugs. Among those present at Grosvenor Square in March was Mick Jagger, who showed up out of a sense of curiosity and captured the mood of the moment perfectly when he told an interviewer afterward that the violence had given him a "buzz."

WITH *MAGICAL MYSTERY TOUR* behind them, the Beatles spent the early winter of 1968 preparing for the trip to India they had postponed in the aftermath of Brian Epstein's death. In the middle of January, George Harrison flew to Bombay, where he spent a week working at the studios of EMI's Indian subsidiary on the soundtrack for *Wonderwall*. The original plan called for Harrison to be joined in India toward the end of the month by the rest of the Beatles and their wives, and for the whole group to proceed to the Maharishi Mahesh Yogi's meditation center in Rishikesh in time for the start of the Guide Course training in February. When the other three Beatles found it impossible to disentangle themselves from their London lives, however, Harrison returned to Britain, and the group wound up spending the first week of February at Abbey

Road, recording several songs for the soundtrack of *Yellow Submarine*, along with a new single scheduled for release while they were away.

The music press in Britain had recently begun to tout the idea of a "rock-'n'-roll revival" as a corrective to the excesses of psychedelia; "Lady Madonna" was the Beatles' endorsement of this incipient trend. The song was based on a barrelhouse piano riff that Paul McCartney retrieved from a Humphrey Lyttleton record (produced by George Martin) called "Bad Penny Blues," which had been a modest hit for Parlophone in 1956. The Beatles updated this riff with fuzz guitars, a saxophone chorus, and sophisticated double-tracked drumming that split the difference between swing and rock by superimposing a snappy straight-time brush beat over a rumbling half-time backbeat. As if to spoof the regressive nature of a "rock-'n'-roll revival," McCartney equipped the song with a lyric cobbled together from a collection of nursery rhymes. With her children at her feet, Lady Madonna sounds like a next-door neighbor to the Old Woman Who Lived in a Shoe, while the release runs through the days of the week in the manner of "Monday's Child." "Thursday night your stockings needed mending," Paul sings, to which a trio of Blind Beatle Mice replies, "See how they run."

A witty, powerful, yet willfully inconsequential track, "Lady Madonna" had all the makings of a classic Beatle B-side, and given the group's on-again, off-again policy of alternating the authorship of singles, the successor to "Hello Goodbye" should rightly have been one of John Lennon's songs. In fact, John had come into the studio with a luminous new ballad called "Across the Universe," which he had written, in part, as a tribute to the Maharishi. (The song's refrain of "Jai Guru Deva Om" was a standard invocation of SRM.) Everyone was taken with the sinuous beauty of the song's melody and its overtly poetic lyric, but John remained dissatisfied with the way the recording turned out. After struggling for several days to find a suitable arrangement—variously adding and subtracting sitar, Mellotron, organ, pedal steel guitar, backward bass and drums, three-part harmonies, and multiple special effects—the Beatles gave up on "Across the Universe," designated "Lady Madonna" as the A-side of the single, and turned for the B-side to a track called "The Inner Light," on which George Harrison came as close as he ever would to achieving the musical synthesis of East and West that had monopolized his creative energies for the past two years. In the end, George accomplished this feat through the simple expedient of going to India to record, for the accompaniment to "The Inner Light" was a by-product of the *Wonderwall* sessions that took place in Bombay in January. Working with Indian studio musicians who were old hands at using traditional instruments in a nontraditional context, Harrison seems to have rediscovered the traditional pop virtues of simplicity, brevity, and clarity. "The Inner Light" is distinguished by a lovely melody and a lyric drawn verbatim from one of the poems in the *Tao Te Ching,* a translation of which had been sent to George by a fan named Juan Mascaró, who was a scholar of Asian languages at Cambridge. In retrospect, Mascaró's selection had a special relevance on the eve of the Beatles' departure for India. "Without going out of my door," the poem begins, "I can know all things on earth / Without looking out of my window / I can know the ways of heaven / For the farther one travels, the less one really knows."

WHILE THE BEATLES were covering their commercial bases in preparation for their upcoming sabbatical from the pop scene, the Maharishi Mahesh Yogi was in New York City on a week-long promotional junket that bore a distinct resemblance to the Beatles' triumphant arrival there in 1964. In the course of this visit (which was organized by the public relations firm of Solters & Sabinson), His Holiness stayed at the Plaza Hotel, lectured at Madison Square Garden, appeared on national television, and bantered in a disarmingly candid and insouciant manner with the New York press. ("People are in poverty because they lack intelligence and because of laziness," the guru noted cheerfully in response to a question about the economic conditions in his homeland. "Transcendental meditation centers will teach them the virtues of selfishness and give them the energy not to be poor anymore.") The official purpose of the trip was the unveiling of the Maharishi's "World Peace Program," a refinement of his original ten-year plan that sought to align the activities of the Spiritual Regeneration Movement with the concerns of the college-age youth who now formed its fastest-growing constituency. Yet it soon became apparent that the Maharishi's idea of a peace movement was something very different from that of most student activists. When asked by reporters about the war in Vietnam, he expressed a complete lack of interest in the political and moral dimensions of the conflict. "Wars,

With the Maharishi, Rishikesh, February 1968

epidemics, famines, and earthquakes are all symptoms of tensions," he explained. By ridding the world of these tensions, the practice of transcendental meditation would "dispel the clouds of war for thousands of years."

Thanks to this prodigious ability to stay "on message," the Maharishi's week-long visit was a promotional boon. In addition to generating profuse coverage in all the New York papers, his presence persuaded the editors of both *Life* and *Look* to feature him prominently in articles on the rising popularity of Eastern spirituality among the young; *Life* went so far as to put His Holiness on its cover and declare 1968 "The Year of the Guru." (It was mainly the underground press, suspicious of the Maharishi's high-powered public relations apparatus and his refusal to speak out against the war, that took a more skeptical view.) At the end of January, in a final flourish of publicity, the Maharishi left New York for India in the company of his newest celebrity-disciple, the starlet Mia Farrow, who had reportedly turned to meditation as a way of coping with the recent breakup of her two-year marriage to Frank Sinatra.

The Beatles joined His Holiness two weeks later, in the middle of February, flying to New Delhi and proceeding from there by taxi to the Maharishi's ashram near the town of Rishikesh, 150 miles northeast of the capital, in the foothills of the Himalayas. "It's as much a holiday as anything," McCartney told reporters as he left London.

Rishikesh (which translates as "Land of the Sages") was an established center of spiritual tourism in India. Many celebrated swamis maintained ashrams in the area, which also supported a large population of the naked, cave-dwelling mendicants Hindus call *sadhus*. The Maharishi's Shankaracharya Meditation Academy occupied a fifteen-acre compound, enclosed by a barbed-wire fence, on a wooded hillside overlooking the fast-flowing Ganges. In addition to the guru's newly built personal residence, the academy provided accommodations for some seventy-five guests, most of whom were housed in simple, well-appointed bungalows.

Nearly all of the Beatles' fellow Guide Course students were well-to-do westerners from North America and Northern Europe, among them Mike Love of the Beach Boys, the folk-rock singer Donovan Leitch, the jazz flutist Paul Horn, and the restless Mia Farrow, who divided her time between the serenity of Rishikesh (where she was joined by her brother and sister) and more secular Indian tourist activities like sunbathing on the resort beaches at Goa. Also on hand was the journalist Lewis Lapham, who was given special access to the ashram in return for his editors' promise of a cover story in *The Saturday Evening Post*.

The stated purpose of the Guide Course was to train the corps of initiators needed to implement SRM's "World Peace Program." The unstated purpose of the course was to provide SRM disciples who had the time, money, and motivation with a chance to immerse themselves in the exoticism of India and the *darshan* (or "aura") of their guru. According to Louis Lapham's published account, the Beatles kept mainly to themselves during their stay at the ashram, attending meals and lectures as a group. Most mornings, they and the other celebrities present were granted a private audience with the Maharishi, who doted on them constantly, to the annoyance of the other disciples. (The Maharishi maintained that they needed the extra attention because they had arrived late for the course.) Evenings they spent in their bungalows, listening to records (it was here that they first heard Bob Dylan's stunning new album, *John Wesley Harding*), smoking pot (notwithstanding the Maharishi's proscription against drugs), and depleting the larder of canned goods and other delicacies that Mal Evans imported each week from New Delhi. Otherwise, John and Paul, joined by their friend Donovan Leitch, passed the time by writing songs. The two of them had not been in such close proximity since the Beatles gave up touring a year and a half before, but few if any of the songs they wrote in India were collaborative efforts. For his part, George Harrison didn't bother to bring a guitar to Rishikesh, though he kept up his practice on the sitar.

Ringo and his wife, Maureen, lasted precisely ten days. He couldn't stomach the food, she couldn't stomach the flies, and they missed their young children at home. "His meditation center is a bit like a Butlin's Holiday Camp," Ringo told reporters upon his return to Britain. Paul McCartney and Jane Asher stuck it out for another month, growing bored with the routine of meditation and uncomfortable with the Maharishi's increasingly high-flown rhetoric. "I get a bit lost in the upper reaches of it," Paul admitted to Lewis Lapham. Adding to his discomfort was the flattery the Maharishi lavished on the Beatles, or "the blessed leaders of the world's youth," as he persisted in calling the group.

The premature departure of their fellow Beatles did not sit well with John and George. In their view, the group's involvement with meditation had fallen into the same pattern as their involvement with LSD, with

Paul and Ringo once again balking on the path to higher consciousness. Though the Spiritual Regeneration Movement was adept at soft-pedaling the cultish aspects of the Maharishi's appeal in its centers around the world, the scene in Rishikesh was another story, and the psychic pressures generated by living for weeks on end in a state of cocoon-like isolation were similar to those of any cult, where one's level of devotion to the leader is held to be the measure of one's well-being. At least some of the Guide Course participants became seriously disassociated as a result of their extended meditations. Mia Farrow's sister Prudence (soon to be immortalized in a Beatle song) seems to have suffered something close to a nervous breakdown during her time at the ashram, staying secluded in her room for days on end, while John Lennon later admitted to feeling "suicidal" for part of the time.

For the two remaining Beatles, these psychic tensions came to a head about three weeks after Paul McCartney's departure, with the arrival of John's friend Alexis Mardas, or "Magic Alex" as he was known, a former television repairman and self-declared electronics expert whom John had summoned from London to keep him company. In no time at all, Mardas initiated a rumor that the Maharishi, who professed to be celibate, had been making advances toward some of the women in the course. This allegation inspired a full-blown crisis of confidence in the minds of John and George, who spent a long night debating the matter before John, on the basis of pure intuition, decided that the rumor must be true. George remained unconvinced, but he was no match for John's certitude. The next morning, without a word of explanation, the two Beatles announced to their mystified spiritual teacher that they and their entourage were leaving immediately. This they did, piling into a fleet of dilapidated taxis for the long drive to New Delhi, during which they indulged in a paranoid fantasy that the Maharishi (like the High Priest in *Help!*) had sent his henchmen after them.

This abrupt and absurd conclusion to the Beatles' stay in Rishikesh was only the final expression of the callowness that had characterized their involvement with the Maharishi at every step of the way—the wonder of it being that it wasn't the banality of his philosophy, or his obvious craving for publicity, or the mercenary practices of his organization, but a childish intrigue involving a rumor of sexual misconduct, that filled their heads with doubt. In any case, the easy indignation with which John responded to Magic Alex's mischief suggests that he was probably looking for a reason to leave. All along, John had been harboring a belief that the Maharishi, at the appropriate moment, was going to reveal the proverbial Answer to him: some jewel of cosmic wisdom that would renew the visionary promise of his early acid trips. But after eight long weeks of dutiful meditation in India, with the heat building and the Guide Course winding down, the most impulsive and impatient member of the Beatles had waited long enough. Like all skilled salesmen, the Maharishi had been selectively forthright in his claims for transcendental meditation. The meditation itself *was* easy. It was the transcendence that came hard.

For George Harrison, the Beatles' experience in Rishikesh left a bitter aftertaste. By the time he returned to London, George was convinced that he and John had been wrong to question the Maharishi's integrity, and angry (not least with himself) at the way the circumstances of their departure seemed to confirm the misgivings that had caused Paul and Ringo to leave early. Though each of the Beatles had gone through periodic bouts of intense interest in various artistic, intellectual, or recreational pursuits, there was no precedent for the sincere and sustained manner in which George had pursued his interest in Indian culture and spirituality. Secure in his own fascination, the youngest member of the group now saw the fickleness with which the others had first embraced and then rejected the Maharishi and his teachings as evidence of a lack of maturity and seriousness on their part. Beyond that, their abandonment of the Maharishi represented the failure of Harrison's principal attempt to assume a leadership role in the group. In the weeks after he returned home, George channeled his frustrations with his bandmates into a new song called "Not Guilty." "Not guilty," he wrote in one of the verses, "for leading you astray on the road to Mandalay."

Though no one could have predicted it at the time, the Beatles' visit to India in the winter of 1968 marked the last occasion on which the four of them would ever travel outside of Britain as a group. As such, their trip to Rishikesh occupies a place in their story analogous to that of their first overseas adventure, their inaugural visit to Hamburg in the fall of 1960. Separated by eight years of once-unimaginable success, these two journeys represented the Beatles' real-life magical mystery tours. On the first, they forged the singular sense of identity and solidarity that would set them apart from all the other musical gangs that haunted the dance halls of Liverpool and catapult them to the attention of fans around world. On the last, they began the painful process by which that singular sense of identity and solidarity, having withstood every form of outside pressure the world could bring to bear, would crack and crumble from within. Though the symbolism and symmetry seem almost too perfect, the mysterious bond that had first been sealed on the stage of a seedy Hamburg nightclub called the Indra would begin to unravel eight years later in the hills of India itself.

> You know, A is for apple, an apple for the teacher, Adam
> and Eve, and apple pie. You can't miss really. I mean you
> don't hate apples anyway. You just hold them in regard,
> even if you don't eat them.
>
> —John Lennon

Having finished with the Maharishi's brand of pop mysticism, the Beatles returned to Britain in the spring of 1968 and plunged headlong into the equally thorny paradoxes of hip capitalism. The basic idea for Apple Corps had been around since the summer of 1967, when Bryce, Hanmer & Co., the accounting firm that represented NEMS, advised Brian Epstein that the most efficient way for the Beatles to shelter their record and film royalties from Britain's onerous personal income tax was by investing those funds in a complex of self-owned companies that would convert personal income into capital gains. Two exploratory divisions of this proposed holding company, Apple Music and Apple Retail, had been operating since the fall. The first was a song publishing company run by Terry Doran, an old friend from Liverpool. Precluded from publishing the Beatles' own music by their contract with Northern Songs, its holdings to date were nominal. Apple Retail, the merchandising division, was responsible for running the boutique on Baker Street, whose finances were already in disarray. Large sums of money had disappeared into the pockets of The Fool, while large quantities of merchandise had disappeared into the pockets of patrons and employees. Just prior to the Beatles' departure for India, Pete Shotton had been relieved as store manager and assigned to a position more suited to his abilities, that of John Lennon's personal assistant. He was replaced by a former NEMS man named John Lyndon, who proved no better than his predecessor at curbing the theft and turning a profit with the store.

By the beginning of April 1968, the structure of Apple Corps was in place and the company had occupied a suite of offices in the center of London, around the corner from EMI's headquarters on Manchester

Square. Neil Aspinall was named managing director, with a pair of former NEMS functionaries, Alistair Taylor and Peter Brown, serving under him. (Taylor had been Brian Epstein's office manager, Brown his personal assistant.) At the Beatles' invitation, Derek Taylor had closed his public relations firm in Hollywood and returned to London to serve as Apple's press officer. Harry Pinsker, a senior member of Bryce, Hanmer & Co., was named as chief financial adviser. A junior Bryce, Hanmer accountant named Stephen Maltz was charged with monitoring the day-to-day operations of the company.

Now, to the existing retail and music publishing divisions were added Apple Records, Apple Films, and Apple Electronics. Apple Records would release recordings by the Beatles and other artists under the auspices of EMI and Capitol; it was headed by a former Liberty Records executive named Ronald Kass. Paul McCartney's prospective brother-in-law, Peter Asher, was hired to serve as the label's head of A&R. Apple Films was headed by Denis O'Dell, a friend of Richard Lester's who had served as associate producer of *A Hard Day's Night* and executive producer of *The Magical Mystery Tour*. O'Dell quickly announced plans for four productions, including a television film based on John Lennon's books and a feature film based on a screenplay by Julio Cortázar, the Spanish writer whose short story had served as the inspiration for *Blow-Up*. Apple Electronics was the sole province of John Lennon's friend Alexis Mardas. Its immediate task was to construct what Lennon described as "one of those massive, big, sort of computerized laboratories they've been trying to invent for years." Mardas would also assist the record division by designing and building a state-of-the-art recording studio in the basement of the five-story Georgian townhouse on Savile Row that Apple had just purchased to serve as its corporate headquarters.

In the middle of May, Lennon, McCartney, and the members of Apple's board of directors flew to New York to present their new company to the world. In their first meeting with reporters since their return from India, the two Beatles began by fielding questions about the Maharishi, who was at that moment touring America with the Beach Boys. "We sort of feel that Maharishi for us was a mistake," Lennon declared. "Meditation we don't think was a mistake. But I think we had a false impression of Maharishi, like people do of us." Turning to the subject of Apple, Lennon and McCartney were suitably vague in their responses to questions about the structure of the company, but expansive about its aims.

"We're in the happy position of not needing any more money," McCartney explained. "So for the first time the bosses aren't in it for the profit. If you come to me and say, 'I've had such and such a dream,' I will say, 'Here's so much money. Go away and do it.' " Paul went on to characterize Apple's business plan as a form of "controlled weirdness, a kind of Western communism." That evening they repeated their pitch for Apple during an appearance on NBC's *Tonight Show*. "We've decided to play businessman for a bit," John told the program's amiable guest host, Joe Garagiola. "So people don't have to go on their knees in an office, you know, begging for a break." Brian Epstein had spent the better part of five years insulating the Beatles from a legion of hustlers and schemers who were eager to exploit their fame; now the two main spokesmen for the group had gone on national television in the United States to announce that they had scads of money to give away to people who had dreams.

Just as millions of teenage girls had fantasized about having a romantic relationship with one or another of the Beatles, by 1968 there were people all over the world who fantasized about having a creative relationship with them. Within days of John and Paul's appeal to the night owls of America, Apple's London offices were deluged with demo tapes, manuscripts, songs, poems, product samples, and hastily improvised grant proposals, all of which were neatly stacked in a back room under the care of the office boy. Other eager applicants simply showed up at the door. "There was a general disposition to be nice to anyone who seemed to be on the trip," recalled Derek Taylor, whose press office served as the reception room for Apple's outreach program. "So if someone came in off the street with an idea and they looked right and felt right and had a nice manner they would get money given to them. It was naïve, it was idealistic, but that's how it was."

Several of the reporters who covered the launch of Apple Corps in New York commented on how poorly John Lennon looked during his visit. ("Too much brown rice at the Maharishi's," one of them surmised.) In fact, Lennon at that moment was in the midst of a personal crisis. Three months after vowing "Nothing's gonna change my world" in the refrain to "Across the Universe," John had set about changing his life with the desperation of a man who feels he has nothing to lose. The agent of this transformation was a thirty-seven-year-old Japanese conceptual artist with whom he had been pursuing an ambiguous yet strangely compelling relationship in the six months prior to his departure for India.

The first casualty of this transformation was his five-year marriage to his wife Cynthia.

Yoko Ono (whose first name translates as "ocean child") was born in Tokyo in 1933, the eldest daughter of a wealthy, Westernized Japanese couple whose marriage effected a merger of two of the country's most prominent commercial families. Her father, Eisuke Ono, was a merchant banker and a member of Japan's small Christian minority. Her mother, the former Isoko Yasuda, was a celebrated Tokyo socialite. Shortly before Yoko's birth, Eisuke was transferred to the San Francisco office of his bank, which meant that he did not actually meet his daughter until 1936, when Yoko accompanied her mother on the first of several extended visits to the United States. Raised by servants on her grandparents' estate, educated at Gakushuin, Tokyo's most exclusive private school, Yoko grew up as a classic poor little rich girl: suffused with wealth and privilege, starved for attention and love. "I was never able to get a hold of my mother without touching her manicure and fur," she later wrote. "My father had a huge desk in front of him that separated us permanently."

During World War II, Eisuke Ono was assigned to his bank's office in Japanese-occupied Hanoi while his wife and three children lived peacefully in Tokyo until the fall of 1944, when the onset of American bombing raids forced them to flee to the countryside. After Japan's surrender, Yoko resumed her studies at Gakushuin, where her classmates now included the Crown Prince Akihito. In 1953, Eisuke was named director of the New York office of the Bank of Tokyo, and the whole Ono family moved to suburban Westchester, where Yoko enrolled at Sarah Lawrence College. There, for next three years, she studied music and writing and steeped herself in the college's *haute* bohemian ambience. In the summer of 1956 she met a young Japanese named Toshi Ichiyanagi, who was studying composition at the Juilliard School; despite the objections of her parents, they were married in the fall. Yoko promptly dropped out of college and moved with Toshi into a loft on Chambers Street in lower Manhattan. In 1958, having completed his studies at Juilliard, Toshi took a course in experimental composition with John Cage at the New School, where he stood out as the only trained musician in a class filled with young painters and poets who were captivated by Cage's Zen-derived theories of artistic indeterminacy. Through Cage—who considered Ichiyanagi to be his prize pupil—Toshi and Yoko became associated with a group of downtown neo-Dadaists that included Alan Kaprow, Robert

Morris, and Jim Dine, all of whom shared an interest in a type of free-form "artist's theater" for which Kaprow had coined the term "happening." In 1960 the Ichiyanagis offered their loft to their friends as a performance space, and several early happenings were staged there. But Yoko's sense of thwarted ambition was taking a toll on their marriage. As she recalled, "It was very hard to make people understand that I was an artist, too. My husband was famous in his own circle, around Juilliard and John Cage and those people. . . . I was having affairs and things like that to compensate, so our relationship deteriorated." Yoko would later attribute her struggle to be taken seriously to the virulent male chauvinism of the New York art scene. But an added problem at this point was that Yoko's art existed mainly in her head. A self-styled "misfit in every medium," she showed no special aptitude for painting, sculpture, or music, and no strong interest in the craft of making art. Instead, Yoko had embraced the Duchampian principle of the artist as thinker, not maker; it was the ideas themselves, not their realization, that mattered most to her. Her most substantial work to date consisted of a series of short, koan-like prose-poems that offered provocative or perplexing suggestions. "Instead of obtaining a mirror, obtain a person. Look into him," read one. "Steal a moon on the water with a bucket. Keep stealing until no moon is seen on the water," read another. She called these pieces "instructionals."

In 1961, Toshi returned to Japan to pursue his musical career. Yoko remained in New York to pursue an affair with a gallery owner named George Maciunas that led to her first show, where she displayed such conceptual oddities as "Painting to Be Stepped On" (a blank scrap of canvas laid on the floor) and "Painting to See the Room Through" (a blank scrap of canvas with a peephole at its center). Later that year, Yoko rented the small recital theater adjoining Carnegie Hall and presented a concert of quasi-musical performance pieces that were heavily influenced by John Cage. Yet neither her gallery show nor her concert elicited much response. Discouraged by her prospects in New York, she decided to rejoin her husband in Tokyo. Toshi welcomed her back, but Yoko's work was rudely received by his fellow avant-gardists in Japan. Devastated by their criticism, she attempted suicide, and spent several months recuperating in a mental hospital. After her release, Yoko and Toshi lived together with a friend of Toshi's from New York, a musician and filmmaker named Tony Cox. This arrangement ended with Yoko becoming pregnant, divorcing Toshi, and marrying Tony Cox. But when her daughter Kyoko was born in the summer of 1963, Yoko felt conflicted about having the child. She quickly initiated another affair with another visiting American, who happened to be her new husband's best friend. Tony returned to New York with Kyoko in the fall of 1964. Yoko followed a few months later, and the couple was reconciled.

Many of the artists Yoko had known from her days on Chambers Street had made a name for themselves during her three-year absence from New York. Jim Dine was now selling his work in uptown galleries; Allan Kaprow was now known as the chief theorist of the "happening"; George Maciunas now presided over Fluxus, a consortium of performance artists with which Yoko became affiliated. In the spring of 1965 she returned to the Carnegie Recital Hall, this time to present a work called "Cut Piece." "Cut Piece" began with Yoko appearing onstage in an evening dress, holding a pair of shears. After enacting a series of ritualistic gestures that suggested to some spectators that she was about to commit hara-kiri, Yoko addressed the audience, inviting them to come up onstage and cut away her dress. Eventually, several of those in attendance overcame their inhibitions and, while the artist knelt impassively, did as they were asked. The performance ended with the severing of Yoko's bra straps, at which point she gasped and covered her breasts with her hands. Though it failed to attract immediate attention, "Cut Piece" became her calling card.

In the meantime, Tony Cox was busy caring for Kyoko and promoting his wife's work. ("I always thought of him as my assistant," Yoko recalled.) During the summer of 1966, thanks to an article Tony had written about her for the English magazine *Art and Artists,* Yoko was invited to participate in a London symposium on the theme of "Destruction in Art." The Coxes arrived in London in September 1966. Yoko performed "Cut Piece" and, for the first time in her career, received enthusiastic reviews. The context clearly helped, since other contributors to the symposium included artists like the English nihilist John Latham, who burned a ten-foot tower of art books outside the British Museum Library, and the Austrian sadist Hermann Nitsch, who staged a ritual sacrifice in which the mutilated carcass of a lamb was paraded around the room. Works like these made "Cut Piece" seem positively genteel, and the London critics, reeling from the smoke and the gore, responded gratefully. "It was impossible to disentangle the compulsion of the audience to cut and Yoko Ono's compulsion to be cut," wrote one. "In cutting off pieces of her clothing, members of the audience show unmistakable signs of artistic striving and she, for her part, is equally unmistakably striving for a kind of nerveless detachment." Among the organizers of the symposium were Barry Miles and John Dunbar, who promptly offered Yoko a show at the Indica Gallery. Heartened by this reception, the Coxes decided to remain in London indefinitely.

First as an artist and later as a celebrity, Yoko Ono would never be shy about straining the credulity of her audience. Yet few things she ever said would inspire such widespread disbelief as her insistence that she didn't know John Lennon from Adam when she was introduced to him by John Dunbar at the preview of her Indica Gallery show. "I didn't know who he was," Yoko later said. "And when I found out, I didn't care. I mean in the art world, a Beatle is—well, you know." Never mind that the Beatles were four of the most famous faces in London, or that their patronage was a cornerstone of the Indica's reputation, or that feigned indifference to the obvious, as epitomized by "Cut Piece," was a theme of Yoko's work. Never mind, for that matter, Allen Kaprow's recollection of a conversation he had with Yoko before she left for London in which she surprised him by expressing a keen interest in the Beatles. As with many of the most brazen prevarications, this one probably sprouted from a tiny seed of truth. At the time of their first meeting, John had just completed his part in *How I Won the War*. His hair was still quite short and he had recently adopted the wire-rimmed spectacles that became his trademark in years to come. The change in his appearance made it quite possible that Yoko didn't recognize him on sight. Once she *did* know who he was, however, it would have been completely out of character for a pair of art-world gypsies like Yoko and Tony Cox to have ignored John's potential as a benefactor. Whatever else he was, even "in the art world," a Beatle was a millionaire.

Yoko's professed ignorance of John's identity was only one aspect of a richly mythologized first encounter that the two of them would eventually reenact in front of movie cameras in 1975. The fact remains that John, if no one else, believed her, and took her apparent indifference as a sign of her integrity. In any case, for a full six months after that first meeting, the link between them lay dormant while Yoko and Tony Cox mounted a relentless campaign of self-promotion. Though the couple was viewed with suspicion in Underground circles (where their New York brand of hustle was felt to be uncool), the mainstream press in Britain found the antics of this eccentric Japanese performance artist with her little-girl voice and her full-grown ego to be richly entertaining. "I was getting very famous," Yoko recalled. "Everything I did was written up, and I was having a kind of love affair with the press. It was really great." In speaking with English journalists, most of whom knew little and cared less about the vagaries of the international avant-garde, Yoko was free to represent herself as a major artist in the United States and Japan. Now it was she who had studied with John Cage; she who had staged the "very first happenings" in their loft on Chambers Street. Her performances at the Carnegie recital theater became her "concerts at Carnegie Hall." So great became the burden of her reputation, Yoko confessed to a reporter, that "I despised myself for being too respected for my work, for being so highly unusual and unique."

Whether she was proposing to wrap a tarpaulin around the lions at the foot of Nelson's Column (after reading a piece about Cristo in *Art and Artists*), presiding over her own personal "Be-In" on Hampstead Heath, or causing a commotion at a psychedelic nightclub with a concert of Cageian "silent songs," Yoko's work in London was anything but unique. Instead, on an even purer level than contemporary art stars like Andy Warhol, she functioned as a true publicity artist, finding her natural medium of expression in the media itself. Her masterpiece in this regard was *Unfinished Film #4,* or *Bottoms* as it came to be known. Shot with the aid of a treadmill, *Bottoms* consisted of several hundred fifteen-second segments, each one showing the tightly framed bare buttocks of a different ambulant individual. The concept originally called for the film to feature the bottoms of people "who represented the London scene," which would have made it a kind of posterior version of David Bailey's *Box of Pin-Ups.* Though nearly all of the representative Londoners Yoko and Tony contacted declined the offer to appear, the invitations alone generated a groundswell of advance publicity for the film. Among those who took the bait was Hunter Davies, who in February 1967 wrote a column in the *Sunday Times* (titled "Oh no, Ono") in which Yoko described *Bottoms* as an act of "social protest . . . it's signing a petition with your behind instead of your signature." When the British Board of Film Censors subsequently gave credence to the protest by banning the film, Yoko became known to the newspaper-reading public as the *"Bottoms* Girl."

The problem for Yoko and Tony was that publicity didn't pay the rent, and by the summer of 1967, the Coxes were deep in debt. It was at this time that Yoko contacted John Lennon directly, sending him a copy of *Grapefruit,* her self-published book of "instructionals," and asking him to underwrite an exhibition of her work at the Lisson Gallery in October. Intrigued by the book, John agreed. Titled "Half Life," the show presented a room full of household furnishings—a bed, a chair, a washbasin, etc.—each of which had been neatly sawed in half and painted white. Also on display were samples of Yoko's "bagwear": large black sacks that were designed to envelop the wearer in a womblike sense of security and well-being. Despite his role as sponsor, Lennon never attended the show.

After "Half Life," Yoko became much bolder in her advances toward John, sending him notes and "instructionals," showing up unannounced at his house, and calling him on the phone. (Cynthia Lennon recalled an evening when Yoko simply hopped into the Lennons' limousine as they were leaving a TM lecture and asked for a ride to her flat.) Increasingly, John encouraged these advances. By February 1968 he was feeling friendly enough toward Yoko to invite her to attend one of the "Lady Madonna" sessions at Abbey Road. During John's two months in India, the tempo of Yoko's correspondence quickened; it was there that he began to feel that he was falling in love with her. While he was away, Yoko scored another publicity coup. Having established herself in New York avant-garde circles as someone who could deliver a convincing aural simulation of an orgasm on demand, she was invited to accompany the jazz saxophonist Ornette Coleman in performing a piece called "Emotion Modulations" at the Royal Albert Hall.

After returning from India in April, John arranged for Cynthia to leave with some friends on a two-week vacation in Greece. He then waited until the very eve of her return before inviting Yoko to visit him in Weybridge. Cynthia Lennon came home the next day to find Yoko wrapped in her bathrobe, sipping tea in the kitchen of her house. Sizing up the situation, Cynthia fled the scene. John brazenly maintained that his relationship with Yoko was purely platonic, but a month later, after a halfhearted attempt at reconciliation, he had Cynthia served with divorce papers accusing *her* of adultery and demanding custody of their son. John moved out of their Weybridge house and into a London flat. Yoko abandoned her husband and daughter and moved in with John. Cynthia hired a lawyer and prepared a countersuit.

John Lennon and Yoko Ono made their first public appearance as a couple in June of 1968, when they arrived arm-in-arm at the National

Theater for the premiere of *In His Own Write,* a one-act play that had been adapted from the material in Lennon's books by the Beatles' friend Victor Spinetti and the American playwright Adrienne Kennedy. The play itself received mixed reviews. But the aesthetic concerns of the critics were completely overshadowed by the prurient concerns of the tabloids, which focused all of their attention on Yoko's appearance with John. "Where's your wife?" reporters shouted at Lennon, who professed to be taken aback at the question. That old standby of the gossip columns, the show-business matrimonial scandal, was one of the few remaining angles on the Beatles' story that had not yet been explored.

45

Well, my version is that I met an interesting guy and we
got together, and suddenly he's got all these in-laws.

—Yoko Ono

For Paul, George, and Ringo, the entry of Yoko Ono into their lives had occurred a few weeks earlier, at the end of May, when the Beatles convened at Abbey Road to begin work on their next LP. In keeping with the band's desire to make themselves at home in the studio, visitors had become more frequent at their recording sessions over the previous year. But while Yoko's mere presence at Abbey Road was not in itself unusual, on this occasion there was nothing mere about Yoko's presence. She sat on a stool at John's right elbow and mirrored his every move. During the intervals when the Beatles weren't actually playing, the two of them, whispering and giggling, withdrew into a private world. As one EMI engineer recalled, she even "went with him to the loo."

At the end of that first long session, a signal event took place. The Beatles had spent nearly twelve hours rehearsing and recording a song called "Revolution" that John had written in response to the recent student uprisings in New York, London, and Paris. On what would prove to be the final take of the night, the band segued from the body of the song into an extended improvisation that eventually degenerated into a maelstrom of guitar feedback, with John repeatedly screaming "all right" at the top of his lungs. At some point during this musical simulation of social chaos, Yoko Ono rose from her seat and did what no visitor to a Beatles recording session had ever done before. Joining John at the microphone, she began to embellish his screams with shrieks and moans and murmured phrases of her own.

Given the charged circumstances, it comes as no surprise that impressions differ concerning the nature of Yoko's reception by the other Beatles. From John's perspective, "Yoko was naïve. She came in and she would expect to perform with them like you would with any group. She was jamming, but there [was] a certain coldness to it." John's account is interesting for its implication that Yoko was indeed some sort of journeyman singer who was accustomed to sitting in with bands. But it is even more interesting for the phrase "a certain coldness," which falls far short of the overt hostility toward Yoko that John would attribute to his band-mates in the years to come. ("A certain coldness" doesn't sound much different from the feeling of exclusion experienced by nearly everyone who ever came into contact with the Beatles as a group.) Yoko herself maintained a firm distinction between the Beatles and their associates in this regard. "I got along with each of them, meaning Paul, George, and Ringo, and none of them was nasty to me. They were pretty civilized about it. But the people around them . . ." she said.

Over time, Yoko's constant and occasionally outspoken presence in the recording studio would unquestionably prompt feelings of annoyance and exasperation on the part of the other Beatles, George Martin, and the staff at Abbey Road. ("Everyone was irritated with her," Martin later said.) At this point, however, all that mattered to the other Beatles was Yoko's monopoly on John's attention and her effect on John's personality. From the start, the insularity of their relationship was remarkable even by the obsessive standards of the newly fallen-in-love: to all outward appearances, they were *never* apart. When Paul McCartney first got together with John in May of 1968 to work on some of the songs they had written in India, Yoko sat in the room with them. After several awkward attempts at collaborating under these conditions, Paul simply backed off.

Beyond the pragmatic problem of John and Yoko's inseparability was Yoko's effect on John's personality, which was like a sudden transfusion of the brash egotism he had managed to suppress over the preceding two years with massive doses of LSD and TM. "I was again becoming as creative and dominant as I had been in the early days, after lying fallow for a couple of years," Lennon recalled. "I was awake again and they weren't used to it." Whether or not the two years during which the Beatles recorded the songs on *Revolver, Sgt. Pepper,* and *Magical Mystery Tour* can plausibly be described as a "fallow" period for Lennon (as opposed, say, to the absolute pinnacle of his career), it was this sudden resurgence of his "dominating" nature that from the spring of 1968 onward transformed relations in the band. To Paul and George especially, John's "awakening" was not unlike that of the classic amnesiac who suddenly comes to his senses and blithely assumes that nothing has changed in the years since he last knew who he was. From their perspective, the John Lennon who awoke in the spring of 1968 was a throwback to the domineering art student of 1960, who had treated their group as an extension of his social circle and therefore assumed that his soul mate Stuart Sutcliffe, though bereft of musical talent, should be taken into the band. Now John had found a new soul mate (one who was also, from their point of view, bereft of musical talent), and he seemed to take it for granted that the creative—and, in due course, commercial—resources of the Beatles should be placed at her command. The big difference between 1960 and 1968, of course, was that the other members of John's group were no longer a gaggle of Liverpool schoolboys, but three of the most accomplished and successful popular musicians in the world.

IN SOME WAYS the Beatles never fully recovered from the shock of that first momentous session at the end of May. In the days that followed, the group repaired to neutral ground, turning their attention to a country song that Ringo had written (or at least had *begun* writing) in 1963 called "Don't Pass Me By." But the tensions in the group were soon played out in a disagreement over "Revolution." John felt that the song made an important political statement and wanted the Beatles to release it as a single right away. Both Paul and George felt that the version they had recorded left something to be desired; they wanted to come up with a better arrangement for the song. Though he eventually deferred to the others and agreed to rerecord the track, John attributed their resistance to personal, not musical, concerns. While this issue simmered, George left on a ten-day trip to California to honor a commitment he had made to appear in a documentary film about Ravi Shankar. Anxious to escape the tensions that were enveloping the band, Ringo accompanied him. During their absence, John and Paul worked in separate studios at Abbey Road: John, together with Yoko, on a collage of tape effects; Paul, by himself, on a haunting acoustic ballad called "Blackbird."

George Harrison's reunion with Ravi Shankar paid an unexpected dividend, stemming from a conversation in which Shankar pressed his most famous pupil about his ambitions on the sitar. After two years of regular practice, during which time he had all but ignored the guitar, Harrison was beginning to realize that the most he could hope to achieve on the sitar was a bare proficiency. Hearing the precocious young students at Shankar's Los Angeles music school confirmed him in this view. Then, on his way home from California, Harrison spent a few days in New York visiting with his friend Eric Clapton, the guitarist in Cream, and Clapton's friend Jimi Hendrix, both of whom were touring the United States with their respective bands. On the basis of his conversations with Shankar, Clapton, and Hendrix, George returned to London resolved to pick up where he had left off on *Revolver,* writing and singing rock songs and playing the electric guitar.

No sooner did he return than Paul McCartney left for Los Angeles to address the sales staff of Capitol Records on the prospects for the new Apple label. When all four Beatles finally reassembled in the studio toward the end of June, John greeted them with a provocatively titled new song "about me and Yoko" called "Everybody's Got Something to Hide Except for Me and My Monkey." (The title was supposedly inspired by some of the hate mail the couple had been receiving.) The Beatles then spent the next two weeks struggling to find a suitable arrangement for an ostensibly carefree song of Paul's called "Ob-La-Di, Ob-La-Da" whose endless, fruitless repetitions drove everyone around the bend. By the middle of July, progress on the album was nearly at a standstill, and the mood in the studio had become so acrimonious that Geoff Emerick, the Beatles' brilliant young engineer, quit after a session in which McCartney and George Martin got into a shouting match after McCartney took exception to Martin's mild critique of his vocal on "Ob-La-Di, Ob-La-Da." "The expletives were really flying," Emerick recalled. "They were falling apart."

BELYING THEIR INNER turmoil, the Beatles appeared to be branching out in all directions during the summer of 1968. The animated film *Yellow Submarine* had its world premiere in London. Apple moved into its handsome new headquarters on Savile Row and closed its boondoggle of a boutique on Baker Street, liquidating the remaining stock in a grand gesture of commercial goodwill by throwing open the doors of the shop and giving it all away. (Cynics pointed out that this was merely an authorized version of what the management had been doing all along.) Paul McCartney had a well-publicized lunch with Lord Poole, chairman of the merchant bank Lazards, to discuss the Beatles' financial situation. "We found Mr. McCartney's whole approach to life very interesting," his lordship told the *Times.* And the Robert Fraser Gallery—recently reopened after Fraser's release from jail—presented an art exhibition by John Lennon titled "You Are Here." The show consisted of a single blank white circular canvas, eight feet in diameter, at the center of which John had scribbled in tiny letters the legend YOU ARE HERE. It hung in a room filled with an assortment of free-standing charity collection boxes (most of them soliciting on behalf of crippled or orphaned children) that Lennon had acquired for the occasion. The show's opening was marked by the release of hundreds of white helium balloons into the sky over London, each balloon carrying a note inviting the recipient to write to John Lennon in care of the Robert Fraser Gallery. Dozens of responses were received; they included an alarming number of obscene and racist remarks directed at Yoko Ono. Simon Taylor of the magazine *Art & Artists* offered a more measured response. Describing the show as "sheer hoko-poko," his review asked Lennon "why a talented composer like yourself should want to waste his time, and ours, in thinking up such self-indulgent and boring gimmickry."

That same summer, Jane Asher revealed during an interview on a pop television program that her engagement to Paul McCartney had broken off. Throughout their five-year run as one of Swinging London's most representative couples, the underlying tensions in their relationship had remained the same. They centered on Paul's misgivings about Jane's commitment to her acting career (including her desire to postpone having children) and Jane's misgivings about Paul's primary ties to the other Beatles. But an additional factor was Paul's promiscuous sex life, about which he managed to be reasonably discreet—if also rather proud. Jane Asher was mistaken if she expected that their formal engagement would cure her fiancé's wandering eye. Their relationship reportedly ended in much the same way that John and Cynthia Lennon's marriage had ended a few months before, with Jane coming home unannounced to find another woman in the house.

> All the great masters have understood that there cannot be great art without the little limited life of the fable, which is always better the simpler it is, and the rich, far-wandering, many-imaged life of the half-seen world beyond it.
>
> —W. B. Yeats

The July premiere of *Yellow Submarine* marked the last gasp of Beatlemania as a public phenomenon in Britain, as thousands of fans brought Piccadilly Circus to a standstill on opening night. At a press conference after the screening, the Beatles were in fine form, cheerfully admitting that, much as they enjoyed the film, they "had nothing to do with it." Strictly speaking, this was true. Their dislike of both the Beatletoon series and its producer, Al Brodax, had caused them to ignore the project until it was nearly done, and it was not until they were shown a rough cut of the film that they agreed to give it their imprimatur by appearing live on camera in a brief epilogue. (The voices of their animated characters were supplied by professional actors.) Yet despite their lack of involvement, the Beatles remained the indispensable element in the film. Not only was the whole production patterned on their personae and inspired by one of their records, but the animation is itself animated by their music; the film comes alive in the songs. There were eleven tunes altogether, including one from *Magical Mystery Tour,* three from *Sgt. Pepper,* two (counting the title track) from *Revolver,* one from *Rubber Soul,* and four tracks that received their debut in the film. These last were all outtakes, recorded over the course of 1967 and early 1968, that had failed to find a place on a single or LP.

Cartoon animation is an even more collaborative and labor-intensive process than conventional filmmaking, and numerous people had a hand in making *Yellow Submarine* a far better picture than Al Brodax and his associates at King Features Syndicate had ever intended it to be. Most of the credit belonged to the film's director, Charles Dunning, and its designer, Heinz Edelmann, whose wildly eclectic artistic imagination became the force behind the film. Most previous efforts at feature-length commercial animation had followed the lead of the Disney Studios by striving for naturalism and stylistic uniformity. Edelmann ignored these conventions in his designs for *Yellow Submarine,* choosing instead to exploit the unique capacity of animation for transforming and juxtaposing visual imagery. The results are almost effortlessly surreal. *Yellow Submarine* is literally swimming with visual quotations, puns, and references to an encyclopedic spectrum of artistic genres and styles: a cartoon history of art and illustration over the preceding hundred years.

Edelmann also made an essential contribution to the story line of the film. The original script, slapped together by Al Brodax and a Hollywood publicist named Lee Mintoff, was little more than an extended Beatletoon. Recognizing that the Beatles needed an antagonist, Edelmann came up with a vision of animated evil, the Blue Meanies, which he then expanded into an entire army of satiric monsters.

Additional credit for the unexpectedly high quality of *Yellow Submarine* belonged, posthumously, to Brian Epstein, who had spent the last few months of his life rejecting the mediocre treatments and screenplays that Al Brodax submitted for his approval. Epstein's intransigence forced Brodax to consult a succession of script doctors, the most influential of whom were the Liverpool poet Roger McGough, who was assigned to give an authentic Scouse flavor to the Beatles' dialogue, and Erich Segal, a young Yale classics professor and budding playwright who was hired to give the screenplay the sort of literary polish that Brodax assumed Brian Epstein was looking for. Bitten by the bug of popular culture, Segal went on to earn fame and fortune as the author of the best-selling novel *Love Story*.

By the time it reached the screen, *Yellow Submarine* had assumed the form of a mock-epic musical fable, set in the pastel paradise of Pepperland, eighty thousand leagues beneath the sea, where life is ruled by an ethos of Beauty, Music, and Love. In the opening scenes of the film, this underwater wonderland is overrun in blitzkrieg fashion by the Blue Meanies, who descend from the hills to enslave the population, silence their music, and banish all joy from the land. The sole survivor of this onslaught is Old Fred, conductor of the national orchestra, Sgt. Pepper's Lonely Hearts Club Band. Making his escape in a yellow submarine, Fred sets sail for Liverpool, where he searches out the Beatles (who bear an uncanny resemblance to the members of his band) and persuades them to return with him to Pepperland. Their voyage back in the submarine (described by Ringo as "a pigment of my imagination") is fraught with adventure. Arriving at last on the silent shores of Pepperland, the Beatles take refuge for the night in a pavilion, where they find the instruments and uniforms of the Lonely Hearts Club Band. At dawn, donning the bandsmen's suits, they strike up the "Sgt. Pepper" theme song, which throws the Blue Meanies into a panic and brings the frozen population of Pepperland surging back to life. The great battle that follows is ultimately decided in single combat between Beatle John, singing a Technicolor version of "All You Need Is Love," and the Meanies' ultimate weapon, the Ferocious Flying Glove, which loses its *G* in the struggle, spelling victory for the forces of Love. The Meanies are routed and renounce their evil ways. Happiness is restored to the people of Pepperland. The film concludes with an appearance by the actual Beatles, who beam madly into the camera and joke lamely about Blue Meanies lurking in the vicinity of the theater.

Despite the Beatles' belief that the press in Britain had soured on them as a result of their involvement with drugs and meditation, the reviews of *Yellow Submarine* were overwhelmingly enthusiastic (apart from a general consensus that the film was overlong). From the tabloids to the trade journals, the picture was praised for its inventiveness and charm and compared to Disney classics like *Fantasia* and *Snow White*. "No feature-length cartoon ever engrossed the ear and eye more harmoniously," declared the congenitally stuffy *Films in Review* (whose critic urged his readers to see the movie more than once, "even if you dislike the whole idea of the Beatles as much as I"). *The Observer* considered it even "more quintessentially Beatle" than their Richard Lester comedies. "A sophisticated work of art for children, and a comic strip for adults, [it is] a constant delight for the eye," concluded the *Daily Express*.

Yet, despite these stirring notices, ticket sales in the weeks following the London premiere fell short of expectations, which caused the film's exhibitors, the Rank Organization, to scale back plans for a general release. Apple Films and United Artists protested this decision vigorously, but Rank was adamant. It had marketed the film as if it were a conventional children's cartoon, timing its release to coincide with the start of the summer school holiday. In place of schoolchildren, however, *Yellow Submarine* was attracting mainly Flower Children, whose presence, especially in the suburban theaters, had the effect of driving the little ones and their parents away. At several London cinemas, Rank replaced the picture with Disney's *Peter Pan*. "At least the children can understand *that*," one theater manager was quoted as saying.

46

They aren't about anything in particular, they're just songs. They're not even particularly connected. We might record all thirty and pick out fourteen, or it could turn out to be two albums or even a three-album pack. We just don't know until we're finished. We're going in with clear heads and hoping for the best.

—Paul McCartney

Throughout the summer, five nights a week, eight to twelve hours a night, the sessions continued at Abbey Road, as the rift between John and the other Beatles broadened into a more generalized mood of frustration and discontent. Toward the end of July, Paul and George got into an argument over George's too-prominent guitar playing on a ballad of Paul's, "Hey Jude." A week later, Harrison retaliated by leading the group through more than a *hundred* desultory takes of his song "Not Guilty." "It was me getting pissed off at Lennon and McCartney for the grief I was catching," he later wrote. "I said I wasn't guilty of getting in the way of their careers." Next, toward the middle of August, after a frustrating session in which he couldn't capture the groove that Paul wanted on a song, Ringo walked out in a huff, feeling unappreciated, vowing to quit the band. Throughout this two-week job action by their drummer, the other Beatles carried on, recording vocal and instrumental overdubs, as well as two new tracks on which McCartney played the drums. No sooner had Ringo returned at the beginning of September than George Martin took off on a vacation he had scheduled months before, leaving a petrified young assistant named Chris Thomas in his stead. (Thomas survived this trial by fire and went on to become one of the top British record producers of the 1970s.)

By now Martin had begun to entertain serious doubts about his future as the Beatles' producer. Slowly but surely, his relationship with the group had deteriorated over the previous year. After the resounding success of *Sgt. Pepper*, he had assumed that the Beatles would be eager to expand upon the lessons they had learned about bringing a sense of form and continuity to their albums. At the start of this latest round of sessions, he had sat down as usual with Lennon and McCartney, listened carefully to the profusion of new songs they had brought back from India, and confessed that he was unimpressed by some of them. He suggested that they start by recording the best of this new material, and then, as they had done on *Sgt. Pepper,* see if they could come up with some kind of organizing theme. Instead the Beatles told Martin that they wanted to record everything they had written, nearly thirty songs. Moreover, they seemed to feel that their next album should be a kind of formal antithesis to *Sgt. Pepper,* on which production and arranging would be downplayed in favor of the sort of raw, unadorned sound that Bob Dylan had used to such startling effect on *John Wesley Harding,* his first new album in a year and a half, whose release in February 1968 had been widely hailed by musicians on both sides of the Atlantic as a much-needed musical antidote to the excesses of acid rock. Underlying these feelings was the Beatles' unspoken resentment at the amount of credit their producer had received for his work on *Sgt. Pepper* and the three astonishing singles they had released in 1967. (*Time*'s reference to "George Martin's new album" had been especially galling to them.) As the sessions dragged on for months, however, with the Beatles effectively rehearsing on tape—recording dozens of takes of each song while they groped for the right feel in the music—Martin grew bored with this back-to-basics approach and dismayed by the band's increasing lack of personal and artistic discipline in the studio.

One of the things that George Martin and the staff at Abbey Road found especially annoying was the Beatles' new practice of interrupting their recording sessions to hold impromptu business meetings at which they would talk, and often argue, about the affairs of Apple Corps. Talk—lubricated by prodigious amounts of drugs and alcohol distributed freely to one and all—remained Apple's principal product during the summer of 1968. While the Beatles poured money into renovating and staffing their new headquarters on Savile Row, in most divisions of the company, the transition from organization to operation had barely begun. At Apple Films, Denis O'Dell was still talking up the same four projects he had announced in the middle of May. At Apple Electronics, Alexis Mardas had already spent thousands of pounds equipping his "massive, sort-of-computerized laboratory." He was now preparing to spend tens of thousands more on the design and construction of the recording studio in the basement at Savile Row. In addition, Mardas had filed dozens of patent applications for inventions that ranged from a home heating and cooling system that ran on ordinary flashlight batteries to a device that made it impossible to tape records off the radio; none of these applications would ever be approved.

Unsurprisingly, the one active and viable division of the company was the record label, which had signed a number of promising artists. These included a journeyman rocker from Liverpool named Jackie Lomax, an unknown American singer-songwriter named James Taylor, and a virginal Welsh folksinger named Mary Hopkins, who had come to Apple's attention as a finalist on the television talent show *Opportunity Knocks*. The label had also signed the estimable American ensemble the Modern Jazz Quartet. In the last week of August, with the release of the first four singles on the Apple label, the Beatles' new company began, for the first time, to make money rather than spend it. Two of these singles, Jackie Lomax's "Sour Milk Sea" (written and produced by George Harrison) and the instrumental "Thingumybob" by the Black Dyke Mills Brass Band (written and produced by Paul McCartney), failed to make the charts. But Mary Hopkins's recording of a wistful Slavic folk tune called "Those Were the Days" (also produced by McCartney) became a major international hit, topping the charts in Britain and rising to number two in the United States, where it was shut out of the number-one spot by the fourth of Apple's inaugural offerings, a new Beatle single that paired the ballad "Hey Jude" with the remake of John Lennon's manifesto, "Revolution." By the end of 1968 the combined sales of "Hey Jude" and "Those Were the Days" totaled 10 million copies worldwide. This made the launch of Apple Records the most commercially spectacular debut of a new label in the history of the recording industry.

The way Paul McCartney told it, "Hey Jude" first occurred to him while he was driving out to Weybridge to visit with Julian Lennon a few weeks after his parents had broken up, with "Jules" becoming "Jude" as the song took shape in his mind. "A bit more country-and-western for me" was Paul's typically unhelpful explanation for why he changed the name. He may have been alluding to the track on *John Wesley Harding* that features a character named Judas Priest, but there's nothing remotely country-and-western about the song McCartney wrote. At the same time, it is hard to imagine that the son of Mary McCartney would have been unaware that in the Roman Catholic church, Jude is the patron saint of lost causes, a connotation that not only fits with the hymnlike feel of the music, but also places the song in the unusual position of offering solace to a saint.

The way John Lennon told it, the first time he heard "Hey Jude," he took it as "Hey John," interpreting some of the lines as Paul's "subconscious" endorsement of his relationship with Yoko Ono. (This also may help to explain why Lennon once described it as the best song McCartney ever wrote.) Yet John was not alone in feeling that the song was speaking to him, for the emotional impact of "Hey Jude" begins with its quality of direct address. Whether or not it is indeed McCartney's best song, it is unquestionably one of his most compelling vocal performances, and when the record was released in August of 1968, it filled the radio airwaves like a benediction for the troubled people of a troubled world.

Indeed, to judge by its sales and its chart performance (including its nine weeks at number one in the United States, or two weeks longer than "I Want to Hold Your Hand"), "Hey Jude" was the most popular single the Beatles would ever release. Its success as a radio song was all the more remarkable for the fact that the record is seven minutes long, with more than half that length taken up by a coda that repeats the same four-bar, three-chord musical phrase upward of eighteen times. Yet so masterful are the pacing and dynamics of the performance that the unprecedented length of the track is hardly noticeable. On its most basic level, "Hey Jude" is a triumph of musical form. It consists of one long crescendo that begins with Paul's solo voice and piano and grows in carefully graduated increments, instrument by instrument, part by part, section by section, into a panoramic arrangement of band and chorus and orchestra that suffuses the track by the end. In its inexorable movement from the personal to the public, the song itself can be said to open its heart to the world.

The lyric to "Hey Jude" has a nice internal rhyme-scheme and a few inspired lines. ("For well you know that it's a fool who plays it cool by making his world a little colder," Paul sings in the first release.) It also contain a number of lines that were originally written as dummy lyrics, including one—"the movement you need is on your shoulder"—that Paul intended to change until John convinced him that this phrase, with its play on the political term "movement" and its wry implication of *Atlas Shrugged*, deserved to stay in the song. But for the most part, the verses are content to restate the theme of forbearance and reassurance in antic-ipation of the point at the start of the coda when the song moves beyond words and enters the realm of pure melodic energy. Cued by a tag of "bet-ter, better, better, better, oh!" that faintly alludes to its forebear on *Sgt. Pepper,* the coda consists of a rising chant of "Nah, nah nah na-na-na-nah, na-na-na-nah, hey Jude" that takes the tiny seed of negation con-tained in the syllable "nah" and turns it, through the force of repetition, into an outsized gesture of affirmation. Though other hit singles (includ-ing Dylan's magisterial "Like a Rolling Stone" and Richard Harris's excru-ciating "MacArthur Park") had lasted nearly as long, none had ever defied its listeners' expectations of finality in the way that this one did. Far from being bored by its seven-minute length, listeners responded to the record as if it cast a spell that they hoped would never end.

On the flip side lay "Revolution," which complements the stately benevolence of "Hey Jude" with an angry musical jolt of retrograde rock 'n' roll. "When I started," John Lennon once said, "rock 'n' roll itself was the basic revolution for people of my age and situation. We needed some-thing loud and clear to break through all the unfeeling and repression that had been coming down on us kids." The pounding beat and heavily distorted guitars of "Revolution" reenact this primitive breakthrough; in a throwback to such violent 1950s classics as "Jailhouse Rock," it was the rawest, angriest track the Beatles would ever release as a single. And yet, though the two songs are musically antithetical, both "Hey Jude" and "Revolution" address the same concern: how best to improve the world? "Open your heart," says "Hey Jude." "Free your mind," says "Revolution." John begins the song by sarcastically acknowledging the desire of every-one, not just self-professed revolutionaries, to change the world. He then proceeds directly to the question of ends and means, singing, "But when you talk about destruction, don't you know that you can count me out." In the verses that follow, he withholds support for people who profess hatred of any kind, and, as the object of a pop personality cult, takes a special delight in skewering the political personality cults that had grown up around such New Left icons as Che Guevara and Chairman Mao.

It is unclear what contact, if any, Lennon and any of the other Beatles might have had with student radicals in Britain and America during the spring of 1968. Though John was still in India at the time of the Grosvenor Square demonstration in March, he and Paul visited New York shortly after the Columbia uprising in April, and radical groups may well have been among those who applied for Apple's philanthropy. But Lennon's skepticism toward student activists went back to his own student days, when he viewed the duffel-coated, trad-jazz-loving supporters of the Committee for Nuclear Disarmament at the Liverpool College of Art as proponents of a competing style of adolescent rebellion that put a sense of moral superiority where its sense of excitement should be.

One thing John need not have worried about was "Revolution" losing its relevance in the six weeks it took for the Beatles to remake and release the record. The May insurrection in France, which paralyzed the country and nearly brought down the government of President Charles De Gaulle, had been followed by violent clashes between police and student demonstrators in cities throughout Europe during the summer of 1968. In Czechoslovakia the social and cultural liberalization symbolized by the "Prague Spring" came to a crushing end in August, when the Soviet Union invaded its Warsaw Pact satellite and reinstituted the repressive policies of the previous hard-line regime. And in the United States, which was still reeling from the assassinations of the Reverend Martin Luther King Jr. and Senator Robert F. Kennedy, the renomination of Richard Nixon and the surging third-party candidacy of the racist firebrand George Wallace, former governor of Alabama, contributed to a widely held perception that the "world's oldest democracy" was coming apart at the seams. In August, at the Democratic Convention in Chicago, the efforts of Jerry Rubin's Yippie (Youth International) Party to mobilize a countercultural army of "Rebels, Youth Spirits, Rock Minstrels, Truth-Seekers, Peacock-Freaks, Poets, Barricade-Jumpers, Lovers, and Artists" to disrupt the convention and protest the nomination of Vice President Hubert Humphrey failed miserably, attracting a mere five thousand demonstrators to the city. But the administration of Mayor Richard Daley, having girded itself for the arrival of up to a million "terrorists," responded to the pinprick provocations of the Yippies with a savage show of force. On the third night of the convention, in full view of television cameras, Chicago policemen removed their badges and name tags and ran riot through the streets and parks of the city, indiscriminately beating and tear-gassing demonstrators, reporters, convention delegates, and anyone else who happened to get in their way. By the time "Revolution" came on the radio at the end of August, the juxtaposed images of Soviet tanks in the streets of Prague and National Guard personnel carriers in the streets of Chicago filled the front pages of newspapers around the world. "Revolution" had been rendered all *too* relevant by the onrushing tide of events.

But in the stunned and bitter aftermath of Chicago, the political wing of the counterculture was scandalized by the song. In America and Britain, student radicals were stung by its sarcasm, its bland assurance that things would be "all right," its failure even to acknowledge the conditions and events that had led them to revolt. Writing in the New Left journal *Ramparts,* Susan Lydon spoke for many of her contemporaries when she accused the Beatles of nothing less than "preaching counter-revolution" to their fans. "To Americans," she wrote, "the defiant spirit of post-Beatles rock 'n' roll seemed so vital, so in tune with what they were feeling, that they wanted desperately to believe it could offer a total world view." But now, Lydon concluded, "it's no longer possible to believe that it's enough just to imitate the buoyant optimism of the Beatles or to live as they do. It is no longer a matter of music but rather one of betrayal."

These views were echoed by other writers in both the mainstream and underground press. "The Beatles have taken refuge in self-righteousness [and] facile optimism," noted Ellen Willis, the newly hired rock critic of *The New Yorker.* "It takes a lot of chutzpah for a multimillionaire to assure the rest of us, 'You know it's gonna be all right.' . . . We may as well face it. Deep within John Lennon there's a fusty old Tory struggling to get out."

Though John Lennon was no stranger to controversy, he was infuriated by the critical response to his song. "You say, 'In order to change the world, we've got to understand what's wrong with the world and then destroy it,'" John wrote in an exchange of letters with a British leftist named John Hoyland that appeared in the radical newspaper *Black Dwarf.* "I'll tell you what's wrong with [the world]. People. So do you want to destroy them?" Compounding John's indignation was the fact that Hoyland and several of the other writers who took the Beatles to task for "Revolution" did so by comparing them, explicitly and unfavorably, to their rivals the Rolling Stones. And the Stones, as if sensing that their star was in the ascendancy, were in the midst of a remarkable musical resurgence in the summer of 1968. With the help of a new American producer named Jimmy Miller, they began their comeback from the artistic nadir of their last album, a woefully misguided imitation of *Sgt. Pepper* called *Their Satanic Majesties' Request,* by releasing a single, "Jumpin'

Jack Flash," that equaled the best of their pre-psychedelic work. They then spent the summer recording an album called *Beggar's Banquet* that confirmed their return to form and included a track called "Street Fighting Man" that celebrated the insurrectionary spirit of 1968. Both John Lennon and Paul McCartney had attended a *Sgt. Pepper*–style listening party for *Beggar's Banquet* in July of 1968, but the release of the album was delayed for months by a dispute between the Stones and Decca Records over the proposed cover art, which consisted of a photograph of a graffitti-strewn restroom wall. In the meantime, Decca's American subsidiary released "Street Fighting Man" as a single in the United States. The record entered the charts in the week of the Democratic Convention and was immediately banned by many Top Forty stations, thereby increasing its cachet on the FM airwaves. For critics and fans who had long seen the Beatles and Stones as the yin and yang of rock, the contrast between "Revolution" and "Street Fighting Man" was stark. The Stones' song, wrote Ellen Willis, "really gets down to the ambiguous relation of rock to rebellion." "The Beatles came late to philosophy," added Susan Lydon. "The Stones, on a very basic level, always had one: sneer, scorn, attack."

47

> We're no better than anyone else. Nobody is. We're all
> the same. We're as good as Beethoven. Everyone's
> the same inside. You need the desire and right
> circumstances, but it's nothing to do with talent, or with
> training or education.
>
> —John Lennon in Hunter Davies's *The Beatles*

In September 1968, the sudden spike of Beatles publicity generated by the popularity of "Hey Jude" and the controversy of "Revolution" was boosted by the publication in Britain and America of Hunter Davies's "authorized biography" of the group. Titled simply *The Beatles,* Davies's book was serialized at length in the *Sunday Times* and *Life* and reviewed in most major literary publications.

If *Yellow Submarine* epitomized the popular perception of the Beatles as modern mythic heroes, Davies's biography expressed the prosaic countermyth to which the group itself subscribed. Drawn from extensive interviews with the principals, their family members, friends, classmates, teachers, and professional associates over the years, the great virtue of the book lay in its concise, anecdotal, and substantially accurate account of the Beatles' individual childhoods and their collective adolescence in Liverpool and Hamburg—a narrative that, for all its minor errors of fact and chronology, has served as the basis for all subsequent biographical writing about the group.

By contrast, the weaker chapters of the book were those dealing with the phenomenon of Beatlemania in Britain and around the world, which Davies dismissed as an incomprehensible and drastically overreported eruption of mass hysteria about which nothing of further interest could possibly be said. In part, this reflected the author's own occupational embarrassment at the excesses of the press. But it also mirrored the view of the Beatles themselves, who turned out to have almost nothing interesting to say about what the experience of mass adulation had meant or felt like to them.

Davies's contract had granted the Beatles and Brian Epstein final approval of the manuscript, and some accommodation and expurgation had occurred as a result. Several direct references to Epstein's homosexuality—which Epstein (to whom the book is dedicated) had sanctioned—were removed at the request of his family. George Harrison asked that more be added about his spiritual beliefs, and Davies (though deeply bored by the subject) had done his best to oblige. John Lennon asked that some unkind remarks he had made about his mother's boyfriend Bobby Dykins be omitted out of concern for the feelings of his half-sisters. John also insisted, to Davies's dismay, that the entire manuscript be shown to his aunt Mimi, who responded by challenging virtually every unhappy or unpleasant memory her nephew had volunteered. Davies was able to placate Mimi by toning down, rather than eliminating, his description of certain events, but the resulting portrait of John's childhood was significantly compromised. (Ironically, it was Lennon who later criticized the book for its lack of candor, though his main objection concerned its failure to report the prodigious amount of casual sex the Beatles had enjoyed on their tours—an omission John seemed to regard as an affront to his reputation as a rock star.)

Still it remained that *The Beatles* was nothing less than the first serious book that had ever been written about a group of rock musicians, and, compared with typical show-business biographies of the period, it gave an exceptionally sober and candid account of the Beatles' lives. If anything, the individual interviews that filled the final chapters of the book were a bit *too* candid in the opinion of several reviewers who found it hard to reconcile their admiration for the Beatles' music with the unflattering portraits of their personalities that emerged. "The overwhelming impression," wrote Philip French in *The New Statesman,* "is that the Beatles are personally rather tiresome and uninteresting, and that what makes them important is the development of their music and the phenomenon of their success, both matters that Davies regards as being outside his brief." Sounding a theme that he would later inflate to pathological proportions in his own biography of John Lennon, Albert Goldman wrote in *Vogue,* "By revealing so candidly the emptiness and banality of the Beatles' lives, this biography, designed to dispel the shadows of mystery, cloaks our most famous musicians in an even darker mystery. How, one asks, have these implacably mediocre youths forged the most compelling symbols of contemporary life?"

That the interviews are banal can hardly be denied. The final third of Davies's biography is yet another installment of "How Does a Beatle Live?" that has been marginally enriched by the participation of the women in their lives. An unavoidable problem was that so much had changed between the time Davies completed his interviews in January 1968 and the appearance of the book in print. John and Cynthia Lennon's marriage, Paul McCartney's relationship with Jane Asher, and the group's involvement with the Maharishi all had come to an end. But the interviews are illuminating, if only for the way they show how much the Beatles, speaking at the height of their post-*Pepper* eminence, privately partook of their own mystique. "The thing is, we're all really the same person," Paul McCartney explains. "We're just parts of the one. We're individuals, but we make up together the Mates, which is one person. If one of us, one side of the Mates, leans over one way we all go with him or we pull him back." "If one experiences something, the others all have to know about it," says Pattie Harrison, picking up the thread. "Even just a mood, they have to rush off and tell each other about it. . . . I didn't realize it when I was first married [but] they all belong to each another. . . . Nobody, not even the wives, can break through it or even comprehend it." When Cynthia Lennon announces that what she would really like is "a holiday on our own . . . just John, Julian, and me," John interjects, "Not even with our Beatle buddies? It's nice to have your mates around." "They seem to need you less than you need them," Cynthia replies.

Philip French's complaint that the book ignored the music was largely justified. Davies did provide an informative, fly-on-the-wall account of the long, ruminative sessions at which several of the tracks on *Sgt. Pepper* were written and recorded. But he was otherwise content merely to note the release of their records in the course of his narrative. Here, too, in his avoidance of musical analysis, he took his cue from the Beatles themselves. "They never discuss or try to evaluate or appreciate their music," Davies wrote. John Lennon's remarks on this subject made for one of the most revealing passages in the book:

> It's nice when people like it, but when they start "appreciating" it, getting great deep things out of it, then it's a lot of shit. It proves what we've always thought about most sorts of so-called art. It's all a lot of shit. We hated all the shit they wrote and talked about

Beethoven and ballet, all kidding themselves it was important. Now it's happening to us. None of it is important. It just takes a few people to get going, and they con themselves into thinking it's important.

We're a con as well. We know we're conning them, because we know people want to be conned. They've given us the freedom to con them. Let's stick that in there, we say, that'll start them puzzling. I'm sure all artists do, when they realize it's a con. I bet Picasso sticks things in. I bet he's been laughing his balls off for the last eighty years. . . . Beethoven was a con, just like we are now. He was just knocking out a bit of work, that was all.

People think the Beatles know what's going on. We don't. We're just doing it. People want to know what the inner meaning of "Mr. Kite" was. There wasn't any. I just did it. I shoved a lot of words together then shoved some noise on.

Lennon's disdain for those who presumed to "appreciate" the Beatles' music recalled the similar attitude he expressed (in Davies's book and elsewhere) for the British jazz scene of the 1950s, with its "rhythm clubs" and "appreciation societies," while his generalized contempt for "so-called art" recalled his resentment of the ambitions and pretensions of his classmates at the Liverpool College of Art. But his philistine bluster about Beethoven "knocking out a bit of work" served mainly to reveal the depth of his insecurity at the fact that the Beatles' music was now being taken so seriously and scrutinized so closely. This was the part of John that had always wanted it both ways: the impressionable teenager whose life had been transformed by the sound of Elvis Presley, and who went on, as a Beatle, to exert a similar influence over the lives of millions of other teenagers, but who still needed to insist that rock 'n' roll was no big thing. It is worth noting that the song John picked to illustrate the lack of "inner meaning" in the Beatles' music, "Being for the Benefit of Mr. Kite!", was a track that had consumed more than thirty hours of studio time, which was about ten times longer than anyone would have even considered devoting to an album track until the Beatles transformed the art of record-making with their own creative ambitions and their obsessive attention to detail. What Lennon had trouble accepting was that, ultimately, he wasn't the one who got to determine the "meaning" of "Mr. Kite," a song sufficiently complex that it has the capacity to mean many different things. For all his intuitive nature, John remained uncomfortable with the intuitive aspect of art. Both as an artist and as a public figure, his ostensibly confessional style masked a desire to retain a tight sense of control over what he revealed about himself. Like Lewis Carroll's "Eggman," he wanted his words to mean just what he chose for them to mean, neither more nor less.

IN BOTH ITS British and American editions, the jacket cover of Hunter Davies's book featured a clever photographic collage in which quadrants of the four Beatles' faces were joined to form a single composite head. In September 1968, another eye-catching photograph began to circulate surreptitiously among journalists in London. This picture—a censored version of which eventually found it way onto the cover of the October 21 edition of *Private Eye*—was a full-length domestic portrait of John Lennon and Yoko Ono, standing in a heap of bedclothes, naked as the day they were born. The couple had taken the picture themselves, using a camera with an automatic shutter; Yoko would later cite this as an illustration of what shy people they were. The photograph was meant to serve as the cover of a forthcoming LP on the Apple label called *Two Virgins*, which John and Yoko had assembled from tapes they made on the night of their first romantic encounter at John's house in Weybridge in the spring.

Yoko maintained that the idea for the cover was John's. But if so, considering the negligible role that nudity had played in the Beatles' work to date, there was every reason to think that John was drawing his inspiration from Yoko, otherwise known as the Bottoms Girl. Until this moment, with the exception of the Fraser Gallery show, the artistic effects of John's involvement with Yoko had been played out behind the scenes. *Two Virgins* thus served as a startling public announcement that theirs was to be a creative collaboration as well as a romantic one. This marked the point where Yoko's exhibitionism—her long-standing desire to call attention to herself by any means necessary—first became imbued with the power of John's fame.

For John, the *Two Virgins* cover was also a way of testing the power of his celebrity, and if he was looking to pick a fight with his record company, EMI was happy to oblige. The company's chairman, Sir Joseph

Lockwood, examined the proposed cover and announced that, Apple or no Apple, EMI and Capitol would have nothing to do with the album. A distribution deal was eventually arranged with a pair of independent labels in Britain and America, both of which packaged the offending cover in a brown paper overwrap. Despite this precaution, at least one imported shipment of the album was seized by U.S. Customs officials and impounded as obscene.

In addition to embarrassing the other Beatles and reinforcing the growing impression on the part of the press and the public that John, under Yoko's influence, seemed to be losing his mind, the flap over the *Two Virgins* album cover had a serious consequence. Sir Joseph Lockwood, it developed, was not the only stodgy corporate type who wanted no part of John and Yoko's latest publicity stunt. Harry Pinsker, the Bryce, Harmer accountant who served as Apple's chief financial adviser, had been appalled for several months at the slipshod manner in which the company was being managed. The *Two Virgins* controversy gave him the out he was looking for. Shortly after the photograph appeared on the cover of *Private Eye,* Pinsker formally severed his relationship with Apple. Within a few weeks his junior colleague, Stephen Maltz, followed suit, resigning in a letter to the Beatles that bluntly summarized their predicament. "After six years' work, for the most part of which you have been at the very top of the musical world . . . what have you got to show for it?" Maltz wrote. "Your personal finances are in a mess. Apple is in a mess." With the resignation of their two accountants, the Beatles and their fledgling company now lacked competent financial management of any kind.

Throughout the summer and into the fall, a similar sense of disorganization and drift had prevailed in the Beatles' musical affairs. Now, confronted by a deadline for fall release, the group scrambled to complete their new (and still untitled) album in a marathon twenty-four-hour mixing and formatting session that ended on October 17. Spurred by George Martin's return and Chris Thomas's continuing participation, the last two weeks of their five-month siege in the studio had been extraordinarily productive, yielding a total of eight new finished tracks. Yet this closing burst of creative energy had done nothing to ease the tensions in the group, for much of the work had been accomplished by individual Beatles working simultaneously in separate studios at Abbey Road. Even before the final mixes were done, Ringo Starr left for Sardinia, where he spent the next few weeks vacationing with his friend Peter Sellers. George Harrison also left early, headed for Los Angeles, where he would spend the next month producing an album by his protégé Jackie Lomax. In his absence, John and Paul churlishly decided to drop "Not Guilty" from the album.

On the day after this final mixing session, the flat where John and Yoko were staying in London was raided by members of the Scotland Yard drugs squad. "Imagine your worst paranoia, because it's here," John told Neil Aspinall over the phone. In fact, the couple had received a tip from a friendly reporter that a raid was possible, and they had spent the previous week disposing of all the drugs they could find. Unbeknownst to the other Beatles, John and Yoko had been taking heroin together for several months. Although the circumstances and extent of their early involvement with the drug remain unclear—Yoko later maintained that they were taking it "in celebration" of themselves as artists—it seems likely that their initiation occurred as a result of their relationship with Robert Fraser, and that it coincided with John's show at the Fraser Gallery in the summer of 1968. As an admitted and convicted heroin user, Fraser was subject to ongoing scrutiny from the police, and it was probably this connection that led them to John and Yoko. As it was, no heroin was found in the raid. But the flat was filled with cartons containing John's possessions from Weybridge, and a thorough search turned up a chunk of hashish that had been packed in a binocular case. Lennon and Ono were arrested, charged with possession of cannabis, and promptly released on bail.

Within days of their arrest, John and Yoko announced that they were expecting a baby, due in February. Expedited by this revelation, Cynthia Lennon's writ for divorce was granted in early November. (Cynthia received an unspectacular settlement of £100,000, along with full custody of Julian, who was provided with a trust fund of £500,000.) Shortly after the divorce was finalized, Yoko entered a London maternity hospital, where, for the next two weeks, doctors monitored her pregnancy. On November 21 she suffered a miscarriage. A few days later John pled guilty to a single count of cannabis possession and paid a modest fine. In return for his guilty plea, the charges against Yoko were dropped, thereby averting the possibility that she could be deported from Britain as an undesirable alien.

All three of the other Beatles had been out of the country at the time of Lennon's arrest. For George Harrison, the six weeks he spent in the

United States during the fall of 1968 represented another enlightening excursion outside the Beatle fold. Assisting him on the Jackie Lomax album were some of the best studio musicians in Los Angeles, who seemed as thrilled to be working with a Beatle as George was to be working with them. The collegial atmosphere that prevailed during these sessions was a far cry from the tension and bickering that had marred the past five months at Abbey Road. After completing his work with Lomax, Harrison accepted an invitation to spend the Thanksgiving holiday with Bob Dylan at his home in Woodstock, New York. There, too, George was impressed by the relaxed and mutually supportive attitude he found among the many resident musicians who were turning the tiny Catskills hamlet into the world's first backwoods pop scene. Harrison was particularly inspired by his contacts with the members of Dylan's former backup group, the Hawks: five bearded musicians of indeterminate age who had spent the two years since Dylan's motorcycle accident holed up in a pink ranch-style house, reinventing themselves as a group of rustic virtuosos called The Band. Their first album, released in the late summer of 1968 under the title *Music From Big Pink,* had astonished musicians on both sides of the Atlantic with its somber timbres, stately tempos, densely conversational singing, and spare instrumental accompaniment. *Big Pink* picked up where *John Wesley Harding* left off in posing a counterweight to the excesses of psychedelia—the Grateful Dead, Jefferson Airplane, Pink Floyd, etc.—and charting a new direction for progressive rock. Among its most fervent admirers was Harrison's friend Eric Clapton, who later cited the album as one of the main reasons he decided to leave the group Cream.

Paul McCartney also paid a fruitful visit to the United States in the fall of 1968. Toward the end of the summer, Paul had contacted an American woman he knew named Linda Eastman and invited her to visit him in London. Linda arrived in September and spent several weeks with Paul at his house in St. John's Wood. As soon as the Beatles completed their album, Paul accompanied her back to New York, where he spent the rest of October staying with Linda and her five-year-old daughter at their apartment on Manhattan's Upper East Side.

Linda Eastman was born in New York in 1943 and raised in the affluent Westchester suburb of Scarsdale. Her mother, Louise, was a department-store heiress from Cleveland. Her father, Lee, was a successful entertainment lawyer, well known in New York legal circles for his autocratic manner and his expertise in the field of copyright law. (The son of Russian Jewish immigrants, he had changed his name from Epstein to Eastman when he graduated from Harvard Law School in 1933.) Doubly endowed with wealth, the Eastmans and their four children lived a cultured, cosmopolitan life. The walls of their homes in Manhattan, Scarsdale, and East Hampton were hung with Matisses and Picassos, along with the work of painters like Robert Rauschenberg and Willem de Kooning, both of whom were clients of Lee's. Linda's older brother, John, attended Stanford and New York University Law School before joining his father's practice (henceforth known as Eastman & Eastman) in 1966. Linda herself was an indifferent student at Scarsdale High School ("Yen for Men" read her yearbook sobriquet). In 1962, during Linda's freshman year at the University of Arizona, her mother was killed when an American Airlines jet crashed into the waters off New York. Lee Eastman soon remarried, and resumed his well-ordered life. Linda was also married shortly after her mother's death, to a geology student named Melvin See, with whom she had a daughter, Heather, born in 1963. But the marriage quickly soured, and in 1965 Linda and her daughter moved back to New York, where she got a job as a receptionist for *Town & Country* magazine. The following year, posing as a photographer, she attended a press reception for the Rolling Stones. After selling some of the pictures she took there, she more or less fell into a career as a pop photographer, relying on her good looks and her undisguised fascination with rock stars to afford her a degree of access to her subjects that more than made up for her lack of professional experience. She first met Paul McCartney in London in 1967, at the listening party heralding the release of *Sgt. Pepper.* They became reacquainted during Paul's trip to New York to announce the formation of Apple Corps.

The two weeks Paul spent with Linda Eastman in New York during the fall of 1968 were a great liberation for him. With his hair slicked back and his face disguised by the scruffy beginnings of a beard, Paul enjoyed an unprecedented taste of freedom, normality, and relative anonymity roaming around the city with Linda, attending clubs and concerts at the Apollo Theater and the Fillmore East. In November, Linda and Heather returned with him to London and took up permanent residence at his house in St. John's Wood.

It is hard to ignore the biographical parallels between the two women John Lennon and Paul McCartney fell in love with in 1968. Both Linda

Eastman and Yoko Ono were foreigners, born to wealth and privilege, who had grown up as the eldest daughters of glamorous mothers and ambitious fathers. Both had entered into ill-fated marriages while still in college; both were the mothers of young daughters; and both had a reputation for being sexually opportunistic in the interests of advancing their careers. Beyond that, however, the similarities between the two women ended. Whereas Yoko's primary identity as an artist had caused her to view every new relationship as an adjunct to her career, Linda had been drawn to photography mainly as a way of making the scene and indulging her yen for men. Whereas Yoko was effectively estranged from her parents and uninvolved with her daughter Kyoko, Linda was close to her family, brimming with maternal instinct, and possessed of a much more emotionally attuned personality. And whereas Yoko, having experienced both mandarin wealth and bohemian poverty, harbored a strong appetite for the sort of luxury a Beatle boyfriend could provide, Linda's tastes, while hardly spartan, were much more down-to-earth. She felt at home in the broken-down palace ambience of McCartney's London townhouse, and she shared Paul's affection for the rustic primitivity of his Scottish farm.

THE COMMERCIAL FAILURE of *Yellow Submarine* in Britain had caused King Features and the film's distributor, United Artists, to delay the American release of the picture until the fall. When the film finally opened in theaters across the country in November 1968, it was an immediate success at the box office, second only to the blockbuster musical *The Sound of Music* in holiday season ticket sales—despite a critical reception that was far more mixed than in Britain. Both *Time* and *Newsweek* soundly panned the picture, with *Time* deciding it was "too square for hippies and too hip for squares" and *Newsweek* describing it as "a huge dismal mess, likely to frustrate Beatle fans and frighten any sensitive child to death." Andrew Sarris of the *Village Voice* was similarly unimpressed, criticizing the visual style as "egregiously eclectic." But other American critics were delighted by the film. "*Yellow Submarine* really fulfills the oft-stated claim—it's for people of all ages," wrote Stanley Kauffman in *The New Republic*. The *New York Times* critic Renata Adler published not one but two reviews in which she praised the film for its visual sophistication and devoted many column inches to cataloging its influences and allusions. Writing in *The New Yorker,* Pauline Kael echoed Andrew Sarris's reservations about the way the animators had "raided" the art of the twentieth century, but confessed that she was nevertheless charmed by the film's "lighthearted, throwaway quality." By December the weight of popular opinion was such that *Time* repeated the critical backflip it had performed with *Sgt. Pepper* and ran a rapturous story about Heinz Edelmann and the "New Magic in Animation."

How to account for the fact that *Yellow Submarine* was so much more popular in the United States than in Britain? As ever, promotion played a part. King Features and United Artists had always considered the United States to be the principal market for the film, and its American release was accompanied by a well-orchestrated publicity and merchandising campaign that flooded stores with Yellow Submarine posters, lunchboxes, sweatshirts, bath toys, and other forms of pop psychedelia that helped draw younger viewers into the orbit of the picture. But the success of the movie in America depended on its appeal to an audience of millions of Beatles fans in their teens and twenties, many of whom, happily stoned, saw it again and again. At least some of this appeal could be attributed to the fact that, by 1968, a great many more young people in America than in Britain really did regard the Beatles as the quasi-mythic figures depicted in the film. The portrayal of John, Paul, George, and Ringo as a quartet of droll, mod, mock-heroic saviors, appearing out of nowhere to free a beleaguered population from the grip of repression and fear—this was precisely the way that many of their fans in America had perceived them all along. And the tragic events of 1968 had only served to renew the charismatic bond that had first linked the Beatles to millions of anxious, rescue-hungry teenagers in the bleak aftermath of John F. Kennedy's death. Now, incredibly, another charismatic Kennedy had been assassinated, together with the living embodiment of America's social conscience, the Reverend Martin Luther King Jr., and with their deaths had died all meaningful hope for the sort of orderly change "within the system" that sympathetic elders had been urging upon the young.

The summer of 1968 had seen the Götterdämmerung of American liberalism in Chicago. The fall had brought the triumph of Richard Nixon—the seminal Kennedy antagonist—who won the presidential election by the narrowest of margins in the first week of November. Young Americans who had identified first with the altruistic rhetoric of the New Frontier and then with the utopian visions of the counterculture could be excused for believing that the Blue Meanies really had taken over. Conceived and written in the midst of the Summer of Love, at a euphoric moment when popular music had truly seemed like a force that was changing the world, *Yellow Submarine* filled American audiences with a yearning for lost innocence that had little resonance for their British counterparts. Where once a shared obsession with the Beatles had revealed a surprising confluence in the sensibilities of British and American teenagers, the different responses to the film now seemed to crystallize the different outlooks and aspirations of young people on opposite sides of the Atlantic. As Nik Cohn wrote of the Beatles in the fall of 1968, "In America and England they have become two entirely different things: in the States, where pop is followed with great solemnity by almost everyone intelligent under the age of thirty, there are still a great many people who take them seriously, who see them as divinities and hang upon their every utterance; in England, where pop remains mostly entertainment, they're seen as cranks, millionaire eccentrics in the grand manner—vaguely regrettable, maybe, but quite harmless."

London, August 1968

48

All you experts listen. None of you can hear. Every track is an individual track; there isn't any Beatle music on it. [It's] John and the band, Paul and the band, George and the band, like that.

—John Lennon

"We tell ourselves stories in order to live," Joan Didion writes at the start of *The White Album,* her acclaimed collection of essays and articles dating from and relating to the end of the 1960s,

> Or at least we do for a while. I am talking here about a time when I began to doubt the premises of all the stories I had ever told myself, a common condition but one I found troubling. . . . I was supposed to have a script, and had mislaid it. I was supposed to hear cues, and no longer did. I was meant to know the plot, but all I knew was what I saw: flash pictures in variable sequence, images with no "meaning" beyond their temporary arrangement, not a movie but a cutting-room experience. . . . I wanted still to believe in the narrative and in the narrative's intelligibility, but to know that one could change the sense with every cut was to begin to perceive the experience as rather more electrical than ethical.

Didion wrote these words to describe a nervous breakdown, signaled by an attack of vertigo and nausea, that she suffered during the summer of 1968. But her tactic as a writer was to make an example of herself ("I offer only that an attack of vertigo and nausea does not now seem to me an inappropriate response to the summer of 1968"), and this elegiac opening was meant to convey the fractured feeling of American life in the midst of that extraordinary year. Music criticism, it can safely be said, was one of the last things on Didion's mind. Yet her description of "flash pictures in variable sequence, images with no 'meaning' beyond their temporary arrangement, not a movie but a cutting-room experience," can hardly be improved upon as a critical insight into the sprawling collection of songs the Beatles released in November 1968 on the double album from which Didion derived the title of her book.

The defining feature of the White Album (as fans dubbed the new release) concerned the way this two-record set stubbornly defied the expectations of "script," "plot," and "narrative" that the Beatles had introduced to rock on *Sgt. Pepper's Lonely Hearts Club Band*. This absence of any narrative structure was especially pronounced for coming at a time when the Beatles' own story, as chronicled by Hunter Davies and mythologized by the makers of *Yellow Submarine*, had reached a new peak of "intelligibility" in the public mind. Long before *Sgt. Pepper*, pop fans had begun to anticipate the "next" Beatles album as the next step in a musical progression that linked the past to the present and pointed the way to the future—just as the changes in how the Beatles themselves looked from one album to the next affirmed a sense of personal transformation in their listeners' lives. "Can the Beatles continue to revitalize all our music in the manner in which they have so far succeeded?" the rock critic John Szwed had written earlier in 1968. "I don't really know. But in all this there is the scary feeling that if the Beatles ever stop making music, we'll all be spiritually dead." The long-awaited release of the White Album, eighteen months after the release of *Sgt. Pepper*, dispelled any fears that the Beatles might stop making music. But buried in the grooves of the new record was ample evidence that, like Joan Didion, the authors of this collection had experienced a breakdown during the summer of 1968 that caused them to doubt the premise of the story they had lived.

The official name of the album was simply *The Beatles*—a default title so uninspired that it was simply ignored by the fans, who renamed the two-record set after the design of its gatefold sleeve. This startlingly unconventional record jacket was conceived, like so much else on the White Album, in direct contrast to *Sgt. Pepper*. In place of the pomp and circumstance of Peter Blake's conclave of cult heroes, the album cover presented a face of perfect blankness—"like a printing error," wrote one reviewer—its square, white surface disturbed only by the name of the group, embossed in small raised lettering near the center, and an eight-digit serial number, stamped at an angle (as if by hand), which seemed to suggest that the album was being issued in a special limited edition of ten million copies or so. The creator of this clever commentary on the work of art in the age of mechanical reproduction was another of the founding fathers of Pop Art in Britain, Richard Hamilton, who, like Peter Blake, had been recommended to the Beatles by his dealer, Robert Fraser. An austerely intellectual artist, Hamilton sought "to avoid competing with the lavish design treatments of most jackets" (in other words, with Blake) by creating a cover "so pure and reticent that it would seem to place it in the context of the most esoteric art publications." His design recalled the empty white canvases with which Robert Rauschenberg had affronted the New York art world in the 1950s and the all-white paintings Bernard Cohen had exhibited in London in 1967. Yet perhaps the strongest and most telling metaphor suggested by Hamilton's cover was that of a clean slate.

The back of the album jacket was left entirely blank, while the inside panels of the gatefold sleeve contained only a listing of the song titles and a small black-and-white photograph of each Beatle. Continuing in the tradition of *Sgt. Pepper* and *Magical Mystery Tour,* souvenirs were included in the package: glossy, eight-by-ten color enlargements of the individual portraits on the record jacket and a poster-sized collage composed of snapshots and contact strips spanning the Beatles' career from Hamburg to the present day. There were pictures of John in bed with Yoko, Ringo dancing with Elizabeth Taylor, George seated at the feet of the Maharishi, and Paul, of all people, in the nude, bisected by a pillar that preserved his modesty. Printed on the back of this poster were the lyrics to all the songs.

The four sides of the White Album contained a total of thirty tracks, or more than twice as many as on any previous Beatle album. Of the twenty-five tracks jointly credited to Lennon and McCartney, twelve were primarily written by John, twelve by Paul, and one, the tape collage called "Revolution 9," was a collaboration between John and Yoko Ono. Of the five remaining tracks, four were written by George and one by Ringo, who also sings the finale, "Good Night," a lullaby written by John. In the manner of *Revolver,* nearly every song on the record has a distinct lead singer, and in every case except "Good Night" it is the Beatle who wrote the song.

The sequencing of the tracks on the White Album has none of the formal organization that characterized *Revolver* and *Sgt. Pepper.* There is little sense of beginning, middle, and end, much less of climax or resolution. While the album contains its share of excellent songs, it contains no one track that has the musical or emotional impact of "Eleanor Rigby,"

"Tomorrow Never Knows," "She's Leaving Home," or "A Day in the Life." (The only song the Beatles recorded during 1968 that belonged in that category was "Hey Jude.") A number of the tracks on all four sides segue smoothly from one to the next (some without missing a beat), and there are several overt jokes of programming, like the juxtaposition of McCartney's down-and-dirty rocker "Why Don't We Do It in the Road" with his romantic ballad "I Will," or the cluster of songs on side two whose titles—"Blackbird," "Piggies," and "Rocky Raccoon"—all refer to animals. By and large, however, the order of the songs was determined by political rather than aesthetic or thematic concerns: no more than two songs by the same singer in a row; one song by George Harrison on each of the four sides, one song sung by Ringo Starr on each of the two records. Combined with the clear lines of authorship, this strict apportionment of tracks suggests the extent to which the White Album was more of a negotiation than a collaboration.

In years to come, John Lennon would positively gloat over the lack of collaboration that went into songs on the White Album, citing this as the quality that caused him to prefer the record to other Beatle albums on which he felt his own contributions could be confused with those of the other three. Lennon was notorious for his revisionist exaggerations about the Beatles' music, but his characterization of the White Album was apt: the lack of collaboration was a defining feature of the songs. At some point during the eighteen months since the collective peak of *Sgt. Pepper,* rock's most remarkable and resilient songwriting partnership had fallen apart. It is customary to date this dissolution from the start of John's relationship with Yoko Ono. But a shift had begun even earlier, as evidenced by the non-collaborative nature of the songs that John and Paul had written in India. In fact, from the end of 1966 onward, with the notable exception of "A Day in the Life," the preponderance of songs on which Lennon and McCartney collaborated most actively (a list of titles that includes "Penny Lane," "A Little Help From My Friends," "Getting Better," "She's Leaving Home," and "Magical Mystery Tour") were songs initiated by Paul. It was this pattern of McCartney soliciting Lennon's involvement that ended abruptly with the arrival of Yoko Ono on the scene. From then on, John and Yoko were together day and night, and because Paul (like everyone else in the Beatles' circle) found the couple's preoccupation with each other to be completely impenetrable, there was no opportunity for him to continue writing with John in the intensive yet informal manner they had perfected over more than a decade of musical friendship. Previously, whether or not they were actively collaborating on a particular song, John and Paul had always served as the primary audience for each other's work. In Yoko, John had found a new sounding board, after which he appeared to lose all interest in Paul's opinion or critique of his songs.

The difference, of course, was that John's new sounding board knew little about music in general and less about rock 'n' roll. Childhood piano lessons had left Yoko with the ability to play a number of classical set pieces, but apart from her orgasmic vocalizing, the musical component of her artistic career had consisted of a handful of quasi-Cagean performance pieces that demonstrated the same disregard for artistic craft as had the work in her gallery shows. Nor was Yoko in any position to be candid with John about his songwriting. As a pair of especially insecure artists united in the first flush of love, John and Yoko tended to function as a mutual admiration society, with each regarding whatever the other did as too marvelous for words. Paul McCartney, by contrast, had been assuaging his partner's insecurities, encouraging his partner's inspirations, and reining in his partner's excesses for many years. Left to his own devices, John tended to write in what he called "bits": short musical phrases that he would play over and over to himself, searching out chords and lyrics, which he would then string together to form verses, choruses, and releases. Because he tended to develop the structure of his songs so empirically, he often got stuck for a line or a chord, and he had particular difficulty coming up with middles and endings. Paul was adept at hearing the musical possibilities suggested by John's bits, and he was often able to suggest a chord, a line, a transition, a countermelody, or, on several memorable occasions, an entire section that meshed with Lennon's work.

McCartney's problem was the opposite of Lennon's. Chords and melodies flowed out of him so easily that his facility as a musician often outstripped his facility as a lyricist. John's role had always been to get Paul to focus more intently on the language and sense of his songs, and to temper his self-acknowledged tendency toward the trite and the sentimental. Though John could be withering in his criticism, most of the time his presence alone had been enough. Over the years Paul began to internalize his partner's editorial role, and his lyric writing was never better than when he was trying to impress John as a way of enlisting his participation in his work.

McCartney responded to the withdrawal of Lennon's participation in his songwriting with a determined display of musical self-sufficiency. Of his twelve tracks on the White Album, fully half are solo or near-solo efforts. On five of them, Paul sings alone and plays all the instruments (supplemented on two by George Martin's arrangement for strings and horns); on another one, Ringo on drums is the only other Beatle on the track. For his part, Lennon also recorded two numbers on which no other Beatle appears: one a solo ballad, and the other a collaboration with Yoko.

Apart from this unprecedented amount of solo material, the absence of collaboration in the Lennon-McCartney songs on the White Album comes across in several ways. Some of the songs, such as John's "Sexy Sadie" and Paul's "Birthday," seem to be based on flimsy or undeveloped ideas; others, such as John's "Glass Onion" and Paul's "I Will" begin strongly and then seem to lose their focus as they go along. By comparison with previous Beatle albums, there's a scarcity of musical surprises on the White Album—fewer of the unexpected chord changes, hooks, and riffs that the presence of a second pair of ears had so often brought to their songs. But the most noticeable effect can be heard in the nature of the singing on the album. One of the reasons that the individuated format of *Revolver* had raised no questions about the unity of the Beatles was that the group vocals on the record had been, if anything, more robust than ever before. On the White Album, by contrast, the vocal harmony, counterpoint, and call-and-response that had produced such masterpieces of group singing as "Taxman," "Eleanor Rigby," "A Little Help From My Friends," and "She's Leaving Home" is nowhere to be found. Not only does every song (but one) have a distinct lead singer, but on the songs where the Beatles do sing together, the relationship between the lead and backing vocals tends to be quite conventional.

THE TWENTY-FIVE LENNON-MCCARTNEY songs on the White Album can be grouped and classed in many different ways, but fully half of them are musical parodies of one sort or another. Setting the standard are the tracks that open and close side one of the album, "Back in the USSR" and "Happiness Is a Warm Gun." Were it not such a witty song, "Back in the USSR" might have been heard as Paul McCartney's answer to "Revolution." Written in India and recorded a few days after the Soviet Union invaded Czechoslovakia in August 1968, the song is a remarkable blend of political and musical satire. With its jet-lagged introduction (complete with engine noise), its accompaniment of driving guitar and pounding piano, and its travelogue motif, the words and music evoke two of pop's great anthems to the American Dream. The title and verses are patterned on Chuck Berry's 1959 single "Back in the U.S.A.," a celebration of his return to the land of freeways, hamburgers, and skyscrapers; the release is patterned on the Beach Boys' 1965 hit "California Girls"—which was itself a variation on the pop geography that Berry had first mapped in "Sweet Little Sixteen" and the Beach Boys had revived in "Surfin' U.S.A." Paul sings it in a husky voice reminiscent of Jerry Lee Lewis, playing the part of a young Russian apparatchik who returns home from an extended stay abroad to find that his view of the Motherland has been transformed by his exposure to the decadent influence of the West. By substituting the U.S.S.R. for the U.S.A., and suggesting that Russians, too, miss the comfort and familiarity of home, the song seems at first to be mocking the chauvinism of Americans abroad. But that's the least of the joke, given the song's origins in a period when the only Russians who were even permitted to travel outside their country did so under KGB surveillance lest they never come home again. The real source of the song's humor involves the ludicrous incompatibility between the totalitarian culture of the Soviet Union and the hedonistic spirit of rock 'n' roll. Though Paul's suggestion that his listeners don't know how lucky they are is ostensibly directed at the singer's Russian countrymen, it applies to his real-life audience as well—all those lucky listeners who took for granted their ability to buy their rock-'n'-roll records over the counter (at a time when a bootlegged copy of *Sgt. Pepper* cost a small fortune on Moscow's black market). In the bridge, where John and George provide a pitch-perfect imitation of the Beach Boys' exuberant vocal counterpoint, Paul sings the praises of Soviet womanhood, region by region, in the manner of "California Girls." "Show me round your snow-capped mountains way down south / Take me to your daddy's farm," he sings, conflating the Beach Boys' "Midwest farmers' daughters" with the Stalinist-era stereotype of Soviet women as tractor drivers. "Come and keep your comrade warm!" Paul adds as George's guitar impersonates an electric balalaika and the jet noise of the introduction returns, sounding now like the wind off the Siberian steppe. Almost in spite of itself, "Back in the USSR" ends up as a backhanded tribute to America's relentless powers of cultural self-aggrandizement: its ability to extol its women, its geography, its music, and its entire way of life with such intensity and imagination as to make its national fantasies compelling to people all over the world.

A disjunction between style and content is only one of the many incongruities in John Lennon's "Happiness Is a Warm Gun," which mixes its verbal and musical metaphors even more freely than "Back in the USSR." "Happiness" is the closest thing on the White Album to a Lennon magnum opus in the line of "I Am the Walrus" or "A Day in the Life," and John, Paul, and George all described it as one of their favorite tracks. An exercise in obscurity, strung together from a series of autonomous "bits," it is a rarity among pop songs for the fact that none of its four drastically asymmetrical sections repeat. It opens in A minor with a dreamy yet ominous passage about a sensuous girl who doesn't miss much and a man in the crowd who's hard to miss, thanks to his mirrored boots, his lying eyes, and his busy hands. In the second section, where the harmony equivocates between A major and A minor and the meter equivocates between 9/8 and 12/8 time, John seems to inhabit this predatory character. "I need a fix 'cause I'm going down," he sings over the undulating melody, "Down to the bits that I left uptown." He then makes a small adjustment in the rhythm and proceeds to dance a little vocal dance on the phrase "Mother Superior jumped the gun," before free-associating his way into a fervent soul-styled testimonial (in C major) to the proposition that "Happiness is a warm gun." (A play on the *Peanuts* comic-strip slogan "Happiness is a warm puppy," this title line was taken from a headline in a gun collectors' magazine whose perversity caught John's eye.) With its plodding 12/8 rhythm, its classic doo-wop chord progression, and its Supremes-style backup chorus, the effect of this final section is to lend the whole track a retroactive air of surreal and sinister comedy. "Happiness" is an example of a song that probably would have been refined or expanded into something more conventional had Yoko Ono not replaced Paul McCartney as John Lennon's sounding board. But it succeeds on the basis of John's brazen confidence, both as a singer and a songwriter, to string together bits and pieces of diffuse imagery and private meaning, no matter how disjointed or obscure.

Though the songs on the White Album show few signs of active collaboration, many of them were written in the same place at the same time, and some of them conform to Lennon and McCartney's established pattern of writing separate songs based on similar lyrics, chords, or themes. There are numerous examples of these companion pieces, beginning with a pair of satiric sing-alongs on side one. Drolly sung by Paul (with just a trace of patois) over an infectious rhythm that combines lilting Jamaican offbeats with stolid English downbeats, "Ob-La-Di, Ob-La-Da" recounts the courtship and marriage of a proper West Indian couple named Desmond and Molly Jones. He's a barrow boy in the town market, she's a nightclub singer. Together they fall in love, build a home, and raise a family under the (literally mollifying) influence of Molly's credo: "Ob-la-di, ob-la-da, life goes on." In addition to playing up the "no problem" stereotype of West Indian equanimity, the song hints at social satire in the way it applies the love-nest sensibility of countless music hall tunes to some of the newest and most reviled members of the English working class. With its big beat and booming chorus, "Ob-La-Di, Ob-La-Da" betrays none of the frustration that went into its recording; it comes across as a distilled expression of high spirits, and the song was such an obvious hit that the Beatles deserved a gold record for *not* releasing it as a single. (The first British group that did so, an unknown quintet called Marmalade, saw it go to number one.)

John Lennon's answer to "Ob-La-Di, Ob-La-Da" was "The Continuing Story of Bungalow Bill," a postcolonial campfire song that enlists a chorus of chirping, childish voices to pose the question "Hey Bungalow Bill, what did you kill, Bungalow Bill?" Inspired by one of the meditators in Rishikesh who took time off from the pursuit of enlightenment to endanger a tiger or two, this Far East version of the Wild West hero Buffalo Bill Cody stalks the savage beast with the help of his overprotective mother and an equally watchful white hunter named Captain Marvel. In addition to a cameo appearance by Yoko Ono, who sings the part of the Mum in her weird soprano, the track is distinguished by a flamenco guitar introduction and a wonderful ending, complete with some spirited regimental whistling, a big round of applause from the chorus, and a dour Mellotron-bassoon that sounds like a refugee from the orchestral cast of *Peter and the Wolf*.

A second set of Lennon-McCartney companion pieces is a pair of chastely affectionate love songs about a couple of shy, old-fashioned girls named Prudence and Martha, who preside over the first two sides of the White Album in a manner reminiscent of Lucy and Rita on *Sgt. Pepper*. Written in honor of Mia Farrow's spaced-out sister, "Dear Prudence" begins with another of John's arpeggiated sunrise openings. "The sun is up, the sky is blue, it's beautiful, and so are you," he sings in the opening verse. Recorded on eight-track equipment during Ringo's hiatus from the band, the accompaniment features inspired performances on piano, bass, and drums—*all* by Paul McCartney, who made the most of Ringo's absence by playing a stunning ten-bar drum solo in the instrumental break that leads to the last refrain, where George Harrison's ascending octaves on guitar (piped through a Leslie speaker) add a note of ethereal urgency to John's efforts to convince this timid girl to be a little less prudent on such a perfect day.

Paul is equally ubiquitous on his own "Martha My Dear," playing piano, bass, drums, and guitar as well as singing the song, which is filled out by George Martin's bittersweet arrangement for brass and strings. A late addition to the White Album, "Martha" is a jaunty tune whose pub piano flavor and subtle harmonization add an undercurrent of yearning to Paul's outwardly jocular attempt to convince this "silly girl" to see that he and she "were meant to be." (Readers of Hunter Davies's biography were in a position to know that Martha was the name of Paul's pet sheepdog, an otherwise distracting biographical detail that gives a wholly different slant to the exclamation "Look what you've done!" in the bridge.)

Some of the parodies on the White Album are aimed at the work of particular artists, others at musical genres. A fine example of the former is "Rocky Raccoon," Paul McCartney's exceedingly artful send-up of Bob Dylan and the outlaw ballad style of *John Wesley Harding*. Set in the Black Hills of Dakota (it was Dylan's home state of Minnesota in an earlier version) and sung with a North Country twang, the song tells of a fateful love triangle involving Rocky, his old flame Lil (better known as Nancy), and his rival Dan. The narrative is packed with Hollywood Western clichés, including the hoedown, the showdown, the flesh wound, and a memorably drunken doctor who staggers into the stricken hero's hotel room and lays *himself* out on the table. George Martin takes a terrific honky-tonk piano break and John Lennon contributes a few bars of wheezy Dylanesque harmonica. Written in India with the help of Donovan Leitch, the song was originally titled "Rocky Sassoon"—a devious pun that alluded to the English poet Siegfried Sassoon (who had died a few months before) in the same way that the pseudonym Bob Dylan alluded to the poet Dylan Thomas.

John Lennon's "Sexy Sadie" was another Rishikesh-inspired satire that picked up a new title along the way. John had originally written the song as an obscenity-laced screed against the Maharishi, basing the lyric on a 1962 B-side by Smokey Robinson and the Miracles called "I've Been Good to You." (Robinson's "Look what you've done / You made a fool out of someone" became Lennon's "Maharishi, what have you done? / You made a fool of everyone.") Having decided to recast the song in a romantic context, John went on to emulate Robinson's vocal style as well, adding falsetto melismas to the story of this world-class seductress who "broke the rules" and "laid it down for all to see." It's not till the last verse that John lets on that he is truly not amused, vowing, "Sexy Sadie, you'll get yours yet / However big you think you are." By that time the song has lost whatever focus it ever had, and John, as if exacting a price from George Harrison for his willingness to spare the Maharishi his wrath, relies on Harrison's Leslified lead guitar to sustain a long and aimless fade-out over the chromatic harmonies of the verse.

Still another of the Rishikesh songs probably began as a parody and then fortuitously overshot its mark. "Mother Nature's Son" is a bucolic acoustic ballad in which Paul assumes the role of "a poor young country boy" who spends his days "sitting singing songs for everyone." (The alliteration carries through to the last verse, where "swaying daisies sing a lazy song beneath the sun.") This character comes across as an affectionate send-up of Donovan, the self-proclaimed "humble minstrel" of pop, who had cornered the market on this sort of pastoral innocence with his own elaborate double album, *A Gift From a Flower to a Garden*. ("We shall fill their days with fairies and elves and pussies and paints, with laughter and song and the gentle influence of Mother Nature," read the album's liner notes.) Yet the chords and melody of "Mother Nature's Son" are so pleasing, and the sound of Paul's voice silhouetted against the sonorous backdrop of George Martin's horns is so affecting, that the song transcends its satiric intentions. Toward the end, Paul runs out of words and simply hums along with the music the rest of way—as if he too were transfixed by the beauty of the tune.

The most entertaining of the genre parodies on the White Album was a pair of songs on side three that satirized the recent trends in rock. "Yer Blues" is a Scouse-inflected send-up of the vicarious misery of the British blues scene, sung with such a convincing air of anguish that many listeners took the song straight. "Yes I'm *lonely*—wanna *die*," John bawls over an undulating guitar riff that sounds like the death moan of a wounded dinosaur. While it echoes the line "You make me so lonely, I could die" from the seminal white blues recording "Heartbreak Hotel," the difference between Presley's "could" and Lennon's "wanna" is the difference between believing that lyrics like these might actually mean something and knowing full well that they don't. "If I ain't dead already," John adds, "girl you know the reason why." The joke is that nobody knows the reason why—or, for that matter, what any of these bluesy poetics are really supposed to mean. "Yer Blues" is a reminder of the cultural realism that distinguished the Beatles from so many of their musical contemporaries in Britain: their acceptance of the idea that, except as a subject of self-parody, certain expressive modes of African-American music lay outside the realm of their experience and hence beyond their emotional range as singers.

McCartney's "Helter Skelter" takes on a related form of musical overstatement by burlesquing the histrionic sexuality associated with guitar heroes like Jimi Hendrix. The song turns the English colloquialism for a fairground ride into a metaphor for the sort of frenzied, operatic sex that adolescent boys of all ages like to fantasize about. "When I get to the bottom I go back to the top of the slide / Where I stop and I turn and I go for a ride / Till I get to the bottom and I see you again!" Paul shouts in a voice so raw-edged and overwrought that many listeners simply assumed it was John singing. "Helter skelter!" he bellows as a juggernaut run on guitar ("look out!") comes skittering down the scale. The cannonade of crashes, crescendos, throbbing machine rhythms and phallocentric guitar riffs that surrounds his outlandish performance is the sound of heavy metal music before the genre got its name. (Specifically, it sounds like a pastiche of effects from a half-dozen Hendrix songs, beginning with "Foxy Lady.") After a ludicrous series of false endings, fade-outs, and fade-ins, the track finally ends in a full-scale smash-up, with Ringo crawling from the wreckage to lodge a formal protest: "I got blisters on my fingers!" he cries. In a song about sexual fantasy, the joke is very rich.

That so many of the Lennon and McCartney songs on the White Album tend toward satire and parody lends a special sweetness and poignancy to the songs that are written and sung straight, without the benefit of a comic or critical twist. This is especially true of the two solo acoustic ballads, one by Paul, the other by John, on side two. Paul's "Blackbird" is a splendid addition to a long line of folk, blues, and pop songs about cuckoos, mockingbirds, diving ducks, bluebirds, robins, nighthawks, swallows, wild geese, whippoorwills, and other feathered friends. It melds a perfectly proportioned melody with an effortlessly poetic lyric: "Blackbird singing in the dead of night / Take these broken wings and learn to fly." Paul's performance is scrupulously understated, while the accompaniment is confined to an acoustic guitar, a steady patter of footfalls, and later, when the verse repeats, a rising chorus of birdcalls.

John Lennon's "Julia" is similar to "Blackbird" in its air of quiet solitude; with its bare acoustic guitar accompaniment, it represented John's first and only entirely solo performance as a Beatle. The title refers to his mother, of course (another biographical reference that readers of Hunter Davies were now in a position to know). But the woman described in the lyrics is a startlingly Oedipal conflation of Julia Lennon and Yoko Ono, the "ocean child" of the refrain. This duality is mirrored in John's delicate, double-track vocal, which shifts seamlessly back and forth between two separate (and, in places, overlapped) performances of the song. The seashore imagery that runs through the lyric affirms the link to Yoko, but it also reflects the fact that the verses of "Julia" were derived from a book of aphorisms called *Sand and Foam* by the Lebanese-American author Khalil Gibran, whose mystical musings on love and life gained a cult following during the late 1960s. Gibran's "Half of what I say is meaningless; but I say it so that the other half may reach you" became John's lovely opening line, "Half of what I say is meaningless, but I say it just to reach you, Julia." And Gibran's "When Life does not find a singer to sing her heart she produces a philosopher to speak her mind," became Lennon's more felicitously phrased "When I cannot sing my heart, I can only speak my mind." The trancelike feeling of John's vocal is enhanced by a melody that hangs on one note in the verse, causing the lyrics to be murmured more than sung, with the only melodic motion falling on the end of the word "Julia" itself. A modest five-bar release provides a break from this monotonality, as well as a gentle allusion to John's earlier dream girl, Lucy in the Sky.

Two of the lesser ballads on the White Album also had clear antecedents in the Beatles' music, in both cases on *Revolver*. "I'm So Tired" is a strung-out, insomniac inversion of "I'm Only Sleeping" that reflects the reorientation of John Lennon's life in the intervening years by substituting romantic obsession for druggy reverie. John sings it with the same limpid delivery he used on the earlier song, wavering over the words "I'm *so-o-oh* tired" before sagging an octave at the mere thought of getting up to fix himself a drink. The second time through the verse, however, having revealed that his "mind is set on you," his voice rises to an anguished shout as he confronts his would-be lover in the bridge: "I'd give you everything I've got for a little peace of mind!" Paul's "I Will," by contrast, was described by its author as "pretty smoochy stuff," and it is best appreciated as the demure punch line to the raunchy parody of "Why Don't We Do It in the Road?", which it follows on side two. Taken on its own terms, the song's lush romanticism and careful construction mark it as an obvious successor to "Here, There, and Everywhere." Unfortunately, "I Will" is so well crafted and smoothly harmonized that it lacks all strong feeling, with Paul professing undying love for a girl (the lyrics tell us) he's never met and whose name he doesn't know. This is one of the few instances in which the restraint Paul typically brought to his ballad singing blanches into something that sounds like simple indifference. "Who knows how long I've loved you?" he asks, and it's tempting to think, "Who cares?"

While John Lennon was correct in characterizing many of the tracks on the White Album as "John with the band, Paul with the band," and so forth, it remains that the Beatles were not just *any* band. The five months they spent at Abbey Road studios recording scores of variations and reiterations on many of these thirty songs amounted to the most protracted period of group rehearsal they had undergone since their days of playing nightly gigs in Liverpool and Hamburg. As a result, much of the ensemble playing on the album is marvelous, nowhere more so than on a pair of tracks on side three, "Birthday" and "Everybody's Got Something to Hide Except for Me and My Monkey," where the heightened levels of personal tension and aggression in the studio seemed to inspire some of the most kinetically powerful music the Beatles would ever record. Both "Birthday" and "Monkey" are primitive rock-'n'-roll dance songs with rudimentary chords, choppy, repetitive melodies, and comically insistent beats. "Birthday" comes across as one of the Beatles' most inexplicably funny songs—the joke of it having something to do with the way that John and Paul, on their one and only attempt to share a lead vocal on the White Album, wind up satirizing their own rivalry by turning a sentiment as innocuous as "Happy Birthday" into a power struggle. "You say it's your birthday," they shout at one another over the charging rhythm of the band. "It's *my* birthday too, yeah!" After allowing their listeners to reflect on this remarkable coincidence for a full eight bars of unaccompanied downbeats on the drums, the birthday boys put on their best New York accents and head off to a "pah-dy, pah-dy" where they proposition each other with an edge of Teutonic insistence: *"I vould like you to dance."* "Everybody's Got Something to Hide Except for Me and My Monkey," the song "about me and Yoko" with which Lennon confronted his fellow Beatles early in the White Album sessions, has an even flimsier pretext. The singing consists of John spewing what sounds in places like a pidgin English translation of the usual dance-hall incitements—"come on is take it easy . . . come on is make it easy" mingled with paradoxical Yokoisms like "the deeper you go, the higher you fly." But the backing is a primer of guitar-group rock, in which downbeats from Ringo and wrenching off-beats from John are overlaid by the sixteenth-note clatter of Paul's over-dubbed cowbell and the angry droning jabber of George's lead guitar. The track ends with a chorus of chattering whose similarity to the "monkey chants" heard in Balinese folk music reflects the Beatles' firsthand experience communing with the rhesus monkeys of Rishikesh.

The ferocious guitar playing on "Birthday" and "Me and My Monkey" highlights one of the great virtues of the White Album, which was George Harrison's vigorous return to form, both as a lead guitarist and as a pop songwriter. George's first track on the album, "While My Guitar Gently Weeps," was virtually a declaration of his recommitment to rock. It was also a gesture of appreciation toward Eric Clapton, whom Harrison invited to play on the song after failing to get the weepy sound he wanted using a tape-reversed guitar. (George also hoped that Clapton's participation would cure the other Beatles of their evident lack of enthusiasm for the track.) The fruit of their collaboration was the most melodically and emotionally stirring pop song Harrison had recorded to date. Characteristically, its only flaw is a spotty lyric that mixes its compassion ("I look at you all, see the love there that's sleeping") with willful banality ("I look at the floor and I see it needs sweeping") and eventually leads George back to his favorite spot at the sickbed of suffering humanity, with his rhyming dictionary ("diverted . . . perverted . . . inverted . . . alerted") in hand. Yet the warmth of his singing offsets the deficiencies of the lyric, and the track's true eloquence is provided by Clapton's lead guitar, which corroborates the song title by answering each line of the verse with an impassioned burst of instrumental commentary. Uncredited yet unmistakable, Clapton's performance ranks with those of Alan Civil on "For No One" and David Mason on "Penny Lane" as an example of the Beatles' ability to summon virtuosity on demand.

Harrison's other contributions are a trio of equally accomplished songs. "Piggies" is an acerbic social satire in the style of "Taxman," on which Chris Thomas's harpsichord and George Martin's strings add a perfect note of mock gentility to an otherwise spare arrangement of bass-note grunts by Paul and tape-looped snorts by John. (This was the only one of Harrison's four tracks on the album to which Lennon made any significant contribution.) Though the song was recorded at a time when student radicals in the United States were expanding the Black Power term "pig" (which originally referred to the police) into an epithet for authority figures in general, Harrison disclaimed this connection, and the distinction he draws in the lyric between the little piggies "crawling in the dirt" and the bigger piggies "in their starched white shirts" comes closer to the creed of the barnyard despots in George Orwell's *Animal Farm*. (If so, Harrison takes Orwell a grisly step further by having his piggy overlords "clutching forks and knives to eat their bacon.") Somewhat more contrived is "Savoy Truffle," a high-spirited soul song with a saxophone chorus and a "found" lyric derived from the contents of a box of brand-name chocolates, the names of which roll off George's tongue like a catalog of life's little pleasures. "But you'll have to have them all pulled out after the Savoy Truffle," he cautions in the bridge, shifting the focus to the karmic cost of tooth decay, then driving the point home with a guitar solo pitched to the register of a dentist's drill. Finally there is "Long Long Long," the darkly beautiful ballad that ends side three. Patterned with worshipful precision on the chords, mood, and meter of Bob Dylan's "Sad-Eyed Lady of the Lowlands" (but a full twenty minutes shorter than its role model), "Long Long Long" was the first real love ballad Harrison had ever recorded. His weary, muted performance was a breakthrough for him as a singer as well: the first time he ever allowed himself to sound humbled by his emotions in a song. "How could I ever have lost you, when I loved you?" he asks, his barely audible singing punctuated by thunderous fills from Starr in the style of "A Day in the Life." Though George would later explain that the words were addressed to God, the question of where he was deriving his affecting new sense of emotional surrender is immaterial to the song.

One of the qualities that made *Revolver* and *Sgt. Pepper* such fully realized albums was the Beatles' success at coming up with suitable material for Ringo Starr to sing. The White Album's installment of "Starr Time," by contrast, was a song that Ringo wrote himself (the publishing credit reads "Starkey"). With a lumbering beat and a scratchy Ozark fiddle, "Don't Pass Me By" is a country-style lament about an anxious guy who's afraid that his girl has stood him up. Apart from some instrumental anomalies (including a skating-rink organ and couple of bone-crushing fills that would have earned any aspiring Nashville drummer a seat on the first bus out of town), the song stays true to type until the last verse, where the lyric veers abruptly from hick angst to sick humor as an apologetic Ringo, having learned the real reason for his girlfriend's absence, delivers the deadpan denouement: "I'm sorry that I doubted you / I was so unfair / You were in a car crash / And you lost your hair."

ULTIMATELY, THE WONDER of the White Album is that it sustains as long as it does. No group of songwriters other than the Beatles could have produced an album with thirty original tracks, and no group of singers other than the Beatles could have succeeded as well at holding their listeners' attention for nearly an hour and a half on record. And still, like most of the double albums released during the heyday of the LP, this one is simply too long. The double-album format requires, if anything, a stronger sense of form and unity, yet it remains that few composers in any musical genre—apart from opera, that is—have been capable of sustaining a piece of music for ninety minutes at a stretch. For this reason, the most satisfying double albums have tended to be recordings of live concerts in which the individual tracks were organized, however loosely, by the format of a performance. *Blonde on Blonde,* the 1966 Dylan album that first established the double LP as a viable format in pop, contains only fourteen songs, which is scarcely more than a conventional pop LP; its extended length is attributable to the length of the individual tracks and to the presence of "Sad Eyed Lady of the Lowlands," which fills the entire fourth side and provides the album with an appropriately weighty ending. By comparison, most of the thirty tracks on the White Album are short, some of them mere fragments, and instead of progressing like *Blonde on Blonde* toward a conclusion whose length and import are commensurate with the scale of the whole production, it ends with what is unquestionably one of the most mediocre—and therefore anticlimactic—sides of music the Beatles would ever release.

Side four of the White Album begins with the original version of "Revolution," here retitled "Revolution 1" and performed as a bluesy shuffle that serves mainly to affirm the judgment of McCartney and Harrison that the Beatles could do better by the song. At the slower, drawling tempo, the singing has an even more sarcastic edge than on the single, the mockery reinforced by a "shooby-doo-wop" backup chorus. But the real distinction of the album version involved John's decision to insert a parenthetical "in" at the end of the line "But when you talk about destruction / Don't you know that you can count me out (in)." Lennon would later point to this as a sign of his own ambivalence about the need for "direct action" in politics. In fact it's a gratuitous gesture—a facile nod to "duality" that runs so counter to the meaning of the lyric as to raise suspicions that the "in" may have been added to the album track *after* the release of the single, in an effort to appease those who took issue with the "counterrevolutionary" message of the song. In years to come, John would consistently attribute the Beatles' reticence about speaking out on controversial issues like the Vietnam War to Brian Epstein's cautious nature. But the album version of "Revolution" demonstrates that John was quite capable of pulling his punches without any help from Epstein.

From this doubtful height of equivocation, side four begins its steady descent into camp, childishness, chaos, and outright kitsch. Paul's "Honey Pie" is an imitation music-hall tune with an old-fashioned recitative introductory verse. As a re-creation of 1920s period sentimentality, it meets or exceeds the standard of "When I'm Sixty-Four." But whereas the earlier track was a charming novelty in the Beatles' work, "Honey Pie" is pure camp in a way that "When I'm Sixty-Four" was not, with Paul adopting an alarming falsetto that sounds like a send-up of Tiny Tim, the freakishly comic novelty singer, ukulele player, and talk-show celebrity whose album *God Bless Tiny Tim* had risen high on the American charts during the summer of 1968. (This makes the track, in effect, a parody of a travesty.) "Honey Pie" is followed by the amusing contrivance of "Savoy Truffle" and then by a trio of John Lennon's songs. Even in 1968, "Cry Baby Cry" sounded badly out of date. A pseudo-

Carrollean nursery rhyme about life in the court of the King and Queen of Marigold, the track was a relic from the bygone era of *Magical Mystery Tour*. Asked about "Cry Baby Cry" in a 1980 interview, Lennon denied having written the song. "Not me. A piece of rubbish," he said. It is followed on the White Album by a great *bin* of rubbish called "Revolution 9," an eight-minute collaboration between John and Yoko that began with a set of tape loops derived from the fateful session in May when Yoko first "jammed" with the Beatles. Onto this base layer they overlaid the sounds of John reading a children's story ("everyone knew that as time went by they'd get a little bit older and a little bit slower . . ."), snatches of conversation, grunting, panting, laughter, church choirs, crowd noise, and a recurrent, disembodied voice with a BBC accent calmly repeating the phrase "Number 9" like a cosmic bingo caller. It ends with choirs singing, machine guns blasting, and sports fans chanting "block that kick." Previously, when the Beatles had experimented with tape effects, they had done so in a way that not only thrilled their listeners but also earned the admiration of composers and aficionados of electronic music. This was not the case with "Revolution 9." Shapeless, formless, gormless, "Revolution 9" is an embarrassment that stands like a black hole at the end of the White Album, sucking up whatever energy and interest remain after the preceding ninety minutes of music. It is a track that neither invites nor rewards close attention, and most listeners preferred to avoid it after one or two hearings, treating "Cry Baby Cry" as the final track.

The actual finale is the lullaby "Good Night," which has been charitably described as a spoof. (William Mann of the *Times,* for one, wrote that it had him "collapsed in laughter.") If so, nobody seems to have mentioned this to Ringo, who dives headfirst into the warm tub of bathos that has been prepared for him by John Lennon's chords and George Martin's strings. He gives the song his all, but his voice is so buried in the lush orchestration that it lacks all character. Previous Beatles albums had ended on their share of high notes ("A Day in the Life," "Tomorrow Never Knows") and low notes ("Everybody's Trying to Be My Baby," "Run for Your Life"). But when Ringo whispers at the end of the White Album, "Good night everybody / Everybody, everywhere," it sounds as if he is the only one left in the studio, and the feeling that lingers is a mixture of banality and sadness.

> Whatever it is or isn't, it is the best album they have ever
> released, and only the Beatles are capable of making a
> better one. You are either hip to it, or you ain't.
>
> —Jann Wenner, *Rolling Stone*

As the first entirely new collection of Beatle songs to be issued in a year and a half, the White Album was snapped up even more hungrily than *Sgt. Pepper*. In Britain, despite the newly imposed sales taxes that further inflated its price, the two-record set spent eight weeks at number one, becoming the first double album ever to top the charts. In America, after a radio buildup modeled on that of *Sgt. Pepper*, with stations authorized to begin airing tracks precisely one week before the album went on sale in stores, Capitol Records reported advance orders exceeding two million copies, and many retailers sold out their entire stock in a single day. FM radio stations played the record continuously; one rock station in San Francisco reported songs from the album occupying the first twenty-nine positions on its playlist. By the end of the year, the White Album had sold nearly four million copies in America. Given the sheer volume of sales, the doubled royalties, and the music publishing bonanza generated by the presence of thirty original songs, the White Album may well have been the single most lucrative release to date in the history of popular recording.

The critical response to the album, on the other hand, ranged from mixed to flat. In marked contrast to *Sgt. Pepper*, which had helped to establish an entire genre of literate rock criticism, the White Album inspired no critical writing of any note. Even the most sympathetic reviewers, including some of the Beatles' most erstwhile champions, clearly didn't know what to make of this shapeless outpouring of songs. *Newsweek*'s Hubert Saal, citing the high proportion of parodies, accused the group of getting their tongues caught in their cheeks. ("This, after rolling the universe into a ball in the immortal 'A Day in the Life'?") Writing in *The Saturday Review*, Ellen Sander complained that "though the album tries to be panoramic in scope, the material is woefully inconsistent, sketchy in content, and the overall feeling is undeniably sloppy and diffuse." William Mann began his review in the London *Times* by heralding the album as "the most important musical event of the year." But beyond his carefully qualified judgment that "nine of the [twenty-five Lennon-McCartney songs] are superbly inventive," Mann gave little indication of why this might be so. The same vagueness applied to a five-thousand-word, track-by-track salute in *Rolling Stone*, written by the magazine's owner and editor, Jann Wenner. Wenner described the White Album as everything it was not: "a far more deliberate, self-conscious, pretentious, organized and structured, coherent and full, *more perfect* album than *Sgt. Pepper's Lonely Hearts Club Band*."

One of the few cogent critical insights came from Michael Wood, a young professor of English at Columbia, who reviewed the album for the progressive Catholic monthly *Commonweal*. Wood described the record as a comprehensive survey of the musical styles generated by the preceding decade of pop—the period that so many of the songs on *Sgt. Pepper* had seemed to reach behind. "*Sgt. Pepper* was nostalgic, a musical gesture toward the past just because it was the past. This album is nostalgic too, but with a sense of purpose and direction. The past here is the Beatles' own—the musical past of their own generation, not that of their parents, or of the old folks they liked. . . . It's as if they had chosen to take possession of their kingdom, run up an inventory of what belongs to them—belongs to us all, since pop has become so popular." Concluding his review with the obligatory literary reference, Wood described the White Album as "a survey of styles, like a chapter from Joyce's *Ulysses*, and done with something of Joyce's energy. It's music by very talented people having a ball, and I'm not sure what else we have a right to ask for. Originality? We're entitled to a rest from that."

49

The saddest thing was actually getting fed up with one
another. It's like growing up in a family. When you get to a
certain age, you want to go off and get your own girl and
your own car, split up a bit.

—George Harrison

The story of the Beatles' formation, rise, and seven-year reign as the
world's most popular, accomplished, and admired rock group remains
unique in the annals of popular music. The story of their dissolution and
demise over the course of 1969, by contrast, is a story that has been
enacted by millions upon millions of frustrated, unhappy families all over
the world.

The metaphor of a family was one that was often invoked by the Beatles themselves. "I'm an only child and they're my brothers," said Ringo
Starr. "From 1962 to around 1969, we were all just for each other. But
suddenly you're older, and you don't want to devote all that time to this
one object." From the start of their success, the Beatles had been perceived as a band of brothers by a public that treated the similarities in
how they looked and dressed and spoke as a form of familial resemblance. Yet for John Lennon and Paul McCartney, the fraternal bond
had evolved, over the years, into something more like a creative marriage. As a result, when they spoke of the group's dissolution, they did so
not in terms of sibling rivalry, but rather in terms of a divorce. "I've compared it to a marriage," John would later say. "The four of us had been
together a long, long time. . . . The whole pressure of it finally got to us,
and we mainly took it out on one another. . . . We could see through one
another and therefore we felt uncomfortable. Because up until then we
really believed intensely in what we were doing, and the product we put
out and everything had to be just right, and we *believed*. Suddenly we
didn't believe. . . . And that was the end of it." In all but name, the Beatles had begun with the friendship of John Lennon and Paul McCartney.

And in all but name, the Beatles ended with the collapse of that artistically fertile yet emotionally fragile friendship over the course of 1969.

LIKE NEARLY EVERY other artistic initiative they had undertaken during the preceding two years, the notion that the Beatles should return to live performing had originated in the restless mind of Paul McCartney. The personal tensions that racked the group over the latter half of 1968 had convinced Paul that the four of them needed to renew their old sense of camaraderie and common purpose. The best way to do this, he believed, was by returning to their roots as a performing band. If nothing else, the White Album had demonstrated that they could still make great music with their original lineup of two guitars, bass, and drums. In Paul's view, all they needed to put things in their proper perspective was to perform together in front of a live audience. Now that the screaming had abated, Paul believed that it was once again possible for the Beatles to play in public like any other band.

The sharpest resistance to McCartney's initiative came from George Harrison, who was categorically opposed to any activity that threatened to revive the frenzied public attention of the Beatlemania years. Harrison's long-standing aversion to publicity had only been strengthened by his recent trip to the States. The time he had spent in Woodstock visiting with Bob Dylan and the members of The Band had exposed him to a vibrant local music scene that seemed, on the face of it, to be completely insulated from the pressures of pop celebrity—a scene in which musicians communed informally and played mainly for the respect and enjoyment of their peers. Having wowed the music world with *John Wesley Harding,* Dylan seemed quite content to remain at home with his wife and children. As the latest beneficiaries of Albert Grossman's mystical style of management, The Band had set a new standard of musical reclusiveness by declining to tour in support of their first LP. In Harrison's view, the music business had reached the point where it was enough for artists to write good songs and make good records without feeling that they owed some indeterminate debt to their fans to appear before them from time to time. If anything, Harrison viewed McCartney's desire to perform in public as the expression of a rather childish need for attention and approval.

John Lennon also had his doubts about the Beatles performing live, though in John's case this reticence was centered on the outlandish expectations he feared would accompany such a move. "There's such a mystique about the Beatles that they'd be expecting God to perform," he told a reporter around this time. Beyond that, Lennon viewed McCartney's suggestion that the Beatles perform a live concert as a prelude to the suggestion that they return to full-fledged touring, and this was about the last thing that Lennon had in mind. In the weeks after Yoko's miscarriage, John and Yoko's heroin use had escalated significantly, which further increased the isolation of their daily existence and amplified John's tendency toward lassitude. "I was stoned all the time," he said later, "and I just didn't give a shit."

Paul McCartney's reaction to his bandmates' reluctance was to propose a compromise. Having learned from the head of Apple's film division, Denis O'Dell, that one of the sound stages at London's Twickenham Studios was available for the month of January, McCartney suggested that the Beatles use the Twickenham facility to rehearse an album's worth of new material, which they would then perform and record onstage before a live audience. Both the rehearsals and the concert would be filmed and made into an hour-long television special; the music from the concert would be released as the Beatles' first live LP. From the beginning, it was unclear whether Twickenham or some more public venue would serve as the site of the actual concert. It also remained unclear whether the rehearsals were being filmed to provide supplementary footage for the television special or for a separate documentary about the making of the album. A year before, the Beatles had turned down an offer by the French director Jean-Luc Godard, who wanted to film them at work in the recording studio as part of a movie he planned to make in London. Denied the Beatles, Godard wound up making the picture (which premiered under the title *One Plus One* at the London Film Festival in December 1968) with the Rolling Stones. But Godard's concept of tracing the evolution of a song through the stages of rehearsal and recording most likely contributed to McCartney's plan to document the process by which the world's foremost recording band transformed its raw material into a finished product.

In an effort to avoid the obvious mistakes they had made with *Magical Mystery Tour,* the Beatles hired a director named Michael Lindsay-Hogg to supervise the filming, leaving the four of them ostensibly free to focus their attention on the music. Like Richard Lester in his pre-Beatle days, Lindsay-Hogg was an expatriate American who had worked mainly as a television director in Britain, most notably on the pop show *Ready Steady Go,* and most recently as the director of the Rolling Stones' "Rock 'n' Roll Circus," a television special that had aired in December 1968. On Lindsay-Hogg's recommendation, several other members of the "Circus" crew were hired to work on the Beatles' film, including Glyn Johns, a well-respected freelance engineer who had worked with the Kinks, the Who, and the Stones, among others, and had recently begun producing records for the Small Faces and the Steve Miller Band. Johns's involvement in the Beatles' film showed how tangled the lines of authority surrounding their recording process had become.

The commercial success of the White Album had done little to assuage George Martin's dissatisfaction with the contentious and ill-disciplined manner in which the record had been made. Martin believed that a threshold had been crossed in the course of those interminable sessions. Contractually speaking, he had been serving at the Beatles' pleasure since the time of *Rubber Soul.* Since then, under his tutelage, the Beatles had become far more knowledgeable about the recording process and far more confident of their own musical ideas. But it was not until the White Album sessions that their collective trust in Martin's musical judgment had seriously begun to erode. This left Martin feeling genuinely doubtful about whether he had any useful role to play in the Beatles' ongoing work. In theory, he liked McCartney's idea of recording a live album composed entirely of new material. It was something that had never been done before in the pop field, and the technical challenge of the project appealed to him. Martin was put off, however, by John Lennon's insistence that the album eschew all "production gimmicks" like overdubbing or editing. This was an extension of the attitude that Lennon had expressed at various points during the White Album sessions. But Martin saw Lennon's insistence on making an "honest" record as an arbitrary form of primitivism that would needlessly compromise the quality of the finished work. In any case, having spent weeks on end during the summer of 1968 sitting idle in the control room at Abbey Road while the Beatles recorded innumerable repetitions of their songs, Martin saw no good reason why he should be present on a daily basis at Twickenham. If the rehearsals had to be recorded for the purposes of the film, Martin was quite content to let Glyn Johns supervise the taping.

Johns, on the other hand, saw Martin's absence as a professional opportunity: "It became fairly clear when I walked in the door that they wanted me to produce, [though] that was never really stated. George Martin wasn't there and I was."

Despite their hiring of a director and their determination to focus their own attention on what they did best, the Beatles set themselves up to repeat at least one of the mistakes of *Magical Mystery Tour*. If the underlying problem with the earlier film (as Paul McCartney told Hunter Davies) was that the group had failed to take the time to do things right, the new project was constrained by an even narrower time frame, owing to Ringo Starr's commitment to appear with Peter Sellers in the screen adaptation of Terry Southern's comic novel *The Magic Christian,* which was scheduled to begin filming at Twickenham in the first week of February. The Beatles' film project, from the first rehearsal to the final (still unspecified) live performance, would have to be completed in exactly one month's time.

On the morning of January 2, 1969, the Beatles convened at Twickenham Studios to begin work on the film and album project that would soon be given the working title of *Get Back.* Accustomed to working at their leisure at Abbey Road, none of the Beatles were happy about having to conform to the unionized, nine-to-five routine at Twickenham. Nor could they get comfortable playing on the low, coldly lit stage that had been set up at one end of the drafty, cavernous room.

On that first day and the next, the Beatles introduced one another to a total of seven nearly completed new songs: two by John, three by Paul, and two by George. As was their custom when recording, the group distracted and entertained themselves by periodically breaking into old favorites like "Lucille" or "Hitchhike." At one point Paul sang a version of John's "I'm So Tired"; John answered with his version of Paul's "Ob-La-Di, Ob-La-Da." Yet the mood in the room remained tense, for there was still a great well of resentment left over from the White Album sessions. Paul was once again inhibited by Yoko's constant presence. John was once again irritated by the "coldness" with which the other Beatles treated Yoko. And George, refreshed from his recent visit to America, was infuriated by his bandmates' lack of enthusiasm for his new songs. If friends like Bob Dylan and Eric Clapton heard something worthwhile in material like "All Things Must Pass" (to cite the most affecting of Harrison's offerings), what besides sheer egotism could account for the air of complete indifference with which Lennon and McCartney first greeted the tune?

A basic tenet of "hipness" holds that not caring at all is almost always preferable to caring too much. In their role as public figures, the Beatles had always maintained a high standard of hipness; as Elizabeth Sutherland noted back in 1964, a large part of their charm came from their way of never pushing too hard. But as John Lennon recalled of the Twickenham sessions, "Paul had this idea that he was going to rehearse us. We would rehearse and then make the album. And of course we're lazy fuckers and we've been playing for twenty years [and] we're not going to sit around rehearsing."

Paul's actual strategy was a bit more complicated. He wanted to use the premise of the Beatles documenting their creative process on film as an opportunity to draw John into collaborating actively with him again. (He may also have been naïvely counting on the presence of the cameras and a director to keep Yoko Ono literally out of the picture.) The first two songs Paul introduced, "I've Got a Feeling" and "Two of Us," were both based on his sharing all or part of the lead singing with John—something that, with the exception of "Birthday," they hadn't done since 1967. "I've Got a Feeling" was actually a joint composition, in the manner of "A Day in the Life," with Paul's verses joined to a release that John had written independently. "Two of Us" had the two of them singing in parallel harmony throughout the verses, and though Paul would later maintain that he wrote the song about his new romance with Linda, it's hard to see how the line "You and I have memories longer than the road that stretches out ahead" could refer to anyone but John and Paul. In the weeks ahead, the Beatles would perform dozens of variations on "Two of Us," which would come to serve as a musical barometer of the emotional climate in the group, expressed in angry versions, tender versions, jokey versions, and impassioned versions of the tune.

After breaking for the weekend, the Beatles resumed on the following Monday with Paul and George getting into an argument about George's playing on "Two of Us." This reprise of their previous dispute over George's playing on "Hey Jude" had an oddly stagy quality, with Paul reveling in the apparent "honesty" of the two of them airing their differences in front of the cameras and George made all the more uncomfortable by the fact that their argument was being filmed. In George's view, the cameras brought out the worst of Paul's self-conscious nature; like the nurse in "Penny Lane," he seemed at times to be playing the part of a musician rehearsing a song. Tense on-camera discussions continued for the rest of the week. Nearly all of them were initiated by McCartney, who continued to act as if he were trying to script the film, raising subjects like the change in the Beatles' outlook since the death of Brian Epstein (whom he unaccountably referred to as "Mr. Epstein"). For his part, John Lennon remained almost completely disengaged from these discussions.

As the week wore on, McCartney stunned his bandmates by introducing a bevy of new songs, including a pair of big ballads, "Let It Be" and "The Long and Winding Road," and a theatrical-sounding number called "Maxwell's Silver Hammer." Yet another new McCartney offering was "Get Back," a blues in the boogie style of John Lee Hooker that started out with a dummy lyric whose refrain of "Get back to where you once belonged" parodied the xenophobic rhetoric of Enoch Powell and his right-wing supporters. (John later claimed that Paul glanced at Yoko every time he sang that line.) On account of its relevance to the Beatles' own efforts to get back to their roots as a performing band, this simple, jammy number was soon adopted as the theme song of the film.

McCartney's outpouring of new songs further exacerbated the tensions in the band. Apart from the two songs he had already shown them, John Lennon had little new material to present. George Harrison, on the other hand, had unveiled a total of four new songs since the rehearsals began. Yet none of them had been received with much enthusiasm by the other Beatles, and John Lennon was particularly scornful of "I Me Mine," whose title and chorus he may or may not have recognized as another of George's musical memos to him and Paul in the style of "Not Guilty." It was especially galling to George that his fellow Beatles could complain about the amount of time they had to spend learning the arrangement for "I Me Mine" and then turn around and submit to a laborious rehearsal of a song like "Maxwell's Silver Hammer," which struck George as a paragon of pop inanity. "The corny one," Paul called it.

By the end of the Beatles' first full week at Twickenham, Harrison had had enough. During a break for lunch on Friday, he got into an argument with John and stormed out, announcing that he was quitting the group. ("See you round the clubs," he said.) The other three Beatles fiddled around for the rest of the afternoon, with John speculating brightly about whom they might pick as a replacement for their lead guitarist. (George's friend Eric Clapton headed the list of nominees.) Another topic of conversation in George's absence was the increasingly dubious question of whether the Beatles still planned to end the film with a live concert and, if so, where that concert should take place. Suggestions ranged from the Tower Ballroom in New Brighton to a reputed Roman amphitheater in Tunisia to the possibility of leasing the newly commissioned Cunard liner *Queen Elizabeth II* and filling it with fans. Michael Lindsay-Hogg was especially keen on finding a spectacular location for the concert to provide a spectacular climax to the film. In a wry allusion to the state of relations in the band, Paul McCartney suggested that they consider performing in the mouth of a volcano.

The Beatles met over the weekend at Ringo's new house in Surrey, where the tensions escalated further. George objected openly to Yoko's constant presence and participation in the group's affairs, John refused to speak, Yoko presumed to speak on his behalf, and George once again left in a huff. The following Monday, neither George nor John appeared at Twickenham; reached by telephone, John showed up late in the afternoon for a desultory rehearsal of "Get Back." Two days later the four Beatles met again at the Apple offices and agreed to end the disastrous sessions at Twickenham and resume filming and rehearsing the following week in the recording studio that Alexis Mardas had been building for the past four months in the basement of the Apple building on Savile Row.

Throughout the sessions at Twickenham, George Harrison had made no secret of his admiration for The Band, whose extended rehearsals in the basement of their house in Woodstock had yielded the songs on *Music From Big Pink*. To some extent, the Beatles' decision to relocate to the basement of Apple was an attempt to cater to George's enthusiasm by turning the foundering film and album project into their own version of Music From Big Green. In a further nod to the gospel-influenced timbres of The Band's music, Harrison asked the American organist Billy Preston to sit in with the group when they began rehearsing at Apple. The Beatles had first met Preston in 1962 when he came to Liverpool as a member of Little Richard's backup band. In the years since, he had played behind the soul stars Sam Cooke and Ray Charles and made several records under his own name. At a recent Ray Charles concert in London, Harrison had recognized Preston, contacted him after the show, and invited him to stop by the Apple offices. By the end of the month, he was signed to the Apple label as well.

. . . .

IN THE MIDDLE of January, while the Beatles struggled to hold them-selves together, EMI released the soundtrack for the film *Yellow Subma-rine*. (The release date had been set back two months so as not to conflict with sales of the White Album.) The first side of the soundtrack LP con-tained six Beatle originals, two of which, the title song and "All You Need Is Love," had been issued previously as *both* singles and album tracks. Of the remaining four originals, one was a sing-along counting-rhyme by Paul called "All Together Now"; two were George Harrison outtakes from 1967, "It's All Too Much" and "It's Only a Northern Song," both of which, with their droning psychedelic accompaniment, sounded utterly anachronistic in the context of 1969; and the last was a piece of literal doggerel called "Hey Bulldog," which featured a cop-show-style piano by John and some expert barking by Paul. (In response to the critical con-sensus that *Yellow Submarine* was too long, UA had cut the entire "Hey Bulldog" sequence from the American version of the film.) The second side of the soundtrack contained a half-dozen orchestrated selections from George Martin's film score, sporting programmatic titles like "Pep-perland Laid Waste" and "March of the Meanies." As a listening experi-ence, the *Yellow Submarine* LP ranked even below the disjointed Capitol soundtracks for *A Hard Day's Night* and *Help!* But the real importance of the album was that with the release of the four new originals, the Beatles had satisfied the sixty-song commitment specified in the contracts they had signed with EMI and Capitol in January 1967.

THE BEATLES HAD planned to start rehearsing and recording in the basement of Apple on Monday, January 20. Prior to that, however, George Martin, Glyn Johns, and a team of technicians from Abbey Road inspected Alexis Mardas's studio and pronounced it completely unus-able. ("All I can remember about it were all of these pretty colors," EMI engineer Alan Parsons recalled of Mardas's handmade mixing board. "It was quite funny, and within a few minutes it was very clear that no music was going to be forthcoming from this machine.") On short notice, George Martin requisitioned an eight-track deck and board from EMI and had them installed in the basement of Apple. By the time the Beatles resumed rehearsals on January 22, all thought of performing a live concert at an exotic location outside of Britain had effectively been abandoned, to the extreme displeasure of Michael Lindsay-Hogg. ("There's lots of good footage, but there's no payoff yet," the director complained.) As it was, only ten days remained before Ringo was due to start work on *The Magic Christian,* and time was running out for the Beatles and their film crew to come up with a climax of any sort. Confronted with a fast-approaching deadline and buoyed by the ebullient presence of Billy Preston, the Beatles managed to stop their bickering and start focusing their attention on the half-dozen new songs they considered suitable for live performance. In the course of that final week of rehearsals, they also found the time to record a pair of songs by George Harrison, "Old Brown Shoe" and "For You Blue," whose lighthearted lyrics and exuberant performances suggested that at least some of the anger in the group had dissipated. Between the pressure of time and the force of inertia, the Beatles decided that virtually the only feasible way of providing Michael Lindsay-Hogg with the cinematic climax he was seeking was by performing their live concert on the roof of the Apple building itself.

Beneath overcast noonday skies on January 30, with the wind gusting and the temperature hovering around forty degrees, the Beatles ascended to the roof of Apple, six stories above Savile Row, and took their places on a makeshift stage of wooden planks that had been laid the day before. Facing the street from right to left stood George Harrison, dressed in a black fur jacket and electric green pants, holding a Fender Telecaster guitar; John Lennon, swathed in a mottled fur coat that matched his mottled brown hair, holding a blond Epiphone guitar; and Paul McCartney, seemingly immune to the January chill, wearing an Epsteinian black suit and playing his old Hofner bass, which still had taped to its body the set list from the Beatles' last concert at Candlestick Park in San Francisco. Seated behind them were Ringo Starr, resplendent in a bright red rain slicker that contrasted sharply with the brass of his cymbals and the light wood finish of his drums, and Billy Preston, all but invisible as he hunched over his electric piano. Seated at stage left was a tiny rooting section consisting of Yoko Ono, Maureen Starkey, and a handful of Apple employees. The Beatles' sound equipment for this open-air performance consisted of the small amplifiers they used for studio recordings, supplemented by the type of public address system a band might use to play a wedding or a small club. Cables from the voice and instrument microphones snaked down the stairway of the Apple building to the basement

studio. The stage area was ringed by lights, cameras, and film technicians; cameras had also been positioned on a nearby rooftop, in the lobby
of the Apple building, and on the street below. From their vantage point,
the Beatles were performing to an audience that consisted mainly of ped-
iments, dormers, and chimney pots. Inadvertently and out of season, they
were reviving a tradition that dated from Tudor times, when town bands
would perform on the roofs of guildhalls on summer evenings.

Except for the fact that they were standing in a line, facing out
instead of in, the Beatles' performance was an extension of the rehearsal
mentality that had prevailed at Twickenham and Apple. They began by
playing two versions of "Get Back," followed by three other guitar-based
numbers: "Don't Let Me Down," "I've Got a Feeling," and "Dig a Pony."
After a brisk revival of their skiffle-era original, "The One After 909," they
performed alternate versions of "I've Got a Feeling" and "Don't Let Me
Down." As the music bounced off nearby buildings and cascaded down
to the street, crowds of people formed on the sidewalks, looking skyward,
trying to locate the source of the sound, and traffic came to a standstill
on Savile Row. Office workers in neighboring buildings leaned out of
open windows; others made their way up to their own rooftops to watch
the show. As the filmmakers had expected, the noise and commotion
attracted the attention of the police, who summoned a vanload of rein-
forcements before knocking on the door of the Apple building. While the
cameras rolled, the bobbies were admitted and directed to the roof,
where they emerged in the middle of the Beatles' third attempt at "Get
Back" and conferred with Mal Evans, the group's road manager. Lennon
and Harrison stopped playing as soon as they caught sight of the police;
McCartney and Starr continued playing and were quickly rejoined by the
other two. Together they finished the song. The "payoff" their director
had hoped for thus devolved into the awkward anticlimax of the London
police politely telling the world's most famous rock group that they would
have to hold it down.

The following day the Beatles returned to the basement of Apple for a
filmed session in which they recorded three more songs that were unsuitable for live performance with the group's standard instrumentation of
electric guitars and drums. These consisted of McCartney's two piano-
based ballads, "Let It Be" and "The Long and Winding Road" (on which
John Lennon played the bass), and "Two of Us," which featured a backing

of acoustic guitars. At the end of this session the film crew packed up and departed, the portable recording equipment was returned to EMI, and the Beatles' *Get Back* film and album project entered the protracted state of limbo it would occupy for the rest of 1969. A week later George Harrison celebrated the end of his worst musical experience as a Beatle by having his tonsils removed.

50

By 1969 it was real madness. We didn't know where we were. . . . Apple was like Toytown and Paul was Ernest the Policeman. We couldn't have gone on and on like that. We had to have a demon king.

—Derek Taylor

In January, while the Beatles were searching for their lost magic in the dark void of Twickenham, an exasperated John Lennon, his mind focused on money matters by the shock of Stephen Maltz's resignation letter and the terms of his own divorce settlement, complained to a reporter from the trade paper *Disc,* "We haven't got half the money people think we have. We have enough to live on but we can't let Apple go on like it is. . . . It doesn't need to make vast profits but if it carries on like this all of us will be broke in the next six months." Lennon's statement was picked up by the wire services and sent around the world. A few days later the *New York Post* quoted him further. "It's been pie in the sky from the start," he said. "Apple's been losing money every week because it needs close running by a big businessman." "When John said we were losing money he was talking about giving too much away to the wrong people," George Harrison added. "We've been too generous and that's going to stop."

Paul McCartney was furious with John for speaking with the press about Apple's financial woes. Though Paul agreed that the company's operations had been spinning out of control, he saw no reason to announce this fact to the world, and he had, in any case, been formulating his own plan to correct the situation. Paul had been impressed by the confidence and sophistication of his girlfriend Linda's father, Lee Eastman, when he met him in New York, and he had since discussed with Eastman the possibility of his becoming involved in the Beatles' business affairs. Eastman's expertise in the field of copyright law and his hard-headed representation of many well-known clients in the arts and entertainment made him an obvious candidate to advise the Beatles. When

McCartney contacted him in January concerning a matter of some urgency, Eastman was all ears.

McCartney's call was prompted not by Lennon's lament, but rather by the fact that Clive Epstein had just informed the Beatles that a firm of merchant bankers called the Triumph Investment Trust had made the Epstein family a substantial offer for the purchase of NEMS. Following the expiration of the Beatles' management contract and the formation of Apple Corps, NEMS had ceased to play an active role in managing the group's affairs. But under the terms of the contracts with EMI and Capitol that Brian Epstein had negotiated in 1967, NEMS continued to receive a 25-percent commission on the Beatles' record royalties. (Though this percentage would almost certainly have been reduced under the terms of any new management contract between Epstein and the Beatles, there was nothing untoward about this arrangement; as a rule, a manager is entitled to his percentage on the contracts he negotiates for an artist, whether he continues to represent the artist or not.) Confronted by the need to pay the substantial death duties owed on his brother's estate, and unnerved by the recent developments at Apple (especially the resignations of Harry Pinsker and Stephen Maltz), Clive Epstein was receptive to Triumph's interest. But he retained a sense of loyalty to the Beatles, and as soon as Triumph had formalized its offer, Epstein met with the group and offered them the opportunity to buy NEMS for themselves. Paul McCartney's first question to Lee Eastman in January 1969 was whether the Beatles should attempt this purchase. After learning that NEMS was entitled to collect a quarter of the Beatles' principal source of income for the next seven years, Eastman was convinced that they should. When Paul asked if he would represent the group in their dealings with Clive Epstein, Eastman said that he would.

Lee Eastman had spent his career representing artists and entertainers, some of whom were decidedly offbeat characters, but he had never felt comfortable in the presence of his daughter's long-haired, pot-smoking, rock-bohemian friends. Eastman had taken his son John into his firm a few years before, and McCartney's summons seems to have struck the father as a perfect opportunity for his son to gain some valuable legal experience. (He may also have assumed that the Beatles would simply be more comfortable dealing with someone their own age.) As a result, it was John Eastman who arrived in London in January 1969 to confer with the Beatles and Clive Epstein. Triumph had made the Epstein family an offer of £1.3 million for their 90-percent share of NEMS, but one-third of that amount was to be paid in two years' time, and was contingent on the receipt of future Beatles record royalties. When John Eastman offered to pay the family £1 million immediately, Epstein accepted without further ado. Eastman and the Beatles then spoke with Sir Joseph Lockwood to request that EMI loan the group the money they needed to buy NEMS. Since EMI already owed the Beatles an equivalent sum in royalties from the skyrocketing sales of the White Album, Lockwood readily agreed. When John Eastman returned to New York toward the end of January, the deal was all but done.

In business as in music, Paul McCartney's inclination was to improve on what had gone before. Whether or not he was aware at this point that the Eastman family name had once been Epstein, what Paul saw in John Eastman was a brasher, more aggressive version of Brian—a suave and self-assured young American whose practical inexperience (unlike Brian's) was amply offset by his wily and tough-minded father. Unfortunately, what John Lennon saw in John Eastman was a *counterfeit* version of Brian—a pretentious, Kennedyesque young American who showed none of Epstein's imagination or sensitivity, much less his personal devotion to the Beatles. (According to one account, Eastman earned Lennon's enmity by attempting to engage the "literary Beatle" in a conversation about Kafka.) Nor did the Eastmans' reputation as art collectors and their representation of successful New York painters sit well with Yoko Ono, who still bore the scars of her rejection by the New York art world. In the sixteen months since Brian Epstein's death, the Beatles had begun referring to the bankers, lawyers, and accountants they were now required to deal with as "suits," and from John Lennon's perspective, the only thing more objectionable than an old "suit" was a young one. John Eastman's apparent success in negotiating with Clive Epstein did little to convince Lennon that he was the "big businessman" the Beatles needed to clean up the mess at Apple. Instead, shortly after Eastman left London, Lennon found the man he thought he was looking for.

Allen Klein was a New York–based accountant and business manager who had been trying to insinuate himself into the Beatles' affairs since the summer of 1964, when he finagled a meeting with Brian Epstein and offered to renegotiate the group's recording contracts with EMI and Capitol in return for 20 percent of any increase in royalties he obtained.

Epstein was as appalled by Klein's presumption as he was by his proposal, and he curtly declined the offer. Denied the Beatles, Klein set out to corner the rest of the market in British Invasion bands. Within a year he was providing his aggressive form of business management to a list of English clients that included the Rolling Stones, the Dave Clark Five, the Animals, Herman's Hermits, and Donovan Leitch. In the fall of 1966, when Brian Epstein was negotiating a new recording contract for the Beatles, Klein flew to London, summoned a group of reporters to his hotel suite, and bluntly declared his intention to add the Beatles to his clientele. Klein's overtures had redoubled in the wake of Epstein's death, but he had never managed to speak with any of the Beatles themselves.

Short and fat, beady-eyed and greasily pompadoured, Allen Klein came across like a figure from *Guys and Dolls*. He spoke in a rattling New York argot, peppered his speech with profanity, and presented himself in a manner that was expressly designed to encourage his adversaries to underestimate him. (His affectations included a fondness for rumpled polo-neck sweaters and the habit of absentmindedly shuffling a deck of playing cards.) Born in Newark, New Jersey, in 1931, the son of a kosher butcher, Klein had spent most of his childhood in an orphanage after his mother died when he was nine months old. After graduating from high school and earning an accounting degree, he got a job in 1956 with a New York firm whose clients included a couple of minor recording stars. The music business, Klein quickly determined, was a den of fiscal iniquity, in which record labels and song publishers routinely defrauded their artists through a byzantine variety of accounting dodges. On the strength of this discovery, Klein made what he later described as "a philosophical decision" to cast his lot with "the little guy, the artist, because that's who I identify with." He soon began to characterize himself as the Robin Hood of Tin Pan Alley, or, as he put it, "Somebody who knows how to give these guys some of their own shit back." His first big client was Bobby Darin, the teen idol turned nightclub singer and movie star. At their first meeting, Klein supposedly told Darin, "I can find you money you never knew you had." This promise became his catchphrase, and his method for making good on it was to demand from record companies the right to perform an independent audit of his client's account. Since it was a foregone conclusion in the record business that any careful accounting would turn up significant irregularities, Klein found that he could often use the mere threat of an audit as a way of persuading a record company to renegotiate the terms of his client's contract. Klein's technique was effective only with established stars—artists who had already earned their record labels large sums of money and promised to earn them more. He knew nothing about the type of personal management practiced by Brian Epstein. "Don't talk to me about 'management,' " went one of his many maxims. "Talk to me about net and gross."

To date, Klein's most successful coup had involved the Rolling Stones. In 1965 he approached the Stones' manager, Andrew Loog Oldham, and offered to help negotiate a new recording contract for the group. The deal they signed with Decca Records was greatly exaggerated at the time; Oldham and Klein claimed that they had won the Stones a "million dollar" advance against royalties. In reality, the contract called for a guarantee, not an advance, to be paid out over ten years, with fully half the money going to Oldham and his new partner Klein. By the end of 1967, Oldham and Klein were suing one another, and all of the Stones' income from recordings and live performances was being paid directly to Klein's office in New York. Klein listed these earnings as assets of his own company and invested them in his own interest (most notably toward the purchase of a large block of stock with which he sought to gain control of the entertainment conglomerate MGM). According to their bassist Bill Wyman, the Stones themselves remained "virtually cashless" during this period. "Our money was still governed by Klein in New York, and sent to all of us on an ad-hoc basis," Wyman recalled.

The Beatles had heard about Klein for years, but none of them had actually met the man until he introduced himself to John Lennon on the set of the Stones' "Rock 'n' Roll Circus" in December 1968. A few weeks later, after reading Lennon's comments about Apple in the New York Post, Klein got through to John on the telephone and arranged to meet him in London toward the end of January. In the meantime, Lennon asked around. "I remember asking Mick [Jagger] what Klein was like, and he said, 'He's all right but it's hard to get your hands on the money.' " Lennon somehow construed this to mean that Klein prevented his clients from squandering their hard-earned wealth.

Klein was characteristically well-prepared for his meeting with Lennon, who came with Yoko Ono at his side. Klein's reading of the Hunter Davies biography had given him a sense of John's psychology and alerted him to the parallels between John's childhood and his own. He now played on those parallels skillfully over the course of an evening in which he demonstrated his knowledge of the Beatles' music (and of John's specific contributions to it) and commiserated with Lennon about the chaos at Apple and the way in which the Beatles had been victimized by the naïve deals Brian Epstein had made. Klein was careful to include Yoko Ono in his presentation, implying that he would get her a film deal with United Artists. John and Yoko were completely smitten by Klein's aura of street smarts and his aggressive New York style. That very evening, John dictated a series of letters to Clive Epstein, Sir Joseph Lockwood, and Dick James, informing them that he had authorized Klein to act on his behalf, and instructing them to provide Klein with any information he requested.

The following day, on the eve of the rooftop concert at Apple, Lennon introduced his new personal manager to the other Beatles. Klein began the meeting by recommending that the group hold off on the purchase of NEMS until he had had a chance to examine their finances. He suggested that the price for NEMS was too high, and that the purchase of the company might not even be desirable. Having solicited the Eastmans' counsel in this matter, Paul McCartney insisted that there was no point in discussing the NEMS deal without them. After Klein suggested that they table the matter until John Eastman could return to London, McCartney left the meeting. In his absence, George Harrison and Ringo Starr agreed informally to let Klein represent their interests as well.

The news of Allen Klein's involvement with the Beatles brought both Lee and John Eastman racing back to London. When they arrived, the three New Yorkers confronted one another in the Beatles' presence. John Eastman laid out the particulars of the NEMS deal, Klein questioned its wisdom, and Lee Eastman responded by attacking Klein's reputation. When the dust had settled, the Apple press office issued a pair of formal announcements, the first stating that Allen Klein had been retained to "look into" the Beatles' finances, the second stating that the firm of Eastman & Eastman had been retained as legal advisers to the group. That same day, Klein met with Clive Epstein and requested that the purchase of NEMS be postponed for several weeks so that he could review the Beatles' finances and, as he put it, ascertain that they could indeed come up with the money for the deal. With mounting trepidation, Epstein agreed to this delay.

Klein returned to New York and spent the first two weeks of February poring over the statements he had obtained from Apple, NEMS, and

EMI. Then, in the middle of the month, John Eastman sent a letter to Clive Epstein. "As you know," it read, "Mr. Allen Klein is doing an audit of the Beatles' affairs vis-à-vis NEMS. When this has been completed, I suggest that we meet to discuss the results of Mr. Klein's audit as well as the propriety of the negotiations surrounding the nine-year agreement between EMI, the Beatles, and NEMS." In two sentences, Eastman managed to inform Epstein that the Beatles' relationship with NEMS—as opposed to the Beatles' ability to purchase NEMS—was the focus of Klein's audit, and that the "propriety" of that relationship was being called into question. With the deadline for payment of his brother's estate taxes fast approaching, Epstein immediately renewed his negotiations with Leonard Richenberg, managing director of the Triumph Investment Group. By the end of February, Triumph owned 90 percent of NEMS.

John Eastman later insisted that he had sent the letter at Klein's request—a claim that Klein denied. But even if Klein had requested it, the letter amounted to a colossal blunder on Eastman's part. Not only did it drive Clive Epstein into the arms of Leonard Richenberg, but it also provided Klein with an opportunity to shine at Eastman's expense. Two days after the sale of NEMS was announced, Klein returned to London and arranged a meeting with Richenberg, whom he subjected to his time-tested tactics of intimidation. His audit, Klein stated, showed that NEMS owed the Beatles a fortune in unreported concert fees from the years 1964–66. Nevertheless, he continued, the Beatles would be willing to forgive this indiscretion if Triumph would simply relinquish its contractual claim to 25 percent of the group's recording royalties. The managing director of Triumph—an economics professor at Oxford and a former adviser to the Macmillan government—was unimpressed. Having sized Klein up as "a nasty little gangster," Richenberg showed him the door.

Unfazed, Klein's next move was to send a letter over the Beatles' signatures to EMI, instructing the company to pay all accrued and future royalties directly to Apple, ignoring the terms of the contract Brian Epstein had signed in 1967. Klein also sent a letter to Richenberg declaring that NEMS was no longer authorized to act in any capacity as the Beatles' agent. Though the letter stopped short of claiming that NEMS was no longer entitled to receive its commission, the implication was clear: Apple, not NEMS, was going to control all future transactions between the two companies. Caught between Allen Klein and Leonard Richenberg, Sir Joseph Lockwood decided that EMI would simply place all the monies it owed the Beatles and/or NEMS in escrow until it could be determined who was entitled to what. Triumph responded by going to court in an effort to freeze the £1.3 million in royalties that EMI owed the Beatles. Noting that the disputed royalties had been securely placed in escrow, the court declined to intervene. However inadvertantly, within a month of his first meeting with John Lennon, Allen Klein had succeeded in cutting the Beatles off from their principal source of income, thereby creating a situation that only he could resolve.

51

It was a choice between the in-laws and the outlaws.

—John Lennon

In March 1969, with their business affairs in turmoil and tensions among the Beatles freshly inflamed by the advent of Allen Klein, Paul McCartney and John Lennon both married the women they had fallen in love with during the previous year. Linda Eastman was four months pregnant at the time of her marriage to Paul, which took place at a local registry office in London. Word of the couple's intentions had been leaked to the newspapers at the last minute, thereby ensuring that a crowd of several hundred people, evenly divided between reporters and fans, was waiting on the street outside when the newlyweds emerged. The McCartneys left immediately for a few days in seclusion at their farm in Scotland, followed by a visit to Linda's family in New York.

None of the other Beatles attended Paul and Linda's wedding, but the day was marred by the suspiciously coincidental arrests of George and Pattie Harrison after a police raid on their home in Esher turned up a sizable cache of hashish. The Harrisons would eventually plead guilty to a charge of cannabis possession and pay a moderate fine. Their arrest was another feather in the cap of a starstruck Drugs Squad detective named Norman Pilcher, who had played a part in the earlier arrests of John Lennon and the Rolling Stones. (In 1973, Pilcher was convicted of perjury and evidence tampering in an unrelated case and sentenced to four years in jail by a judge who accused him of "deliberately poison[ing] the wells of criminal justice.")

One week after Paul and Linda's wedding, John and Yoko followed suit. (Yoko's divorce from Tony Cox had been finalized in February.) In an effort to avoid the crush of publicity that surrounded the McCartney nuptials, the couple traveled first to Paris and then to the Crown colony of Gibraltar to be married in a private civil ceremony. ("Miss Ono is an actress, painter, and maker of a film on human bottoms," the *Times* of London reported, straight-faced.) From Gibraltar they made their way back to Paris and then to Amsterdam. There, having had their fill of privacy, John and Yoko installed themselves in a suite at the Hilton Hotel, declared their stay to be a "Bed-In for Peace," and invited the international press to join them on their honeymoon. For the next week, lounging in bed in their white pajamas, flanked by enormous baskets of flowers and a pair of hand-lettered signs that read "Hair Peace" and "Bed Peace" (puns on the titles of Yoko's works like "Cut Piece"), they received a succession of sheepish reporters, whose initial prurient curiosity, primed by the *Two Virgins* cover, soon yielded to a series of repetitive and often sardonic questions about the nature of a "Bed-In" and its purpose in the larger scheme of things.

John and Yoko had collaborated on any number of joint projects during their first year together, but the Amsterdam Bed-In marked a new stage in their careers as publicity artists. "It's the best idea we've had yet," John boasted. "We're doing a commercial for peace on the front pages of newspapers around the world instead of a commercial for war." From the Lennons' perspective, they were turning the tables on the press's intrusive fascination with celebrities like themselves to extol the politics of consciousness and gesture over the politics of confrontation. "We're trying to sell peace, like a product, and sell it like people sell soap or soft drinks," John explained. He and Yoko were "trying to communicate, through the communications media, press, and TV, to try to tell people, who are interested in protesting, to try and do something about it, instead of sitting home talking about it." John and Yoko saw themselves as media activists, using their mastery of public relations to effect a greater good. Others, beginning with spokesmen for the media itself, took a less generous view. "Beatle John and his charmer Yoko have now established themselves as the outstanding nut cases of the Western world," declared the *Daily Express*. The Lennons were variously dismissed as cynical self-promoters, using the cause of peace to call attention to themselves, and fatuous dilettantes, vastly underestimating the political realities that contributed to war. (Asked how she would have dealt with the threat of a megalomaniacal figure like Hitler, Yoko replied, "I would have gone to bed with him. In ten days I would have changed his mind.") But under the narcissistic logic that derived from the marriage of Yoko's exhibitionism to John's celebrity, there was nothing incompatible about combining a well-meaning political gesture with an act of blatant self-advertisement, while the couple's courting of rejection and ridicule only worked to strengthen their bond. As John explained it,

"Yoko and I are quite willing to be the world's clowns if by doing so it will do some good. I know I'm one of those 'famous personalities.' For reasons known only to themselves, people do print what I say. And I'm saying peace."

After spending a week in Amsterdam, John and Yoko flew to Vienna, where they invited reporters to interview them while they huddled together inside a black sack. The purpose of their visit was to publicize the premiere on Austrian television of a remarkable film called *Rape*, which they had commissioned in November 1968, shortly after their arrests for cannabis possession. Based on a one-sentence "script" by Yoko, *Rape* is a chilling extension of the theme of victimization that Yoko first explored with "Cut Piece," and is universally regarded as her most artistically successful film.

AT THE END of March, the honeymoons of both Beatles came abruptly to an end with the announcement in the London newspapers that the Associated Television Corporation (ATV), an entertainment conglomerate headed by Sir Lew Grade (a.k.a. "the most powerful man in [British] show business"), was seeking to purchase Northern Songs, the publicly traded music publishing company that owned the copyrights on the entire Lennon-McCartney catalog. In the opening move of this takeover bid, ATV had acquired the shares of Northern's president, Dick James, and its chairman, Charles Silver. Like Clive Epstein, Dick James had been growing increasingly nervous at the turmoil surrounding Apple and the signs of disunity among the Beatles. Northern Songs had Lennon and McCartney under contract until 1973, but as the only publicly traded music publishing company in Britain, the value of its stock was subject to investors' perceptions regarding the future of its prime asset, the Lennon-McCartney partnership. For Dick James, the involvement of Allen Klein in the Beatles' affairs represented the last straw, for James was a music business insider, and he was well aware of Klein's reputation.

The Beatles were understandably furious with James for selling his shares in Northern Songs without informing them of his plans. Even before Lennon and McCartney could return from their honeymoons, George Harrison confronted James and accused him of betraying the band that had made him a multimillionaire. (Although Harrison had allowed his own contract with Northern Songs to lapse in 1968, he and

Ringo continued to own stock in the company.) From James's perspective, of course, he had failed to inform the Beatles for fear of alerting Allen Klein. But his "business is business" stance was galling nonetheless. Though Northern Songs had done a capable job of servicing the Lennon-McCartney catalog, the company's efforts at promotion paled beside those of the Beatles themselves, whose records and films had made their music ubiquitous throughout the world. Unlike Brian Epstein or George Martin, both of whom made critical contributions to the Beatles' success, Dick James was simply one of the luckiest men in show business, and it was no overstatement to say that he owed the Beatles his entire career as a music publisher.

Allen Klein was also on vacation when the news of the ATV bid was announced, but he quickly arrived in London raring to do battle on the Beatles' behalf. In the wake of the NEMS fiasco, Klein welcomed another chance to show the group how aggressive and effective he could be. Over the next two weeks Klein put together a counteroffer worth more than £2 million that was designed to secure the Beatles a controlling interest in Northern Songs by purchasing an additional 20 percent of the company's shares on top of the 31 percent they already collectively owned. Their counteroffer was underwritten by a loan of £1.25 million from the merchant bankers Henry Ansbacher & Co., and it was sweetened by a promise from Lennon and McCartney to extend their contract with Northern for two additional years beyond its expiration in 1973. The loan was necessary because £1.3 million of the Beatles' money was frozen as a result of their dispute with the Triumph Investment Trust. The collateral for the Ansbacher loan consisted of John Lennon's shares in Northern Songs plus 45,000 shares of MGM stock that was pledged by the Beatles' new business partner, Allen Klein. Klein's participation was necessary because Paul McCartney, acting on the advice of his brother-in-law, John Eastman, had refused to put up his own shares in Northern Songs as collateral for the loan.

EARLY IN APRIL, as the battle for control of Northern Songs was being fought, John Lennon and Paul McCartney met with Glyn Johns at Olympic Sound Studios in West London to mix two of the tracks the Beatles had recorded at Apple in January, "Get Back" and "Don't Let Me Down," for release as the group's first single of 1969. Shortly after the

Apple sessions had ended, Johns had taken it upon himself to review the tapes and create a rough mix of a highly unconventional album. "As the Beatles had proven themselves to be masters of the 'produced' record," he explained, "I thought it would be a pretty neat idea to release something that was completely the opposite of what everybody had come to expect from the band." Accordingly he had constructed "an album of rehearsals, with chat and jokes and bits of general conversation in between the tracks." Initially the Beatles had been indifferent to this idea, but after hearing Johns's rough mix, Lennon and McCartney told him to go ahead with the project. Johns collected the tapes of the *Get Back* sessions from the vault at Abbey Road and spent the next month at Olympic Sound putting the album together by himself.

Two weeks later Apple released "Get Back" b/w "Don't Let Me Down." The eight months since the release of "Hey Jude" had been the longest span between singles the Beatles had ever allowed, and the public responded by buying this catchy, upbeat record at a rate that caused it to become the first record ever released in Britain to *enter* the charts at number one. From its origins as a parody of Powellism, "Get Back" had evolved into a sketchy narrative about the wanderings of a pair of characters named Jojo and Loretta (who "thought she was a woman, but she was another man"). Paul sings it brightly over the scampering rhythm of Ringo's snare and Billy Preston's electric piano, enjoining one and all to "get back to where you once belonged" while the band drives the words home with the simplest of hooks: three evenly phrased accents on the three chords (A, D, G) that carry the A major tune, followed by a pair of additional slashing syncopations on the tonic chord. That "Jojo" sounds like an obvious conflation of John and Yoko may have caused some paranoia on their part, although John himself had a hand in the verse about Loretta, whose gender issues may have reflected a comment he made to *Melody Maker* that, intellectually, "Yoko's like a man." In keeping with its jammy origins, the track features the most extensive instrumental playing of any Beatle single. Both Billy Preston and John Lennon perform extended solos—John having taken over the lead guitar chair after George Harrison walked out during the rehearsals at Twickenham.

The B-side of the single, "Don't Let Me Down," was John's one substantial contribution to the January sessions at Apple. The song has a dreamy, love-soaked feel and a fine, minimalist lyric that answers the impassioned "don'ts" of the title and refrain with a trio of droll verses that practically conjugate the verb "to do" ("She do me . . . she does me . . . she done me"). Though the simple chord progression seems to have been modeled on the then-recent instrumental "Albatross" by Fleetwood Mac, the overall sound of the arrangement—the weary tempo, the loose phrasing of Paul's harmony, and the groundswells of bass, Leslie-toned guitar, and electric piano that answer John's voice in the chorus—were strongly suggestive of The Band.

A few days after the release of "Get Back," John and Paul, accompanied by George Martin and Geoff Emerick, returned to Abbey Road studios for the first time since the completion of the White Album. There, with Martin producing, Emerick engineering, and the other two Beatles absent, they recorded a song called "The Ballad of John and Yoko," in which John marked his return to married life by chronicling in five narrative verses the itinerary of his and Yoko's wedding and honeymoon excursion from London to Paris to Gibraltar to Amsterdam to Vienna and back to London, complete with press commentary ("The newspapers said, she's gone to his head / They look just like two gurus in drag"). John provided the lead vocal and guitar, while Paul expertly simulated the rest of the band, playing bass, drums, piano, percussion, and singing harmony. The travelogue lyric and the chugging accompaniment were sung and played in the style of Chuck Berry. By starting the chorus with the exclamation "Christ!" and ending with the line "They're gonna crucify me," John revived some of his old demons as an expression of the persecution complex that had sealed his relationship with Yoko as firmly as any wedding band. For his part, Paul McCartney's enthusiastic participation in this session, together with his endorsement of the record's release as a single a mere six weeks after "Get Back," demonstrated how strongly Paul continued to believe that the future of the Beatles rested on his ability to revive his musical relationship with John.

"The Ballad of John and Yoko" marked the beginning of two weeks of sessions in which the Beatles recorded the basic tracks for five new songs, including two by Harrison ("Old Brown Shoe" and "Something") and one each by Lennon ("I Want You"), McCartney ("Oh! Darling"), and Starr ("Octopus's Garden"). Though these sessions were nominally overseen by George Martin's assistant Chris Thomas, they were effectively produced by the Beatles themselves. (At this point, the idea of artists producing their own recordings was simply too much for the corporate bureaucracy of EMI.) While the Beatles were recording this new material at Abbey Road, across town at Olympic Sound, Glyn Johns continued his work on the "rehearsal album" he was assembling from the tapes of the sessions at Apple. Johns's version of *Get Back* now consisted of twelve Beatle originals along with cover versions of the Drifters' hit "Save the Last Dance for Me" and a bawdy Liverpool folk song called "Maggie Mae." When the Beatles heard the album, they were enthusiastic enough about it to commission a cover that drew an explicit connection to the only other ostensibly "live" album they had ever made, *Please Please Me*. Using the same photographer, the four of them posed on the stairwell of the EMI Building at Manchester Square in a precise re-creation of the cover of their first LP. While the lines of the building were unchanged, the contrast in the Beatles' appearance in the two photographs was almost as striking as the contrast between the waxwork Moptops and the psychedelic vaudevillians on the cover of *Sgt. Pepper*. What had passed for long hair on the fresh-faced lads of 1963 now looked like something out of a grammar-school graduation photograph compared with the thickly tressed and (with the exception of Paul McCartney) mustachioed men of 1969. John Lennon in particular was almost unrecognizable compared with his former self, his features entirely obscured by a full beard that grew high on his cheekbones, round, wire-rimmed spectacles, and a dense thicket of shoulder-length hair, parted like Yoko's in the middle, that cascaded down his forehead and across both sides of his face.

In the meantime, the takeover struggle for Northern Songs was gaining momentum amid daily speculation and intrigue in the financial press concerning the efforts of ATV and the Beatles to woo the support of a consortium of institutional investors who controlled nearly 15 percent of the shares in the company. Another significant player was the Triumph Investment Trust, which had acquired a 5-percent interest in Northern Songs through its purchase of NEMS. A major concern of both the consortium and Triumph was that Allen Klein have nothing to do with the management of Northern Songs if the Beatles did succeed in gaining control of the company. This concern was heightened in the last week of April when Klein held a press conference at Apple to announce formally that he was taking over "representation" of the Beatles' companies. When asked at this press conference about his role in securing the Ansbacher loan for the Beatles, Klein insisted, "Whatever arrangement I have with the Beatles has nothing to do with Northern Songs."

In fact, Klein's participation in the fight for Northern Songs had *everything* to do with his desire to manage the Beatles, for his willingness to back them up with his own money impressed John Lennon, George Harrison, and Ringo Starr as a definitive gesture of good faith. Shortly after the press conference at Apple, Klein presented the group with a three-year management contract that entitled him to 20 percent, off the top, of everything they earned. Knowing that the other Beatles were prepared to agree to these terms, Paul McCartney pressed to reduce Klein's percentage to 15 percent and limit his commission to any new contracts he negotiated on behalf of the group. Eventually a compromise was reached that gave Klein 20 percent of any new contracts he negotiated and 20 percent of any increase he obtained on the Beatles' old contracts. The contract also gave him 10 percent of the gross earnings of Apple Records, 10 percent of George Harrison and Ringo Starr's music publishing income, and 25 percent of the Beatles' income from merchandising. Apple was also obligated to pay all living and travel expenses for Klein and his staff in London. In what amounted to a purely symbolic gesture, McCartney continued to register his displeasure by refusing to sign his copy of the contract, prompting a furious argument between him and the other three Beatles in the middle of a recording session on May 5. The following day, when the group returned to the studio, Paul unveiled a new song he had written that began with the words "You never give me your money / You only give me your funny papers. . . ."

Within days of placing the Beatles under contract, Klein summarily fired most of the Apple management staff. He began with Alistair Taylor, the former NEMS stalwart who served as office manager of Apple (and whom Klein described as "literally a spy for NEMS"). Next on the list was Ron Kass, the head of Apple Records and the company's most capable (and hence, in Klein's view, most threatening) executive, whose label had sold more than 16 million singles and albums in its first eight months of existence. (Kass's departure was followed a month later by the voluntary resignation of his A&R chief, Peter Asher, who wound up taking his principal discovery, James Taylor, along with him.) Klein then worked his way down through the corporate hierarchy of Apple, sparing only Neil Aspinall, Peter Brown, and Derek Taylor, all of whom were effectively demoted to the role of personal assistants to the Beatles. A Klein functionary named Peter Howard was installed at Savile Row to oversee all of the company's financial expenditures. In an ugly reprise of the cowardice they had shown toward Pete Best in 1962, the Beatles offered not a word of regret or appreciation to any of their former employees—some of whom, like Alistair Taylor, had literally existed at their beck and call since 1963. Within days of Ron Kass's departure, John and Yoko appropriated his large ground-floor office to serve as the nerve center of their own private company, Bag Productions. The Lennons also celebrated Allen Klein's appointment as the Beatles' manager by purchasing a thirty-room Georgian mansion called Tittenhurst Park, which stood on a manicured seventy-acre estate near Ascot.

By the middle of May, the battle for control of Northern Songs appeared to be tilting in the Beatles' favor. Bruce Ormond, the managing director of Ansbacher, had structured a deal whereby the consortium of institutional investors would ally with the Beatles to replace the current management of Northern with a new board of directors under an arrangement that would place the voting interests of both the consortium and the Beatles in the hands of independent trustees. Having gained the consent of the consortium, Ormond presented the deal to Allen Klein and the Beatles, only to have John Lennon reject the idea of relinquishing control to a trustee. "I'm not going to be fucked around by men in suits sitting on their fat arses in the City," John reportedly told Ormond. With that, the consortium's own men in suits began to reconsider. On Friday, May 17, the headline in the London *Times* had read, ATV DEFEAT IN BID FOR NORTHERN SONGS. On the following Monday, the *Times* headline read, ATV WINS NORTHERN SONGS. Over the weekend, the consortium had signed a letter of agreement with Sir Lew Grade. The rift between John Lennon and Paul McCartney over Allen Klein had cost them control of the single most lucrative music publishing asset in the era of rock 'n' roll.

52

Of course there is no question of us splitting up. There are some people who would like to see our friendship break up, but this is a physical and spiritual impossibility. The thing people don't understand about the Beatles is that we've known each other for so long and our level of communication is something others don't understand. We are all influencing each other. I don't question anything John does anymore. I know why he does it. I understand.

—George Harrison (April 1969)

At the end of May, Apple Records rush-released "The Ballad of John and Yoko" as the Beatles' second single of the year. (In the United States, a number of Top Forty stations banned the song on account of its references to Christ and crucifixion.) At a moment when "Get Back" was still at the top of the charts in Britain and the United States, the release of the record had less to do with commercial considerations than with the staging of John and Yoko's second week-long Bed-In for Peace at the Queen Elizabeth Hotel in Montreal, Canada. The Lennons had originally planned to bring their peace campaign to the United States, but John's conviction for cannabis possession had given the American immigration authorities all the excuse they needed to refuse him a visitor's visa. After traveling first to the Bahamas, which turned out to be much hotter and farther from the United States than John had imagined, they settled on Montreal, which had the desired proximity to American media outlets. (As the principal destination for young Americans fleeing the military draft, Canada was viewed as a peace-friendly nation.) During their week in Montreal, John and Yoko were visited by several dozen American reporters and gave numerous telephone interviews to American radio stations. They also received a succession of countercultural celebrities, including Timothy Leary, Allen Ginsberg, and Dick Gregory, some of whom participated in a hastily organized hotel-room recording session of a new song John had written called "Give Peace a Chance." The song was a sing-along anthem in the mold of "All You Need Is Love," with formulaic, fill-in-the-blank verses ("everybody's talking 'bout . . .") resolving in the simple "all we are saying" of the refrain. Two months later, when Apple released this recording of "Give Peace a Chance" as a single, the publishing credit read Lennon-McCartney, but the name of the artist was listed as the Plastic Ono Band.

The Beatles spent the entire month of June on vacation. The McCartneys traveled to Greece, the Harrisons to Sardinia, and the Starrs to the South of France. Prior to his departure, Paul McCartney telephoned George Martin to ask Martin if he would be willing to work with the Beatles on a new album that they wanted to record over the summer. Allen Klein had just decided to postpone the release of *Get Back* until he had a chance to approach United Artists about the possibility of releasing Michael Lindsay-Hogg's film as a theatrical feature, and Klein was eager for the Beatles to release an album by the end of the year. That Paul felt a need to ask Martin about his availability dramatized how much the Beatles' professional situation had changed since the start of the year. Working with the group had become a "miserable experience" for Martin: "After [*Get Back*], I thought it was the end of the road for all of us. I didn't really want to work with them anymore because they were becoming unpleasant people—to themselves as well as to other people. . . . I was quite surprised when Paul rang me up and asked me to produce another record for them. I said, 'If I'm really allowed to produce it, I will. If I have to go back and accept a lot of instructions which I don't like, then I won't do it.'" One of Martin's conditions was that the record be made at Abbey Road. Martin also requested that Geoff Emerick be brought in to engineer the album. (In the spring, Emerick had quit his job at EMI and gone to work for Apple, where he designed and built a genuine state-of-the-art recording studio in the basement at Savile Row.) Armed with McCartney's assurances, Martin went ahead and booked a block of time for the Beatles at Abbey Road from the first of July to the end of August.

John and Yoko remained in London for most of June, making television and radio appearances on behalf of their peace campaign and overseeing the extensive renovations they had commissioned on Tittenhurst Park. Toward the end of the month, they took John's son, Julian, and Yoko's daughter, Kyoko, on a driving vacation that included visits to John's aunt Mimi in Liverpool and his aunt Elizabeth in Edinburgh. John had rarely driven a car since getting his license in 1964; four days into the trip, he steered his rented Austin headlong into a ditch. Rushed by ambulance to a hospital in Glasgow, John, Yoko, and Kyoko were treated for serious cuts and bruises. (John reportedly required seventeen stitches to close a gash on his head.) Cynthia Lennon and Tony Cox quickly arrived to whisk their frightened children away. After nearly a week in the hospital, John and Yoko were returned to London by helicopter. When it was determined that Yoko was once again pregnant, her doctors advised her to remain in bed for the time being.

Two days after the Lennons' road accident, Brian Jones of the Rolling Stones was found dead in the swimming pool of his home. A coroner's inquest subsequently attributed Jones's death to "drowning associated with alcohol, drugs, and severe liver deterioration." But, as with Brian Epstein, there were rumors of suicide. Barely a month before his death, Jones had been forced to "resign" from the band he had founded and had been replaced by a baby-faced guitarist named Mick Taylor. His departure from the Stones marked the end of a bitter power struggle between Jones and Mick Jagger that had divided the group for years, and it was sealed by Jones's flagrant drug and alcohol abuse, which had ravaged his mind, sapped his energy, and saddled him with an arrest record that made it impossible for the Stones—who, like the Beatles, were seeking to return to their roots as a performing band—to obtain the visas they would need to tour in the United States.

On the weekend after Jones's death, the Stones performed a free concert in Hyde Park that was attended by an estimated quarter of a million people. Sponsored and filmed by Granada Television, the concert had been planned for more than a month, but the band turned the occasion into a memorial service for their former guitarist. Mick Jagger read an elegiac passage by Shelley in his best mock-Cockney accent, and hundreds of white butterflies were released from cages at the front of the stage. (Instead of rising as intended in a photogenic cloud, most settled on the ground and were trampled underfoot.) Though the Stones themselves were embarrassed by the sloppiness of their first live performance in more than two years, the event was like a gigantic London version of the free concerts that were a hallmark of the rock scene in San Francisco. Adding to the authenticity was the presence of a security detail composed of English Hell's Angels, a group of former Rockers who had taken their fascination with mechanized machismo to the next stage, modeling themselves on the California-based motorcycle outlaws with the same precision of style and absence of substance with which many English flower children had emulated their American counterparts.

IT IS UNCLEAR to what extent Paul McCartney had informed the other Beatles of the assurances he gave to George Martin to assuage Martin's concerns about working with the group again. What is certain is that the July sessions got off to an inauspicious start. July 1 was the date of John Lennon's car crash in Scotland, which suggests that John felt no strong obligation to be making a record in London that day; it would be several weeks before he was in any condition to record. (His and Yoko's recovery from their injuries was seriously compounded by the symptoms of heroin withdrawal.) As a result, Paul was the only Beatle to show up at Abbey Road on the first day of the sessions, where he spent several hours refining his lead vocal on "You Never Give Me Your Money." On the second day, George and Ringo joined him, and for the next three weeks they more or less functioned as a three-piece band, recording three new songs from scratch, and adding vocal and instrumental overdubs to three of the basic tracks they had recorded in April. John did make a brief appearance nine days into the sessions, though the nature of his visit did nothing to rekindle a sense of harmony in the group. Because Yoko had been told to remain in bed, and because John felt incapable of going anywhere without her, his arrival at Abbey Road was preceded by that of a double bed, which was set up amid the instruments and amplifiers in the main room of the studio. John and Yoko followed in an ambulance, whose attendants carried Yoko into the studio and tucked her into the bed. Whether by accident or design, the Beatles spent the entire afternoon recording Paul's "Maxwell's Silver Hammer," a song that John despised. John remained an elusive presence at Abbey Road until the third week in July, when, once again accompanied by Yoko and her bed, he unveiled a new song called "Come Together" whose title was suggested by the slogan ("Come together! Join the Party!") of Timothy Leary's latest publicity stunt, his recently announced campaign for the governorship of California.

In keeping with McCartney's commitment to giving George Martin a free hand as producer, the two of them had discussed the possibility that the new album might conform to a formal musical plan. Martin envisioned something even more thematically ambitious than the music-hall-bill-with-epilogue structure of *Sgt. Pepper*. He proposed an album that would consist of "a continuously moving piece of music," which would lead the Beatles "to try to think in symphonic terms." When John Lennon joined the sessions, however, he made it clear that he had no interest in this kind of symphonic thinking. John's idea of a suitable format for the album was to put all of his songs on one side and all of Paul's songs on the other. McCartney resolved this disagreement by proposing another compromise. The first side of the album would conform to Lennon's vision and, in the style of *Revolver*, present each of the Beatles in a highly individualized form. The second side of the album would conform to Martin's vision. By now, both John and Paul had accumulated their usual store of half-finished bits and pieces, which, in prior years, they would have worked together to refine into finished songs. Given that active collaboration was now out of the question, McCartney and Martin came up with the idea of arranging a half-dozen or so of these half-finished songs into a medley or suite that would employ some of the harmonic and thematic linkages that Martin had in mind. On this basis, the Beatles settled down in the weeks after Lennon's return for a series of sessions in which the four of them would work together only when they had to. In the words of the tape-operator John Kurlander (who went on to become a senior engineer at EMI), "When just one of the Beatles was on a session it would be absolutely great; with two of them it would be okay; with three of them the atmosphere would get a bit tense; and when the four of them were together it would occasionally be unbearable."

ALLEN KLEIN, MEANWHILE, spent the summer of 1969 attending to the shambles he had helped to make of the Beatles' business affairs. Desperate to free up the record royalties that EMI had been holding in escrow since the spring, Klein began by reopening negotiations with his nemesis Leonard Richenberg at the Triumph Investment Trust. Dispensing with his usual bluster, Klein agreed to a settlement that would pay the new owners of NEMS their full share (£325,000) of the £1.3 million in royalties that had been placed in escrow by EMI, an additional £800,000 in lieu of record royalties for next three years, and 5 percent of the royalties due over the final four years (1972–76) of the Beatles' recording contract. As an adjunct to this deal, the Beatles received stock in Triumph in return for relinquishing the 10-percent interest they held in NEMS, and Triumph received a roughly equivalent amount of cash from the Beatles in return for the 5-percent interest NEMS held in Northern Songs.

With the NEMS matter settled, Klein turned his attention to the thing that he did best. The standard approach to contract renegotiations in the record business has always turned on the simple fact that a record label cannot *compel* a disaffected artist to make records (provided the artist is willing to suffer the loss of income from remaining idle). In the Beatles' case, Brian Epstein had already included a built-in basis for renegotiation in the nine-year deal he signed in 1967 with EMI and Capitol by casting the Beatles' commitment not in terms of records but rather in terms of tracks. This approach was typical of Epstein. Rather than broaching the subject of a renegotiation with a stated or implied threat to withhold "product," it would have allowed him to sit down with EMI and Capitol having already fulfilled the commitment he had made on behalf of the group. Now it was Klein, whose standard opening move consisted of the double-barreled threat to withhold product and audit his client's account, who benefited from Epstein's more decorous approach.

In the three years since the Beatles had signed their last contract with EMI, many of the benchmarks that had governed the royalty structure of the record business in Britain and America had been swept away. A historical shift was occurring throughout the entertainment industry whereby, for the first time, the economics of the industry would take the primacy of the performer into account. In the music business, the rise of independent production and "lease taping" had demystified the actual costs involved in recording, manufacturing, distributing, and promoting a record, turning the indeterminate expense of "grooming" talent into a straightforward matter of pounds and pence, dollars and cents. Established, top-selling artists were no longer willing to acquiesce to a royalty structure in which they were expected, in effect, to subsidize the often unsuccessful efforts of record companies to sign and promote new talent, while the ready access to the means of record production had turned the sale of records into a series of distribution deals.

As a result, when Allen Klein sat down with Sir Joseph Lockwood of EMI and Victor Gortikoff, the new president of Capitol, in the summer of 1969, the only questions to be decided were how much more EMI and Capitol were going to have to pay the Beatles in royalties and how much more product EMI and Capitol were going to be able to get from the group. The new royalty rate that Klein secured for the Beatles was the equivalent of 25 percent of the wholesale price of a record for the first three years remaining on their contract, rising to 33 percent for the last four years of the deal. In return, the Beatles agreed to produce a minimum of two albums and three singles a year. EMI/Capitol also gained the right to reissue and repackage the group's old records. Having played a leading role in helping to transform the record business from a scruffy sidelight of the entertainment industry into a billion-dollar enterprise, the Beatles were finally positioned to reap the full rewards of their success.

Next on Allen Klein's to-do list was reaching an accord with his other nemesis, Sir Lew Grade. After signing a letter of agreement with the consortium of stockholders whose support had given ATV control of Northern Songs, Grade had spent the entire summer haggling with the consortium's representatives over the price of a buyout deal. In September the two sides finally came to terms. Aware that ATV's goal was to gain complete ownership of the company, Klein initially made Grade a complex offer that would have given Lennon and McCartney a lucrative package of cash and ATV stock in return for their shares, extended their contract with Northern, and given the company the rights to publish the songs of George Harrison and Ringo Starr as well. But John Eastman, on behalf of Paul McCartney, categorically rejected this deal. In the end, Klein agreed to sell the Beatles' 31-percent interest in Northern Songs to ATV for the same price ATV had paid the consortium for its shares, netting Lennon and McCartney a cash payment of more than £2 million.

> "Higher!" Sly shouted into the crowd. "Higher!" they boomed back with the force of half a million voices at their loudest. He threw up his arms in a peace sign and the audience responded, shouting "higher" in unison and raising their arms and fingers into the air, joyously, desperately, far as a huge searchlight could pick out, arms and hands and fingers raised in peace signs, heads and voices crying out into the night, crying the anguished plea of the Sixties: Higher, higher!
>
> —Ellen Sander

On a Monday evening in the second week of August, as the sessions at Abbey Road drew to a close, John, Paul, and George spent several hours recording vocal overdubs on a song John had written about his relationship with Yoko called "I Want You (She's So Heavy)." Their work consisted of chanting the phrase "she's so *heavy*" over and over onto multiple tracks. Though all four of the Beatles would play with one another in various configurations during the months and years ahead, that evening, and those words, marked the last time that the three founding members of the group would ever sing together on a song. The following Friday, George Martin and the Beatles spent the afternoon and evening supervising overdubs by a thirty-piece orchestra onto four of the album's tracks.

That same day the Woodstock Music and Art Fair opened its gates on the grounds of a six-hundred-acre dairy farm in upstate New York. By nightfall the gates and the fences that linked them had been trampled down by the first waves of a crowd of more than half a million people who converged on the festival from all over the Northeast, creating what *Rolling Stone* described as a *"cosmic* traffic jam" that eventually closed the country roads of Sullivan County for fifteen miles in all directions. Tens of thousands of people turned back in disappointment. Tens of thousands simply abandoned their cars and spent the weekend camped out in the adjoining woods, fields, and hamlets, prevailing on the generosity of the local population for the necessities of life. But hundreds of thousands more pressed on, streaming along the roads and across the rolling countryside toward the festival site, drawn by the promise of an event that had been promoted in the underground press as "a three-day orgy of music, dope, and communal experience." They had come to see and hear a bill of thirty musical acts, the same as at Monterey. But in the two years since the Summer of Love, the size of the crowd had increased by a factor of ten. By the following day, torrential rains, ninety-degree heat, and the astonishing incompetence of the promoters had combined with the presence of this great multitude to turn the Woodstock festival into an undeclared disaster area, beset by the shortages of food, water, shelter, and sanitation commonly associated with floods and earthquakes.

Early press reports of the event anxiously sounded this theme of a disaster in the making. But over the course of the weekend, and in the days afterward, the focus of the coverage shifted to the extraordinarily peaceful, resourceful, and cooperative behavior of the crowd. Satiated by an abundant supply of drugs, sex, and rock 'n' roll, the hundreds of thousands of festivalgoers seemed determined to make the best of what was potentially a very bad situation. "Notwithstanding their personality, their dress, and their ideas," a local police chief told the press, "they are the most courteous, considerate, and well-behaved group of kids I have ever been in contact with." On the basis of these reports, a cultural myth was born.

In many ways, Woodstock was a culmination of a spirit and an ethos that had first broached the popular mainstream in Britain and America with the advent of Beatlemania in 1963: an unmanageably large crowd of young people, bound together by their shared love of rock and their lion-ization of the musicians who played it, finding enough safety and power in numbers to create a fleeting state of community where the usual rules were momentarily suspended to allow for the expression of ecstatic feel-ings and uninhibited behavior that had no place in the normal scheme of things. As was true of Beatlemania, the music at Woodstock—much of it badly played by exhausted and strung-out musicians who had waited for hours past their scheduled starting times to go onstage—was secondary to the participatory feeling of the event as a whole. (At Monterey the audience had paid while the bands played for free; at Woodstock the bands were paid while most of the audience was admitted for free.) Coming at a time when the utopian dreams of the 1960s seemed to be foundering in the cities as the decade drew to a close, the Woodstock fes-tival held out the promise that the gentler, more hopeful values of the counterculture might yet prevail, if not in the country as a whole, then at least in the rural countryside.

A minor irony of the festival was that while Woodstock derived its name and its initial cachet from its association with the small town that had become an unlikely center of the rock world thanks to Bob Dylan's reclusive residency, the event itself took place sixty miles from the actual town of Woodstock, and the promoters were unsuccessful in their efforts to persuade Dylan to perform. Two weeks later, however, Dylan gave his first major live performance in more than two years at a slightly smaller but otherwise similar rock festival that was held in Britain on the Isle of Wight. Nearly the entire rock aristocracy of London turned out for this second coming, along with 200,000 fans. All of the Beatles attended except Paul McCartney, whose daughter Mary had been born three days before. Dylan went on almost three hours late on the last night of the fes-tival and played for barely an hour, accompanied by The Band. Though his performance was, in John Lennon's estimate, "reasonable, albeit slightly flat," most people were disappointed, and his set ended with fans chanting angrily for more. "I don't ever want to perform in England again," Dylan told reporters the following day.

Two weeks after the Isle of Wight, it was John Lennon's turn. Sitting in his office at Apple, Lennon received a last-minute phone call from a Canadian promoter inviting him to attend still another festival, billed as a "Rock 'n' Roll Revival" and featuring performers like Chuck Berry and Little Richard, that was taking place in Toronto the following day. Invited to attend, Lennon impulsively told the delighted promoter that he wanted to perform. Within a few hours, a backup band was recruited consisting of Eric Clapton on guitar, the Beatles' old friend Klaus Voorman on bass, and a drummer named Alan White. (Though Lennon asked George Harrison to accompany him, Harrison declined.) There was no time for rehearsal; the next day everyone got on a plane, flew to Toronto, and went straight to the festival site. Having recently started on methadone, John was sick with nerves before his performance. Once onstage, he led the group (which was billed as the Plastic Ono Band) through a set that included "Blue Suede Shoes," "Money," "Yer Blues," "Cold Turkey" (a new song inspired by his heroin withdrawal), and "Give Peace a Chance." From a musical standpoint the performance was a complete fiasco, with John forgetting the words to most of the songs and the band stumbling through the rudimentary arrangements. The set ended with a screeching number by Yoko, accompanied by feedback from John's guitar and a chorus of voices from members of the audience who were screaming at her to get off the stage.

Though the music was dreadful, John was exhilarated by the experience of performing live. ("It was bloody marvelous," he told a reporter, to which Yoko added with unintended irony, "It was one of those things where nobody could come on afterwards.") On the return flight to London, Lennon told Clapton, Voorman, and Allen Klein that he had decided to leave the Beatles and form a new group. Aware of John's impulsiveness, Klein pleaded with him, if not to reconsider, then at least to keep his decision to himself for the time being. Klein explained that any suggestion of a breakup would have a disastrous effect on the complex web of financial arrangements he had been making on behalf of the group. Lennon agreed to keep quiet until all the papers were signed.

In the third week of September the Beatles met with Allen Klein at Apple headquarters to sign their new recording contracts with Capitol and EMI. Their new album was scheduled for release in a matter of days, and with advance orders for the record surging, Klein and the Beatles were looking forward to reaping the rewards of their new recording deal. Unsurprisingly, the act of signing a contract that committed them to providing their record company with a minimum of two albums and three singles a year prompted some discussion about the future. Undeterred by the debacle of *Get Back* (and no doubt hoping to capitalize on John's enthusiasm for his appearance in Toronto), Paul McCartney restated his belief that the best thing for the group would be a return to performing live. This time Paul suggested that they consider "a series of surprise one-night stands in unlikely places—just letting a hundred or so people into the village hall, so to speak, and then locking the doors." John's response to this suggestion was succinct. "I think you're daft," he told Paul, adding, "I'm leaving the Beatles. I want a divorce." Though both George and Ringo had announced at different points during the preceding year that they were quitting the group, everyone in the room knew that the words meant something different coming from John. Once again, Klein prevailed on Lennon and the others to make no public statements about the dissolution of the group. But, unbeknownst to the rest of the world, by the time their new album went on sale on September 26, 1969, the Beatles were teetering on the brink of extinction.

Abbey Road, London, August 1969

53

I just can't get any complete impression of *Abbey Road*.
With *Pepper* and even the White Album, I got an overall
image of the complete product. But with this one, I'm still
at a loss. I think it's a bit like *Revolver,* but I still feel very
abstract about it. I just can't see it as a whole entity yet.
To me, listening to *Abbey Road* is a bit like listening to
someone else. It doesn't feel like the Beatles.

—George Harrison (September 1969)

In the hierarchy of Beatles album cover iconography, Iain Macmillan's color photograph on the front of *Abbey Road* ranks third in impact and importance behind Robert Freeman's side-lit portrait on *With the Beatles* and Peter Blake's crowd of cult heroes on *Sgt. Pepper's Lonely Hearts Club Band.* Based on a sketch by Paul McCartney, the cover pictures the Beatles as literal pedestrians, striding purposefully across the broad white bands of a crosswalk on the tree-lined residential street that runs in front of the EMI studio complex in St. John's Wood. The roadway behind them is bisected by a broken white line that recedes into the distance, almost but not quite reaching as far as the patch of blue suburban sky that descends from the top of the picture. The emphasis on perspective links the cover of the Beatles' tenth and last true album to the photograph of the group on the ascending staircase at EMI headquarters that served as the cover of their first Parlophone LP. Yet while there the movement was up, here, tellingly, the movement is out and away.

In contrast to the uniform front they had heretofore shown the world, the Beatles dressed for the cover of *Abbey Road* in a manner that seemed designed to highlight their differences. Walking in a line from left to right, John Lennon leads the way, his lionlike mane of chestnut-brown hair cascading over the shoulders of the immaculate white suit that John had adopted as a signature over the course of 1969, when he and Yoko, like Stuart and Astrid in Hamburg, had taken to dressing identically as a way of affirming their love. Immediately behind him is Ringo, in a suit as black as John's is white, the cut and drape of his jacket harking back to his days as a Teddy Boy. Next comes Paul, a study in casual conservatism in an open-necked white shirt and a dark gray double-breasted suit with his jacket unbuttoned, a cigarette in his hand, and his feet bare. Bringing up the rear is George, who is dressed not as a British rock musician but rather as an American hippie with chest-length hair and in blue denim from head to toe.

The suggestion to name the album *Abbey Road* came, like the idea for the cover, from Paul McCartney. An earlier proposal to call the record *Everest* was rejected as too pretentious—though not before the Beatles had entertained a pipe dream of traveling to Tibet to have themselves photographed in front of the world's highest peak. The title *Abbey Road* seems to have been chosen more as a result of inertia than of inspiration. *Everest* had been considered because it was the name of the brand of cigarettes that Geoff Emerick happened to smoke, which brings to mind the rather desperate image of the Beatles looking around the control room of EMI Studios for some hint or sign of a suitable title until Paul finally glimpsed the forest through the trees and came up with the notion of naming the record after the studio itself. At the time it was chosen, the title was an obscure reference. Though the informal name of EMI's London studio complex has since become immortalized on account of its association with the Beatles, it was not a term that many people outside of the record business in Britain would have recognized in 1969.

The Beatles' decision to name the album after the site of their greatest artistic triumphs was one of many indications that they were aware during the summer of 1969 that they could well be making their last record together. And that *Abbey Road* should be named after a professional recording studio was especially germane, for the quality of the album was a tribute to the Beatles' ability to function—at the last minute, when all else had failed—as a professional recording band. Until now, their reluctance to professionalize their attitude toward making records had been a cornerstone of their greatness. It had encouraged the ruminative approach and the insistence on treating the studio as a playground for their musical whims that had revolutionized both the sound and the business of popular music in the years since 1963. "Hobby work" was a term that Paul McCartney had used on more than one occasion to describe the Beatles' attitude toward both songwriting and recording. Those activities, for all their intensive nature, had often seemed less like work than play after years of nightly club dates, theater concerts, and international tours.

But the sessions that produced *Abbey Road* had none of the leisurely pace and little of the ruminative quality that had marked the Beatles' approach to the studio since the time of *Rubber Soul*. With the basic instrumental tracks to five of the songs on the album already completed, the sessions in the summer of 1969 had involved a little over a month of active recording, with John Lennon absent from the studio for more than half of that time. Following his return, the Beatles relied extensively on the practice they had adopted during the White Album sessions of working individually in the separate studios at Abbey Road—to the point where the four of them played, sang, or otherwise communed with one another only when it was absolutely necessary. The psychological conditions under which the album was recorded were thus unprecedented for them. Virtually the only way the Beatles could now interact as a group was to play music with one another, and that is what they did on *Abbey Road*, with an intensity and sensitivity that, given the emotional context, can seem both heroic and heartbreaking at times. Their friendships may have been seriously compromised, but their dedication to their work allowed them to rise above the wreckage of their personal relations to create an album of which they could all be proud.

While the Beatles had always been, in Paul McCartney's words, "a great little band," the magisterial quality of their singing, songwriting, and record production from 1965 onward had tended to overshadow their ability as instrumentalists, especially after the advent of such flamboyantly virtuosic groups as the Jimi Hendrix Experience and Cream. Yet for all their tense nature, the sessions for the White Album and *Get Back* had gone a long way toward restoring the Beatles' confidence in their basic musicianship, and on *Abbey Road*, the entire band seemed to take a step forward as ensemble players.

As the most widely respected instrumentalist in the group, Paul McCartney had been helping to redefine the role of the bass guitar in rock music since the time of *Rubber Soul*. On *Abbey Road* he added a bold melodic fluidity in the upper register of the bass that gave his playing the prominence of a lead instrument at times. This was particularly apparent on John Lennon's "I Want You (She's So Heavy)" and George Harrison's "Something," two tracks on which Paul seemed to be channeling all of his frustrated collaborative energy into his bass playing. In the past, Ringo Starr had relied mainly on studio production techniques to create the distinctive drum sounds heard on the Beatles' records. On *Abbey Road,* Ringo followed the example of Levon Helm, the highly influential drummer in The Band, and began using a drum set equipped with old-fashioned calfskin heads whose exceptionally round, deep tones caused him to favor his tom-toms as never before. ("Tom-tom madness" was the way he later characterized his playing on the album.) For his part, John Lennon contributed some uncharacteristically polished lead guitar to his own "I Want You (She's So Heavy)" and Paul's "You Never Give Me Your Money." But the true musical star of the album was George Harrison, whose facility and confidence as a lead guitarist had improved dramatically since his reconversion to rock in the summer of 1968—so much so that George seemed to inhabit an entirely new instrumental persona on *Abbey Road.* By piping his guitar through a rotating Leslie speaker almost as a matter of course, and incorporating the use of a "bottleneck" slide into his playing, Harrison achieved a piquant, lyrical tone that sounded, more than ever, like a distinct melodic voice. His other major instrumental contribution to the album was his introduction of the Moog synthesizer into the Beatles' sonic repertoire. Harrison first heard and acquired one of these first-generation keyboard synthesizers during his stay in Los Angeles producing Jackie Lomax. Adopted as the Beatles' newest musical toy, the Moog eventually found its way onto a half-dozen of the songs on *Abbey Road.*

THE FIRST SIDE of the album, as George Harrison told the press, is something like *Revolver,* and something like the White Album, in that each track is strongly identified with an individual Beatle. There are two songs each from John and Paul, one song each from George and Ringo. The six tracks are arrayed with mandala-like symmetry, with John holding down the ends, Paul holding down the middle, and George and Ringo providing the connection—or buffer—between the other two.

"Come Together" opens the album with a song by John that was thoroughly transformed in the studio by Paul's contribution to its arrangement. (This makes it the last gasp of a permutation of the Lennon-McCartney collaboration that produced such gems as "Ticket to Ride.") John originally wrote "Come Together" as an up-tempo blues in the style of Chuck Berry, with a chugging rhythm guitar and an opening line derived from one of Berry's car songs, "You Can't Catch Me." After hearing him play it, Paul suggested that they minimize the similarity to the Berry song by slowing the tempo down. This transformed the feeling of "Come Together" as dramatically as George Martin's suggestion that they speed the tempo up had transformed the feeling of "Please Please Me" in 1962. At the slower tempo, with the whole track drenched in echo, the song seems to creep and slink to the accompaniment of Paul's levitational bass, which rises an augmented ninth in the span of every bar, and Ringo's muffled drums, which whisper and scurry through the four-bar introduction to each verse before merging under the singing with the sullen eighth-note pattern of John's muted rhythm guitar. Both the tempo and overall timbre of the arrangement owed a debt to the "swamp-rock" style of Mac Rebennack, the New Orleans–born studio musician and songwriter whose impersonation of a singing voodoo "conjure man" named Dr. John the Night Tripper had yielded several eccentric albums that were popular with the late-1960s underground. Rebennack and most of his band were junkies, and their musical vocabulary reflected the heroin experience in much the same way that the music of the Beatles, Jimi Hendrix, and the California groups had reflected the psychedelic experience. In its murky interplay of tones and textures, "Come Together" is suffused by a thick narcotic haze.

Although the opening line ("Here come old flat-top") was taken verbatim from "You Can't Catch Me," the rest of the lyric bears little relation to Berry's song. Instead the verses present a catalog of surreal images to describe the song's pariah-like protagonist, whose attributes include "juju eyeballs," "ono sideboards," and "toe-jam football." At the time, some fans theorized that each of the four verses of "Come Together" described a different Beatle. But the grotesque tone of the imagery remains consistent throughout the song, and it seems more likely that John was painting another sardonic self-portrait in the style of "I Am the Walrus." Repeating the formal pattern of "Walrus" and "All You Need Is Love," he offset the enigmatic verses with a simple refrain based on the song title: "Come together right now . . . over me." The line took the puerile double-entendre of Timothy Leary's campaign slogan and applied it to the burgeoning martyr complex that John had revealed in "The Ballad of John and Yoko." If that was the crucifixion, "Come Together" is more like the holy communion, with hard drugs replacing wine and wafer as the elements of the sacrament. Reduced to a sibilant sound effect by the slap-back echo on his voice, the phrase that John repeats again and again in the introduction to the verses is *"shoot* me." Impeccably recorded, this ominous opening track introduces the stark economy that characterizes most of the instrumental accompaniment on *Abbey Road,* with Paul's sultry electric piano and George's ghostly guitar joining the song only as needed, dividing up the solo that follows the third verse, then resurfacing in the coda, where John's incantations of "Come together" are set against the backwash of Ringo's cymbals and George's eerie, answering fills.

As TIME WOULD tell, there was only one member of the Beatles who would benefit conclusively from the breakup of the group. George Harrison's two stunningly accomplished tracks on *Abbey Road* are the work of a late-blooming singer-songwriter who is finally coming into his own. "Something," on the first side of the album, would go on to earn a reputation as one of the classic love songs of the rock era. Like "Yesterday," it has been covered by hundreds of singers, including Ray Charles, James Brown, Smokey Robinson, Elvis Presley, and, most famously, Frank Sinatra, who described it on numerous occasions as his "favorite Lennon-McCartney song." In the Beatles' canon, it stands with the best work of Lennon ("In My Life") and McCartney ("Here, There, and Everywhere") as a mature expression of requited love. The chords and melody of "Something" were written during the White Album sessions, and the first line of lyric was taken from the title of a James Taylor song called "Something in the Way She Moves." After searching for months for an answering line, Harrison finally hit upon the words "attracts me like no other lover," which struck a fine balance between innocence and experience and formed the template for the later verses. (Unlike Morris Levy, the litigious head of Roulette Records who held the copyright on "You Can't Catch Me" and sued John Lennon for his appropriation of its lyric, Taylor and his publisher did not take issue with Harrison's song.)

The popularity of "Something" as a vehicle for other singers was all the more remarkable for the fact that the song, as written, is essentially a duet between Harrison's voice and his lead guitar. Though it gives the impression of being highly melodic, the tune in the verse is actually very narrow, moving in a range of five notes, which allows George to sing it with great relaxation and force. What gives the song its melodic flavor is the pining electric guitar riff that introduces the verse and the bridge (and whose effect is amplified as the song progresses by George Martin's unobtrusive arrangement for strings). This memorable hook not only adds "top" to the tune; it also provides a tangible expression of the "something" that the lyric wisely leaves unsaid (much as McCartney's extraordinarily active and expressive bass line suggests an undercurrent of powerful emotion beneath the self-possessed surface of the song). As a further sign of Harrison's bursting self-confidence, his final contribution to "Something" was to play a superbly understated guitar solo over the full eight bars of the verse. It is the first extended solo the Beatles' lead guitarist had taken on a song of his own since "Don't Bother Me," his debut as a composer back in 1963.

PAUL MCCARTNEY FIRST became passionate about playing the guitar in the wake of his mother's death, and one of the roles that music had always played in his life was to provide him with a source of comfort and a means of escape. During the *Get Back* sessions, Paul had evoked his mother by name in the opening verse of the hymnlike ballad "Let It Be," drawing a connection between the grief he felt at her loss and the sense of sorrow he was experiencing in the current "times of trouble," as the musical band of brothers that had formed the core of his personal and professional life threatened to fall apart. Compared with "Let It Be," Paul's first two tracks on *Abbey Road* are expressions of the escapist side of his musical nature. But given the deteriorating state of relations among the Beatles, both of these songs—the one an exceedingly enthusiastic account of a triple murder, the other a 1950s-style spoof of romantic abandonment—can also be seen as significant acts of sublimation on McCartney's part.

At one point during the *Get Back* sessions, Paul referred to "Maxwell's Silver Hammer" as a "Tom Lehrer–type song." A brilliant satirical songwriter, Lehrer retired from the music business in the early 1970s, leaving behind such blackly comic gems as "Poisoning Pigeons in the Park" and "Irish Ballad," which tells of a fair-haired maid who "not only [did] her family wrong, she did every one of them in." Another source of inspiration may have been the Weill-Brecht-Blitzstein standard "Mack the Knife," with "Max" standing in for "Mackie." (John Lennon actually sang a few bars of "Mack the Knife" during a run-through of "Maxwell's Silver Hammer" at Twickenham Studios.) Perfected over days of relentless rehearsal, first in January and then again in July, the song is a preternaturally catchy music-hall number in the line of "When I'm Sixty-Four," "Your Mother Should Know," and "Honey Pie." It features a flawless arrangement of Paul on piano and Moog, George on bass and guitars, and Ringo on drums and anvil chorus. Paul sings the articulate lyric with an air of relentless good cheer, describing in three verses how Maxwell Edison—medical student, class clown, and homicidal maniac—literally knocks off his girlfriend, his teacher, and the judge who presides at his trial. Like many high-profile serial killers, Maxwell has his fans, led by Rose and Valerie, shouting from the gallery of the courtroom for his release. From a musical standpoint, the signature of the song is the pounding double accent from Ringo's anvil that accompanies the words "bang bang" in a chorus that recounts how Maxwell's murderous medical hammer came down on his victims' heads. By the end of the song, that hammer has begun to take a toll on the heads of its listeners as well.

For reasons having more to do with its cheerful demeanor than its grisly content, "Maxwell's Silver Hammer" became a benchmark of the Beatles' discontent over the course of 1969. In September, a few weeks prior to John Lennon's announcement that he wanted a "divorce" from the group, Lennon's assistant, Anthony Fawcett, recorded a conversation between John and Paul at Apple in which John expressed his resentment at the way Paul had managed to monopolize the A-sides of the Beatles' singles over the previous two years. John went on to complain about Paul's tendency to write catchy, upbeat songs like "Ob-La-Di, Ob-La-Da" and "Maxwell's Silver Hammer" and then flog them to death in the studio in an effort to turn them into hit singles, even though none of the Beatles regarded them as anything more than promising commercial properties. According to Fawcett, Paul did not offer much of a rebuttal to John's remarks. From a pragmatic perspective, McCartney's continuing efforts to produce hit singles on behalf of the Beatles could be seen as an expression of his admirable work ethic and his undiminished professional ambition. But it also represented a certain failure of artistic nerve and imagination on Paul's part, given the level of cultural and commercial power the Beatles commanded by now. Left to his own devices by Lennon's abdication from their creative partnership, McCartney was regressing to a more traditional concept of popular music as a form of "light entertainment"—precisely the concept that the Beatles, in their prime, had done so much to explode. The sorriest aspect of "Maxwell's Silver Hammer" is thus the way it demonstrates how Paul's workmanlike tendency to build on his past successes had caused him to translate the genuinely charming novelty and subversive parody of "When I'm Sixty-Four" into a personal subgenre of glibly clever songs that had devolved in the two years since *Sgt. Pepper* into a form of musical *shtick*.

Grouped with "Maxwell's Silver Hammer" in the middle of side one, "Oh! Darling," is a much more satisfying expression of McCartney's penchant for tongue-in-cheek. The song is a carefully crafted replica of a familiar type of rhythm-and-blues ballad, set to the distinctive 12/8 meter that migrated into popular music during the 1950s from New Orleans piano blues and provided the rolling rhythmic accompaniment for numerous hits of the time, including the Platters' "Great Pretender," James Brown's "Please Please Please," and Little Richard's "Send Me Some Lovin'." (The displaced exclamation point in the title is taken from Richard's "Ooh! My Soul.") The period flavor and the parodistic exaggeration of the arrangement—as epitomized by George's neck-wringing squawks on the offbeats and his deranged staccato of octave-wide arpeggios in the bridge—give Paul the critical distance he needs to banish all sense of self-consciousness about imitating an overtly black style. He responds by throwing himself totally into the performance, singing in a hoarse, fulsome shout that simultaneously summons and sends up the melodramatic emotionality of 1950s doo-wop and rhythm and blues. Apart from its wonderfully nuanced lead vocal, "Oh! Darling" is an expression of musical minimalism. It matches a relentlessly simple accompaniment with a relentlessly repetitive lyric that offers a promise of good behavior ("I'll never do you no harm") as the prelude to a desperate plea ("If you leave me, I'll never make it alone"). Given the state of relations among the Beatles during this time, it is hard to imagine that Paul's rendering of this heartbroken sentiment, however satiric, did not have some basis in his sense of rejection by John. Years later, Lennon expressed great admiration for "Oh! Darling," though he couldn't help adding that he felt McCartney should have let him sing it, since it was more his type of song. In fact, Paul's performance is so edgy and raw that many otherwise astute listeners, including the critics Nik Cohn and Ellen Sander in their published reviews of *Abbey Road,* blithely assumed that it was John who was singing the song.

. . . .

PAUL MCCARTNEY WAS not the only Beatle to worry about his ability to "make it on his own." At least some of the sense of desperation that prompted John Lennon to go public with the group's financial woes in January 1969 had stemmed from John's fear that the mismanagement of Apple was creating a situation in which he might not be able to *afford* to leave the Beatles even if he wanted to. Yet any concerns that John or Paul may have had about their financial futures as ex-Beatles paled beside those of Ringo Starr. From the start of their careers as recording artists, Lennon and McCartney had consistently earned more from their song publishing royalties than the Beatles as individuals had earned from the millions of records they sold. This began to change in 1967 after Brian Epstein renegotiated their contracts with Capitol and EMI, but the Lennon-McCartney catalog, which had grown to include nearly 175 songs, continued to generate an enormous amount of income that went directly to John and Paul. George Harrison's royalties on the twenty or so songs he had published since 1963, while only a fraction of the amount earned by the other two, still provided him with a significant source of independent income. Starr had none of this to fall back on, and his decision to try his hand at songwriting, beginning with "Don't Pass Me By" on the White Album, was largely inspired by a desire to share more fully in the wealth of the world's most popular band.

His self-written contribution to *Abbey Road,* "Octopus's Garden," is a spirited, country-flavored children's song that derives a certain poignancy from the eagerness with which Ringo, embracing his role as the Beatles' ambassador to the depths of the sea, returns to the scene of his first great triumph in "Yellow Submarine." Inspired by a Mediterranean vacation he took during his two-week hiatus from the White Album sessions, the song is a wishful fantasy of "joy for every girl and boy," whose visions of being "warm below the storm" and having "no one to tell us what to do" clearly reflected its author's disenchantment with the turmoil among the Beatles at the time. In this sense, however, the true poignancy of "Octopus's Garden" comes from the way the track suffers by comparison with the boisterous camaraderie of "Yellow Submarine." Instead of being set in the present ("We all live . . ."), Ringo's return to the seabed is set in the conditional tense ("I'd like to be . . ."). And though the Beatles did their best to liven up the track with a sing-along chorus and a cheerful overlay of whooping guitar from George, rinky-tink piano from Paul, and burbling hydraulics from Ringo (who accompanies George's solo with the help of a microphone, a glass of water, and a straw), the ingredient that is conspicuously missing from the recording is the manic humor and crazed theatricality with which John Lennon had turned the sessions that produced "Yellow Submarine" into a second coming of the Goons. (Though John played rhythm guitar on the backing track when it was recorded in April, he was nowhere to be found when the vocal and instrumental overdubs were added in July.) In his absence, Ringo's song comes across as an inadvertent reminder of how little of the Beatles' once incomparable spirit of fun and fellowship remained in their music by the time of *Abbey Road,* when the octopus in their garden, more often than not, was missing a few of its arms.

FROM GEORGE MARTIN's perspective, one of the odd things about the disdainful attitude John Lennon adopted toward the use of studio production techniques from the White Album sessions onward was that, historically, John's songs had generally been the tracks that required the greatest expenditures of time, effort, and production expertise in the studio. "I Want You (She's So Heavy)" took this paradox to a new level. As the first song the Beatles recorded in the aftermath of the *Get Back* sessions, and the last song they worked on for *Abbey Road,* the group returned to it a half-dozen times during the spring and summer of 1969, adding vocal and instrumental overdubs to a basic track that was itself an edited composite of three separate takes. This long and involved genesis placed "I Want You" in the company of such major production numbers as "Tomorrow Never Knows," "Strawberry Fields Forever," and "A Day in the Life," not to mention McCartney's "Hey Jude," which it surpassed by half a minute as the longest Beatles song on record. Yet, compared to these earlier masterworks, "I Want You" is notable mainly for the willful one-dimensionality of its words and music. By confining itself to a single verse of nine words (three fewer than "Love Me Do"), it represents John's attempt to monumentalize his feelings for Yoko Ono while adhering to the minimalist aesthetic that Yoko herself extolled. The result is a strange brew of laconic blues realism and narcissistic grandiosity that sounds, by the end, like a collaboration between Phil Spector and Gertrude Stein.

After a brief, arpeggiated introduction in 12/8 time, the song begins with John singing the ten-bar verse, phrasing and rephrasing the lyric, "I want you so bad / It's driving me mad," against the unaccompanied melody line of his own guitar. He then spends the next seven and a half minutes seeing what he and his fellow Beatles, ably assisted by Billy Preston on organ, can make of this stark declaration of desire. For the first four minutes of the track, their efforts center on multiple vocal and instrumental reiterations of the verse over a brooding "blues rhumba" (inspired by Booker T. & the MGs) that alternates with a refrain based on the arpeggiated chords and plodding 12/8 meter of the introduction, whose only lyric is the song's parenthetical subtitle, "She's so heavy!" The relentless repetition of the words and music has the effect of calling attention to the exceptionally nuanced nature of John's conjoined vocal and lead guitar and the rich textural variations in the accompaniment, as McCartney's quicksilver runs generate great groundswells of sound in the transitions between the verses, and Preston's organ fills the pause that John inserts between the words "She's so" and "heavy" with a strident two-bar glissando that lends a tormented, Phantom-of-the-Opera ambience to the refrain.

On the eighth and final rendition of the unchanging verse, John answers the line "it's driving me mad" with an anguished scream that strongly suggests the words are not meant to be taken metaphorically. Then the song enters an extended instrumental coda in which the arpeggiated refrain in D minor is repeated without variation no fewer than fifteen times, setting the stage for one of the darkest and strangest interludes in all of the Beatles' work: a three-minute simulation of romantic obsession that teeters between the tiresome, the affecting, and the absurd. While Lennon's and Harrison's multiply double-tracked guitars cycle mechanically through the five-bar sequence of chords, a growing windstorm of white noise (generated by the Moog synthesizer) begins to envelop the music, lending an obliterating, almost nightmarish, quality to the track. In its final moments, "I Want You (She's So Heavy)" seems to pass directly from the realm of the musical into the realm of the psychological, to end with a brutalist gesture, as Lennon instructed Geoff Emerick to physically cut the tape.

THE FIFTEEN-MINUTE SEQUENCE of eight songs (and song fragments) that concludes the second side of *Abbey Road* was not identified as a medley or a suite on the album cover or the record label. The titles are listed individually, and in the early going, the transition from one song to the next feels no different from that of the preceding tracks. Nor are the themes or the lyrics of the songs that constitute the medley interrelated in any obvious way. As a result, the entire second side of *Abbey Road* is best heard as a sequence of loosely related songs whose emotional intensity and overall pacing gradually build to a climax as the album nears its end.

The side begins with a second astonishment from George Harrison, the impact of which is only enhanced by the ponderous nature of the track that precedes it at the end of side one. "Here Comes the Sun" is a study in lightness and brightness—two qualities that had rarely been associated with Harrison's music in the past. (The closest precedent is "If I Needed Someone" on *Rubber Soul*.) Introduced by a chiming I-IV-V progression on an acoustic guitar, the body of this simple, folk-like tune is embellished with an understated arrangement for synthesizer, wood- winds, and strings that delicately shadows the melody. The three well- written verses, all beginning with the tender phrase "Little darling," evoke the siege of winter, the thaw of spring, and the warmth of "smiles returning to the faces." Each resolves in a refrain in which the title line is sung three times in three-part harmony, rounded off by George's interjec- tion, "And *I* say . . . It's *all* right," the phrasing of which sets up an accented pattern of three against four that is echoed over the next two bars by arpeggiated triads on guitar. This pattern is then extended and elaborated further in the song's release, where cascading lines of "Sun! sun! sun! here it comes!" are sung in triplet rhythm over arpeggiated tri- ads while the meter of the music shifts seamlessly between bars in 2/4, 3/8, 5/8, and 4/4 time. Anchored by Ringo's somersaulting fills, this com- pound meter serves as a metaphor for the lyric, with the tripletted accents in 3/8 and 5/8 cutting across the underlying quarter-note pulse of the music like the rays of the sun cutting across the melting ice of winter, generating a tension that builds and then yields on the phrase "here it comes" to the comforting symmetry of 4/4 time. The cumulative effect is one of true release: of coming through a long and arduous experience and emerging whole at the end.

As THE CHILD of a wealthy, westernized Japanese family, Yoko Ono had been taught the piano in childhood, and she retained the ability to play a number of classical set pieces as an adult. One of these was the Moonlight Sonata (by the noted con artist Ludwig van Beethoven), whose first movement, according to John Lennon, inspired the arpeggiated chords of the ballad "Because." Because the influence of Yoko's sensibility on John is apparent in the lyrics as well, this iridescently beautiful song, which was the last complete track the Beatles recorded for *Abbey Road,* can be heard as her parting gift to the group of "in-laws" with whom she clashed in so many ways.

Whether or not the Beatles were aware at the time they recorded "Because" that it was truly their swan song, their singing on the track, skillfully arranged in three-part harmony by George Martin, represents the most intricate and rhapsodic blend of their voices on record. Set, like the Beethoven sonata, in the key of C-sharp minor, the entire production of words and music, singing and accompaniment, has a classical elegance that verges on formal perfection. So as to focus all of the listeners' attention on the complex blend and grain of the vocal harmonies, the other aspects of the song are rendered as simply as possible. The arpeggiated lines of the electric harpsichord and electric guitar that voice the chords remain rhythmically static throughout; they are bolstered in the song's brief release by George Martin's brass, and later, in the coda, by the recorder-like sound of the Moog. Each of the three verses is introduced by melismatic "Ahhhs" that form a D major triad (sounding a distinctive flatted II chord that figures prominently in the Moonlight Sonata as well) before reverting to the C-sharp-minor tonic. In a format that could serve as the basis of a children's book, the lyric to each verse consists of a single line, beginning with the word "Because," in which an aspect of nature ("the world . . . the wind . . . the sky") is converted by means of its description ("is round . . . is high . . . is blue") into an emotion ("it turns me on . . . blows my mind . . . makes me cry"). The result is some of the gentlest, most poetically accessible wordplay John Lennon ever wrote. As the first instance of shared lead singing on *Abbey Road,* "Because" comes as a reminder that, far more than the playing or songwriting on their early records, it was the utterly distinctive blend of the Beatles' voices that set them apart from the start.

"Because" ends on its flatted II chord, which leaves the harmony hanging and sets up the opening of Paul's "You Never Give Me Your Money," the first of the eight songs and song fragments that comprise the concluding, fifteen-minute medley that marked the end of the Beatles' eight-year career as a recording band. These eight songs were arranged and recorded in five segments—or, to apply the symphonic metaphor, movements—the basic instrumental accompaniment of which was rehearsed and performed live by the Beatles in the studio. The segments were then linked to one another—in some cases by edits at predetermined points of musical transition, in other cases by means of mixing-board "crossfades" in which the end of one track was blended with the start of the next.

The sequence opens with Paul's most ambitious and affecting song on the entire album, "You Never Give Me Your Money," which is itself a kind of mini-suite that encapsulates and foreshadows many of the motifs that are played out in the medley as a whole. The song's four musically distinct sections, set in different keys, are organized by a kind of dream logic and linked by a series of pivot points in the music and lyrics. (The only previous Beatles song to employ this sort of nonrepeating, episodic structure was John's "Happiness Is a Warm Gun.") The track begins quietly with Paul singing alone at the piano, the wistful insistence of his A minor melody ably matched to a lyric whose allusions to "funny papers" and "negotiations" are an epitaph for his clashes with the rest of the group regarding Apple and Allen Klein. Over the course of the first verse, the other Beatles seem to drift into the music—John's guitar here, Ringo's cymbals there—until a thumping drum fill rouses the whole band into an eight-bar passage based on a classic boogie-woogie piano riff (backed by half-time drumming reminiscent of "Lady Madonna"), with words and music that seem to be coming from another time and place—a memory, from the sound of it, whose references to "out of college, money spent" and "see no future, pay no rent" are evocative of the Beatles' lives in Liverpool at the start of their musical careers. In the following section, these dead-end vistas are transformed, as the boogie beat drops out and the phrase "nowhere to go" is recast as a "magic feeling" of freedom and possibility in a chorus of wordless "Ahhhs" that float over another round of the ringing arpeggios on guitar that recur in song after song on *Abbey Road*. By now Paul's piano has disappeared from the accompaniment, and it is George's guitar that steers the band into a driving, Chuck Berry–style riff in A major that forms the stirring finale of the song. "Soon we'll be away from here," Paul promises, recounting a scenario of escape-by-limousine whose relevance to the frenzied days of Beatlemania is reinforced by his acknowledgment that "One sweet dream came true today."

The track then fades with a chorus of Beatles repeating the familiar play-ground "choosing" rhyme, "One, two, three, four, five, six, seven, all good children go to heaven"—a variation of "eeeny meany miney mo" that ends this shadowy recapitulation of the Beatles' saga on a note of child-ishness that obscures the rhyme's traditional function as a way of deter-mining who is in and who is out.

The long fade of "You Never Give Me Your Money" ends in a hush of tape-looped night sounds, peepers, and wind chimes that set the stage for the burbling guitar, muffled cymbals, and thumping rhythm of "Sun King," which rises like the mist on a lake. As the first of the three con-tiguous song fragments John Lennon contributed to the medley, "Sun King" is almost a parody of "Because." It applies the same dreamy tempo, gentle chordal melody, and rapt vocal harmonies to a lyric describing the arrival of an Apollonian figure whose mere presence leaves "everybody" glowing with laughter and happiness. Since the effect of this Apollonian figure is precisely the same as that of the Beatles on their fans, the song, while merely a fragment, revives the theme of the charismatic trickster that John expressed so mordantly in "I Am the Walrus." For when the Sun King finally begins to speak, he does so in a language that no one can understand: a blend of pidgin Italian and Spanish in which random words like "paparazzi," "mi amore," and "corazon" are strung together in a stream of mellifluous yet utterly meaningless nonsense.

After the phrase "cake and eat it carousel," the pretense of "Sun King" is punctured by a funky little drum fill that sets up the rigorous soul groove of a second Lennon fragment about a storybook miser ("sleeps in the park, shaves in the dark") named "Mean Mr. Mustard," whose chief form of recreation consists of accompanying his shop-girl sister Pam to public appearances by the Queen, where he "always shouts out some-thing obscene." "Such a dirty old man," John repeats as the band careens into a 3/4 passage that carries a distant echo of the dance of Henry the Horse, only to be brought up short by the intrusion (in stop time) of a trio of spiky guitar chords and the onset of a pounding double-time rhythm from the drums that shifts the focus back onto sister Pam, whose sobri-quet "Polythene" suggests some unusual recreational interests of her own. "Well you should see Polythene Pam," John sings in a cackling Scouse accent, "She's so good-looking but she looks like a man." He goes on to describe a jackbooted girl with a passion for plastic who's a real killer when she's dressed to the hilt. Though the song was written in

India as part of the same fictional litter that yielded Bungalow Bill and Sexy Sadie, "Polythene Pam" sounds like something the Beatles might have written during their days on Hamburg's Reeperbahn. John finishes off his sketch of this fetishistic temptress with a string of sardonic "yeah, yeah, yeahs" that make Paul's quotation of "She Loves You" at the end of "All You Need Is Love" sound heartfelt by comparison, whereupon Ringo and George take off on an exhilarating instrumental jag whose pistonlike tom-toms and graceful, arching guitar lines segue via a smooth descent from the key of E to A major (and a shout of "Look out!" from John) into Paul's contribution to the trio of dubious character sketches that form the up-tempo midsection of the medley, "She Came in Through the Bathroom Window," which derives some of its churning half-time feel and narrative flavor from the Rolling Stones' recent B-side, "You Can't Always Get What You Want." Various autobiographical explanations have been offered for the song's haphazardly obscure lyric, but the first verse, in which Paul introduces an unnamed female housebreaker who "sucks her thumb and wonders by the banks of her own lagoon," sounds in the context of the Beatles like an undisguised jab at Yoko Ono, who had recently commissioned the construction of a man-made lake at her home in Tittenhurst Park. "Didn't anybody tell her?" Paul asks in the bridge, against the ringing phrases of George's guitar. "Didn't anybody *see*?"

"She Came in Through the Bathroom Window" eventually comes to a full stop on an A major chord, which reverts to a somber A minor for the opening of "Golden Slumbers." This exceedingly tender, melancholy number was based on a lullaby by the Elizabethan playwright Thomas Dekker that Paul found in a piano songbook and set to a tune of his own. It was recorded during John Lennon's absence from the *Abbey Road* sessions in July, when it was combined with another McCartney fragment called "Carry That Weight" and a thematic reprise of "You Never Give Me Your Money"—thereby enabling McCartney and George Martin to present the "symphonic" concept of the medley as a fait accompli to Lennon upon his return. "Once there was a way to get back homeward," Paul muses quietly in the opening bars, his voice supported by a gently rocking figure on piano and Martin's swelling arrangement for strings. "Sleep pretty darling, do not cry," he offers, "And I will sing a lullaby." His promise is answered by a stop-start drum fill that propels the song with unexpected force into the text of Dekker's poem—"Golden slumbers fill your eyes / Smiles awake you when you rise"—set to a melody in C major whose stentorian delivery and straining harmony (an F^9 chord sounds behind the words "slumbers" and "awake") defy all expectations of what is meant by the term "lullaby." Then the music subsides and Paul repeats the homeward-looking verse, which is followed again by Ringo's fill. Only this time, instead of the promised lullaby, Paul, George, and Ringo join in a rousing chant of "Boy, you're gonna carry that weight / Carry that weight a long time!" Singing in unison (with Ringo's voice predominating) and sounding less like the harmonized angels of "Because" and "Sun King" than like the crowd at a soccer match, they repeat this dour prophecy until a chorus of horns lets loose with the opening strains (in A minor) of "You Never Give Me Your Money." The melodic allusion is followed by a new verse of the song itself, which Paul concludes with the line "And in the middle of the celebrations, I break down." A downbeat of truly symphonic proportions from the brass (on a pivotal G^7 chord) then plunges the music back into the chorus of "Carry That Weight," which is played and sung with immense power, accompanied this time by arpeggiated chords on guitar. While the bass descends the scale from C to B to A, the broken chords ascend from C to G to A, their accented tonic notes subdividing the stately 4/4 rhythm into groups of three, as the musical motifs of the medley seem to be sounding together in preparation for a grand finale that feels as if it is just moments away.

George Martin had hoped to enlist the Beatles in making an album that would go beyond *Sgt. Pepper* in its thematic structure and unified form. But Martin was a musician in the traditional sense, and he conceived of surpassing the Beatles' acknowledged masterpiece as an essentially musical challenge. As a group of popular artists *par excellence*, however, the Beatles understood intuitively—and in the case of John Lennon, gratefully—that surpassing *Sgt. Pepper* was no longer within the realm of possibility for them, because *Sgt. Pepper*, like *Revolver, Rubber Soul*, and the seven other Beatles albums that preceded it, was the work of a group of collaborative singers and songwriters that had subsequently ceased to exist. No one understood this better than Paul McCartney, whose earnest, energetic, and at times overbearing efforts to cajole his bandmates into soldiering on after the triumph of *Sgt. Pepper* and the tragedy of Brian Epstein's death were based on his conviction that nothing the Beatles might ever achieve as individuals could possibly compare with what they had accomplished—and might still accomplish—as a group. The enthusiasm with which McCartney embraced Martin's suggestion that they try to surpass *Sgt. Pepper* was not based on his belief that they would succeed; rather it was based on his stubborn hope that by trying once again to outdo themselves, the Beatles might rekindle the musical camaraderie and collaborative genius that had placed them in a league of their own. To that end, Paul reserved all of his best material for the concluding medley (unlike John, who contributed nothing but odds and ends). And he used all of his considerable powers of persuasion and organization to enlist the other Beatles' participation in this project as well.

Ultimately, however, Paul's loyalty to the Beatles was stronger than his loyalty to George Martin or anyone else, and so, rather than end the album with the sort of grand "symphonic" gesture that Martin had in mind, he came up with the last of the Beatles' great surprises, a final, brilliant twist that was, in its own way, closer to the inspired spirit of *Sgt. Pepper* than anything else on *Abbey Road*. Just as the booming chorus and ringing arpeggios of "Carry That Weight" combine to create the expectation that the album is coming to a close, the music seems to jump right out of its skin: the tempo surging, the orchestra fleeing, the harmony changing direction in a series of wrenching guitar chords that leap first from A to D, then from B to E, in both cases landing hard on the beat, and then again from A to D, this time in a pair of jarringly syncopated accents that bring the band up short. Ringo leaps into the breach with a rackety two-bar fill and the sequence of chords repeats over a brisk, *Sgt. Pepper*–style backbeat. "Oh *yeah!*" Paul shrieks. "All *right!* . . . *Are* you going to be in my dreams . . . tonight?"

In the blink of an eye, the musical setting has shifted from the orchestral uplift of strings and brass to the rawest variety of rock 'n' roll. Instead of a grand symphonic ending, McCartney had chosen—at the last possible moment—to bring the Beatles and their listeners back to the place where it all began: before the marathon recording sessions, before the stadium concerts and provincial package tours, before the grueling one-nighters in dance halls and cellar dives—to the simple setting of John, Paul, and George, sawing away on their three guitars, as they had done in hotel rooms, dressing rooms, and before that in bedrooms, from the time George joined the Quarry Men eleven years before. The one concession to the whole incredible saga that had elapsed between then and now was the presence of Ringo Starr, the steady, solid drummer the Beatles had always lacked during their years of musical apprenticeship in Liverpool and Hamburg. In recognition of this, the next eight bars are given over to Ringo for his only drum solo on record, a barrage of brawny tom-tom figures (each of them followed by a moment in which he seems to pause for the approval of the others) underlain by the time-keeping pulse of his bass drum. Then a crescendo of steady eighth-notes orchestrates the reentry of the bass and rhythm guitar, vamping in flatted-seventh chords on an elementary tonic-subdominant cadence in A major. "Love you" the Beatles chant, until the bare alternation of A^7 and D^7 chords is joined by the four-note pickup of a searing lead guitar and the start of an instrumental round-robin composed of nine two-bar solo breaks in which Paul, George, and John (in that order) trade licks, with each guitarist playing off or building on his predecessor's effort. Recorded live in the studio, these rotating two-bar solos are like little musical character sketches, in which each of the Beatles assumes his customary role: Paul the initiator, George the embellisher, John holding out for the last word. (At the same time, the solos are uncredited, and between the speed of the transitions and the similarities in the timbre and content of the different parts, it is by no means clear how many guitarists are playing, much less the identity of the player at any given point.) Paul opens with a characteristically fluid and melodically balanced line that sounds a high A before snaking an octave down the scale; George responds by soaring to an even higher D and sustaining it for half a bar before descending in syncopated pairs of sixteenth notes; John then picks up on the pattern of George's sixteenths with a series of choppy thirds that hammer relentlessly on the second and flatted seventh degrees of the scale. The second time through, Paul answers John's bluesy flatted sevenths with bluesy minor thirds and then proceeds to echo George's earlier line, spiraling up to that same high D; George responds with some minor thirds of his own, while mimicking the choppy rhythm of John's part; John then drops down two octaves to unleash a growling single-note line. On his final two-bar solo, Paul plays almost nothing *but* minor thirds and flatted sevenths in a herky-jerky rhythm that ends with a sudden plunge to a low A; George then reaches for the stars with a steeply ascending line that is pitched an octave above any notes heard so far; and John finishes with a string of insistent and heavily distorted fourths, phrased in triplets, that drag behind the beat and grate against the background harmony.

Finally, as abruptly as this old-fashioned rave-up began, it ends, with the band stopping short, leaving only the faint eighth-note pulse of a piano sounding tinny A major chords. "And in the end . . ." Paul sings, his voice rising. A pair of lightning-quick guitar licks sound a sixteenth note apart, as John and George join in a three-part harmony on the shallow arc of melody with which the Beatles deliver the line that would serve as their epitaph: "The love you take . . . is equal to the love you make." The inverted chords behind their voices enact a slow chromatic descent across four bars of 3/8 meter to arrive in the key of C major on the phrase "the love you make." This long-awaited resolution (which was prefigured by the opening of the medley in the key of A minor) is first softened by the reentry of George Martin's strings, then deepened by the return of the drums. As George Harrison's lead guitar plays an extended arpeggio that rises two octaves up the scale, the singers add a final curtain of "Ahhs" as the harmony lifts from C to D to E flat to F. Ringo's tom-toms provide a final nudging emphasis, and with a gentle plagal cadence, the song, the medley, and the album come to rest on a common C major chord.

EPILOGUE

> And when the Sieve turned round and round, and every-
> one cried, "You'll all be drowned!" They called aloud, "Our
> Sieve ain't big, but we don't care a button! we don't care a
> fig! In a Sieve we'll go to sea!"
>
> —Edward Lear, "The Jumblies"

For its sheer ingenuity, the long medley on the second side of *Abbey Road* marked a high point of Paul McCartney's efforts to serve as the motivator and organizer of the Beatles' creative energies since the time of John Lennon's dreamy withdrawal into the realm of psychedelic experience in the spring of 1966. The task that Paul had set himself was formidable: to create a musical situation that would pique the interest and participation of his bandmates, particularly John, and at the same time, if worse came to worst, provide the Beatles' endangered recording career with an ending of which they could all be proud. As things turned out, they had little choice *but* to do the medley, since, apart from the songs that had already been recorded for the *Get Back* project, the Beatles simply did not have enough new material to fill both sides of an LP.

So it was that *Abbey Road* became the only one of the ten albums the Beatles had released to date to end with a song by McCartney. The title of the last track, which runs from the start of the rock-'n'-roll rave up through the couplet "the love you make," was listed as simply "The End." Having orchestrated an opportunity for the Beatles to revisit their humble beginnings as a "great little band," Paul's final contribution was to write an epitaph for the album that could serve, if necessary, as an epitaph for the Beatles' career. (Years later he said he got the idea for the ending from the couplets that Shakespeare and other Elizabethan playwrights placed at the ends of their plays.) And the simple moral calculus of the "the love you make," which echoes the Hindu doctrine of karma and the biblical Golden Rule, serves this function admirably.

At the same time, however, McCartney felt a need to hedge his bet, for *Abbey Road* was recorded at a time when the end of the Beatles was nigh, but by no means certain. So thirty seconds after the last plaintive strains of George Harrison's guitar and George Martin's strings have faded, the album bursts back to life with the sound of Paul—yet again—singing a music-hall ditty: "Her Majesty, she's a very nice girl but she doesn't have a lot to say." The joke, coming from the mouth of a Beatle, was that this working-class term of domestic endearment could as easily refer to the Monarch herself. The addition of "Her Majesty" turned "The End" into the first in a long series of false, deferred, and inconclusive endings to the Beatles' story that would play out over the next ten years.

Abbey Road was released in the last week of September 1969. Reviews of the album in both the mainstream and music press were mixed—more so than those of any preceding Beatles album. The medley on the second side was widely praised for its dash and excitement, but the overall tenor of the critical response suggested that the Beatles, two years after they virtually willed the rock press into being with *Sgt. Pepper,* were now being reviewed like any other band. Sales of the album, on the other hand, were nothing short of spectacular. In the Aquarian afterglow of the Woodstock Festival, *Abbey Road* topped the charts for a total of seventeen weeks in Britain, eleven in the United States, and sold an estimated four million copies by the end of 1969.

The lackluster response of the press to the music on *Abbey Road* may have been attributable, in part, to the inordinate amount of attention paid to a bizarre rumor that surfaced in the United States about two weeks after the album's release. The gist of it was that Paul McCartney had been killed in an automobile accident outside London in the fall of 1966, and that the Beatles had secretly replaced their dead bassist with a look-alike whose entry into the group had been shrewdly masked by the overall change in their appearances at the time of *Sgt. Pepper* and by their decision to forgo live performances, which enabled George Martin to compensate for the loss of McCartney by using a sound-alike singer in the studio. Of necessity, other people besides the surviving Beatles, their manager, and their producer had been in on the ruse—among them Jane Asher, who had overcome her grief and agreed to masquerade as the surrogate McCartney's girlfriend and fiancée until the summer of 1968, when the new Paul fell in love with Linda Eastman (who presumably thought she was falling in love with the real thing).

The basis for this rumor was found in an elaborate subtext of visual and aural clues that the surviving Beatles—for some inexplicable reason—had gone to great lengths to plant on their records and album covers. The trail of evidence began with a slurry voice saying "I buried Paul" that some listeners discerned in the coda of "Strawberry Fields Forever." It went on to include the funereal cover of *Sgt. Pepper,* the reference to the accident victim in "A Day in the Life," and various album tracks that, when played backwards or slowed down, seemed to re-create the sound of a car crash. The most recent and overt piece of the puzzle was the cover of *Abbey Road,* which depicted the white-suited John as a priest, the black-suited Ringo as an undertaker, the barefoot Paul as a corpse, and the denim-clad George as a gravedigger. "Come together over me," declared the album's opening track, which went on to give the game away with the line "one and one and one is three."

The Paul-is-dead rumor first surfaced in October 1969 in an anonymous phone call to a Detroit disc jockey, who repeated the information over the air. Two days later the University of Michigan *Daily* published a review of *Abbey Road* beneath the banner headline MCCARTNEY IS DEAD: NEW EVIDENCE BROUGHT TO LIGHT. Accompanied by a grisly photograph that purported to show Paul's decapitated head, the piece, written by "Fred LaBour," was an obvious spoof. But by appearing to corroborate the radio broadcast, it released the rumor of Paul's death into a jungle telegraph of FM radio stations, underground newspapers, and excited word of mouth that soon spilled over into the mainstream press. By the beginning of November, *Life* magazine could justify putting a photograph of Paul and his family on its cover with the caption PAUL IS STILL WITH US. Interviewed in the accompanying article, McCartney issued a somewhat cryptic statement of his own. "We make good music and we want to go on making good music," he said. "But the Beatle thing is over. It has been exploded, partly by what we have done and partly by other people."

If the Paul-is-dead hoax was one expression of the popular fantasy that the Beatles had encoded their records with esoteric messages directed at a cognoscenti of studious fans, a far more sinister version of that same belief came to light in Los Angeles in the fall of 1969. The summer before, residents of the city had been stunned by the news of a horrifying multiple murder at a house in the Hollywood Hills. The victims included the film star Sharon Tate, her unborn child, and four other people whose bodies were found stabbed, shot, and strewn around the residence that Tate rented with her husband, the director Roman Polanski. Adding to the horror were reports that "revolutionary" graffiti had been painted on the walls of the house in the victims' blood. In the fall, the police arrested the members of a hippie "family" headed by a demonic-looking career criminal named Charles Manson, and charged them with the crime. Since his most recent release from prison in 1967, Manson had assembled a cultlike gang of several young men and nearly a dozen young women, most of them runaways he had recruited in the Haight-Ashbury and Hollywood. As police and prosecutors sought to determine a motive for the killings, they learned that the Manson Family subscribed to an apocalyptic vision based on their belief that the Beatles represented the Four Horsemen of the Apocalypse described in the Book of Revelation, and that their songs, particularly those on the White Album, were filled with personal messages directed at Manson and his followers, instructing them on how to go about fulfilling the prophecy. The murders were part of this plan.

"Many people I know in Los Angeles believe that the Sixties ended abruptly," Joan Didion noted in *The White Album,* "at the exact moment when the word of the murders on Cielo Drive traveled like brushfire through the community. . . . The tension broke that day. The paranoia was fulfilled." For countless other people, in Los Angeles and elsewhere, the symbolic end of the 1960s came a few months after the Manson murders at a concert in Altamont, California, by the Rolling Stones, who in November 1969 set out on their first American tour in almost three years. The Stones by now were well aware that the Beatles were on the verge of breaking up, and they saw their return to the concert stage as an opportunity to assume the mantle, as their tour publicity described it, of "The World's Greatest Rock 'n' Roll Band."

The news that Britain's second-biggest group would be returning to the United States was greeted with great anticipation by American fans. "In the year of Woodstock, *Tommy, Abbey Road,* [and] the Isle of Wight," wrote Ellen Sander, "the Rolling Stones tour could blow the whole pop scene wide open with an explosion of energy and a tidal wave of rejuvenation." For their part, the Stones rose magnificently to the occasion, filling large arenas with an unsurpassed mixture of musical grit and theatrical flair. Thrilled by the success of their early shows, the group hired the filmmakers Albert and David Maysles to document the remainder of the tour. As the Beatles had discovered with *Get Back,* the addition of cameras generated a narrative pressure that cried out for some form of climax. Accordingly the Stones hastily improvised a plan to end their tour by staging a massive free concert on the outskirts of San Francisco. Evoking the spirit of Woodstock, Mick Jagger informed the press archly that this concert was intended to create "a sort of microcosmic society which sets an example for the rest of America as to how one can behave in large gatherings." Organizational support was provided by the San Francisco rock establishment, led by the Grateful Dead, whose management suggested that the Hell's Angels motorcycle gang be hired to provide security around the stage. The Dead's link with the Hell's Angels went back to their early association with Ken Kesey and the Merry Pranksters, who had lured the Angels into an uneasy alliance with the counterculture by inviting them to some of the first "acid tests." Since then, despite their thuggish behavior and their fascist political beliefs, the Angels had been romanticized as a band of righteous outlaws by hippies and radicals throughout Northern California. The Stones had already used a group of English Hell's Angels to provide security at their concert in Hyde Park; they had no idea of the difference between the British impersonators and the American sociopaths.

Drawn by a roster of acts that included the Dead, the Jefferson Airplane, Crosby, Stills & Nash, and other top California bands, a crowd of 300,000 people gathered at the Altamont Speedway on December 6, 1969, for a concert that was touted as "Woodstock West." Charged with the superfluous task of maintaining order around the stage, a contingent of a hundred Hell's Angels, stoned on beer and barbiturates, fulfilled their role with a sadistic zeal that escalated over the course of the afternoon into the systematic brutalization of fans and musicians alike. By the time the Stones were ready to take the stage, darkness had fallen, dozens of people had been badly beaten, and a pall of fear and foreboding hung over the crowd. Three songs into the Stones' set, a gang of Hell's Angels wielding knives and clubs attacked a tall, conspicuously dressed black teenager who had spent most of the day dancing near the stage with his white girlfriend. When the terrified youth pulled out an unloaded revolver, he was brutally stabbed and beaten to death in front of the band.

The symbolism of this murder, which seemed to embody so many of the cultural contradictions of the decade that was coming to an end, was so powerful and inescapable as to generate a wave of revulsion throughout the counterculture. The events of that day were widely understood to mark the death knell of the utopian spirit of the 1960s as surely as Woodstock marked its apotheosis. More than any other white entertainers of their generation, the Rolling Stones had built their careers on the conscious emulation of black music, black style, and black sensibility. Now, in the interests of providing a spectacular climax for their tour and their film, they had sponsored and performed at a concert where a young black man had been viciously murdered by a group of racist thugs who had been hired, unnecessarily, to protect the band from its own audience. On the eve of the Altamont concert, the Stones released a new album, engineered by Glyn Johns. After hearing from Johns about his work on the *Get Back* project, the title they gave this new record was a riposte to the title of the Beatles' unreleased ballad, "Let It Be." They called it *Let It Bleed*.

THE COMMERCIAL SUCCESS of *Abbey Road* marked the beginning of a financial bonanza that Allen Klein had dreamed about since he first set his sights on the Beatles in 1964. Klein's response to John Lennon's announcement that he wanted a "divorce" from the group was first to suppress it and then to ignore it. The idea that the most lucrative act in the history of the record business, having reached the peak of its earning power, might truly and permanently disband over creative and personal differences was almost inconceivable to a man whose credo was "Don't talk to me about 'management'; talk to me about net and gross."

In November 1969, Klein concluded a deal with United Artists to release the still-unfinished film of *Get Back* as a theatrical feature in the spring of 1970, thereby satisfying the original three-picture contract the Beatles and Brian Epstein had signed in 1963. The film and its soundtrack album would enable Klein to maintain the illusion that the Beatles were still a viable group through the middle of 1970. That was plenty of time, in his view, to turn the personal situation around. Klein believed that the financial incentives, combined with his own powers of persuasion, could convince the Beatles not only to stay together, but also, like the Stones, to mount a major tour in the year ahead. Having gained the trust of John, George, and Ringo, his hopes for reuniting the group depended on bringing Paul around, and his strategy for doing this included lending his support to Paul's desire for the Beatles to tour.

John Lennon and Yoko Ono spent the fall of 1969 promoting their Peace Campaign with activities that included John's well-publicized decision to return his MBE medal to Buckingham Palace as an act of protest against British involvement in the wars in Biafra and Vietnam, and the sponsorship of large billboards in New York, Paris, Rome, Berlin, Tokyo, and a half-dozen other major cities reading "War Is Over! If You Want It—Happy Christmas from John & Yoko." With Allen Klein's encouragement, Ringo Starr spent the fall recording tracks for a solo album called *Sentimental Journey,* on which he commissioned a dozen noted pop arrangers to produce lushly orchestrated versions of Tin Pan Alley standards, including "Night and Day," "Stardust," and "Love Is a Many-Splendoured Thing." In December, George Harrison accepted an invitation from Eric Clapton and toured for several weeks in Britain and Europe as part of an all-star pickup band fronted by a pair of white American soul singers named Bonnie and Delaney Bramlett. For his part, Paul McCartney shook off the rumors of his death and the gloom prompted by his alienation from the other Beatles by getting down to work, recording tracks for a solo album at his home in St. Johns Wood.

By the end of 1969, Michael Lindsay-Hogg had completed his post-production work on the Beatles film. The final cut of the picture had been shaped by Allen Klein's directive that the film focus exclusively on the four Beatles, which required the director to dispense with nearly all of the dialogue and interaction between the band and their friends and the crew. An exception to this Beatles-only policy was a scene in which John and Yoko were shown waltzing around the sound stage at Twickenham Studios to the cabaret-like strains of George Harrison's "I Me Mine." The use of the song in the film called for its inclusion on the soundtrack album. But because "I Me Mine" had never been properly recorded during the rehearsals at Twickenham, three of the Beatles—George, Paul, and Ringo—agreed to meet on the first weekend of the new decade at Abbey Road, where they spent nine hours recording a full-band version of the song. This session marked another provisional ending to the Beatles story: the last time they would ever officially record as the Beatles. That Harrison had written "I Me Mine" as a commentary on the selfishness of John and Paul, and that the purpose of the track was to provide the musical accompaniment to a dance by John and Yoko, only added to the poignancy of this final recording date, which took place eight years to the day from the Beatles' disastrous audition at Decca Records in 1962.

John Lennon spent the New Year's holiday vacationing in Denmark, where he and Yoko celebrated the end of the 1960s by having their hair cropped short. When John was informed of the "I Me Mine" session, he elected not to attend. Toward the end of January, however, backed by George Harrison and the rhythm section from the Plastic Ono Band, John recorded a new song called "Instant Karma." The record was produced by Phil Spector, whom the Beatles had first met in Britain in 1964 and whose reentry into their professional lives was arranged by Allen Klein.

In February 1970, Ringo Starr completed his *Sentimental Journey,* and Paul McCartney booked time under a pseudonym to mix and master his solo album at Abbey Road. In March, Apple released McCartney's hymn-like ballad from the *Get Back* sessions, "Let It Be," as the Beatles' first single of 1970. Produced by George Martin and cast in the stately, inspirational mold of "Hey Jude," "Let It Be" fell short of the formal perfection of its model. But on the strength of Paul's singing and George's eloquently understated guitar solo, "Let It Be" became the Beatles' last great record, a plea for acceptance and forbearance on behalf of all the "brokenhearted people living in the world." The single entered the American charts at number six, the highest position of entry ever recorded, but its rise to number one was delayed for two weeks by the presence of Simon and Garfunkel's blockbuster ballad, "Bridge Over Troubled Water." In Britain the popularity of the Simon and Garfunkel song caused "Let It Be" to peak at number two.

In the meantime, impressed with Phil Spector's uncharacteristically spare production on "Instant Karma," John Lennon and Allen Klein hired the eccentric American to remix the soundtrack album for the Beatles film, which was now scheduled for release in May under the new title of *Let It Be.* Having never been impressed with Glyn Johns's original concept of an informal "album of rehearsals," Klein instructed Spector to make the record sound "more commercial."

Paul McCartney completed the tracks for his solo album in March. Up to this point, the very existence of the record, which was titled simply *McCartney,* had been a closely kept secret. Now Paul made the arrangements to have the album pressed and released directly with EMI, bypassing Apple and Allen Klein. A release date was set for the middle of April. When Klein finally heard about this, he objected strongly, arguing that Paul's album would compete with the release of Ringo's *Sentimental Journey,* which was set for the beginning of April, and the *Let It Be* soundtrack, which was set for the middle of May. At Klein's request, Lennon, Harrison, and Starr signed a letter instructing EMI to postpone the release of *McCartney;* they then sent Ringo to speak with Paul and persuade him to go along. Ringo's attempt to do so ended with Paul, in a fury, throwing him out of his house. This confrontation pushed the tensions in the Beatles past the breaking point.

On April 10, a week before the official release of *McCartney,* Paul personally sent out review copies to the press. The accompanying promotional packet contained a self-written "interview" in which he answered questions about the album and its relation to his work with the Beatles. To the question "Is this album a rest away from the Beatles or the start of a solo career?" Paul replied, "Time will tell." To the question "Is your break with the Beatles temporary or permanent?" Paul replied, "I don't know." To the question "Do you foresee a time when Lennon-McCartney becomes an active songwriting partnership again?" Paul answered simply, "No." And to the question "Did you miss the other Beatles and George Martin?" Paul repeated, "No." One week later, Apple issued a press release confirming that "Paul McCartney has left the Beatles due to personal, musical, and business differences."

McCartney's announcement made headlines in newspapers and magazines all over the world. Its most immediate effect was to turn both the film and album of *Let It Be* into postscripts to the Beatles' career. The film had its world premiere in New York in the middle of May; it opened in London and Liverpool a week after that. None of the Beatles attended any of the openings. The soundtrack album was released at the same time.

As the work of a television director who was making his first featurelength film, *Let It Be* was harshly criticized on both technical and conceptual grounds. "This isn't a motion picture," wrote the critic for *Films in Review,* "merely 16mm photography." But most reviewers glossed over the mediocrity of Michael Lindsay-Hogg's direction to comment, in the wake of McCartney's announcement, on the sad spectacle of exhaustion, frustration, and dissolution that was depicted on the screen. "Watching an institution such as the Beatles in their film *Let It Be* is rather like watching the Albert Hall being dismantled into a block of National Coal Board offices," suggested the Sunday *Telegraph.* Penelope Gilliatt, who had written with such appreciation about the Beatles in *A Hard Day's Night,* described *Let It Be* as "a very bad film and a touching one . . . about the breaking apart of this reassuring, geometrically perfect, once apparently ageless family of siblings."

On a more positive note, several reviewers noted that some of the performances in the film sounded better than the equivalent tracks on the *Let It Be* soundtrack album, citing Paul McCartney's ballad "The Long and Winding Road" as the prime example of this. In the film, Paul is shown singing the song at the piano to the understated accompaniment of Ringo on drums, John on bass, Billy Preston on organ, and George on electric guitar. On the album, Phil Spector had effectively overwritten the Beatles' version with a Hollywood-style arrangement for strings, horns, and a full choir of female voices. It was only the most egregious example of Spector's misguided production, which included a mangled remix of "Let It Be" and a slowed-down version of John Lennon's unreleased ballad "Across the Universe" that Spector scored for strings and choir and, with Alan Klein's blessing, added to the LP. With *Let It Be,* the Beatles' recording career came full circle. Their last album was made the way that albums had been made before they revolutionized the politics of the recording studio and the record business, by a producer who took it upon himself to decide how best to present their music without consulting them—a producer who, uncoincidentally, hadn't had a hit since 1965.

BY THE END of 1970, all four former members of the Beatles had released solo albums. *Sentimental Journey* was so roundly panned by critics that Ringo offered the lame excuse "I made it for my Mum," but he followed it in September with *Beaucoups of Blues,* a country album recorded in Nashville that earned respectable reviews. In November, George Harrison released *All Things Must Pass,* an expansive three-record collection of songs. Despite its inordinate length and Phil Spector's murky production, the overall quality of the musicianship and songwriting made the album not just the beginning, but also, arguably, the high point of Harrison's career as a solo artist. A month later, Apple released *John Lennon/Plastic Ono Band,* an ambitious, uncompromising, and genuinely edgy album on which John's anguished singing and overtly autobiographical songwriting were influenced by his and Yoko's involvement with a form of "primal" psychotherapy developed by the American psychologist Dr. Arthur Janov. Together with *McCartney,* these albums marked the end of the Beatles as a unified creative force and the start of four distinct solo careers.

December 1970 brought another provisional ending, as Paul McCartney, acting on the advice of his attorney John Eastman, filed a lawsuit in High Court, London, against John Lennon, George Harrison, Richard Starkey, and Apple Corps Ltd. The purpose of the suit was to dissolve the partnership Beatles & Co., under the terms of which the four of them had agreed to share equally in their earnings from concerts, records, and films. From McCartney's perspective, extricating himself from this agreement was the only way he could keep the money he made from his solo career out of the hands of Allen Klein. In the spring of 1971, the court found in McCartney's favor and placed Beatles & Co. in receivership. (McCartney's case was not hurt by the fact that Klein, whose testimony the trial judge likened to that of a "second-rate salesman," was convicted in New York on tax reporting charges in the midst of the High Court proceeding.) This was the beginning of a legal saga that would continue for seven years. What began as a case of *McCartney v. Lennon, Harrison, & Starkey* would shift, from 1973 onward, into a series of suits and countersuits that pitted Lennon, Harrison, and Starr against Klein. Eventually, in 1977, Apple would pay Klein a final settlement of more than $4 million to stay out of his former clients' lives.

IN THE DECADE to come, John Lennon would release four more solo albums, along with a collection of rock-'n'-roll cover tunes whose cover featured one of Jurgen Vollmer's photographs of John as a young rocker in Hamburg. His first two solo albums, *Plastic Ono Band* and *Imagine,* were by far his best. The former was distinguished by a concluding track called "God" on which John declared "the dream is over" and renounced a long list of former idols, icons, and heroes, to end with the lines "I don't believe in Beatles, I just believe in me . . . Yoko and me." *Imagine* was made memorable by its title cut, which went on to serve as the iconic theme of Lennon's whole solo career. The album was made notorious by "How Do You Sleep," a bitter screed directed at Paul McCartney that included the line "The sound that you make is Muzak to my ears."

Following the release of *Imagine,* Lennon's nonmusical activities and personal life tended to overshadow his career as a recording artist. After moving to New York City in the summer of 1971, John and Yoko immersed themselves in various left-wing political causes. Their activism eventually inflamed the paranoia of the Nixon administration, which tried to revoke John's residency visa in 1973. Soon afterward, he and Yoko went through a well-publicized breakup, which ended with their reconciliation in 1974. The following year, Yoko gave birth to their son Sean, John's immigration case was resolved in his favor, and he was granted U.S. citizenship. At that point he withdrew completely from the public eye, and devoted the remainder of the 1970s to family life.

Not surprisingly, Paul McCartney's career as a solo artist during the 1970s was the most dynamic and commercially successful of all the former Beatles'. From 1970 to 1980, in one guise or another, Paul released an album a year. Seven of these records, including the critically acclaimed 1973 album *Band on the Run,* were made with the group Wings, which he formed with his wife, Linda, in 1971. All of McCartney's albums sold in the millions; many of them topped the charts in Britain and the United States; and virtually every one of them produced a number-one single as well. ("Mull of Kintyre," released in 1977, became the best-selling single in the history of the British record business.) Though Wings was never perceived as anything but a vehicle for its leader, the band developed a following in its own right, and toured regularly from 1973 onward. By the end of the 1970s, Paul McCartney was well on his way to becoming the most commercially successful musician in the history of the music business.

Apart from a pair of arrests for marijuana possession in Scotland and Japan, McCartney's personal life remained shielded from public view throughout the 1970s. He and Linda had a total of three children together; by all accounts, their devotion to one another was such that they rarely spent a day apart.

George Harrison followed *All Things Must Pass* with five more studio albums during the 1970s. All but the last two, released on his own Dark Horse label, were commercially successful, though few if any of the songs on these records fulfilled the promise of "Something" and "Here Comes the Sun." Harrison's most artistically acclaimed musical effort during those years was the Concert for Bangladesh, which was organized to raise money and public awareness for the humanitarian crisis caused by the outbreak of civil war in East Pakistan. The first rock benefit of its kind, the concert was held at New York's Madison Square Garden in August 1971 and featured fine performances by Harrison and an all-star band that included Eric Clapton, Billy Preston, and Ringo Starr. The high point of the show was a surprise appearance by Bob Dylan, his first since the Isle of Wight. Harrison had originally envisioned turning the concert into an impromptu Beatles reunion, but Paul McCartney declined his invitation to appear, and John Lennon, after originally accepting, backed out after Yoko Ono took offense at George's insistence that she not perform.

Shortly after the Beatles disbanded, George's wife, Pattie, fell in love with his close friend Eric Clapton, and the couple ended their marriage on amicable terms. George was remarried in 1978 to an American named Olivia Arias; their son Dhani was born the same year.

Ringo Starr released five additional albums during the decade that followed the Beatles' breakup. The first two, *Ringo* (1973) and *Goodnight Vienna* (1974), were musically entertaining and commercially successful records that enlisted the participation of the other former Beatles, individually, as songwriters and musicians. The last three albums, made without the help of his former bandmates, were unequivocal artistic and commercial failures. Ringo's best work on record during this period came on a pair of hit singles, "It Don't Come Easy" (1971) and "Photograph" (1973), both of which he co-wrote with George Harrison.

Starr also appeared in several films during the 1970s, earning critical praise for his portrayal of a Teddy boy in the 1973 picture *That'll Be the Day*. His marriage to Maureen ended in divorce in 1975, and he spent the remainder of the decade living somewhat peripatetically on the international celebrity circuit. Asked by an interviewer if he had any unfulfilled ambitions, Ringo responded, "My one ambition was to have been in the audience when the Beatles played. It must have been great."

Through it all, no matter where they went or what they did, the four former Beatles remained inexorably linked to one another in the minds of millions of fans in countries around the world. At regular intervals, prompted by the published comments of one or another, or by some promoter's offer of an astronomical sum, the rumor would resurface that they were preparing to reunite.

THE CONCLUSIVE END of the Beatles story came on December 8, 1980, when John Lennon was murdered on the street outside his New York apartment building by a deranged fan whose blank, thick face, as it appeared in newspaper photographs, was rendered less malevolent by the mop of Beatle hair that framed it. At the time he was arrested, Mark David Chapman carried a handgun, a complete collection of Beatles tapes, and a copy of *The Catcher in the Rye*. He reportedly told his court-appointed attorney that he had killed Lennon because "I understood his words but I didn't understand his meaning." At the time of his death, John had just emerged from semiretirement to release, with Yoko, his first album of new material in more than six years. Inevitably, his return to active duty as a singer and songwriter had inspired a new wave of speculation that the Beatles might reunite. His murder ended that speculation once and for all.

Paul McCartney was in London in December 1980, recording his first album with George Martin as producer and Geoff Emerick as engineer since *Abbey Road*. The day after Lennon's murder, McCartney arrived at the studio, determined to work. Asked to comment on John's death, Paul betrayed his anguish with the inadequacy of his response. "It's a drag," he said. In the weeks and months to come, the hagiography of John Lennon went into overdrive, spurred by the grief of his widow and the efforts of the press to satisfy and capitalize on the feelings of millions of brokenhearted Beatles fans around the world. The apparent flippancy of McCartney's remark would attach to his public image and be seen by some to epitomize the shallowness of his personality.

McCartney's real response to the loss of his former best friend and close collaborator came sixteen months later, in April 1982, with the release of the album he had been recording at the time of Lennon's death, now called *Tug of War*. Faced with a photograph that showed Paul with his hands pressed against a pair of monitor headphones in a way that made it look as if he was cradling his head in his arms, the new album was widely praised as containing his best work on record since *Band on the Run*—or possibly even *Abbey Road*. In addition to the contributions of George Martin and Geoff Emerick, Ringo Starr plays drums on one track, the Beatles' old guitar hero Carl Perkins sings and plays on another, and much of the music carries stirring echoes of the past. A song called "Wanderlust" features dazzling multitracked vocals that recall the contrapuntal refrains of "Eleanor Rigby" and "She's Leaving Home." A rousing rocker called "Ballroom Dancing" evokes the seedy dance halls the Beatles played in Liverpool and Hamburg ("in the time of Davy Crockett"); another track called "Take It Away" recounts their first encounter with Brian Epstein at the Cavern Club, "a self-important impresario [with] a message for the band." In a eulogistic ballad called "Here Today," scored for strings in the style of "Yesterday," Paul addresses

John directly, singing, "I am holding back the tears no more: I love you." But the jewel of the album is the title cut, where McCartney, having hit on the perfect metaphor of two people whose struggle with each other depends on each of them retaining his grip on the rope, outdid himself in composing a tribute to the life and times and creative genius he shared with his old best friend. "We expected more," Paul sings in a voice whose dry, weary elegance harkens back to his greatest performances on *Revolver* and *Sgt. Pepper*, "but with one thing and another, we were trying to outdo each other in a tug-of-war." "In another world," he continues, as the simple chords of the song's release open out onto an almost limitless vista of musical space and time, "we could stand on top of the mountain with our flag unfurled."

In another world, they had done just that.

NOTES

PROLOGUE

p. 1   *They went to sea in a Sieve*   Lear (1947), 71.

p. 2   *Won't you please sing*   Braun (1964), 94.

p. 3   *I don't want to talk to them*   A. Aronowitz in Braun (1964), 98.

p. 3   *I don't want to interview them*   G. Cameron in Braun (1964), 97.

p. 5   *How did you propose*   transcript of New York press conference, 10 February 1964.

p. 5   *Obviously, these kids*   Braun (1964), 111.

p. 6   *And what do you do?*   R. Starr in Braun (1964), 123.

p. 6   *I loved it*   Mrs. N. Rockefeller, *New York Herald Tribune,* 13 February 1964.

p. 6   Billboard *estimated*   *Billboard,* 4 April 1954.

p. 10   *The very cut of their limbs*   Morris, *The Saturday Evening Post,* 27 August 1966.

p. 13   *I keep seeing pictures*   P. McCartney in C. Salewicz, *Q,* October 1986.

CHAPTER I

p. 17   *You've got to keep in mind*   S. Phillips in *Hold* (1989), 131.

p. 20   *I never sang like that*   E. Presley in *Jet,* 1 August 1957.

p. 22   *I heard Elvis Presley*   J. Lennon in R. York, *Rolling Stone,* 28 June 1970.

p. 22   *A disconcerting mixture*   Osborne (1977), 8.

p. 22   *It's such a long time*   Osborne (1977), 13.

p. 23   *A sturdy old plant*   Osborne (1977), 67.

p. 23   *A hostage*   Osborne (1977), 43.

p. 23   *The belief that life*   A. Alvarez (1962), 25.

p. 23   *The salient thing*   Tynan (1961), 192–93.

p. 24   *Working-class scholarship boy*   see Hoggart (1957).

p. 25   *The first moment in history*   Hewison (1981), 127.

p. 25   *The social revolution of 1945*   Sampson (1962), 636–37.

p. 25   *The most compelling social characteristic*   Cooke (1988), 122.

p. 25   *A tremendous romance about America*   Gosling (1962), 24.

CHAPTER 2

p. 26   *I was bored on the 9th*   Lennon (1964), back cover.

p. 27   A. Lennon account, see Davies (1968), 6–8.

p. 28   *Sporadically*   J. Lennon in Sheff (1981), 173.

p. 29   *Wilde and Whistler*   J. Lennon in Sheff (1981), 167.

p. 29   *She's a real Boticelli*   Carpenter (1984), 571.

p. 29   *He did not share*   Coleman (1984), 44.

p. 34   *Eminently likeable*   A. Durband in Salewizc (1986), 30.

p. 34   *The need to soldier on*   McCartney (1981), unpaged.

p. 34   *A passport to popularity*   McCartney (1981), unpaged.

CHAPTER 3

p. 36   *It was a port*   J. Lennon in Wenner (1971), 18.

p. 37   *Extent and solidity*   Melville (1986), 229.

p. 38   *The death of a prime minister*   *The Spectator,* 14 January 1949.

p. 39   *A decaying corpse*   Brophy (1946), 137.

p. 39   *Walking arm in arm*   Melville (1986), 277.

p. 40   *In the role of missionaries*   Mays (1964), 57.

p. 41   *A curious cult of Northernness*   Orwell (1958), 110.

p. 42   For Scouse dialect, see Wright (1976); Trudgill (1990); Trudgill (1978); Shaw (1966); and Shaw (1971).

p. 42   *Intonation in Liverpool*   Wright (1976), 46–7.

p. 43   *To understand Liverpool*   Owen, *The Spectator,* 5 February 1965.

p. 43   *I was born in Liverpool*   Redfern (1984), 1.

CHAPTER 4

p. 45   *One of the things I realized*   P. McCartney in Baird (1988), 38.

p. 45   *He was the fairground hero*   P. McCartney in Postscript to Davies (1985), 370.

p. 47   *College pudding*   P. McCartney in Davies (1968), 25.

p. 48   *But good gracious*   Saki (H. H. Munro) (1961), "The Baker's Dozen."

p. 48   *Whatever sociological thing*   J. Lennon in Sheff (1981), 170.

p. 48   *I was aggressive because*   J. Lennon in Davies (1968), 13.

p. 49   *A constant conflict*   L. E. Sissman, *The New Yorker,* 24 December 1973.

p. 50   *I was twelve*   J. Lennon in *The New York Times Book Review,* 30 September 1973.

p. 50   *The refuge of the bright*   Melly (1971), 146.

p. 52   *We dressed in Teddy boy style*   J. Lennon in *New York Post,* 14 August 1964.

p. 55   *It was a brand new house*   L. Harrison in Davies (1968), 38.

p. 56   *I think it was awful*   G. Harrison (1980), 21 and Davies (1968), 39.

p. 56   *I cannot tell you*   G. Harrison (1980), 22.

p. 57   *A bloody kid*   J. Lennon in Wenner (1971), 160.

CHAPTER 5

p. 58 *We started off imitating Elvis*   P. McCartney in Palmer (1976), 237.

p. 60 *Saga of perfect decline*   Guralnik (1979), 137.

p. 61 *If I ever have to write*   J. Leiber in Guralnick (1994), 449.

p. 63 *Bigger than religion*   J. Lennon in Cleave, *The Observer,* 4 January 1981.

p. 63 *A ridiculous favorite*   P. McCartney in Wyndam, *London Life,* December 1965.

p. 63 *He really wrote his own stuff*   J. Lennon in Wenner (1971), 168.

CHAPTER 6

p. 69 *A disconcerting mixture*   Osborne (1977), 8.

p. 70 *I was in a sort of blind rage*   J. Lennon in Davies (1968), 53.

p. 72 *wouldn't compete to become*   A. Durband in Salewicz (1986), 63.

p. 75 *The music of every sideburned delinquent*   Kelley (1986), 254.

CHAPTER 7

p. 78 *Many people ask*   J. Lennon in *Mersey Beat,* 6 July 1961.

p. 78 *Monomyth*   see Campbell (1968), 3–46.

p. 80 *Our role in life*   P. McCartney in Smith (1988), 200.

p. 82 *Where are your tanks*   J. Lennon in Coleman (1984), 119.

p. 84 *Fascinated by Teddy boys*   A. Kirchherr in Davies (1968), 83.

p. 84 *Edgar Allan Poe*   A. Kirchherr in Norman (1981), 91.

p. 87 *When someone is trying to be natural*   G. Mann, intro. to Sander (1973).

CHAPTER 8

p. 90 *There was a feeling*   G. Harrison (1980), 33.

p. 90 *The new legislation*   Levin (1970), 280.

p. 91 *The same sort of impact*   T. Richardson, *Films & Filming,* February 1959.

p. 92 Lady Chatterley *trial*   see Rolphe (1961) and Levin (1970).

p. 92 *Unbridled sex*   Rolphe (1961), 210.

p. 93 *I was not embarrassed*   *Daily Telegraph,* 3 November 1960.

p. 93 *We have with us this evening*   Bennett et al. (1963), 93.

p. 94 *Something desperate about Stuart*   Paolozzi in Willet (1967), 166.

CHAPTER 9

p. 99 *Pop Art is*   Richard Hamilton in Hewison (1986), 42.

p. 100 *Back in the catbird seat*   Cohn (1969), 96.

CHAPTER 10

p. 108 *This was the real thing*   B. Wooler, *Mersey Beat,* 31 August 1961.

p. 108 *Our original intention*   G. Harrison, *Rolling Stone,* 5 November 1987.

p. 110 *Liverpool children are the noisiest*   Turner (1967), 146–47.

p. 110 On gang culture and beat music   see C. Fletcher, *New Society,* 20 February 1964.

p. 112 *I think the Beatles are No. 1*   B. Wooler, *Mersey Beat,* 31 August 1961.

p. 113 *Throughout my schooldays*   Epstein (1964), 25.

p. 114 *Procuring people's confidence*   B. Epstein in Taylor (1984), 129.

p. 114 *There was a sort of wistfulness*   H. Lindsey in Geller (2000), 13.

p. 114 *A really promising student*   RADA report, in Geller (2000), 18.

p. 114 *I fancy Rome*   B. Epstein in Geller (2000), 35.

p. 115 *I had never seen anything like the Beatles*   B. Epstein in Coleman (1984), 154.

p. 115 *Everything about the Beatles*   B. Epstein in *The Observer,* 17 May 1964.

p. 116 *Middle-class commercialism*   B. Epstein in *The Observer,* 17 May 1964.

p. 120 *An unusual quality of sound*   Martin (1979), 122.

p. 121 *A live eel in my hands*   Martin (1979), 28.

CHAPTER 11

p. 124 *I was the new boy*   R. Starr in *Melody Maker,* 14 November 1964.

p. 125 *Just ordinary poor working-class*   R. Starr in Davies (1968), 141.

p. 125 *A quiet thoughtful type*   Davies (1968), 147.

p. 127 *It's how I'm built*   R. Starr in Braun (1964), 38.

p. 127 *To be so aware*   J. Lennon in Braun (1964), 37.

p. 129 *Subconsciously we knew*   C. Stamp in Oldham (2000), 83.

p. 132 *The new arty-crafties*   R. Gosling in *Queen,* September 1961.

p. 135 *The first bluesy thing we tried to do*   P. McCartney in Lewisohn (1988), 7.

p. 136 *Tact is the* sine qua non   Martin (1979), 44.

p. 136 *Another of your funny ones*   G. Martin in Smith (1988), 203.

p. 138 *Why did you talk like that*   P. McCartney (1981), unpaged.

CHAPTER 12

p. 141 *Sexual intercourse began*   Larkin (1974).

p. 143 *Great Britain has lost an empire*   D. Acheson in *The Times* (London), 6 December 1962.

p. 143 *Philip of Spain, Louis XIV*   H. Macmillan in *The Times* (London), 8 December 1962.

p. 143 *It is the nature of nations diminished*   *The Spectator,* 14 December 1962.

p. 144 *Britain's Troubled Mood*   *Time,* 28 January 1963.

p. 144 *The old ethos was molded*   Sampson (1962), 638.

p. 145 *Why the Beatles create all that frenzy*   M. Cleave, *Evening Standard,* 2 February 1963.

p. 150 *A minor mythology*   Hoggart (1957), 160.

p. 152 *Like a Hollywood movie*   B. Bilgorri in *The Sunday Times Magazine,* 4 March 1983.

p. 153 On the Profumo Affair, see Denning (1963), Irving (1963), Levin (1970), and Booker (1969).

p. 158 *Getting a really loud rhythm sound*   Martin (1979), 120.

p. 159 *Four Frenzied Fauntleroys*   *Daily Mirror,* 10 September 1963.

CHAPTER 13

p. 161 *Within the last century*   Boorstin (1978), 47.

p. 161 *We risk being the first people in history*   Boorstin (1978), 240.

p. 161 Pseudo-events, see Boorstin (1978), 9–76.

p. 162 *Brian had more fans*   G. Marsden in Geller (2000), 64.

p. 162 *The Beatles are famous*   B. Epstein in Bailey (1969), 73.

p. 163 *Does it irk you*   B. Epstein in K. Harris, *The Observer*, 17 May 1964.

p. 163 *The biggest theatrical attraction*   B. Epstein in Braun (1964), 47.

p. 164 *Screaming like an animal*   *Daily Mail*, 21 October 1963.

p. 164 *A horde of screaming Beatle fans*   *Daily Mirror*, 28 Oct 1963.

p. 164 *Most of the 5,000 hysterical youngsters*   *Sunday Times*, 27 October 1963.

p. 166 *This hysteria presumably fills heads*   editorial in *Daily Telegraph*, 2 November 1963.

p. 166 *Is it true that Decca turned you down*   These quotations are drawn from Braun (1964); V. Mulchrone, *Daily Mail*, 21 October 1963; and M. Cleave, *New York World Telegram*, 27 December 1963.

p. 167 *Nothing is more English*   Chesterton (1953), 213.

p. 167 *A nice personality bit*   J. Lennon and D. Mather, BBC interview, 12 December 1963.

p. 168 *Rattle your jewelry*   J. Lennon, ATV broadcast, 10 November 1963.

p. 168 *In seven successive Royal shows*   *Daily Telegraph*, 5 November 1963.

p. 169 *Anatomy of Beatlemania*   *Sunday Times*, 3 November 1963.

p. 169 *Roots of Beatlemania*   *Observer*, 10 November 1963.

p. 169 *I think I'll invite them down*   Viscount Montgomery in Braun (1964), 69.

p. 169 *An agreeable bunch of kids*   F. Newton, *The New Statesman*, 8 November 1963.

CHAPTER 14

p. 170 *Anarchy is too strong a word*   R. Lester in DiFranco (1978), 5.

p. 171 *We don't believe in our fame*   P. McCartney in Braun (1964), 54.

p. 171 *We're kidding everyone*   J. Lennon in Cameron, *Life*, 21 February 1964.

p. 171 *We won't do a rags to riches story*   in S. Watts, *New York Times*, 26 April 1964.

p. 171 *I don't feel like I imagine an idol*   P. McCartney in Braun (1964), 33.

p. 171 *Paul does, the rest of us don't*   J. Lennon in Braun (1964), 111.

p. 172 *Don't forget that music*   J. Lennon in *Melody Maker*, 3 August 1963.

p. 172 *This isn't show business*   J. Lennon in Braun (1964), 52.

p. 172 *It is devotion to the extraordinary*   Weber in Gerth (1946), 249.

p. 172 Weber on charisma, see Gerth (1946), Eisenstadt (1968), Lindholm (1993).

p. 175 Freud on charisma, see Freud (1950), Freud (1959), Smelser (1963), Smelser (1998), and Becker (1973).

p. 176 *We have only to think of the troop*   Freud (1959), 52.

p. 181 *God Save the Queen*   Braun (1964), 20.

p. 181 *You don't have to be a genius*   *Sunday Times*, 3 November 1963.

p. 181 *For the girls who participated in Beatlemania*   Ehrenreich (1986), 19, 35.

p. 184 *I've never seen them alive before*   Braun (1964), 23.

p. 185 *They who are causing the storm*   *Daily Mail*, 21 October 1963.

CHAPTER 15

p. 187 *The outstanding English composers* W. Mann, *The Times* (London), 27 December 1963.

p. 192 *He's got the most perfect voice* J. Lennon in Cott, *Rolling Stone,* 23 November 1968.

CHAPTER 16

p. 195 *New York can destroy an individual* White (1949), 9.

p. 195 *The Queen mother beamed* *Time,* 15 November 1963.

p. 196 On Epstein and Ed Sullivan, see Bowles (1980), 179–88.

p. 198 *A most discouraging revolution* D. Dexter in Martland (1997), 234.

p. 200 *They are not phony* B. Epstein in *The New Yorker,* 28 December 1963.

p. 203 *International understanding* S. Bernstein in Braun (1964), 130.

CHAPTER 17

p. 204 *In the modern world* Goodman (1960), 137.

p. 204 *A vast seismograph* P. Brodeur, *Show,* December 1964.

p. 205 *The dream of violence* in "The Un-Angry Young Men," Fiedler (1963).

p. 206 *It was a hero America needed* N. Mailer, *Esquire,* November 1960.

CHAPTER 18

p. 211 *So this is America* R. Starr in Braun (1964), 95.

p. 211 *Britons Succumb to Beatlemania* *New York Times,* 1 December 1963.

p. 211 *Front page of the show-business weekly* *Variety,* 4 December 1963.

p. 212 On the publicity campaign Capitol Records memo dated 23 December 1963.

p. 213 *Sweet-sour* *Vogue,* December 1963.

p. 213 *Having missed the Beatle thing* P. Brodeur, *Show,* December 1964.

p. 214 *High pitched, loud beyond reason* *Newsweek,* 18 November 1963.

p. 214 *The pretext of a connection* J. Gould, *New York Times,* 10 February 1964.

p. 216 *He was so living* Wolfenstein (1965), 224.

p. 217 *These words are drawn* see Wolfenstein (1965), 224–33.

p. 218 *Mourning at a distance* Wolfenstein (1965), 71.

p. 221 *Their ye-ye is the worst* *France-Soir* in Braun (1964), 79.

p. 221 *The Mozart of rock 'n' roll* *Variety,* 18 September 1963.

p. 221 *They've got their own groups* P. McCartney in Braun (1964), 91.

CHAPTER 19

p. 223 *Britain is in a revolutionary situation* A. Brien, *The Spectator,* 22 May 1964.

p. 223 *England exploded* P. McCartney in Wyndam, *London Life,* December 1965.

p. 224 For press coverage of Mod-Rocker violence, see Cohen (2002), 40, 87.

p. 224 *Excuse for rage* H. Fairlie in *The Spectator,* 22 May 1964.

p. 227 *I feel as if snakes* Orton (1986), 166.

p. 228 *I'm very conscious of it* M. Forster in Aitken (1967), 264.

p. 228 *I'm received as the Duke of Cockney* M. Caine in Aitken (1967), 268.

CHAPTER 20

p. 229 *On that first day I met the Beatles*   R. Lester in DiFranco (1978), 5.

p. 230 *A job for a dilettante*   R. Lester, *The New Yorker*, 28 October 1968.

p. 232 *The structure of the script*   R. Lester in DiFranco (1978), 3.

p. 233 *A literal menagerie of characters*   M. Wood, *New Society*, 27 June 1968.

p. 233 *Never seen or heard the Beatles*   C. Curran in Thomson (1987), 47.

CHAPTER 21

p. 238 Beatles in Australia, see Baker (1985).

p. 240 *The things I wanted to say*   A. Owen in Walker (1974), 265.

p. 243 On Gilbert Taylor, see Walker (1974), 269.

p. 244 *The legitimacy of the Beatles*   *Newsweek*, 24 August 1964.

p. 244 *This is going to surprise you*   B. Crowther, *New York Times*, 12 August 1964.

p. 244 *The Citizen Kane of jukebox musicals*   A. Sarris, *Village Voice*, 27 August 1964.

p. 244 *Conspiracy of delinquency*   A. Schlesinger Jr., *Show*, November 1964.

p. 245 *The stoicism of clowns*   P. Gilliatt in Byron (1977), 248–49.

p. 245 *A litter of perfectly groomed*   I. Quigley, *The Spectator*, 10 July 1964.

p. 245 *Four successful young men*   E. Sutherland, *The New Republic*, 18 August 1964.

CHAPTER 22

p. 249 *Go ahead and let yourselves go*   J. Lennon in Aronowitz, *New York Post*, 26 August 1964.

p. 251 *They were doing things nobody was doing*   B. Dylan in Scaduto (1971), 175.

p. 253 Meeting with Dylan, see Aronowitz, *Q*, May 1994.

p. 253 *When you're with another tea smoker*   L. Armstrong in Hammond (1977), 109.

CHAPTER 23

p. 255 *You could call our new one*   John Lennon in *Melody Maker*, 19 December 1964.

p. 256 *Material's becoming a hell of a problem*   J. Lennon, *Melody Maker*, 17 October 1964.

CHAPTER 24

p. 262 *Most nights this new aristocracy*   in Cohn (1969), 186.

p. 263 *The immediate rewards of quick money*   F. Wyndham in Bailey (1965), intro.

p. 263 *We were like kings of the jungle then*   J. Lennon in Wenner (1971), 88.

p. 268 *It was me singing "help" and I meant it*   J. Lennon in Wenner (1971), 115.

CHAPTER 25

p. 270 *Jesus El Pifco was a foreigner*   in Lennon (1965), 95.

p. 271 *Azue orl gnome*   in Lennon (1965), 122.

p. 272 MBE Controversy, see Thomson (1987), 53–57; Sampson (1962), 268–74; Sampson, *The Observer*, 5 January 1964.

p. 273 *Colonel Wagg from Dover* *The Times* (London), 17 June 1965.

p. 273 *I don't care if Mr. Dupuis eats his medal* R. Starr, quoted by N. Hentoff in Eisen (1969).

p. 274 *I said in a more fatuous moment* R. Lester in French, *Movie*, no. 14, 1965.

p. 274 *We enjoyed making* Help! P. McCartney in Wyndam, *London Life*, December 1965.

p. 275 *Its innovatory character* P. French, *Movie*, no. 14, 1965.

p. 275 *It's commercially safer* P. Kael in Byron (1977), 250.

p. 276 *The chief problem with the second film* S. Kauffman, *The New Republic*, 25 September 1965.

p. 277 *Is that all there is?* A. Livingston in Dexter (1976), 182.

CHAPTER 26

p. 281 *I asked about Beatlemania* A. Levy, *Good Housekeeping*, July 1965.

p. 283 Meeting with Elvis, see Gulralnik (1999), 210–12; Goldman (1981), 374–78.

p. 284 *Hey Beatle* S. Booth in Eisen (1969), 48.

p. 286 *A love of pot and the Beatles* C. Hillman in notes to the Byrds CD Collection.

CHAPTER 27

p. 289 *Coming into the studio* Martin (1994).

p. 290 *Oh, that's my D shape* G. Martin in *Stereo Review*, February 1971.

p. 290 *I've changed from being a gaffer* G. Martin in Davies (1968), 280.

p. 291 *A lot of my experience* P. Ramone in Smith (1988), 412.

CHAPTER 28

p. 295 *We've got some comedy songs* P. McCartney in Wyndam, *London Life*, December 1965.

p. 297 *I was trying to be sophisticated* J. Lennon in Sheff (1981), 188.

p. 300 *It must be about somebody* G. Harrison (1980), 88.

CHAPTER 29

p. 307 *The difference in the way* P. Townshend in *Rolling Stone*, eds. (1971), 119.

p. 307 Cleave interviews, *Evening Standard* 4 March, 11 March, 18 March, 25 March 1966.

p. 312 *But Paul McCartney worries* P. Townshend in *Rolling Stone*, eds. (1971), 119.

p. 315 *Clark Kent of the Underground* Green (1989), 45.

p. 315 Ginsberg birthday party, see Miles (1989), 370.

p. 315 *Miles was a great catalyst* P. McCartney in Green (1989), 77.

CHAPTER 30

p. 316 *This is how one ought to see*   Huxley (1960), 34.

p. 316 *We were cackling in the streets*   Wenner (1971), 73–74.

p. 317 *It was like opening the door*   G. Harrison in *Rolling Stone,* 5 November 1987.

p. 317 *It was more of a visual thing*   Wenner (1971), 78.

p. 319 *Pre-mortem death-rebirth experience*   Leary (1964), 30.

p. 319 *You see, I go the message on acid*   Wenner (1971), 77.

p. 319 *Something else I'm going to do*   J. Lennon in Cleave, *Evening Standard,* 4 March 1966.

p. 320 *One must surrender consciously*   Jung (1968), 167.

p. 320 *One sometimes feels that the unconscious*   Jung (1968), 164, 170.

p. 321 *He seemed to oscillate between extremes*   R. Freeman (1983), 10.

p. 321 *I have to see the others*   J. Lennon in Davies (1968), 295.

p. 321 *I did some drawings at the time*   J. Lennon in Wenner (1971), 140.

p. 322 *I don't know whether poets think*   P. McCartney in Cleave, *Evening Standard,* 25 March 1966.

p. 323 *I like first-person music*   J. Lennon in Wenner (1971), 52.

p. 324 *I was suddenly struck by great visions*   J. Lennon in Davies (1968), 289.

p. 324 *Eternity in a flower*   Huxley (1960), 36–7.

CHAPTER 31

p. 328 *There's a lot of random*   P. McCartney in Aldridge, *The Observer,* 26 November 1967.

p. 332 *Very paranoid*   J. Lennon in Cott, *Rolling Stone,* 23 November 1968.

p. 333 *A hymn to youth*   B. Wilson in *Melody Maker,* 21 May 1966.

p. 335 *Simply amazed*   P. McCartney in *Musician,* August 1980.

CHAPTER 32

p. 336 *We were just sort of going on there*   G. Harrison in *Holiday,* February 1968.

p. 338 *I don't feel tycoonish today*   B. Epstein in Cleave, *Evening Standard,* 1 April 1966.

p. 339 *Imelda Stood Up*   *Manila Times,* 5 July 1966.

p. 339 *A few weeks to recuperate*   G. Harrison in *The Saturday Evening Post,* 27 August 1966.

p. 339 *Old Beatles—A Study in Paradox*   M. Cleave, *The New York Times Magazine,* 3 July 1966.

p. 340 *We just felt it was so absurd*   T. Charles in *New York Times,* 4 August 1966.

p. 340 *Municipal facilities be used*   *Newsweek,* 22 August 1966.

p. 340 *Some subjects must not be dealt with*   *L'Osservatore Romano,* quoted in Norman (1981), 266.

p. 340 *Contempt for hypocrisy*   *New York Times,* 6 August 1966.

p. 340 *Lennon was simply stating*   *America,* 20 August 1966.

p. 341 *It seems a nerve*   R. Pitman, *Daily Express,* 15 August 1966.

p. 341 *A band of evangelists*   *Newsweek,* 24 February 1964.

p. 341 *Lo! Beatles descend*   *Variety,* 26 August 1964.

p. 341 *They have become a religion*   J. Miller, *Partisan Review,* Summer 1964.

p. 341 *Cripples threw away their sticks*   D. Taylor in *The Saturday Evening Post,* 8 August 1964.

p. 342 *We are in the fight*   Noebel (1965).

p. 343 *The first time we started to see*   P. McCartney in *Rolling Stone,* 5 November 1987.

p. 345 *You could party hop*   Perry (1984), 38.

p. 345 *The Yellow Submarine was first proposed*   Rossman (1971), 161–63.

p. 346 *People with certain religious beliefs*   B. Epstein in *Time,* 12 August 1966.

p. 346 *If I had said television*   J. Lennon, Chicago press conference, 11 August 1966.

p. 346 *The Beatles are about to enter*   *New York Times,* 23 August 1966.

p. 346 *There are more people*   J. Lennon in *New York Times,* 23 August 1966.

Chapter 33

p. 351 *I don't think there's ever been a better song*   J. Leiber in Smith (1988), 122.

p. 351 *Pop had come of age*   Melly (1971), 85.

p. 351 *A hang-up for my dad*   P. McCartney in Aldridge, *The Observer,* 26 November 1967.

p. 357 *We've all of us grown up*   P. McCartney in Davies, *Sunday Times,* 27 January 1967.

p. 357 *Self-sufficient cosmology*   Barthes (1972), 65.

p. 358 *This guy who I didn't really know*   J. Lennon in Wenner (1971), 78; Sheff (1981), 190.

p. 359 *Bird is a favorite Sinatra word*   G. Talese, *Esquire,* April 1966.

p. 362 *People got introduced to Dr. Roberts*   Cherry Vanilla in Stein (1982), 213–17.

Chapter 34

p. 367 *We sort of half hope for the Downfall*   J. Lennon in Cleave, *The New York Times Magazine,* 3 July 1966.

p. 367 *A savage anti-militaristic cartoon*   *The Times* (London), 16 November 1967.

p. 368 *He's the interpreter*   P. McCartney in *Sunday Times,* 27 January 1967.

p. 369 *The great sitar explosion began*   Shankar (1968), 92.

p. 369 *Sparkle and easy fame*   Shankar (1968), 72.

p. 369 *Very charming and polite*   Shankar (1968), 92.

p. 369 *I am trying not only to teach*   Shankar (1968), 89.

p. 370 *The difference over here*   G. Harrison in *New York Times,* 12 December 1966.

p. 370 *The Beatles ended three months*   *New York Times,* 26 November 1966.

p. 370 *Last week it emerged*   *Sunday Times,* 13 November 1966.

p. 371 *We'll work together only if*   P. McCartney in *Sunday Times,* 27 January 1967.

p. 371 *Beatles Breaking Up*   *Variety*, 25 January 1967.

p. 371 *I did try to go my own way*   J. Lennon in Davies (1968), 299.

p. 375 *A big, definitive, serious book*   Davies (1985), xviii.

CHAPTER 35

p. 377 *Personally, I don't think*   B. Wooler in S. Reynolds, *The Guardian*, 8 October 1963.

p. 380 *Then in 1914 it begins to rain*   Bennett (1969), 28.

p. 381 *We always had fun at Strawberry Fields*   J. Lennon in Sheff (1981), 166–75.

p. 382 *You can fix it, George*   J. Lennon in Martin (1979), 200.

CHAPTER 36

p. 385 *Man is least himself*   Wilde (1969), 389.

p. 385 *I thought it would be nice to lose our identities*   P. McCartney, *Playboy*, December 1984; Smith (1988), 201.

p. 387 *Not only a self-portrait*   Melly (1971), 127.

p. 387 *The Beatles insisted everything on Sgt. Pepper*   G. Emerick in notes on *Sgt. Pepper* CD (1987).

p. 388 *After having had the experience*   G. Harrison (1980), 108.

p. 388 *It was peer pressure of the highest variety*   P. McCartney in Green (1989), 182.

p. 389 *When I came back after five months*   J. Asher in Davies (1968), 309.

p. 390 *The most clamorous morning after furor*   Walker (1974), 376.

p. 391 *We realized for the first time*   P. McCartney in Aldridge, *Observer*, 26 November 1967.

p. 391 *Pioneer of Pop Art*   J. Russell, *Sunday Times*, 4 February 1962.

p. 391 *Paul explained it was like a band*   Blake in Taylor (1987), 33.

p. 392 *All legends, all mythologies*   Abel Gance in Benjamin (1968), 222.

p. 393 *Diana Dors has no drawers*   Opie (1960), 108.

p. 395 *New music from the Beatles*   in Marcus (1969), 66.

p. 396 *The summer of 1967 was spent*   P. Williams, *Mademoiselle*, November 1968.

CHAPTER 37

p. 397 *From the moment when the conductor*   W. L. George in Cheshire (1974), 80.

p. 402 *It's a much younger girl*   P. McCartney in Aldridge, *Observer*, 26 November 1967.

p. 405 *I got dozens of old steam organ tapes*   G. Martin in *Melody Maker*, 28 August 1971.

p. 409 *An outright piece of garbage*   J. Lennon in Sheff (1981), 193.

p. 412 *Inspired village band*   J. Cocteau in Crosland (1972), 328.

p. 412 *The chief theme of Parade*   Steegmuller (1970), 161.

p. 414 *Don't try to stay together*   Martin (1979), 210.

p. 415 *There are 4,000 holes in the road*   *Daily Mail*, 17 January 1967.

CHAPTER 38

p. 418 *It was the summer of 1967*   Sander, *Trips* (1969), 89.

p. 419 *They are here*   D. Taylor in Sander, *Trips* (1969), 95.

p. 420 *The New Far-Out Beatles*   *Life*, 16 June 1967.

p. 420 *A masterpiece*   *Newsweek*, 26 June 1967.

p. 420 *Mix-master to the Beatles*   *Time*, 16 June 1967.

p. 420 *Talk of the Town*   *The New Yorker*, 24 June 1967.

p. 421 *Salute to Sgt. Pepper*   *Christian Science Monitor*, 17 July 1967.

p. 421 *Literature and criticism*   *Saturday Review*, 19 August 1967.

p. 421 *The Messengers*   *Time*, 22 September 1967.

p. 421 *I and my colleagues*   N. Rorem, *The New York Review of Books*, 18 January 1968.

p. 421 *The Beatles and the Beatless*   J. Peyser, *Columbia Forum*, Fall 1967.

p. 422 *The two mainstreams of music*   F. Grunfeld, *Horizon*, Winter 1968.

p. 422 *Sgt. Pepper was genuinely a breakthrough*   Cohn (1969), 144.

p. 422 *If being a critic*   R. Goldstein, *Village Voice*, 20 July 1967.

p. 422 *An album of special effects*   R. Goldstein, *New York Times*, 16 June 1967.

p. 423 *A complete celebration of LSD*   T. Leary in *Look*, 8 August 1967.

p. 423 *We write songs*   P. McCartney in Aldridge, *The Observer*, 26 November 1967.

p. 424 *The image of this female*   J. Lennon in Sheff (1981), 191.

p. 424 *Learning from the Beatles*   R. Poirier, *Partisan Review*, Fall 1967.

CHAPTER 39

p. 426 *In London in 1967*   Neville (1970), 30.

p. 426 *Basic English*   *The Times* (of London), 19 May 1967.

p. 427 *It became almost fascinating*   G. Melly, *The Observer*, 2 July 1967.

p. 427 *A vast exercise in electronic rhetoric*   S. Hood, *The Spectator*, 30 June 1967.

p. 427 *This is Steve Race*   BBC-TV broadcast, 25 June 1967.

p. 429 *Secrets of the Pop Stars Hideaway*   *News of the World*, 5 February 1967.

p. 430 *I might take LSD again*   *Daily Mirror*, 19 June 1967.

p. 430 *What one cannot and should not forget*   M. Furlong in Taylor (1987), 111.

p. 430 *Who breaks a butterfly*   *The Times* (of London), 1 July 1967.

p. 431 *The verdict of one generation*   *The Observer*, 2 July 1967.

p. 431 *The law against marijuana is immoral*   *The Times* (of London), 24 July 1967.

p. 431 *I get bored like everyone else*   R. Starr in Connolly (1983), 37.

p. 432 *I gotta turn George on*   see *Melody Maker*, 19 August 1967.

p. 432 *This was the first thing*   G. Harrison, *David Frost Programme*, 29 September 1967.

p. 433 *I can't see in retrospect*   M. McClure in Perry (1984), 274.

p. 434 *An immensely successful career*   M. Hennessey, *Melody Maker*, 5 August 1967.

p. 434 *Incautious self-overdose*   *The Times* (of London), 9 September 1967.

p. 435 *I am certain that they would not agree*   B. Epstein in M. Hennessey, *Melody Maker*, 5 August 1967.

p. 436 *Essentially a gentleman businessman*   *The Times* (of London), 28 August 1967.

p. 436 *His part in it all has tended to be put down*   G. Martin in Southhall (1982), 101.

p. 436 *They are certainly not where they are*   B. Epstein in *Melody Maker,* 5 August 1967.

p. 437 *We loved Brian*   Beatles on Epstein, see *New Musical Express,* 2 September 1967.

p. 437 *I really didn't have any misconceptions*   J. Lennon in Wenner (1971), 52.

CHAPTER 40

p. 438 *In all the time he managed them*   Cohn (1969), 159.

p. 440 *Making films in sound*   G. Martin in *Holiday,* February 1968.

p. 440 *A record is sound and a film is visual*   P. McCartney in *Sunday Times,* 24 December 1967.

p. 440 *A disgusting example of the nastiness*   *Films in Review,* November 1967.

p. 441 *What the Beatles should do*   R. Lester in *Rolling Stone,* 14 December 1967.

p. 442 *Well, they can take them apart*   J. Lennon in *Rolling Stone,* 23 November 1968.

p. 443 *The first line was written on one acid trip*   J. Lennon in Sheff (1981), 194–95.

p. 444 On the Walrus and the Eggman, see Carroll (1960), Chapters 4 and 6.

CHAPTER 41

p. 446 *I can't understand their interest in religion*   P. Best in Davies (1985), xxxvi.

p. 446 *The appearance of this man*   Needleman (1970), 133.

p. 447 *The much-discussed surrender*   J. Mortimer, *The New Statesman,* 29 September 1967.

p. 447 *Preposterous . . . almost puerile*   P. Worsthorne in *New York Times,* 11 September 1967.

p. 448 *A technique to live a spiritual life*   Maharishi in *Listener,* 21 September 1967.

p. 448 *Natural state of man is joy*   Maharishi in Horn, *Look,* 6 February 1968.

p. 450 *There's high, and there's high*   G. Harrison in *Holiday,* February 1968.

p. 450 *A world from which all limits*   Martin (1981), 156.

p. 450 *Alas, the mind can be expanded*   Mehta (1979), 90.

CHAPTER 42

p. 452 *The closest Western Civilization*   L. Winner in Marcus (1969), 52.

p. 455 *Chaotic . . . A colossal conceit*   *Daily Mirror, Daily Mail,* 27 December 1967.

p. 455 *I cannot ever remember*   J. Thomas, *Daily Express,* 27 December 1967.

p. 456 *Well-meaning, good-humored anarchy*   H. Raynor, *The Times* (London), 27 December 1967.

p. 456 *A kind of fantastical morality play*   K. Dewhurst, *Guardian,* 4 January 1968.

p. 456 *The criticisms of* Magical Mystery Tour   J. Cott, *Rolling Stone,* 10 February 1968.

p. 457 *The unconscious magical element*   C. Marowitz, *Village Voice,* 4 January 1968.

p. 457 *You're the first person I've spoken with*   P. McCartney in Connolly (1983), 32.

p. 457 *Very thick*   *The Times* (London), 28 December 1967.

p. 457 *Was it really so bad*   P. McCartney, *David Frost Programme,* 27 December 1967.

p. 457 *We knew we weren't taking time*   P. McCartney in Davies, 308.

p. 457 *There was nobody*   N. Aspinall in McCabe (1972), 106.

CHAPTER 43

p. 458 *The hippies were there in great number*   Mailer (1968), 91.

p. 459 *From protest to resistance*   see Gitlin (1987), 242–60.

p. 459 *The plain and obvious fact*   Nuttall (1968), vii.

p. 460 *The youth of the world*   R. Poirier, *The Atlantic Monthly,* October 1968.

p. 461 *Playing with fire*   *International Times,* 19 April 1968.

p. 461 *A buzz*   M. Jagger in Melly (1971), 135.

p. 463 *Without going out of my door*   see G. Harrison (1980), 118.

p. 463 *People are in poverty*   Maharishi in *Rolling Stone,* 9 March 1968.

p. 463 *Wars, epidemics, famines*   Maharishi in *New York Times,* 22 January 1968.

p. 465 *It's as much a holiday*   P. McCartney in Connolly (1983), 33.

p. 466 *His meditation center is a bit like a Butlin's*   R. Starr in *Melody Maker,* 9 March 1968.

p. 466 *I get a bit lost*   P. McCartney in Lapham, *The Saturday Evening Post,* 13 May 1968.

CHAPTER 44

p. 470 *You know, A is for apple*   J. Lennon in *Business Week,* 18 May 1968.

p. 471 *One of those big, sort of computerized*   J. Lennon in *Business Week,* 18 May 1968.

p. 471 *We sort of feel that the Maharishi*   J. Lennon in CBS Radio interview, May 1968.

p. 472 *We're in the happy position*   P. McCartney, New York press conference, 14 May 1968.

p. 472 *We've decided to play businessman*   J. Lennon, *The Tonight Show,* 14 May 1968.

p. 472 *There was a general disposition*   D. Taylor in Green (1989), 225.

p. 472 *Too much brown rice*   L. Sweeney, *Christian Science Monitor,* 20 May 1968.

p. 473 *I was never able to get a hold*   Y. Ono, *New York Times,* 24 February 1973.

p. 474 *It was hard to make people understand*   Y. Ono in *Esquire,* December 1970.

p. 474 *Instead of obtaining a mirror*   Y. Ono (1970), unpaged.

p. 475 *It was impossible to disentangle*   see Hopkins (1986), 60–61.

p. 476 *I didn't know who he was*   Y. Ono, *Look,* 18 March 1969.

p. 476 *For* Allen Kaprow conversation, see Hopkins (1986), 58.

p. 477 *I was getting very famous*   Y. Ono in *Look,* 18 March 1969, and *Rolling Stone,* October 1981.

p. 477 *I despised myself for being so well respected*   Y. Ono, *Esquire,* December 1970.

p. 477 *Social protest*   H. Davies, *Sunday Times,* 5 February 1967.

p. 478 *Cynthia Lennon recalled*   Twist (1978), 182.

CHAPTER 45

p. 480 *Well, my version*   Y. Ono in Sheff (1981), 155.

p. 480 *Yoko was naïve*   J. Lennon in Wenner (1971), 69.

p. 481 *I got along with them*   Y. Ono in Sheff (1981), 155.

p. 481 *I was again becoming as creative and dominant*   J. Lennon in Sheff (1981), 197.

p. 483 *The expletives were really flying*   G. Emerick in Lewisohn (1988), 143.

p. 483 *We found Mr. McCartney's*   Lord Pool in *The Times* (London), 3 July 1968.

p. 484 *Sheer hoko-poko*   S. Taylor, *Art and Artists,* August 1968.

p. 484 *All the great masters*   Yeats (1961), 216.

p. 485 *Nothing to do with it*   P. McCartney in *Newsweek,* 19 August 1968.

p. 487 *No feature length cartoon*   *Films in Review,* August 1968.

p. 487 *More quintessentially Beatle*   T. Milne, *The Observer,* 21 July 1968.

p. 487 *A sophisticated work of art*   *Daily Express,* 18 July 1968.

p. 487 *At least the children can understand that*   *Newsweek,* 19 August 1968.

CHAPTER 46

p. 488 *They aren't about anything*   P. McCartney in *Melody Maker,* 8 June 1968.

p. 488 *It was me getting pissed off*   G. Harrison in *Musician,* November 1987.

p. 490 *A bit more country and western*   P. McCartney in *Rolling Stone,* 31 January 1974.

p. 492 *When I started*   J. Lennon in *Red Mole,* 8 March 1971.

p. 494 *Preaching counter-revolution*   S. Lydon, *Ramparts,* 30 November 1968.

p. 494 *The Beatles have taken refuge*   E. Willis, The *New Yorker,* 1 February 1969.

CHAPTER 47

p. 496 *We're no better than anyone else*   J. Lennon in Davies (1968), 291.

p. 497 *The overwhelming impression*   P. French, *The New Statesman,* 4 October 1968.

p. 497 *By revealing so candidly*   A. Goldman, *Vogue,* October 1968.

p. 498 *We're all really the same person*   P. McCartney in Davies (1968), 300.

p. 498 *If one experiences something*   G. Harrison in Davies (1968), 324.

p. 498 *Not even with our Beatle buddies*   J. and C. Lennon in Davies (1968), 285.

p. 498 *They never discuss or try to evaluate*   Davies (1968), 283.

p. 498 *It's nice when people like it*   J. Lennon in Davies (1968), 284.

p. 501 *After six years' work*   S. Maltz in Brown (1983), 329.

p. 502 *Imagine your worst paranoia*   J. Lennon in Brown (1983), 318.

p. 502 *In celebration*   Y. Ono in *Rolling Stone,* 1 October 1981.

p. 505 *Too square for hippies*   *Time,* 22 November 1968.

p. 505 *A huge dismal mess*   *Newsweek,* 25 November 1968.

p. 505 *Egregiously eclectic*   A. Sarris, *Village Voice,* 14 November 1968.

p. 505 *For people of all ages*   S. Kauffman, *The New Republic,* 16 November 1968.

p. 506 *Lighthearted, throwaway quality*   P. Kael, *The New Yorker,* 30 November 1968.

p. 506 *New Magic in Animation*   *Time,* 27 December 1968.

p. 507 *In American and England*   Cohn (1969), 161.

CHAPTER 48

p. 509 *All you experts listen*   J. Lennon in *Rolling Stone,* 14 May 1970.

p. 509 *We tell ourselves stories*   Didion (1979), 11–13.

p. 510 *Can the Beatles continue*   J. Szwed in *Jazz & Pop,* January 1968.

p. 510 *Like a printing error*   H. Saal, *Newsweek,* 9 December 1968.

p. 511 *To avoid competing*   Hamilton (1982), 104.

p. 527 *Not me, a piece of rubbish*   J. Lennon in Sheff (1981), 209.

p. 527 *Collapsed in laughter*   W. Mann, *The Times* (London), 22 November 1968.

p. 528 *Whatever it is or isn't*   J. Wenner, *Rolling Stone,* 21 December 1968.

p. 528 *After rolling the universe in a ball*   H. Saal, *Newsweek,* 9 December 1968.

p. 528 *Though the album tried to be panoramic*   E. Sander, *Saturday Review,* 28 December 1968.

p. 528 *Most important musical event*   W. Mann, *The Times* (London), 22 November 1968.

p. 529 *A far more deliberate*   J. Wenner, *Rolling Stone,* 21 December 1968.

p. 529 *Sgt. Pepper was nostalgic*   M. Wood, *Commonweal,* 27 December 1968.

CHAPTER 49

p. 530 *The saddest thing*   G. Harrison in Smith (1988), 261.

p. 530 *I'm an only child*   R. Starr in *Rolling Stone,* 30 April 1981.

p. 530 *I've compared it to a marriage*   J. Lennon in Solt (1988), 139.

p. 532 *There's such a mystique*   J. Lennon in D. Wigg, *The Beatles Tapes* (CD, 1996).

p. 532 *I was stoned all the time*   J. Lennon in Wenner (1971), 118.

p. 534 *It became fairly clear*   G. Johns in Buskin (1999), 144.

p. 535 *Paul had this idea*   J. Lennon in Wenner (1971), 118.

p. 536 *See you round the clubs*   G. Harrison in Sulpy (1999), 174.

p. 538 *All I can remember about it*   A. Parsons in Buskin (1999), 195.

p. 539 *There's lots of good footage*   M. Lindsay-Hogg in Russell (1985), 109.

CHAPTER 50

p. 542 *By 1969 it was real madness*   D. Taylor in Green (1989), 278–80.

p. 542 *We haven't got half the money*   J. Lennon in Coleman, *Disc and Music Echo,* 17 January 1968.

p. 542 *It's been pie in the sky*   J. Lennon in *New York Post*, 16 January 1969.

p. 544 On Allen Klein, see *New York Daily News*, 4 August 1969; *New York Times*, 21 May 1969.

p. 545 *A philosophical decision*   A. Klein in *Playboy*, November 1971.

p. 545 *Somebody who knows how*   A. Klein in *Playboy*, November 1971.

p. 546 *Don't talk to me about "management"*   A. Klein in McCabe (1972), 138.

p. 546 *Virtually cashless*   B. Wyman in Wyman (1990), 478.

p. 546 *I remember asking Mick*   J. Lennon in *Hit Parader*, December 1975.

p. 548 *As you know, Mr. Klein*   see McCabe (1972), 112.

p. 548 *A nasty little gangster*   L. Richenberg in McCabe (1972), 115.

CHAPTER 51

p. 550 *It was a choice*   J. Lennon in *Time*, 31 May 1976.

p. 550 *Miss Ono is an actress*   *The Times* (London), 21 March 1969.

p. 551 *It's the best idea we've had yet*   J. Lennon on *David Frost Programme*, 14 June 1969.

p. 551 *Trying to communicate*   J. Lennon on Eamon Andrews, ATV, 3 April 1969.

p. 551 *Beatle John and his charmer*   *Daily Express*, quoted in Hopkins (1986), 100.

p. 551 *I would have gone to bed with him*   Y. Ono in Hopkins (1986), 100.

p. 552 *Yoko and I are quite willing*   J. Lennon in Hopkins (1986), 101.

p. 554 *As the Beatles had proven themselves*   G. Johns in Buskin (1999), 144.

p. 554 *Yoko's like a man*   J. Lennon in *Melody Maker*, 26 April 1969.

p. 556 *Whatever arrangement I have*   A. Klein in *Newsweek*, 12 May 1969.

p. 557 *Literally a spy for NEMS*   A. Klein in *Rolling Stone*, 29 November 1969.

p. 558 *I'm not going to be fucked around*   J. Lennon in McCabe (1972), 141.

CHAPTER 52

p. 559 *There is no question of us splitting up*   G. Harrison in *Sunday Times*, 6 April 1969.

p. 560 *Miserable experience*   G. Martin in Buskin (1999), 64.

p. 563 *A continuously moving piece of music*   G. Martin in Buskin (1999), 65.

p. 563 *When one of the Beatles was on a session*   J. Kurlander in Buskin (1999), 146.

p. 565 *Higher! Sly shouted into the crowd*   Sander (1973), 156–57.

p. 566 *Cosmic traffic jam*   *Rolling Stone*, 20 September 1969.

p. 566 *A three-day orgy*   in E. Willis, *The New Yorker*, 6 September 1969.

p. 567 *Notwithstanding their personality*   *Rolling Stone*, 20 September 1969.

p. 568 *Reasonable, albeit slightly flat*   J. Lennon in Shelton (1986), 408.

p. 568 *I don't ever want to perform in England*   B. Dylan in Shelton (1986), 408.

p. 568 *It was bloody marvelous*   J. Lennon in *Rolling Stone*, 18 October 1969.

p. 569 *A series of surprise one-night stands*   P. McCartney in R. Meryman, *Life*, April 1971.

p. 569 *I want a divorce*   J. Lennon in R. Meryman, *Life*, April 1971.

CHAPTER 53

p. 571 *I just can't get any complete impression*   G. Harrison in *Rolling Stone,* 18 October 1969.

p. 572 *Hobby work*   P. McCartney in Davies (1968), 301.

p. 574 *Tom-tom madness*   R. Starr in Weinberg (1984), 185.

p. 578 *Anthony Fawcett recorded a conversation*   Fawcett (1981), 92–95.

EPILOGUE

p. 592 *And when the Sieve turned round and round*   Lear (1947), 71.

p. 594 MCCARTNEY IS DEAD   *University of Michigan Daily,* 14 October 1969.

p. 594 PAUL IS STILL WITH US   *Life,* 7 November 1969.

p. 595 *Many people I know in Los Angeles*   Didion (1979), 47.

p. 595 *In the year of Woodstock*   E. Sander, *Saturday Review,* 29 November 1969.

p. 596 *A sort of microcosmic society*   Mick Jagger, quoted by S. Booth in notes to *Gimme Shelter* (DVD 2000).

p. 600 *This isn't a motion picture*   *Films in Review,* August/September 1970.

p. 600 *Watching an institution such as the Beatles*   *Sunday Telegraph,* 24 May 1970.

p. 600 *A very bad film*   P. Gilliatt, *The New Yorker,* 6 June 1970.

p. 602 *Second-rate salesman*   McCabe (1972), 186.

p. 604 *Unfulfilled ambitions*   R. Starr in Weinberg (1984), 189.

p. 605 *I understood his words*   M. Chapman in J. Rosen, *The Guardian,* 10 December 1980.

BIBLIOGRAPHY

Aitken, Jonathan. *The Young Meteors*. New York: Atheneum, 1967.

Alloway, Lawrence, et al. *Modern Dreams: The Rise and Fall and Rise of Pop*. Cambridge: MIT Press, 1988.

Alvarez, A., ed. *The New Poetry*. Hammondsworth: Penguin (1962).

Amis, Kingsley. *Lucky Jim*. London: Penguin, 1961.

———. *One Fat Englishman*. New York: Harcourt, Brace & World, 1964.

Auden, W. H. *Collected Poems*. London: Faber & Faber, 1976.

Aughton, Peter. *Liverpool: A People's History*. Preston, England: Carnegie, 1990.

Ayerst, David. *Understanding Schools*. London: Penguin, 1967.

Bacon, David, and Norman Maslov. *The Beatles' England*. San Francisco: 910 Press, 1982.

Bailey, David. *David Bailey's Box of Pin Ups*. London: Weidenfeld & Nicholson, 1965.

Bailey, David, and Peter Evans. *Goodbye Baby and Amen*. New York: Coward-McCann, 1969.

Baird, Julia. *John Lennon: My Brother*. New York: Henry Holt, 1988.

Baker, Glenn A. *The Beatles Down Under: The 1964 Australia and New Zealand Tour*. Ann Arbor, MI: Pierian, 1985.

Barnouw, Erik. *A History of Broadcasting in the United States*. New York: Oxford, 1966–70.

Barrow, Tony. *P. S. We Love You: The Beatles Story 1962–63*. London: Mirror, 1982.

Barthes, Roland. *Mythologies*. New York: Noonday, 1972.

———. *The Eiffel Tower*. New York: Hill & Wang, 1979.

Bayles, Martha. *The Hole in Our Soul*. New York: Free Press, 1994.

Beatles, The. *The Beatles Complete Scores*. London: Wise Publications, 1989.

———. *Anthology*. San Francisco: Chronicle, 2000.

Becker, Ernest. *The Denial of Death*. New York: Free Press, 1973.

Belchem, John. *Merseypride: Essays in Liverpool Exceptionalism*. Liverpool: Liverpool University Press, 2000.

Bender, Marylin. *The Beautiful People*. New York: Coward-McCann, 1967.

Benjamin, Walter. *Illuminations.* New York: Harcourt, Brace & World, 1968.

Bennett, Alan, Peter Cooke, Jonathan Miller, and Dudley Moore. *Beyond the Fringe.* New York: Random House, 1963.

Bennett, Alan. *Forty Years On.* London: Faber, 1969.

Berry, Chuck. *The Autobiography.* New York: Harmony, 1987.

Best, Pete. *Beatle: The Pete Best Story.* New York: Dell, 1985.

Bird, Brian. *Skiffle.* London: Hale, 1958.

Blake, Andrew. *The Land Without Music.* Manchester, England: Manchester University Press, 1997.

Bogdanor, Vernon. *The Age of Affluence: 1951–1964.* London: Macmillan, 1970.

Booker, Christopher, Richard Ingrams, and William Rushton. *Private Eye's Romantic England.* London: Weidenfeld & Nicholson, 1963.

Booker, Christopher. *The Neophiliacs.* London: Collins, 1969.

Boorstin, Daniel J. *The Image.* New York: Vintage, 1987.

Bowles, Jerry. *A Thousand Sundays: The Ed Sullivan Show.* New York: Putnam, 1980.

Braudy, Leo. *The Frenzy of Renown.* New York: Oxford, 1986.

Braun, Michael. *Love Me Do: The Beatles' Progress.* London: Penguin, 1964.

Briggs, Asa. *A Social History of England.* New York: Viking, 1983.

Bronson, Fred. *The Billboard Book of Number One Hits.* New York: Billboard, 1985.

Brophy, John. *City of Departures.* London: Collins, 1946.

Brown, Jacqueline Nassy. *Dropping Anchor, Setting Sail.* Princeton, NJ: Princeton University Press, 2005.

Brown, Peter, and Steven Gaines. *The Love You Make.* New York: McGraw-Hill, 1983.

Buskin, Richard. *Inside Tracks.* New York: Spike, 1999.

Byron, Stuart, and Elisabeth Weis. *Movie Comedy.* London: Penguin, 1977.

Campbell, Joseph. *The Hero with a Thousand Faces.* Princeton, NJ: Princeton University Press, 1968.

Cantwell, Robert. *When We Were Good: The Folk Revival.* Cambridge, MA: Harvard University Press, 1996.

Carpenter, Humphrey, and Mari Prtitchard. *The Oxford Companion to Children's Literature.* New York: Oxford, 1984.

Carroll, Lewis. *The Annotated Alice.* Edited by Martin Gardner. New York: New American Library, 1960.

Chanan, Michael. *Repeated Takes: A Short History of Recording and Its Effects on Music.* New York: Verso, 1995.

Chandler, George. *Liverpool.* London: B. T. Batsford, 1957.

———. *Liverpool and Literature.* Liverpool: Rondo, 1974.

Chapple, Steve, and Reebee Garofalo, *Rock 'n' Roll Is Here to Pay.* Chicago: Nelson-Hall, 1977.

Cheshire, David F. *Music Hall in Britain.* Newton Abbot: David & Charles, 1974.

Chesterton, G. K. *A Handful of Authors.* New York: Sheed & Ward, 1953.

Church, Richard. *Across the Bridge.* New York: Dutton, 1956.

Clarke, Donald. *The Rise and Fall of Popular Music.* New York: St. Martin's Griffin, 1995.

Clarke, Peter. *Hope and Glory: Britain 1900–1990.* New York: Penguin, 1996.

Cohen, Stanley. *Folk Devils and Moral Panics*. 3rd edition. London: Routledge, 2002.

Cohn, Nik. *Awopbopaloobop alopbamboom*. New York: Grove, 1969.

Coleman, Ray. *Lennon*. New York: McGraw-Hill, 1984.

Connolly, Ray. *Stardust Memories*. London: Pavilion, 1983.

Cooke, Alistair. *America Observed*. New York: Knopf, 1988.

Cording, Robert, Shelli Jankowski Smith, and E. J. Miller Laino. *In My Life: Encounters with the Beatles*. New York: Fromm, 1998.

Cornelius, John. *Liverpool 8*. London: J. Murray, 1982.

Cott, Jonathan, and Christine Doudna, eds. *The Ballad of John and Yoko*. Garden City, NY: Rolling Stone, 1982.

Crompton, Richmal. *Just William*. London: Macmillan, 1990.

Crosland, Margaret, ed. *Cocteau's World*. New York: Dodd, Mead, 1972.

Cunningham, Mark. *Good Vibrations: A History of Record Production*. Chessington: Castle Communications, 1996.

Davies, Hunter. *The Beatles: The Authorized Biography*. New York: McGraw-Hill, 1968.

———. *The Beatles: The Authorized Biography*. 2nd revised edition. New York: McGraw-Hill, 1985.

Davis, Clive. *Clive: Inside the Record Business*. New York: Ballantine, 1974.

Delany, Shelagh. *A Taste of Honey*. New York: Grove Press, 1959.

Denning, Lord Alfred. *John Profumo and Christine Keeler*. London: Stationery Office, 1963.

Dent, H. C. *Secondary Education for All*. London: Routledge, 1949.

Dexter, Dave. *Playback*. New York: Billboard, 1976.

Didion, Joan. *The White Album*. New York: Pocket Books, 1979.

———. *Slouching Toward Bethlehem*. New York: Washington Square Press, 1981.

Diefendorf, Jeffry M. *In the Wake of War: The Reconstruction of German Cities After World War II*. New York: Oxford, 1993.

DiFranco, J. Philip, ed. *The Beatles in Richard Lester's A Hard Day's Night*. New York: Penguin, 1978.

DiLello, Richard. *The Longest Cocktail Party*. Ann Arbor, MI: Pierian Press, 1983.

Douglas, Susan J. *Where the Girls Are: Growing Up Female with the Mass Media*. New York: Times Books, 1994.

Durgnat, Raymond. *A Mirror for England*. London: Faber & Faber 1970.

Ehrenreich, Barbara, Elizabeth Hess, and Gloria Jacobs. *Re-Making Love*. Garden City, NY: Doubleday, 1986.

Ehrlich, Cyril. *The Music Profession in Britain Since the Eighteenth Century*. Oxford: Clarendon, 1985.

Eisen, Jonathan. *The Age of Rock: Sounds of the American Cultural Revolution*. New York: Vintage, 1969.

Eisenstadt, S. N., ed. *Max Weber on Charisma and Institution Building*. Chicago: University of Chicago, 1968.

Emerick, Geoff. *Here, There and Everywhere*. New York: Gotham, 2006.

Epstein, Brian. *A Cellarful of Noise*. London: Souvenir Press, 1964.

Erikson, Erik H. *Childhood and Society*. New York: Norton, 1986.

Escott, Colin, and Martin Hawkins. *Good Rockin' Tonight: Sun Records and the Birth of Rock 'n' Roll*. New York: St. Martin's Press, 1991.

Evans, Mike. *The Art of the Beatles*. New York: Beech Tree, 1984.

———. *The Beatles Literary Anthology*. London: Plexus, 2004.

Evans-Wentz, W. Y. *The Tibetan Book of the Dead*. New York: Oxford, 1960.

Everett, Walter. *The Beatles as Musicians: Revolver Through the Anthology*. New York: Oxford, 1999.

———. *The Beatles as Musicians: The Quarry Men Through Rubber Soul*. New York: Oxford, 2001.

Fawcett, Anthony. *John Lennon: One Day at a Time*. Revised edition. New York: Grove, 1981.

Feldman, Gene, and Max Gartenberg. *The Beat Generation and the Angry Young Men*. New York: Dell, 1958.

Fiedler, Leslie. *No! In Thunder: Essays on Myth and Literature*. London: Eyre & Spottiswoode, 1963.

Fitzgerald, F. Scott. *The Jazz Age*. New York: New Directions, 1996.

Ford, Boris, ed. *Modern Britain*. Cambridge, England: Cambridge University Press, 1992.

Forem, Jack. *Transcendental Meditation: Maharishi Mahesh Yogi and the Science of Creative Intelligence*. New York: Dutton, 1973.

Fornatale, Peter, and Joshua C. Mills. *Radio in the Television Age*. New York: Overlook, 1980.

Forrester, Helen. *Lime Street at Two*. London: Bodley Head, 1985.

Freeman, Robert. *Yesterday: The Beatles 1963–1965*. New York: Holt, Rinehart & Winston, 1983.

———. *The Beatles: A Private View*. New York: Big Tent, 2003.

Freud, Sigmund. *Totem and Taboo*. New York: Norton, 1950.

———. *Group Psychology and the Analysis of the Ego*. New York: Norton, 1959.

Frith, Simon. *Sound Effects*. New York: Pantheon, 1981.

Frith, Simon, and Howard Horne. *Art into Pop*. London: Methuen, 1987.

Frith, Simon, and Andrew Goodwin, eds. *On Record*. New York: Pantheon, 1990.

Furia, Philip. *The Poets of Tin Pan Alley*. New York: Oxford, 1990.

Gabler, Neil. *An Empire of Their Own*. New York: Crown, 1988.

Gambaccini, Paul, Tim Rice, and Jonathan Rice, eds. *British Hit Singles*. Enfield, England: Guinness, 1991.

———. *British Hit Albums*. Enfield, England: Guinness, 1992.

Geller, Debbie. *In My Life: The Brian Epstein Story*. New York: St. Martin's Press, 2000.

George, Nelson. *The Death of Rhythm & Blues*. New York: Dutton, 1989.

Gerth, H. H., and C. Wright Mills. *From Max Weber: Essays in Sociology*. New York: Oxford, 1946.

Gessner, Robert. *The Moving Image*. New York: Dutton, 1968.

Gibran, Kahlil. *Sand and Foam: A Book of Aphorisms*. New York: Knopf, 1973.

Gifford, Denis. *British Animated Films*. Jefferson, NC: McFarland, 1987.

Gilbert, James. *A Cycle of Outrage*. New York: Oxford, 1986.

Gillett, Charlie. *The Sound of the City: The Rise of Rock and Roll.* New York: Pantheon, 1970.

Gilliatt, Penelope. *To Wit: Skin and Bones of Comedy.* New York: Scribner's, 1990.

Gitlin, Todd. *The Sixties: Years of Hope, Days of Rage.* New York: Bantam, 1987.

Gleason, Ralph J. *The Jefferson Airplane and the San Francisco Sound.* New York: Ballantine, 1969.

Golby, J. M., and A. W. Purdue. *The Civilization of the Crowd.* New York: Schocken, 1984.

Goldman, Albert. *Elvis.* New York: McGraw-Hill, 1981.

———. *The Lives of John Lennon.* New York: W. Morrow, 1988.

Gorer, Geoffrey. *Exploring English Character.* New York: Criterion, 1955.

Gosling, Ray. *Sum Total.* London: Faber & Faber, 1962.

Green, Jonathon. *Days in the Life: Voices from The English Underground.* London: Minerva, 1989.

Green, Martin. *A Mirror for Anglo-Saxons.* New York: Harper, 1961.

———. *Transatlantic Patterns.* New York: Basic Books, 1977.

Greenwood, Walter. *Love on the Dole.* London: Jonathan Cape, 1935.

Grein, Paul. *Capitol Records Fiftieth Anniversary: 1942–1992.* Hollywood, CA: Capitol Records, 1992.

Grundy, Bill. *That Man: A Memory of Tommy Handley.* London: Elm Tree, 1976.

Guralnik, Peter. *Lost Highway.* Boston: Godine, 1979.

———. *Last Train to Memphis: The Rise of Elvis Presley.* Boston: Little, Brown, 1994.

———. *Careless Love: The Unmaking of Elvis Presley.* Boston: Little, Brown, 1999.

Hadju, David. *Positively 4th Street.* New York: Farrar Straus & Giroux, 2001.

Hall, Stuart, and Paddy Whannel. *The Popular Arts.* New York: Pantheon, 1965.

Hall, Stuart, and Tony Jefferson, eds. *Resistance Through Rituals: Youth Subcultures in Postwar Britain.* London: Hutchinson, 1975.

Halsey, A. H. *Change in British Society: From 1900 to the Present Day.* New York: Oxford, 1995.

Hamilton, Richard. *Collected Words.* New York: Thames & Hudson, 1982.

Hamm, Charles. *Yesterdays: Popular Song in America.* New York: Norton, 1979.

Hammond, John. *John Hammond on Record.* New York: Summit, 1977.

Harrison, George. *I Me Mine.* Guildford, Surrey: Genesis, 1980.

Harry, Bill, ed. *Mersey Beat: The Beginnings of the Beatles.* New York: Omnibus, 1977.

Hayes, Harold, ed. *Smiling Through the Apocalypse: Esquire's History of the Sixties.* New York: McCall, 1969.

Hebdige, Dick. *Subculture: The Meaning of Style.* London: Methuen, 1979.

Henri, Adrian, Roger McGough, and Brian Patten. *The Mersey Sound.* New York: Penguin, 1983.

Hertsgaard, Mark. *A Day in the Life.* New York: Delacorte, 1995.

Hewison, Robert. *Under Siege: Literary Life in London 1939–45.* New York: Oxford, 1977.

———. *In Anger: Culture in the Cold War 1945–60.* New York: Oxford, 1981.

————. *Monty Python: The Case Against.* New York: Grove Press, 1981.

————. *Too Much: Art and Society in the Sixties.* New York: Oxford, 1986.

Hitchens, Christopher. *Blood, Class, and Nostalgia: Anglo-American Ironies.* New York: Farrar Straus & Giroux, 1990.

Hoffman, Dezo. *With the Beatles.* New York: Omnibus, 1982.

Hoggart, Richard. *The Uses of Literacy.* New York: Oxford, 1957.

Hold, Sid, ed. *The Rolling Stone Interviews: The 1980s.* New York: St. Martin's Press, 1989.

Hollingshead, Michael. *The Man Who Turned On the World.* New York: Abelard-Schuman, 1974.

Holloway, David, ed. *The Daily Telegraph: The Sixties.* New York: Simon & Schuster, 1992.

Hopkins, Harry. *The New Look.* Boston: Houghton Mifflin, 1964.

Hopkins, Jerry. *Yoko Ono.* New York: Macmillan, 1986.

Howlett, Kevin. *The Beatles at The BEEB: The Story of Their Radio Career.* Ann Arbor, MI: Pierian, 1983.

Huber, David Miles, and Robert E. Runstein. *Modern Recording Techniques.* Boston: Focal Press, 2001.

Huxley, Aldous. *The Doors of Perception [and] Heaven and Hell.* London: Chatto & Windus, 1960.

————. *Island.* New York: Harper & Row, 1962.

Irving, Clive, Ron Hall, and Jeremy Wallington. *Anatomy of a Scandal.* New York: M. S. Mill & William Morrow, 1963.

Isherwood, Christopher. *My Guru and His Disciple.* London: Eyre Methuen, 1980.

Johnson, John A. *American Bandstand.* New York: Oxford, 1984.

Jones, Dylan. *Haircults: Fifty Years of Styles and Cuts.* New York: Thames & Hudson, 1990.

Jonnes, Jill. *Hep-Cats, Narcs, and Pipe Dreams.* Baltimore: Johns Hopkins, 1996.

Jung, Carl G., ed. *Man and His Symbols.* New York: Dell, 1968.

Kael, Pauline. *I Lost It at The Movies.* Atlantic Monthly Press, 1965.

————. *Deeper into Movies.* Boston: Little, Brown, 1973.

————. *For Keeps: 30 Years at the Movies.* New York: Dutton, 1994.

Kahn, E. J., Jr. *The Voice: The Story of an American Phenomenon.* New York: Harper & Brothers, 1947.

Kaiser, Charles. *1968 in America.* New York: Grove Press, 1988.

Kater, Michael H. *Different Drummers: Jazz in the Culture of Nazi Germany.* New York: Oxford, 1992.

Kavanagh, Ted. *Tommy Handley.* London: Hodder & Stoughton, 1949.

————. *The ITMA Years.* London: Woburn Press, 1974.

Kelley, Kitty. *His Way: The Unauthorized Biography of Frank Sinatra.* New York: Bantam, 1986.

Kennan, Kent Wheeler. *The Technique of Orchestration.* 2nd edition. Englewood Cliffs, NJ: Prentice-Hall, 1970.

Kerr, Madeline. *The People of Ship Street.* London: Routledge & Kegan Paul, 1958.

Kesey, Ken. *Demon Box.* New York: Penguin, 1986.

Klein, Joe. *Woody Guthrie: A Life.* New York: Ballantine, 1980.

Koestler, Arthur, ed. *Suicide of a Nation?* London: Macmillan, 1964.

Kramer, Daniel. *Bob Dylan.* New York: Citadel Press, 1967.

Lahr, John. *Prick Up Your Ears: The Biography of Joe Orton.* New York: Knopf, 1978.

Lane, Tony. *Liverpool: City of the Sea.* Liverpool: Liverpool University Press, 1997.

Larkin, Colin, ed. *The Virgin Encyclopedia of Sixties Music.* London: Virgin Books, 2002.

Larkin, Philip. *High Windows.* London: Faber & Faber, 1974.

Laurie, Peter. *The Teenage Revolution.* London: A. Blond, 1965.

Lawrence, D. H. *Lady Chatterley's Lover.* London: Penguin, 1960.

Lear, Edward, and Holbrook Jackson, ed. *The Complete Nonsense of Edward Lear.* London: Faber & Faber, 1947.

Leary, Timothy, Ralph Metzner, and Richard Alpert. *The Psychedelic Experience.* New York: Citadel, 1964.

Leigh, Spencer. *Let's Go Down the Cavern.* London: Vermilion, 1984.

Lennon, John. *In His Own Write.* London: Jonathan Cape, 1964.

———. *A Spaniard in the Works.* London: Jonathan Cape, 1965.

———. *Skywriting by Word of Mouth.* New York: Harper & Row, 1986.

Lerner, Alan J. *My Fair Lady.* New York: New American Library, 1956.

Levin, Bernard. *The Pendulum Years.* London: Pan, 1970.

Lewis, David. *Illustrated History of Liverpool's Suburbs.* Derby, England: Breedon Books, 2006.

Lewis, Vic. *Music and Maiden Overs.* London: Chatto & Windus, 1987.

Lewisohn, Mark. *The Beatles Live!* New York: Henry Holt, 1986.

———. *The Beatles Recording Sessions.* New York: Harmony, 1988.

———. *The Complete Beatles Chronicle.* London: Hamlyn, 2000.

Lindholm, Charles. *Charisma.* Cambridge, MA: Basil Blackwell, 1993.

Liverpool Echo. *Images of Merseyside.* Derby, England: Breedon Books, 1994.

Lucie-Smith, Edward. *The Liverpool Scene.* Garden City, NY: Doubleday, 1968.

———. *British Painting and Sculpture 1960–1970.* London: Tate, 1970.

MacDonald, Ian. *Revolution in the Head.* New York: Henry Holt, 1994.

MacInnes, Colin. *Absolute Beginners.* London: MacGibbon & Kee, 1960.

———. *England Half English.* New York: Random House, 1961.

———. *Sweet Saturday Night.* London: MacGibbon & Kee, 1967.

Mackay, Charles. *Extraordinary Popular Delusions and the Madness of Crowds.* New York: Harmony, 1980.

Mailer, Norman. *The Armies of the Night.* New York: New American Library, 1968.

Marcus, Greil. *Rock and Roll Will Stand.* Boston: Beacon, 1969.

———. *Mystery Train.* New York: Dutton, 1975.

Marcus, Steven. *Engels, Manchester, and the Working Class.* New York: Norton, 1974.

Martin, Bernice. *The Sociology of Contemporary Cultural Change.* Cambridge, MA: Basil Blackwell, 1981.

Martin, George. *All You Need Is Ears.* New York: St. Martin's Press, 1979.

———. *With a Little Help from My Friends.* Boston: Little, Brown, 1994.

Martland, Peter. *Since Records Began: EMI the First 100 Years.* Portland, OR: Amadeus Press, 1997.

Marwick, Arthur. *Britain in Our Century.* New York: Thames and Hudson, 1984.

————. *British Society Since 1945.* New York: Penguin, 1982.

Mason, Paul. *The Maharishi.* Rockport, MA: Element, 1994.

Mays, John Barron. *Growing Up in the City.* Liverpool: Liverpool University Press, 1964.

————. *The Young Pretenders.* London: M. Joseph, 1965.

McCabe, Peter, and Robert D. Schonfeld. *Apple to the Core: The Unmaking of the Beatles.* New York: Pocket Books, 1972.

McCartney, Mike. *The Macs: Mike McCartney's Family Album.* New York: Delilah, 1981.

McKibben, Ross. *Classes and Cultures: England 1918–1951.* New York: Oxford, 1998.

McLuhan, Marshall. *Understanding Media: Extensions of Man.* New York: McGraw-Hill, 1965.

Mehta, Gita. *Karma Cola: Marketing the Mystic East.* New York: Simon & Schuster, 1979.

Mellers, Wilfrid. *Twilight of the Gods: The Music of the Beatles.* New York: Schirmer, 1973.

Mellor, David. *The Sixties Art Scene in London.* London: Phaedon, 1993.

Melly, George. *Revolt into Style: The Pop Arts.* Garden City, NY: Anchor, 1971.

————. *Scouse Mouse.* London: Weidenfeld & Nicholson, 1984.

Melville, Herman. *Redburn.* New York: Penguin, 1986.

Metzner, Ralph. *The Ecstatic Adventure.* New York: Macmillan, 1968.

Miles, Barry. *Ginsberg.* New York: Simon & Schuster, 1989.

Miles, Barry. *Paul McCartney: Many Years from Now.* New York: Henry Holt, 1997.

Miller, Karl, ed. *Writing in England Today: The Last Fifteen Years.* London: Penguin, 1968.

Milligan, Terrence A. *Silly Verse for Kids.* London: Dobson, 1959.

————. *Goon Show Scripts.* London: Woburn Press, 1972.

Moers, Ellen. *The Dandy: Brummell to Beerbohm.* New York: Viking, 1960.

Moorhouse, Geoffrey. *The Other England.* London: Penguin, 1964.

Morgan, Kenneth O. *The People's Peace: British History 1945–1989.* New York: Oxford, 1990.

Motion, Andrew. *The Lamberts: George, Constance and Kit.* New York: Farrar Straus & Giroux, 1986.

Mulvach, Jane, ed. *Vogue History of 20th Century Fashion.* New York: Viking, 1988.

Murray, Albert. *Stomping the Blues.* New York: Vintage, 1982.

Needleman, Jacob. *The New Religions.* Garden City, NY: Doubleday, 1970.

Neises, Charles P., ed. *The Beatles Reader.* Ann Arbor, MI: Pierian, 1984.

Neville, Richard. *Play Power.* New York: Random House, 1970.

Noebel, David A. *Communism, Hypnotism and the Beatles.* Tulsa, OK: Christian Crusade Publications, 1965.

Norman, Philip. *Shout: The Beatles in Their Generation.* New York: Fireside, 1981.

————. *Symphony for the Devil: The Rolling Stones Story.* New York: Simon & Schuster, 1984.

Nuttall, Jeff. *Bomb Culture.* New York: Delacorte, 1968.

O'Brien, Geoffrey. *Dream Time: Chapters from the Sixties.* New York: Viking, 1988.

O'Grady, Terence. *The Beatles: A Musical Revolution.* Boston: Twayne, 1983.

O'Mara, Pat. *Autobiography of a Liverpool Slummy.* New York: Vanguard, 1933.

O'Neill, William L. *Coming Apart: An Informal History of America in the 1960s.* Chicago: Quadrangle, 1971.

Ochs, Michael. *Rock Archives.* Garden City, NY: Doubleday, 1984.

Oldham, Andrew Loog. *Stoned: A Memoir of London in the 1960s.* New York: St. Martin's Press, 2000.

Ono, Yoko. *Grapefruit: A Book of Instructions.* London: Owen, 1970.

Opie, Iona and Peter. *The Lore and Language of Schoolchildren.* Oxford: Clarendon, 1960.

Orton, Joe. *The Orton Diaries.* New York: Harper & Row, 1986.

Orwell, George. *The Road to Wigan Pier.* New York: Harcourt Brace, 1958.

———. *Essays.* Everyman's Library, New York: Knopf, 2002.

Osborne, John. *Look Back in Anger, The Entertainer, [and] Epitaph for George Dillon.* New York: Bantam, 1977.

Owen, Alun. *Three TV Plays: No Trams to Lime Street, After the Funeral, Lena Oh My Lena.* New York: Hill & Wang, 1963.

Palmer, Tony. *All You Need Is Love: The Story of Popular Music.* New York: Grossman, 1976.

Perrett, Bryan. *Liverpool: City at War.* London: Hale, 1990.

Perry, Charles. *The Haight-Ashbury: A History.* New York: Random House, 1984.

Petkov, Steve, and Leonard Mustazza, eds. *The Frank Sinatra Reader.* New York: Oxford, 1995.

Poirier, Richard. *The Performing Self.* New York: Oxford, 1971.

Pritchard, David, and Alan Lysaght. *The Beatles: An Oral History.* New York: Hyperion, 1998.

Quant, Mary. *Quant by Quant.* New York: Putnam, 1967.

Rachlin, Harvey. *The Encyclopedia of the Music Business.* New York: Harper & Row, 1981.

Rank, Otto. *Art and Artist.* New York: Norton, 1989.

Redfern, Walter. *Puns.* Cambridge, MA: Basil Blackwell, 1984.

Reisman, David, Nathan Glazer, and Reuel Denney. *The Lonely Crowd.* Garden City, NY: Anchor, 1953.

Revill, David. *The Roaring Silence: John Cage, A Life.* London: Bloomsbury, 1992.

Riley, Tim. *Tell Me Why.* New York: Knopf, 1988.

Rimler, Walter. *Not Fade Away.* Ann Arbor, MI: Pierian Press, 1984.

Roberts, Robert. *The Classic Slum.* New York: Penguin, 1973.

Robinson, John A. T. *Honest to God.* Philadelphia: Westminster Press, 1963.

Rogan, Johnny. *Starmakers and Svengalis.* London: Macdonald, 1988.

Rolling Stone, eds. *The Rolling Stone Interviews.* New York: Paperback Library, 1971.

Rolphe, C. H. *The Trial of Lady Chatterley's Lover.* London: Penguin, 1961.

Rorem, Ned. *Setting the Tone: Essays and a Diary.* New York: Coward-McCann, 1983.

Rosenberg, Deena. *Fascinating Rhythm: George and Ira Gershwin.* New York: Dutton, 1991.

Ross, Andrew. *No Respect: Intellectuals and Popular Culture*. London: Routledge, 1989.

Rossman, Michael. *The Wedding Within the War*. Garden City, NY: Doubleday, 1971.

Roszak, Theodore. *The Making of a Counterculture*. Garden City, NY: Doubleday, 1969.

Rothwell, Catherine. *Liverpool (Britain in Old Photographs)*. Gloucestershire, England: Sutton, 1996.

Rudd, Natalie. *Peter Blake*. London: Tate Publishing, 1993.

Russell, Ethan A. *Dear Mr. Fantasy: Diary of a Decade*. Boston: Houghton Mifflin, 1985.

Ryback, Timothy W. *Rock Around the Block*. New York: Oxford, 1990.

Said, Edward W. *Orientalism*. New York: Random House, 1978.

Saki (H. H. Munro). *The Best of Saki*. New York: Viking, 1961.

Salewicz, Michael. *McCartney*. New York: St. Martin's Press, 1986.

Sampson, Anthony. *Anatomy of Britain*. London: Hodder & Stoughton, 1962.

Sandbrook, Dominic. *Never Had It So Good*. London: Abacus, 2006.

Sander, August. *Photographs of an Epic*. New York: Aperture, 1980.

Sander, Ellen. *Trips: Rock Life in the Sixties*. New York: Scribner's, 1973.

Sanjek, Russell, and David Sanjek. *American Popular Music Business in the 20th Century*. New York: Oxford, 1991.

Sawyer, Roger. *Spike Milligan: A Celebration*. London: Virgin Books, 1995.

Scaduto, Anthony. *Mick Jagger: Everybody's Lucifer*. New York: Berkley, 1974.

———. *Bob Dylan: An Intimate Biography*. New York: Grosset & Dunlap, 1971.

Scherman, Tony. *Backbeat: Earl Palmer's Story*. Washington: Smithsonian, 1999.

Schickel, Richard. *Intimate Strangers: The Culture of Celebrity*. New York: Fromm, 1986.

Seago, Alex. *Burning The Box of Beautiful Things*. New York: Oxford, 1995.

Sennett, Richard. *The Fall of Public Man*. New York: Knopf, 1977.

Shankar, Ravi. *My Music, My Life*. New York: Simon & Schuster, 1968.

Shaw, Arnold. *Honkers and Shouters*. New York: Macmillan, 1978.

Shaw, Frank, Fritz Spiegl, Stan Kelly. *Lern Yerself Scouse*. Liverpool: Scouse Press, 1966.

———. *My Liverpool*, Gallery Press, 1971.

Sheff, David. *The Playboy Interviews with John Lennon and Yoko Ono*. New York: Playboy Press, 1981.

Shelton, Robert. *No Direction Home: The Life and Music of Bob Dylan*. New York: William Morrow, 1986.

Shotton, Peter. *John Lennon in My Life*. New York: Stein & Day, 1983.

Sillitoe, Alan. *Saturday Night and Sunday Morning*. New York: Knopf, 1958.

Sinyard, Neil. *The Films of Richard Lester*. London: Croom Helm, 1985.

Sissons, Michael, and Philip French, eds. *The Age of Austerity*. London: Hodder & Stoughton, 1963.

Smelser, Neil J. *The Theory of Collective Behavior*. New York: Free Press, 1963.

———. *The Social Edges of Psychoanalysis*. Berkeley: University of California Press, 1998.

Smith, Joe. *Off the Record: An Oral History of Popular Music.* New York: Warner, 1988.

Solderbergh, Steven. *Getting Away with It.* London: Faber & Faber, 1999.

Solt, Andrew, and Sam Egan. *Imagine: John Lennon.* New York: Macmillan, 1988.

Somach, Denny, Kathleen Somach, and Kevin Gunn, eds. *Ticket to Ride.* New York: William Morrow, 1989.

Sontag, Susan. *Against Interpretation.* New York: Farrar Straus & Giroux, 1986.

Southall, Brian. *Abbey Road.* Cambridge: Patrick Stephens, 1982.

Spitz, Bob. *The Beatles.* Boston: Little, Brown, 2005.

Stannard, Neville. *The Beatles' Long and Winding Road: A History of the Beatles on Record.* New York: Avon, 1982.

Steegmuller, Francis. *Cocteau: A Biography.* Boston: Little, Brown, 1970.

Stein, Jean. *Edie: An American Biography.* New York: Dell, 1982.

Stevens, Jay. *Storming Heaven: LSD and the American Dream.* New York: Harper & Row, 1988.

Stewart, Susan. *On Longing.* Baltimore: Johns Hopkins University Press, 1984.

Sulpy, Doug, and Ray Schweighardt. *Get Back: The Unauthorized Chronicle of the Beatles Let It Be Disaster.* New York: St. Martin's Griffin, 1999.

Taylor, Alistair. *A Secret History.* London: John Blake, 2001.

Taylor, Derek. *As Time Goes By: Living in the Sixties.* Ann Arbor: Pierian, 1983.

———. *Fifty Years Adrift.* Guildford, Surrey: Genesis, 1984.

———. *It Was Twenty Years Ago Today.* New York: Simon & Schuster, 1987.

Taylor, John Russell. *Anger and After.* London: Methuen, 1962.

Thomas, Denis. *Challenge in Fleet Street.* Truth, 1957.

Thomson, Elizabeth, and David Gutman, eds. *The Lennon Companion.* New York: Schirmer, 1987.

Tiffen, Herbert J. *A History of the Liverpool Institute Schools.* Liverpool: Liverpool Institute Old Boys' Association, 1935.

Tomkins, Calvin. *Duchamp: A Biography.* New York: Henry Holt, 1996.

Trilling, Lionel. *Sincerity and Authenticity.* Cambridge, MA: Harvard, 1971.

Trudgill, Peter. *The Dialects of England.* Cambridge, MA: Basil Blackwell, 1990.

———. *Sociological Patterns in British English.* London: E. Arnold, 1978.

Turner, Graham. *The North Country.* London: Eyre & Spottiswoode, 1967.

Twist, Cynthia. *A Twist of Lennon.* New York: Avon, 1978.

Tynan, Kenneth. *Curtains.* New York: Atheneum, 1961.

———. *Tynan: Left and Right.* New York: Atheneum, 1968.

Vollmer, Jurgen. *Rock 'n' Roll Times.* New York: Overlook Press, 1983.

Walker, Alexander. *Hollywood UK.* New York: Stein & Day, 1974.

Weinberg, Max. *The Big Beat: Conversations with Rock's Great Drummers.* Chicago: Contemporary, 1984.

Wenner, Jann. *Lennon Remembers.* New York: Popular Library, 1971.

Whitburn, Joel. *The Billboard Book of Top 40 Hits.* New York: Billboard, 1985.

———. *Top R&B Singles 1942–1988.* Menomonee Falls, WI: Record Research, 1988.

Whitcomb, Ian. *After the Ball: Pop Music from Rag to Rock.* New York: Simon & Schuster, 1972.

————. *Rock Odyssey: A Musician's Chronicle of the Sixties.* Garden City, NY: Doubleday, 1983.

White, Charles. *The Life and Times of Little Richard.* New York: Pocket Books, 1984.

White, E. B. *Here Is New York.* New York: Harper, 1949.

Whittemore, Katharine, ed. *The Sixties: Recollections of the Decade from Harper's Magazine.* New York: Franklin Square, 1995.

Whittington-Egan, Richard. *Liverpool Roundabout.* Liverpool: Philip, Son & Nephew, 1957.

————. *Liverpool Soundings.* Liverpool: Gallery, 1969.

Wilde, Oscar. *The Artist as Critic.* Chicago: University of Chicago, 1969.

Wilder, Alec. *American Popular Song: The Great Innovators.* New York: Oxford, 1972.

Willett, John. *Art in the City.* London: Methuen, 1967.

Williams, Alan. *The Man Who Gave the Beatles Away.* New York: Macmillan, 1975.

Williams, Francis. *The American Invasion.* New York: Crown, 1962.

Williams, Paul. *Outlaw Blues.* New York: New York: Dutton, 1969.

Williams, Raymond. *Culture and Society: 1780–1950.* New York: Columbia University Press, 1983.

Williams, Richard. *Out of His Head: The Sound of Phil Spector.* New York: Outerbridge & Lazard, 1972.

Willis, Paul E. *Profane Culture.* London: Routledge & Kegan Paul, 1978.

Willmott, Peter. *Adolescent Boys of East London.* London: Routledge & Kegan Paul, 1966.

Wills, Gary. *The Kennedy Imprisonment: A Meditation on Power.* Boston: Little, Brown, 1981.

Wilmut, Roger. *The Goon Show Companion.* New York: St. Martin's Press, 1976.

————. *From Fringe to Flying Circus.* London: Methuen, 1982.

Wilson, Colin. *The Outsider.* Boston: Houghton Mifflin, 1956.

Wolfe, Tom. *The Kandy-Kolored Tangerine Flake Streamline Baby.* New York: Noonday, 1965.

————. *The Pump House Gang.* New York: Farrar Straus & Giroux, 1968.

————. *The Electric Kool-Aid Acid Test.* New York: Farrar Straus & Giroux, 1968.

Wolfenstein, Martha, and Gilbert Kliman, eds. *Children and the Death of a President.* Garden City, NY: Doubleday, 1965.

Wood, Charles. *Dingo.* New York: Grove Press, 1967.

Wright, Peter. *Lancashire Dialect.* Dalesman, 1976.

Wyman, Bill. *Stone Alone.* New York: Viking, 1990.

Yeats, W. B. *Essays and Introductions.* London: Macmillan, 1961.

Yogananda, Paramahansa. *Autobiography of a Yogi.* New York: Philosophical Library, 1946.

Young, Michael. *The Rise of the Meritocracy.* New York: Thames & Hudson, 1958.

Acknowledgments

This book was written over the course of many years, during which a great many people made important contributions to its initiation, development, and completion. Some of those contributions were knowing and direct, others were unknowing and indirect. It would be impossible to name and acknowledge everyone, but I would like to offer my profuse and heartfelt thanks to the following mentors, colleagues, friends, and lovers:

To my esteemed former teachers at Cornell University, Carol Greenhouse, Robert Ascher, Larry Moore, and James McConkey, some of whom read early, tentative chapters of the manuscript and offered me invaluable advice and encouragement at a time when the book was but a gleam in my eye, and to the late Henry Adams at the Collegiate School, who instilled in me a lifelong respect for the written word.

To my musical mentor, the late Alan Dawson, who taught me more about the rudiments of both drumming and living than I will ever be able to put into practice.

To my old friends and former bandmates Milt Reder and Bill Lane, with whom I first discovered and experienced so much of the music I have written about in this book, and to my dear friends Jeremy Alderson, Richard Edelmen, Joan Ades, Sam Hood, Judy Upjohn, and Bill Benson, who have served as a constant source of comfort and diversion over the years.

To Jacob Brackman, who lent me a little bit of his chutzpah many years ago, and to Terry Funk-Antman, who helped me see the forest through the trees.

To Gay Leonhardt, whose support and companionship sustained me during much of the time I was working on this book.

To my friend and agent, Kenneth Wapner, who soothed my nerves and championed my interests at every step of the way.

To the late William Shawn, who served as my first editor on this book and offered incalculable forms of guidance, encouragement, and inspiration during the years we worked together on it.

To my editor, John Glusman, who inherited this book from Shawn and came to treat it as his own, supplementing his own calm disposition, dry wit, and incisive intelligence with levels of patience and dedication that, by the standards of modern publishing, verged on the pathological at times. And to John's colleagues at Harmony Books, Kate Kennedy, Dan Rembert, Lauren Dong, Linnea Knollmueller, Mark McCauslin, and David Wade Smith, who ably assisted in the beautiful design and production of the book.

And finally, with a full heart, I wish to acknowledge the contribution of Lisa Corinne Davis, whose love, support, and fierce determination inspired and challenged me, at long last, to finish what I had started.

PHOTOGRAPH CREDITS

INDEX

Italicized page numbers indicate photos

Jonathan Gould is a writer and a former professional musician who studied with the eminent jazz drummer Alan Dawson and spent many years working in bands and recording studios. In addition to writing and playing music, Gould has raised a family, served in local politics, and taken an active role in the life of the upstate New York community where he has lived for the past twenty-five years. He currently divides his time between New York City and Willow, New York.